Dear Valued Customer,

We realize you're a busy professional with deadlines to hit. Whether your goal is to learn a new technology or solve a critical problem, we want to be there to lend you a hand. Our primary objective is to provide you with the insight and knowledge you need to stay atop the highly competitive and ever-changing technology industry.

Wiley Publishing, Inc., offers books on a wide variety of technical categories, including security, data warehousing, software development tools, and networking — everything you need to reach your peak. Regardless of your level of expertise, the Wiley family of books has you covered.

- For Dummies® – The ***fun*** and ***easy*** way™ to learn
- The Weekend Crash Course® – The ***fastest*** way to learn a new tool or technology
- Visual – For those who prefer to learn a new topic ***visually***
- The Bible – The ***100% comprehensive*** tutorial and reference
- The Wiley Professional list – ***Practical*** and ***reliable*** resources for IT professionals

The book you now hold is part of our new *60 Minutes a Day* series which delivers what we think is the closest experience to an actual hands-on seminar that is possible with a book. Our author team are veterans of hundreds of hours of classroom teaching and they use that background to guide you past the hurdles and pitfalls to confidence and mastery of XML in manageable units that can be read and put to use in just an hour. If you have a broadband connection to the Web, you can see Linda and Al introduce each topic — but this book will still be your best learning resource if you download only the audio files or use it strictly as a printed resource. From fundamentals to security and Web Services, you'll find this self-paced training to be your best learning aid.

Our commitment to you does not end at the last page of this book. We'd want to open a dialog with you to see what other solutions we can provide. Please be sure to visit us at www.wiley.com/compbooks to review our complete title list and explore the other resources we offer. If you have a comment, suggestion, or any other inquiry, please locate the "contact us" link at www.wiley.com.

Finally, we encourage you to review the following page for a list of Wiley titles on related topics. Thank you for your support and we look forward to hearing from you and serving your needs again in the future.

Sincerely,

Richard K Swadley

Richard K. Swadley
Vice President & Executive Group Publisher
Wiley Technology Publishing

Bible

FOR DUMMIES

Wiley Publishing, Inc.

more information on related titles

XML in 60 Minutes a Day

Linda McKinnon
Al McKinnon

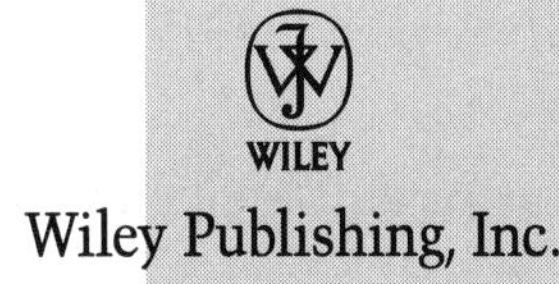

Wiley Publishing, Inc.

Executive Publisher: Robert Ipsen
Vice-President and Publisher: Joseph B. Wikert
Senior Editor: Ben Ryan
Editorial Manager: Kathryn A. Malm
Developmental Editor: Jerry Olson
Production Editor: Vincent Kunkemueller
Media Development Specialist: Kit Malone
Text Design & Composition: Wiley Composition Services

Published by Wiley Publishing, Inc., Indianapolis, Indiana
Published simultaneously in Canada

Library of Congress Cataloging-in-Publication Data:

ISBN: 0-471-42254-1

Printed in the United States of America

10 9 8 7 6 5 4 3 2 1

A Note from the Consulting Editor

Instructor-led training has proven to be an effective and popular tool for training engineers and developers. To convey technical ideas and concepts, the classroom experience has been shown to be superior when compared to other delivery methods. As a technical trainer for more than 20 years, I have seen the effectiveness of instructor-led training firsthand. *60 Minutes a Day* combines the best of the instructor-led training and book experience. Technical training is typically divided into short and discrete modules, where each module encapsulates a specific topic. Each module is then followed by "questions and answers" and a review. *60 Minutes a Day* titles follow the same model: each chapter is short, discrete, and can be completed in 60 minutes a day. For these books, I have enlisted premier technical trainers as authors. They provide the voice of the trainer and demonstrate classroom experience in each book of the series. You even get an opportunity to meet the actual trainer: As part of this innovative approach, each chapter of a *60 Minutes a Day* book is presented online by the author. Readers are encouraged to view the online presentation before reading the relevant chapter. Therefore, *60 Minutes a Day* delivers the complete classroom experience—even the trainer.

As an imprint of Wiley Publishing, Inc., Gearhead Press continues to bring you, the reader, the level of quality that Wiley has delivered consistently for nearly 200 years.

Thank you.

Donis Marshall
Founder, Gearhead Press
Consulting Editor, Wiley Technology Publishing Group

Contents

Acknowledgments xvii

About the Authors xix

Introduction xxi

Chapter 1 XML Backgrounder 1

Why Do We Need a History Lesson Chapter? 2
Basics: From Documents to Markup and Metalanguages 3
What's a Document? 3
What Is Markup? 4
XML Is a Markup Language and a Metalanguage 6
Markup Languages 6
Metalanguages 7
The Evolution of XML 7
The Advent of Generic Coding 7
GML Led the Way 8
Other Typesetting Developments 10
SGML: Parent of HTML and XML 12
HTML: The Older Sibling of XML 15
The Arrival of XML 17
XML-Related Applications 22
The World Wide Web Consortium and XML 25
Possible XML Issues: "Nobody's Perfect (Yet)" 27
Lab Exercises: Instructions and Conventions 28
A Brief Introduction to Space Gems, Inc. 29
Chapter 1 Labs: Web Exploration 29
Summary 32

Chapter 2 Setting Up Your XML Working Environment **39**
Hardware Requirements 40
Web Servers 40
Web Browsers 43
XML Authoring Tools 45
Simple Text Editors 45
Graphical Editors 47
Use Only the Latest Versions of Microsoft Word for HTML/XML Creation 49
Integrated Development Environments 52
Converting HTML Documents to XML 55
Chapter 2 Labs: Creating an XML Authoring Environment 56
Computer System Requirements 56
Operating System Requirements 56
Creating Your XML Environment: Overview 56
Summary 62

Chapter 3 Anatomy of an XML Document **67**
What Are XML Documents? 67
XML Document Processing 68
Applications 68
XML Parsers 69
Document Errors 70
The Structure of XML Documents 70
The Logical Structure 71
The Prolog 71
The Data Instance 77
The Physical Structure: Entities 92
Entities Are Parsed or Unparsed 93
Entities Can Be Internal or External 93
General Entities versus Parameter Entities 94
Preserving Characters from Parser Misinterpretation 97
Predefined Entities 97
Numeric Character References 98
CDATA Sections 100
What Is a Well-Formed XML Document? 101
What Is a Valid XML Document? 104
Chapter 3 Labs: Anatomy of an XML File 105
Summary 112

Chapter 4 Document Type Definitions **117**
What Are Document Type Definitions? 118
Why Use Document Type Definitions? 119
Creating DTDs—General 120
DTD Types and Locations 121
Internal DTD Subsets 122
External DTD Subsets 122

Private External DTDs 123
External DTD Subsets Located at Web Sites 124
Remote External DTDs with Public Access 125
Internal DTDs Combined with External DTDs 126
DTD Declarations: General 127
Element Type Declarations 128
The Content Model 129
Elements Containing Parsed Character Data 129
Element Types Containing Other Element Types 130
Element Types Containing Mixed Content 130
Empty Element Declarations 131
Elements with "Any" Content 132
Element Content Operators 132
Attribute List Declarations 134
Attribute Declarations to Preserve White Space 137
Language ID Attribute Declarations 138
Entity Declarations 139
General Entity Declarations 139
Parameter Entity Declarations 140
Notation Declarations 143
Non-XML Data Introduced with an Attribute 143
Non-XML Data Introduced as an Entity 145
Declaring Namespace Attributes in the DTD 146
Default Namespace Declarations 147
Prefix Namespace Declarations 148
Limitations of DTDs with Respect to Namespace Declarations 149
Normalization 149
Chapter 4 Labs: Creating a DTD 149
Summary 155

Chapter 5 XML Schemas 161
What Are Schemas? 162
XML Schema 1.0: A Two-Part W3C XML Schema Recommendation 163
The XML Schema Abstract Model 164
The Logical Structure of a Sample XML Schema 166
The Prolog 168
The <Schema> Element: Namespaces and Qualified or Unqualified Locals 170
Namespace Declarations 170
Target Namespaces 171
The minedata.xsd Document as a Support Schema 172
Global and Local References: Qualified and Unqualified Locals 173

Element Type Declarations 175
The <sg1:diamonds> Element Declaration: Complex Data Types 176
The <sg1:gem> Element Declaration 178
Compositors 181
Empty Element Content 181
The <sg1:catalog> Element: Simple Data Types 182
Mixed Content Elements 183
Using Facets to Define Data More Precisely 184
Schema Document Structures 186
The Nesting Structure 186
The Flat Catalog Structure 188
Using Schemas and DTDs Together 190
Chapter 5 Labs: Creating Simple Schemas 191
Summary 200

Chapter 6 XHTML 205
HTML Review 206
A Brief History of HTML and XHTML 206
HTML Shortcomings 208
XHTML Definition and Background 209
Advantages of XHTML 211
XHTML Is Related to XML 211
XHTML Is Extensible 212
XHTML Is Modular 213
XHTML Is Portable 214
XHTML 1.0's Three Variants, DTDs, and Schemas 214
The XHTML 1.0 Strict Variant 215
The XHTML 1.0 Transitional Variant 216
The XHTML 1.0 Frameset Variant 217
XHTML Syntax 218
The Logical Structure of an XHTML Document 218
The Prolog 219
The Data Instance 219
XHTML Follows XML's Strict Syntax Rules 220
XHTML Element Types Must Be Properly Nested 220
All HTML-Related Tag Names Must Be Lowercase 221
All XHTML Elements Must Be Closed 221
Attribute Names Must Be Lowercase; Attribute Values Must Be Quoted 223
Attribute Minimization Is Forbidden 223
The name Attribute Has Been Replaced by the id Attribute 224
Start Moving to XHTML Soon! 225
Converting Web Sites to XHTML 225
XHTML Utilities and Services Provided by W3C 226
W3C's HTML Validation Service 226
Amaya, W3C's Editor and Browser 227

Other XHTML Utilities and Services 229
HTML Tidy 229
HTML-Kit 229
Chapter 6 Labs: Creating XHTML Documents 230
Summary 234

Chapter 7 XML and Cascading Style Sheets 239
Overview of Cascading Style Sheets 240
CSS and the World Wide Web Consortium 240
Dave Raggett's Adding a Touch of Style Web Site 241
W3C's CSS Validation Service 241
Coping with CSS Issues 242
Specifying Styles for HTML and XML Documents 242
Inline Style Specifications 242
Internal Style Sheet Specifications 243
Internal Style Sheet Specifications for HTML and XHTML 243
Internal Style Sheet Specifications for Other XML-Related Language Documents 244
Affiliating Documents with External Style Sheets 245
Affiliating HTML and XHTML Documents with External Style Sheets 245
Affiliating Other Types of XML Documents with External Style Sheets 246
CSS and the Parsing Process 247
Creating CSS Style Rules 249
Basic Style Rule Syntax 249
Selectors 249
Declarations 251
Displaying Inline versus Block Elements 251
Selectors with Pseudo-Elements 253
Grouping Selectors by Classes 256
Grouping Selectors by Pseudo-Classes 258
Combining Pseudo-Classes with Other CSS Classes 260
Grouping Selectors by the ID Attribute 263
Inserting Images as Backgrounds 264
Inserting Images as Discrete Elements 266
Drawing Borders around Elements 268
Text Alignment, Margins, and Indentations 269
Absolute and Relative Positioning 269
Example: Absolute Positioning 269
Example: Relative Positioning 271
The Cascading Nature of Cascading Style Sheets 272
Chapter 7 Labs: Applying CSS 273
Summary 278

Chapter 8	**XLinks**	**283**
	XLink: The XML Linking Language	284
	The W3C and XLink	284
	XLink and XPointer Implementations	285
	Basic XLink Concepts	285
	Resources	285
	Link Traversal, Arcs, and Link Direction	286
	XLink Logical Structures	286
	Declare an XLink Namespace	287
	Naming XLink Links	287
	XLink's Global Attributes	287
	A Linking Element Needs a type Attribute	289
	Other Important Attributes: show and actuate	291
	Combining XLink Type Elements and Attributes: Two Restrictions	292
	Example: Simple-Type XLink	294
	Example: Extended-Type XLink	295
	Combining XLink, XPath, and XPointer to Access Subresources	300
	The XML Path Language (XPath)	300
	XPath Expressions, Location Paths, and Location Steps	301
	XPath Expressions and Location Paths	301
	Location Steps	303
	Axes	304
	Node Tests	306
	Predicates	307
	XPath Expressions Can Contain Functions	308
	The XML Pointer Language Extends XPath	311
	Pointers Address a Document's Internal Structure	312
	XPointer Basics: Points, Ranges, and Locations	313
	XPointer Points	313
	Node-points	313
	Character-points	314
	XPointer Ranges	314
	Browser Display of XLink Links and Syntax	315
	Chapter 8 Labs: Using XLink, XPath, and XPointer	316
	Summary	325
Chapter 9	**XML Transformations**	**331**
	Why Transform XML Data?	332
	The W3C and Transformations	333
	The Extensible Stylesheet Language (XSL)	333
	XSL Parsers	334
	The XSL Transformation Language (XSLT)	334
	XML Path Language (XPath)	335

Sample XML Transformation: Tabulating a List of Diamonds 336
The XML Source Document 337
The XSLT Style Sheet 341
Node 5: Begin Transformation Using Query Contexts and First Template Rule 346
Nodes 6 through 12: Creating Elements Using <xsl:element> 348
Node 13: Building an HTML Table with XSLT Element Types 348
Node 14: Processing Continues on the Source <gem> Node 349
Node 15: The Current Template Rule and a Template Rule for <gem> 349
Node 16: Creating the First Row in the HTML Table 349
Node 17: More Template Patterns Fill Out the Table Row 350
Nodes 23 through 25: Filling Out the Individual Name Table Cell 350
Nodes 18 through 22: Filling Out the Other Cells in the Table Row 350
Filling In the Other Rows in the Table 351
Chapter 9 Labs: Using XML Transformation Software 351
Summary 368

Chapter 10 XML Data Binding 373
What Is Data Binding? 374
Performing Data Binding 376
Data Placeholders: Data Consumer Elements 376
The <div> Element 378
The <span> Element 380
The <table> Element 380
Data Source/Data Fields: The datasrc and datafld Attributes 385
Data Nesting and the Two-Level Rule 387
Data Island Storage of XML Data 389
External Data Islands 389
Internal XML Data Islands 391
Data Binding and Table Repetition Agents 392
Data Source Objects (DSOs) 393
Navigating Recordsets 396
Chapter 10 Labs: Data Binding with XML 401
Summary 409

Chapter 11 VML 415
Basic Digital Imaging Technologies 416
Bitmap Graphics 416
Vector Graphics 418
VML Development 419
What Is VML? A Definition 420
Creating VML Documents 421
Logical Structure: A Prolog and an <html> Element 422
Namespace Declarations 422

Behavior Declarations 423
VML Elements in the <body> Element 424
The <shape> Element 425
Creating Graphic Objects Using the path Attribute or <path> Element 426
VML's Predefined Shapes 430
The <shapetype> Element for Frequently Used Custom Figures 435
Figure Placement 435
Altering the Appearance of VML Figures 440
Grouping Shapes Together 444
Scalable Vector Graphics (SVG) 446
Chapter 11 Labs: Creating VML Documents 447
Summary 450

Chapter 12 SMIL 455
What Is Streaming Media? 455
What Is the Synchronized Multimedia Integrated Language? 456
The W3C and SMIL 457
SMIL 1.0 457
SMIL 2.0 458
XHTML+SMIL Profile 459
Viewing and Creating SMIL Documents 459
Creating SMIL Documents 459
The Prolog 460
The SMIL 1.0 DTD 460
The Root Element: <smil> 461
The <head> Element 462
The <layout> Element 462
The <root-layout> Element 463
The <region> Element 465
When Media Object Dimensions Don't Match Region Dimensions 466
The <meta> Element 469
The <switch> Element 469
The <body> Element: Content, Temporal, and Linking Information 470
Synchronizing Media Objects with the <par> and <seq> Elements 470
The SMIL Media Object Elements 472
The <switch> Element 477
SMIL's Hyperlinking Elements 479
Chapter 12 Labs: Getting Started with SMIL 483
Summary 491

Chapter 13 RDF **497**
Web Search and Publication Issues 498
Metadata Is the Key to the Solution 499
The W3C, PICS, and RDF 500
RDF Defined 502
The Semantic Web and Recent RDF Developments 504
RDF Implementations 506
RDF Concepts and Syntax 507
Statements 507
Resources 508
Properties 508
Values 509
RDF Graphs 509
The Logical Structure of an RDF Document 510
The Prolog 510
The <RDF> Root Element, Namespaces, and Content Models 510
Resource Descriptions Are Nested within <Description> Elements 512
Property Elements 513
Abbreviating RDF 515
Substituting Our Own XML Data into Others' Data Content Models 515
Using the resource Attribute 516
Chapter 13 Labs: Creating and Validating RDF 516
Summary 523

Chapter 14 CDF **529**
Basic Communication Concepts 530
Basic Webcasting and Managed Webcasting 531
What Are Channels? 532
The User's Side of CDF: Accessing Channels 534
Investigating Available Channels 534
Adding a Web Site Channel to Your Favorites List 536
Adding a Channel from a Web Site That Does Not Provide a CDF Subscription 536
Adding a Channel from a Web Site That Offers CDF Subscription 539
Channel Synchronization: Setup and Activation 542
Viewing a Channel Offline 543
Development of the CDF Specification 544
CDF Resources 544
Channel Definition Format: A Definition 545
The Publisher's Side of CDF: Creating CDF Channels 546
Designing the Channel 547
Creating Logo Images 549

The Logical Structure of a CDF Document 549
The Prolog 549
The <channel> Element 550
Other CDF Elements 552
Special Characters and Character Encoding 563
Test Your Comprehension with a Sample CDF File 564
Posting the CDF File to the Web Server 564
Providing Access to the Channel 564
Chapter 14 Labs: Getting Started with CDF 567
Basic CDF File for Web Pages 568
Summary 574

Chapter 15 SOAP 579
What Are Web Services? 580
The UDDI : Organization, Project, Specification, and Registry 581
The Web Service Description Language (WSDL) 585
WSDL Development 585
A Real WSDL File at Work: The GetLocalTime Web Service 586
WSDL File Structure 588
A Sample WSDL Document File: GetLocalTime 588
The Prolog 589
The <definitions> Root Data Element 589
The <types> Element 589
The <message> Element 590
The <portType> Element 591
The <binding> Element 592
The <service> and <port> Elements 593
The Last Line 594
The Bottom Line 594
What Is SOAP? 594
Development of the SOAP Specification 595
Basic SOAP Message Construct 597
The SOAP Envelope 598
The SOAP Header 599
The role Attribute 600
The mustUnderstand Attribute 600
The encodingStyle Attribute 601
The SOAP Body 602
SOAP Request Example 602
SOAP Response Example 603
SOAP Faults 603
Values for the <Value> Element within the <Code> Element 604
Example SOAP Fault Message 605
Chapter 15 Labs: Accessing Web Services with SOAP 605
Summary 609

Chapter 16 MathML **615**
Mathematical Expression Issues 616
Early Visual Presentation Solutions 618
The W3C and MathML 619
The W3C Math Working Group 620
MathML Design Goals 620
MathML Implementations 621
What Is MathML? 622
The Logical Structure of a MathML Document 623
The Prolog 623
MathML DTDs or Schemas 623
MathML and Style Sheets 625
MathML Markup Specifications 625
The <math> Element 626
MathML and Namespaces 628
MathML Attributes 629
Bases, Scripts, Characters, and Symbols 629
Presentation Markup 630
Content Markup 633
Prefix Notation 636
Combining Presentation and Content Markup 637
Two Basic Math-Expression Creation Techniques and Concepts 637
Abstract Expression Trees 638
Layout Boxes 638
Chapter 16 Labs: Getting Started with MathML 640
Summary 649

Appendix About the 60 Minutes Web Site **655**

Index **659**

Acknowledgments

We teach several courses in several information technology curricula. This book is dedicated to all those students who, no matter what their level of expertise, spoke out in class or approached us on the side to ask us about basic XML concepts. It is difficult, we know, to find time to become familiar with the basic concepts of a new and unfamiliar technology like XML, especially when our colleagues already seem to be "in the know." We thank them for their courage and dedication, and for pointing us in the right direction regarding topics to present in this book.

There are many others to thank. A big thanks to Donis Marshall of Gearhead Press for providing this opportunity, for providing support and direction, and for being patient beyond measure. Thanks, too, to J.W. (Jerry) Olsen, our project manager, who suffered with us the most, along with two editors he managed, Sydney Jones and Joann Woy. This is a far better product because of their efforts, flexibility, and adaptability. Thanks to Ben Ryan, Kathryn Malm, and Vincent Kunkemueller at Wiley Publishing, Inc., for their support and patience, too.

Finally, thanks to our friends and family. In the future (well, at least until the next project), we promise not to be so preoccupied and to put in more "face time" with them.

About the Authors

Linda McKinnon has a Mass Communications degree and has worked for more than 20 years in computing science and information technology. She has performed increasingly advanced work—design, development, implementation, database management, data control, and system security—on large corporate computer systems across various platforms. At the same time, her duties have also included user administration and assistance, and troubleshooting both mainframe and personal computer systems and networks.

Since 1990, Ms. McKinnon has been president and senior consultant for Skills in Motion Inc. In that capacity, she has been responsible for providing, and occasionally developing, instruction on the installation, configuration, and administration of various platforms, such as AIX, Linux, other Unix flavors, Novell NetWare, and Windows NT/2000, 9x, and XP. She is also an expert at TCP/IP addressing and configuration. More recently, Linda has been responsible for the installation, implementation, and administration of many IBM p-Series (RS/6000) SP2 systems. Because of her background in Java, JavaScript, and XML programming, as well as Web services and other Web development, she also teaches those curricula on IBM's WebSphere Server Application Development systems.

Al McKinnon is an engineer, technical author, and trainer who assists clients throughout North America in the areas of network design, installation, and auditing. He has been a contributing author to national standards and has written manuals, specifications, provincial policies, procedures, regulations, legislation, magazine articles, and editorials.

Al and Linda are headquartered in Calgary, Canada.

Introduction

Welcome to *XML in 60 Minutes a Day*! If you're interested in learning about XML, this is a good place to start. Or if you're interested in building a simple XML-based Web site, you can also start here.

We know there are several XML books available already: textbooks, handbooks, pamphlets—you name it. If you are in a bookstore or library, you are probably surrounded by them. You may even have one or more already at your workstation or office, at home, or in your study carrel. Plus, there are also plenty of Internet sites where you can learn almost everything about XML, from a quick overview to an explanation of the finest syntactic or semantic details.

So, why should you choose this book? In the next few sections, we hope to tell you why, to convince you that this book is a good introductory textbook, a good reference manual, and a good investment in your future. It may even entertain you.

Overview of the Book and Technology

Development of XML and its related standards, specifications, and vocabularies is proceeding at an almost explosive rate, with simultaneous progress on many fronts and with ever-evolving objectives. Those who want or need to learn about XML quickly need answers to questions like these: What is XML? Where did it come from? How do I get started? What do I concentrate on? What can I learn that's useful to me *now*? How long is it going to take to be productive with XML?

We can help to answer those questions. We wrote this book for several reasons:

- It reflects what our colleagues and students have requested for years: an easily read text that introduces and explains what they need to know now to get up to speed with XML in a Windows environment. Meanwhile, the companion Web site, discussed in Appendix A, will help those who work in a Linux environment.
- Although there are many XML books on the market, we wanted to create one that would allow you to be up and running with XML in a proper order and according to an optimal schedule.
- This book contains material comparable to what you would find in a good introductory XML course. The price of this book is pretty attractive compared to what you would pay at any technical institute, college, or university for a comparable XML intro course.
- This book also makes a great companion for almost anyone's introductory XML course. Its definitions, explanations, lab exercises, and review questions supplement material in others' courses. In fact, we take the time to explain some concepts that, because of scheduling or prerequisite assumptions, instructors tend to gloss over or omit.
- If you follow the lab procedures in this book, you can actually build your own XML-oriented Web site, quickly and inexpensively.
- This book will also help you if you are pursuing XML certification. We want to help you get ahead. Our quiz questions are comparable to those you will eventually find on an XML certification test. But please don't look for *everything* you will need to know for an XML certification test. This is, after all, an introductory-level book.
- Finally, the book is written as an invitation to you to get involved with XML development. You may already have knowledge, experience, interest, or even the enthusiasm to help with the XML revolution. Or you may be just around the corner from it. If there is a topic that you find interesting or exciting, it's never too late to volunteer. In almost every chapter, you will see several opportunities to contact those who are continually developing XML standards and vocabularies.

What a challenge it is to be as up-to-date as possible! XML-related standards are constantly being updated. To help you keep pace, we provide Web site references in every chapter so that you can check for the latest developments. When you check the Web sites, you'll see that the changes are overwhelmingly for the better.

How This Book Is Organized

From the outset, we knew that the outline for our book would be part rigid, part flexible. What does that mean? Well, the first five chapters of this book provide the most basic and fundamental XML information and open the door to the topics in the rest of the book. The latter chapters address several related XML standards and languages, and provide you with other real-world XML information and capabilities. As an initial strategy, then, we suggest that you start with Chapter 1 and proceed right through to Chapter 16. That way, you will receive the information in what we consider to be an optimal and cumulative order, and you will be able to construct your version of the example Web site in the proper sequence.

Alternately, if you are not intending to perform the lab exercises and construct a Web site, you might start with Chapter 2 and proceed to the end of Chapter 5 to get the basics. Then, you could examine the other chapters as you need to or your curiosity guides you. In that case, you can also go to the book's site at www.wiley.com/compbooks/60minutesaday and download various source or solution files to examine their content and structure, or go to the Space Gems, Inc. Web site and examine the source code of the documents you find there.

You probably want to know what's in our book. Like many introductory courses and textbooks, this one begins with a discussion of the technology it will introduce; that is, it explains the origins of XML and shows you where it fits into the information technology world and into the development of the World Wide Web.

In Chapter 1, we go right back to basics. We explain basic document and markup concepts. After that, we define XML as a markup language and a metalanguage. That is followed by a brief history of XML and its ancestor technologies. The World Wide Web Consortium (the W3C) is essential to XML development, so we discuss that organization, its principles, and its objectives, too.

Chapter 2 explains how to create an XML working environment, since we are anxious to get up and running quickly, so that we can begin creating our sample Web site. It starts by specifying hardware requirements and then discusses Web server, Web browser, and XML authoring applications. The lab exercises provide step-by-step instructions for installing, configuring, and using the applications we will use for the remainder of the book.

In Chapter 3, we begin to discuss XML documents and their processing. We talk about XML-related applications, XML processors (also called parsers), and XML errors. Then we discuss the physical and logical structure of a generic XML document. Chapter 3 continues with an introduction to the basic components of an XML document: element types, attributes, namespace declarations, and entities. It concludes with definitions of two important concepts: the well-formedness and validity of XML documents.

Chapters 4 and 5 discuss two methods for defining (the official XML term is *declaring*) the components of XML-related documents for purposes of document validation: the use of the more traditional document type definitions (DTDs) and the newer-technology XML schemas. A knowledge of DTDs and schemas is essential if you will eventually be creating your own specific XML vocabularies.

In Chapter 6, we introduce the largest of the XML-derived languages developed so far, XHTML. XHTML resembles HTML Version 4 and is expected to replace HTML eventually. We discuss the conversion of existing HTML documents to XHTML and the creation of XHTML documents from scratch. We also list some free utilities that facilitate those activities.

We introduce the Cascading Style Sheet language (CSS) in Chapter 7. Not only do cascading style sheets allow designers to control data semantics and structure they facilitate the transformation of XML data into an appealing presentation as well.

Chapter 8 shows you how to create XML-related hyperlinks and even how to integrate them with your existing Web page projects. We discuss three XML-related standards that provide linking capability: the XML Linking language (XLink), the XML Path language (XPath), and the XML Pointer language (XPointer). Together, they overcome the inadequacies in classic HTML linking.

In Chapter 9, we discuss another method for transforming XML documents, using the Extensible Stylesheet Language (XSL) family of XML-related standards. But unlike the display-oriented style sheets discussed in Chapter 7, the Chapter 9 style sheets prepare XML data for further processing.

Chapter 10 presents XML as both data sources and as data retrieval documents. We discuss basic XML-related data binding concepts and the agent applications that synchronize and retrieve data in an XML environment.

Chapters 11 and 12 are a little more fun than the transformation and data binding chapters. Chapter 11 introduces the Vector Markup Language (VML), the prevailing XML-related graphics language. Chapter 12 introduces SMIL (the Synchronized Multimedia Integration Language), which is used for adding multimedia to Web page documents.

In Chapter 13, we discuss the Resource Description Framework language (RDF), which allows us to include appropriate meta data in our Web page documents to describe the information in those documents clearly and accurately. RDF will eventually make our systems seem "smarter," since it will make our Web searches faster and provide the information we really want.

Chapter 14 explains the Channel Definition Format language, which allows Web users and publishers to obtain or provide, respectively, regularly updated Web site information. We bet you've already used CDF without knowing its name or how valuable it can be.

Chapter 15 introduces the Simple Object Access Protocol (SOAP), which has become the most popular protocol for exchanging messages with and otherwise accessing Web services. In this chapter, we discuss Web services in general, the Universal Description, Discovery, and Integration service in particular, and the construction and use of SOAP messages.

Chapter 16 takes us back almost to the roots of XML. The Mathematical Markup Language (MathML) has been developed to help us share mathematical and scientific expressions across the Web. MathML allows us to not only display the various numbers and symbols in our equations, but also to transmit their actual meaning.

The Appendix contains information about what you can expect to find on the three *XML in 60 Minutes a Day* companion Web sites. One will provide instructional audio and video presentations. The second will provide downloadable resource and solution files to help you complete the lab exercises found in this book.

The third companion Web site is the Web site that belongs to the fictitious Space Gems, Inc. company. When we began this book, we thought it would be instructive and fun to help you the reader create your own real, operating Web site. So we created an imaginary gemstone exploration and marketing company called Space Gems, Inc. When you perform the lab exercises, you can perform tasks that the Space Gems Web site designer and administrator would perform.

Who Should Read This Book

We wrote our book for several audiences, including:

- The experienced HTML Web site designer, developer, or Web site administrator who faces a transition from HTML to XML
- The manager who faces updating or upgrading an Internet service
- The student who faces an introductory XML course or who has been fast-tracked into an intermediate-level course and isn't quite sure about having the prerequisite knowledge and experience to keep up with the instructor or other students
- The work-at-home or small business professional whose firm never seems to have enough funds for training, yet who needs to stay current with Web technology

You don't need a lot of experience to understand and use this book. It is geared toward the XML newcomer. Granted, it might be beneficial if you already have a background in HTML or Web site publishing or administration, but that's not necessary. (An old "discount bin" HTML manual is usually sufficient.)

Occasionally, we mention some advanced concepts, but we don't dwell on them. We mention them mostly to stimulate your curiosity.

Tools You Will Need

In Chapter 2, "Setting Up Your XML Working Environment," and in the Appendix, we describe the hardware you will need to perform the lab exercises and to access and use the three companion Web sites to *XML in 60 Minutes a Day*. Thereafter, we suggest you install Windows XP Professional or Windows 2000 Professional as a base operating system, with Internet Explorer as your base Web browser application. In Chapter 2, we describe all the applications you will need to perform your lab exercises. If additional or different applications are required for later exercises, we tell you where the applications are located and how to install them. We have tried to find online sources that are free or that provide trial periods that are long enough for you to complete the relevant exercises.

As we mentioned in the earlier *Overview of the Book and Technology* section, copies of our lab exercises that are oriented to the Linux operating system are available at www.wiley.com/compbooks/60minutesaday. Although we used the Red Hat distribution of Linux to create the exercises, any version of Linux will suffice to perform them.

Please be aware that some of the Linux XML labs still require you to use Internet Explorer to test the procedures. On those occasions, you will need both a Windows system and a Linux system. To help you share files between the two systems, we have provided additional technical solutions at our (the authors') Web site at www.skillsinmotion.com.

Summary

We hope you'll enjoy this introduction to XML. Once you've worked your way through the book, you'll have enough background to begin creating many XML documents and to contribute to almost any HTML or XML-related Web site. Plus, you will have enough basic knowledge to tackle an intermediate-level XML course or text.

Besides being a good introductory course, this book also is a good reference manual and a good investment in your future. Good luck! And thanks for selecting our book!

XML Backgrounder

The past five or six years have witnessed an explosive growth of Extensible Markup Language (XML) as more individuals and organizations link their computer systems together to exchange data and create usable information, and as more vendors convert their electronic commerce Web sites to provide goods and services. XML has matured quickly and now is capable of providing a standard for the structure, transmission, and interchange of data, whether that data travels within the same computer system, through a local network, or clear across the globe, and whether the applications and operating systems processing the data are identical or different. All of the major software companies—most notably the Web browser developers such as Microsoft, Netscape, Mozilla, Konqueror, and Opera—are enthusiastic about XML. Promoting the use of XML standards is the next step in the evolution of the World Wide Web.

This book introduces you to XML and shows you why XML is becoming so popular. It also introduces you to several XML-related languages and standards as we teach you to develop a simple e-commerce Web site. You will build this Web site yourself over the course of several laboratory exercises.

In this first chapter, we provide an overview of some basic document processing concepts and then discuss the context of XML's development and the development of its predecessors. We'll define and discuss markup, markup languages, and metalanguages, too. We'll then discuss the need for standards, the role of XML as a standard, and the role of the World Wide Web Consortium (W3C) in the development of the World Wide Web, XML, and other Web-related technologies.

By the end of this chapter, you should be familiar with basic markup concepts and be able to participate in any general conversation about XML as a metalanguage and a markup language.

Why Do We Need a History Lesson Chapter?

We swear that the exchange in the accompanying Classroom Q & A actually took place just before we began this book. The question is verbatim, but we've paraphrased our answer a little.

Classroom Q & A

Q: I was in the bookstore yesterday and I was looking at some XML books. Why do so many XML books begin with some sort of history lesson? Why should we care about XML's history? Why not just get at it?

A: It's true that this first chapter is a combination of concepts and history, but there are several reasons for chapters like this:

- XML's development process is meaningful to your understanding of its concepts and its open, independence-oriented culture.
- The XML story is interesting and even heroic. The fact that you're reading this means you are about to become a character in the story, too. And many of its heroes are among us—some of them you can actually contact with just a few mouse clicks and keystrokes. They're fighting the good fight, and they'd be happy to have you assist them.
- XML didn't just happen yesterday, and it didn't happen all at once. It's not just another flavor of the month. It has evolved from its predecessors over the past 40 years or more, and it's expanding and evolving constantly.
- We'll show you how XML draws from its heritage, how it constantly evolves to cope with ever-growing needs, and how it pays dividends for the worlds of communication and commerce.

Meanwhile, to illustrate the evolving nature of XML, from the time we began drafting this book until the time we finished it, we had to revise several chapters to keep the information current. By the time you read this book, no doubt even more changes will have occurred. That's why we provide Web site and other references so that you can get the latest XML information and updates.

Several chapters introduce XML-derived and -related markup languages. Because each language came along at a different time and because each has a rather unique heritage and evolution, there will be a brief historical summary in each of those chapters, too.

Let's start our background and history chapter with a discussion of some basic concepts that will appear several times throughout this book.

Basics: From Documents to Markup and Metalanguages

This section examines some basic concepts and then uses those concepts to build a definition of XML.

What's a Document?

Outside the IT world, we encounter all sorts of hard-copy documents: letters, forms, books, newspapers, magazines, invoices, maps, birthday cards, leaflets, posters, sticky notes, and many others. The concept of the hard-copy document evolved almost without notice. When we encounter new types of hard-copy documents in our homes, offices, classrooms, libraries, stationery stores, or local newsstands, we seem to accept them unconsciously. Meanwhile, within the IT world, the concept of the electronic document has evolved, too.

Let's start with a more basic definition first: the definition of text. Text is generally considered to consist of words, sentences, lines, paragraphs, and even pages. Typically, the term *text* also refers to electronic text stored as only simple character codes (for example, American Standard Code for Information Interchange, or ASCII, codes)—that is, without any formatting.

At one time, the electronic document was only considered to be a text file created with applications called text editors or word processors. You could almost use the terms text and document interchangeably. However, as developments occurred on many IT fronts, the concept of the electronic document expanded to contain tables, graphics, charts, and other objects, in a manner that parallels the evolution of hard-copy documents. Now, in the IT world, documents are considered to be electronic files of any size for any media (for example, text, audio, video, and graphics), created by any application. So now, the definition of text is a subset of the definition of the document.

In their Extensible Markup Language 1.0 Recommendation, which is recognized as the official XML standard, the W3C defines an *XML document* as a "data object if it is well-formed, as defined in (Extensible Markup Language Recommendation). . . . Each XML document has both a logical and a physical structure." (We discuss the W3C in more detail in *The World Wide Web Consortium and XML* section later in this chapter.)

That definition might appear obscure at this point, but don't worry. We discuss and expand on that definition in Chapter 3, "Anatomy of an XML Document," when we discuss XML documents in more detail. Actually, we discuss some form of XML-related document or another in almost every chapter, but Chapter 3 provides the most essential and basic discussion of document components and structure.

Related to the discussion of documents is the term *document processing*, which is the discipline that deals with creating applications that allow you to deal with documents of all types. Document processing is split into creating or manipulating those documents destined for human viewing and consumption (people-oriented processing), as well as those that are destined for computer consumption (machine-oriented processing). Documents of the former type were comparatively long-lived (examples: specifications, drawings, procedures, charts, and memos). Documents of the latter type tend to have shorter lives because their data may be manipulated, transformed, or combined on the fly to create or add to different documents.

As you'll see, XML descends from a rich document-processing heritage.

What Is Markup?

The concept of markup is important. After all, it's the M in XML. But what does it mean? Basically, it's a way to add information about data to the data itself.

You may not have had much experience with other markup languages, but you have probably used markup in one form or another. For example, have you ever:

- Underlined or highlighted words or passages on a hard-copy document to indicate important information?
- Marked up a draft hard copy of a document with symbols indicating "new paragraph here," "bold this," or "remove this"?
- Made marks on a map indicating where you want to turn, or where specific features are located?
- Numbered bits of information, such as steps, in an otherwise unnumbered procedure?

Those and similar activities involve marking up data. All the symbols, notes, numbers, designated actions, or highlights—all of which qualify as some sort of markup—emphasize or convey something about the data: what it means or what you are supposed to do with it.

A significant paper titled "Markup Systems and the Future of Scholarly Text Processing," by James H. Coombs and Allen H. Renear of Brown University and Steven J. DeRose of Electronic Book Technologies, describes six types of markup:

- Punctuational, which consists of the use of defined marks (examples: spaces, periods, and commas) to provide primarily syntactic information about written utterances. Punctuation has been around so long that we take it for granted.
- Presentational, which we use to group our materials for order and clarity. Examples include horizontal and vertical spacing, page breaks, numbering, chapter and section breaks, justification, and lists.
- Procedural, which is a characteristic of whatever system will be used to create presentations. Often grouped with what we call file formats, it tells someone or something (such as a formatter with a set of installed drivers) about the size and format of a document (examples: letter, legal, and portrait and landscape views), fonts, and other production information.
- Descriptive, which allows authors to identify certain elements of their data as belonging to a specific family of text. The common word-processing tag BT (for basal text) is an example: When a text formatter encounters that code, it consults, and then follows, a predefined set of rules that tell it what to do to display or print the characters associated with that code. If changes become necessary, you only need to change the rules, not each BT tag in the document.
- Referential, which refers to separate physical or electronic entities (that is, located external to the document being processed) that will be imported and placed in the proper sequence during document processing. In Chapter 3 and elsewhere in this book, you will see how to incorporate audio, video, and other files into XML documents by using this type of markup.
- Metamarkup, which provides the ability to control the definition and interpretation of markup tags, and to extend the vocabulary of derivative markup languages. Metadata, the concept of information about information, is related to this concept.

If you would like to read the Coombs, Renear, and DeRose paper that the preceding definitions were taken from, you can find it online at www.oasis-open.org/cover/coombs.html#Figure1.

Markup, in summary, is the inserting of characters or symbols into a document to indicate the document's physical and logical structure, to indicate how the information in a document should appear, or to provide some other form of instruction. The primary goal of markup is to separate the treatment (for example, the appearance or structure) of a document from the actual data in the document.

XML Is a Markup Language and a Metalanguage

There are over two dozen categories of computer languages; you are probably familiar with some of them already. For example, machine languages consist entirely of numbers and are only understood by computers; assembly languages are symbolic representations of the machine language of a specific computer; programming languages such as COBOL, C++, Java, and Fortran instruct computers to do specific tasks; and fourth-generation languages, whose syntax is closer to human languages.

Some language categories are separate and discrete, dedicated to specific functions; some languages are subsets of others; and some are hybrids of other languages.

For a more comprehensive listing of computer languages and their respective definitions, consult the The Language List Web site, maintained by Bill Kinnersley of the Computer Science Department, University of Kansas, at http://cui.unige.ch/OSG/info/Langlist/intro.html.

XML doesn't fall into any of the categories previously listed, but it falls into two other categories: It's a markup language *and* a metalanguage.

Markup Languages

Extrapolating the definition of markup, markup languages are those that allow us to create documents consisting of plaintext data and other entities, plus markup codes that define the logical components and structure, as well as describe the appearance or other aspects of the data. The markup codes, called *tags*, are located adjacent to their respective data. In addition, the data and tags are usually composed of common text characters, so they can remain independent of platform and operating system.

Why use markup languages? These days, with the proliferation of computer networks across the world, with their myriad of applications, operating systems, and proprietary network devices, the data transmitted over the wire, through the air, and through space must include all the information necessary for automated systems (such as computers, routers, firewalls, and hubs) to transmit, receive, and otherwise deal with the data. The receiver needs the markup tags to interpret the message: the format and content of database data, multimedia graphic files or audio files, debit card transactions, credit card authorizations, or any other various document types.

Metalanguages

In the *What Is Markup?* section, we provided a listing of markup types. One of the types was called metamarkup, which provides the capability to control the definition and interpretation of markup tags, and to extend the vocabulary of derivative markup languages. That is consistent with the definition found at Mr. Kinnersley's Web site, where he defines a metalanguage as a "language used for formal description of another language." It is also consistent with other definitions of metalanguages, which describe them as languages that provide for conformance-proving mechanisms.

XML permits developers to create their own specialized derivative languages, but all of those languages have one thing in common: They meet XML specifications. If languages and documents contravene the XML specifications, the XML processors in their respective applications may or may not process them. Even if they do, they will likely generate error messages.

The Evolution of XML

Until the late 1960s, it was accepted practice that electronic manuscript files would contain macros or control codes (referred to as *specific coding*) to prescribe how the manuscript documents should be rendered. Plus, the format of the document files, and the applications that manipulated them, were often proprietary to the publishers.

Also, document processing applications were of a black-box nature. Users couldn't get at all the coding to examine and possibly modify it; therefore, document coding was not open source. It was also nonstandard: Tags and other coding from one application were not identical or interchangeable with those from another application. Documents created with one application were usually not compatible with other applications.

The Advent of Generic Coding

There are several good historical summaries of the state of document processing prior to the development of generic coding, upon which XML and its predecessors are based. This section paraphrases from several sources, especially, from those found at Charles F. Goldfarb's SGML Source home page at www.sgmlsource.com, in his SGML History Niche at www.sgmlsource.com/history/. (SGML stands for Standard Generalized Markup Language; we look at SGML more closely later in this chapter.) Documents there are recommended reading.

We have already mentioned the proprietary nature of early document processing technologies. A number of movements began in the late 1960s that would lead to a substantial change from that philosophy, including the following:

- New York book designer Stanley Rice advocated the development and adoption of standard style macros based on the structural elements of publications (examples: parts and chapters).
- William Tunnicliffe of the Graphic Communication Association (GCA; now known as the International Digital Enterprise Alliance) advocated "the separation of information content of documents from their format." This was the concept of generic coding at its embryonic stage.
- In 1969, IBM began research on an integrated processing project: the application of computers to the legal profession. The project involved the integration of a text editing application with a database information retrieval system and a document composition application.

There was intellectual cross-pollination among the initiatives, which bore fruit for the GCA, IBM, and, eventually, for all of us.

For further information on IDEAlliance (formerly the GCA), consult www.idealliance.org/.

GML Led the Way

As the IBM team worked on their integrated document project, they recognized that their eventual product language would have to reflect three features:

- Markup in general would have to be the common language (the developers refer to it as the *lingua franca*) for data description, structure, and communication, and it would have to be readable and writable by all relevant computer applications.
- The markup would have to be extensible, not related to just one industry, because an infinite variety of information types might eventually be created. In other words, they saw that their technology might and should be applied to all professions.
- The documents common to the information in each different area would need some sort of description mechanism or rules, against which the documents could be checked for conformity—that is, proofed.

The IBM team called the first version of the product they developed in 1969 the *Text Description Language*. Development continued and its name was changed in 1971 to the Generalized Markup Language. The name was chosen deliberately, so that its acronym, GML, could serve as a reminder of the GML's original creators: Charles **G**oldfarb, Ed **M**osher, and Ray **L**orie.

With GML, IBM removed specific formatting instructions from the content of the document itself. GML's markup was based only on the identification of the different types of structural components in a document. With GML, an author could assign descriptive tag names to the sections of data. After the various sections were thus identified, any application could be written to manipulate the data as long as it contained the appropriate tag references.

GML was first released under its own name as part of Advanced Text Management System in 1973. It became an integral part of several IBM publishing systems, most notably IBM Script.

Table 1.1 lists some basic GML codes.

The following is a sample of GML markup:

```
:h2.Definitions:
:ol.
     li.1. noun, a gem variety of corundum in transparent or translucent
          crystals of a color other than red; especially, a transparent
          rich blue
     :li.2. noun, a gem of such corundum
     :li.3. noun, a deep purplish blue color
     :li.4. adjective, made of or resembling a sapphire gem
     :li.5. adjective, having the color of a blue sapphire
:eol.
```

Table 1.1 GML Tag Examples

TAG	EXPLANATION
:title	Document title
:h0-:h6	Zero level through sixth-level titles
:ul / :eul	Begin and end unordered lists
:ol / :eol	Begin and end ordered lists
:li	Item that appears following a "begin list" tag
:hp1 / :hp2 / :hp3	Start highlight level 1, 2, or 3 (where 1=underscore, 2=bold, and 3=both)
:ehp1 / :ehp2 / :hp3	End highlight level 1, 2, or 3
:lq / :elq	Begin and end a long quote (also called a block quote)

Let's examine the sample coding. Notice that a GML tag begins at the left margin (that's why they're called flush left) and that the tag name is preceded by a colon. The colon is the GML *delimiter*, which instructs the application (presumably a text formatter) to begin processing a tag. Immediately following the delimiter is the descriptive tag h2, which indicates that the content, when encountered, is to be formatted according to the predefined rules for a second-level title. The tag is followed by a *content separator* (the period), which tells the processor to stop processing the tag and to, instead, process the text data that follows according to the h2 rules. Finally, the data (that is, the word Definitions followed by a colon) appears.

GML's descriptive generic coding makes a document more portable because the content can be printed or displayed in different ways according to an application's interpretation of the tag without making any changes to the original document file. Plus, the author doesn't have to supply the formatting details. So, using one application, the h2-tagged definitions might be printed in a Times font at 30-point size, while the list items (that is, the content on the :li lines) might be printed in Times at 12 points. With another application, definitions might appear on-screen in a bolded sans serif font at 24 points, while the list items appear in sans serif at 10 points.

GML development didn't stop with its release in 1973. As the SGML history documents indicate, Mr. Goldfarb "continued research on document structures . . . short references, link processes, and concurrent document types . . . . By far the most important was the concept of a validating parser that could read a document type definition and check the accuracy of markup without actually processing a document."

Document type definitions, which would fulfill the third required feature of the three listed earlier in this section, had been in development since the beginning of the work on GML.

In 1975 to 1978, IBM introduced their Document Composition Facility (DCF), based on the IBM Script product of the 1960s but with upgrades like GML support. With DCF, GML left the essentially research-only domain and became commercially available.

Other Typesetting Developments

As we stated previously, until the late 1960s computer text processing applications were proprietary in nature. GML's creators showed the document processing world that there was merit in creating a portable, machine-independent system of encoding.

The development of generic coding and other document processing technologies, however, did not cease with the appearance of GML. The GCA had initiated their System X project, which would later be called GenCode. Work on that project would continue through the 1970s.

Other automated typesetting technologies prevalent or being developed simultaneously with (and even later than) GML and System X/GenCode, but in different areas, include the following:

Mainframe publishing applications. Expensive, esoteric, and requiring mainframe systems, these were still fairly powerful; however, most dealt with data display and did not reflect the direction shown by GML.

Desktop publishing (DTP) applications (also called formatting markup applications). As personal computers became more powerful and less expensive, desktop publishing applications appeared more frequently. They are used for producing newsletters, books, and other documents that used to require professional typesetters.

DTP applications are advantageous for large, detailed reports. Often, they're freely available, powerful, and used throughout the world (an example is the TeX family of DTP applications: TeX, LaTex, MikTeX, and others). They're often platform-independent and have powerful facilities for mathematical and scientific equations and other expressions (better than word processing applications, which we discuss in the next bullet point), as well as section and chapter numbering. But they are primarily display-oriented rather than data-oriented. Plus, there is no instant feedback or instant modification. In fact, additional applications are required to translate a DTP rendition file to a presentation format that is human-readable, including Device Independent (DVI), PostScript (PS), Portable Document Format (PDF), and HyperText Markup Language (HTML). After that, a specific viewer application (for example, a DVI viewer) must be activated to view the final results. Only after the document file is displayed can you finally print it.

Word processor applications. From a user interface perspective, word processor applications are an improvement over desktop publishing applications. These applications create renditions, but they provide a nicer user interface to create and manipulate them. The interface is designed to look similar to the presentation: the finished paper product or screen layout. That's why using these applications is called What You See Is What You Get (WYSIWYG, pronounced "wizzywig") publishing. WYSIWYGs are becoming more sophisticated and more like desktop publishing applications.

But WYSIWYG applications have their drawbacks, too: They still don't have all the sophistication of desktop publishing applications, especially when it comes to rendering mathematical or scientific expressions. Also, with most, their features are generally inserted into the document file with nonstandard markup codes. Plus, the codes are only visible to the application during processing, but not to the user during document creation or editing. Thus, with most WYSIWYGs (there are exceptions), all you see in the user interface (that is, on-screen) is the effect of the codes that the applications have inserted, not the codes themselves. However, some WYSIWYGs allow you to save a document in HTML format, allowing those applications to compete with Web page design applications. So the codes have become somewhat more standard and, after a fashion, visible, but again, these applications emphasize data display rather than data semantics, and not all of them are platform-independent.

Simple text editors (also called plaintext applications). Simple text editors are scaled-down (compared to WYSIWYG) applications for creating plaintext documents. That is, they create documents consisting of ordinary text. After that, most do not allow you to apply even the simplest typesetting features, including page breaks. But the applications are small, use few resources, and come already installed on almost every operating system.

SGML: Parent of HTML and XML

With all these developments in their respective arenas, two facts became apparent:

- For markup languages to be truly portable and useful to the myriad of eventual users in several environments on many networks around the world, a standard would have to be developed to list all acceptable and valid markup tags.
- Any eventual standard must clearly define the meaning and syntax of the markup tags.

Further, any information intended for public use could not be proprietary. That is, it couldn't be restricted to one technology and certainly not to one make, model, or manufacturer of such a technology.

In addition, public-oriented information should be in a form that could be reused in many different ways to optimize time and effort. Proprietary data formats, no matter how well documented or publicized, would be unacceptable.

To meet the challenge, the American National Standards Institute (ANSI), in 1978, established the Computer Languages for the Processing of Text committee, which began work on a standard text description language. That language was to be based on GML. The GenCode committee of the GCA provided several people (including the aforementioned Mr. Tunnicliffe; he would come to play a vital role) dedicated to the task of developing the SGML standard. Mr. Goldfarb, one of the three original GML creators, also participated.

The committee published its first working draft of the Standard Generalized Markup Language standard in 1980. After several drafts, the United States Internal Revenue Service and the United States Department of Defense adopted SGML. Many national and international organizations, notably other defense organizations in North America and elsewhere, subsequently adopted SGML, too.

By 1984, the SGML project had also been authorized by the International Organization for Standardization (ISO), which established its own SGML development team; however, alignment between the ANSI and ISO teams was maintained by Mr. Goldfarb, who served as project editor for both.

In 1986, the Standard Generalized Markup Language (ISO 8879:1986)—an international standard describing markup for the structure and content of different types of electronic, machine-readable documents—was approved.

SGML was not designed as a document encoder on its own. Its power comes from its use as a standard by which other, more specific languages, tailored to the specific requirements of any organization or industry, can be developed. SGML became the overarching standard metalanguage and would be used to facilitate the creation of many derivative markup languages—most notably, HTML and XML.

The derivative languages and their respective documents may then be processed, without changes or losses, for varying purposes and in different forms by any appropriately written program that can process SGML. The documents might be transmitted or displayed on a PC, on laptop or handheld computers, in print, or via projection without fear of information being lost or misinterpreted.

SGML-related languages separate the three aspects of a typical document (the data structure, content, and style) and deal mainly with the relationship between structure and content. To that end, the concept of a separate but related document called the document type definition (or DTD, the subject of Chapter 4, "Document Type Definitions"), which had been born with GML, was formalized with SGML.

SGML thus became an extremely powerful and extensible tool, and it led to the cataloging and indexing of data in many important and complex industries (examples: defense, as mentioned, plus medical, financial, aerospace, telecommunications, and entertainment). Table 1.2 lists several SGML-based languages.

Table 1.2 Examples of SGML-Based Languages

LANGUAGE	DESCRIPTION
HyperText Markup Language (HTML)	Perhaps the most famous; used to create hypertext documents. In use over the World Wide Web since 1990.
Extensible Markup Language (XML)	Used to create other industry-specific or organization-specific languages; the scaled-down, Internet-oriented version of SGML.
Continuous Acquisition and Lifecycle Support (CALS)	Formerly called Computer-aided Acquisition and Logistics Support. More recently called Commerce at Light Speed. Used for documenting complex military equipment.
Text Encoding Initiative (TEI)	An international standard that allows libraries, museums, publishers, scholars, and others to represent texts for online research and teaching.
The Standard Music Description Language (SMDL)	Used to define timing and user-defined functions for pitches, chords, and instrumental and vocal sounds.
News Industry Text Format (NITF)	For describing information for the News Distribution Industry.

A longer list of SGML-related languages can be found at the Oasis Cover Pages Web site at http://xml.coverpages.org/gen-apps.html.

The following is an example of SGML markup. Notice that start tags and end tags (terms enclosed in angle brackets and located before the beginning and after the end of the data, respectively) are used to identify elements (contrast that to GML's *left-flush* tags). Everything from the start tag <sect_title> to the end tag </sect_title>, including those tags, is part of the <sect_title> element.

```
<section>
    <sect_title><No. 29 - Sapphire</sect_title>
    <pronunciation>Pronounced: &apos;sa-&quot;fIr</pronunciation>
    <origin>Origin: Middle English <src_wd>safir</src_wd>, from Old
       French via Latin <src_wd>sapphirus</src_wd>, via the Greek
       <src_wd>sappheiros</src_wd>; may be of Semitic origin;
       similar to Hebrew <src_wd>sappIr</src_wd>; dates back
       to the 13th century AD
    </origin>
    <definitions>
       <subhead1>Definitions</subhead1>
```

```
        <defn_list>
          <defn>1. noun, a gem variety of corundum in transparent or
                   translucent crystals of a color other than
                   red; especially, a transparent rich blue
          <defn>2. noun, a gem of such corundum
          <defn>3. noun, a deep purplish blue color
          <defn>4. adjective, made of or resembling a sapphire gem
          <defn>5. adjective, having the color of a blue sapphire
        </defn_list>
     </definitions>
</section>
```

Full SGML systems are applied to large, complex document situations (it's no wonder they're used for the aerospace industry and military installations) that can make use of the full standard, that likely won't require frequent Web access, and that can otherwise justify the expense of installing, configuring, and maintaining the systems needed to process SGML-related documents.

Despite its advantages, however, there are also some disadvantages to SGML. It's a big and complex standard, and its page count numbers in the hundreds. Fully SGML-compliant languages are generally big and resource-intensive and are usually too cumbersome for Web browser-related functions. Web browser manufacturers have stated that their products do not and will not fully comply with SGML. Further, adding SGML capability to a word processor application, to save documents to SGML specifications, doubles or triples the application's price.

HTML: The Older Sibling of XML

The HyperText Markup Language (HTML) was developed at the Conseil Européen pour la Recherche Nucléaire (CERN, the European Organization for Nuclear Research), which was the original home of the World Wide Web, in the early 1990s. HTML's original purpose was to provide a platform-independent mechanism to hyperlink-related documents, whether those documents were on the same local area network or situated across the world. The Internet was already a mature technology, supported by government, academic institutions, and large corporations, and HTML could help them by providing a universal means to link and display basic business-style documents.

The HTML standard was first defined under the Internet Engineering Task Force (IETF) Network Working Group's Request for Comments (RFC) No. 1866, in November 1995. It was authored by Tim Berners-Lee of CERN. (He would later move to the Laboratory for Computer Science at the Massachusetts Institute of Technology. Mr. Berners-Lee was also the inventor and architect of the World Wide Web.) As the Network Working Group approved RFC 1866, the then newly formed World Wide Web Consortium also adopted it as their HTML 2.0 Recommendation.

HTML was developed as a derivative language of SGML. Any fully conformant SGML applications can read HTML documents. Commonly, however, HTML source code is interpreted and displayed by a Web browser application. We define Web browsers more fully in Chapter 2, "Setting Up Your XML Working Environment," but basically they are HTML processing applications that conform to HTML standard display rules but are not robust enough to be fully SGML-compliant. That doesn't matter, though, because HTML is a much simplified version of SGML with a fixed and limited set of predefined markup components. HTML contains basic tags and attributes for headings, paragraphs, lists, illustrations, hyperlinks, some multimedia, and some other features.

Because it was free, simple, and widely supported, HTML quickly became popular. It sparked a Web publishing phenomenon because it allowed ordinary people to create a Web presence. The vast majority of Web pages are now written in HTML.

One major complaint about HTML is that most Web page designers are concerned only with how their documents look. This overwhelming concern for display quality seemed to slow the progress toward extensibility, especially with respect to data semantics.

Equally annoying was the limited and strictly predefined set of HTML components such as its elements and attributes, which resulted in something of a limited and restricted—that is, nonarbitrary from a developer's standpoint—set of document structure options. The same set of markups must be used in all HTML documents, and their meanings cannot be altered. For example, the <ul> tag always specifies that an HTML application has to display an unnumbered list, but the tag doesn't allow you to describe the items being listed. Similarly, the <li> tag instructs the HTML processing application to treat the subsequent content as an item in the list. Again, no hint is given as to what the item might actually be. Developers in various fields have to manipulate their data to fit it into HTML document models. Often there is no fit, or the fit is extremely difficult and clumsy.

The W3C has made attempts to incorporate some extensibility into HTML in recent years. Revised versions of HTML have been released periodically since 1994, but the inconsistent implementation of the new features from Web browser to Web browser has disappointed many designers. They're unsure at times whether their extensible HTML coding will be supported. Meanwhile, individual browser manufacturers, most notably Microsoft, have supplemented HTML through proprietary extensions to their browsers. Although important for execution and admittedly extensible and flexible, the supplemental code tends to violate the open source aspects that most developers regard so highly in SGML-related languages.

The Arrival of XML

Most World Wide Web-related developers, especially those concerned with the semantics and structure of data, knew that the fundamental components of HTML—its tagging, simple hypertext linking, and hard-coded presentation—would not scale up to meet future needs. They felt that nothing except an SGML-based solution would work in the long run.

In 1996, the World Wide Web Consortium sponsored a team of SGML experts whose goal was to develop a markup language with the power and extensibility of SGML, but with the simplicity of HTML. These SGML experts did not want to see the Web of the future as being prone to multiple confusing data standards, to standards controlled by a single vendor or nation, or to proprietary tools, utilities, and applications.

The work progressed quickly. The team was able to draw from the work of its sponsors—the W3C, the United States Defense Advanced Research Projects Agency (DARPA), and the European Union—and the work of other developers who were seeking to solve similar problems. They removed the nonessential, unused, cryptic parts of SGML to leave a smaller, more easily and simply implemented, Web-friendly markup and metalanguage, which they named the Extensible Markup Language (XML).

The Extensible Markup Language 1.0 specification, which we call XML 1.0 throughout this book, was endorsed by the W3C as a Recommendation (their version of an international standard) on February 10, 1998. The XML specification is only a couple of dozen pages long, compared to the much longer ISO SGML standard at a couple of hundred pages. Here is the definition of XML that appears in the Recommendation: "The Extensible Markup Language (XML) is a subset of [the Standard Generalized Markup Language. . .whose] goal is to enable generic SGML to be served, received, and processed on the Web in the way that is now possible with HTML. XML has been designed for ease of implementation and for interoperability with both SGML and HTML."

Development of XML continues. XML 1.0 (Second Edition) was accepted as a W3C Recommendation on October 6, 2000.

For further information regarding the nature of XML development activity, look at the W3C Web site at www.w3.org, or turn to the discussion of the W3C near the end of this chapter.

Many industries, such as academia, insurance, and aerospace, and even individual organizations, are writing XML-based languages and standards that everyone in their specific community can use, so that sharing their high volumes of data over the Internet becomes easier and faster.

XML was designed, like HTML, to be a derivative language of SGML (that is, to be an *SGML application*) for use on the World Wide Web or on intranets. XML can provide the same functionality as SGML for print, hypertext, and content management, but it is simpler and easier to develop with, and it works in conjunction with a number of related XML core standards, some of which we'll discuss later in this book.

Its SGML heritage gives XML several advantages:

- Similar to SGML, XML is categorized as both a markup specification language and a metalanguage.
- As a metalanguage, it acts as a standard by which developers can create specific customized subset languages (complete with their own unique sets of tags, attributes, and entities that describe the structure and semantics of the languages) and respective documents to benefit their respective organization or industry. This ability to create arbitrary XML components is augmented by the ability to develop specific document type definitions or XML schemas that work with the XML languages and their XML documents, to define components, and to proof the documents. These principles form the bases of XML's extensible nature. Programming languages, however, must still be used to create the applications that will manipulate the subset languages and documents.
- Every valid XML document is also a valid SGML document. Any fully conformant SGML system will also read XML documents.
- XML imposes no limits on a user wishing to define markup. Markup needs only to be character-based and human-legible. SGML- and XML-tagged data can be used to create, manage, and maintain large collections of complex information.
- XML is platform- and software-independent, so the same document files may be used with a wide variety of operating systems, as well as in authoring and publishing environments.
- XML was developed as a public format, as an open standard. It is not a proprietary development by any company or nation.
- XML's ease of implementation has fostered inexpensive, occasionally free XML processing tools; for example, parsers, validators, and document format converters.
- As more XML subset languages are developed, and as these languages tend more toward data processing than document publishing, the number of dynamically generated XML documents is increasing. These documents will be dynamic and short-lived because they will be created by computer programs, used almost simultaneously by other computer

programs, and then destroyed. Humans won't ever have to see many of the generated documents. We may just get an inkling of their fleeting existence from transaction summaries or logs.

So with XML a designer can concentrate on using tags and other components to define a document's contents and structure as accurately as possible. Formatting the contents is secondary and, if at all, occurs later, likely through the use of display or transformation style sheets (which are discussed in Chapter 7, "XML and Cascading Style Sheets," and Chapter 9, "XML Transformations," respectively).

XML doesn't seem to make much sense on its own. Its sensibility becomes readily apparent when you create other standards, vocabularies, and documents with it. Plus, an XML-related document cannot do anything by itself; rather, one or more specific programs must be developed to interact with it.

A major advantage of XML over SGML is that it does not require a system that is capable of understanding full SGML. Nevertheless, XML is still SGML-related, and XML files may still be parsed and validated (those concepts will be discussed in Chapter 2) the same as any other SGML file. Think of XML as being "SGML-minus," not "HTML-plus."

But XML is not expected or intended to replace SGML in every environment. Full SGML systems are still extremely valuable because they provide solutions for large, complex problems that justify their development and expense. Again, consider the complex nature of the defense or aerospace industries, or the complex nature of government. SGML is at home there and contributes immeasurably. XML lacks several features that make SGML a more satisfactory solution for the creation and long-time storage of complex documents or for the use of high-end typesetting applications.

XML, on the other hand, is designed to deliver structured content over the Web. Fortunately, SGML-related languages can be designed to be compatible with XML, so their corporate or organizational environments need not be mutually exclusive. In this way, occasionally the advantages of both can be provided. In many organizations, filtering SGML to XML (that is, using XML as an output format for an SGML installation) would be the standard procedure for Web-based delivery.

Because XML and HTML both were derived from SGML, some consider them siblings. There are even similarities between them. For instance, they are both text-based, and both use tags, elements, and attributes. So they appear similar.

XML, however, was designed to describe data semantics and, so, to focus on what the data actually is and how it is structured. HTML, as we've stated before, was designed to display content and to focus on how the content looks.

So HTML processing reflects the people-oriented processing we discussed earlier in this chapter, while XML reflects more machine-oriented processing.

There are only a fixed number of HTML tags, and their names and purposes are predefined in the HTML standard. There can be no variation, so the arbitrary (in XML's case, *arbitrary* takes on a positive slant because it means that designers can assign whatever names and properties to an XML component that they want) and customized meaning of the XML tag <fan.20cmblade.pt_no>, for example, would not be interpreted by an HTML application.

Figures 1.1 and 1.2 illustrate a comparison of samples of HTML source code and XML source code respectively. Notice how, in the HTML document in Figure 1.1, the tags are in uppercase, a common practice with HTML. (HTML isn't case-sensitive.)

The XML document in Figure 1.2, with its descriptive tags, provides more flexibility and reusability. It already looks more sophisticated than the HTML document, simply because it has more descriptive elements. But this document pales in comparison to what a more comprehensive XML document might contain, with all the appropriate descriptive elements, attributes, and entities.

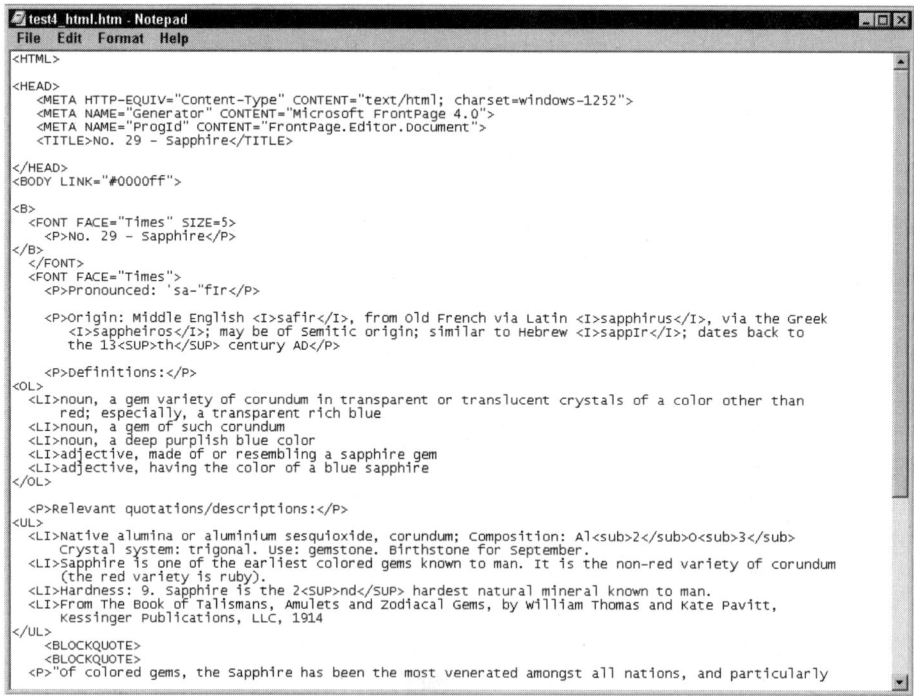

```
<HTML>

<HEAD>
   <META HTTP-EQUIV="Content-Type" CONTENT="text/html; charset=windows-1252">
   <META NAME="Generator" CONTENT="Microsoft FrontPage 4.0">
   <META NAME="ProgId" CONTENT="FrontPage.Editor.Document">
   <TITLE>No. 29 - Sapphire</TITLE>

</HEAD>
<BODY LINK="#0000ff">

<B>
  <FONT FACE="Times" SIZE=5>
    <P>No. 29 - Sapphire</P>
</B>
  </FONT>
  <FONT FACE="Times">
    <P>Pronounced: 'sa-"fIr</P>

    <P>Origin: Middle English <I>safir</I>, from Old French via Latin <I>sapphirus</I>, via the Greek
       <I>sappheiros</I>; may be of Semitic origin; similar to Hebrew <I>sappIr</I>; dates back to
       the 13<SUP>th</SUP> century AD</P>

    <P>Definitions:</P>
<OL>
  <LI>noun, a gem variety of corundum in transparent or translucent crystals of a color other than
      red; especially, a transparent rich blue
  <LI>noun, a gem of such corundum
  <LI>noun, a deep purplish blue color
  <LI>adjective, made of or resembling a sapphire gem
  <LI>adjective, having the color of a blue sapphire
</OL>

  <P>Relevant quotations/descriptions:</P>
<UL>
  <LI>Native alumina or aluminium sesquioxide, corundum; Composition: Al<sub>2</sub>O<sub>3</sub>
      Crystal system: trigonal. Use: gemstone. Birthstone for September.
  <LI>Sapphire is one of the earliest colored gems known to man. It is the non-red variety of corundum
      (the red variety is ruby).
  <LI>Hardness: 9. Sapphire is the 2<SUP>nd</SUP> hardest natural mineral known to man.
  <LI>From The Book of Talismans, Amulets and Zodiacal Gems, by William Thomas and Kate Pavitt,
      Kessinger Publications, LLC, 1914
</UL>
    <BLOCKQUOTE>
    <BLOCKQUOTE>
  <P>"Of colored gems, the Sapphire has been the most venerated amongst all nations, and particularly
```

Figure 1.1 An example of HTML coding.

test4_xml.xml - Notepad

File Edit Format Help

```
<html>

<head>
   <meta http-equiv="Content-Type" content="text/html; charset=windows-1252">
   <title>No.
      <cat_no>29</cat_no> - <gem_name>Sapphire</gem_name>
   </title>

</head>
<body link="#0000ff">

<b>
  <font face="Times" SIZE=5>
    <p>No. 29 - Sapphire</p>
</b>
  </font>
  <font face="Times">
    <p>Pronounced:
       <pronounce>&apos;sa-&quotfIr</pronounce>

    <p>Origin: Middle English <me>safir</me>, from Old French via Latin <ltn>sapphirus</ltn>, via the Greek
       <grk>sappheiros</grk>; may be of Semitic origin; similar to Hebrew <hbw>sappIr</hbw>; dates back to
       the 13<sup>th</sup> century AD</p>

    <p>Definitions:</p>
<defn_list>
  <defn>noun, a gem variety of corundum in transparent or translucent crystals of a color other than
      red; especially, a transparent rich blue</defn>
  <defn>noun, a gem of such corundum</defn>
  <defn>noun, a deep purplish blue color</defn>
  <defn>adjective, made of or resembling a sapphire gem</defn>
  <defn>adjective, having the color of a blue sapphire</defn>
</defn_list>

  <p>Relevant quotations/descriptions:</p>
<desc_list>
  <desc>Native alumina or aluminium sesquioxide, corundum; Composition: Al<sub>2</sub>O<sub>3</sub>
       Crystal system:trigonal. Use: gemstone. Birthstone for September.
  </desc>
  <desc>Sapphire is one of the earliest colored gems known to man. It is the non-red variety of corundum
       (the red variety is ruby).
  </desc>
  <desc>Hardness: 9. Sapphire is the 2<sup>nd</sup> hardest natural mineral known to man.
  </desc>
  <desc>From The Book of Talismans, Amulets and Zodiacal Gems, by William Thomas and Kate Pavitt, Kessinger
      Publications, LLC, 1914
  </desc>
</desc_list>
    <blockquote>
    <blockquote>
  <quote>"Of colored gems, the Sapphire has been the most venerated amongst all nations, and particularly
```

Figure 1.2 An example of XML coding.

The arbitrariness and extensibility of XML data allow for more precise data searches and, especially, better commerce transactions. It's also more scalable and provides a more robust infrastructure.

More, and more sophisticated, XML editing tools are constantly being developed, but you can still do XML design and development with simple text editors. Because XML tags describe data and so are used as part of business transactions and research, XML syntax requires more precision and strict adherence to its grammar rules (for example, XML is case-sensitive). XML grammar can't be dealt with loosely the way HTML grammar has relaxed over the past few years. But observing XML's stricter grammar rules will actually benefit you in the long run, providing for well-formed, valid, and reliable languages and documents.

HTML pages usually constitute a static library. There are exceptions, of course: At some sophisticated Web sites, the developers have written or adapted powerful (read: expensive) Web servers whose subroutines can generate HTML pages on the fly. With XML, pages are more easily—and so, more likely to be—generated dynamically from data found on a site's Web servers, on its enterprise databases, and on other Web sites. If it is structured according to XML principles, then that information can be accessed, analyzed, extracted, sorted, styled, and otherwise manipulated to create customized documents for people or machines, with long or short lives. In this manner, XML data becomes smarter, and Web pages actually become Web services. XML thus contributes to the World Wide Web Consortium's goal of the *Semantic Web,* where computer dumbness is reduced somewhat as systems begin to emulate a kind of rudimentary understanding of the data they share.

As the World Wide Web continues to develop, XML will increase its share of data description-, structure-, and semantic-oriented languages and documents. Meanwhile, HTML will likely continue to be used to format and display portions of the same data. So XML would only replace HTML when HTML can't provide sufficient retrieval precision or data reusability; otherwise, XML and HTML could—and already do, in many cases—coexist with and complement one another. A contradiction to this peaceful coexistence arises, however, when we read about the future of XHTML, which is the subject of Chapter 6, "XHTML." XHTML is an XML-related standard that, at first glance, resembles HTML. It has been touted as a future replacement for HTML. Many XML proponents say, "The sooner, the better."

XML-Related Applications

XML applications are languages derived from the XML standard. Although we use the terms XML derivative language or XML application interchangeably throughout this book, several more terms can be used to describe the same concept: dialect, application profile, standard, vocabulary, abbreviated version, restricted form, subset, distillation, protocol, instance, and extension. Likely there are even more. In the XML world, these terms are considered to be similar in meaning. In certain contexts, though, one may be more accurate than another. Hypothetically, for example, if some people developed a ToyML (that is, a toy markup and metalanguage) and they expected that, eventually, a HulaHoopML might be derived from ToyML, then ToyML might be considered to be a vocabulary *and* a standard, while HulaHoopML might be just a vocabulary. Whatever name they go by, though, XML applications are derived and extended from XML, and conform to the XML 1.0 Recommendation. But XML applications must not be confused with applications, which are programs developed with computer programming languages.

XML applications are being developed constantly, and hundreds of them are now in use in many organizations and industries around the world. The XML-related applications whose names appear in the spherical-looking circles in Figure 1.3 are those that you will be introduced to during the course of this book.

The upcoming XML-related vocabularies are listed in Table 1.3.

There are many other XML-related languages, most of which are relevant to specific industries or organizations. The list of available languages will continue to grow as XML becomes more widely accepted as a Web technology, and as more browsers support XML-based markup more comprehensively.

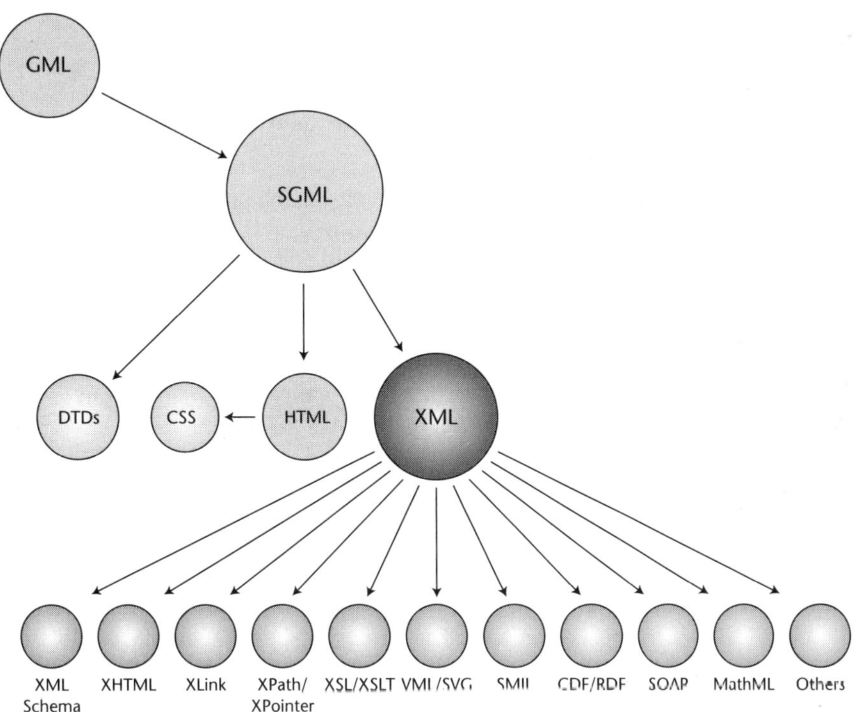

Figure 1.3 Relation of XML to its predecessors and to XML-related standards.

Table 1.3 Examples of XML-Related Languages

XML-RELATED LANGUAGE	DESCRIPTION
XML Schema	Two-part standard that facilitates the development of better XML data descriptions and the definition of XML vocabularies; predicted to replace DTDs in the future.
XHTML	HTML rewritten as an XML vocabulary; predicted to replace HTML.
XLink	Language for linking among XML documents (generally for linking to a specific whole document).
XPointer	Language for linking to specific locations within the same or other documents.
XSL	Extensible Stylesheet Language is the style standard for XML; it specifies the presentation and appearance of an XML document.
XSLT	Extensible Stylesheet Language Transformation is used to transform (that is, reformat) one type of XML document into other types of XML documents.
VML	The most widespread of the XML-related graphic languages; used for encoding of vector information to describe how that information may be displayed and edited; intended to help developers address the problems and disadvantages of bitmap graphics.
SVG	W3C's open-standard XML-related vector graphics standard; has its own mature DTD; not yet widely implemented, but gaining popularity; intended to make Web browsers compatible with drawing tools like CorelDRAW, Adobe Illustrator, and others.
SMIL	Synchronized Multimedia Integration Language was designed to integrate multimedia objects into a synchronized presentation.
CDF	Channel Definition Format; an open specification that permits automatic delivery of updated Web information to compatible receiver programs; has only achieved W3C Note status.
RDF	The W3C Resource Description Framework Model and Syntax Specification; provides a more general treatment of metadata than CDF.

Table 1.3 *(continued)*

XML-RELATED LANGUAGE	DESCRIPTION
SOAP	An XML-related network protocol specification for invoking methods on servers, services, components, and objects; also used for representing method parameters, return values, and exceptions.
MathML	Mathematical Markup Language; a language for depicting mathematical expressions while maintaining the functionality of the expressions; an early driving force behind XML development.

For a more comprehensive list of XML vocabularies and to monitor W3C activities, consult the W3C's Web site at www.w3.org or the XML Road Map at IDEAlliance's Web site at www.idealliance.org/.

The World Wide Web Consortium and XML

We have already referred to the World Wide Web Consortium (W3C) several times in this chapter. Here's a short explanation of this important organization.

In October 1994, Tim Berners-Lee, inventor and architect of the W3C (also mentioned previously as the author of the first HTML RFC), founded the W3C at the Massachusetts Institute of Technology, Laboratory for Computer Science in collaboration with funding from the United States Defense Advanced Research Project Agency (DARPA) and the European Union. In their own words, "The purpose of the W3C is to develop interoperable technologies (specifications, guidelines, and applications) to promote the Web as a forum for information, commerce, communication, and collective understanding."

Membership in the W3C has grown to more than 500 organizations from around the world, and the W3C is hosted by three organizations: Massachusetts Institute of Technology (MIT) in the United States, the French National Institute for Research in Computer Science and Control (INRIA) in France, and Keio University in Japan.

For more information about the W3C, check the About Us Web page at www.w3.org/Consortium/. From there, you can link to other pages that describe their membership, policies, activities, and processes.

If you aren't aware of the W3C yet, note that they have indeed been a major player in the development of World Wide Web technologies. In later chapters, we'll tell you how their teams have developed important XML-related vocabularies and other standards, have succeeded in stopping or delaying otherwise shortsighted (if not downright wrongheaded) initiatives, and have opened up the development of what otherwise might have been proprietary standards and applications. There should be no underestimating their influence and achievements.

The first phase of the W3C's XML Activity started in June 1996 and culminated in the February 1998 Recommendation titled Extensible Markup Language (XML) 1.0. That Recommendation, which we'll refer to many times in this book as XML 1.0, was revised in October 2000.

Here are some XML-related goals and best practices as enunciated by the W3C in the XML 1.0 Recommendation. (The specification contains more detailed descriptions.)

1. It shall be straightforward to use XML over the Internet. End users must be able to display XML documents and view the respective source coding as easily as they display and view HTML. XML shall also support a wide variety of authoring, browsing, and analysis applications.
2. XML shall be compatible with SGML. XML was designed with the World Wide Web in mind. It has to be compatible with existing standards, but it still must cope with the bandwidth and time constraints of Web communication.
3. It shall be easy to write programs that process XML documents. The W3C promotes a first-glance philosophy: They state that it should only take about two weeks for a competent computer science graduate student to build a program capable of processing XML documents.
4. The number of optional features in XML is to be kept to an absolute minimum, ideally zero. Optional features can lead to compatibility problems, confusion, and frustration.
5. XML documents should be human-legible and reasonably clear. Even if you don't have an XML browser or one of the sophisticated XML editors, you should still be able use a text editor to examine XML content.
6. XML design should be prepared quickly. With XML derivative languages and documents, the emphasis should be on quicker problem solutions. The final product may be complex, but the design stage should proceed with little delay.
7. The design of XML shall be formal and concise (that is, it should adhere strictly to XML grammar and vocabulary).

8. XML documents shall be easy to create. Although there are several sophisticated editors available to create XML documents, it still must be possible to create XML documents with alternate methods, like simple text editors, WYSIWYG text applications, or simple scripts.
9. Terseness in XML markup is of minimal importance. It's true that several SGML features were designed to minimize a developer's typing, but those features are not supported in XML. Emphasize human legibility and understanding.

The W3C provides a quick synopsis of XML for newcomers, managers, or executives who find themselves thrust into XML-related decision making. It is called "XML in 10 Points" and can be found at www.w3.org/XML/1999/XML-in-10-points.

Meanwhile, there has been and continues to be a constant parade of Web-related developments, resulting in the production of many W3C Recommendations and other documents. Several W3C Working Groups constantly conduct XML-related development work in parallel. Almost every day, the W3C announces progress on one XML front or another on their Web site at www.w3c.org. IDEAlliance also lists XML applications at their Web site at www.idealliance.org/standards_vocab.asp.

Possible XML Issues: "Nobody's Perfect (Yet)"

In a book that promotes the use of XML and XML-related standards, it may seem odd that we are listing two possible issues that may arise from the use of XML over other possible solutions. However, these issues arise mostly from XML's fast-paced and leading edge development and, as you can readily see, can be overcome with appropriate planning and implementation. At any rate, here are two concerns that you should be aware of if you are contemplating the adoption or adaptation of XML in your organization:

- XML is a rapidly growing technology with development going on in several different areas at once (for example, graphics, multimedia, Web protocols), and the development of applications (browsers included) lags behind it. The latest versions of Microsoft Internet Explorer, Konqueror (a Unix KDE-based open source Web browser), Mozilla/Gecko, and Netscape are XML 1.0-compatible, but may not be as consistently compliant with the additional XML-related core standards (especially when we note the speed at which new standards are developed and existing standards are updated).

- Your specific needs may not be met by an XML application. Perhaps because of the complexity of your data you might consider moving to SGML (remember the examples presented previously: the air transport industry, the telecommunications industry, and others). However, even if you do not adopt XML as your organizational standard, you may still be able to use an XML vocabulary for Web transactions or other output.

Lab Exercises: Instructions and Conventions

All of the examples, instructions, and other conventions contained in this book use Microsoft Windows 2000 Professional as a base operating system; however, the lab exercises will also work if you are using Microsoft Windows XP Professional and Linux.

Instructions for the Windows 2000 and XP environments are documented in this book. The comparable instructions for Linux can be found on this book's Web site as noted in the book's introduction.

The lab exercises are divided into logical sections, and each section has its own title and short introduction. The step-by-step instructions for the lab exercises are numbered consecutively for each logical section. For example, Steps 1 through 10 might compose the first logical section. In the next logical section, the steps will begin, again, at Step 1.

While we were creating the steps, we made certain assumptions regarding prerequisite experience and skill sets. We tried not to be too redundant when describing mouse or window clicks. On the other hand, we were careful to add what we thought would be helpful hints, tips, notes, and even cautions. If we thought that further explanation was required, we added substeps or hints.

Here is an example of our approach to creating lab exercise steps:

1. This would be the basic step. We may include some text regarding what you are attempting to do at this step, to maintain a conceptual flow. Substeps for performing this instruction may be included as a., b., and more.
    a. If the step involves more than one activity or maneuver, we would itemize them here as substeps.
    b. Also, if we think it is necessary to bring something to your attention or advise you to watch for a tricky issue, that advice might also be included as one or more substeps.

In the foregoing example, there is just one basic step: Step 1. Assistance for Step 1 was listed in Steps a and b.

At all times, read the entire basic Step 1, including all substeps, before executing that step.

A Brief Introduction to Space Gems, Inc.

As you progress through the lab exercises in this book, you will be assuming the role of the Web site developer for a fictitious company named Space Gems, Inc., headquartered on Earth. In that capacity, you will help them to become an enterprise on the World Wide Web. Space Gems' business is gemstone exploration and sales throughout that great final frontier, space. We'll follow Space Gems' activities on Earth and Mars (in our own solar system, which we nickname Sol), as well as their frontier activities on other (again, fictitious) worlds in other planetary systems near our galaxy. Those far-flung planets revolve around the following stars, which, according to the United States' National Aeronautics and Space Agency, are already known to have planets:

- 70 Virginus in the constellation Virgo.
- 47 Ursae Majoris in the constellation Ursa Major (the Big Bear). (Ursa Major is the larger overall constellation that contains the smaller but more familiar Big Dipper.)
- 51 Pegasi, just outside the Great Square of the constellation Pegasus.
- 55 Cancri in the constellation Cancer.
- HD49674 in the constellation Auriga.

Chapter 1 Labs: Web Exploration

We haven't really taught you too much about the mechanics of XML yet, so the labs for this chapter are almost trivial. However, they are also instructive to some extent.

Lab 1.1: Looking Locally for XML Files

In this lab, you'll use Windows Explorer to look for XML files that were installed with your operating system with your applications or that have been downloaded to your system while you've explored the Internet.

To perform the lab exercises in this book, we are presuming you have installed and configured Microsoft Windows 2000 Professional, Windows XP Professional, or Linux as your base operating system. Chances are, then, that this first lab exercise will be successful. If you also have access to a computer system with an older operating system, it might be enlightening, for comparison purposes, to perform a similar search of its resources. We'll bet that your search won't be as successful.

1. On your Windows desktop, click Start, Programs, Accessories, Windows Explorer.
2. When the Windows Explorer window opens, the My Documents folder will be highlighted already. Click the plus sign (+) next to My Computer; then highlight the C: drive (which may or may not have a descriptive name).
3. Click Search on the toolbar.
4. When the Search pane appears, type the following into the Search for files or folders named: dialog:

   ```
   *.xml
   ```

5. Ensure that Local Hard Drives (C:) is selected in the Look in: dialog box, and click the Search Now button.

A Search Results pane appears on the right side and displays a list of XML files that Explorer encounters as it scans the C: drive. If you have configured Microsoft Windows 2000 Professional, Windows XP Professional, or Linux as your base operating system, chances are you'll see several files listed. They may have been found in the following directories, and maybe more:

- C:\Program Files\name of application\
- C:\TEMP\
- C:\WINDOWS\
- C:\WINNT\

You may not have found all of the XML-related files. Not all have .xml as their filename extensions. Whether they do often depends on the intentions of their creators.

Meanwhile, if you have performed the search on a computer system with an older operating system, you may or may not have found any files at all. If you did, they were probably in the \Program Files\name of application or \TEMP\ directories, and not in any operating system-related files.

Lab 1.2: Examining an XML File

Presuming that during Lab 1.1 you were successful searching for files with .xml as their filename extensions, you will now examine the contents of one of the files.

We presume that Windows Explorer found several XML files in the C:\Windows\system32\icsxml folder on our system. Let's take a quick look at the contents of one of those files.

In this part of the exercise, ensure that you only look at the file. Do *not* make any permanent changes to it. (In other words, if you make any changes, even just to alter the structure in order to make the file easier to read, do *not* click File, Save.)

1. With the Search Results window displayed, highlight the name of the file you want to look at.
2. Right-click the filename, scroll down to Open with, and click Notepad (this is one example where a simple text editor can make file examination quick and convenient).
3. Try to determine what the function of the file might be. Look for comment lines that begin with <!— and end with —>. Failing that, the names within the markup tags, denoted by < and > brackets, may provide a clue. You'll find that, as you progress through *XML in 60 Minutes a Day*, analyzing XML files becomes easier.
4. When you are finished examining the file, click File, Exit, or simply click the Close (X) button in the top right corner.

Lab 1.3: Visit Some Web Sites to See How Many Use XML

In this lab, you will check various Web sites to see if they use XML extensively or whether they have incorporated just some XML.

1. We'll first visit the W3C Web site, where, we can safely wager, we'll find Web pages containing XML coding.
   a. From your Windows Desktop, click Start; then scroll up to Programs, and click your Web browser application (it might be

Internet Explorer, Netscape Navigator, Mozilla, Opera, or any of a number of available browsers). For this exercise, let's presume you are using Internet Explorer.

b. In the locator bar, type the following and then press Enter:

```
http://www.w3.org
```

2. When the home page for the World Wide Web Consortium's Web site appears, go up to the toolbar and press and hold View; then scroll down to Source, and release the mouse button there. A new window appears, which shows you the beginning of the code that went into creating the W3C site. The first couple of lines will look like this:

```
<?xml version="1.0" encoding="us-ascii" ?>
<!DOCTYPE html PUBLIC "-//W3C//DTD XHTML 1.0 Transitional//EN"
    "http://www.w3.org/TR/xhtml1/DTD/xhtml1-transitional.dtd" >
<html xmlhs= ... etc.
```

The W3C Web site does, indeed, contain code written to the specifications of XML Recommendation 1.0, as well as to the other core standards—notably, the XHTML standard (which we discuss in Chapter 6). Again, as you progress through *XML in 60 Minutes a Day*, you will become more familiar with this type of coding.

3. If you have the time, check out other Web sites, such as those who provide XML tutorials (to find them, try entering something like "XML tutorials" in a Web search engine, and then follow the links). You'll probably find several right away that have incorporated at least a little XML coding. When you view their source, you'll see that the first few lines will resemble those in Step 2.

Summary

Before you move on to Chapter 2, review these key concepts that we discussed in Chapter 1:

- Documents are electronic files of any size for any media (text, audio, video, graphics, and so on) created by any application. Document processing is the discipline that deals with creating applications that allow you to deal with documents of all types. It is split into creating or manipulating those documents destined for human viewing and consumption (people-oriented processing) and into creating and manipulating documents destined for computer consumption (machine-oriented processing).

- Markup, in summary, is the inserting of characters or symbols into a document to indicate the document's physical and logical structure, to indicate how the information in a document should appear, or to provide some other form of instruction. The primary goal of markup is to separate the treatment (such as the semantics, structure, or appearance) of the document from the data in the document.
- Six types of markup have been defined: punctuational, presentational, procedural, descriptive, referential, and metamarkup. XML mostly uses descriptive, referential, and metamarkup.
- SGML was developed from 1978 to 1986. It has been a standard by which other, more specific languages tailored to the specific requirements of any organization or industry can be created. SGML has facilitated the cataloging and indexing of data in many important and complex industries. XML and HTML are both offsprings of SGML, but SGML-compliant languages are big and resource-intensive, usually too cumbersome for Web browser-related functions. Brower manufacturers admit that their products do not and will not fully comply with SGML.
- HTML, developed in the early 1990s, is a simplified version of SGML with a fixed and limited set of predefined markup components. HTML contains format-oriented markup only. Because it was free, simple, and widely supported, HTML sparked a Web publishing phenomenon and made the Web available to ordinary people. Its markup components are fixed and do not lend themselves to describing what data is, only to describing how it should be displayed.
- The Extensible Markup Language (XML) was developed from 1996 to 1998 as a derivative of SGML. Development continues today on XML and many XML-related standards and vocabularies. XML is a markup language, so it allows developers to create documents consisting of plaintext data and other entities, and markup codes that define the logical components and structure, as well as describe the appearance or other aspects of the data. XML is also a metalanguage, so it provides the capability to control the definition and interpretation of markup tags, and for extending the vocabulary of derivative markup languages.
- XML can provide similar print, hypertext, and content management functionality as SGML, but is lightweight enough for use on the World Wide Web or on intranets.
- XML's arbitrary and extensible nature allows for more precise data searches and better commerce transactions. It's also more scalable and provides a more robust data infrastructure.

- XML-related derivative languages are being developed constantly, and hundreds of them are now in use in many organizations and industries around the world. More and more XML development tools are appearing, which is a testament to XML's growing popularity.
- XML still has two minor issues. Because it is a rapidly growing technology, the development of related applications (browsers included) lags behind it. And XML may not meet the needs of large and complex data sets as well as SGML. For those who still choose SGML languages as their solutions, however, they may still be able to use an XML vocabulary for Web-related data or other transactions.
- The World Wide Web Consortium is a major player in the development of World Wide Web technologies. It is also at the hub of XML development; new standards are being developed constantly. Its XML-related goals and best practices are worth remembering.

Review Questions

1. True or false? Documents are considered to be electronic files of any size, for any media, created by any application.
2. Which of the following is *not* a type of markup?
   a. Punctuational
   b. Descriptive
   c. Referential
   d. Extensible
   e. Metamarkup
   f. None of the above
3. What are two disadvantages of HTML compared to XML?
4. What type of computer language is XML?
   a. Referential language
   b. Extensible language
   c. Metalanguage
   d. Programming language
   e. Markup language
   f. All of the above
5. What is the name of the document mechanism that is used to prove conformance of a language derived from SGML or XML?
6. If something is developed as a public format and is not proprietary in any way, what is the term given to it?
   a. Open source
   b. World Wide
   c. Extensible
   d. Generalized
   e. Standardized
   f. None of the above
7. Place the following in order of date of development: HTML, XML, SGML, GML, and GenCode.
8. What are two issues concerning XML?

9. True or false? One man is credited with architecting and inventing the World Wide Web, and with inventing HTML.
10. Which of the following XML-derived languages is destined to replace HTML?
    a. SVG
    b. SMIL
    c. RDF
    d. ESPN
    e. NPR
    f. None of the above

Answers to Review Questions

1. True.
2. **d.** The six types of markup are listed and described in the *What Is Markup?* section.
3. Choose any two of the following:
   - **a.** It is only display-oriented.
   - **b.** It has a limited set of predefined markup components.
   - **c.** It can't tell you *about* the data.
   - **d.** It does not lend itself well to machine-oriented, dynamic document creation, although it can be done.
4. **d.** and **e.** Please refer to the *XML Is a Markup Language and a Metalanguage* section.
5. A document type definition (DTD). Schemas only apply to languages derived from XML, not SGML.
6. **a.** For further information regarding open source, visit www.opensource.org.
7. From earliest to latest, they are: GML, GenCode, SGML, HTML, and XML.
8. Here are two disadvantages to XML:
   - **a.** XML development is going on so rapidly, on so many fronts, that commercial applications are lagging behind.
   - **b.** XML is not as robust as SGML for large and complex data structures.
9. True. His name is Tim Berners-Lee. (Bravo!)
10. **f.** XHTML is the XML application that many expect to replace HTML eventually.

Setting Up Your XML Working Environment

Chapter 1, "XML Backgrounder," discussed XML's document processing heritage. Chapter 2 shows you how to prepare for the creation of XML documents (or, if you prefer, XML instances). It has been developed in response to these questions, voiced by our students while doing their lab exercises: How are these systems configured? What do we need to install before we can create XML documents?

In this chapter we discuss what constitutes a basic XML authoring environment, namely, computer hardware and the associated software: Web servers, Web browsers, and XML authoring applications. We introduce the three fundamental categories of XML authoring tools and list several of the prominent tools, including where to go to get your own copies. The lab exercise provides detailed instructions for installing and configuring your own XML authoring environment in a Microsoft Windows environment. (We'll also tell you where to get similar instructions for installing one in a Linux environment.)

By the end of this chapter, you will be set up and ready to begin creating and viewing your own XML documents.

Hardware Requirements

A large system is not required to perform the lab exercises at the end of each chapter in this book. Here are the basic system requirements for the lab exercises:

- A personal computer with at least 64 MB of RAM and a 500-MB hard disk.
- An Internet connection.
- A copy of the Microsoft Windows 2000 or XP Professional operating system on CD-ROM.
- A copy of Microsoft's Internet Information Services (IIS) software for the Microsoft Windows environment or Apache for the Linux (or several other Unix variations) environment.
- A copy of a current Web browser application. At this writing, we suggest Microsoft Internet Explorer Version 6 or higher, or Netscape 6 for the Windows environment; or Netscape 6, Mozilla 1 or Konqueror 2 for the Linux/Unix environment.
- A copy of your choice of XML authoring software. (We'll also refer to it as editing software and other equivalent terms.) We are suggesting TIBCO Software Inc.'s Turbo XML editor for the lab exercises, but there is a vast array of choices, from sophisticated integrated development environments (IDEs) to the simplest text editors.

Meanwhile, for the purposes of this book, neither the Web server nor the XML editor will use much CPU or RAM. (Full industrial-scale integrated development environments would require far more, naturally.) Although the physical system requirements for this book are conservative, you will still require a fairly robust connection to the Internet to download software and source files, as well as to participate in related online activities.

Web Servers

Web servers go by several similar names: Web server, HTTP server, and World Wide Web server. There are two basic ways to define the term Web server. One definition is the software installed on a server-class computer system that will enable that system to transmit Web pages upon request from an end user's browser. The other definition refers to the computer system itself, after the software has been installed and configured. You can make any computer system a Web server by installing the appropriate software and then connecting the system to the Internet. Every electronic commerce operation depends on its Web servers.

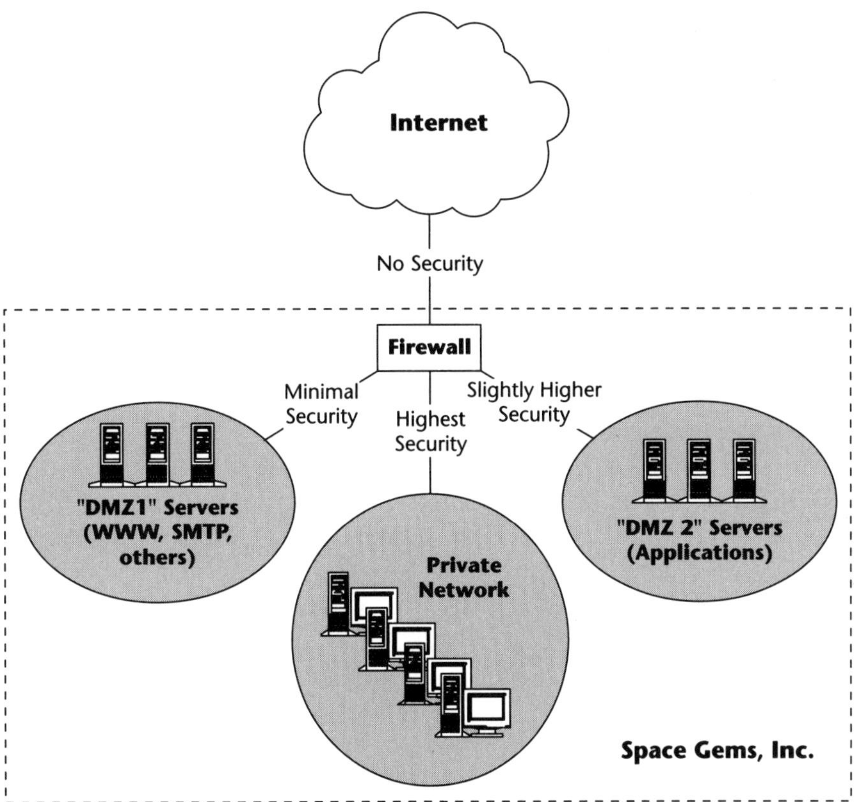

Figure 2.1 Space Gems' network schematic.

After it's installed, Web server software is configured such that the computer will have an IP address and, usually, a domain name. Figure 2.1 shows a schematic for the Space Gems, Inc. computer network. It is fairly typical for a small- to medium-sized enterprise.

Behind its firewall, Space Gems has three network segments. (In other words, it has three zones.)

Space Gems' Private Network. This consists of employee systems and data servers, intended solely for Space Gems' employees. This will be given the highest security designation when one or more firewalls are configured.

Demilitarized Zone 1 (DMZ1). A group of servers and systems on a lower-security network segment, that provide Space Gems with the capability to respond to requests from the Internet (the Internet servers are referred to in Figure 2.1 as WWW), to send and receive email messages (referred to as SMTP), and maybe to provide other low-risk, low-security services. Web servers are often located in DMZs like this to prevent hackers, who would try to access the network through the Web server, from gaining access to the higher-security application servers or, especially, to the private segment of an organization's network. DMZs are occasionally sacrificed to hackers, but at least the private networks remain safe.

Demilitarized Zone 2 (DMZ2). A group of servers on an intermediate security network segment, that provide applications and services intended for Space Gems' employees and their most trusted clients, suppliers, and so on.

In this case, all of Space Gems' DMZ1 and DMZ2 systems likely have Web server software installed on them. There may also be Web server software installed on some private network systems.

Now, if an end user somewhere on the Internet enters the www.spacegems .com URL in his or her browser's location bar, a request will be sent to the server that has been configured with the domain name *spacegems* (that server is probably in DMZ1 here). After the server receives the request, it responds by transmitting a page document designated by Space Gems, to the requester's browser.

Several domain names may be mapped to the same physical computer. This concept is called *virtual hosting*, and the computer is called a *virtual server*. Virtual hosting allows you to provide several different Web sites, each with its own domain name and even IP address, using the same Web server system. Requests sent to these different sites will be routed by IP address, hostname, or browser language setting to the correct virtual host (that is, to its own respective Web site). Virtual hosting is a technique that will be illustrated in the lab exercises later in this chapter.

Individual virtual hosts have unique Web root directories (or folders), directory (or folder) hierarchies, default filenames, and error files and restricted access files.

On the other hand, the different virtual host Web sites will likely share system caching, plug-ins, security realms, and other features.

Many Web server software applications are available. The following are the most prominent:

Public domain software. HTTPd is public domain software that can be downloaded from the National Center for Supercomputing Applications (NCSA, located at the University of Illinois at Urbana-Champaign, Illinois). Their HTTPd Web site is http://hoohoo.ncsa.uiuc.edu/docs/Overview.html.

Apache Web Server. Developed by the Apache Software Foundation, a membership-based, not-for-profit corporation that provides various kinds of support for Apache open source software projects. Information and downloads are available from http://httpd.apache.org/.

Microsoft Internet Information Server (IIS). Usually included with Windows server software; IIS is integrated at the Windows operating system level. Check Microsoft's IIS Web site at www.microsoft.com/windows2000/server/evaluation/features/web.asp for features, support, and downloads.

Sun ONE Web Server (formerly iPlanet Web Server, Enterprise Edition). Developed by the Sun Microsystems, Inc.- Netscape Alliance. Under the iPlanet brand name, the Sun-Netscape Alliance is producing new versions of Netscape products. Further information and a trial download can be found at Sun's Web site at wwws.sun.com/software/products/web_srvr/home_web_srvr.html.

IBM HTTP Server. Part of IBM's WebSphere line. Further information and downloads are available at IBM's Web site at www-3.ibm.com/software/webservers/httpservers/.

Web Browsers

Web browsers (also called Internet browsers) are software applications that locate, request, and display Web pages and navigate from one Web site or page to another. They also contain email and chat clients. Almost all browsers are graphical browsers (they can display text and graphics), although some text-only browsers are still around. Also, most browsers present multimedia information—sound and video are the most predominant—although they usually require plug-in utilities for some multimedia formats. Basically, browsers act as client applications to those server applications on remote Web server systems. They usually use the HTTP protocol but also use FTP and others.

To read XML, a browser application must contain another application called an *XML parser* (also called an XML processor), which conducts a preliminary check on XML documents. If the documents meet criteria for what are termed well-formedness and validity, the XML parser restructures the data in the documents and then passes the restructured data to the application (that is, to the browser) proper. More explanations regarding parsers, well-formedness and validity can be found in Chapter 3, "Anatomy of an XML Document."

Browsers are generally judged according to how they measure up to the following questions:

- Is the browser free or at least inexpensive? Are updates or upgrades free or inexpensive?
- Is installation easy and trouble-free? How about configuration?
- Is the interface easy to look at and use?

- How does the browser perform? For example, does it load pages quickly? Is it stable or does it crash occasionally—and why? Can you see the same information on Web sites with one browser as you can with another?
- What about its other features? For example, can you customize its appearance? Can you customize its behavior? Does it have integrated email and chat client programs? Does it support XML?
- Are service and support available? Are they free?

Here are the most prominent Web browsers:

Internet Explorer. The browser against which other browsers are usually compared. IE 4.0 was the first Web browser to implement XML. Microsoft provides two parsers: one nonvalidating and one validating. Supports DHTML, CSS1, DOM1, SMIL, Microsoft XML 3.0, and a .NET Web service behavior that allows XML/SOAP database queries. Further information and downloads are available from the Microsoft Web site at www.microsoft.com/windows/ie/default.asp.

Netscape. Supports XML, HTML 4, and Cascading Style Sheets. Available for Windows, Linux, and Mac OS. More information and downloads are available from the Netscape Web site at http://channels.netscape.com/ns/browsers/default.jsp.

Konqueror. An open source KDE desktop environment-related (thus, available for Linux and other Unix variations) Web browser that complies with HTML 4 and supports Java applets, JavaScript, Cascading Style Sheets Recommendation 1 and (partially) 2. It is also compatible with Netscape plug-ins. It uses XML documents for configuration and other functions. More information and downloads are available from the Konqueror Web site at www.konqueror.org/.

Mozilla. Developed by the Mozilla Organization, a virtual organization that makes their Mozilla browser a successful open source project and product. Mozilla is fast and stable, and it allows you to disable many pop-up ads. Mozilla supports XML, but its parser is nonvalidating. More information and downloads are available from the Mozilla Web site at www.mozilla.org/.

Opera. Developed by Opera Software. Available for Windows, Linux, Macintosh, Symbian, QNX, and OS/2 operating systems. XML viewing capability became available with the Version 4.0 beta. Further information and downloads are available from the Opera Web site at www.opera.com/.

Other browsers are available. As time goes by, more will be developed, and more will support XML.

XML Authoring Tools

If you become an XML developer, your authoring or editing applications will probably become your most important XML software. We'll refer to these applications as XML authoring tools or XML editors. Because XML is an open standard, it doesn't restrict you to one editor or another (or one classification or another), even after you get started. If you find an editor is too restrictive, or you find yourself occasionally in a situation or location where you can't use your customary editor, you can often switch to another, and your documents will still function. However, your options may be limited by software costs, licensing, and other factors. Meanwhile, your choice of editor will probably influence the look, structure, and interoperability of your XML documents, at least during the initial creation stages. For example, some applications require the creation of other components (such as DTDs or style sheets) prior to document creation.

There are three basic XML authoring tool classifications, each with several authoring applications. In order of complexity, starting with the least complex, the three basic XML authoring tool classifications are as follows:

- Simple text editors
- Graphical editors
- Integrated development environments

We'll discuss each classification in turn and then list a few representative editing tools from each. Note that these classification boundaries are becoming blurred as the tool developers add to or modify the features in their respective applications. They do so by adopting or adapting features that were previously available in applications in the higher categories or by becoming more interoperable with other types of applications (for example, graphics, audio, or video applications) or other document editors.

As mentioned in Chapter 1, XML is being adopted by more and more Web developers; therefore, we can expect other types of Web-based applications—especially HTML editors, database software, and e-commerce software—to incorporate XML support and, with it, some level of XML creation capability. In the near future, these other application types will likely form their own category of XML creation tools.

Simple Text Editors

Simple text (also called plaintext) applications are small and uncomplicated, so they're easy on computer system resources. Consequently, plaintext editors have shipped and installed with personal computer operating systems since the 1980s. With some Unix operating systems, they've been around since the 1970s. You can find one on virtually any computer you boot up.

Text editors have few features and are limited in their display capabilities. Some use only one font; some only let you use a few different colors. You can't really change the look and feel of your text with these programs, but because they allow you to write ASCII (but not usually Unicode) text, they are still good enough to create modest XML documents—XML tags generally use the symbols and characters found on a standard keyboard. They are not recommended for creating complex documents in larger structures, but if you know what you're doing and you want to make only a few changes, they can still be used to modify any existing XML document. Following are some examples:

Microsoft Notepad. Notepad installs with the Windows operating system. It is not resource-intensive, typically using less than 1 MB of RAM and just a few CPU cycles when activated. A few menu-driven options are available in Notepad—just enough to accomplish simple text editing.

vi (found on virtually every Unix system, including Linux). Unix users likely recognize vi, although they may know it by its other names, like *vim* or other variations on the *vi* name. vi is the Unix equivalent to Notepad: It is the ubiquitous text editor in the Unix world. It, too, is a modest application, so it is likely to continue to be installed on almost every Unix system. Several vi variants are customizable and can recognize XML tags, so they can highlight those tags in different colors, indent, and perform other functions to facilitate XML creation and editing. A Unix version of vi is available from SourceForge.net's vimonline Web site at http://vim.sourceforge.net/. A version of vi called WinVi (vi with a Windows wrapper interface) is available from Raphael "Ramo" Molle at www.winvi.de/en/.

Microsoft WordPad. Another application that installs on almost every Windows system, WordPad provides more features than Notepad such as different fonts and font sizes, toolbars, and more sophisticated margin and tab stop controls. WordPad provides a slightly better user interface and more appealing-looking documents without the necessity of Microsoft Word.

Emacs (found on more and more Unix systems). At one time, the equivalent of WordPad in the Unix environment, but now somewhat more sophisticated.

SimpleText. SimpleText ships with every Macintosh system. It limits the size of a document that you can create, but you can use a drag-and-drop feature, record sounds, and use QuickDraw (though with minimal support).

As limited as they are, simple text editors are far from extinct. Their advantages stem from their simplicity to learn and use, their capability to get the job done, the few system resources they use, the convenience of finding them on virtually every system, and the fact that you don't have to install a separate and much larger WYSIWYG application or an office suite of applications to create simple text documents. Witness how easy it was to examine the sample XML files found by Windows Explorer in the lab exercises for Chapter 1.

Consequently, simple text editors are still among the most popular text manipulation tools, especially if the document being created or modified is not large or complex. Some developers are capable of, and comfortable with, creating whole documents with simple text editors. Throughout this book, you will see several examples of basic documents created with simple text editors.

Graphical Editors

Despite our glowing words for them, simple text editors can be slow when producing XML and XML-related documents, such as style sheets, DTDs, and schemas.

Many dedicated XML editors, complete with graphical user interfaces (GUIs), are now available that behave similarly to word processor applications with which we are familiar. In addition to simple text editing, the features of graphical XML editors include, but may not be limited to, the following:

- tags that are color-highlighted
- capability to hide tags, combined with immediate application of style sheets to provide a WYSIWYG document view
- menus of options
- drag-and-drop editing
- click-and-drag highlighting
- other special mechanisms for manipulating markup
- checking for well-formedness
- validity checking
- macro creation to save steps
- menus of only those elements that are declared and defined within DTDs or schemas

The last feature, also referred to as *structure checking*, is popular. The editor can resist the addition of any element that doesn't belong. That way the editor can prevent the author from making syntactic or structural mistakes. Keep in mind, however, that structure checking can also hinder someone from experimenting with different element orderings by forcing the author to stop and figure out why one or another of those maneuvers was rejected.

Unlike SGML editors, which by nature are more complex and expensive, simpler and more affordable editors are being created for XML. Here are some examples of graphical editors for XML. Some provide the features described previously, while others are in transition from graphical text editing to more of an integrated development environment discussed later in this chapter:

Microsoft XML Notepad. Its interface consists of a two-pane display: elements, attributes, comments, and text are added to the XML document via the tree structure in the left pane; values for those components are entered in the corresponding text boxes in the right pane. For additional information and to download a copy of XML Notepad, go to the Microsoft Developer Network (MSDN) Web site (http://msdn.microsoft.com/library/) and enter "xml notepad" in the search engine there.

XAE (XML Authoring Environment for Emacs). Developed by Paul Kinnucan, XAE is add-on software that enables you to use Emacs (or XEmacs) and your Unix system's HTML browser to create, transform, and display XML documents. For further information and to download a copy, go to http://xae.sunsite.dk/.

Peter's XML Editor. This is a modest, but effective, XML development tool. For further information and to download a copy, go to the Web site at www.iol.ie/~pxe/index.html.

Adobe FrameMaker. Enterprise-class authoring and publishing software, FrameMaker is a WYSIWYG application that is evolving into an IDE. For further information or for trial software, go to the Adobe Web site at www.adobe.com/products/framemaker/main.html.

Conglomerate. This is a hybrid word processor-style editor that is moving toward becoming an IDE. Conglomerate is free-software licensed under the GNU General Public License. It consists of a GUI and a server-database combination that performs storage, searching, version control, transformation, and publishing. The code base is apparently still unfinished but reasonably stable, and it will be rewritten. Source code for Unix and Windows is available. Further information and a downloadable copy are available through the Web site at www.conglomerate.org/.

Emilé. Developed by Media Design In-Progress for the Macintosh environment, Emilé is a customizable XML editor that supports DTDs and comes with a validating parser. Color highlighting allows you to see the hierarchical structure and the content. It can be extended with other plug-in components. For further information and to download a test copy, see the Media Design In-Progress Web site at http://in-progress.com/emile/.

Microsoft FrontPage 2002. FrontPage 2002 has an option called *Apply XML Formatting Rules* to automatically reformat the HTML tags on an HTML page to make them XML-compliant. For further information, go to the Microsoft Office Assistance Center Web site at http://office.microsoft.com/assistance/default.aspx and search for "frontpage xml".

Microsoft Word. See the comments that follow in the next section.

Use Only the Latest Versions of Microsoft Word for HTML/XML Creation

No doubt about it, Microsoft Word is one of the most well-known and well-used word processing applications in modern publishing. If, however, you're going to use Word to eventually generate XML (such as by creating a Word document, converting it to HTML, and converting that HTML document to XML), you should be aware of the drawbacks of using older versions of Word—in particular, any versions up to and including Word 97. Newer Word versions have better compatibility with Web page formats.

Earlier versions of Microsoft Word add many extraneous tags and other information into their documents. The extra information and tags risk confusion with the tags and data you might create in your XML documents. Here's an example you can try:

1. If you have a system with, for example, Word 97, click Start, Programs, Microsoft Word.
2. Click File, New and Blank Document, and OK.
3. When the new document window appears, type in a simple yet unique word or phrase as shown in Figure 2.2.

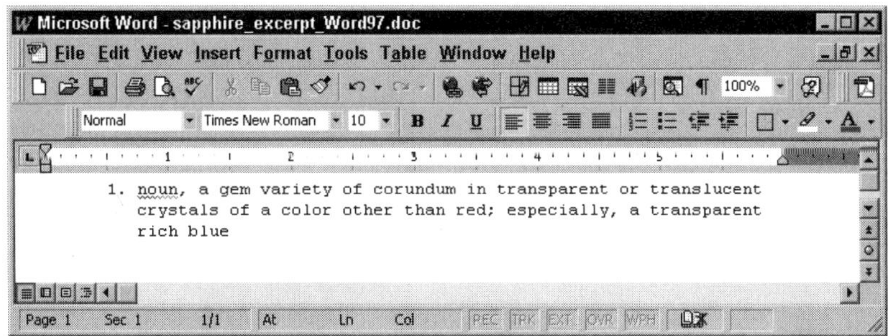

Figure 2.2 A test document named sapphire_excerpt created with Word 97.

4. Click File, Save As, and in the Save As dialog box give the file an appropriate filename (in our example, you can see that the document has been named sapphire_excerpt_Word97). In the Save as Type field, click the down arrow to open the drop-down menu, click Rich Text Format (*.rtf), and click Save. The simple Word document is now in RTF format.
5. Click the File menu button again, and click Save as HTML Document. In the Save as HTML dialog box, give the file an appropriate filename. In the Save as Type field, accept the default HTML document and then click Save.
6. Open the Notepad application by clicking Start, Programs, Accessories, Notepad.
7. When Notepad has started, click File and Open. In the Open dialog box, browse through the Look In field's directory structure until you find the RTF file you saved in Step 4. You may have to click the down arrow in the Files of Type field to open the drop-down menu and then select All Files.
8. When your file is displayed, you will see that your actual text (in the example, the sapphire description) begins near the end of the file. Meanwhile, look at all the tags Word 97 has inserted. Take a look at Figure 2.3 to see what happened with our sapphire excerpt example.

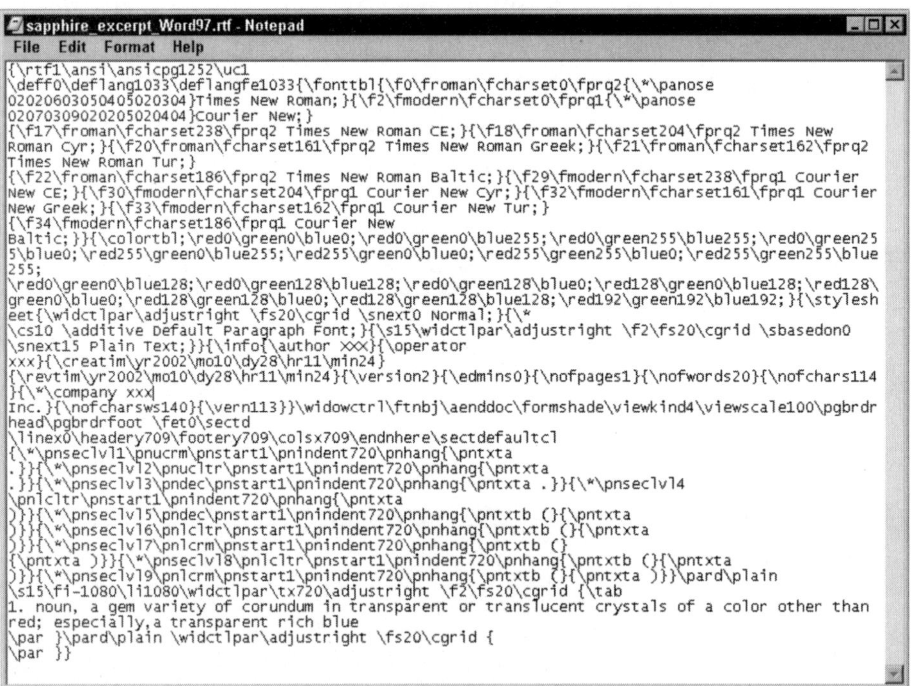


```
{\rtf1\ansi\ansicpg1252\uc1
\deff0\deflang1033\deflangfe1033{\fonttbl{\f0\froman\fcharset0\fprq2{\*\panose
02020603050405020304}Times New Roman;}{\f2\fmodern\fcharset0\fprq1{\*\panose
02070309020205020404}Courier New;}
{\f17\froman\fcharset238\fprq2 Times New Roman CE;}{\f18\froman\fcharset204\fprq2 Times New
Roman Cyr;}{\f20\froman\fcharset161\fprq2 Times New Roman Greek;}{\f21\froman\fcharset162\fprq2
Times New Roman Tur;}
{\f22\froman\fcharset186\fprq2 Times New Roman Baltic;}{\f29\fmodern\fcharset238\fprq1 Courier
New CE;}{\f30\fmodern\fcharset204\fprq1 Courier New Cyr;}{\f32\fmodern\fcharset161\fprq1 Courier
New Greek;}{\f33\fmodern\fcharset162\fprq1 Courier New Tur;}
{\f34\fmodern\fcharset186\fprq1 Courier New
Baltic;}}{\colortbl;\red0\green0\blue0;\red0\green0\blue255;\red0\green255\blue255;\red0\green25
5\blue0;\red255\green0\blue255;\red255\green0\blue0;\red255\green255\blue0;\red255\green255\blue
255;
\red0\green0\blue128;\red0\green128\blue128;\red0\green128\blue0;\red128\green0\blue128;\red128\
green0\blue0;\red128\green128\blue0;\red128\green128\blue128;\red192\green192\blue192;}{\stylesh
eet{\widctlpar\adjustright \fs20\cgrid \snext0 Normal;}{\*
\cs10 \additive Default Paragraph Font;}{\s15\widctlpar\adjustright \f2\fs20\cgrid \sbasedon0
\snext15 Plain Text;}}{\info{\author xxx}{\operator
xxx}{\creatim\yr2002\mo10\dy28\hr11\min24}
{\revtim\yr2002\mo10\dy28\hr11\min24}{\version2}{\edmins0}{\nofpages1}{\nofwords20}{\nofchars114
}{\*\company xxx
Inc.}{\nofcharsws140}{\vern113}}\widowctrl\ftnbj\aenddoc\formshade\viewkind4\viewscale100\pgbrdr
head\pgbrdrfoot \fet0\sectd
\linex0\headery709\footery709\colsx709\endnhere\sectdefaultcl
{\*\pnseclvl1\pnucrm\pnstart1\pnindent720\pnhang{\pntxta
.}}{\*\pnseclvl2\pnucltr\pnstart1\pnindent720\pnhang{\pntxta
.}}{\*\pnseclvl3\pndec\pnstart1\pnindent720\pnhang{\pntxta .}}{\*\pnseclvl4
\pnlcltr\pnstart1\pnindent720\pnhang{\pntxta
)}}{\*\pnseclvl5\pndec\pnstart1\pnindent720\pnhang{\pntxtb (}{\pntxta
)}}{\*\pnseclvl6\pnlcltr\pnstart1\pnindent720\pnhang{\pntxtb (}{\pntxta
)}}{\*\pnseclvl7\pnlcrm\pnstart1\pnindent720\pnhang{\pntxtb (}
{\pntxta )}}{\*\pnseclvl8\pnlcltr\pnstart1\pnindent720\pnhang{\pntxtb (}{\pntxta
)}}{\*\pnseclvl9\pnlcrm\pnstart1\pnindent720\pnhang{\pntxtb (}{\pntxta )}}\pard\plain
\s15\fi-1080\li1080\widctlpar\tx720\adjustright \f2\fs20\cgrid {\tab
1. noun, a gem variety of corundum in transparent or translucent crystals of a color other than
red; especially,a transparent rich blue
\par }\pard\plain \widctlpar\adjustright \fs20\cgrid {
\par }}
```

Figure 2.3 RTF results from the Word 97 version of sapphire_excerpt.

9. Open another Notepad instance. Again, use Start, Programs, Accessories, Notepad.
10. When Notepad has started this time, click File and then Open. In the Open dialog box, navigate the Look In field's directory structure until you find the HTML format file you saved in Step 5. Again, you may have to click the down arrow to open the drop-down menu in the Files of Type field and then select All Files.
11. When the HTML version of the file is displayed, you will see your text, but the HTML tags have been altered and several extra tags have been inserted by Word again. Figure 2.4 illustrates what happened with our sapphire excerpt example. For a small and simple file such as this, the conversion to HTML seems acceptable. For larger, complex documents, it could cause headaches.

It should be clear from the results displayed in Figure 2.3 why old versions of Microsoft Word, despite all its document production benefits in many other contexts, is not as good a tool for XML document creation as other HTML-specific applications.

Meanwhile, if you had used Notepad to view the file in DOC format, or even in TXT format, you would have seen that additional information had been added to the sapphire file, but the extra characters would have been unreadable. At least in the RTF and HTML formats you can see what Word 97 was trying to convey. Do you understand now why the size of the HTML version of the file is approximately 1 KB, while the RTF version is 3 KB? And Word 97's DOC version is 19 KB!

```
sapphire_excerpt_Word97.htm - Notepad
File  Edit  Format  Help
<HTML>
<HEAD>
<META HTTP-EQUIV="Content-Type" CONTENT="text/html; charset=windows-1252">
<META NAME="Generator" CONTENT="Microsoft Word 97">
</HEAD>
<BODY>
<DIR>
<DIR>
<DIR>

<FONT FACE="Courier New" SIZE=2><P>&#9;1. noun, a gem variety of corundum in
transparent or translucent crystals of a color other than red; especially, a
transparent rich blue</P>
</FONT><FONT SIZE=2></DIR>
</DIR>
</DIR>
</FONT></BODY>
</HTML>
```

Figure 2.4 The sapphire_excerpt document after being saved in HTML format looks like this figure.

Integrated Development Environments

In general, any integrated development environment looks like a single application, but it is much more than that. IDEs are a combination of text editors, compilers, debuggers, GUI developers, version tracking and control, and even document databases. They may be standalone applications, may be a base application with plug-ins for extensibility, or may come already bundled as a number of compatible applications. Some examples of IDEs that you may already be familiar with and that provide a fairly user-friendly framework are Microsoft's Visual Basic and IBM's Visual Age for Java for programming languages, and Macromedia, Inc.'s Dreamweaver or Microsoft's FrontPage for HTML development.

XML IDEs not only enable you to create and edit XML documents, they also usually include the functions listed in the previous paragraphs plus all the major aspects of XML design and editing, such as document authoring, editing, and validation; DTD or schema editing, and validation; and Extensible Stylesheet Language editing and transformation (the latter topic is discussed in detail in Chapter 9, "XML Transformations").

A sophisticated IDE environment facilitates large project development and coordination by teams of developers who may be side by side on the same network or even around the world from each other. Some IDEs even provide shared file repositories with check-in and check-out control, where two developers cannot modify the same file at the same time.

Some IDE tools provide version control where, at certain points in the development cycle, the developer or team may decide to save the whole project in its state at that time to create a particular intermediate version of the project.

Take a look at Figure 2.5, where several developers are working independently on their respective documents and each developer's workstation is equipped with an instance (the developer's own copy, perhaps, or a network copy) of the IDE software.

The documents or other physical entities on which they are working are likely located inside a repository structure on one or more servers inside—or even outside—the company intranet. This is achieved by setting up directory or filesystem shares, and by the IDE software keeping track of the locations of the entities in a small database of its own.

According to a schedule, the developers will close and *version* their code; then the network administrator (or Webmaster) will move their files into a development or staging environment for testing. That testing environment is modeled after the production environment but is usually smaller scale. After the documents and other entities are tested and all necessary corrections are made, the files are then promoted by the Webmaster on to the Web servers in a DMZ—that is, into the production environment—where they can be accessed by end users.

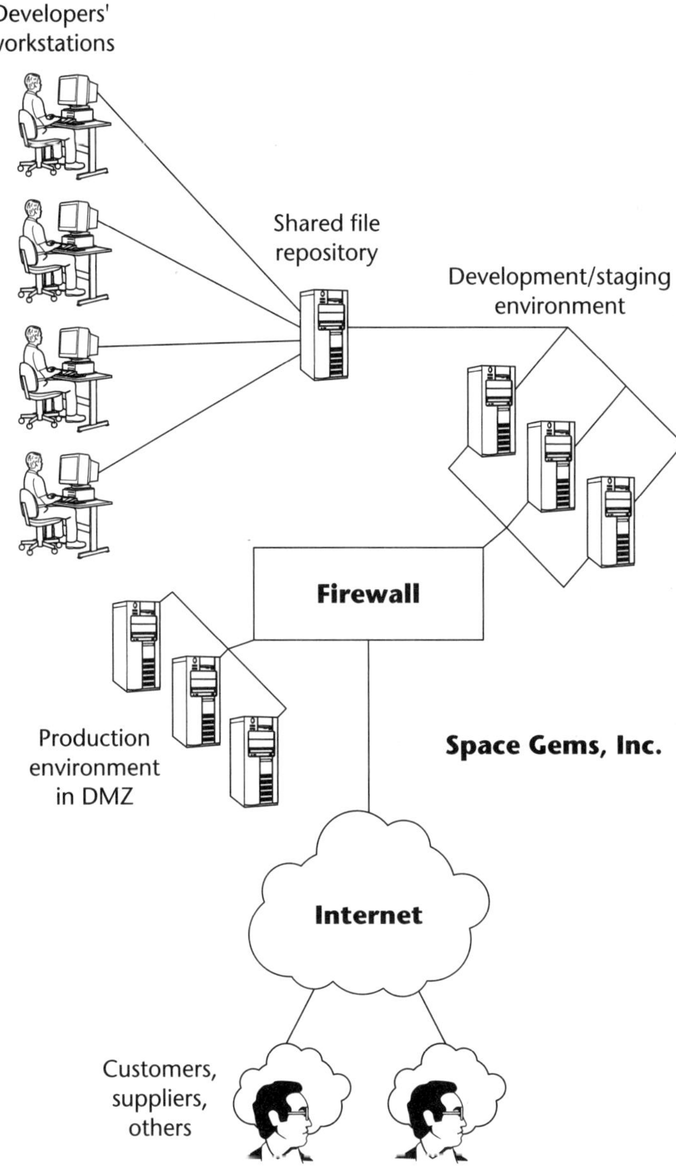

Figure 2.5 One possible IDE configuration.

Moving documents directly from a developer's desktop directly into the production environment is *not* a recommended practice.

Classroom Q & A

Q: Occasionally, when our colleagues back at the office have used IDEs, they've encountered the phrase "save the document to the project" or something similar. Is that the same as the old familiar "save the file"?

A: No, it means something quite different. Saving to a project means creating an entry in the project database to show the IDE where a document or other entity is located so that it might be properly retrieved and rendered with the rest of the documents that pertain to the project. It is *not* the same as saving a file, which must still be done in addition to saving to a project. So it is a two-step operation: Save the document (in other words, create a permanent copy in the repository); then save the document to the project (tell the IDE where in the repository, the permanent copy of the document can be found).

Several XML IDEs are available. Here are a few popular examples:

TurboXML. Developed by TIBCO Software Inc., TurboXML is an IDE that supports DTDs and schemas for XML document creation and project management. You can investigate TurboXML and other TIBCO XML software as well as download a trial version of TurboXML at the TIBCO Web site, www.tibco.com/solutions/products/extensibility/turbo_xml.jsp. This Java-based Integrated Development Environment is available for the following operating systems: Windows 95/98/2000 and NT, Mac OS X, Linux x86, Solaris SPARC, Solaris x86, HP-UX 11.0 and 11i, and other Unix platforms.

Corel XMetaL. This is another application that has evolved from a graphical editor to an IDE. It provides integration between the WYSIWYG authoring tool, content repositories, databases, and other workflow systems. It also provides the capability to convert documents from other formats (including Microsoft Word and Excel) to XML. You can download a trial version of XMetaL from the SoftQuad Web site at www.xmetal.com/top_frame.sq.

Xeena. Xeena is a visual editor developed by IBM that is more "IDE-minus" than "editor-plus." Xeena takes an existing DTD or schema and builds a context-sensitive palette of elements defined by those documents to help ensure validity from the start. You can work on more than one document at once. Xeena can be integrated with other document management systems, repositories, and versioning regimes. For further information on Xeena, or to download a trial version, go to its Web site at www.alphaworks.ibm.com/tech/xeena.

XML Spy. Developed by Altova GmbH (Austria)/Altova, Inc. (United States) and first released in February 1999, Spy is a Windows application that supports Unicode and all major character-set encodings, DTDs, and XML schemas. Its editor provides five different document views. It can import text files, Word documents, and data from Access, Oracle, and SQL Server databases. For further information and to download a free 30-day evaluation version, go to Altova's Web site at www.xmlspy.com.

Komodo. Developed by ActiveState Corporation, Komodo is a multilanguage IDE with an integrated debugger, leading-edge XSLT support, and other significant IDE features. It is available for Windows and Linux environments. For further information, or to download a trial version, go to the ActiveState Web site at www.activestate.com/Products/Komodo/pricing_and_licensing.plex.

Arbortext Epic. Designed by Arbortext, Inc. for creating XML and SGML content, Epic supports DTDs, schemas, and other core XML standards. Arbortext offers many additional and powerful "integrations" (their term). It's available for Windows and Sun Solaris Unix. For information regarding Epic's many features, visit Arbortext's Web site at www.arbortext.com/html/epic_editor_datasheet.html.

Converting HTML Documents to XML

For documents that are already in non-XML formats, such as Microsoft Word or other word processing formats, HTML, and others, there are non-XML conversion applications (also called N-converters) available to convert those files to XML.

Several Web sites contain links to non-XML to XML and vice versa converters. Here are a few:

- HTML Tidy, a command-line program, found at www.w3.org/People/Raggett/tidy/.
- TidyCOM, a Windows interface wrapper utility that allows you to use Tidy in a Microsoft Windows environment, found at http://perso.wanadoo.fr/ablavier/TidyCOM/.
- Lars Garshol's Web site titled "XML tools by category: A part of Free XML Tools" at www.garshol.priv.no/download/xmltools/cat_ix.html.
- Go to the XML software Web site at www.xmlsoftware.com/ and then click Technical, Conversion tools. Navigate to a page that, at this writing, has an amazing 47 conversion applications of various descriptions.

Other conversion applications can be found through World Wide Web search engines. Further, some of the graphical text and IDE applications also provide conversion utilities.

Chapter 2 Labs: Creating an XML Authoring Environment

As we mentioned in Chapter 1, most of the labs in this book revolve around Space Gems, Inc., our fictitious intergalactic precious gem dealer. You will be assuming the role of their Web developer. This section summarizes the hardware and software requirements for the Chapter 2 labs and provides an overview about creating your XML environment.

Computer System Requirements

As mentioned in the *Hardware Requirements* section earlier in this chapter, a large computer system is not required to perform the labs contained in this book. Neither the Web server nor the XML editor will use much CPU or RAM. For a list of system requirements, please refer to that section.

Operating System Requirements

As mentioned briefly in Chapter 1, all of the instructions and conventions in this book presume that you are using Microsoft Windows 2000 Professional as a base operating system. These exercises will also work using Windows XP Professional and Linux. Instructions for using both Windows 2000 and XP are documented within this book.

If you have installed—or will be installing—Linux as your operating system, you will find instructions for installing the Apache Web server and TurboXML at the *XML in 60 Minutes a Day* Web site as noted in the book's introduction.

Creating Your XML Environment: Overview

Once a version of the Windows operating system has been installed, there are still two basic steps to complete before the XML environment is created. They are as follows:

- Installing a Web server
- Installing an XML editor

In Lab 2.1, you will install Microsoft Internet Information Services (IIS) as the Web server. Linux users, on the other hand, will have to install and configure the Apache Web server software that comes with Linux. Again, all of the necessary instructions for configuring Apache on Linux are available on the *XML in 60 Minutes a Day* Web site.

In Lab 2.2, you'll install TIBCO Software, Inc.'s TurboXML as the XML editor. With little effort, this lab could also be performed with other XML editing tools, such as Altova Inc./Altova GmbH's XML Spy; however, we recommend that you perform the steps using the TurboXML editor prior to adapting the steps for any other editor. If you attempt to install another editor with the Lab 2.2 instructions, be prepared for conversions, substitutions, and troubleshooting.

Lab 2.1: Installing Microsoft's IIS Web Server

In this first lab, you will install, configure, and test Microsoft's IIS Web server as the first component of your XML working environment.

There are four basic steps to installing and configuring a Microsoft IIS Web server:

- Installing and starting the Microsoft Internet Information Services (IIS)
- Creating a Web server root directory
- Configuring IIS (that is, creating a virtual host and installing content files in its Web server root directory)
- Testing IIS

Lab 2.1, therefore, has been split into four sections: one for each of those Web server installation steps.

Installing Internet Information Services (IIS)

These instructions presume that you have installed Windows 2000 or XP Professional. Before you proceed, ensure that you have tested your Internet connection. An active connection to the Internet is required to download some HTML Web server content that has already been generated for you and is stored on the *XML in 60 Minutes a Day* Web site in a file called SG_webcontent.zip. We did this to save you time and effort. You will be working with and modifying these files throughout this book.

Also, ensure that you have your Windows 2000 or XP Professional installation CD nearby. You'll need it because during the configuration of IIS, you will be prompted to insert the CD so it can copy some additional dynamic link library (DLL) files into the operating system directories.

Windows 2000 or XP Professional versions come with either IIS or Personal Web Services. Unfortunately, neither IIS nor Personal Web Services is available for Windows XP Home.

As you install, configure, and test the IIS Web server, you will also create a virtual host called SpaceGems. The Web server root is C:\WWW\SpaceGems\. You will then be ready to install the XML editor.

To install IIS, perform these steps:

1. Log on as an Administrator.
2. Click Start, Settings, Control Panel.
3. Double-click Add/Remove Programs.
4. Click Add/Remove Windows Components.
5. Click the check box next to the Internet Information Services (IIS) component, and then click Next.
6. Insert the Windows product CD-ROM when appropriate. You should now have an IIS Admin Service running on the system.
7. Click Start, Settings, Control Panel, Services. Look for the IIS Admin Service, and make sure that it is started.

Creating a Web Server Root Directory

Before configuring your IIS Web server, you first have to create a directory (folder) to hold the Web server content. Later, during the configuration of the Web server, you have to provide the folder name and the path to it to indicate where the Web content will reside. We encourage you to use the same pathing convention so the links within the supplied content files will function without editing.

To create a Web server root directory, perform these steps:

1. In the next section of Lab 2.1, you will create a virtual host called SpaceGems. In preparation for that, create a folder called C:\WWW\SpaceGems. This folder will be the Web root for the Web service.

You can use any appropriate drive letter to represent the hard disk drive as long as you keep track of it and use it consistently. By default, this book will use C: as the hard disk convention.

2. Download the SG_webcontent.exe file from the *XML in 60 Minutes a Day* Web site, and expand the files into the C:\WWW\SpaceGems folder so that the index.html file will reside in the SpaceGems folder.

Configuring Internet Information Services

Microsoft Internet Information Service's default parameters are not quite suitable for the environment that we are trying to create, so we will create a new virtual host called SpaceGems with a separate Web root defined as C:\WWW\SpaceGems.

1. On the Windows Desktop, right-click My Computer.
2. Click Manage.
3. Expand Services and Applications, Internet Information Services.
4. Right-click Default Web Site and then choose New, Virtual Directory on the context menu. Click Next to continue.
5. Enter SpaceGems as the Alias, and click Next.
6. Browse to the C:\WWW\SpaceGems folder inside the Virtual Directory Creation Wizard dialog box, and click Next.
7. Check all of the boxes to enable all functions inside the Access Permissions Window; then click Next, Yes, and Finish.

The only reason we are enabling all features is because this is a development environment. This would not be proper practice for a production environment.

8. Right-click SpaceGems, and then choose Properties.
9. Click Documents, and click Add.
10. Enter index.html as the Default Document Name; then click OK.
11. Use the up arrow to move index.html document to the top of the list, and then click OK.
12. Refresh the service for the new parameters to take effect. Right-click Default Web Site again, and then choose Stop to stop the Web service. After it has stopped, press Start to refresh the service.

You now have a functional Web service that will serve an index page for http://localhost/spacegems. You have no doubt noticed that, at present, the index page is very basic. We will be adding functionality to the index page and the rest of the Web site as we develop the Space Gems scenario throughout the book.

Testing Internet Information Services

To test your IIS installation, perform these steps:

1. Perform a ping test on http://localhost/spacegems.
   a. On your desktop, click Start, Programs, Accessories, Command Prompt to open a command window.
   b. At the prompt, type the following command:

      ```
      ping localhost
      ```

      The response should be 127.0.0.1.

2. Open a browser and, in the location bar, enter the following URL:

```
http://localhost/spacegems
```

The displayed index page should look similar to the presentation in Figure 2.6.

Figure 2.6 Space Gems' index page, viewed in Internet Explorer.

You have now created your starting point for the Space Gems case study. This modest Web site will be further developed as we move through the lab exercises in this book.

This concludes the first part of the creation of your XML environment. In the next lab, you will install the TurboXML editor.

Lab 2.2: Installing TurboXML

In Lab 2.2, you will install a 30-day evaluation version of TIBCO Software, Inc.'s XML editor called TurboXML. This is the second of the two major components in your XML working environment.

After the product is installed, you will require a 30-day trial code to enable the editor. A trial code can be obtained by visiting either TIBCO's Web site at www.tibco.com/solutions/products/extensibility/turbo_xml.jsp or this book's Web site, as noted in its introduction, and clicking the TurboXML link. As you access the download link for TurboXML, you will be asked to register. After registering with TIBCO, you will receive a complete link with a registration product code containing a complete set of instructions on how to download the TIB_turboxml_2.3.0_w32.exe by email. The system will only take a minute to generate the email message for you.

After you have received the link and code by email from TIBCO, perform these steps:

1. Download the TIB_turboxml_2.3.0_w32.exe file, and then double-click the file to initiate the installation.
2. Accept all of the defaults by clicking Next for the installation.
3. Open the TurboXML editor, and fill out the TurboXML Registration dialog box.
4. Enter the registration code that TIBCO sent you in the email, and click Continue Trial. You will be presented with a small TurboXML window like the one shown in Figure 2.7.

   TurboXML will be used as the XML editor for all the lab exercises in this book. Using a professional XML editor such as TurboXML will allow us to introduce some advanced and sophisticated techniques without having to subject you to too much coding.
5. Close the TurboXML window.

This concludes the installation of your XML editor. You have now installed a typical XML development environment for a small Web site. In future lab exercises, we'll show you how to use these tools.

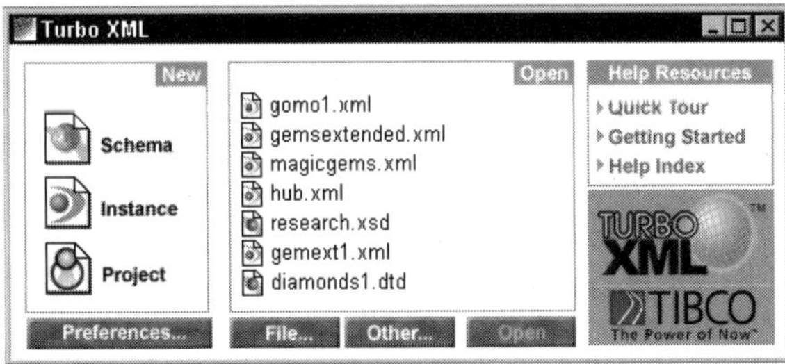

Figure 2.7 TurboXML introductory window.

Summary

Before you move on to Chapter 3, take a moment to review these key concepts from Chapter 2. Some of the Chapter 2 information will serve you in other Internet-related areas, too.

- A minimal XML working environment consists of a personal computer with a current operating system (with the installation files nearby on hard disk or CD-ROM), a robust Internet connection, a copy of current Web server software, a copy of current Web browser software, and a copy of XML authoring software.
- A Web server is a computer system with the appropriate software installed to allow it to respond to Internet requests. The Web server is generally located on a lower-security segment of an organization's network (the segment is often referred to as a demilitarized zone, or DMZ) and connected through a firewall to the Internet.
- Virtual hosting allows you to create more than one Web site on one Web server system. Each Web site, however, will still have its own domain name and IP address.
- A Web browser is a client application that is used to locate, request, and display Web pages and to navigate from one Web site or page to another. It usually also contains email and chat clients. Almost all browsers are graphical in nature. To read XML, though, a browser must also contain an XML processor.
- There are three basic categories of XML authoring tools: simple text editors, graphical text editors, and integrated development environments (IDEs).
- Because XML is an open standard, it doesn't restrict you to a single editor or even a single kind of editor. You can work on a document with one type at first and then later switch to another.
- Simple text editors are small, uncomplicated, and easy on computer system resources. That's why they ship and install with the base operating systems. They don't have many editing features, but they are still widely used to examine and create XML documents.
- Graphical XML editors have several more features and provide a GUI display. Many word processors and other business suite applications, as well as HTML editors, have been modified to provide XML support.

- Integrated development environments often look like a single application program with sophisticated features. However, they are often a combination of two or more applications: editors, compilers, debuggers, repositories, and version control applications.
- Conversion applications are available, such as the command line-oriented HTML Tidy or the Windows-oriented TidyCOM, which will convert non-XML documents (such as Microsoft Word documents and HTML documents) into XML documents. Some of the IDE tools also provide conversion capability.

Review Questions

1. What are the four software components that compose an XML authoring environment?
2. Why would a Web server be located in a demilitarized zone segment of an organization's network?
3. Which of the following would be shared by all Web sites on a server in a virtual hosting environment?
   a. Web root directories
   b. Default filenames
   c. Caching
   d. File directory or folder hierarchies
   e. Plug-ins
   f. Error files and restricted access files
   g. Security realms
4. To read XML, a browser application must contain an____________________ (also called an ________________).
5. True or false? After you begin authoring an XML document, you must use the same authoring tool to edit that document.
6. Why should you be wary of using earlier versions of Microsoft Word for creating XML documents?
7. What are N-converters?
8. In your lab exercise, what were the four steps to installing the IIS Web server?
9. After you have configured the Microsoft Web server, what do you have to do to ensure that the parameters become effective?
10. What two-step procedure did you use to test the Web server?

Answers to Review Questions

1. The four software components that compose an XML authoring environment are as follows:
   a. An operating system
   b. A Web server
   c. A Web browser
   d. An XML authoring application
2. A Web server might be located in a demilitarized zone segment of an organization's network to keep outside hackers from accessing the higher-security private segment of an organization's network.
3. In a virtual hosting environment, the Web sites would share **c.**, **e.**, and **g.**
4. To read XML, a browser application must contain an XML parser (also called an XML processor).
5. False. XML is an open standard. You can edit any XML document with nearly any editor. Restrictions might be applied if some tools can't see a defining DTD or schema, though. When in doubt, use a simple text editor, although it can be inconvenient for large files or extensive edits.
6. Earlier versions of Microsoft Word add extraneous information and tags, which introduce the risk of confusion with the descriptive tags you might have created in the same documents.
7. N-converters are applications that assist you in converting non-XML format documents to XML.
8. The four basic steps to installing a Microsoft IIS Web server are as follows:
   a. Installing and starting the Microsoft Internet Information Services (IIS)
   b. Creating a Web server root directory
   c. Configuring IIS (that is, creating a virtual host and installing content files in its Web server root directory)
   d. Testing IIS
9. Refresh the Web service: Stop the Web service, and then, only after the system has indicated that the Web service has indeed stopped, start the Web service.
10. To test the Web server, we first performed a ping test on http://localhost/*Websitename* (in the lab exercise, the Web site name was spacegems) from a command window. After that part was successful, we started our browser application and then went to the http://localhost/*Websitename* URL.

Anatomy of an XML Document

Many XML-related languages, applications, and Web sites have appeared since XML development began in the mid-1990s. The pace of development is accelerating, too, but without properly constructed XML documents, none of them can be effective.

In previous chapters, we explained where XML comes from and how to set up an XML working environment. Now we're ready to begin building some XML documents. In this chapter, you will learn a little about applications, XML parsers, an XML document's logical and physical structure and its components, and the principles of well-formedness and validity.

By the end of this chapter, you will know what an XML document is, how it sends instructions to an application and parser, and how to create and structure an XML document.

What Are XML Documents?

In Chapter 1, "XML Backgrounder," we discussed how documents have evolved from files created by text applications to electronic files of any size for any media (for example, text, audio, video, and graphics) created by any application. As noted, the XML 1.0 Recommendation defines an *XML document* as a "data object if it is well-formed, as defined in (Extensible Markup Language Recommendation). Each XML document has both a logical and a physical structure."

Expanding that definition, each XML document contains a unique instance of logically structured data, plus additional instructions for the parser and the application. The data instance portion contains data components with unique values. All the components and their respective values must conform to definitions in the language's conformance-checking mechanisms—in other words, a document type definition or schema. After being processed by an XML parser, the data in a document is structured and then passed to the application.

But the W3C has drawn a bit of a boundary around XML documents when they refer to them as data objects. They are not quite the same as, say, Java objects, which can contain a combination of data and procedures to manipulate the data. With XML, manipulation is left to the parsers and applications.

As you progress through this chapter, you will begin to understand why those who think XML documents are just text documents—mostly because, on the surface, text is all they seem to contain—tend to underestimate XML's capability to structure and integrate data of all types.

XML Document Processing

XML documents can't do anything on their own. Applications must be written to process the data contained in them. Here is an overview of the process by which applications call for and use XML documents.

Applications

Used alone, the term *application* means a program or group of programs intended for end users and designed to access and manipulate data (in our case, the data in XML documents). Don't confuse this term with *XML application*, which is one of several terms used to refer to a derivative markup language created according to XML 1.0.

To clarify, consider the following comparison: A Web browser is an *application* that can access and display the information from XML documents. But the Synchronized Multimedia Integration Language (SMIL), discussed in Chapter 12, "SMIL," is an XML application because it is its own language, developed using XML 1.0 specifications.

It is not our intention to show you how to create applications; however, in the lab exercises later in this chapter, you will use applications to help you create an XML document or to display the results of your XML document creation labors. Meanwhile, to process XML documents, the applications must have XML parsers integrated within them.

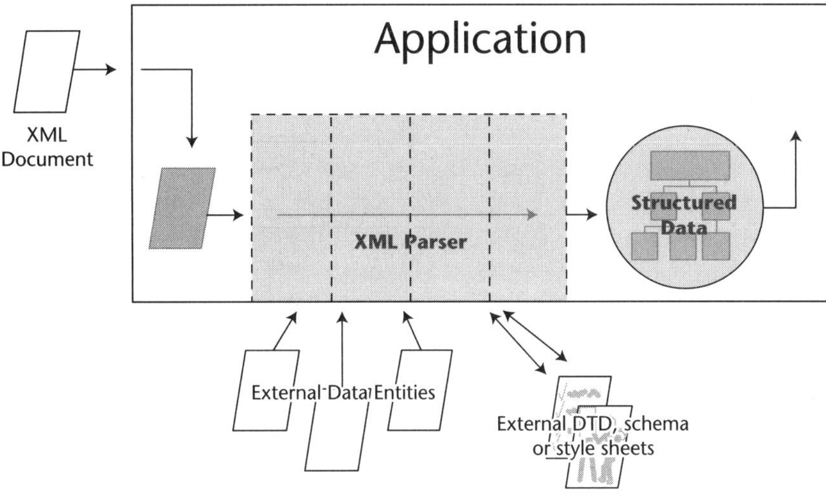

Figure 3.1 An XML parser translates XML entities into a data structure.

XML Parsers

XML processors—more commonly called XML parsers—are reusable pieces of code that are integrated with computer applications. Application developers can write their own parsers, but they don't need to; several are available—for free, on the Internet—which they can include in their applications. Later when an application calls for an XML document, the parser is activated, reads the XML document, and screens it on behalf of the application. *Screening* means the parser performs checks on the document, creates a data structure, and passes the structured data to the application. Figure 3.1 illustrates the process.

XML parsers are of two general types: those that check only for well-formedness and those that check for well-formedness *and* validity. The second type, which consults DTDs or schemas to check the document for conformance to the respective XML-related language, is called a *validating parser*.

Parsers generally contain four basic types of operators:

A content handler. Turns the document's string of characters into a sequence of events that are then translated into a treelike data structure (illustrated in Figure 3.1), which it then provides to the application.

An error handler. Determines the nature of any errors in the XML document and then acts accordingly. (Document errors are discussed in the section that follows.)

A DTD and schema handler. Examines the DTD or schema and then checks the XML document for conformity with the DTD or schema. This operator only appears in validating parsers.

An entity resolver. Incorporates any data referenced within the XML document's referential markup that is located outside the XML document entity itself or that is not intended to be parsed in a customary manner.

Several parsers are available, including expat (at www.jclark.com/xml/expat.html or http://sourceforge.net/projects/expat/), the Apache Software Foundation's Xerces (at http://xml.apache.org/), IBM's XML Parser for Java (at www.alphaworks.ibm.com/tech/xml4j), and Microsoft's MSXML (at http://support.microsoft.com/default.aspx?scid=fh;en-us;msxml).

Document Errors

Parsers occasionally encounter errors in XML documents. The W3C classifies errors in two ways: nonfatal and fatal errors. A nonfatal error is a violation of the rules of XML 1.0. For these errors, the W3C does not define specific penalties. They leave that up to the respective parser and application developers. They just say that "conforming software may detect and report an error and may recover from it."

Fatal errors are a different matter. The W3C stipulates that a conforming XML parser must be able to detect fatal errors and must then report them to the application, which can then produce its own error message. It is up to the application developer to code that in. The W3C goes on to say if a parser detects a fatal error, it may continue processing, but only to look for more errors; it is not allowed to continue normal content processing.

In the section *What Is a Well-Formed XML Document?* later in this chapter, we discuss XML 1.0's well-formedness constraints. For now, we'll state that violations of those constraints, among others, constitute fatal errors. (For a more comprehensive explanation of errors and fatal errors, consult the XML 1.0 Recommendation.)

The Structure of XML Documents

XML 1.0 states that XML documents have two kinds of structure: a logical structure and a physical structure. Although we will discuss the basic physical structure of an XML document in this chapter, later chapters will tend to discuss logical structure predominantly. There are two reasons:

- It's the easiest way to give you an idea of how the languages and their respective documents are supposed to work—that is, to show you how to create and structure components to achieve your objectives.
- The logical approach provides a good model for understanding, comparing, and even combining XML-related vocabularies and documents.

The physical structure of XML documents tends not to stray far from the basics we'll show you in this chapter. However, if important physical structure or other concerns arise during the discussions of the other XML-related languages, we address them, too.

Before we begin discussing the logical structure, though, let's fine-tune three of our fundamental definitions. Here we've paraphrased the text, markup, and character data definitions listed by the W3C in XML 1.0:

- Text consists of intermingled markup and character data.
- Markup consists of the following:
  - In the prolog: XML declarations, processing instructions, document type declarations, comments, and any white space.
  - In the data instance (that is, within the scope of the root element): start tags, end tags, empty element tags, attributes entity references, character references, and CDATA section delimiters.
- Character data is all text that is not markup.

The Logical Structure

The basic logical structure of an XML document consists of the following:

- The prolog
- The data instance (that is, the root element and any elements contained in the root element)

The Prolog

The prolog is a preface or introduction to the XML document. It is the first major logical component of an XML document and, because of its content, must be inserted prior to the next major logical component, the data instance. The prolog provides initial advice to the application, the parser, and any human reader about the document and, especially, prepares the parser to better handle the data instance.

The prolog may contain up to five types of components:

- An XML declaration
- Processing instructions
- A document type declaration
- Comments
- White space

Refer to the simple XML document gems_excerpt_02.xml in Figure 3.2. It has a five-line prolog right at the beginning, consisting of an example of each of the five components listed previously. In fact, there are two comments. The use of white space may not be so obvious to you, but if there were no spaces or end-of-line indicators in the prolog of this document, we would have trouble recognizing the components easily and quickly; they would all run together. Don't worry about white space yet, though. We discuss it in more detail in the *White Space* section later in this chapter.

The XML Declaration

The XML 1.0 Recommendation suggests that every XML document should begin with an XML declaration that states, basically, that the document is indeed an XML document. The declaration (also called the header) must be on the document's first line. XML 1.0 also states that all prolog components are optional, but that a well-formed XML document should begin with an XML declaration.

We strongly recommend that you include an XML declaration at the beginning of every XML document to help ensure that it is well formed.

```
<?xml version="1.0" encoding="UTF-8" standalone="no"?>
<?xml-stylesheet type="text/css" href="diamonds2.css"?>
<!DOCTYPE diamonds SYSTEM "diamonds2.dtd">
<!-- Gems Version 2 - Space Gems, Inc. -->
<!-- filename: gems_excerpt_02.xml -->
<diamonds>
        <gem>
                <name>Sparkler</name>
                <carats>105</carats>
                <color>F</color>
                <clarity>IF</clarity>
                <cut>Super Ideal</cut>
                <cost>126000</cost>
                <reserved />
        </gem>
        <gem>
                <name>Merlin</name>
                <carats>41</carats>
                <color>D</color>
                <clarity>FL</clarity>
                <cut>Ideal</cut>
                <cost>82000</cost>
        </gem>
</diamonds>
```

Figure 3.2 A simple XML document containing a five-line prolog.

Let's examine the XML declaration statement from Figure 3.2. The basic tag for an XML declaration statement is <?xml ... ?>. XML 1.0 specifies that *xml* must be lowercase. The XML declaration is actually a kind of processing instruction (discussed next); that is, it talks to the *application*, not to the parser. What it says, in a way, is "activate the XML parser; this is an XML document" and then provides additional information about the document for use by the application and the parser. The information appears in three pseudo-attributes: the XML version number (version="1.0"), the document's language encoding designation (encoding="UTF-8"), and the standalone pseudo-attribute specification (standalone="no").

We discuss pseudo-attributes and attributes in detail later in this chapter. They're similar concepts, but not identical. In the meantime, remember to enclose the value portion of all XML pseudo-attributes and attributes in quotation marks (double quotes are normally used, but single quotes are acceptable, too).

In the XML declaration, the XML version pseudo-attribute refers to the version of the XML Recommendation whose specifications the document has been written to. It is mandatory to state the version number. Currently, there is only Version 1.0, corresponding to the W3C's XML Recommendation 1.0, so *1.0* is the value that must be specified.

The encoding pseudo-attribute is optional. XML supports several character sets listed on the Internet Assigned Numbers Authority's Official Names for Character Sets Web site at www.iana.org/assignments/character-sets. Several values can be specified for the encoding pseudo-attribute. If you do not specify a value, the parser will use the UTF-8 default value. That value will suffice for everything we do in this book.

The third part of the declaration, the standalone pseudo-attribute, is also somewhat optional. If the document will be parsed by itself—that is, if there will be no need to refer to any external entities like DTDs or schemas that contain declarations for the components in the XML document—the standalone value should be yes (which is the default value if the standalone pseudo-attribute does not appear). If there are declarations in such external entities, however, and they must be enlisted by the XML parser before it can process the document, specify no.

Processing Instructions

The second line of Figure 3.2 is an example of a processing instruction (PI). PIs are instructions passed by the XML processor to the application and, so, are rather frowned on by XML purists. Processing instruction syntax looks similar to the following:

```
<?piname pseudo-attributes?>
```

Similar to the XML declaration statement, a single question mark appears at the beginning and the end of a processing instruction. The *piname*, also called the PI name or PI target, tells the application what type of PI it is. It is up to the application developers to code in which PI targets will be recognized.

The second line of Figure 3.2 is a common PI that is recognized by browsers like Internet Explorer and Netscape Navigator. The PI name is the fairly common xml-stylesheet; we're telling the application that we are associating a style sheet with this document. The type pseudo-attribute tells the application to look for a text-type cascading style sheet that will instruct it how to display the components found in the XML document. The style sheet uniform resource identifier (URI) is simply diamonds2.css, meaning the name of the style sheet document is diamonds2.css and is found locally on the system because the URI contains no additional pathing information.

Later, in Chapter 9, "XML Transformations," you will see a PI similar to the following:

```
<?xml-stylesheet type="text/xsl" href="gems1.xsl"?>
```

This PI points the application to a different type of style sheet, one that will help transform an XML document to an HTML document.

If you are coding any other type of PI, don't use PI names beginning with the characters "XML," "xml," or similar. They have been reserved by the W3C for future XML standardization.

The Document Type Declaration

XML does not require the inclusion of the document type of declaration in all circumstances. The document type declaration (also called a DOCTYPE definition) tells the parser what function the document's author expects the document to play: That is, it tells the parser what *type* of document it is, then indicates to the parser how the document's components will be defined and related to one another. Let's look at the declaration on the third line of Figure 3.2.

The opening keyword DOCTYPE tells the XML parser that this statement is indeed a document type declaration. "Diamonds" indicates that the name of the class that the document belongs to is diamonds; that the document is a diamonds *type* of document. The class name is arbitrarily specified by the document developer and often coincides with the name of document element, which we will discuss in the section titled *The Data Instance* later in this chapter. For example, a developer who is writing a book might name the class of the basic document book and then import other XML documents, whose class names might be chapter, section, or whatever, into the book document.

Let's deviate from the Figure 3.2 example for a moment. If a developer chooses to provide the appropriate component declarations and then have the parser validate the document as well as check the document for well-formedness, the DOCTYPE definition statement is the place where the declarations would be inserted. For the Figure 3.2 document components, the document type declaration, complete with the inserted declarations, would resemble the following:

```
<!DOCTYPE diamonds [
     <!ELEMENT diamonds (gem)*>
     <!ELEMENT gem (name,carats,color,clarity,cut,cost,reserved?)>
     <!ELEMENT name (#PCDATA)>
     <!ELEMENT carats (#PCDATA)>
     <!ELEMENT color (#PCDATA)>
     <!ELEMENT clarity (#PCDATA)>
     <!ELEMENT cut (#PCDATA)>
     <!ELEMENT cost (#PCDATA)>
     <!ELEMENT reserved (EMPTY)>
]>
```

Notice that if the DOCTYPE definition (to use the alternate name) lists these declarations within its own confines, the developer must place the declarations between an opening square bracket and a closing square bracket. Doing so creates an *internal DTD*. If such an internal DTD is constructed, the standalone pseudo-attribute in the XML declaration would have to be standalone="yes".

Returning to the Figure 3.2 example, the keyword SYSTEM indicates to the parser that the declarations for the document's components will not be found in the Figure 3.2 document, but within an external document. Further, the parser should be ready to look for that external document on the local system and then check the Figure 3.2 document for validity against the declarations in the external document. But which external document and where is it? That is specified next in the URI that appears in quotation marks. The parser is to look for an external document named diamonds2.dtd.

If that external document is located even further remotely, the full path to the document would have to be specified in the URI instead of just the filename.

Classroom Q & A

Q: So you're saying that the declarations can be located in the XML document *or* in that other external document, right?

A: Not quite. We realize that, at this point, we have left you with that impression. However, declarations can exist in both places and work together. Your XML document may contain extra components in addition to those declared in the external document. Or maybe, for this document, you want to alter one or more of the component declarations from those in the external document. To do so, you would declare the additional or updated components right there in the Figure 3.2 document—in what is termed an *internal subset*—and rely on the external document—that is, the *external subset*—to provide the declarations for the rest of the components. The combination of the internal subset and the external subset is what you would correctly call the document type definition. In other words, both portions would form the complete DTD. We discuss this again in Chapter 4, "Document Type Definitions."

Even though document type declarations are optional, one is required if the developer intends the parser to validate the document by internal or external markup declarations. As a best practice to avoid ambiguity, we recommend always including a document type declaration in the prolog.

The various keywords, declarations, and the nature of internal and external DTDs are explained in detail in Chapter 4.

Comments

The purpose of adding comment statements to an XML document is not to provide instruction to the parser or to the application, because comments are ignored by the parser. Here are three purposes for comments:

- To say something to anyone who will later examine the XML document
- Combined with white space, to break a document into sections
- To temporarily disable sections of the document

XML uses the same comment syntax as HTML. The following are two examples:

```
<!-- Gems Version 1 - Space Gems, Inc. -->
<!-- filename: gems_excerpt_04.xml -->
```

Properly constructed, comments can be placed anywhere in a document; however, it is considered bad form to place a comment before the XML declaration statement.

After you have begun a comment, be careful not to use the literal string "--" (that is, two hyphens in a row) anywhere in it except at the very end. The XML parser will otherwise see the string and presume that the comment has ended, then create errors based on any remaining characters in the rest of the intended comment.

The Data Instance

The data instance portion of an XML document follows the prolog and consists of one or more elements. Elements are an XML document's data containers and are the basic building blocks of XML data instances.

Element Types, Tags, and Names

Each element begins and ends with its *element type* (also referred to as an element name), contained in a tag (some refer to tags as tag names, but purists prefer tags). There are three kinds of tags. *Start tags* (also called opening tags), appear at the beginning of an element, and *end tags* (or closing tags) appear at the end of an element. Also, a sort of hybrid tag introduces *declared-empty elements* (elements that are not intended to contain any data). Here is an excerpt from Figure 3.2, which illustrates all three kinds of tags:

```
<cost>126000</cost>
<reserved />
```

The <cost> tag is a start tag, the </cost> tag is an end tag, and <reserved /> is a declared-empty element tag. Notice that each tag is delimited by a left angle bracket (<) at the beginning and a right angle bracket (>) at the end. The end tag always has a slash immediately after the left angle bracket before its name. The empty element tag also has a slash, but it appears immediately before the ending angle bracket after the name. In the empty element tag, the /> combination tells the parser not to expect a classic end tag for this particular element.

We'll revisit declared empty elements later in this chapter when we discuss element content. Meanwhile, here are some rules for naming element types:

- They can begin with a letter, a colon, or an underscore, but they can't begin with a number.
- Subsequent characters may include letters, numbers, underscores, hyphens, colons, and periods, but they can't contain certain XML-specific symbols. Examples: the ampersand (&), the "at" symbol (@), and the less-than symbol (<).
- The names can't contain white space (a departure from SGML); they must be one continuous string of characters. If white space appeared in the name, the XML parser would treat the portion following the white space as an improperly constructed attribute. This is one reason why you occasionally see descriptive multiple word tags composed of a mixture of upper- and lowercase characters such as <elementType>.
- Names can't contain parenthetical statements to describe contents or intentions.

The element type is also called the element's generic identifier (GI). It's that *type* that is actually being declared (defined) in the DTD or schema. Thus, whenever an author inserts one or more elements with a given name, that author creates one or more instances of that type of element.

We concur with those who recommend that when you are creating names for element types, you should make them as descriptive of their contents as possible. This best practice facilitates human legibility, and the uniqueness of the name also facilitates the ability to search through a document quickly using text strings.

The Extent of an Element

An element extends from the first left angle bracket in its start tag through the start tag, through the element's content, and then through the end tag to the last right angle bracket. Here's an example of a complete element:

```
<name>Sparkler</name>
```

The upcoming section of this chapter, *Structuring Data with Nested Elements*, discusses how elements can be placed wholly (that is, nested) within other elements. That nesting increases the extent of the surrounding element. Here is an example:

```
<gem>
      <name>Sparkler</name>
      <reserved />
</gem>
```

In this case, the <gem> element extends from the first left angle bracket in the <gem> start tag, all the way through the complete <name> and <reserved /> elements, to the last right angle bracket in the </gem> end tag.

Elements Can Have Different Kinds of Content

As shown in the previous example, it is possible to locate elements wholly within other elements. In Figure 3.2, the <diamonds> element contains two <gem> elements and they, in turn, contain other elements. The <diamonds> element is the *document element* (also called the root element) because it contains the document's data instance. So <diamonds> serves two logical purposes: It is the root element, and it is the direct parent element of two elements—the two <gem> elements. And because <diamonds> contains two elements, but apparently does not contain any character data, it has *element content.*

The two sibling <gem> elements are the direct child elements of <diamonds>. Similar to <diamonds>, the <gem> elements also have element content because each contains child elements of its own.

Notice, however, that the child elements of the <gem> elements do not have element content. Because they contain character data strings (for example, names, numbers, and descriptive acronyms) instead, we say they have *data content*. The discussions of DTDs and XML schemas in their respective Chapters 4 and 5 expand upon these concepts.

It is also possible for elements to contain both elements and data, that is, to have *mixed content*. For example, Space Gems might have a child element called <saleDate> located inside a <gem> element, and its content might be character data describing the date that a gem was sold. Or its content may tell the parser to insert the contents of a <salePending> element and, consequently, display a message that states "sale of this gem has not yet been finalized" or something similar.

Additionally, an element can have content designated as *any*. That is, you can declare that an element will be valid as long as it contains *something*. A practice such as this, at first glance, probably seems imprecise, even risky. But it can be handy if you are trying to retrofit a new DTD to existing documents. This is discussed further in Chapter 4.

Empty Elements

In addition to containing several types of content, elements can also be empty. There are two types of empty elements:

Declared-empty. Elements that are intended to remain empty and so are defined that way in the document's DTD or schema.

Elements with no content. Elements whose DTD or schema declarations indicate that they *may* contain content. But, in certain cases, the start and end tags may appear, with no data between them, or the tags may not appear at all.

Declared-empty elements are often intended to function as a kind of marker, to indicate a point where, during the course of the execution of the application, something specific is supposed to happen. Or they may be used as document search criteria. For example, you may write a script that searches for and then somehow manipulates all documents, parent elements, or whatever, that contain certain specified elements.

Here, again, is the now-familiar declared empty <reserved> element:

```
<reserved />
```

When the XML parser encounters a tag with that syntax, it will recognize it and will not expect to encounter an end tag like </reserved>.

Here is the syntax for an element that has no content:

```
<cost></cost>
```

Chapter 4 shows you how to insert the appropriate declarations for these and declared empty elements in a DTD. Chapter 5, "XML Schemas," shows you similar syntax, but for a schema.

It is legal in XML to use empty element start tag and end tag syntax in a document, such as <reserved></reserved>, for elements declared to be empty, as well as for those elements that are eligible to contain data but have no content at the time. We recommend, however, that the best approach is still to use empty-element tag syntax (for example, <reserved />) for declared empty elements.

Attributes

Elements may, but don't necessarily have to, contain attributes, also known as attribute specifications. Attributes are another type of descriptive metadata (that is, data about data) that you can specify for your elements. Attributes take the form of name:value pairs, and you add them to your start tags immediately after the element name but separated from the name by at least a single space. Applications can be coded to look for them in XML documents, and to then manipulate the data in the elements that the attributes appear in.

Whether or not attributes are inserted, as well as their nature, is left to the discretion of the document author. When might you use them? Table 3.1 contains examples.

As you can see from Table 3.1, you can specify names for attributes and insert more than one attribute in a start tag. Be advised, though, that some applications are written to tolerate only a fixed few attributes.

Table 3.1 Examples of Attributes in Action

ELEMENT CONTAINING ATTRIBUTE	TRANSLATION
<gem location="Sol">	Gems that originate in the Sol system.
<gem catPublish="no">	Gems that will not appear in the catalog.
<gem location="Auriga" catPublish="yes">	Gems from the Auriga constellation that will appear in the catalog.
<gem status="loaned" return_exp="04-30-2049">	Inventory gems that are currently loaned to someone and are effectively not for sale at this time. Expect return on April 30, 2049.

There are concerns about the necessity for attributes, especially when child elements might work as well or better. The choice of whether and when to use attributes versus elements is contextual and must be left to the developer and the perceived needs at the time of development (for example, flexibility of the needed structure, processor power available, and the ability of developers and their applications to comprehend and manipulate the components in the structure). Here are some guidelines:

- Some applications may limit the number of attributes they will select.
- Attributes can't contain elements; if you want the information to be displayed or otherwise manipulated, it should appear in an element.
- Attributes can't be nested (that is, they can't contain other attributes), so attribute information must be simple and limited in descriptiveness.
- From a system and network performance standpoint, remember that smaller documents are processed more quickly by parsers. Using elements with attributes might enhance system performance.
- Similarly, performance might be enhanced if you avoid using default attribute values, which would likely be specified in external DTDs or schemas. With default values, the parser has to consult the external documents more often.
- Attribute names follow the same rules as element names.
- For any element, its attribute names must be unique.
- Remember that XML is case-sensitive. So an attribute named *location* is not the same as one named *Location* or *LoCaTiOn*.
- In XML, you must always assign values to your attributes; otherwise, XML parsers will treat HTML-like standalone attributes as errors.
- All attribute values must be surrounded by quotation marks; single and double are both acceptable.

The use of quotation marks can be complicated if the attribute value contains quotation marks of its own. Consider the following:

```
<msg_logistix text='From Logistics: "Asteroid activity causes shipment
delays at that time of year."'/>
```

In this example, the use of single quotes around the whole value preserves the value, which is double-quoted shipping advice from the Logistics group. Without the single quotes, the parser would have cut the message off prematurely and issued an error message. On the other hand, if the Logistics message had been in single quotes, the whole value could have remained in normal double quotes, which is the usual technique.

There are cases when an attribute value contains both single *and* double quotes. Consider this example, which uses XML named entities (discussed later in this chapter) to describe a display case that is 2 feet long, 6 inches wide, and 2-½ inches deep. The &apos is substituted in place of a single quote and " is substituted twice in place of double quotes.

```
<display_case size="2&apos; long/6&quot; wide
                    /2-&frac12&quot; deep">
```

Thus, *2' long* means 2′ *long*, while *6"wide* means 6″ *wide*, and *2-½" deep* means 2-½″ *deep*.

For further details about attributes, consult XML 1.0 at the W3C's Web site at www.w3.org/TR/2000/REC-xml-20001006.

Classroom Q & A

Q: Earlier, with respect to the XML declaration, you mentioned "pseudo-attributes." Are they the same as or different from attributes?

A: Pseudo-attributes look similar to attributes, but they're different. Pseudo-attributes appear in prologs, not in the data instance. And they describe an overall document (the XML document or a related external entity document), not an element or the data in it.

White Space

Ordinarily, white space, such as spaces, tabs, carriage returns, and blank lines, is used during document development to organize a document or to facilitate human legibility. After the document is built, the developer may only care that some basic white space is preserved—for example, single spaces between the individual words that constitute the parsed character data. Beyond that, normal XML data documents don't require additional white space preservation.

Meanwhile, when XML parsers examine documents and see all the extra tabs, spaces, and carriage returns inserted by the developers for organization and legibility, they don't issue error messages. Their white space normalization algorithms (for details regarding those algorithms, see XML 1.0) render the documents so that the parsers and applications can live with them and the data.

But there are some documents, such as those containing song lyrics, certain types of technical specifications and procedures, performance scripts, meeting minutes, poems, recipes, and similar documents, whose benefits depend on more than basic normalized white space treatment. They need their original customized character and "significant" white space structures, so their authors do care about parser and application treatment. Consider the following:

```
<poem>
     <title>Oh Diamond, Mine!</title>
     <stanza number="1">You dazzle us, you're brilliant!
                        Yet hard and so resilient
                        Symbol of love, loyalty and light
                        Sought after, day and night!
                        Oh diamond, mine!
     </stanza>
     <stanza number="2"> ...
     ...
</poem>
```

The XML parser would normally process this poem document as if it were one long string, such as the following:

```
<poem><title>Oh Diamond, Mine!</title><stanza number="1">You dazzle us,
you're brilliant!Yet hard and so resilient Symbol of love, loyalty
     and light Sought after, day and night!Oh diamond, mine!</stanza>
     <stanza number="2"> ... </poem>
```

How do we ensure that significant white space survives to the final output? An attribute named xml:space can be used for elements containing significant white space. There are only two value options for xml:space: *default*, which means, roughly, "let the application do what it would normally do," or *preserve*.

So the preceding poem's white space would be treated by the parser in a manner similar to the following:

```
<poem xml:space="preserve">
<title>Oh Diamond, Mine!</title>
     <stanza number="1">You dazzle us, you're brilliant!
                        Yet hard and so resilient
                        Symbol of love, loyalty and light
                        Sought after, day and night!
                        Oh diamond, mine!</stanza>
<stanza number="2"> ...
</poem>
```

Of course, the ultimate appearance of the poem would depend on the declarations in style sheets and other external documents, but the stanza would remain intact—the way the poet designed it.

Structuring Data with Nested Elements

Recall the data instance from the gems_excerpt_02.xml file in Figure 3.2:

```
<diamonds>
     <gem>
          <name>Sparkler</name>
          <carats>105</carats>
          <color>F</color>
          <clarity>IF</clarity>
          <cut>Super Ideal</cut>
          <cost>126000</cost>
     </gem>
     <gem>
          <name>Merlin</name>
          <carats>41</carats>
          <color>D</color>
          <clarity>FL</clarity>
          <cut>Ideal</cut>
          <cost>82000</cost>
     </gem>
</diamonds>
```

The root element is named <diamonds>. In the data instance portion of an XML document, the root element is the parent element of all other elements, because all the elements in the XML document have been placed in it. Typically, the root element is not considered to *have* a parent, though it will (almost) always *be* a parent. Why almost? If it contained data only and no other elements, it would likely spark a semantic debate. One side says, "It contains all the data, so it is still a parent element." The other side counters, "If there are no child elements, there can be no parent element." Pick whatever side you like, as long as you grasp the concept.

Conversely, as the root <diamonds> element is the parent of all the other elements, all other elements are children of the root element, either directly or indirectly.

The concept of placing one element within another is called *nesting*. Thus, elements can be nested within other elements. In gems_excerpt_02.xml, <diamonds> is the direct parent of two specific elements, both of which are called <gem>. In other words, the two <gem> elements are nested within <diamonds>.

Each of the two <gem> elements is a direct child element (also called a subelement) of the parent <diamonds> element. The two <gem> elements are also called *sibling elements* (some call them sister elements) to one another because they are both contained *within* the same parent element. Siblings are considered to be on the same level in the structure.

Meanwhile, each non-root element in the document can have only one parent element. As illustrated in gems_excerpt_02.xml, each child element must be wholly contained within the extent of its parent element and must not overlap with any sibling element. That constraint is vitally important with respect to the concepts of well-formedness and validity, which are discussed later in this chapter. To explain the statement by example, look at the <clarity> element in either <gem> element. The <clarity> element is contained in its respective <gem> only. No part of <clarity> appears outside of its own <gem>.

The two <gem> elements are also parent elements because they, in turn, contain their own child elements. The children of the top <gem> element have identical names to the child elements in the other <gem>; therefore, the child elements found in the top <gem> element are siblings to one another. Similarly, the child elements in the bottom <gem> are also siblings to one another; however, the child elements in the top <gem> are not siblings to the children of the bottom <gem> element. They do not have a common parent element.

Careful planning, as well as proper grammar and other proper construction techniques, provide developers the ability to make the best of parent-child logical structure concepts, no matter how small or large the XML documents become.

Namespaces

As XML development expands, everyone is going to be free to create XML-related languages and documents. The probability increases that many of us are going to create element types and attributes with identical names. Many applications are going to encounter name collisions as they try to sort out exactly which collections of data they are supposed to draw their referenced elements and attributes from, of the potentially millions out there.

Consider, for example, Figure 3.3, which depicts a document named gem_desc_29.xml that lists several descriptive details about a diamond named Smokey from the Ursae Majoris star system. Notice that there are four occurrences of *name:* twice as an element type name (providing the name of the gemstone and also the name of the mine where it was found), and twice as an attribute specification (in the <diamonds> element, where it indicates that Ursae Majoris is the value for the name of a star system, and in the <catalog> element, where it indicates the name of a catalog).

Imagine that an application is supposed to access this document and activate the parser to structure data that, it has been told, has a *name* component. How would it know which *name* it encounters is the appropriate one? In other words, how would it know it found the *name* component in the correct data set? Clearly, none of the occurrences of *name* in this document is truly unique, and so data manipulation would be troublesome. A parser would be lost if it didn't get some sort of additional information.

One strategy that is growing in popularity in the XML world is the use of XML *namespace declarations*. Take a look at the document named gem_desc_30.xml, depicted in Figure 3.4.

```
<?xml version="1.0" encoding="UTF-8" standalone="no"?>
<?xml-stylesheet type="text/css" href="diamonds2.css"?>
<!DOCTYPE diamonds SYSTEM "diamonds3.dtd">
<!-- Gems Version 2 - Space Gems, Inc. -->
<!-- filename: gem_desc_29.xml -->
<diamonds name="Ursae Majoris">

        <gem>
                <name>Smokey</name>
                <carats>1003</carats>
                <color>F</color>
                <clarity>IF</clarity>
                <cut>Ideal</cut>
                <cost>2250000</cost>
        </gem>
        <mine>
                <name>Ice Mountain 2 </name>
                <region>Montis Glacialis</region>
                <planet> Capitan </planet>
        </mine>
        <reserved />
        <catalog name="SpaceGems Diamonds" publish="yes" />

</diamonds>
```

Figure 3.3 An XML document that is subject to name collisions.

Notice that, in Figure 3.4, the start tag for the root element type <sg1:diamonds ...> contains several different attributes, each resembling *xmlns:sgx="http://www.SpaceGems.com/xxxxx/2047/."* Each of these attributes is called a *namespace declaration*. Namespace declarations create uniqueness for their respective element type names and attributes. Declaring them in the root element means that they will all apply throughout the extent of the root element—that is, throughout the data instance. Now, when the different instances of *name* appear, each has a different sgx: prefix (for example, *sg1:name* in <sg1:diamonds>). According to the declarations in the root element, each sgx: prefix represents a different namespace. Consequently, each *name* will be unique because each will have a different universal name. Here's a dissection of one of the namespace declarations:

xmlns This text string indicates to the parser that the attribute is an XML namespace declaration and that the element types and attributes will conform to the specifications in the W3C Recommendation titled Namespaces in XML, dated January 1999.

```
<?xml version="1.0" encoding="UTF-8" standalone="no"?>
<?xml-stylesheet type="text/css" href="diamonds2.css"?>
<!DOCTYPE diamonds SYSTEM "diamonds4.dtd">
<!-- Gems Version 2 - Space Gems, Inc. -->
<!-- filename: gem_desc_30.xml -->
<sg1:diamonds
        xmlns:sg1="http://www.SpaceGems.com/2047/"
        xmlns:sg2="http://www.SpaceGems.com/gems/2047/"
        xmlns:sg3="http://www.SpaceGems.com/mines/2047/"
        xmlns:sg4="http://www.SpaceGems.com/catalogs/2047/"
                        sg1:name="Ursae Majoris" >
        <sg2:gem >
                <sg2:name>Smokey </sg2:name>
                <sg2:carats>1003</sg2:carats>
                <sg2:color>F</sg2:color>
                <sg2:clarity>IF</sg2:clarity>
                <sg2:cut>Ideal</sg2:cut>
                <sg2:cost>2250000</sg2:cost>
        </sg2:gem>
        <sg3:mine >
                <sg3:name> Ice Mountain 2</sg3:name>
                <sg3:region>Montis Glacialis</sg3:region>
                <sg3:planet>Capitan</sg3:planet>
        </sg3:mine>
        <sg1:reserved />
        <sg4:catalog
                sg4:name="SpaceGems Diamonds" sg4:publish="yes" />
</sg1:diamonds>
```

Figure 3.4 XML document containing prefix namespaces.

: A colon is used as a delimiter between the *xmlns* text string and the prefix that follows. It indicates that a prefix will be used and that the text string appearing between the colon and the subsequent equal sign (=) is the prefix.

sg2 This text string is the prefix to be used in this example. It is an abbreviation that will be substituted for the whole namespace URI identifier when the time comes to create qualified names (discussed later in this chapter) for the element types and attributes. We will also discuss some occasions when a namespace is declared, but no prefix is specified or used in name creation (for example, when default namespaces or empty string namespaces will be specified).

http://www.SpaceGems.com/gems/2047/ This is the namespace URI identifier that qualifies the element type name or attribute name, and so ensures that an element type name or attribute name will be unique. It is also called the namespace name. It is the extra information that is provided to the parser to let the parser recognize the correct element type or attribute. In most cases, the URI takes the form of a URL, such as this one. Using URLs is recommended by the W3C Namespaces in XML Recommendation: They will add the uniqueness that you need, and they won't be rejected by parsers or applications on the basis of syntax because their syntax is well known. In the meantime, the parser will not bother to access this URL, so you do not have to install any documents at that location. In fact, the URL doesn't really even have to physically exist; the URL is only being used as a *logical device* to add uniqueness to an element type or attribute name.

Although it is not necessary for the Web site designated by the namespace URI identifier to exist, we do recommend creating one. It will allow you to maintain control over the URL itself (that is, it would be very unlikely anyone else would use the URL if you are the one who owns it). Also, as you see in the example, the year has been incorporated into the URL, too, to help ensure even more uniqueness.

In other words, in XML, a namespace is a logical device that represents a unique collection of declarations for element types and attributes. A namespace declaration is a signal to a parser that the component belongs to such a unique collection. The XML definition varies from the typical computing science definition of namespace, which is an actual physical collection of names in a data set.

The namespace declaration, in effect, creates what is called a *universal name* for an element type or attribute. In this case, the universal name tag for *name* would look like *<{http://www.SpaceGems.com/gems/2047/}name>*. The universal name is thus composed of *{http://www.SpaceGems.com/gems/2047/}*, which is called the *qualifying URI*, and *name*, which is called the *local part*.

The reason we say the universal name is *created in effect* and not just *created* is that the whole universal name isn't really created at all as such. A complete universal name, with the braces (that is, the curly brackets), dots, slashes, and other odd characters that potentially could be used to create the URL found in it, would cause trouble for the parser.

There are several kinds of namespace declarations:

- Prefix namespace declarations
- Default namespace declarations
- Empty string namespace declarations

Prefix Namespace Declarations

The examples shown in Figure 3.4 are prefix namespace declarations. We stated that the *sg2* text string is an abbreviation that is used instead of the whole namespace URI identifier when creating qualified names for element types and namespaces.

The start tag *<sg2:gem>* is an example of a qualified name, which consists of the prefix *sg2*, the colon (:) delimiter, and the *gem* local part. The prefix performs these functions:

- It identifies the name as being part of the declared namespace.
- It substitutes for the actual URI/URL, whose characters might otherwise run afoul of the parser.
- It is an abbreviation and thus saves keystrokes.

In the gem_desc_30.xml document in Figure 3.4, four different prefix namespace declarations, each with its own logical namespace, have been inserted in the root element so that each *name* will be unique. As you can see, the qualified names appear in the respective start tags, end tags, and declared empty tags.

Now let's examine a different, but just as effective, approach to prefix namespace declarations, as depicted in the document named gem_desc_31.xml in Figure 3.5.

```
<?xml version="1.0" encoding="UTF-8" standalone="no"?>
<?xml-stylesheet type="text/css" href="diamonds2.css"?>
<!DOCTYPE diamonds SYSTEM "diamonds4.dtd">
<!-- Gems Version 2 - Space Gems, Inc. -->
<!-- filename: gem_desc_31.xml -->
<sg1:diamonds xmlns:sg1="http://www.SpaceGems.com/2047/"
                                    sg1:name="Ursae Majoris">
        <sg1:gem xmlns:sg1="http://www.SpaceGems.com/gems/2047/">
                <sg1:name>Smokey</sg1:name>
                <sg1:carats>1003</sg1:carats>
                <sg1:color>F</sg1:color>
                <sg1:clarity>IF</sg1:clarity>
                <sg1:cut>Ideal</sg1:cut>
                <sg1:cost>2250000</sg1:cost>
        </sg1:gem>
        <sg1:mine xmlns:sg1="http://www.SpaceGems.com/mines/2047/">
                <sg1:name> Ice Mountain 2</sg1:name>
                <sg1:region>Montis Glacialis</sg1:region>
                <sg1:planet>Capitan</sg1:planet>
        </sg1:mine>
        <sg1:reserved />
        <sg1:catalog xmlns:sg1="http://www.SpaceGems.com/catalogs/2047/"
                sg1:name="SpaceGems Diamonds"sg1:publish="yes" />
</sg1:diamonds>
```

Figure 3.5 Alternative approach to prefix namespaces.

In this case, the author apparently did not want different prefixes simply to show that as long as the namespace URI is different for each declaration, the prefix can remain the same. In gem_desc_31.xml, therefore, the sg1: namespace is defined first in the <sg1:diamonds> tag and then redefined in each of the <sg1.gem>, <sg1:mine>, and <sg1:catalog> tags. The namespace declaration for the <sg1:diamonds> element type would be inherited by all the child elements unless it is redefined and overridden in one or another element. In the gem_desc_31.xml document, the namespace declaration is redefined in all the child elements under <sg1:diamonds>. Meanwhile, the namespace declaration for <sg1:gem> would only be effective for <sg1:gem> and its child elements, if it had any, and would not apply to <sg1:gem>'s sibling elements (that is, it would not apply to <sg1:mine>, <sg1:reserved>, or <sg1:catalog>.

Notice that because there is no explicit namespace declaration for the <sg1:reserved> element, it will inherit the namespace declaration from its parent element <sg1:diamonds>.

Remember that you cannot use prefixes that begin with xml, XML, xMl, or any such combination. They are reserved for use by XML and XML-related specifications.

Default Namespace Declarations

The principles discussed in the latter part of the preceding section apply to default namespace declarations, too. The reasoning behind default namespace declarations is simple: "If a namespace isn't explicitly declared for a specific section of a document, then, by default, the namespace will be. . . ."

There is usually one default namespace declaration per document or, at most, a few, but there are no restrictions. Figure 3.6 illustrates the use of three such declarations, as well as an empty string namespace declaration in the <gems> element. Those declarations are discussed in the next section.

In the <diamonds>, <mine>, and <catalog> start tags, there are namespace declarations similar to prefix namespace declarations, but they are missing the colon and the prefix. In these cases, each declaration tells the parser: "Throughout this element and any child elements, the namespace for any element type names that do not start with a prefix will be *http://www.SpaceGems.com/2047/xxxx/*, unless the declaration is overridden." For example, the element <name> within <mine> may not have a prefix, but it still has, in effect, the two-part universal name *{http://www.SpaceGems.com/2047/mines/}name*. So it is still unique.

You can see that the <diamonds> default namespace is overridden for the <gem> element (we discuss that declaration in the next section), as well as for the <mine> and <catalog> elements, but the declaration still holds for the empty <reserved /> type element. Its universal name is the unique *{http://www.SpaceGems.com/2047/}reserved*.

```
<?xml version="1.0" encoding="UTF-8" standalone="no"?>
<?xml-stylesheet type="text/css" href="diamonds2.css"?>
<!DOCTYPE diamonds SYSTEM "diamonds5.dtd">
<!-- Gems Version 2 - Space Gems, Inc. -->
<!-- filename: gem_desc_32.xml -->

<diamonds xmlns="http://www.SpaceGems.com/ 2047/"name="Ursae Majoris" >
        <gem xmlns="">
                <name>Smokey</name>
                <carats>1003</carats>
                <color>F</color>
                <clarity>IF</clarity>
                <cut>Ideal</cut>
                <cost>2250000</cost>
        </gem>
        <mine xmlns="http://www.SpaceGems.com/mines/2047/">
                <name>Ice Mountain 2</name>
                <region>Montis Glacialis</region>
                <planet> Capitan </planet>
        </mine>
        <reserved />
        <catalog xmlns="http://www.SpaceGems.com/catalogs/2047/"
                        name="SpaceGems Diamonds" publish="yes" />
</diamonds>
```

Figure 3.6 Document with default and empty string namespace declarations.

Meanwhile, for the <mine> element type, the default namespace (again, there is no colon or prefix in the declaration) has been specified as http://www.SpaceGems.com/2047/mines/. The <mine> element's children (that is, the <name>, <region>, and <planet> elements) will inherit the <mine> element's namespace because there is no namespace declaration in any of their respective start tags that would override it.

Finally, a default namespace has also been declared for the empty <catalog> element: Its declaration states that the default namespace will be http://www.SpaceGems.com/2047/catalogs/. You can see that the ensuing attributes do not have prefixes; they are simply name="SpaceGems Diamonds" and publish="yes". But the default namespace would also appear in their respective universal names, too.

The advantages to default namespaces are the reduction of typing and the resulting structure "cleanliness."

Empty String Namespace Declarations

In the gem_desc_32.xml document in Figure 3.6, the namespace declaration for the <gem> element type is xmlns="". Because there are no characters between the quotation marks, this is called an *empty string namespace declaration*. Empty string namespace declarations basically "erase" any previously established namespace declarations, leaving a universal name with no universal qualifying URL. The local part *gem* is the only component of the name.

While <gem>'s parent, <diamonds>, uses its own namespace, <gem>'s siblings, <mine> and <catalog>, also have their own respective namespaces. Meanwhile, <gem>'s sibling, <reserved />, has inherited <diamonds>' namespace, but <gem> itself has no specified namespace. So its children (<name>, <carats>, <color>, and the others) also have no declared namespace because they inherit from <gem> and they have no namespace declarations of their own. What names they have, then, are those shown in Figure 3.6. There is no qualifying URI component to them.

In the Figure 3.6 case, all four names still have unique names. Three have fully developed and unique two-part universal names, while the <name> type element under <gem> has just a one-part universal name. Empty string namespace declarations are a commonly used device for erasing previous namespaces for particular element types.

The advantages to empty string declarations are similar to default namespace declarations: a cleaner-looking structure and less typing. Without a namespace, however, there is still a chance of name collisions.

Namespace Declarations and Inheritance

As illustrated in the previous sections, the scope of every namespace declaration is restricted to the extent of the element in whose start tag it has been declared. They can be declared in the root element and so be effective throughout the entire data instance. Or they can be declared in elements that are children of other elements and so be applicable throughout their own respective extents and the extents of their own children unless and until one or more of those children contains its own namespace declaration.

If a namespace is declared in an element, it can't be inherited by a sibling element (that is, by an element on the same level) or by a parent element (in other words, by an element above them).

As shown previously, empty string declarations can be used to turn off an inherited namespace declaration and prevent it from being inherited.

The Physical Structure: Entities

Physically, every XML document is composed of data storage units called *entities*. Entities reflect XML's referential markup aspects, as defined in Chapter 1, and are used for several reasons:

- To keep track of and provide, during the parsing process, the data that makes up the XML document.
- To refer to often-repeated data (so that you don't have to do as much data entry keyboarding).

- To refer to data that changes occasionally. When certain data changes, you don't have to keep "breaking open" all the documents that contain that data—just the source document (again, in a manner of speaking, using entities will save keystrokes).
- To include data located in documents outside of the XML document (that is, to break up otherwise very large documents).

Depending on the context, entities can be categorized in any of three ways. Let's discuss these various methods of categorization.

Entities Are Parsed or Unparsed

Entities are categorized a number of ways. One way is according to whether they are parsed or unparsed data resources. (Although we will follow the XML convention of *parsed* and *unparsed*, our students have found "parseable" and "unparseable" to be more descriptive.) Each entity is one or the other.

Parsed entities contain XML format text characters that can represent markup or content data and are intended to be processed by an XML parser. Unparsed entities, on the other hand, are resources that are not intended to be parsed by an XML parser. The entity is to be passed as is to an application. The contents of an unparsed entity may or may not be text, and may or may not be in an XML format. Examples of non-XML format entities are binary documents such as graphic, audio, and video files, or selections of program code in other formats. During the parsing process, an XML parser will read the entity reference and then substitute the actual data or data document into the XML data structure instead of the entity reference.

Entities Can Be Internal or External

Another way to categorize entities is according to their location with respect to the XML document that references them. Entities that are located within the XML document are called *internal entities*. Internal entities range from individual well-formed XML-format text characters to strings of such characters.

Each XML document contains at least one internal entity: the root element that contains the document entity. To quote the W3C, "[The *document entity*] serves as the starting point for the XML processor and may contain the whole document."

An external entity is a data source located outside the XML document being parsed. External entities may be non-XML format documents, so they would be unparsed (for example, binary documents such as graphics, audio, and video), or they may even be other XML documents. Outside documents are included during the parsing process by the inclusion of specific entity references in the XML document.

Entities other than the document entity, whether internal or external, must be given names by the developer so that references can be constructed to call for the data in those entities.

The reference to the external entity usually includes a form of a URI that points to its location. When the parser reads the reference, it will retrieve the entity referred to, parse it if required to do so, and pass its data to the application.

General Entities versus Parameter Entities

Another way to categorize entities is as follows:

General entities. Declared in DTDs or schemas and used for constructing related XML documents.

Parameter entities. Declared in DTDs or schemas, but used for constructing the DTDs or schemas themselves.

We discuss general entities in the next section and discuss parameter entities in Chapters 4 and 5.

General Entity References

All entities are given specific names by the developer. With the exception of the document entity, all entities used in an XML document must first be defined as entities in an internal or external DTD, or in a schema. The declaration assigns the unique name to the entity and provides the data, or a reference to the location of the entity that will eventually be substituted into the data structure by the parser. Later, within the appropriate element in the logical structure of the document, the entity is referenced by the name declared for it.

Notable exceptions to the "must declare rule" are XML's five predefined general entities. Even without being declared in DTDs or schemas, XML parsers will automatically recognize them and treat them accordingly. They are discussed in more detail later in this chapter.

Figure 3.7 illustrates the use of an internal entity named constellation, whose value is *Ursae Majoris* and which is called from an element named <location>. The general entity syntax follows. It's important to ensure that both the ampersand at the beginning of the reference and the semicolon at the end of the reference are *not* omitted.

```
<elementname>&entityname;</elementname>
```

The entity declaration syntax takes the form:

```
<!ENTITY entityname entitydata>
```

"constellation" → entity declared

"constellation" → entity at work

```
<?xml version="1.0" encoding="UTF-8" standalone="yes"?>
<?xml-stylesheet type="text/css" href="diamonds1.css"?>
<!DOCTYPE diamonds [
<!ELEMENT diamonds (location,gem)*>
<!ELEMENT location (#PCDATA)>
<!ELEMENT gem (name,carats,color,clarity,cut,cost)>
<!ELEMENT name (#PCDATA)>
<!ELEMENT carats (#PCDATA)>
<!ELEMENT color (#PCDATA)>
<!ELEMENT clarity (#PCDATA)>
<!ELEMENT cut (#PCDATA)>
<!ELEMENT cost (#PCDATA)>
<!ENTITY constellation "Ursae Majoris">
]>
<!-- Gems Version 1 - Space Gems, Inc. -->
<!-- filename: gems_excerpt_04.xml -->
<diamonds>
	<location>&constellation;</location>
	<gem>
		<name>Smokey</name>
		<carats>1003.29</carats>
		<color>F</color>
		<clarity>IF</clarity>
		<cut>Ideal</cut>
		<cost>2250000</cost>
	</gem>
</diamonds>
```

Figure 3.7 This XML document contains an internal entity.

Consider the following external variation of this example. Suppose a parsed file named constellation.xml contains the location where a gem was found. Look at Figure 3.8 to see how it is accessed by the XML parser and combined with the original XML document. Notice how the entity declaration has been changed to include the keyword SYSTEM to indicate that an external entity, located on the local system, is about to be declared.

If an unparsed entity were being referenced, the reference would be the same except that *that* document's filename (and path, if applicable) would appear instead of the XML document named constellation.xml.

For further information about general entities, check the XML 1.0 Recommendation at the W3C's Web site at www.w3.org/TR/REC-xml#sec-intro.

Occasionally, users and authors mix the terms *entity* and *entity reference*. Actually, the confusion arises when someone refers to an entity reference as the entity. Just remember that entities are the actual physical storage units for data, and entity references are the method for referring to them. For an entity to play a role in any XML document, an entity reference must appear in that document.

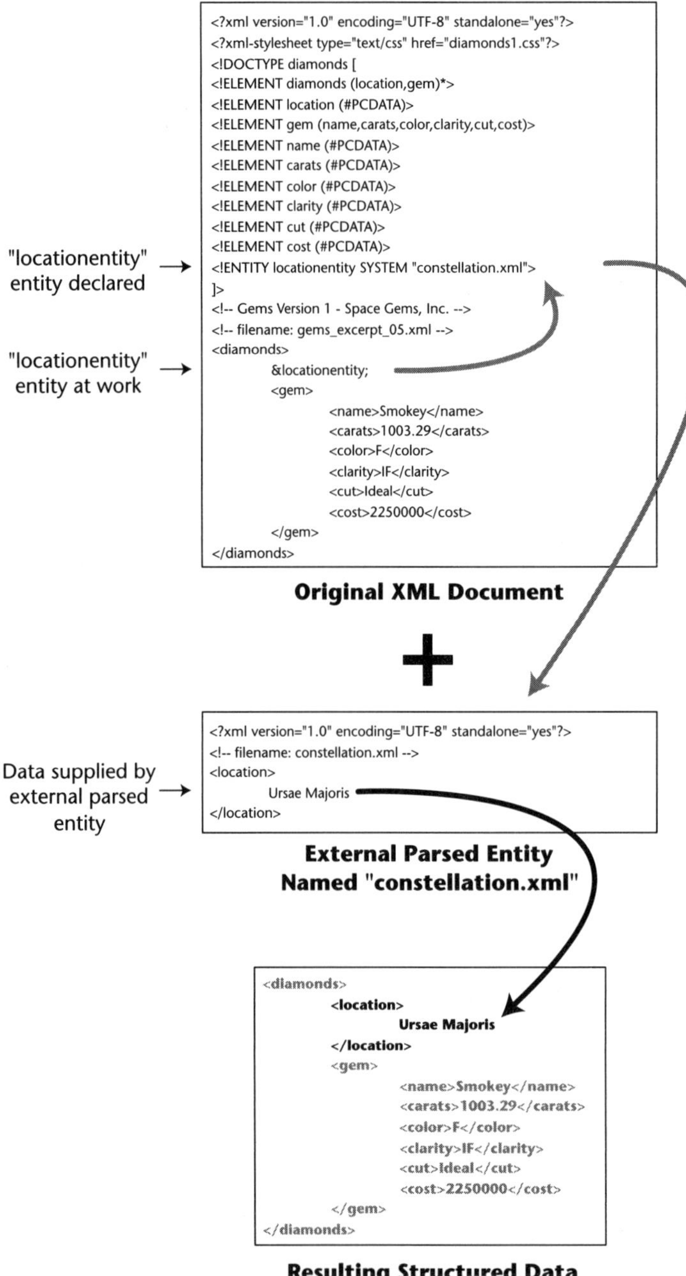

Figure 3.8 Using another XML document as an external parsed entity.

Preserving Characters from Parser Misinterpretation

Some characters have been reserved by XML for use with markup. When they are encountered by the parser, the parser will always interpret them as introducing markup instructions (for example, tags, attribute values, and named entities). The five reserved characters are as follows:

- The left angle bracket, or less-than symbol (<)
- The right angle bracket, or greater-than symbol (>)
- The quotation mark (")
- The apostrophe (')
- The ampersand (&)

But there may be occasions when we want to pass such characters directly to the application without parsing them or we may want to insert these characters into an XML document as data. So we have to find a way to represent them so that the XML parser won't view them as markup indicators and, thereafter, create errors.

To resolve this difficulty, XML provides three methods:

- Predefined entities
- Numeric character references
- CDATA sections

Predefined Entities

In Table 3.2, you can see the alternative coding that XML provides for the five reserved characters. Each code is called a predefined (named) entity reference, or simply a *predefined entity*.

Table 3.2 XML's Predefined Entity References

RESERVED CHARACTER	ENTITY REFERENCE	DESCRIPTION
<	<	Left side angle bracket, or less-than symbol
>	>	Right side angle bracket, or greater-than symbol
"	"	Quotation mark
'	'	Apostrophe
&	&	Ampersand, or "and" symbol

Notice that their specific entity references are similar to their names. That's why entities that take this form are called *named entities*. Similar to all entities, they begin with the ampersand (&) and end with a semicolon.

The predefined nature of these entity references makes them exceptions to the "need to declare" rule: You don't need to define them in your document or in a DTD or schema, although that is still recommended. Later, when you substitute any of them in your data content, the originally intended characters will be displayed or printed and you will not receive parser errors. For example, the following tip would run afoul of the parser:

```
<tip>
     Remember! When evaluating diamonds, look for the "5 C's":
     Color, carats, cut, clarity, & cost!
</tip>
```

Normally, the XML parser would encounter the quotation marks, the apostrophe, and the ampersand (&), and then interpret them accordingly as markup indicators. Subsequently, if the parser did not signal errors, the application would probably create an unusual and incorrect rendering.

To preserve the quotation marks, the apostrophe, and the ampersand in their intended form, you could alter the coding by inserting the corresponding predefined entities. The tip would look similar to the following:

```
<tip>
     Remember! When evaluating diamonds, look for the
            &quot;5 C&apos;s&quot;:
     Color, carats, cut, clarity, &amp; cost!
</tip>
```

It looks a little confusing to us, maybe, but it's acceptable to the parser.

Numeric Character References

Commonly called character references, *numeric character references* are a special kind of entity reference. They are used to insert foreign language or other unusual characters—those that can't be typed directly on your keyboard—into an XML document. There are two formats for character references:

Decimal references. Take the form &#*nnn*; where *nnn* is the decimal number assigned to the character.

Hexadecimal references. Take the form &#x*hhh*; where *hhh* is the appropriate hexadecimal number.

Table 3.3 lists several common character references that may come in handy when you're coding XML documents. Again, these are entities: They begin with ampersands and end with semicolons.

Table 3.3 Common Decimal and Hexadecimal Character References

CHARACTER	DECIMAL CODE	HEXADECIMAL CODE	NAMED ENTITY	DISPLAY
Currency—Euro sign	€	€	€	€
Currency—Pound sterling sign	£	£	£	£
Currency—Yen (Yuan) sign	¥	¥	¥	¥
Ampersand	&	&	&	&
Less than sign (LH angle bracket)	<	<	<	<
Greater than sign (RH angle bracket)	>	>	>	>
Quotation mark	"	"	"	"
Apostrophe	'	'	'	'
Copyright symbol	©	©	©	©
Registered trademark symbol	®	®	®	®
En space (half as wide as it is tall)				n/a
Em space (as wide as it is tall)				n/a
Nonbreaking space				n/a
Horizontal tab			&tab;	n/a
Linefeed
n/a	n/a
Carriage return
n/a	n/a

Although the semicolon can be omitted if the character reference is followed by a white space, as a best practice, we recommend including the semicolon at the end of the character references.

Although there is still more support for the decimal coding (it's been around since HTML appeared) in the common browsers, support is growing for the Unicode Standard hexadecimal references. If checking the display, try to check with at least two different browser applications.

If you use your Windows calculator in scientific mode, you can easily convert the decimal (Dec) format to hexadecimal (Hex) format or vice versa.

For further information about the Unicode Standard and its hexadecimal characters as well as an extensive set of character charts, visit the Unicode Consortium Web site at www.unicode.org/charts/. For additional help with decimal or hexadecimal coding, you can also visit the W3C's HTML Web site at www.w3.org/TR/REC-html40/charset.html or the Web Design Group's Web site at www.htmlhelp.com/reference/html40/entities/.

Here is what the tip would look like with numeric character references in hexadecimal format:

```
<tip>
     Remember! When evaluating diamonds, look for the
          &#x22;5 C&#x27;s&#x22;:
     Color, carats, cut, clarity, &#x26; cost!
</tip>
```

CDATA Sections

Predefined entity references provide an alternate coding solution for elements that contain several reserved characters, but as we saw in the previous example, the results, at first glance, can be a little confusing.

As an alternate method to the occasionally messy predefined entity reference solution, you could use a character data (CDATA) section. It would tell the parser to ignore the markup aspect of the characters between the CDATA section's two special delimiters, and to pass those characters to the application as text.

The special delimiters are the CDStart indicator <![cdata[and the CDEnd indicator]]>. The preserved data is situated between them. All that data is passed directly to the application as text characters and parsing goes into a sort of "off" mode until the CDEnd indicator is encountered.

Here is the previous tip recoded with a CDATA section:

```
<tip>
     <![cdata[
     Remember! When evaluating diamonds, look for the "5 C's":
     Color, carats, cut, clarity, & cost!
     ]]>
</tip>
```

Following are a few things to remember about CDATA sections:

- Any white space you insert between the delimiters will remain intact.
- Don't nest CDATA sections. After the parser finds the first CDEnd indicator, it considers the CDATA section ended and will return to normal parsing mode. Errors would occur for CDATA code that followed.
- Be careful if you are including a string of text (especially program code) that coincidentally contains a string that resembles a CDEnd indicator. That text string would trigger the parser to return to normal parsing mode, too.
- If you intend to include any markup indicators between the CDATA delimiters (in other words, if you want to include tags, comments, or other components), those markups will not be properly interpreted by the parser because it has been instructed to turn off normal parsing for the duration of the CDATA section.

What Is a Well-Formed XML Document?

So far in this book, numerous references have been made to well-formed XML documents. Well-formed documents conform to the well-formedness constraints of XML 1.0. Now that we've introduced the basic XML document components, it will be easier to discuss and illustrate those constraints and, therefore, to define well-formed documents.

Here are the grammatical, logical, and structural rules that compose XML 1.0's well-formedness constraints:

- The document must contain at least one element.
- Each parsed entity (for example, the style sheet document or schema) that is referenced directly or indirectly within an XML document must also be well formed.
- An XML document can have only one root element—or, if you prefer, the document element—and all other elements must be nested in it. No part of the root element may appear within the content of any other element in the document.
- For all the other non-root elements, if their start tag appears in the content of one element, then the corresponding end tag must also be in the content of the same element. In other words, the elements must nest properly within each other and cannot "overlap"; and any one element cannot have more than one parent element.

- Every start tag must have a corresponding end tag.
- Element names must obey XML naming conventions (listed earlier in this chapter).

You have seen several well-formed documents already in this chapter. Figure 3.9 illustrates a simple well-formed document.

Notice how the root element is called <diamonds> and how proper nesting occurs within <diamonds> and within the two <gem> elements. Now look at Figure 3.10, which is the same document as that shown in Figure 3.9, except that some (incorrect) changes have been deliberately made to it, for illustration purposes, to make the document *not* well formed.

In gems_excerpt_03.xml, within both <gem> elements, there are other elements that violate one or more of the well-formedness constraints listed earlier:

- An overlap in the <color> and <clarity> elements: The start tag of the <clarity> element is encountered before the end tag of the <color> element.
- In both <gem> elements, it appears that the <cost> element content has, in effect, two parents (<gem> and <cut>).
- In the first <gem> element, the <cut> element has no end tag.
- In the second <gem> element, the <cut> element has an end tag, but it is misspelled as </cult>, which looks like the name of another element entirely.

```
<?xml version="1.0" encoding="UTF-8" standalone="yes"?>
<?xml-stylesheet type="text/css" href="diamonds1.css"?>
<!-- Gems Version 1 - Space Gems, Inc. -->
<!-- filename: gems_excerpt_01.xml -->
<diamonds>
    <gem>
        <name>Sparkler</name>
        <carats>105</carats>
        <color>F</color>
        <clarity>IF</clarity>
        <cut>Super Ideal</cut>
        <cost>126000</cost>
    </gem>
    <gem>
        <name>Merlin</name>
        <carats>41</carats>
        <color>D</color>
        <clarity>FL</clarity>
        <cut>Ideal</cut>
        <cost>82000</cost>
    </gem>
</diamonds>
```

Figure 3.9 A well-formed XML document.

```
<?xml version="1.0" encoding="UTF-8" standalone="yes"?>
<?xml-stylesheet type="text/css" href="diamonds1.css"?>
<!-- Gems Version 1 - Space Gems, Inc. -->
<!-- filename: gems_excerpt_03.xml -->
<diamonds>
	<gem>
		<name>Sparkler</name><carats>105</carats>
		<color>F<clarity></color>IF</clarity>
		<cut>Super Ideal<cost>126000</cost>
	</gem>
	<gem>
		<name>Merlin</name><carats>41</carats>
		<color>D<clarity></color>FL</clarity>
		<cut>Ideal<cost>82000</cost></cult>
	</gem>
</diamonds>
```

Figure 3.10 An XML document that is not well-formed.

These violations reflect what was at one time called "freeform XML." Freeform practices such as this have been tolerated in HTML (allowing for them is one reason that HTML applications such as browsers have become bloated with otherwise unnecessary logic), but HTML is concerned primarily with document appearance, while XML is overwhelmingly concerned with the description and structure of data.

In the past, such freeform practices in XML may have just been considered bad practice, but they were not considered fatal errors. However, there is more at stake in the XML world of databases and commercial transactions, so more XML processors are being developed that conform strictly to the W3C well-formedness constraints. Consequently, freeform XML has become grounds for fatal error in accordance with the W3C's intent. We recommend strongly that freeform XML not appear in any of your documents.

Classroom Q & A

Q: In the file gems_excerpt_03.xml, one line had two elements on it, but you didn't mention it as an error. Is that OK?

A: Yes, with XML it is acceptable to place more than one element on a line. XML parsers, unless specifically programmed to do so, are not concerned with this kind of white space manipulation or lack thereof.

What Is a Valid XML Document?

A valid XML document is a well-formed XML document that also conforms to the declarations, structures, and other rules defined in the document's respective DTD or schema. Consider the examples in Figure 3.11.

The file on the left, gems_excerpt_01.xml, is a well-formed XML document. On the right is another well-formed version of the same file, namely gems_excerpt_02.xml, which contains the same information but also contains a document type declaration (bolded just for illustrative purposes) that specifies an external DTD document called diamonds2.dtd. In this case, we can safely presume that gems_excerpt_03 conforms to diamonds2.dtd. That is, a validating parser has been activated by its application and, then, has:

- Imported an instance of the DTD file and examined the declarations therein
- Compared the elements in the data instance of gems_excerpt_03.xml to those declarations
- Found that the elements conform to their respective declarations

So, gems_excerpt_03.xml is a valid XML document, too.

```
<?xml version="1.0" encoding="UTF-8" standalone="yes"?>
<?xml-stylesheet type="text/css" href="diamonds1.css"?>

<!-- Gems Version 1 - Space Gems, Inc. -->
<!-- filename: gems_excerpt_01.xml -->
<diamonds>
      <gem>
            <name>Sparkler</name>
            <carats>105</carats>
            <color>F</color>
            <clarity>IF</clarity>
            <cut>Super Ideal</cut>
            <cost>126000</cost>
            <reserved />
      </gem>
      <gem>
            <name>Merlin</name>
            <carats>41</carats>
            <color>D</color>
            <clarity>FL</clarity>
            <cut>Ideal</cut>
            <cost>82000</cost>
      </gem>
</diamonds>
```

Well-Formed XML Document

```
<?xml version="1.0" encoding="UTF-8" standalone="no"?>
<?xml-stylesheet type="text/css" href="diamonds2.css"?>
<!DOCTYPE diamonds SYSTEM "diamonds2.dtd">
<!-- Gems Version 2 - Space Gems, Inc. -->
<!-- filename: gems_excerpt_02.xml -->
<diamonds>
      <gem>
            <name>Sparkler</name>
            <carats>105</carats>
            <color>F</color>
            <clarity>IF</clarity>
            <cut>Super Ideal</cut>
            <cost>126000</cost>
            <reserved />
      </gem>
      <gem>
            <name>Merlin</name>
            <carats>41</carats>
            <color>D</color>
            <clarity>FL</clarity>
            <cut>Ideal</cut>
            <cost>82000</cost>
      </gem>
</diamonds>
```

Well-Formed and Valid XML Document

Figure 3.11 Comparison of a well-formed document and a valid document.

Chapter 3 Labs: Anatomy of an XML File

As mentioned in Chapter 2, "Setting Up Your XML Working Environment," you can use a simple text editor to create an XML document. For a small XML document, that may be totally satisfactory, but when the requirements for XML files become more complex, working with a simple text editor can be too cumbersome and you could deviate from the correct XML standard requirements and create syntax typographical errors. The labs that follow in this chapter have three goals:

- To familiarize you with the TurboXML editor's behavior by creating a simple XML document.
- To illustrate the importance of good planning. We show you how to "accidentally" code yourself into a corner. At that point, we will revisit the design and fix it.
- After you have created an XML data instance, to have you work with the document using a regular text editor (which will probably give you a real appreciation for tools such as TurboXML; it will be a sort of "XML editor appreciation moment").

We won't introduce a DTD or a schema at this time. We will work with them in the next two chapters. For this lab, the editor will indicate an error when it says it cannot find the document's schema. This is an advisory error only. For now, just ignore any error messages related to not being able to locate the DTD or schema; however, be advised that some editors in the industry would not be so forgiving. They won't even open or create an instance without the prior existence of a schema or DTD of some description.

Lab 3.1: Create a Simple XML Data Instance with Elements

The best way to describe a diamond's qualities is to describe what's known as its five C's. The five C's are carat, color, clarity, cut, and cost. Space Gems specializes in large, expensive diamonds and doesn't stock many smaller ones. Table 3.4 lists all the diamonds that are for sale. We will design a simple XML instance to itemize all these diamonds and their characteristics. The document we create in Lab 3.1 will contain elements only to describe the data. Lab 3.2 presents an alternate design that uses both elements and attributes.

Table 3.4 List of Space Gems' Premium Diamonds

NAME	WEIGHT (CARATS)	COLOR	CLARITY	CUT	COST (USD)
Sparkler	105	F	IF (Internally Flawless)	Super Ideal	126000
Merlin	41	D	FL (Flawless)	Ideal	82000
Cullinan	3106	H	VS1, VS2 (Very Slightly Imperfect)	Rough	2174200
Dark	500	J	SL1, SL2 (Slightly Imperfect)	Rough	450000

1. Open the TurboXML editor. Click Continue Trial, if necessary.
2. Click Instance.
3. The Untitled–XML Instance dialog box appears with a <root> element called root. This window also indicates that there is an error. The error makes it look as though we are off to a bad start, but this is OK. The editor is just advising us that there is no governing schema for this instance, which is correct at this time. We are going to ignore all related messages at this time.
4. Rename the <root> element to <diamonds>. Place the cursor over the <root> element and then right-click. Choose Rename, and enter "diamonds".
5. Add six additional elements called <name>, <carat>, <color>, <clarity>, <cut>, and <cost>.
   a. Click Insert on the bottom toolbar, which is also called the factory toolbar (alternatively, click the blue diamond icon located to the immediate right of Insert on the same bottom bar). A new empty element space appears, waiting input. Type the first element called <name>, and then press Enter.
   b. Another new empty element space appears, waiting for input.
   c. Click the Position as Child button (Hint: It's the button with the yellow arrow, third from the left on the toolbar that appears when you click Insert. The arrow points to the right and then hooks downward. When you place the mouse pointer over it, its name appears) to create <carat> as a child element to <name>.
   d. Type the second element called <carat> and press Enter. Another new empty element space appears, waiting for input.

e. Type the third element called <color> and press Enter.

f. Repeat the instructions for <clarity>, <cut>, and <cost>.

If your element is not positioned properly, you can drag and drop it by placing the cursor over the blue icon next to the element name inside the tag area on the left. Using the left mouse button, drag it. A little black line will appear indicating the target area.

6. The final view should look like Figure 3.12. You can see the seven new elements arrayed on the left-hand side.

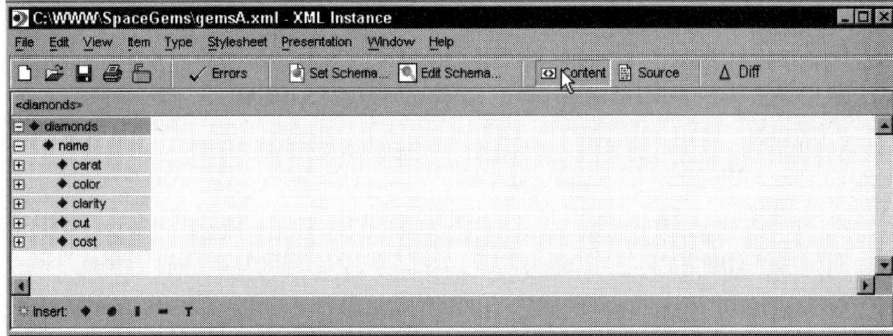

Figure 3.12 GUI view of the new XML instance during development.

7. Click View on the top menu bar, and then click Source.

8. Click View on the top menu bar, and then click Content.

9. Enter the data values from Table 3.4 into the XML data instance called diamonds.

   a. Try to click the space to the right of the <carat> element. You should be able to enter a value. Enter the data value "105".

   b. Now click the space to the right of the <name> element. Problem! You should not be able to enter a value or, if you examine the source, the data value may be misplaced. The reason is that, by default, the <name> element is only allowed to contain other elements.

10. To remedy this situation, rename this parent element called <name> to <gem>; then create a new child element within this <gem> element called <name>.

11. Click View on the top menu bar, and then click Source. The solution should look like Figure 3.13. Notice the eight new elements.

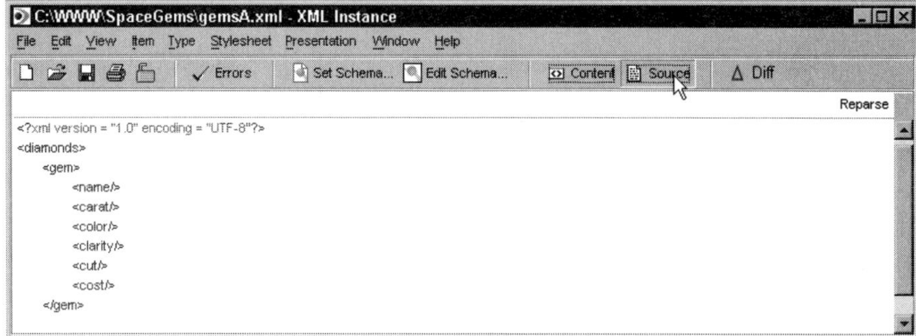

Figure 3.13 Source view of the new XML document.

12. Now enter all of the data values from Table 3.4.
    a. Click View on the top menu bar, and click Content.
    b. Click the space to the right of the <name> element, and enter "Sparkler".
    c. Click the space to the right of the <carat> element, and enter "105".
    d. Click the space to the right of the <color> element, and enter "F".
    e. Click the space to the right of the <clarity> element, and enter "IF".
    f. Click the space to the right of the <cut> element, and enter "Super Ideal".
    g. Click the space to the right of the <cost> element, and enter "126000".
13. To enter the second diamond, use the copy feature. Highlight the <gem> element and then click Edit, Copy.
14. Highlight the <diamond> element, and click Edit, Paste on the top menu bar. Make sure that you have copied the entire <gem> element, including the </gem> end tag.
15. Proceed to replace the data values for the next three diamonds. Work at the file until it looks like the following code:

```
Solution gems1.xml file.
<?xml version = "1.0" encoding = "UTF-8"?>
<!--Gems Version 1-->
<diamonds>
      <gem>
            <name>Sparkler</name>
            <carat>105</carat>
            <color>F</color>
```

```
            <clarity>IF</clarity>
            <cut>Super Ideal</cut>
            <cost>126000</cost>
        </gem>
        <gem>
            <name>Merlin</name>
            <carat>41</carat>
            <color>D</color>
            <clarity>FL</clarity>
            <cut>Ideal</cut>
            <cost>82000</cost>
        </gem>
        <gem>
            <name>Cullinan</name>
            <carat>3106</carat>
            <color>H</color>
            <clarity>VS1,VS2</clarity>
            <cut>Rough</cut>
            <cost>2174200</cost>
        </gem>
        <gem>
            <name>Dark</name>
            <carat>500</carat>
            <color>J</color>
            <clarity>SI1,SI2</clarity>
            <cut>Rough</cut>
            <cost>450000</cost>
        </gem>
    </diamonds>
```

If you are having difficulty editing the Lab 3.1 file with TurboXML, save the file and use Microsoft Notepad. The XML editor has no schema definitions to rely on, so it may be stubborn. This will go away.

16. Insert a comment at the top of the instance that identifies this as gemsA.xml.

   a. Highlight the <diamond> element.

   b. Click the Insert New Comment icon on the bottom menu bar.

   c. Drag the comment to the top of the file. Place the cursor over the blue icon next to the comment. Using the left mouse button, drag it to the top of the file. If you cannot get it right to the top, place it under the root element.

17. Save the file as gemsA.xml to the C:\WWW\SpaceGems folder.

Lab 3.2: Creating an XML Instance Using Elements and Attributes

This lab uses the same diamond data as the previous example but also uses attributes in the instance to describe some of the data. We will show you how to develop the new instance using the same information to illustrate that two XML developers may not necessarily come up with the same design.

1. Open the TurboXML editor. Click Continue Trial, if necessary.
2. Click Instance.
3. Rename the root element to <diamonds>.
4. Create a new element called <gem>.
5. Create a new attribute for <gem> called <name>. Click the blue dot, not the diamond to create an attribute.
6. Create five more new attributes for <gem> called <carat>, <color>, <clarity>, <cut>, and <cost>.
7. Both the Content and Source views of the new file should look like Figures 3.14 and 3.15. Notice how each view depicts the two new elements and six new attributes.
8. Make three more copies of the <gem> element for the data values.
   a. Using the Shift key, select the <gem> element as well as all the attributes.
   b. On the main application toolbar, click Edit Copy and then Edit Paste. As if by magic, the application will insert another <gem> element under the highlighted <gem> element. If you did not highlight all of the items, the </gem> end tag will be omitted.

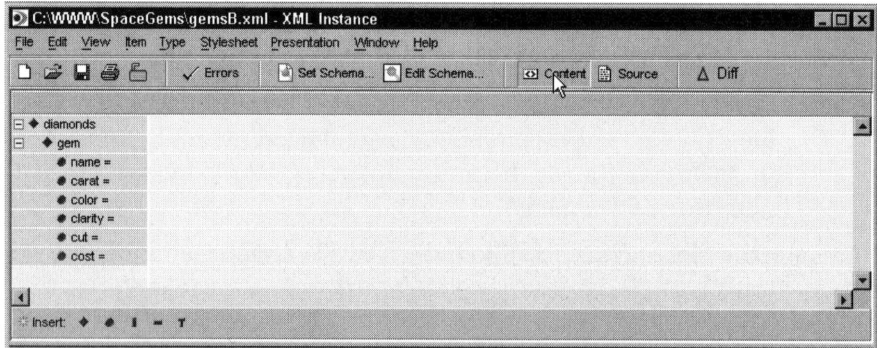

Figure 3.14 GUI view of the new XML instance: elements and attributes.

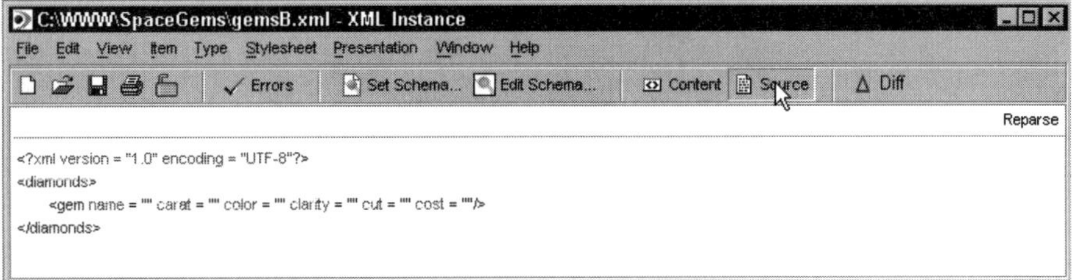

Figure 3.15 Source view of the new XML elements and attributes.

9. Enter the data from Table 3.4 into the XML instance called diamonds.
10. Work with the file until it looks like the following code. Ignore the line breaks between the attributes, which are inserted here to make it printable.

```
Solution gemsB.xml file.
<?xml version = "1.0" encoding = "UTF-8"?>
<diamonds>
     <gem name = "Sparkler" carat = "105"
          color = "F" clarity = "IF"
          cut = "Super Ideal" cost = "126000"/>
     <gem name = "Merlin" carat = "41"
          color = "D" clarity = "FL"
          cut = "Ideal" cost = "82000"/>
     <gem name = "Cullinan" carat = "3106"
          color = "H" clarity = "VS1,VS2"
          cut = "Rough" cost = "2174200"/>
     <gem name = "Dark" carat = "500"
          color = "J" clarity = "SL1,SL2"
          cut = "Rough" cost = "450000"/>
</diamonds>
```

11. Insert a comment at the top of the instance that identifies this file as gemsB.xml.
12. Save the file as gemsB.xml to the C:\WWW\SpaceGems folder.

Lab 3.3: Design Your Own XML Instance

Given the information in Table 3.5, design a new instance on your own. When it's finished, save the instance file as gemsC.xml in the C:\WWW\SpaceGems folder.

One possible solution for this challenge can be found at this book's Web site, as noted in its introduction.

Table 3.5 Space Gems' Largest Rough, Uncut Diamonds

NAME	WEIGHT (CARATS)	DISCOVERY DATE (YEAR)	LOCATION
Great Mogul	787.50	1650	Sol–Earth (India)
Excelsior	995.20	1893	Sol–Earth (South Africa)
Reitz (aka Jubilee)	650.80	1895	Sol–Earth (South Africa)
Cullinan	3,106.75	1905	Sol–Earth (South Africa)
Jonker	726.00	1934	Sol–Earth (South Africa)
El Presidente Vargas	726.60	1938	Sol–Earth (Brazil)
Woyie River	770.00	1945	Sol–Earth (Sierra Leone)
Star of Sierra Leone	968.80	1972	Sol–Earth (Sierra Leone)
Zale	890.00	1984	Sol–Earth (uncertain; Sierra Leone?)
Inukshuk	952.37	2009	Sol–Earth (Canada)
Ares	620.14	2024	Sol–Mars (Tharsis Montes)
Smokey	1003.29	2035	Ursae Majoris–Capitan (Montis Glacialis)
The Dancer	1841.16	2043	Pegasi–Patella Regina (Profundum Atrum)

Summary

We have discussed a lot of important concepts in this chapter—concepts to be remembered no matter which of the subsequent chapters you read. Before you move on, ensure that you have a grasp of the following basic key concepts.

- The W3C defines an XML document as a "data object if it is well formed, as defined in (Extensible Markup Language Recommendation). . . . Each XML document has both a logical and a physical structure." This chapter expanded on that definition.
- An application is a program or a group of programs designed to access and manipulate XML documents. The term should not be confused with the term XML application.

- XML parsers are reusable pieces of code that developers can obtain and then include in their applications. When an application calls for an XML document, the parser is activated and screens the XML document on behalf of the application, then passes structured data to the application.
- The W3C says that a conforming XML parser must be able to detect fatal errors and must then report them to the application.
- The prolog begins with an XML declaration (or header) and can also contain processing instructions, a document type declaration (also called a DOCTYPE definition), comments, and white space.
- Element names reflect the element type (also called the element's generic identifier or GI). Element names have strict rules.
- Elements can contain data, other elements, both data and other elements, or nothing. There are two types of empty elements: declared empty elements and elements with no content.
- Attributes are another type of descriptive metadata that you can specify for your elements. If performance is an issue, consider using attributes instead of simple subelements.
- In the data instance portion of an XML document, the root element is the parent element of all other elements. Placing one element within another is called nesting. Nesting relationships form the structure of the data instance.
- Namespace declarations are the mechanisms by which namespace collisions are prevented in XML documents. There are three kinds: the prefix namespace declaration, the default namespace declaration, and the empty string namespace declaration.
- The physical structure of an XML document consists of entities, which may be parsed or unparsed and internal or external, and they may range in size from single text characters to whole documents. General entities deal with constructing XML documents. Parameter entities deal with constructing DTDs or schemas.
- You can use three techniques to prevent a parser from misinterpreting characters: predefined entities, character references, and CDATA sections.
- To be well formed, an XML document must meet six grammatical, logical, and structural constraints imposed by the W3C XML 1.0 Recommendation.
- A valid XML document is a well-formed XML document that also conforms to the declarations, structures, and other rules defined in the document's respective DTD or schema.

Review Questions

1. What is the difference between an *application* and an *XML application*?
2. What are the names of the four basic operators in a validating parser?
3. What are the two most fundamental components of an XML document?
4. Match the following:

a. Comments	i. Speak to the application
b. Processing instructions	ii. Speak to the parser
c. Document type declarations	iii. Speak to human beings

5. What are the two types of empty elements?
6. What is the difference between attributes and pseudo-attributes?
7. What are the components of a qualified name resulting from a prefix namespace declaration?
8. Which namespace declaration "turns off" previous namespace declarations?
   a. Prefix
   b. Empty string
   c. Default
   d. None of the above
9. General entity references deal with entities used for constructing ______________________, while parameter entity references deal with entities used for constructing ______________________.
10. What are the five characters reserved for markup characters in XML, and what are their corresponding predefined entities?
11. What are the six W3C well-formedness constraints?
12. What is the definition of a valid XML document?

Answers to Review Questions

1. Used alone, the term *application* means a program or group of programs intended for end users and designed to access and manipulate XML documents. An *XML application* is one of several terms used to refer to a derivative markup language created according to XML 1.0.
2. The four basic operators in a validating parser are a content handler, an error handler, a DTD and schema handler, and an entity resolver.
3. The two most fundamental components of an XML document are the prolog and the data instance.
4. **a.** and **iii.**; **b.** and **i.**; **c.** and **ii.**
5. Those that are termed *declared empty* and those that are termed *elements with no content*.
6. Attributes appear in the data instance component within the start tags of elements. They provide additional description of an element or its data. Pseudo-attributes look similar to attributes but appear in declarations or instructions in the prolog component. Their descriptions pertain to a whole document.
7. The components are the prefix, the colon delimiter, and the local part of the name.
8. **b.** There are two considerations here. As discussed in the text, the latest namespace declaration overrides previous namespace declarations. Also, when an empty string is specified as a prefix, the subsequent relevant names only need the local part to qualify as universal names; they don't need qualifying URLs. The effect is to "shut off" namespace declarations for the extent that the empty string namespace is in effect.
9. General entity references deal with entities used for constructing XML documents, while parameter entity references deal with entities used for constructing DTDs or schemas.
10. The five reserved characters and their predefined entities are as follows:
    a. The left angle bracket, or less-than symbol (<); its entity is <
    b. The right angle bracket, or greater-than symbol (>); its entity is >
    c. The quotation mark ("); its entity is "
    d. The apostrophe ('); its entity is '
    e. The ampersand (&); its entity is &

11. The six well-formedness constraints are as follows:
    a. An XML document must contain at least one element.
    b. Each parsed entity referenced directly or indirectly within an XML document must also be well-formed.
    c. An XML document can have only one root element and all other elements must be nested within it.
    d. Non-root elements must nest properly within each other and cannot "overlap."
    e. Every start tag must have a corresponding end tag. The declared empty start tag is not a classic XML start tag, so it is an exception.
    f. Element names must obey XML naming conventions.
12. A valid XML document is a well-formed XML document that also conforms to the declarations, structures, and other rules defined in the document's respective DTD or schema.

Document Type Definitions

Chapter 1, "XML Backgrounder," explains that XML is derived from SGML and that many markup and metalanguages have been derived, in turn, from XML.

New XML-based markup languages are created by developers who can't find an existing XML language to meet their industry or organizational needs. They want to create one or more specific types of documents, with specific components related to one another and combined in specific ways. Thus, they have two basic requirements: a way to define the structure and content of their new markup language, and a way to link the relevant documents they will eventually create back to that markup language for validation purposes.

The second requirement—creating and linking relevant documents—will probably turn out to be the easier task. But that first one—defining the new markup language—can be a long and involved process. Whole books have been written on that topic. Nevertheless, after you have developed a robust, comprehensive, and extensible document type definition, and when you see that the well-formed and valid documents based on it are properly processed by your applications, you will conclude that those rewards are worth the effort.

Presently, XML provides two methods for defining new markup languages: the document type definition (DTD) and the schema. In this chapter, we introduce you to basic DTD concepts and syntax. In the next chapter, we introduce you to XML schemas, which are becoming increasingly popular, but which differ significantly from DTDs in a number of areas.

By the end of this chapter, you will know how to create small, simple DTDs and how to create simple, relevant documents based on those DTDs. You will also see how the guided editing capability of the XML editor used in your lab exercises really comes in handy.

What Are Document Type Definitions?

Each XML-related language is a unique markup solution that meets the specific needs of an organization, industry, group, or even individual. So each language varies from all the others in scope and intent. That is, the names of their document types, element types, and other components are unique and different. But they all have several aspects in common. Each is written according to the XML 1.0 specifications, which makes all of them members of the same extended markup family. Each is readable by any XML-compliant browser. Each language must be built according to a consistent set of rules, structures, and semantics. After that consistent set has been developed, related XML documents can be created.

Document type definitions have historically been the most common method for defining an XML-related language and, thereafter, for developing the related documents. They are a form of metamarkup, which we defined in Chapter 1, that was born during the development of GML in the late 1960s and, later, made part of the ISO's SGML standard (ISO 8879:1986). XML inherited the DTD, with its distinctly non-XML vocabulary, grammar, and syntax, from SGML.

DTDs define (the W3C's term is *declare*, which is the term we'll use most often) all of the components that an XML language or document is allowed to contain, as well as the structural relationships among those components. Thus, each unique XML vocabulary, along with its related XML documents, will be created according to the content and structure rules declared within its respective DTD or schema. (Each language can have only one of those documents, and that one document must be either a DTD or a schema.) DTDs are composed of the following:

- An internal subset of declarations located within an XML document
- An actual separate, external document that contains such declarations
- A combination of both

If there is only one set of declarations and it is found within the XML document, the declarations are called an *internal DTD*. If the declarations are in a separate document, they are called an *external DTD*. If there is a combination of internal and external declarations, each is called a *subset* and, together, they are considered to be the DTD.

To define document types, a DTD must contain several kinds of information (each is discussed in detail in this chapter):

Element type declarations. You can't create just any element types in your XML documents. All element types have to be declared in the DTD, too, and so become part of the DTD's set of allowed element types (that is, part of the language's vocabulary).

Attribute declarations. Similarly, a DTD declares the set of attributes that can be included in the start tag for each element. Each attribute declaration defines the name, default values, and behavior of the attribute.

Entity declarations. DTDs contain the specified name and definitions for general and parameter entities. Often, entities are declared in the internal subsets (which we'll define soon) as well as in the external subsets.

Notation declarations. Notation declarations are labels that specify various types of nonparsed binary data (and text data, too, occasionally).

Other information. This type of information consists of the XML declaration at the beginning of the document, as well as comments and white space that help to structure the document and communicate other relevant information.

These declarations are discussed in detail later in this chapter. We'll see how their syntax defines the relationships among the components they define. These relationships form the content model—that is, the nesting aspects, order, number, frequency, and required or optional nature of the components—and, thus, the XML-related language's grammar. They are so important that a large portion of the W3C XML Recommendation is dedicated to defining the various declarations that are allowed in DTDs.

Why Use Document Type Definitions?

We've discussed already how XML is powerful, because with it you can create your own unique element types with meaningful tags. Furthermore, it is possible—but not recommended—to write XML in a freeform style, where elements can occur in a fairly arbitrary order and where elements can be properly nested or overlap. However, the vast majority of XML-related applications are not able to process your documents if the elements occur in an arbitrary order or if they overlap. To ensure that an XML document always communicates what the author intends, there should be some structure and content rules (also called constraints). Those rules are manifested in DTDs and schemas.

Classroom Q & A

Q: So, when would you use a DTD or schema?

A: On several occasions you would consider using DTDs. Here are some examples: when you want to specify default values for attributes or when you want to use style sheets or transformation style sheets. Also, the use of DTDs and schemas would lead to the development of smaller-size XML-related browsers, unlike those HTML browsers that have to carry extra logic in order to "guess" the meaning of bad HTML coding. Or when you want to conduct commerce transactions, it would be important for all parties to use applications and documents that recognize common components. Or when you are a member of a user community (that is, within an organization or an industry) that shares data.

The declarations within a DTD communicate meta information about the DTD and its related documents to an XML parser. That meta information includes the type, frequency, sequencing, and nesting of elements; attribute information; various types of entities; the names and types of external files that may be referenced; and the formats of some external (non-XML) data that also may be referenced.

Creating DTDs—General

In this chapter, we show you how to create the declarations found in a basic DTD. But we won't be discussing DTD design in detail. Detailed design—that is, the best content model; the number and semantics of element types, attributes, and other components; the jurisdiction over DTDs; and many other aspects—depends on the specific challenge and context facing the developer. However, we will make a few general comments.

XML DTDs must be designed to comply with the XML well-formedness and validity constraints. The job of the DTD is to ensure validity, so it must be well formed and valid itself. However, a DTD must not contain any SGML features that are not allowed in XML.

The design and implementation of DTDs—at least, those used by an organization, industry, society, or other data-sharing group—can be a complex process, rivaling the management of any complex project. So, like project management, the process usually involves several stages: planning and design; creation and testing (some call it validating or verification); deployment and commissioning; and finally, documentation. Please recognize that there may eventually be an extension phase—that is, a revisit to the definition of the language to add components—based on experience gained during the initial use of the XML-related language and its documents. So it is important to design a DTD for extensibility.

We recommend that, during the documentation stage, DTD developers provide complete and detailed documentation with every DTD suite (XML documents, relevant DTDs, and other referenced entities). The documentation should be designed for use by XML novices and experts, and it should detail the syntax, proper use, and client-specific definition for each element in a DTD. Additional relevant information about each element, such as probable audio/visual presentation, should also be included as comments. You should also produce documentation for all other XML documents (including all of their relevant DTDs and other documents) that will interoperate with the subject XML document and DTD suite. An XML application isn't considered complete or stable until it is fully documented.

If you are working on the development of an XML application or on the development of individual DTDs or schemas, consult one or more of the several books dedicated to DTD design on the market. This chapter can only provide an introduction and overview to the syntax, components, and processes.

For any mature XML application, its DTDs are usually referenced by more than one document. So DTDs should be designed to be flexible, reusable, and practical. The more detailed the DTD, the more detailed the related documents' structures, element types, and attributes will be. Consequently, there is a greater likelihood that, when the related applications access XML documents, they will obtain the data they need from them. But remember that the development of each DTD and document component costs time and money.

DTD Types and Locations

As we learned in Chapter 3, "Anatomy of an XML Document," a valid XML document is a well-formed XML document with a document type declaration that contains or refers to a DTD or schema and that conforms to the declarations found in that DTD or schema. The respective W3C Recommendations for XML and XML schemas identify all of the criteria in detail.

In Chapter 3, we also discussed how the structure of a conforming XML document consists of two major parts: the prolog and the data instance (which contains the root element and other components). A document type declaration statement (also called a DOCTYPE definition) should always be included in the prolog. That declaration states what class or type the document is and may also refer to internal and external DTD declarations to which the document must adhere to be valid.

As we stated earlier, then, within its document type declaration statement, there may be an internal set of declarations (an internal DTD or internal subset), the name and location of an external document containing declarations (an external DTD or an external subset), or both. In other words, there may be a standalone internal DTD, an external DTD, or a combination of an internal DTD plus a reference to an external DTD.

To determine whether a document is valid, the XML processor must read the entire document type definition, including internal and external subsets. For some applications, however, validity may not be required, and it may be sufficient for the processor to read only the internal subset.

Internal DTD Subsets

Figure 4.1 is an example of an XML document that contains an internal DTD subset. In Figure 4.1, the standalone pseudo-attribute states standalone="yes", so we can say that the document contains only an internal DTD. The value "yes" indicates that the components in the document need to be validated against the internal declarations only; no external DTD subset needs to be consulted.

Because the standalone specification is "yes", the parser looks for an internal DTD in the document type declaration statement, between the opening and closing square brackets ([and]).

Internal DTDs are handy during early development stages. An author can check validity and save time and resources without installing applications or altering server or directory systems. A validating parser, which merely has to check a document against the document's own internal declarations, is all that is needed.

A developer is not restricted to using either an internal DTD or an external DTD. Developers can combine internal declaration subsets with external DTD subsets. In combination cases, the value of standalone is set to "no". The parser would then consult the declarations in the internal subset and in the external subset.

External DTD Subsets

DTD declarations can be stored in an external document, which is referred to in the DOCTYPE definition of one or more XML documents. There are three types of external DTDs:

- Private external DTDs
- External DTDs located at Web sites
- External DTDs with public access

```
<?xml version="1.0" encoding="UTF-8" standalone="yes"?>
<?xml-stylesheet type="text/css" href="diamonds1.css"?>
<!DOCTYPE diamonds [
<!ELEMENT diamonds (location,gem)*>
<!ELEMENT location (#PCDATA)>
<!ELEMENT gem (name,carats,color,clarity,cut,cost,reserved)>
<!ELEMENT name (#PCDATA)>
<!ELEMENT carats (#PCDATA)>
<!ELEMENT color (#PCDATA)>
<!ELEMENT clarity (#PCDATA)>
<!ELEMENT cut (#PCDATA)>
<!ELEMENT cost (#PCDATA)>
<!ELEMENT reserved EMPTY>
]>
<!-- Gems Version 1 - Space Gems, Inc. -->
<!-- filename: gems_excerpt_04.xml -->
<diamonds>
	<location>Ursae Majoris</location>
	<gem>
		<name>Smokey</name>
		<carats>1003.29</carats>
		<color>F</color>
		<clarity>IF</clarity>
		<cut>Ideal</cut>
		<cost>2250000</cost>
		<reserved />
	</gem>
</diamonds>
```

Figure 4.1 A simple XML document with an internal DTD subset.

Private External DTDs

Figure 4.2 illustrates another XML document, whose standalone pseudo-attribute has been set to "no" in the XML declaration statement. In the DOCTYPE definition statement, the parser is told that an external DTD subset must be consulted. In this case, the external subset can be called the external DTD, because it alone contains the declarations. In the figure, the name of the external DTD document is diamonds2.dtd. The XML document must follow the syntax and structure rules found in diamonds2.dtd.

There is an indication that the physical location of the diamonds2.dtd document is on the local system, because the keyword SYSTEM has been inserted after the class specification diamonds. In fact, the diamonds2.dtd document appears to be in the same directory as the XML document itself, because there are no additional paths (that is, folders or directories) specified with diamonds2.dtd.

```
<?xml version="1.0" encoding="UTF-8" standalone="no"?>
<?xml-stylesheet type="text/css" href="diamonds1.css"?>
<!DOCTYPE diamonds SYSTEM "diamonds2.dtd">
<!-- Gems Version 1 - Space Gems, Inc. -->
<!-- filename: gems_excerpt_05.xml -->
<diamonds>
        <location>Ursae Majoris</location>
        <gem>
                <name>Smokey</name>
...
```

Figure 4.2 A simple XML document with a reference to a private external DTD subset.

It is not necessary for the external DTD subset document name to have a .dtd file extension. It is convenient, though, even if it just indicates the nature of the document's contents to others.

The diamonds2.dtd DTD is termed *private*, because it is available only to the user of the system or to those who are able to access the system over a local network, not to those outside the network. The benefit of a private DTD derives from the fact that the developer has control over its content declarations. The document itself is found in the developer's network and so can be modified or extended in-house. The significance of such privacy will become evident as you read about public DTD documents later.

External DTD Subsets Located at Web Sites

Figure 4.3 shows another example of an XML document with an external DTD. Again, the standalone pseudo-attribute has been set to "no", and, in the DOCTYPE definition statement the parser is told that an external DTD subset must be consulted. However, this time the DTD document, although the word SYSTEM still appears, is located in the part of the developer's network that hosts the developer's Web site. The Web site is identified by its URL, and an additional path, indicating a specific directory where the DTD is located, is appended to the URL. When the XML parser reads the document type declaration statement, it sends a request in the form of the URL plus the relative path address, to the specified Web site to access the external DTD subset. At the Web site, the Web server software takes the relative path portion and adds it to the address of the Web site's document directory, which it knows because that directory is already configured in its software. The Web server software knows exactly where to go in its own directory structure to retrieve the DTD and returns a copy of the DTD to the requester (that is, to the parser in the application that accessed the XML document), even though the requester only knew the Web site address and the relative path.

```
<?xml version="1.0" encoding="UTF-8" standalone="no"?>
<?xml-stylesheet type="text/css" href="diamonds1.css"?>
<!DOCTYPE diamonds SYSTEM
        "http://www.SpaceGems.com/dtds/diamonds3.dtd" >
<!-- Gems Version 1 - Space Gems, Inc. -->
<!-- filename: gems_excerpt_06.xml -->
<diamonds>
        <location>Ursae Majoris</location>
        <gem>
                <name>Smokey</name>
...
```

Figure 4.3 A simple XML document containing a reference to an external DTD at a URI or URL.

After the parser receives a copy of the DTD, it validates the document against the declarations in the DTD. If the document is valid, the parser passes the data in the document to the application.

The diamonds2.dtd DTD is termed *public,* because it is available to users who are outside the organization's local network. However, the developer and organization still have control over the DTD's content, because the DTD is still found in the developer's network and so can be modified or extended in-house.

Remote External DTDs with Public Access

So far we have seen how to access an organization's private network DTD and a DTD that is located at a Web site belonging to a private organization. But if a DTD is considered a standard for an XML language and is intended for public use by all those individuals, organizations, or societies that want to share common data, there is a different method for referring to it. Figure 4.4 shows an example of this type of reference. The document now refers to a DTD named gemstones3.dtd located at a Web site belonging to the Galactic Jewelry and Gemstone Association.

```
<?xml version="1.0" encoding="UTF-8" standalone="no"?>
<?xml-stylesheet type="text/css" href="diamonds1.css"?>
<!DOCTYPE diamonds PUBLIC "-//GJGA//gemstones.dtd Version 3.0//EN"
        "http://www.GJGA.com/dtds/gemstones3.dtd" >
<!-- Gems Version 1 - Space Gems, Inc. -->
<!-- filename: gems_excerpt_07.xml -->
<diamonds>
        <location>Ursae Majoris</location>
        <gem>
                <name>Smokey</name>
...
```

Figure 4.4 A simple XML document containing a reference to a public external DTD.

Notice that, in the document type declaration statement in the document in Figure 4.4, the reference has been changed to resemble the following basic syntax:

```
<!DOCTYPE documenttype PUBLIC fpi URL>
```

The keyword PUBLIC replaces the keyword SYSTEM that we saw in previous external DTD references. In Figure 4.4, the coding immediately following the PUBLIC keyword (that is, "-//GJGA//gemstones.dtd Version 3.0//EN") is called the Formal Public Identifier, or FPI.

The "-" in the first field of the FPI indicates that the DTD is defined by a private individual or organization, not one approved by a nonstandards body (in which case, you would use a "+") or by an official standard (in which case, you would reference the relevant standard itself, for example, ISO/IEC 10646). In the second field, you see the text "GJGA", which is a unique name that indicates the owner and maintainer of the DTD. The third field contains the text "gemstones.dtd Version 3.0", which describes the type of DTD document and provides a unique identifier. This is a gemstones type of DTD document and is the third version of this external DTD to be created. The two-letter specification "EN" in the fourth field indicates that the DTD document is written in English.

The DOCTYPE definition continues, providing the URL for the Web site at which the DTD is found, along with a relative directory path to pass to the Web server at that Web site so that the DTD document can be found. Thus, when an XML parser encounters this information in the XML document, it consults the PUBLIC DTD at that Web site as it processes the XML document.

The external DTD in this case is within the jurisdiction of the Galactic Jewelry & Gemstones Association (GJGA). It is not within the SpaceGems network. Thus, changes to the DTD can only be made through the cooperation of the GJGA and its other member organizations. We see this type of external DTD at work when we discuss XHTML in Chapter 6.

Internal DTDs Combined with External DTDs

If a document refers to an external DTD subset, most of the declarations will appear inside that external subset document. However, if a document requires the definition of additional components (usually entities representing graphics or other nonparsed documents) and it is not possible to add them to the external DTD document, it is possible to add them to the specific XML document. Figure 4.5 displays an example of an XML document that provides a small internal DTD subset, but that also refers to an external DTD subset. As shown in Figure 4.5, standalone has been set to "no" in the XML declaration statement.

```
<?xml version="1.0" encoding="UTF-8" standalone="no"?>
<?xml-stylesheet type="text/css" href="diamonds1.css"?>
<!DOCTYPE diamonds  PUBLIC "-//GJGA//gemstones.dtd Version 3.0//EN"
  "http://www.GJGA.com/dtds/gemstones3.dtd" [
  <!ENTITY constellation "Ursae Majoris">
  ]>
<!-- Gems Version 1 - Space Gems, Inc. -->
<!-- filename: gems_excerpt_08.xml -->
<diamonds>
        <location>&constellation;</location>
        <gem>
                <name>Smokey</name>
...
```

Figure 4.5 This simple XML document contains an internal subset plus a reference to a public, external DTD.

Combination DTDs are used when a document author wants to introduce a special component and perhaps show its relationship to the other components (like the entity shown in Figure 4.5; presumably, the definitions of all the element types appear in the external DTD subset). The declarations in the internal subset of the DTD are added to the declarations in the external subset DTD. Collectively, then, they compose the DTD.

It is not recommended to override an existing declaration in the external subset by making a contradictory declaration in the internal subset. (The internal declarations are parsed before those in the external subset, so the more appropriate term is preempted.) More than likely, if there are such contradictory declarations in the internal subset, processing stops—although it is impossible to predict how every application will react—and an error message may be issued.

Some manuals state that the internal declarations will prevail over the external declarations, because of precedence, but that is not necessarily the case. Occasionally, some commercial applications allow the internal declaration to override the one in the external subset. If you are creating your own applications or parsers, that may not be a problem. If you aren't, your testing stage should include relevant checks.

DTD Declarations: General

Earlier, in the *What Are Document Type Definitions?* section, we listed the four kinds of declarations found in DTDs. We discuss them in more detail in this section. Before we proceed, however, remember when composing DTDs to pay attention to the ordering of the declarations. If you include the same declaration more than once, the first one preempts the ones that follow.

Also, any names used in DTD declarations—for element types, attribute lists, entities, or notations—must adhere to XML naming conventions:

- An element type name can begin with a letter, a colon, or an underscore, but not with a number.
- Subsequent characters in the name may be alphanumeric, underscores, hyphens, colons, and periods.
- The name can't contain certain XML-specific symbols, such as the ampersand (&), the at symbol (@), or the less than symbol (<).
- The name can't contain white space.
- The name can't contain parenthetic statements, such as words enclosed in parentheses or brackets.

Element Type Declarations

Element type declarations specify the names of the element types that appear in related documents and describe the content of those element types. Every element type you intend to use must be declared in the DTD. If it is not declared in the DTD, a validation error will eventually occur. Each declaration statement defines only one element type. Thus, the DTD must contain as many element type declarations as there are intended element types.

Here is a sample element type declaration:

```
<!ELEMENT diamonds (location,gem)*>
```

The declaration begins with a left angle bracket, called a start indicator. It is followed by an uppercase keyword (in this case, ELEMENT), which identifies the type of declaration. The combination of the start indicator and the keyword is called a *declaration identifier*. No white space is allowed between the start indicator and the keyword. The keyword is reserved, meaning that there are only so many of them and you must use them as they are intended. So, to declare an element type, you must use the keyword ELEMENT.

If you are developing an XML language or XML documents, it is a best practice for the developers to agree on a style convention for component names and then to conform to that convention throughout document or language creation. Some developers prefer lowercase. This is the convention we use in this book, although we acknowledge that it can occasionally create confusion with attributes (attributes are discussed later in this chapter). That's why, in the text of this book, we surround element type names with angle brackets (for example, <color>). Occasionally, though, we'll use generic names (that is, elementname, documenttype, or similar) when we discuss basic syntax.

Element type names are case-sensitive. If an element name is specified in the DTD as being in title case (initial capital characters), it must also be specified in title case in related documents and applications. Otherwise, the document will not pass a parser's validity check.

The Content Model

In any element type declaration, the information that follows the element type name is called the *content model* (or content specification). In its simplest application, the content model defines which child element types a single parent element type may contain. Those child element types are listed in parentheses.

Meanwhile, the content model in total is more than just a list of contents in any one element type. The combination of element types and their contents describes the whole structure of the XML-related language for which the DTD is being designed.

The following sections describe how various element types are declared in DTDs.

Elements Containing Parsed Character Data

If you are creating a declaration for an element type that is intended to contain parsed character data, you insert the reserved uppercase keyword #PCDATA in the content model position, similar to the following example:

```
<!ELEMENT location (#PCDATA)>
```

Instances of this element type contain character data, and that data is intended to be checked by the XML parser. The term character data refers to plaintext characters but does not include XML's predefined entity reference symbols (the left-hand bracket, the ampersand, the semicolon, or quotation marks). However, the term character data is general: It does not indicate whether the content is alphabetic or numeric, for example. By contrast, XML schemas, which will be discussed in more detail in the next chapter, provide for additional, more precise specifications, such as integers, date format, and floating-point decimals.

If an entity reference appears in the element, the parser retrieves the referenced data and replaces the reference with the actual entity values. However, the entities must not contain elements of their own.

Purists consider this element type to be an example of a mixed content element type. It's true, but for the beginner, the concepts should be discussed separately, because they are a little easier to grasp a step at a time.

Element Types Containing Other Element Types

As stated in Chapter 3, "Anatomy of an XML Document," element types that contain other elements have what is called *element content*. The declaration resembles the following general syntax:

```
<!ELEMENT elementname (childelement1, ... childelementn)>
```

This is the most basic syntax for element content declarations. We show you how it can be modified as we progress. However, in this basic syntax, the names of any child elements are inserted between parentheses following the name of the parent element type. If there is more than one child element type, all the element type names are sequenced within the one set of parentheses and each name is separated from the others by a comma.

Meanwhile, a separate element declaration must also appear in the DTD for each child element listed in the content model of a parent element type. The content models of those declarations describe the content of the respective child elements.

We suggest declaring the child elements in the DTD in the same order as they appear in the parent element declaration, although XML 1.0 does not mandate that. Such a strategy makes it easier and more orderly for the DTD author and for any other analysts or troubleshooters who examine the DTD in the future.

Developers who build a content model with more than one element type and want to specify the exact cardinality (that is, the order, sequence, and frequency of the appearance) of the element types in the related documents can use specific operator symbols, which are discussed later in this chapter.

Element Types Containing Mixed Content

Element types that contain character data *and* child elements are said to contain mixed content. A mixed content element type declaration has the following basic syntax:

```
<!ELEMENT parentelement (#PCDATA | childelement1 | childelementn)*>
```

If a developer intends for an element type to contain mixed content, then within parentheses in the appropriate declaration, the developer specifies the following:

- The keyword #PCDATA, indicating that the element type can contain parsed data.
- The names of the relevant child elements, separated by vertical lines (also called pipes).

When using a mixed content declaration, you cannot use element operator symbols (discussed later in this chapter) inside the parentheses. They can be used only inside the parentheses when you create declarations for element types that contain element content only. You are also not allowed to specify the frequency or the order of appearance of the child element types. Thus, avoid mixed content declarations if you can. Although they're used to translate simple documents into XML, there isn't much use for them otherwise.

Here is a simple example of a mixed content element declaration:

```
<!ELEMENT invStatus (#PCDATA | orderMsg )*>
```

This declares an inventory status element type, which might contain the number of items in stock or might, alternately, provide a message that indicates order status. Notice two things:

- There must be white space on either side of the vertical bar.
- There must be an asterisk (*) on the outside of the last parenthesis to show that either data or a child element type must occur within the parent <invStatus> element type.

Empty Element Declarations

In Chapter 3, "Anatomy of an XML Document," we introduced the concept of declared empty elements. They are different from element types whose DTD declarations indicate that they *may* contain content but for various reasons occasionally do not. The latter element types are simply called *elements with no content*. Here is an example of the declaration syntax for declared empty element types:

```
<!ELEMENT reserved EMPTY>
```

This example is taken from Figure 4.1, where it forms part of the internal DTD subset, and from the other figures, too, where it is presumed to be part of the external subset. With this type of declaration, the only requirement is to add the reserved uppercase keyword EMPTY after the name of the element type which, in this case, is <reserved>.

These declared empty element types are often used as markers to indicate that some action can or will take place during execution by the application. For example, the application may initiate a search for documents or parent elements containing the empty element type and then may execute additional prescribed steps with or on the other related element types.

In Figures 4.1 through 4.5, for example, the Smokey diamond seems to be "reserved," whatever that means (perhaps no purchase will be allowed or someone already has bid on it or purchased it or whatever). So maybe an application will or will not display Smokey in a catalog, or will not add Smokey's value to the other Space Gems assets. Meanwhile, the <reserved> element type could not be inserted properly, and the XML document would not be valid, unless the declared empty <reserved> declaration appears in the DTD.

Although these elements will not be permitted to contain data, their tags can be assigned attributes, as we discuss later in this chapter.

Elements with "Any" Content

As we discussed briefly in Chapter 3, "Anatomy of an XML Document," element types can be declared to contain a kind of content called *any content*. In the DTD, the declaration says, basically, that the element is valid as long as it contains any kind of data. Thus, there are no content restrictions on the element types or their instances. This declaration indicates to an XML validating parser that it doesn't have to perform a check on the specified element type's content. Here is the basic syntax:

```
<!ELEMENT elementname ANY>
```

All you need to do is insert the reserved uppercase keyword ANY after the name of the element type. Although such a no-restrictions approach to element types seems imprecise at best and risky at worst, an ANY declaration can be beneficial if you are creating a DTD to retrofit to existing documents or if it is used during document conversion. Time and processor resources can be saved when content doesn't need to be validated all the time. An ANY specification should eventually be changed to something more precise and descriptive to provide better control over structure and content.

Element Content Operators

A content model that contains more than one element name usually uses specific operator symbols to indicate the cardinality (that is, the order and frequency of appearance) of element types. These operators include the following:

- The comma (,)
- The vertical line, or pipe (|)
- The question mark (?)
- The plus sign (+)
- The asterisk (*)

These symbols can be used singly or in combination. If you want to specify that element types can be used in combination, nest their element type names in parentheses. With parentheses, element types can be nested to whatever depth you require.

The Comma

The comma allows you to specify a required sequence of child elements. It also serves as an AND operator. The use of a comma in an element content declaration is shown in the following example:

```
<!ELEMENT gem (name,carats,color,clarity,cut,cost)>
```

This declaration tells the parser that there is an element type named <gem> that contains one of each of the following child element types: <name>, <carats>, <color>, <clarity>, <cut>, *and* <cost>, in that order.

The Vertical Line

The vertical line, or pipe, allows you to specify a list of candidate child element types, only one of which can occur in an instance of the parent element type. So the pipe serves as an OR operator. Here is an example:

```
<!ELEMENT price (msrPrice | discPrice)>
```

This declaration says that there is an element type named <price> that contains one of two possible element types: either the manufacturer's suggested retail price <msrPrice> or the discounted price <discPrice>. As mentioned previously, the vertical line must have white space on both sides of it.

The Question Mark

The question mark allows you to specify that the child element is optional; whether it is included is decided by the XML document author. A question mark is used in the following example:

```
<!ELEMENT gem (name,carats,color,clarity,cut,cost,reserved?)>
```

This declaration is actually more accurate in its definition of the <gem> element type compared to the previous comma example. It says that there is an element type named <gem> that will contain one of each of the following child element types: <name>, <carats>, <color>, <clarity>, <cut>, and <cost>, in that order, and they may or may not be followed by a <reserved /> element type (in our examples, we are using <reserved /> as a declared empty element type).

The Plus Sign

The plus sign operator specifies that at least one instance of the child element types will appear in an instance of the parent element type, but there is no restriction on the number of times that any of the specified child element types can appear. There is also no restriction on the order of their appearance. Here is an example:

```
<!ELEMENT saleGems (diamond | ruby | sapphire | emerald)+>
```

This declaration says that there is an element type named <saleGems> that contains at least one instance of a child element type and that the instance can be either a <diamond>, <ruby>, <sapphire>, or <emerald> element type. Thus, child elements within <saleGems> could be:

- Just one <sapphire>
- A collection, such as <emerald> <diamond> <diamond> <emerald> <ruby> <sapphire>
- Two <diamond>s
- Some other combination of child elements

The Asterisk

The asterisk operator specifies that zero or more of the child element types may appear in an instance of the parent element type. There is no maximum or minimum number of instances of each child element type that may appear. Here is an example:

```
<!ELEMENT saleCatalog (#PCDATA | diamond | emerald | ruby | sapphire)*>
```

This example illustrates a mixed content element type declaration that we discussed earlier in this chapter.

We also mentioned earlier that the "character data only" element type declaration is actually an example of the mixed content element type declaration. This example declaration states that there is an element type named <saleCatalog> that may contain one or more child element types. If it does, the child element type can be parsed character data or parsed character data interspersed with one or more <diamond>, <emerald>, <ruby>, or <sapphire> child element types. Thus, there may not be any child elements, there may be any combination of the listed child element types, or there may be character data with or without child element types.

Attribute List Declarations

As we discussed in Chapter 3, attributes provide you with the capability to provide additional information about your element types. They appear as name:value pairs inside start tags immediately after the name of the element type.

Here is a quick reminder of the basic syntax for an attribute in an XML document (not in a DTD):

```
<gem location="Sol">
```

This example is re-created from Table 3.1. The attribute name is location, and its value is specified to be "Sol". We'll revisit this example when we discuss declarations.

Meanwhile, as we stated in Chapter 3, you can freely add attributes to your XML documents, but those documents cannot be valid unless the attributes also have been declared in the document's DTD. Attributes are declared in DTDs by the use of attribute list declarations. The following is the basic syntax for an attribute list declaration:

```
<!ATTLIST elementtypename     attributename1  attType  defaultvalue1
                                . . .
                                 attributenamen  attType  defaultvaluen>
```

Each declaration starts with the uppercase keyword ATTLIST and then provides the name of the element type to which the declared attribute applies. Then the name of the attribute itself is provided. After that, there is a keyword (represented by our generic term *attType* in the preceding syntax) description of the attribute's type—that is, the nature of the data that will eventually be specified as the value for the attribute in the XML attributes for that element. Finally, a default value for the attribute is specified for those occasions when none is specified by the DTD author.

As you can see from this syntax, you can insert more than one attribute declaration in a single ATTLIST. You can also create more than one ATTLIST per element type. However, you cannot mix attributes from more than one element type in a single ATTLIST.

Here is a simple example of an attribute list declaration:

```
<!ATTLIST gem location CDATA #REQUIRED>
```

In this example, the element is named <gem>, the name of its attribute is location, the type of values that may be specified for the attributes is CDATA (character data string), and the default value for the attribute is #REQUIRED. #REQUIRED indicates that no default value exists. Eventually, the XML parser reads the DTD as it validates the XML document and passes the attribute specification data to the application.

CDATA is one of XML's 10 possible attribute types. Table 4.1 lists all the attribute types available.

Table 4.1 Attribute Types

ATTRIBUTE TYPE	VALUE SPECIFICATION
CDATA	Value is a character string. Any text is allowed except XML's reserved characters (for them, use predefined entity references).
ENTITY	Value is the name of a single entity. The entity must also be declared in the DTD.
ENTITIES	Value may be multiple entity names, separated by white space.
ID	Value is a proper, unique XML name (that is, a unique identifier). Each ID value in a document must be different. Each instance of an element type can have only one ID attribute.
IDREF	Value is the value of a single ID attribute on some element instance in the document (usually an element to which the current element is related).
IDREFS	Value contains multiple IDREF values, separated by white space.
List of names	This attribute type is also called *enumerated*. Value must be taken from a list of names that appears in the declaration. The possible values are explicitly enumerated in the declaration.
NMTOKEN	This is a restricted form of string attribute (they begin with a letter). The value consists of a single word or string with no white space.
NMTOKENS	Value may contain multiple NMTOKEN values, separated by white space.
NOTATION	Value consists of a sequence of name tokens, but matches one or more notation types (instructions for processing formatted or non-XML data).

In the example attribute declaration, the specification for the nature of any default value specified for the <gem> location is #REQUIRED. Then in our example XML documents, the specified value for the location attribute in the <gem> tag was "Sol". You may ask how they are related. Table 4.2 explains the four possible default values that you can specify for attributes in their respective declarations.

Table 4.2 Attribute Default Values

DEFAULT VALUE	INTERPRETATION
#REQUIRED	The XML document author must specify a value for the attribute for every occurrence of the element type in the document.
#IMPLIED	The document author does not have to specify a value and no default value is provided. However, the author may specify a value. If a value is not specified, the XML parser must proceed without error.
"value"	In the declaration, any legal value can be specified as the attribute's default. However, in related documents, the document author may override the default value but is not required to do so. Note, though, that if a value is not specified by the document author, then the default value found in the declaration will be used.
#FIXED "value"	There is a fixed, nonvarying default value in the declaration. In this case, document authors are not required to insert the attribute in the related element types, but if they do, the attribute must have that specified default value anyway. If it is not present, the element type will be treated as though it has that attribute and its value is the default value specified in the DTD declaration.

Based on Table 4.2, whenever the element <gem> appears, a value for the location must be specified by the document author. That's why, in our document example, the location attribute in <gem> was given the value "Sol".

Attribute Declarations to Preserve White Space

As we discussed in Chapter 3, during XML document and DTD development, white space is added so that the developer can visualize the document's structure and functions. Maintenance of that white space during subsequent processing by the parser and the application program isn't usually a concern. Sometimes, though, depending on the task facing the document author, the creation or maintenance of white space may be significant. White space is also a consideration in mixed content element types (that is, the interspersing of text with elements). In those cases, the developer must be aware of the content model of the elements in question.

White-space maintenance requires two steps: inserting the xml:space attribute in the relevant element start tags, and the corresponding declaration of the attribute in the DTD. Both of these are needed to advise the parser to maintain white space.

Remember that the only legal values for XML:space are *preserve* and *default*. The value default indicates that the author does not mind whatever processing the application will apply to the element. On the other hand, for any element whose start tag includes the attribute specification xml:space="preserve", all white space in that element (and within child elements that do not explicitly reset XML:space) is considered significant and is maintained.

Here is the example that you first saw in Chapter 3:

```
<poem xml:space="preserve">
<title>Oh Diamond, Mine!</title>
     <stanza number="1">You dazzle us, you're brilliant!
                        Yet hard and so resilient
                        Symbol of love, loyalty and light
                        Sought after, day and night!
                        Oh diamond, mine!</stanza>
     <stanza number="2">
                     ......
</poem>
```

Now, all we need is the syntax for the xml:space attribute declaration. Here is an example, based on the preceding poem stanza:

```
<!ATTLIST poem xml:space (default | preserve) default>
```

As you can see, in a DTD the XML:space attribute must be declared as an item list type (also called an enumerated type) with only the two values as choices, followed by whatever default value the author prefers (in the current example, the default value chosen by the author is default).

Language ID Attribute Declarations

In Chapter 3, we mentioned how some applications benefit from information about the original language in which a document is written. The attribute XML:lang is used to specify the language.

Here again are the examples from Chapter 3:

```
<cost xml:lang="en-us">25000 dollars</cost>
```

and

```
<cost xml:lang="x-cancri-au">*%+|||</cost>
```

For them to be effective, declarations for xml:lang must appear in the DTD. Respectively, the declarations for the two examples might look like:

```
<!ATTLIST cost xml:lang NMTOKEN 'en-us'>
```

and

```
<!ATTLIST cost xml:lang NMTOKEN 'x-cancri-au'>
```

In each case, the names are character strings that begin with a letter. In each case, too, there is a default value specified between quotation marks.

Entity Declarations

We learned in Chapter 3 that entities are the physical storage units for the parsed and unparsed data that compose every XML document. They are references that are passed along to the application by the XML parser, at which time the parser expands them (that is, accesses the entities, structures data, and passes the data to the application). Because of what they represent, entities are powerful content management devices. But, like element types and attributes, for entities to be effective and for the documents containing them to be valid, there must be matching declarations for them in their respective internal or external DTD subsets. Basically, those declarations specify names for the entities and then define what the entities represent.

In Chapter 3, the discussion of entities centered on general entities, which are used for developing element types in XML documents. Discussion of the other type, parameter entities, was delayed until this chapter, because they are relevant to the development of the declarations in DTD subsets.

General Entity Declarations

As we saw in Chapter 3, general entities are found in XML documents. They are of two types:

Internal. The entity is found in the same document where the entity reference appears.

External. The entity is found in a separate document from the one in which the entity reference appears.

Because they are slightly different, their syntax is different. The following example is a general internal entity representing a specific date. First, here is an example of an entity reference that appears in the XML document:

```
<discoveryDate>&date;</discoveryDate>
```

We know it is an entity reference by the presence of the ampersand at the beginning and the semicolon at the end of the entity name. Now, here is the corresponding entity declaration that appears in the DOCTYPE definition statement in the prolog of the same XML document between the opening square bracket and the closing square bracket (for further details, please consult Chapter 3):

```
<!ENTITY date "May 16, 2047">
```

The declaration is fairly straightforward: an uppercase keyword ENTITY followed by the name of the entity and then the value for the entity in quotation marks.

The next example is a general external entity representing a document containing a photograph or some other type of graphic. Here is the entity reference that appears in the XML document:

```
<gemLogo>&xhrylliteSmall;</gemLogo>
```

The syntax for the external general entity reference is the same as for the internal general entity reference. The difference is in where the entity declaration is located.

Now, here is the entity declaration that appears in the respective DTD document that would be referenced in the DOCTYPE definition of the XML document:

```
<!ENTITY xhrylliteSmall SYSTEM "\logos\xhrylliteSm_04.jpg">
```

Again, we see the uppercase keyword ENTITY followed by the entity name. Then we are told that the entity document is on the local system at the end of the relative path.

Parameter Entity Declarations

Parameter entities are different from general entities. Where general entities are used for building XML document components, parameter entities are used for building declarations in DTD subsets. Parameter entities, however, may also appear in XML documents, because they can be used in internal DTD subsets. The parameter entity references are expanded as the XML parser reviews the DTD. In this way, the data contained in the entity is brought into the process as the XML document or language is being validated rather than later when the XML processor passes the document data to the application (as is the case with general entities).

Parameter entities are also of two types:

Internal. The entity and entity reference are found in the internal DTD subset of an XML document.

External. The entity and entity reference are found in the external DTD subset document.

Parameter entity declaration syntax is similar to that for general entity declarations, but also resembles the syntax for attribute specifications, discussed earlier in this chapter. To use the parameter entity reference, insert the name of the entity, surrounded by a percent sign (%) and a semi-colon, into an element declaration, as you see in the following generic syntax:

```
<!ELEMENT %entityname;>
```

Internal Parameter Entities

An application of an internal parameter entity is shown in Figure 4.6. Note how, in the figure's "before" scenario, the <gem> element type is composed of <diamond>, <emerald>, <ruby>, and <sapphire> element types. In turn, each of those four child element types is composed of <name>, <carats>, <color>, <clarity>, <cut>, <cost>, and perhaps <reserved/> element types. Thus, the element type declarations for <diamond>, <emerald>, <ruby>, and <sapphire> are identical. A parameter entity reference would be handy for this situation.

In the "after" scenario, we see a declaration for a parameter entity named gemInfo. That parameter entity is composed of references to the <name>, <carats>, <color>, <cut>, <cost>, and <reserved /> element types. Additionally, in the internal DTD subset, the declarations for the <diamond>, <emerald>, <ruby>, and <sapphire> include the reference to the parameter entity *gemInfo*.

You can see that this is a two-step operation, too. First, you create the entity declaration, which looks like:

```
<!ENTITY % entityname "entitydefinition">
```

Notice the extra percent symbol (%) inserted before the entity name, which indicates to the parser that this is a parameter entity.

Then you insert the parameter entity references into the element type declarations, which now resemble:

```
<!ELEMENT elementname %entityname;>
```

Notice that the parameter entity reference starts with the percent symbol, not the ampersand as you saw with other entity references.

One advantage to the parameter entity reference is the savings of keystrokes without jeopardizing any accuracy. The second advantage, perhaps not so apparent at first, is this: If you create several parameter entities and want to change the references in them, you only need to modify the parameter entities or create new ones. There is no need to change all the element type declarations.

```
<?xml version="1.0" encoding="UTF-8" standalone="yes"?>
<?xml-stylesheet type="text/css" href="diamonds1.css"?>
<!DOCTYPE inventory      [

<!ELEMENT gem (diamond,emerald,ruby,sapphire)*>
<!ELEMENT diamond (name,carats,color,clarity,cut,cost,reserved?)>
<!ELEMENT emerald (name,carats,color,clarity,cut,cost,reserved?)>
<!ELEMENT ruby (name,carats,color,clarity,cut,cost,reserved?)>
<!ELEMENT sapphire (name,carats,color,clarity,cut,cost,reserved?)>
<!ELEMENT name (#PCDATA)>
<!ELEMENT carats (#PCDATA)>
<!ELEMENT color (#PCDATA)>
<!ELEMENT clarity (#PCDATA)>
<!ELEMENT cut (#PCDATA)>
<!ELEMENT cost (#PCDATA)>
<!ELEMENT reserved EMPTY>
]>
<!-- Gems Version 1 - Space Gems, Inc. -->
<!-- filename: gems_excerpt_10.xml -->
<gem>
        <diamond>
                <name>Smokey</name>

...
```

BEFORE

```
<?xml version="1.0" encoding="UTF-8" standalone="yes"?>
<?xml-stylesheet type="text/css" href="diamonds1.css"?>
<!DOCTYPE inventory      [
<!ENTITY % gemInfo "(name,carats,color,clarity,cut,cost,reserved?)">
<!ELEMENT gem (diamond,emerald,ruby,sapphire)*>
<!ELEMENT diamond %gemInfo;>
<!ELEMENT emerald %gemInfo;>
<!ELEMENT ruby %gemInfo;>
<!ELEMENT sapphire %gemInfo;>
<!ELEMENT name (#PCDATA)>
<!ELEMENT carats (#PCDATA)>
<!ELEMENT color (#PCDATA)>
<!ELEMENT clarity (#PCDATA)>
<!ELEMENT cut (#PCDATA)>
<!ELEMENT cost (#PCDATA)>
<!ELEMENT reserved EMPTY>
]>
<!-- Gems Version 1 - Space Gems, Inc. -->
<!-- filename: gems_excerpt_11.xml -->
<gem>
        <diamond>
                <name>Smokey</name>

...
```

AFTER

Figure 4.6 Example of an internal parameter entity.

External Parameter Entities

Parameter entities can be added to external DTD subsets in a manner similar to the way the internal parameter entity example appears in Figure 4.6. Parameter entity advantages are multiplied if you add them to external DTDs, especially if each of several DTDs are accessed by several XML documents.

Notation Declarations

We've mentioned that XML documents can contain parsed text data and unparsed data (for example, audio, video, and other document files). In Chapter 3, "Anatomy of an XML Document," we showed you how to incorporate XML data. Now we show you how to incorporate non-XML data.

There are two basic methods for incorporating non-XML data into XML documents: providing references to the specific non-XML documents through a series of attributes in a start tag, and providing entity-type attributes (often in their own dedicated element types). However, for the non-XML data references to be validated, we must include appropriate notation and other declarations in the respective DTD. The following sections discuss each method.

Non-XML Data Introduced with an Attribute

To illustrate this method, let's use an example. Presume we want to add an existing Graphics Interchange Format (GIF) logo, called diamond.gif, to an XML document so that when the XML document is called by its application the graphic image displays. Let's say that we also want to install the reference to the graphic document as an attribute in the start tag for the <diamond> element type in Figure 4.6. For our first attempt, we would probably assume (incorrectly) that all we have to do is add a simple attribute to the <diamond> element start tag in the XML document, like this:

```
<diamond logo="diamond.gif" >
     <gem> Smokey</gem>
```

Unfortunately, the addition of that simple attribute is insufficient. With XML, more information is required, because the parser and application won't recognize the GIF format automatically. The start tag actually has to be something like this:

```
<diamond logo="diamond.gif" logo_type="gif" >
     <gem> Smokey</gem>
```

That seems simple enough. (We are presuming that the document diamond.gif is located in the same directory as the XML document; if it is located elsewhere, more path information would be required.) And it is simple as far as the XML document is concerned. But by itself it doesn't solve the binary format recognition issue. We now have to turn our attention to the DTD (the internal *or* external subset, wherever you want to place the appropriate declarations), because of the attributes and values we have introduced. First, we have to advise the parser what the logo_type="gif" attribute really means because, after all, we have arbitrarily chosen the attribute name and value. Let's start with the gif value. It requires a notation declaration in the DTD subset, like this:

```
<!NOTATION gif SYSTEM "image/gif" >
```

As you can see, notation declarations apply labels, such as gif in this example, to specific types of nonparsed binary data. The generic syntax is:

```
<!NOTATION notationLabel SYSTEM "identifier" >
```

The declaration begins with the upperclass keyword NOTATION followed by the arbitrary label name (author's choice). Then the keyword SYSTEM commonly appears, followed by a term that identifies a file, an application, a formal specification, or other information source that provides the application with the capability to display or otherwise manipulate the binary data document. When the binary format is fairly common, such as the Multipurpose Internet Mail Extension (MIME) types such as image/tif (image being the primary media content type, whereas tif is the content subtype), image/jpg, or image/gif, the keyword SYSTEM is sufficient. Following SYSTEM is the actual name of the file, application, or other information. In this case, the combined content/subcontent MIME binary media name is required as the external identifier.

For a complete list of MIME media types, check the University of Southern California's Information Sciences Institute Web site at www.isi.edu/in-notes/iana/assignments/media-types/media-types. There you will see a list of individual MIME types along with references to the IETF Requests for Comments that define those types.

We may also want the capability to add graphics with other common graphic formats (for example, Joint Photographic Experts Group [JPEG] and tagged image file format [TIFF]) to our XML document. So let's also provide notation declarations for them in the DTD. As you can see, their external identifiers indicate that they, too, are MIME media types:

```
<!NOTATION jpg SYSTEM "image/jpg" >
<!NOTATION tif SYSTEM "image/tif" >
```

If you want to use other public binary formats besides the most common ones, such as MIME types, you may have to use the keyword PUBLIC instead of SYSTEM in the declaration and provide a Formal Public Identifier (FPI) reference to the location of the other application or information that is required to manipulate the unparsed data document.

After the labels are declared, attribute declarations must be included in the DTD. By now, the following should be familiar:

```
<!ATTLIST diamond
     logo NMTOKEN #IMPLIED
     logo_type NOTATION (gif | jpg | tif) #IMPLIED>
```

The necessary DTD declarations are now in place. Previously, we included the attributes in the start tag of the <diamond> element type. Now, for everything to work, the application developers have to create the code for manipulating the data. Typically, we rely on browser applications, which contain such code.

Non-XML Data Introduced as an Entity

We'll use an example to illustrate this second method. This time, presume that we want to add an existing JPEG format logo, called diamond.jpg, to an XML document. In this case, though, when the XML document is called by its application, the graphic image will be treated as an entity even though, on the surface, it still looks like an attribute in the start tag of a declared empty <diamond_logo /> element type. Here's what the attribute specification in the XML document might look like:

```
<diamond>
     <diamond_logo logo="diamond_pix01" />
          <gem>Smokey</gem>
```

As you can see, the attribute syntax is simpler than the earlier example, because only one attribute specification is needed. We are using a declared empty element type, although the attribute could appear in any element type; it doesn't have to be empty.

Now we need to focus on the respective DTD. First, ensure that there is a declaration for our empty element:

```
<!ELEMENT diamond_logo EMPTY>
```

Second, insert a declaration for the attribute specification:

```
<!ATTLIST diamond_logo logo ENTITY #IMPLIED>
```

See how the attribute name, logo, is tied to the element type name, diamond_logo. The declaration tells the parser that the attribute type is a single entity and that the XML document author can supply a specification if desired; none is compulsory and there is no default value.

Now it is time to define or declare the entity itself. So the following must also be added:

```
<!ENTITY diamond_pix01 SYSTEM "diamond.jpg" NDATA jpg >
```

This tells the parser that, when it sees the value diamond_pix01 specified for an entity type attribute, it should access the document named diamond.jpg on the local system. Furthermore, the diamond.jpg document is unparsed data (indicated by the NDATA) of jpg format.

The parser at this point still doesn't know what *jpg* format means, so a notation declaration is still necessary. Here it is:

```
<!NOTATION jpg SYSTEM "image/jpg" >
```

The parser learns that *jpg* is a MIME media type whose primary content is an image and whose subcontent type is JPEG. If you want, you could add declarations for TIFF, GIF, or other formats here, too.

Now the XML document and its respective DTD subsets are ready. The parser checks the document, accesses and reads the declarations in its DTD subsets, accesses the graphic document, structures all the data, and passes it to the application. It's up to the application to know what to do next.

Our examples focused on nontext unparsed data. But notation declarations can also play a role with text data. You can use them to label text data that has specific formats (for example, date formats such as ISO's mm/dd/yy or European dd/mm/yy).

Table 4.3 lists some examples of identifiers for such text data. (The last one is fictitious but indicates the format you might use for a customized data format.) However, since no one has developed a universally accepted standard identifier scheme, the list in Table 4.3 may be of limited utility.

Declaring Namespace Attributes in the DTD

In Chapter 3, we learned how namespace declarations are a specialized form of attribute specifications. Thus, for their documents to be valid, declarations for namespaces must also appear in DTDs and schemas. A declaration must appear for each namespace. But just as default namespaces differ from prefix namespaces, their declarations also differ. The next sections describe the specific approaches to declaring the types of namespaces in DTDs.

Table 4.3 Examples of External Identifiers Used with Notation Declaration

EXTERNAL IDENTIFIERS	DESCRIPTION
SYSTEM "ISO 4217:1995"	ISO standard for world currencies.
SYSTEM "ISO 8601:1998"	ISO Standard for date formats.
SYSTEM "..\winnt\system32\ notepad.exe"	Microsoft Notepad can be used to manipulate or display the data.
PUBLIC "-//SpaceGems// notations graficRez//EN" "http://SpaceGems.com/ graphics/gifPix.htm"	This is an FPI for the Space Gems online graphic document resource that is needed to manipulate the data.

Default Namespace Declarations

Creating the appropriate declarations for a default namespace attribute is fairly straightforward. Consider the following example:

```
<diamonds xmlns="http://www.SpaceGems.com/2047/" name="Ursae Majoris" >
     <gem>
          <name>Smokey</name>
          <carats>1003</carats>
          <color>F</color>
          <clarity>IF</clarity>
          <cut>Ideal</cut>
          <cost>2250000</cost>
     </gem>
</diamonds>
```

The <diamonds> element type contains the child element <gem>. So the respective DTD document would contain an element type declaration for each of <diamonds> and <gem>.

After the <diamonds> element type declaration is created, what would the declaration for the default namespace in its start tag look like? We would be correct if we created the following attribute declaration:

```
<!ATTLIST diamonds xmlns CDATA #FIXED "http://www.SpaceGems.com/2047/" >
```

The declaration states that in the extent of any instance of the <diamonds> element type, an attribute named xmlns appears, whose value contains parseable character data. The value does not change; it is fixed at http://www.SpaceGems.com/2047/.

Prefix Namespace Declarations

As we saw in the previous section, creating a default namespace declaration in a DTD can be fairly straightforward. Creating declarations for prefix namespaces, on the other hand, is a little more complex. Consider the following example, which is just the previous example modified to include a prefix namespace instead of a default namespace:

```
<sg:diamonds xmlns:sg="http://www.SpaceGems.com/2047/"
     sg:name="Ursae Majoris" >
     <sg:gem>
          <sg:name>Smokey</sg:name>
          <sg:carats>1003</sg:carats>
          <sg:color>F</sg:color>
          <sg:clarity>IF</sg:clarity>
          <sg:cut>Ideal</sg:cut>
          <sg:cost>2250000</sg:cost>
     </sg:gem>
</sg:diamonds>
```

Here, the <sg:diamonds> element contains the child element <sg:gem>. But now in the DTD the declaration for the <sg:diamonds> element has not changed from what it was for the default namespace example:

```
<!ELEMENT diamonds (gem)* >
```

This time, a different declaration must be created for the xmlns attribute in the <sg:diamonds> start tag. That declaration will look like:

```
<!ATTLIST sg:diamonds xmlns:sg CDATA #FIXED
"http://www.SpaceGems.com/2047/" >
```

This declaration states that, within the extent of an element type named <sg:diamonds>, there is a prefix namespace attribute named xmlns:sg. Furthermore, the value for that attribute contains parseable character data. Its value is fixed at http://www.SpaceGems.com/2047/. In element type names in the extent of <diamonds>, the value for the namespace is represented by the namespace prefix sg:. All element types that begin with the sg: prefix are treated as though the value of the attribute was appended to the beginning of the local part of their name. (For example, the unique universal name for sg:color would effectively be <{http://www.SpaceGems.com/2047/}color>.)

If you will be inserting more than one prefix namespace into an XML document, ensure for validity that you also install a separate attribute declaration for the additional namespaces into the respective DTD.

Limitations of DTDs with Respect to Namespace Declarations

Because the concept of DTDs predates the development of the W3C namespaces in the XML Recommendation, among other reasons, DTDs do not provide the same level of support for namespaces that XML schemas do. Schema specifications were developed at approximately the same time as the W3C namespace specifications, so they are more flexible and comprehensive, as you will see in the next chapter.

Normalization

At the appropriate time during processing, the XML parser also performs a process called *attribute normalization*. That is, just before the validation stage, the parser uses an algorithm specified in section 3.3.3 of the W3C's XML 1.0 (Second Edition) Recommendation to replace attribute references and entity references with actual data and to resolve white space. If you would like more information on normalization, refer to the XML 1.0 Recommendation.

Chapter 4 Labs: Creating a DTD

In the Chapter 3 lab exercises, you created an XML document whose data instance consisted of a structure of several elements containing the names and relevant characteristics of several diamonds. That document was created to introduce you to the nature of XML data structuring and formatting. In practice, though, a DTD is created first and then is used as a template to create XML documents (TurboxXML calls them instances). So the labs in this chapter represent a restart. In the first lab, you construct a DTD that declares the properties of several diamond-related components. In the second, you create an XML data instance from that DTD. That instance is identical to the lab exercise data instance, using the same data that was given to you in the Chapter 3 lab exercises.

Lab 4.1: Creating a Simple External DTD

The file you create describes the same series of precious diamonds that was introduced in Chapter 3. For the design of this first DTD, we'll pursue these basic goals:

- To allow more than one <gem> to be listed. This is achieved by ensuring that the <gem> element is repeatable.
- To ensure that all of the five C's are present for all diamonds. Later in the lab, you improve upon some of the logic inside the DTD and retest your work by creating a new XML instance from it.

The difference between wanting the <gem> element to be repeatable by using an asterisk (meaning "zero to many times") in the declaration, or the plus sign (meaning "one to many times") is subtle. In this specific case, a data instance without at least one <gem> element would not make sense. So we use the plus sign. But in a case where there were several elements besides <gem> to choose from, it would make better sense to use an asterisk, because another element might be able to replace <gem>. Another point we want you to remember for this example is that the five C's have to be entered in a specific order. Trying to reorder any of the five C's should result in an error when the XML document is validated.

In this lab, we start to work with a graphical user interface. We chose the GUI to emphasize the terminology used, rather than the syntax. But the syntax is still important. If you want to check the syntax, you can change the TurboXML view from *elements* to *source* and back again at any time during the lab. Now let's get started.

1. Open the TurboXML editor. Click Continue Trial if necessary.
2. Click Instance.
3. Click File, New, DTD. A new window appears with a new root element; at this time, it is called unnamed. Using the edit bar at the top of the bottom frame, rename this <diamonds>.
4. Now, for the newly named <diamonds> element type, click the cell called Content.
5. From the drop-down list, change the Content Type to Elements. This specifies that the new root element called <diamonds> will contain more elements (that is, it will have element content and be a parent element). An example of this step is demonstrated in Figure 4.7.

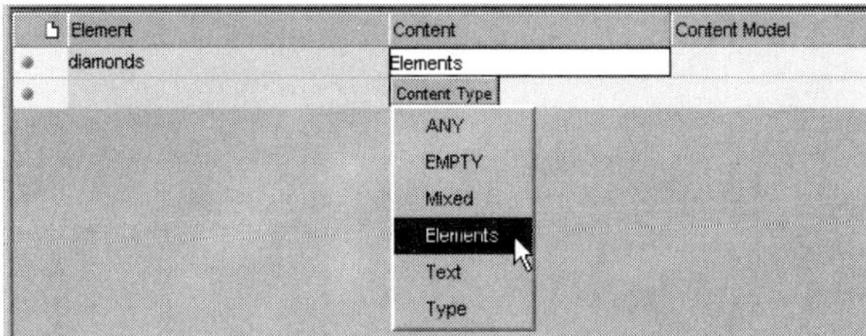

Figure 4.7 TurboXML editor indicating candidate content types.

6. Click the cell under the <diamonds> element, and create a new element called <gem>.
7. Click the <gem> element's Content cell.
8. From the Content Type drop-down list, specify Elements for the <gem> element. The <gem> element will be able to contain elements of its own now, making it a parent element as well.
9. Go back to the <diamonds> element and click its Content Model cell.
10. Place the cursor inside the parentheses ().
11. Select <gem> from the drop-down list.
12. Click Repeatable. An example of this step is demonstrated in Figure 4.8. You can see how the TurboXML editor can be used to build the correct syntax and nesting structure. However, you still have to check the Source view to ensure that the expected syntax appears.

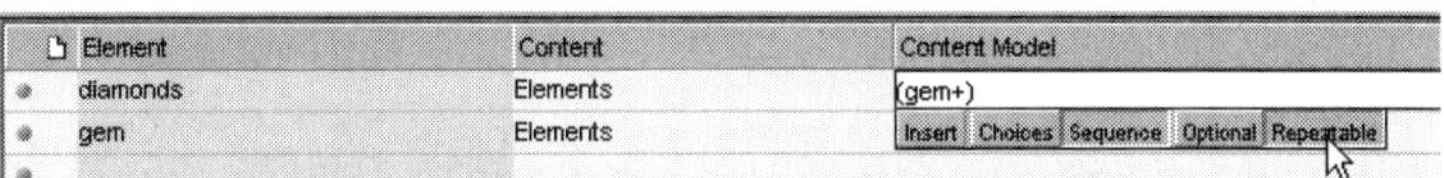

Figure 4.8 TurboXML editor facilitates content model construction.

13. If you place the cursor on <diamonds>, the view should resemble Figure 4.8. The view will vary depending on where the cursor was last clicked. The Figure 4.9 view resulted from clicking on <diamonds> and the Content Model column heading.

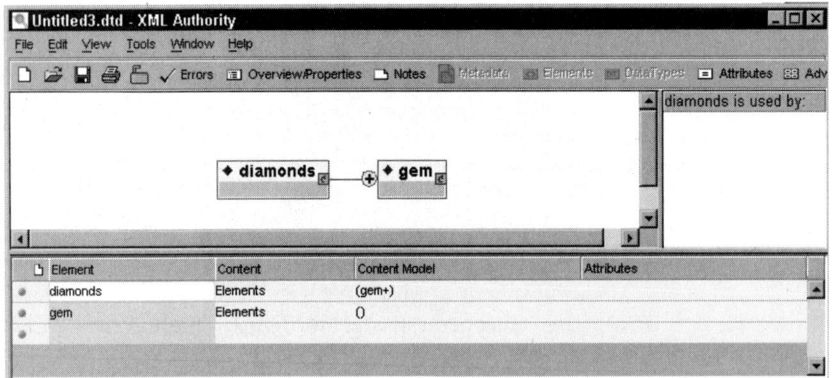

Figure 4.9 Adding element types.

14. Add six new element types called <name>, <carat>, <color>, <clarity>, <cut>, and <cost>. To do so:
    a. Click the next empty cell under the Element column, and type "name".
    b. Click the Content cell beside the element type, and choose Text from the drop-down list.
    c. Repeat **a.** and **b.** to add declarations for the carat, color, clarity, cut, and cost element types.
15. Go back to the <gem> element type and click its Content Model cell. Then click Insert, and add name, carat, color, clarity, cut, and cost.
16. If you place the cursor on <diamonds>, the view should now look like Figure 4.10.

At any time you can alternate the views between the GUI and Source. Click View on the top menu bar, and choose Elements/Types for the GUI. Choose View, Source to see the code.

17. Click the Errors item on the top menu bar. Address any errors. If there are errors, feel free to fix them with either the GUI or the Source view.
18. Save the file as diamonds1.dtd to the C:\WWW\SpaceGems folder.
    a. Change the Save as Type to DTD(*.dtd).
    b. Enter the filename as diamonds1, and click Save.

1. Click here to position the view in the top frame.

2. Click here to expand the list of elements.

3. Click here to sort the elements by Content Model.

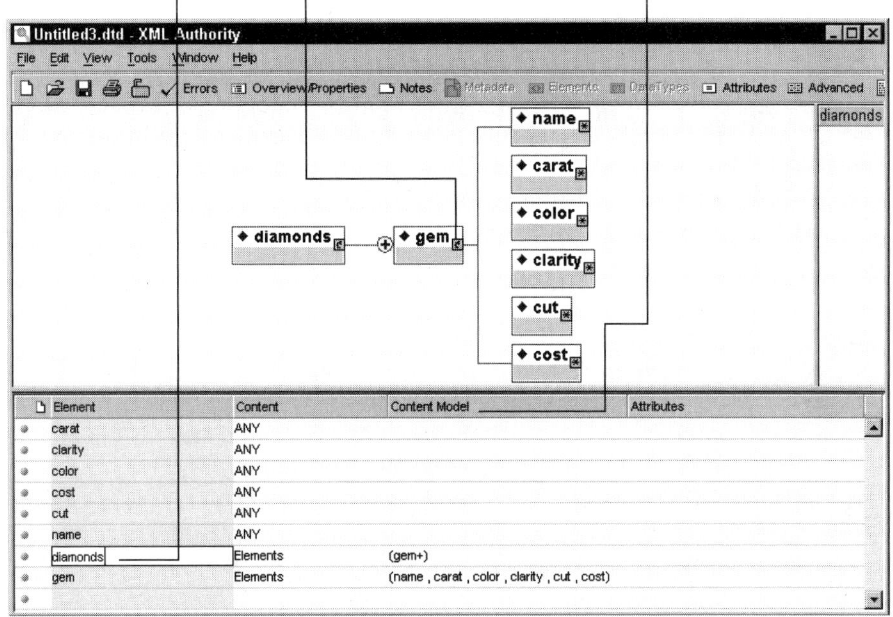

Figure 4.10 GUI view of the DTD under development.

Lab 4.2: Creating a New Instance from the DTD

Now we'll have you create a new XML document (again, TurboXML calls XML documents *instances*) using the DTD you just built. By the end of this exercise, you will see how handy this technique is.

1. Open the TurboXML editor.
2. Click Instance.
3. Click File, Set Schema. Then choose diamonds1.dtd, and click Open.
4. A dialog box asks you, "What element type should serve as the root for the document?" Choose diamonds and click OK.

5. Enter the data from Table 4.4 into the XML instance. If you need to add another <gem> element, click Insert on the bottom menu bar and click gem. This inserts another <gem> element with all of its child elements. (Although it is always important to check your work, to ensure that you are getting the desired effects, don't worry too much about getting 100 percent accuracy with the Table 4.4 values. If, for example, you want to enter "IF", instead of "IF – Internally Flawless", for clarity, it will not impact the functionality of the labs at this time.

6. When you're done entering the Table 4.4 data, click the Errors item on the top menu bar to check the validity of the new document. Address any errors.

Table 4.4 List of Top Diamonds for Galaxy Gems

NAME	CARAT	COLOR	CLARITY	CUT	COST
Sparkler	105	F	IF-Internally Flawless	Super Ideal	126000
Merlin	41	D	FL-Flawless	Ideal	82000
Cullinan	3106	H	VS1, VS2 – Very Slightly Imperfect	Rough	2174200
Dark	500	J	SL1, SL2 – Slightly Imperfect	Rough	450000

7. Save the file as gems1.xml in the C:\WWW\SpaceGems folder.

Additional Labs

For additional lab exercises, visit the *XML in 60 Minutes a Day* Web site that is described in this book's introduction. There you'll find these additional labs:

- Refining the DTD
- Creating a New XML Instance from diamonds2.dtd
- Using Attributes and Entities
- Creating a New XML Document from diamonds3.dtd

- Calling the External DTD: URL vs. Local File
- Combining Internal and External DTDs
- Using Namespaces in DTDs

If your objective is to complete the Space Gems Web site, then you'll find these additional labs to be essential.

Summary

We can't overemphasize the importance of DTDs to the creation of XML languages and documents. Before you move on to Chapter 5, "XML Schemas," ensure that you have a grasp of the following concepts. They'll serve you well as you learn about schemas and as you learn about the other XML-related languages we discuss in subsequent chapters of this book.

- Document type definitions (DTDs) are a form of metamarkup. They were first developed with GML in the late 1960s and later made part of the ISO's SGML standard. They have historically been the most common method for defining XML-related languages. But the vocabulary, grammar, and syntax of a DTD are not like XML.
- DTDs contain several kinds of information: element type declarations, attribute declarations, entity declarations, notation declarations, and other information.
- DTDs are included or referred to in an XML document's document type declaration statement. To be valid, the document must adhere to its DTD declarations.
- DTD declarations can be located in several locations: in the XML document, on the local system or network, or on Web servers anywhere on the Internet.
- In a DTD, element type declarations provide the basis for the content model of an XML language and its related documents.
- If a content model contains more than one element name, it will probably use specific operator symbols (that is, a comma, vertical line, question mark, plus sign, or asterisk) to indicate the order and frequency of appearance of element types.
- In Chapter 3, we learned that general entities are used for developing element types in XML documents. In this chapter, we learned that parameter entities are used to develop DTD declarations.

- There are two basic methods for introducing non-XML data into XML documents: through a series of attributes and through single entity-type attributes (often in their own dedicated element types). Neither method is really straightforward, and both involve combinations of declarations in a DTD.
- DTDs support namespaces, which are a specialized form of attribute. For their documents to be valid, declarations for namespaces must also appear in DTDs and schemas. Because DTD concepts predated XML, DTDs do not provide the same flexibility and comprehensiveness for namespaces that XML schemas do.

Review Questions

1. What are the four types of declarations found in DTDs?
2. True or false? As long as a DTD contains SGML features and meets SGML specifications, its declarations can be used in an XML environment.
3. DTD subsets can be located:
   a. Externally at publicly accessed Web sites
   b. Internally in an XML document
   c. On a private computer network
   d. On a company's own Web site
   e. All of the above
4. A complete DTD consists of declarations found in ______________ or in ________________, if there is one.
5. True or false? Element type names can begin with letters, numbers, colons, or underscores.
6. Match the content operator symbols to their meanings.

a. Comma	i. Choose one from a list
b. Vertical line	ii. At least one
c. Question mark	iii. Zero or more
d. Plus sign	iv. Required sequence
e. Asterisk	v. Optional

7. Which of the following is *not* an attribute type?
   a. CDATA
   b. ENTITY
   c. NDATA
   d. IDREFS
   e. "list of names"
   f. None of the above
8. Which of the following are legal values for the XML:space attribute? (Be careful: there may be more than one correct answer.)
   a. Include
   b. Preserve
   c. Maintain

d. Ignore

e. Default

9. General entities are used for building ________________________ and parameter entities are used for building ________________________ .

10. Provide the syntax for the following declaration: In the event of any instance of the <diamonds> element type, an attribute named xmlns will appear, whose value will contain parseable character data. The value will not change; it is fixed at www.SpaceGems.com/2047/.

Answers to Review Questions

1. The four types of declarations found in DTDs are as follows:
    a. Element type declarations
    b. Attribute declarations
    c. Entity declarations
    d. Notation declarations
2. False. Not all SGML features are used by XML.
3. **e.** As discussed in the text, a document's DTD can be located at any of those four locations. Check the text for the appropriate syntax.
4. A complete DTD consists of declarations found in an internal subset and/or in an external subset, if there is one.
5. False. Numbers are not allowed.
6. **a.** and **iv.**; **b.** and **i.**; **c.** and **v.**; **d.** and **ii.**; **e.** and **iii.**
7. **c.** You can find the others listed in Table 4.1 of the text. NDATA is just a made-up acronym that may look familiar but doesn't really exist in the XML world.
8. **b.** and **e.** These answers are readily found in the *Attribute Declarations to Preserve White Space* section of the text.
9. General entities are used for building XML document components, and parameter entities are used for building declarations in DTD subsets. Developing a declaration is covered in the section titled *Declaring Namespace Attributes in the DTD*.
10. Answer:

```
<!ATTLIST diamonds xmlns CDATA #FIXED
"http://www.SpaceGems.com/2047/" >
```

XML Schemas

The purpose of any XML document model is to provide a means to validate an XML document at machine speed. The earlier, faster, and more easily you transact business, the better your business will be. In a large-scale environment, where vast amounts of information are received from many and varied sources and sent to many and varied destinations, the ability to check document validity at high speed is an important business consideration. No one wants to process content if it is prone to errors. So no one wants to process documents that do not adhere to their prescribed models or aren't valid.

In Chapter 4, "Document Type Definitions," we showed you how DTDs provide a mechanism for describing the content and structure—the model—of XML-related languages and documents. However, since DTDs predated XML, several DTD shortcomings were already known by the time XML 1.0 became a W3C Recommendation in February 1998.

Several XML-related modeling languages, most notably XML Schema, were developed to overcome the limitations of DTDs. In this chapter, we briefly introduce the W3C Schema Recommendation, which is the standard by which XML schemas will be composed in the future. Then, we review several basic schema components, along with some options and alternative methods.

By the end of this chapter, you will also be acquainted with how to make simple XML schema documents, how to create XML documents from a schema, how to tell an XML parser to consult with a schema document, and even how to create a new schema from an existing schema.

We will only scratch the surface of XML schema functionality. If you need to use schemas, we recommend consulting the W3C Web site. Several excellent online tutorials and printed texts are available, dedicated to XML Schema theory and practice.

What Are Schemas?

The term schema is borrowed from database technology. There, a schema determines the structure and relationships among data in relational database tables. In the XML world, schemas in general define the various models for an XML-related language (one schema exists for each class of documents that make up the language). The models prescribe the arrangement of element types, attributes, and other data in a valid document.

Using this broad definition, we can see that DTDs qualify as schemas, too. The DTD concept was developed to model the content of languages and documents derived from GML and SGML. DTDs became the official schema mechanism for SGML, and XML inherited DTD concepts and constructs from SGML.

Although DTDs are currently the most widely used tool for defining document types, they have several shortcomings, among which are the following:

- They have their own syntax, which differs from XML. It would be more efficient, and it would make learning easier, if the tools used to process XML documents could also process the document models with little or no alteration.
- DTDs have a limited ability to describe the data in elements and attributes. For example, it is difficult or impossible to indicate the nature of some character data (numbers, date formats, currencies).
- DTDs are not flexible or extensible enough to take full advantage of namespaces (they can't define or restrict the content of elements based on context sensitivity, which is illustrated later in this chapter).

DTDs have other shortcomings, but discussion of those shortcomings is beyond the introductory nature of this book. Meanwhile, the DTD modeling language could be revised or extended, but not without impacting many, if not all, existing SGML-related languages, their respective descendants, and all the related documents. Thus, several alternative modeling languages were developed to overcome some shortcomings of DTDs: XML Schema, Document Content Description (DCD), Regular Language description for XML (RELAX), BizTalk, Schema for Object-oriented XML (Schematron), and others.

It is predicted that XML Schema models will eventually replace DTDs. But they have some catching up to do first, since DTDs have been around officially since the 1986 SGML standard and enjoy advantages like existing tool support (all SGML-related tools and many XML-related tools can already process DTDs), extensive deployment (many document types are already defined with DTDs), and the widespread existing expertise and applications.

XML Schema 1.0: A Two-Part W3C XML Schema Recommendation

The shortcomings of DTDs were well known even when the W3C endorsed the first edition of the Extensible Markup Language (XML) 1.0 Recommendation in February 1998. In fact, in 1998, as part of the W3C's XML activity, it formed the XML Schema Working Group, charged with developing a new XML Schema Definition language (XSD), which they envisioned becoming the most powerful, flexible, and extensible type of schema available. By May 2001, the Working Group developed the two-part XML Schema Recommendation 1.0. Part 1 of the Recommendation is dedicated to schema structures; Part 2 to pertinent data types.

If you are interested, you can find Part 1 of the Schema Recommendation at www.w3.org/TR/xmlschema-1/. Part 2 can be found at www.w3.org/TR/xmlschema-2/. Part 0, which is a primer for using XML schemas, is worth examining, too. It's located at www.w3.org/TR/xmlschema-0

The two-part XML Schema Recommendation was developed as a content modeling language and application of XML, not as an application of SGML. It is a large, complex standard that lets you specify almost any kind of XML relationship, but it requires a lot of familiarity and practice to implement comprehensively. In this book, we usually refer to it as XML Schema 1.0 (some also call it XSchema). From this point, we refer to individual schema document models developed according to XML Schema as schemas, schema documents, or schema models.

As of this writing, a notice is posted on the W3C's XML Schema Web site that states: "The XML Schema WG is currently working to develop a set of requirements for XML Schema 1.1, which is intended to be mostly compatible with XML Schema 1.0 and to have approximately the same scope, but also to fix bugs and make whatever improvements we can, consistent with the constraints on scope and compatibility." The notice invites participation in the project from the Web community.

XML schemas were developed to overcome the shortcomings of, and eventually replace, DTDs. Since XML Schema pertains only to XML and XML-related languages, it follows then that XML schemas pertain to XML-related languages and documents.

Classroom Q & A

Q: Wait! Sorry to interrupt, but I'm a little confused. Are they capital S *Schemas* or noncapital s *schemas*?

A: Don't worry, it's an issue that arises for many XML schema newcomers. When we refer to the W3C XML Schema Recommendations, we use the capital S reference. For example, in the paragraph preceding your question, we say that "Since XML Schema pertains . . . "; this is a reference to the W3C Recommendation. By contrast, the individual documents that are created by developers according to XML Schema 1.0 or 1.1 rules are called *schemas* or *XML schemas*. In the same paragraph, the first sentence begins "XML schemas were developed to . . . " This is a reference to schemas in general.

The XML Schema Abstract Model

The W3C states that all XML schemas can be described in terms of one basic abstract data model. That model serves to create schemas that specify the structure and content of data to be provided to a conforming XML parser. But, as we see later, the XML Schema abstract model is conceptual only. It does not dictate any specific structure or style for subsequent schemas or documents. It just provides a vast selection of components to choose from when building schemas and prescribes how the components should be combined. The W3C defines 13 kinds of schema components, in three major groups. They are listed in Table 5.1.

In this chapter, we discuss all primary components and some secondary components. We will especially create and manipulate element declarations. Table 5.2 lists the XML Schema predefined elements in the two-part Schema 1.0 Recommendation. These elements are commonly used to construct element declarations in schema models (schema documents whose filenames contain the .xsd extension).

Table 5.1 XML Schema Major Component Groups

NAME OF COMPONENT GROUP	COMPONENTS IN GROUP
Primary components	Simple type definitions Complex type definitions Attribute declarations Element declarations
Secondary components	Attribute group definitions Identity-constraint definitions Model group definitions Notation declarations
"Helper" components	Annotations Model groups Particles Wildcards Attribute Uses

For example, to declare an element, we use <xs:element>. Similarly, to declare attributes, we use <xs:attribute>. Elements that contain child elements, attributes, or both are said to be *complex* content types (also called complex data types or just complex types), whereas elements that contain numbers or other character strings but do not contain child elements are called *simple* content types. Attributes, meanwhile, are always simple types. New complex types are defined using a combination of <xs:element> and <xs:complexType>, whose definitions typically contain element declarations, element references, and attribute declarations. New simple types are defined by <xs:element> or <xs:attribute> in combination with <xs:simpleType>.

Table 5.2 XML Schema Elements Used to Construct Schema Models

ELEMENT NAME	ELEMENT NAME	ELEMENT NAME
xs:schema	xs:complexType	xs:complexContent
xs:simpleContent	xs:extension	xs:element
xs:group	xs:all	xs:choice
xs:sequence	xs:any	xs:anyAttribute
xs:attribute	xs:attributeGroup	xs:unique
xs:key	xs:keyref	xs:selector
xs:field	xs:include	xs:import
xs:redefine	xs:notation	

From another perspective, new XML schema models are defined in terms of constraints. A constraint defines what can appear in a given language or document. The two kinds of constraints are as follows:

Content model constraints. Define element types that can appear in a document. They establish the vocabulary for an XML language and its documents. They also describe the pattern of appearance—the number and type of components, the order they appear in, and whether they are required or optional. In that capacity, they also determine the grammar of the language and documents.

Data type constraints. Describe the appearance and numbers of data types that the schema will accept as valid—such as minOccurs, maxOccurs, use, fixed, and default, which, when used with elements and attributes, govern the frequency of appearance and data associated with the respective components.

The development of XML Schema 1.0 brought no change to the definition of well-formedness and only a slight change to the definition of validity. With XML schemas, a valid document is any well-formed document that conforms to its schema's constraints.

The Logical Structure of a Sample XML Schema

Figure 5.1 shows a simple XML document, named gems_excerpt_62.xml, alongside its respective DTD document. The content and structure of both should be familiar. We've included the DTD here because it helps us to see the types of components that the schema documents are modeling and to interpret the schema declarations.

From the DTD document, you can see that its respective conforming or valid XML documents will each have a root element type named <sg1:diamonds> and that the root element, as a parent element, will contain at least one sequence of child element types named <sg1:gem>, <sg2:mine>, and <sg1:catalog>, indicated by the plus sign outside the parentheses containing those element type names in the <sg1:diamonds> declaration. The <sg1:diamonds> declaration also contains a list of attributes: two are namespace attributes—xmlns:sg1 and xmlns:sg2—and the third is sg1:catPublish, which indicates whether the <sg1:diamonds> data will be published in a catalog (the default is apparently Y for yes).

```
<?xml version = "1.0" encoding="UTF-8"?>
<!-- filename: diamonds05.dtd - ->
<!ELEMENT sg1:diamonds      (sg1:gem,sg2:mine,sg1:catalog)+>
<!ATTLIST sg1:diamonds
        xmlns:sg1 CDATA #FIXED "http://www.SpaceGems.com/2047/gemdata"
        xmlns:sg2 CDATA #FIXED "http://www.SpaceGems.com/2047/minedata">
<!ELEMENT sg1:gem                (sg1:name,sg1:cost?,sg1:reserved?)+>
<!ELEMENT sg1:name               (#PCDATA)>
<!ELEMENT sg1:cost               (#PCDATA)>
<!ATTLIST sg1:cost
        catPublish  ( Y | N )  #IMPLIED "Y" >
<!ELEMENT sg1:reserved                EMPTY  >
<!ELEMENT sg2:mine               (sg2:name,sg2:system,sg2:planet)+>
<!ELEMENT sg2:name               (#PCDATA)>
<!ELEMENT sg2:system             (#PCDATA)>
<!ELEMENT sg2:planet             (#PCDATA)>
<!ELEMENT sg1:catalog            (#PCDATA)>
```

DTD Document

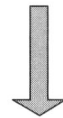

```
<?xml version="1.0" encoding="UTF-8" standalone="no"?>
<?xml-stylesheet type="text/css" href="diamonds2.css"?>
<!DOCTYPE diamonds SYSTEM "diamonds05.dtd" >
<!-- Gems Version 2 - Space Gems, Inc. -->
<!-- filename: gems_excerpt_62.xml -->
<sg1:diamonds xmlns:sg1="http://www.SpaceGems.com/gemdata"
        xmlns:sg2="http://www.SpaceGems.com/minedata">
        <sg1:gem>
                <sg1:name>Smokey</sg1:name>
                <sg1:cost sg1:catPublish="N">2,250,000</sg1:cost>
                <sg1:reserved />
        </sg1:gem>
        <sg2:mine>
                <sg2:name>Capitan Uno</sg2:name>
                <sg2:region>Ursae Majoris 47</sg2:region>
                <sg2:planet>UMa 47 F</sg2:planet>
        </sg2:mine>
        <sg1:catalog>Annual 2047</sg1:catalog>
</sg1:diamonds>
```

Corresponding XML Document

Figure 5.1 A sample DTD and its conforming document.

The <sg1:gem> element types will contain and be a parent element to <sg1:name>, <sg1:cost>, and <sg1:reserved />. Thus, every time an <sg1:gem> element occurs, it will contain one <sg1:name> element type and perhaps, because the question marks after their names indicate that they are optional, <sg1:cost> and <sg1:reserved /> element types, too. The <sg1:name> and <sg1:cost> element types will contain parsed character data, whereas the <sg1:reserved /> element type is declared empty.

The <sg2:mine> element type will contain a sequence of element types, too: its own version of a <name> element called <sg2:name>, plus <sg2:system> and <sg2:planet> element types. All these child element types will contain parsed character data. The <sg1:catalog> element will simply contain parsed character data.

We can see by the respective prefixes in the element tags that these various element types belong to two namespaces. The existence of two namespaces allows both the <sg1:gem> and <sg2:mine> element types to contain their own respective versions of a <name> element.

The XML document in Figure 5.1 adheres to its DTD specifications. Figure 5.2 illustrates the result of converting the Figure 5.1 DTD to two simple XML schema documents. It could easily have been converted to a single schema document (and a simpler one to boot), but we want to show you how two schema documents can work together. Note the .xsd extension at the end of the documents' respective filenames. The extension indicates that these files are XML schema documents.

Let's examine these documents in some detail.

The Prolog

The first two lines of each schema document are their respective prologs. By now, you recognize the first lines as XML declarations. In a schema document, the XML declaration is the only required prolog component. As with most XML application documents, it should be the first line at the top of the document; nothing should precede it. If you need to refresh your memory regarding the XML declaration, please refer to Chapter 3, "Anatomy of an XML Document."

The second line in each document is a comment line. Although not essential, each has probably been inserted by its author to indicate to a reader what the respective schema documents are named (that is, gemdata.xsd and minedata.xsd).

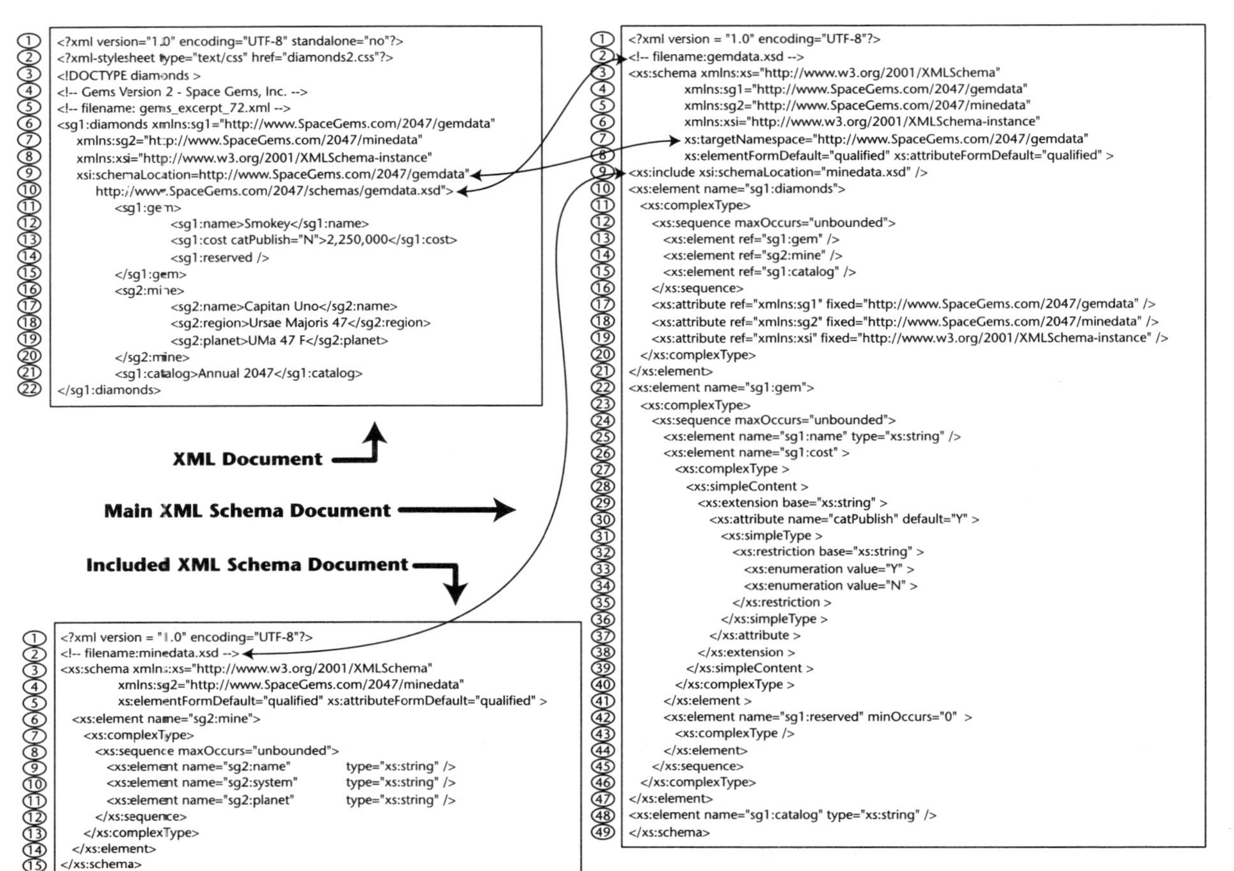

Figure 5.2 An XML document and its two corresponding schema documents.

The <Schema> Element: Namespaces and Qualified or Unqualified Locals

The third line of each schema, beginning with "<xs:schema...", is the start tag for the <schema> element, which is the first element of the schema data model and is equivalent to the root element of an XML document. The <schema> element is the parent element of all other elements in the schema document.

In the case of the gemdata.xsd schema, the <xs:schema ... > start tag also includes several attribute specifications for the namespaces and the qualified or unqualified local elements.

Namespace Declarations

In the <xs:schema...> start tag, the first namespace declaration is xmlns: xs="http://www.w3.org/2001/XMLSchema". This tells the parser that, when it encounters data types preceded by the prefix xs:, the meaning of those data types will be identical to the definition found for them in the W3C Schema 1.0 Recommendation. Thus, they have standard definitions and so require no further definition in this schema document before they are processed.

As a reminder, do not be misled or confused by references to URLs used in namespaces; although URLs are readily identified as Web addresses, they are simply used to add uniqueness to the names used in the schema.

The first namespace in the schema document is used, and the xs: prefix is subsequently added to the XML schema-defined components, to easily identify those Schema 1.0 components. This makes it easier to keep track of them among all the other schema document components being defined by the designer.

In other schema-related textbooks, Web sites, and documents, the prefix used for this first type of namespace is *xsd*. We use xs: because it is specified by default by several DTD-to-schema conversion software applications, including two we used during the preparation of this book. If you read other references and encounter <xsd:schema> or similar, don't worry. It means the same thing to the parser. In fact, you could assign any prefix, or not use one at all, as long as your choice is consistent between the namespace and the component names.

Two more namespace declarations, whose prefixes are sg1: and sg2:, follow the xs: namespace declaration in the gemdata.xsd document. However, just the sg2: namespace declaration appears in the minedata.xsd document. Those namespace declarations appear because various element types that begin with those prefixes will be declared in each schema.

Another namespace declaration, whose prefix is xsi:, appears in gemdata.xsd. It is discussed in the next section.

Target Namespaces

By now, we are familiar with the XML validation process, whereby a parser attempts to validate an XML data instance document against the declarations in its schema documents. But how will the parser know which schema documents to consult? A method must exist that tells the parser which schema document to access. The concept of target namespaces provides that method.

Look at lines 8 through 10 of the gems_excerpt_72.xml XML document in Figure 5.2. We've already briefly mentioned the namespace declaration xmlns:xsi="http://www.w3.org/2001/XMLSchema-instance" in line 8. It tells the parser that when it sees any component that begins with the xsi: prefix, the associated component is defined in what is called the XML Schema instance namespace and requires no extra declaration to define it.

On line 9, we see the beginning of the two-value attribute called xsi:schemaLocation. Here, we're introducing a component from the XML Schema instance namespace; in fact, it's the only one introduced in gemdata.xsd. Its first value is http://www.SpaceGems.com/2047/gemdata, which is a target namespace. When the parser reads this value, it knows that when it eventually encounters a schema document that contains an attribute named targetNamespace, whose value is identical to this URL, it will have found the appropriate schema document.

On line 10 of the XML document, a URI/URL is provided to tell the parser exactly where to go to find the schema document it needs.

Let's review the gemdata.xsd schema document. On line 7, within the <schema> element start tag, a targetNamespace attribute appears:

```
targetNamespace="http://www.SpaceGems.com/2047/gemdata"
```

Once the parser reads this attribute, it knows that it has found the schema document referred to in the XML document. The parser can then examine the XML document and compare its components against the declarations in this schema document.

The targetNamespace attribute is usually placed within the root <schema> element, as it is here. However, this is not a universal rule or practice. Depending on the intent of the schema designer, the attribute specification may be placed within any element declaration.

To recap: During the parsing and validating process, the parser examines the XML instance document, reads the URI/URLs in the schemaLocation attribute specification, and looks for the schema document whose <schema> start tag contains the identical URI/URL specified as the value for its targetNamespace attribute. This targeting process gives the process its name.

As an alternative to the combination of the xsi:schemaLocation and targetNamespace attributes, we could use the following attribute in the XML document:

```
xsi:noNamespaceSchemaLocation=
    "http://www.SpaceGems.com/2047/schemas/gemdata.xsd"
```

The difference here is that this attribute provides the parser with the URI/URL location of the appropriate schema document, but also tells the parser that that document does not contain a targetNamespace attribute.

The minedata.xsd Document as a Support Schema

Although the examples and projects presented in this book are simple, typical schemas in an e-commerce environment may actually use element types and attributes from multiple schemas accessed via different namespace-related methods. That's why we split our sample schema declarations between two schema documents: to show how a schema designer or author can create several schema documents, all of which share a common umbrella namespace.

The main schema document (the gemdata.xsd document) will be specified in the XML document, and the targetNamespace attribute in the main schema document will correspond to that specification. But the main schema document contains an additional element type, either:

```
"<xs:include schemaLocation="nameOfSupportSchemaDoc.xsd"/>"
```

or

```
"<xs:import namespace="http://www.SpaceGems.com"
        schemaLocation="nameOfSupportSchemaDoc.xsd"/>"
```

On line 9 of the gemdata.xsd main schema document, we provide the simpler of the two element types, the <xs:include ...> element that tells the parser to include minedata.xsd as an additional schema document. When the parser encounters the element type, it reads the value of the schemaLocation attribute, accesses that schema document, and treats it as a support schema. The declarations in the included schema documents are added to those in the main schema document, and they are all regarded as a combined schema model.

These combinations of schema documents can provide great flexibility in design, but you must be diligent with regard to element type declarations. If you examine an otherwise schemalike document (a document containing declarations and an .xsd filename extension) and you don't see a targetNamespace attribute, you may be looking at a support schema (also called a support namespace or a chameleon namespace).

Global and Local References: Qualified and Unqualified Locals

Figure 5.3 is almost identical to Figure 5.2, but here we have emphasized different features. On line 8 of gemdata.xsd and on line 5 of minedata.xsd, within the respective <schema> element tags, two attributes occur: elementFormDefault and attributeFormDefault, both of whose values are specified as *qualified*. Before we can explain the impact of these attribute specifications, a couple of other concepts must be explained.

Element types or attributes declared within the extent of the <schema> element type are called globally declared, global references, archetypes, or globals. In Figure 5.3, <sg1:diamonds> (line 10 in gemdata.xsd), <sg1:gem> (line 23 in gemdata.xsd), <sg2:mine> (line 6 in minedata.xsd), and <sg1:catalog> (line 34 in gemdata.xsd) are globally declared, as are the namespace attributes represented by the prefixes xs:, sg1:, sg2:, and xsi:. These have been italicized for emphasis, as have their respective elements and attributes in the XML document on the left of Figure 5.3.

By contrast, local or locally declared schema elements and attributes are those declared within the extent of child elements of the <schema> element. In Figure 5.3, we have boldfaced the declarations for <sg1:name> (line 25 in gemdata.xsd), <sg1:cost> (line 26 in gemdata.xsd), <sg1:reserved /> (lines 31 to 33 in gemdata.xsd), <sg2:name> (line 9 in minedata.xsd), <sg2:system> (line 10 in minedata.xsd), and <sg2:planet> (line 11 in minedata.xsd), as well as the sg1:catPublish attribute (line 28 in gemdata.xsd). Corresponding elements and attributes in the XML document appear in bold on the left of Figure 5.3.

During the schema and document design phases, for various reasons, the schema and document designers must decide whether they want the namespace prefixes to be displayed (or exposed) in the tags of locally declared elements tags in their XML documents. Choosing to have the prefixes appear in the tags qualifies the locally declared elements. When prefixes appear, these tags have "exposed the identity" of the namespaces pertaining to those local element types.

Whatever their decision, the designers then incorporate the elementFormDefault and attributeFormDefault attributes into their schema documents, as a sort of binary on/off switch to illustrate their choice. Only two options are available for either attribute: qualified or unqualified. If the value is specified as qualified, the prefixes appear in the tags of the local elements in the XML documents (the global elements are unaffected). The value for both has been specified as qualified in line 8 of gemdata.xsd and in line 5 of minedata.xsd (the values don't have to be identical in multiple schema documents, incidentally). So, in the XML document in Figure 5.3, we see that the prefixes appear in the tags for the locally declared elements (those elements have been bolded for emphasis).

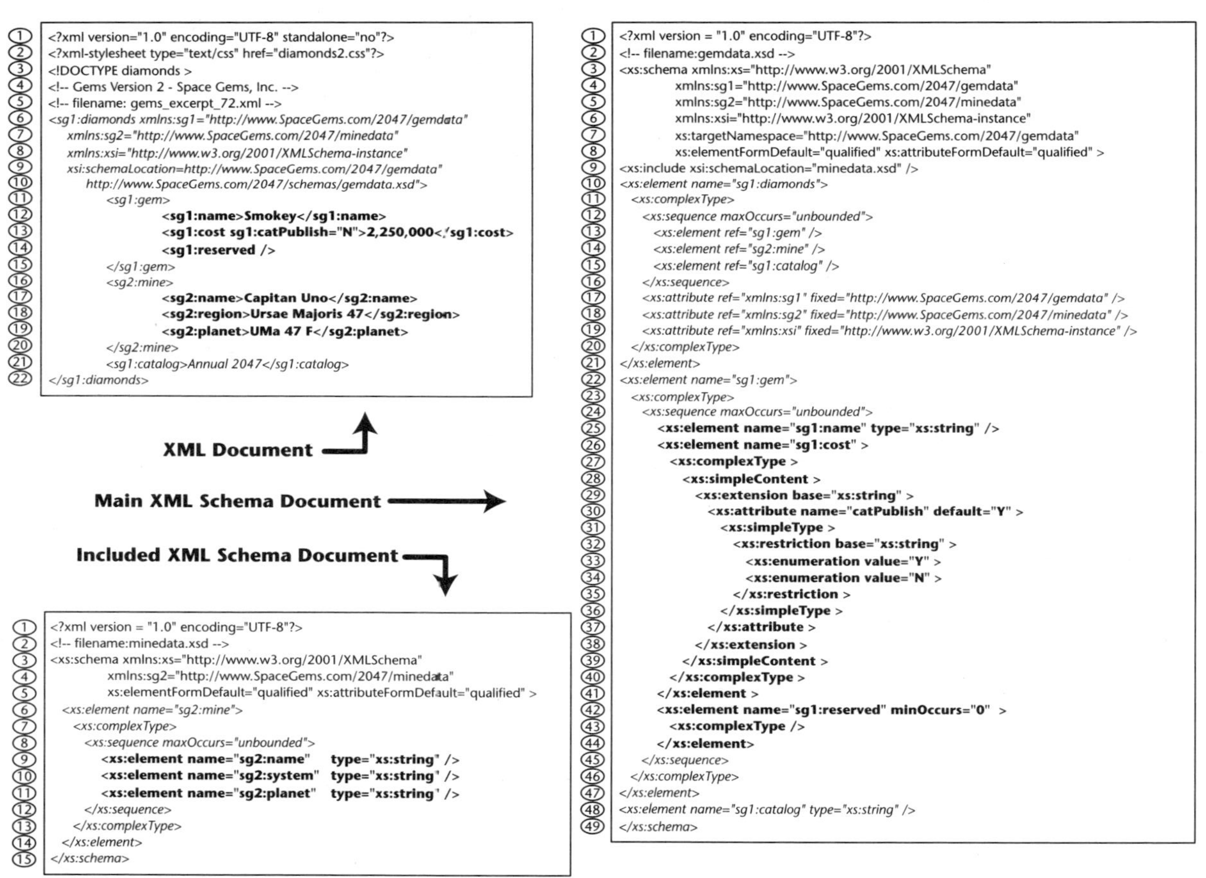

XML Document

```
<?xml version="1.0" encoding="UTF-8" standalone="no"?>
<?xml-stylesheet type="text/css" href="diamonds2.css"?>
<!DOCTYPE diamonds >
<!-- Gems Version 2 - Space Gems, Inc. -->
<!-- filename: gems_excerpt_72.xml -->
<sg1:diamonds xmlns:sg1="http://www.SpaceGems.com/2047/gemdata"
  xmlns:sg2="http://www.SpaceGems.com/2047/minedata"
  xmlns:xsi="http://www.w3.org/2001/XMLSchema-instance"
  xsi:schemaLocation=http://www.SpaceGems.com/2047/gemdata"
    http://www.SpaceGems.com/2047/schemas/gemdata.xsd">
      <sg1:gem>
            <sg1:name>Smokey</sg1:name>
            <sg1:cost sg1:catPublish="N">2,250,000</sg1:cost>
            <sg1:reserved />
      </sg1:gem>
      <sg2:mine>
            <sg2:name>Capitan Uno</sg2:name>
            <sg2:region>Ursae Majoris 47</sg2:region>
            <sg2:planet>UMa 47 F</sg2:planet>
      </sg2:mine>
      <sg1:catalog>Annual 2047</sg1:catalog>
</sg1:diamonds>
```

Main XML Schema Document

```
<?xml version = "1.0" encoding="UTF-8"?>
<!-- filename:gemdata.xsd -->
<xs:schema xmlns:xs="http://www.w3.org/2001/XMLSchema"
        xmlns:sg1="http://www.SpaceGems.com/2047/gemdata"
        xmlns:sg2="http://www.SpaceGems.com/2047/minedata"
        xmlns:xsi="http://www.w3.org/2001/XMLSchema-instance"
        xs:targetNamespace="http://www.SpaceGems.com/2047/gemdata"
        xs:elementFormDefault="qualified" xs:attributeFormDefault="qualified" >
<xs:include xsi:schemaLocation="minedata.xsd" />
<xs:element name="sg1:diamonds">
  <xs:complexType>
    <xs:sequence maxOccurs="unbounded">
      <xs:element ref="sg1:gem" />
      <xs:element ref="sg2:mine" />
      <xs:element ref="sg1:catalog" />
    </xs:sequence>
    <xs:attribute ref="xmlns:sg1" fixed="http://www.SpaceGems.com/2047/gemdata" />
    <xs:attribute ref="xmlns:sg2" fixed="http://www.SpaceGems.com/2047/minedata" />
    <xs:attribute ref="xmlns:xsi" fixed="http://www.w3.org/2001/XMLSchema-instance" />
  </xs:complexType>
</xs:element>
<xs:element name="sg1:gem">
  <xs:complexType>
    <xs:sequence maxOccurs="unbounded">
      <xs:element name="sg1:name" type="xs:string" />
      <xs:element name="sg1:cost" >
        <xs:complexType >
          <xs:simpleContent >
            <xs:extension base="xs:string" >
              <xs:attribute name="catPublish" default="Y" >
                <xs:simpleType >
                  <xs:restriction base="xs:string" >
                    <xs:enumeration value="Y" >
                    <xs:enumeration value="N" >
                  </xs:restriction >
                </xs:simpleType >
              </xs:attribute >
            </xs:extension >
          </xs:simpleContent >
        </xs:complexType >
      </xs:element >
      <xs:element name="sg1:reserved" minOccurs="0" >
        <xs:complexType />
      </xs:element>
    </xs:sequence>
  </xs:complexType>
</xs:element>
<xs:element name="sg1:catalog" type="xs:string" />
</xs:schema>
```

Included XML Schema Document

```
<?xml version = "1.0" encoding="UTF-8"?>
<!-- filename:minedata.xsd -->
<xs:schema xmlns:xs="http://www.w3.org/2001/XMLSchema"
        xmlns:sg2="http://www.SpaceGems.com/2047/minedata"
        xs:elementFormDefault="qualified" xs:attributeFormDefault="qualified" >
  <xs:element name="sg2:mine">
    <xs:complexType>
      <xs:sequence maxOccurs="unbounded">
        <xs:element name="sg2:name"    type="xs:string" />
        <xs:element name="sg2:system"  type="xs:string' />
        <xs:element name="sg2:planet"  type="xs:string' />
      </xs:sequence>
    </xs:complexType>
  </xs:element>
</xs:schema>
```

Figure 5.3 Globally and locally declared components.

```
<?xml version="1.0" encoding="UTF-8" standalone="no"?>
<?xml-stylesheet type="text/css" href="diamonds2.css"?>
<!DOCTYPE diamonds >
<!-- Gems Version 2 - Space Gems, Inc. -->
<!-- filename: gems_excerpt_82.xml -->
<sg1:diamonds xmlns:sg1="http://www.SpaceGems.com/2047/gemdata"
   xmlns:sg2="http://www.SpaceGems.com/2047/minedata"
   xmlns:xsi="http://www.w3.org/2001/XMLSchema-instance"
   xsi:schemaLocation=http://www.SpaceGems.com/2047/gemdata"
      http://www.SpaceGems.com/2047/schemas/gemdata.xsd" >
         <sg1:gem>
                  <name>Smokey</name>
                  <cost catPublish="N"> 2,250,000</cost>
                  <reserved />
         </sg1:gem>
         <sg2:mine>
                  <name>Capitan Uno</name>
                  <region>Ursae Majoris 47</region>
                  <planet>UMa 47 F</planet>
         </sg2:mine>
         <sg1:catalog> Annual 2047</sg1:catalog>
</sg1:diamonds>
```

Figure 5.4 Unqualified locals.

If the values of the elementFormDefault and attributeFormDefault attributes are unqualified, the XML document may resemble Figure 5.4. There, the sg1: and sg2: prefixes do not appear. The document is cleaner looking and requires fewer keystrokes to create. Figure 5.4 illustrates how, using schemas, you can create identical context-sensitive tags. For example, <name> looks identical in the both the <gem> and <mine> element types in the same document, but the difference appears in the respective declarations in the schema model documents. However, the globally declared element types remain unaffected.

Element Type Declarations

The discussion in this section revolves around Figure 5.5, which depicts the XML document named gems_excerpt_72.xml (referred to as "the XML document"), the top portion of the corresponding schema document named gemdata.xsd, and the corresponding DTD document named diamonds05.dtd. The

DTD will not be used as the document model for the XML document, but is presented here because it is useful for illustrating, by comparison, some schema concepts we'll discuss. Meanwhile, lines 6 through 15 in the XML document illustrate several different types of elements.

The <sg1:diamonds> Element Declaration: Complex Data Types

The first element type, <sg1:diamonds> is the XML document's root element, the parent element for the document's actual data instance. Figure 5.5 illustrates <sg1:diamonds> in its XML document, as well as in its corresponding DTD and schema. Lines 10 through 24 of the gemdata.xsd schema document provide the model for <sg1:diamonds>. Line 10 provides its name. Often, element types only require a single-line declaration. However, since <sg1:diamonds> contains other element types, it is called a complex data type (or complex content type), and it requires an <xs:complexType> element to complete the element type declaration.

To repeat what we said earlier, complex data types are element types that contain other element types, attributes, or both. Simple data types contain no attributes or child elements, just character data. Attribute specifications are typically simple types.

The <xs:complexType> element in Line 11 indicates the beginning of the definition for the <sg1:diamonds> complex data type.

In line 3 of the DTD document, we see that <sg1:diamonds> must be composed of a sequence of three other element types: <sg1:gem>, <sg2:mine>, and <sg1:catalog>, and because of the plus sign in the names of those elements, every <sg1:diamonds> element type must contain that sequence, in that order. The plus sign indicates the cardinality of the sequence—the number of times the sequence may occur in the related XML documents. It indicates that the sequence must occur at least once, but that there is no limit to the number of times it may occur.

Line 12 in the gemdata.xsd schema document starts the sequence declaration. The <xs:sequence ...> element is called a *compositor* (discussed later in the *Compositor* section). It tells the parser that the complex data type <sg1:diamonds> contains a sequence of element types. As we create a plus-sign equivalent instruction in the schema, we would normally substitute the appropriate schema attributes to indicate the cardinality of the sequence: minOccurs (the minimum number of occurrences) and maxOccurs (the maximum number of occurrences). A specification for maxOccurs is present, but minOccurs has not been specified because there is no need for it here. The plus sign in the DTD indicated "at least once" and minOccurs' default value is once.

```
<?xml version="1.0" encoding="UTF-8" standalone="no"?>
<?xml-stylesheet type="text/css" href="diamonds2.css"?>
<!DOCTYPE diamonds >
<!-- Gems Version 2 - Space Gems, Inc. -->
<!-- filename: gems_excerpt_72.xml -->
<sg1:diamonds xmlns:sg1="http://www.SpaceGems.com/2047/gemdata"
    xmlns:sg2="http://www.SpaceGems.com/2047/minedata"
    xmlns:xsi="http://www.w3.org/2001/XMLSchema-instance"
    xsi:schemaLocation=http://www.SpaceGems.com/2047/gemdata"
        http://www.SpaceGems.com/2047/schemas/gemdata.xsd">
            <sg1:gem>
                        <sg1:name>Smokey</sg1:name>
                        <sg1:cost catPublish="N">2,250,000</sg1:cost>
                        <sg1:reserved />
            </sg1:gem>
            <sg2:mine>
                        <sg2:name>Capitan Uno</sg2:name>
                        <sg2:region>Ursae Majoris 47</sg2:region>
                        <sg2:planet>UMa 47 F</sg2:planet>
            </sg2:mine>
            <sg1:catalog>Annual 2047</sg1:catalog>
</sg1:diamonds>
```

XML Document

```
<?xml version = "1.0" encoding="UTF-8"?>
<!-- filename: diamonds05.dtd - ->
<!ELEMENT sg1:diamonds     (sg1:gem,sg2:mine,sg1:catalog)+>
<!ATTLIST sg1:diamonds
            xmlns:sg1 CDATA #FIXED
                        "http://www.SpaceGems.com/2047/gemdata"
            xmlns:sg2 CDATA #FIXED
                        "http://www.SpaceGems.com/2047/minedata">
<!ELEMENT sg1:gem           (sg1:name,sg1:cost?,sg1:reserved?)+>
<!ELEMENT sg1:name          (#PCDATA)>
<!ELEMENT sg1:cost          (#PCDATA)>
<!ATTLIST sg1:cost
            catPublish  ( Y | N )  #IMPLIED "Y" >
<!ELEMENT sg1:reserved        EMPTY >
<!ELEMENT sg2:mine          (sg2:name,sg2:system,sg2:planet)+>
<!ELEMENT sg2:name          (#PCDATA)>
<!ELEMENT sg2:system        (#PCDATA)>
<!ELEMENT sg2:planet        (#PCDATA)>
<!ELEMENT sg1:catalog       (#PCDATA)>
```

DTD Document

```
<?xml version = "1.0" encoding="UTF-8"?>
<!-- filename:gemdata.xsd -->
<xs:schema xmlns:xs="http://www.w3.org/2001/XMLSchema"
            xmlns:sg1="http://www.SpaceGems.com/2047/gemdata"
            xmlns:sg2="http://www.SpaceGems.com/2047/minedata"
            xmlns:xsi="http://www.w3.org/2001/XMLSchema-instance"
            xs:targetNamespace="http://www.SpaceGems.com/2047/gemdata"
            xs:elementFormDefault="qualified" xs:attributeFormDefault="qualified" >
<xs:include xsi:schemaLocation="minedata.xsd" />
<xs:element name="sg1:diamonds">
  <xs:complexType>
    <xs:sequence maxOccurs="unbounded">
      <xs:element ref="sg1:gem" />
      <xs:element ref="sg2:mine" />
      <xs:element ref="sg1:catalog" />
    </xs:sequence>
    <xs:attribute ref="xmlns:sg1"
            fixed="http://www.SpaceGems.com/2047/gemdata" />
    <xs:attribute ref="xmlns:sg2"
            fixed="http://www.SpaceGems.com/2047/minedata" />
    <xs:attribute ref="xmlns:xsi"
            fixed="http://www.w3.org/2001/XMLSchema-instance" />
  </xs:complexType>
</xs:element>
<xs:element name="sg1:gem">
  <xs:complexType>
    <xs:sequence maxOccurs="unbounded">

• • •
```

Main XML Schema Document

Figure 5.5 The <sg1:diamonds> element declaration.

The default value for maxOccurs is also once, but since the sequence is specified to occur at least once, the default value would be insufficient. So the value of maxOccurs has been specified as "unbounded" for its maximum occurrence value (otherwise, the value for maxOccurs' specifications could be any positive integer). Unbounded indicates the schema designer's intent that the sequence can occur as many times as the document author wants.

Lines 13 through 15 tell the parser which three element types compose the <sg1:diamonds> sequence. In this case, all three element types are globally declared, so the <xs:element ...> declarations contain the reference attribute ref="elementtypename", which tells the parser to look for globally declared definitions within the extent of the <xs:schema> element, where their definitions are actually declared, and not here.

At points like this, the designer always has a choice of whether to provide local declarations here, or to create global declarations under the <xs:schema ...> element and then provide references to them here. We chose the latter strategy.

The elements <sg1:gem>, <sg1:mine>, and <sg1:catalog> will only occur once for each time an <sg1:diamonds> element appears. Their default minOccurs="1" and maxOccurs="1" values are sufficient. Although you could specify values for minOccurs and maxOccurs for those element types, it is not necessary to do so.

Line 16 signals the end of the definition of the sequence of element types. Lines 17 through 19 define the three namespace attributes. Here, the "ref=" indicates that these definitions are also globally declared. In this case, they are found within the <xs:schema ...> start tag. This is the customary approach to declaring namespaces. Line 20 signals the end of the complex data type definition; line 21, the end of the <sg1:diamonds> element type definition.

The <sg1:gem> Element Declaration

Lines 22 through 47 define and declare the various components within the <sg1:gem> element type. These lines are depicted in the XML schema document in Figure 5.6.

Like <sg1:diamonds>, <sg1:gem> is a complex data type. As you can see from line 9 of the DTD document, any <sg1:gem> element type must also contain a sequence of its own: a mandatory <sg1:name> element and two optional elements, <sg1:cost> and <sg1:reserved>. Lines 10 through 13 of the DTD document tell you that: <sg1:name> and <sg1:cost> are element types that will contain parsed character data. In addition to data, <sg1:cost> will contain the catPublish attribute, for which an author may (the use of catPublish is not required) specify a "Y" or "N" value; otherwise, the parser will presume the default value "Y". Line 14 declares that the <sg1:reserved /> element type is empty.

```
<?xml version="1.0" encoding="UTF-8" standalone="no"?>
<?xml-stylesheet type="text/css" href="diamonds2.css"?>
<!DOCTYPE diamonds >
<!-- Gems Version 2 - Space Gems, Inc. -->
<!-- filename: gems_excerpt_72.xml -->
<sg1:diamonds xmlns:sg1="http://www.SpaceGems.com/2047/gemdata"
   xmlns:sg2="http://www.SpaceGems.com/2047/minedata"
   xmlns:xsi="http://www.w3.org/2001/XMLSchema-instance"
   xsi:schemaLocation=http://www.SpaceGems.com/2047/gemdata"
      http://www.SpaceGems.com/2047/schemas/gemdata.xsd">
         <sg1:gem>
               <sg1:name>Smokey</sg1:name>
               <sg1:cost catPublish="N">2,250,000</sg1:cost>
               <sg1:reserved />
         </sg1:gem>
         <sg2:mine>
               <sg2:name>Capitan Uno</sg2:name>
               <sg2:region>Ursae Majoris 47</sg2:region>
               <sg2:planet>UMa 47 F</sg2:planet>
         </sg2:mine>
         <sg1:catalog>Annual 2047</sg1:catalog>
</sg1:diamonds>
```

XML Document

```
<?xml version = "1.0" encoding="UTF-8"?>
<!-- filename: diamonds05.dtd - ->
<!ELEMENT sg1:diamonds     (sg1:gem,sg2:mine,sg1:catalog)+>
<!ATTLIST sg1:diamonds
          xmlns:sg1 CDATA #FIXED
                     "http://www.SpaceGems.com/2047/gemdata"
          xmlns:sg2 CDATA #FIXED
                     "http://www.SpaceGems.com/2047/minedata">
<!ELEMENT sg1:gem          (sg1:name,sg1:cost?,sg1:reserved?)+>
<!ELEMENT sg1:name         (#PCDATA)>
<!ELEMENT sg1:cost         (#PCDATA)>
<!ATTLIST sg1:cost
          catPublish   ( Y | N )  #IMPLIED "Y" >
<!ELEMENT sg1:reserved        EMPTY  >
<!ELEMENT sg2:mine         (sg2:name,sg2:system,sg2:planet)+>
<!ELEMENT sg2:name         (#PCDATA)>
<!ELEMENT sg2:system       (#PCDATA)>
<!ELEMENT sg2:planet       (#PCDATA)>
<!ELEMENT sg1:catalog      (#PCDATA)>
```

DTD Document

```
...
<xs:element name="sg1:gem">
  <xs:complexType>
    <xs:sequence maxOccurs="unbounded">
      <xs:element name="sg1:name" type="xs:string" />
      <xs:element name="sg1:cost" >
        <xs:complexType >
          <xs:simpleContent >
            <xs:extension base="xs:string" >
              <xs:attribute name="catPublish" default="Y" >
                <xs:simpleType >
                  <xs:restriction base="xs:string" >
                    <xs:enumeration value="Y" >
                    <xs:enumeration value="N" >
                  </xs:restriction >
                </xs:simpleType >
              </xs:attribute >
            </xs:extension >
          </xs:simpleContent >
        </xs:complexType >
      </xs:element >
      <xs:element name="sg1:reserved" minOccurs="0" >
        <xs:complexType />
      </xs:element>
    </xs:sequence>
  </xs:complexType>
</xs:element>
<xs:element name="sg1:catalog" type="xs:string" />
</xs:schema>
```

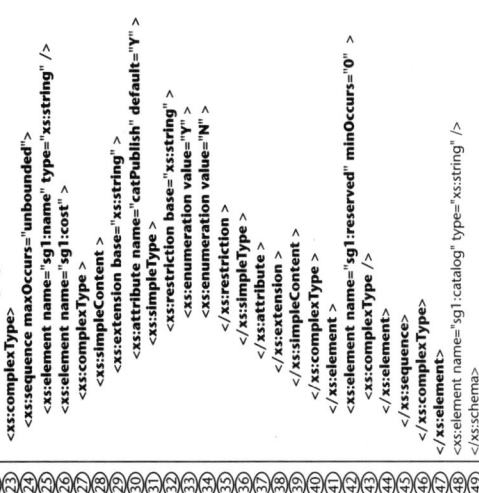

Main XML Schema Document "gemdata.xsd"

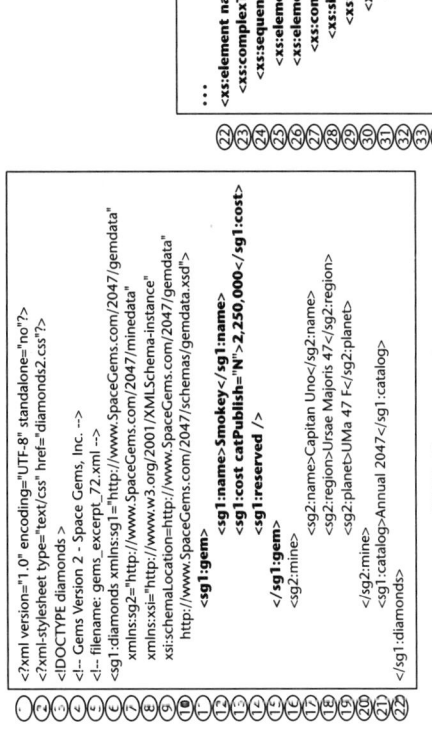

Figure 5.6 The <sg1:gem> element declaration.

In the gemdata.xsd schema document, line 22 identifies the beginning of the <sg1:gem> element type and line 23 marks the beginning of the definition of <sg1:gem> as a complex data type. Line 24 indicates the beginning of the sequence of components to be included in <sg1:gem>. Similar to the sequence in <sg1:diamonds>, no limit is set on the number of sequences that can be included in an <sg1:gem> element type.

The designer has chosen to provide a single-line local declaration here for the <sg1:name> element type. You can tell it is locally declared by the presence of the name="sg1:name" attribute specification (a global component would contain a "ref=" attribute). The type="xs:string" attribute indicates to the parser that the content of the element type will be a string of text characters, as defined in the Schema 1.0 Recommendation.

The <sg1:cost> element type is a complex data type, too. Although it will not contain any child element types, it will contain an attribute specification. However, line 28 labels <sg1:cost> as a simple content element, since, as an element type, it will contain no child elements, only character data.

To add an attribute to a simple content element, the schema designer must create an extension to the element. Line 29 advises the parser that an extension will be created but doesn't yet state the nature of the extension. That instruction comes in line 30, where the parser is advised that an attribute named catPublish is to be included. The value of this attribute may be specified by the document author, but if it isn't specified, then the "Y" default value will prevail. Since the attribute's name, catPublish, does not have an xs: prefix, it is not defined in the XML Schema Recommendation. Thus, a definition must be provided.

By line 13, the DTD seems to be more complete in its definition. Here the DTD explicitly states that catPublish is #IMPLIED, meaning a document author may, but doesn't necessarily have to, provide a value for the attribute. The schema document, however, doesn't explicitly state that. That's how it works: If it doesn't say use="required" in the schema's attribute declaration, then providing a value is left to the document author. If it does say use="required", this is the schema equivalent of the DTD's #REQUIRED specification.

The values we can specify for the use= attribute are as follows:

Required. A value for the attribute must be specified in a valid XML document.

Optional. The attribute does not have to appear; whether it does, and any specification for its value, is left to the XML document author.

Fixed. The attribute's value is fixed; when use="fixed" appears in the schema document, another attribute named value="xxx" must follow it and the schema designer must substitute the fixed value for the xxx.

Because the catPublish attribute is going to be slightly customized, it must be defined for the parser. Line 31 indicates that <sg1:cost>'s catPublish attribute will be a simple data type as expected. But because the designer wants to restrict the choices that the document author will have with respect to the attribute values, a restriction is imposed on the normal character string in line 32.

The restriction is defined in lines 33 and 34: The <xs:enumeration ...> declarations say that the allowed text strings will be restricted to either a Y (from line 33) or an N (from line 34).

From the <xs:enumeration> tag, we recognize that the term is defined in the XML Schema Recommendation. The enumeration is a data type called a *facet* (discussed in more detail later). It is used here to specify the values from which we can choose whether to publish information in a merchandise catalog.

It's worth mentioning that the <xs:extension ...> and <xs:restriction ...> declarations both indicate a certain amount of inheritance in data types, originating from their XML Schema 1.0 properties. Approach it this way: If you are going to customize a typical data type declaration by adding or reducing features, then you have to think in terms of <xs:extension ...> and <xs:restriction ...> elements, respectively.

Lines 35 to 41 signal an end to the restricted list of candidate text strings, the attribute's simple content definition, the attribute definition, and the extension to the <sg1:cost> element's simple content and complex data definitions.

Compositors

The <xs:sequence ...> element tells the parser that declarations for a specific sequence of element types will follow immediately. The <xs:sequence ...> is called the *sequence compositor*. Compositors are specialized XML Schema elements that define groups of elements and attributes within a schema. Three types of compositors exist: sequence compositors, of which we have already seen two examples; <xs:choice ...> compositors, which indicate one or more choices of element types for a document author; and <xs:all ... > compositors, which indicate that one or more of the ensuing elements can appear in the XML document in any order.

Empty Element Content

Schemas also allow a designer to declare empty element types. These are declared by using the <xs:complexType> element type, but deliberately omitting the definition of any child elements within the complex data type. Several methods can be used to declare an empty element type. This first one is identical to that found in lines 42 through 44 in gemdata.xsd:

```
<xs:element name="sg1:reserved">
      <xs:complexType />
</xs:element>
```

This method actually uses an empty <xs:complexType /> element in the <sg1:reserved> element declaration. The only difference between this example and that shown in Figure 5.6 is that the Figure 5.6 <sg1:reserved> element is constrained by the minOccurs="0" attribute, which indicates that the element type is optional and thus does not have to appear within the extent of the <sg1:gem> element type. The next method declares an empty element type:

```
<xs:element name="sg1:reserved">
      <xs:complexType>
      </xs:complexType>
</xs:element>
```

Instead of using an empty element, this method uses <xs:complexType> start and end tags, with nothing declared between them.

The <sg1:catalog> Element: Simple Data Types

The declaration for <sg1:catalog>, the last child element type under <sg1:-diamonds>, is found on line 48 of gemdata.xsd. The declaration indicates that this element type must contain parsed character data only, with no subelements and no attributes. Therefore, <sg1:catalog> is a simple data type and the length of its declarations should be a single line.

In lines 30 through 37, we declared another simple data type: the catPublish attribute, whose value choices are Y or N. Like <sg1:catalog>, the base data type for catPublish was a text string. We chose the text string here because they are the most common simple data types and we wanted to show how to create extensions and restrictions based on them. However, Table 5.3 lists other simple types defined in XML Schema 1.0 (for a comprehensive listing, please refer to the XML Schema 1.0 Recommendation itself). Note that, when you refer to a simple type found in XML Schema 1.0, the name of the type is usually preceded by a namespace prefix, such as the xs: we use in this book. The document designer can assign whatever prefix he or she chooses to the namespace or can avoid using a prefix through the use a default namespace declaration.

Table 5.3 Simple Types Defined in W3C XML Schema Recommendation

SIMPLE TYPE	DEFINITION
binary	Contains binary values (e.g., 1001, 11101).
boolean	Contains values like True or False, 1, or 0.
date	Contains a date in YYYY-MM-DD format.
decimal	Contains a decimal value, positive or negative.
ENTITY, ENTITIES	Contains an ENTITY or ENTITIES attribute type, as described in the W3C XML Recommendation.

Table 5.3 *(continued)*

SIMPLE TYPE	DEFINITION
ID	Contains an ID attribute type, as described in the W3C XML Recommendation.
int, integer	Contains an integer.
language	Contains a language identifier (e.g., en-US, de, fr).
Qname	Contains an XML qualified name (i.e., contains a namespace reference plus a local name, separated by a colon).
string	Contains a string of text characters.
time	Contains a time reference (e.g., 08:13:47.639).
anyURI	Contains a Uniform Resource Identifier reference; the value can be absolute or relative.

Mixed Content Elements

Although neither the gemdata.xsd nor minedata.xsd documents contain examples of mixed content element types, these are still important to a schema designer. Where DTDs cannot exert control over the order of the child elements or over the number of times they appear, schemas *can*, because they have more complete syntax. For example, following is a portion of a schema that contains a mixed content element: a request letter to Space Gems Inc. mine managers advising them that they can obtain new equipment as long as a specific form is sent in by a given deadline. Naturally, because the element will contain other elements as well as text, the element will be a complex type. An attribute named mixed is included in the complexType element start tag; its value is specified as true.

```
<xs:element name="eqptRequest" >
   <xs:complexType mixed="true" >
      <xs:sequence >
         <xs:element name="mineMgr" type="xs:string" />
         <xs:element name="gemTestEqpt" type="xs:string" />
         <xs:element name="system" type=xs:string" />
         <xs:element name="formNo" >
            <simpleType >
               <restriction base='xs:string'>
                  <xs:pattern value= "[A-Z]{3} \s [1-9]{4}-[0-9]{2}"/>
               </restriction>
            </simpleType>
         </xs:element>
```

```
            <xs:element name="deadlineDays" >
               <xs:simpleType base="xs:integer" >
                  <xs:maxInclusive value="30" />
               <xs:/simpleType>
            </xs:element>
            <xs:element name="budgetSupvr" type="xs:string" />
         </xs:sequence >
      </xs:complexType>
   </xs:element>
```

Here is what the data instance of a conforming XML document might look like:

```
<eqptRequest>
To <mineMgr>Stu D. Duque</mineMgr>:
Our records show that, in the past, your staff have
requested a/an <gemTestEqpt>polariscope</gemTestEqpt>
for your facility. The 2047 Q3 budget for the
<system>Auriga</system> system has been approved and we
are pleased to inform you that the requested equipment
can now be purchased but, first, you must verify the
request by submitting an updated
<formNo>GTR 2040-29</formNo> form within
<deadlineDays>15</deadlineDays> Sol-Earth days.
Thank you in advance for your cooperation.
<budgetSupvr>Lotta Cash</budgetSupvr>
```

Using Facets to Define Data More Precisely

In Figures 5.5 and 5.6, the gemdata.xsd schema document used inheritance (<xs:restriction> or <xs:extension> elements) to describe attribute values more precisely. It also illustrated how the facet <xs:enumeration> could be used to limit the text string values available for the catPublish attribute to Y or N. Facets provide a means for more precise definition of data contained within a simple type element or attribute. Their generic syntax is fairly simple:

```
<facetname value="facetvalue"/>
```

In the *Mixed Content Elements* section, another facet (xs:maxInclusive) was used to limit the time during which an Auriga mine manager could submit a particular form to Space Gems' headquarters. A facet named <xs:pattern> prescribed the syntax for the company form to be submitted.

Facets like <xs:maxInclusive>, <xs:minInclusive>, <xs:enumeration>, and <xs:pattern> are popular and valuable to a schema designer. In fact, <xs:pattern> is used for the designation of Universal Product Codes (UPCs), International Standard Book Numbers (ISBNs), stock keeping units (SKUs), and other inventory-control numbers.

More facets available with XML Schema 1.0 are described briefly in Table 5.4. For a comprehensive listing of all XML Schema 1.0 facets, please refer to XML Schema Part 2: Datatypes.

Table 5.4 XML Schema 1.0 Facet Examples

FACET NAME	DESCRIPTION
Length	Specifies the length of a value. Limited to the value 2147483647. Items larger than this limit will not be validated correctly.
minLength	Specifies the minimum length of a value.
maxLength	Specifies the maximum length of a value. Also limited to 2147483647. Items larger than that limit will not be validated correctly.
maxExclusive	Defines a maximum exclusive upper bounds of a data type value. Example: "less than 3" would require a maxExclusive value of 3 or a maxInclusive of 2.
minExclusive	Defines the exclusive lower bounds of a data type value. Example: "at least seven" would require a minExclusive value of 7.
duration	Specifies a time period. The value is a six-dimensional space designating a Gregorian year, month, day, hour, minute, and second. The number of seconds can include decimal digits. An optional preceding minus sign (-) can indicate a negative duration. If the sign is omitted, a positive duration is presumed. Example: To indicate a duration of 3 years, 6 months, 9 days, 12 hours, and 15 minutes, state P3Y6M9DT12H15M. Minus 24 hours, by comparison, this looks like -P24H.
totalDigits	Defines the maximum number of digits in the value of a given data type. The value specified for totalDigits must be a positive integer.
fractionDigits	Specifies the maximum number of digits in the fractional part of a value of a given data type. The value of fractionDigits must be a non-negative integer.
whiteSpace	Value must be one of preserve, replace, or collapse, depending on data type. When "xs:string" is specified, white space is usually "preserved" by default.

Be careful when specifying facets with simple data types. Not all facets apply to all data types. Check the XML Schema 1.0 Recommendation to see which facets go with which simple data types.

Schema Document Structures

There are almost as many ways to create a logical structure for a schema document as there are schema documents. But they are all variations or combinations of two basic approaches: the nesting approach or the flat catalog approach.

The Nesting Structure

The nesting structure is based on a predominance of locally declared data types (Figure 5.7 uses element type declarations as examples). Figure 5.7 illustrates the element type hierarchy of a nesting approach.

A full element declaration is inserted every time an element type is needed. Notice that in Figure 5.7, there are no ref="elementxx" declarations. Figure 5.8 depicts the schema document that reflects the hierarchy presented in Figure 5.7.

In the generic schema document depicted in Figure 5.8, the element type named <element6> appears within four other element types (<element2>, <element4>, <element5>, and <element7>). It is fully declared within each one, and in each case, the declaration is identical. Many programmers call this structure the nesting doll or Russian doll structure, since the element declarations are cloaked one within another, reminiscent of those festive hollow dolls that act as containers for identical but smaller dolls.

Among the advantages to the nesting structure are the ease with which you can create context-sensitive element tags. However, compared to the flat catalog (discussed in the next section), the XML parser uses more resources when processing this type of schema. Further, if a designer wants to make changes to, for example, the <element6> declaration in Figure 5.7, then those changes must be made to the <element6> declarations in all four locations. This takes time and may introduce the risk of mistakes in one or more of the <element6> declarations. That may not be a big issue for a small schema, but it could be problematic for larger schemas.

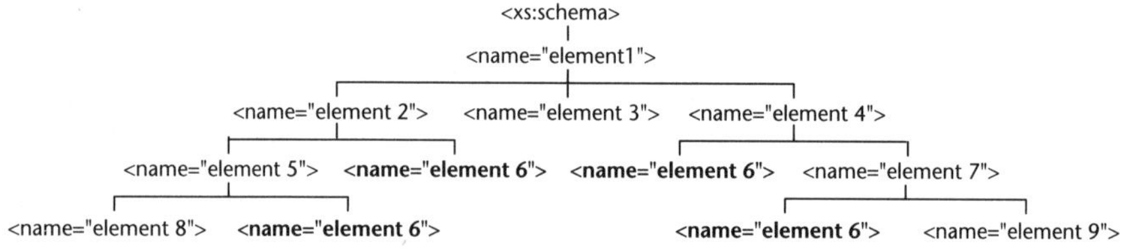

Figure 5.7 Nesting hierarchy.

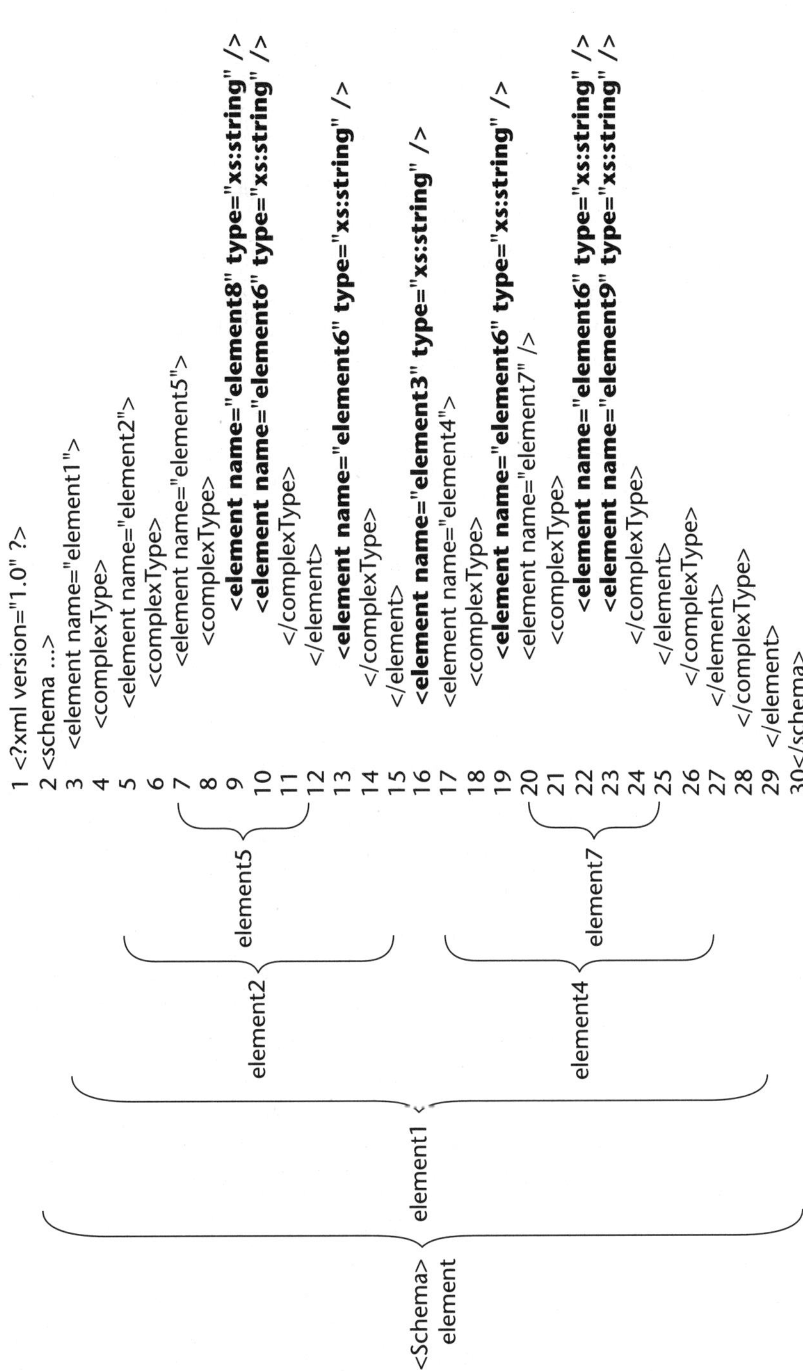

Figure 5.8 Nesting structure within the schema document.

The Flat Catalog Structure

Figure 5.9 illustrates a flat catalog approach to the same schema shown in Figures 5.7 and 5.8. The flat catalog provides declarations within the <schema> element and then employs global references to those declarations elsewhere in the document. The flat catalog creates a flatter schema structure. In Figure 5.9, the ref="element6" element type declarations within the declarations of <element2>, <element5>, <element4>, and <element7> all point to the name="element6" declaration within <schema>. The parser reads the "ref=" declarations, looking for definitions in the corresponding "name=" declaration.

In the flat catalog structure, the full <element6> element type declaration needs to appear only once. Then, in any relevant child element types, the simpler "ref=" syntax is used to refer to the <element6> declaration. The advantages to the flat catalog approach include the following:

- Keystrokes are usually saved, especially if the full declaration is complex in nature (the simple examples in this text don't really show that advantage, but they are readily seen in larger schema documents).
- Less likelihood exists for typographical or syntactic errors.
- A programmer can group all the common simpleType elements together in one location, immediately within the <schema> element.
- The schema's hierarchy is inherently flatter and, thus, easier to code and interpret.
- Programmer and processor resources are saved.
- If a change must be made to one common element, then it need only be made in one location, thus reducing the risk of nonuniform changes to elements. The references inherit the changes automatically.

At this point, you may be curious about the structure of the gemdata.xsd and minedata.xsd example schema documents used. Figure 5.10 illustrates that gemdata.xsd is a combination of both nesting and flat catalog structures, but that minedata.xsd has a simple nesting structure.

The gemdata.xsd schema could easily be changed to a flat catalog structure, but then certain advantages might be lost (for example, the context-sensitive element naming, as well as our ability to demonstrate more types of schema coding for you). Most DTD-to-schema conversion applications prefer the flat catalog structure for those schema documents they facilitate.

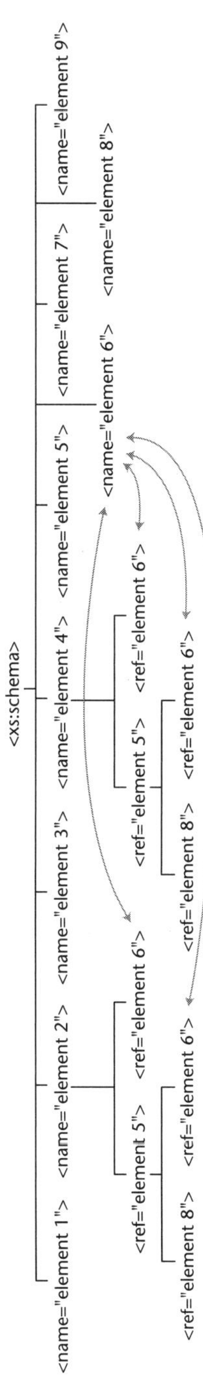

Figure 5.9 Flat catalog hierarchy.

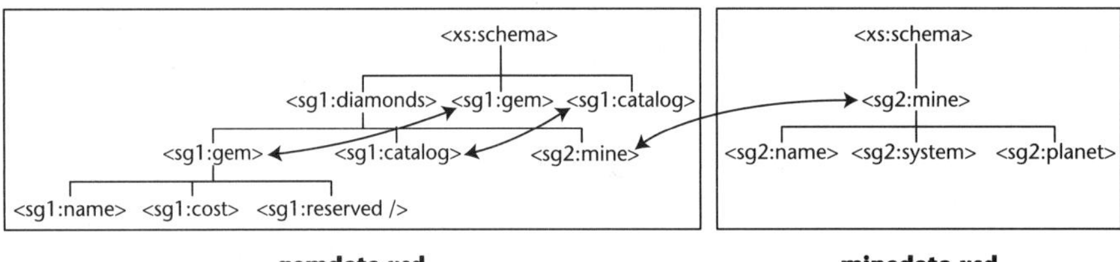

Figure 5.10 Structures of example schema documents.

Using Schemas and DTDs Together

One of the shortcomings of schemas is that they don't easily support character reference entities (discussed in Chapter 3, "Anatomy of an XML Document"). If you normally want to use XML Schema validation but will also use character reference entities in your XML documents (the classic example is the Euro currency sign, €, the character entity for which is *€*), then you might consider combining DTD validation and XML Schema validation.

The strategy is two-fold: First, refer to the DTD in the DOCTYPE definition in the prolog, and second, "call" the appropriate schema in the root element of the XML document. (We get a little ahead of ourselves here, by using as our example the development of an XHTML document; XHTML is the subject of the next chapter.) Trouble arises when you want to include the xsi:schemaLocation attribute, which is not defined in any of the three XHTML DTDs. So, if you want to use both DTD and XML Schema validation, then the attribute must be included by declaring it in the internal DTD subset of your document. The document type declaration in the document must resemble this:

```
<!DOCTYPE html PUBLIC "-//W3C//DTD XHTML 1.0 Strict//EN"
     "http://www.w3.org/TR/xhtml1/DTD/xhtml1-strict.dtd"[
<!ATTLIST html
     xmlns:xsi CDATA #FIXED
     "http://www.w3.org/2001/XMLSchema-instance"
     xsi:schemaLocation CDATA #IMPLIED >
]>
```

This example presumes that you will be using the Strict variant of XHTML. As you will see in Chapter 6, XHTML allows the option of using one of three variants: Strict, Transitional, and Frameset. The choice is reflected at two points in the document type declaration. These concepts are covered in Chapter 6.

Once the internal DTD declaration has been inserted into the document type declaration, we can adjust the start tag for the XHTML root <html> element:

```
<html xmlns="http://www.w3.org/1999/xhtml"
     lang="en" xml:lang="en"
     xmlns:xsi="http://www.w3.org/2001/XMLSchema-instance"
```

```
    xsi:schemaLocation="http://www.w3.org/1999/xhtml
    http://www.w3.org/2002/08/xhtml/xhtml1-strict.xsd">
...
</html>
```

The combination of the modified DOCTYPE definition in the prolog, plus the modified root <html> element start tag, allows us to combine DTD and Schema validation.

Chapter 5 Labs: Creating Simple Schemas

In the lab exercises for Chapter 4, "Document Type Definitions," we created some basic DTDs. Here we create basic XML schemas using the same content model that we used in Chapter 4. The first procedure instructs you on how to create a simple schema. The ensuing procedures help you to add more sophisticated constraints to create data instance documents from your schema and then introduce more complex data element types. If you are interested, and we hope you are, two more schema exercises are included at this book's Web site, at the URL provided in the book's introduction.

Lab 5.1: Create a Basic Schema

The file you create in this first exercise will describe the same series of diamonds that were introduced in the last chapter. The design of this first schema is based on the previous DTD, which had only two goals in mind. The first goal was to allow more than one <gem> to be listed. This was achieved by ensuring that the <gem> element type was repeatable or unbounded. The second goal was to ensure that all of the five C's (carats, color, clarity, cut, and cost) are present for all diamonds.

In this lab, as in the Chapter 4 labs, we work with our software's GUI view, and so we will tend to emphasize schema terminology rather than syntax. However, syntax is still important. So, to become familiar with schema syntax, please change the TurboXML view from the GUI element view to the source code and back periodically throughout the lab.

1. Open the Turbo XML editor. Click Continue Trial, if necessary.
2. Click Schema.
3. Click Overview/Properties to change the view inside the editor.
4. Rename the unnamed element to diamonds.
5. Change the Content of <diamonds> to Elements.

6. Place the cursor inside the parentheses ( ) for the Content Model for <diamonds>, and type "gem" and click Repeatable. Exit the cell using the Tab key.
7. Click the button for Globally defined inside the Auto Create dialog box. Click Create.
8. Change the Content of <gem> to Elements.
9. Place the cursor inside the parentheses () for the Content Model for <diamonds> and type "name,carat,color,clarity,cut,cost" (include the commas, but with no spaces between the element type names). Exit the cell using the Tab key.
10. Click the button for Globally defined inside the Auto Create dialog box. Click Create.
11. Check for errors.
12. Save the file as diamonds1.xsd. Your view should resemble Figure 5.11.

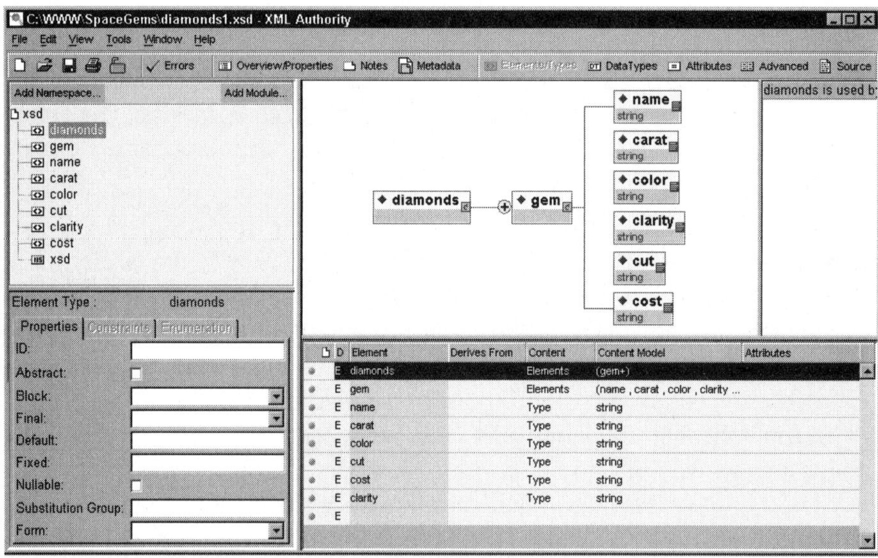

Figure 5.11 Schema layout for diamonds1.xsd.

Lab 5.2: Add Constraints to the Basic Schema

The diamonds1.xsd does not take advantage of the many constraints that are available to refine the schema. In this exercise, you will add some specific constraints to the schema that allow us to progress to a more complex model. In fact, these constraints provide more sophistication than we could have achieved with the DTDs in Chapter 4.

1. Open the TurboXML editor.
2. Click diamonds1.xsd to open.
3. Click the Data Type for the <carat> element, click Constraints, click Insert, and choose More, positiveInteger.
4. Click the Data Type for the <color> element. Choose String. You can refer to Figure 5.12 for help with the following steps.
5. Click the Data Types item on the top menu bar. Type "color.type" in the Name cell and "string" in the BaseType cell. Tab over to the Options cell.
6. Move to the new Element Type: color.type pane on the left side of the frame. Click the enumeration menu tab, and create the enumeration list by adding the values shown in Figure 5.12.

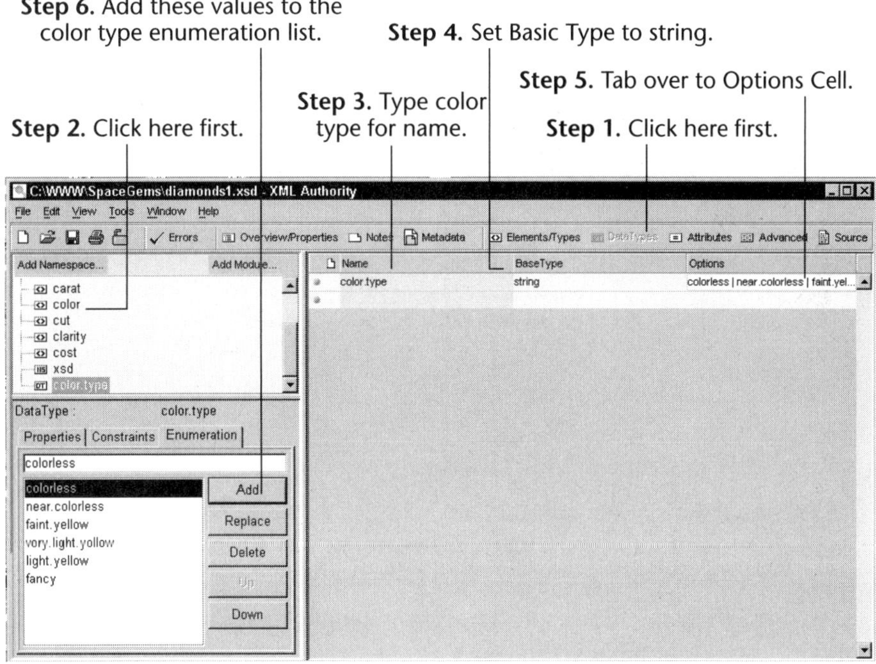

Figure 5.12 Creating the color.type data type for the <color> element.

7. Return to the Element/Types view by clicking Element/Types on the top menu bar.
8. Click the Data Type cell for the <color> element, choose Insert user-defined type, and choose color.type. The view should resemble Figure 5.13.

D	Element	Derives From	Content	Data Type	Attributes
E	diamonds		Elements	(gem+)	
E	gem		Elements	(name , carat , color , clarity ...	
E	name		Type	string	
E	carat		Type	Insert / Insert user-defined type / Constraints / Edit Enums	
E	color		Type	color.type	
E	clarity		Type	string	
E	cut		Type	string	
E	cost		Type	decimal	
E					

Figure 5.13 Changing the data type of the <color> element.

9. Using the same process, create a user-defined data type called clarity.type for the <clarity> element:
   a. Click Data Types on the top menu bar.
   b. Enter clarity.type for Name.
   c. Enter string for Base Type.
   d. Tab over to Options.
   e. Click the Enumeration menu tab on the pane on the left side of the frame.
   f. Create the enumeration list by adding the values shown in Figure 5.14.

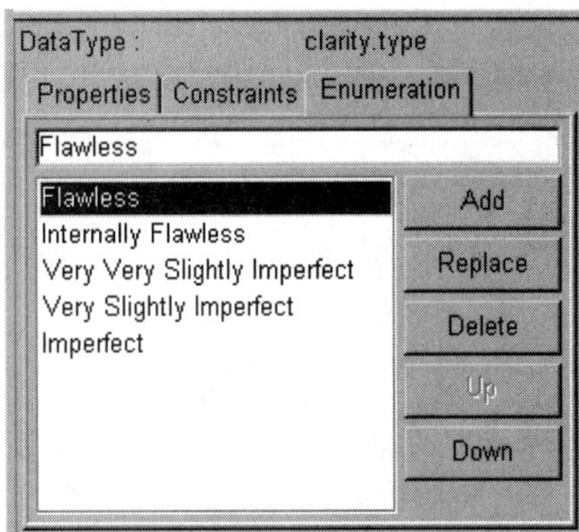

Figure 5.14 List of enumeration values for clarity.type.

   g. Return to the Element/Types view by clicking Element/Types on the top menu bar.
   h. Click the Data Type cell for the <clarity> element, choose Insert user-defined type, and choose clarity.type.

10. Click the Data Type cell for the <cost> element. Then choose More, Decimal.

11. Check for Errors.

12. Save the file as diamonds2.xsd.
13. Click Source to examine and study the code line by line. You could have entered this all by hand if you wanted. Ah, the power of a good XML schema editor!

Lab 5.3: Create a New Instance from diamonds2.xsd

The improved schema should make data documents easier to create and manipulate, and provide more sophistication and precision than the Chapter 4 DTDs. In this third exercise, you will create a new XML instance document from your schema document.

While you are performing the next few steps, feel free to test the schema and the software by (1) trying to enter numbers inside an element defined as string and (2) trying to enter alpha characters in an element defined as positiveInteger.

1. Open the Turbo XML editor.
2. Click Instance.
3. Click File, Set Schema. Then choose diamonds2.xsd and choose diamonds as a root element. Click OK.
4. Create four <gem> elements, and enter the data shown in Table 5.5 into the instance.
5. Check for errors.
6. Save the file as gems3.xml.

Table 5.5 List of Top Diamonds for Galaxy Gems

NAME	CARATS	COLOR	CLARITY	CUT	COST, $
Sparkler	105	Near colorless	IF Internally Flawless	Full-cut brilliant	126000
Merlin	41	Colorless	FL Flawless	Point cut	82000
Cullinan	3106	Faint yellow	VS1, VS2 Very Slightly Imperfect	Rough	2174200
Dark	500	Near colorless	SI1, SI2 Slightly Imperfect	Rough	450000

Lab 5.4: Use Complex Types in Schemas

This procedure allows you to create a slightly more complex schema, one that concentrates on a design issue that we wrestled with at the end of the DTD lab in Chapter 4. In this case, we illustrate how you can reuse elements. This lab starts by separating some gem data common to both diamonds and other precious gems. Then only those elements that are unique to either diamonds or precious gems will be added when the common elements are extended from the generic gem data. There are many ways this model could have been made. After working through this lab once, you may want to try and create a model based on different assumptions and approaches. Meanwhile, we start by creating the gemdata element type and adding a namespace to the schema to separate it from any other schema that may be out there.

1. Open the TurboXML editor.
2. Click Schema.
3. Change the view by clicking Overview/Properties.
4. Add a namespace to differentiate the schema.
   a. Highlight the xsd object at the top left-hand pane in the frame.
   b. Click File, Schema Properties from the top menu bar.
   c. Type *gemdata* in the Prefix area on the Schema Properties dialog box.
   d. Type *http://www.spacegems.com/stones* in the Target Namespace area on the Schema Properties dialog box.
   e. Click OK.
5. Create the complex type <gemdata> element.
   a. Enter *gemdata* as the element name in the element cell.
   b. Click the first field called D of the second row, below the unnamed element, and set the Decl Type to Complex Type.
   c. Change the Content of the <gemdata> element to Elements.
   d. Place the cursor inside the parentheses () of the <gemdata> Content Model and type *name*, *image*, *origin*, *clarity*, *shape*, and *cost*. Exit the cell using the Tab key.
   e. Click the button for Globally defined inside the Auto Create dialog box. Click Create.

If you find you have an element named *unnamed*, please delete it.

6. Create two Data Types called shape.types and clarity.scale.
   a. Click Data Types on the top menu bar.
   b. Type "shape.types" inside the Name area.
   c. Type "string" in the Base Type area.
   d. Tab over to the Options area.
   e. Move to the new Element Type: shape.types pane on the left side of the frame. Click the enumeration menu tab, and create the enumeration list by adding the following values:
      - Round
      - Emerald
      - Heart
      - Marquise
      - Oval
      - Pear
      - Princess
   f. Move back to the Data Types pane on the right side of the frame.
   g. Type "clarity.scale" inside the Name area.
   h. Type "string" inside the Base Type area.
   i. Tab to the Options area.
   j. Move to the new Element Type: clarity.scale pane on the left side of the frame. Click the enumeration menu tab and create the enumeration list by adding the following values:
      - Flawless-Internally Flawless
      - Very Very Slightly Imperfect
      - Very Slightly Imperfect
      - Slightly Imperfect
      - Imperfect
7. Modify the Content Model values for the following listed elements.
   a. Click Element/Types on the top menu bar.
   b. Change the Data Type for the <clarity> element to clarity.scale.
   c. Change the Data Type for the <cost> element to positiveInteger.

   d. Change the Data Type for the <shape> element to shape.types.
   e. Leave the Data Type for the <name>, <image>, and <origin> elements set to string.
8. Check for Errors.
9. Save the file as diamonds3.xsd.

Lab 5.5: Create a Complex <diamonds> Element to Extend <gemdata>

The new <diamonds> element will extend the existing <gemdata> element so that it can use the existing elements defined inside <gemdata>. We create only three new elements for <diamonds>: <carat>, <color>, and <cut>. Unlike using DTDs, with schemas we can easily extend an existing element without having to create new <elements>, because the elements inside <gemdata> were described as global, not private.

1. Open the TurboXML editor.
2. Open diamonds3.xsd.
3. Change the view by clicking Overview/Properties.
4. Create another complex type element called <diamonds>:
   a. Enter diamonds as the element name in the element cell.
   b. Click the field called D, and set the Decl Type to Complex Type.
   c. Click the Extends cell in the Derives from cell and click Extends, then Select. Then choose the <gemdata> element. The editor will add an e_ to the name of the element that will signify that it is extended.
   d. Change the Content to Elements.
   e. Place the cursor inside the parentheses () for the Content Model for <diamonds>, and type the three new elements as carat, color, and cut. Exit the cell using the Tab key.
   f. Click the button for Globally defined inside the Auto Create dialog box. Click Create.
5. Check for Errors.
6. Save the file back again as diamonds3.xsd.

Lab 5.6: Create One More Complex <precious.gems> Element to Extend <gemdata>

The <precious.gems> element extends the existing <gemdata> element as well. We create three more new elements for <precious.gems>: gem.type, weight, and size. The procedure is almost identical to the previous set. The goal here is two-fold: (1) to create a file of source code for you to review and compare to the course notes and (2) to create two independent complex types.

1. Open the Turbo XML editor.
2. Open diamonds3.xsd.
3. Change the view by clicking Overview/Properties.
4. Create another complex type called <precious.gems>.
   a. Click the field called D and set the Decl Type to Complex Type.
   b. Click the Extends cell and click Extends, then Select. Choose the <gemdata> element. The editor will add an e_ to the name of the element that will signify that it is extended.
   c. Change the Content to Elements.
   d. Place the cursor inside the parentheses () for the Content Model for <precious.gems>, and type the three new elements as gem.type, weight, and size. Exit the cell using the Tab key.
   e. Click the button for Globally defined inside the Auto Create dialog box. Click Create.
5. Create one Data Type called type.of.gem.
   a. Click Data Types on the top menu bar.
   b. Type type.of.gem inside the Name area.
   c. Type string in the Base Type area.
   d. Tab over to the Options area.
   e. Move to the new Element Type: type.of.gem pane on the left side of the frame. Click the Enumeration menu tab, and create the enumeration list by adding the following values:
      - Sapphire
      - Ruby
      - Emerald

6. Return to the Element/Types view by clicking Element/Types on the top menu bar.
7. Click the Data Type cell for the <gem.type> element, choose Insert user-defined type, then choose type.of.gem.
8. Check for errors.
9. Save the file back again as diamonds3.xsd.
10. Click Source to examine and study the code created by the schema editor.

Summary

XML schemas represent a powerful and flexible step forward in the world of XML. In upcoming chapters, we will see how some XML languages now have new definitive (that is, "W3C official") schemas, as well as their established DTDs. Many XML proponents predict that schemas will replace DTDs in just a few short years. As we move on to Chapter 6, here are some important facts to remember about XML schemas.

- The shortcomings of DTDs were well known by the time XML 1.0 was endorsed and led to the development of XML Schema 1.0 as a content modeling language that is also an application of XML.
- The XML Schema abstract model consists of 13 kinds of schema components in three major groups. We discussed all the primary components in Chapter 5, as well as some of the secondary and helper components.
- Because of its XML heritage, a schema document consists of two major portions: a prolog and a data instance. The only requirement in the prolog is an XML declaration. The root element type in the data instance is the <schema> element type.
- Namespace declarations and target namespaces are the mechanisms by which an XML data document informs a parser to use its schema document for validation.
- More than one schema document can be used to validate an XML document. In e-commerce environments, that strategy is used often. The document calls a target schema that in turn can call one or more support schema documents.

- The concepts of global and local references, coupled with qualified and unqualified references, provide schemas with a capability to create context-sensitive element type names.
- Complex data types are element types that contain other element types or attributes. Simple data types are the converse: They do not contain other element types or attributes, just character data.
- Three types of compositor element types exist: <sequence>, <choice>, and <all>. These are used to define groups of element types or attributes within a schema document.
- Facets are element types used to provide precise data definitions within simple type data and attributes.
- Two basic schema structure strategies are used: the nesting structure and the flat catalog structure. Because of their respective advantages, they are frequently combined in the same schema document.
- Schemas don't handle character reference entities easily. If you are using such references, consider combining a schema and a DTD for document validation.

Review Questions

1. Which of the following is *not* an advantage of DTDs?
   a. They have their own style of syntax.
   b. They handle character reference entities more easily.
   c. More utilities and applications are available to use them.
   d. They are extensively deployed already.
   e. Widespread expertise is "out there" already.
2. True or false? DTDs fall within the classic definition of schema, too.
3. Which of the following are true?
   a. Complex data types can contain elements and attributes only.
   b. Simple data types contain attributes and character data.
   c. Simple data types contain character data only.
   d. Complex data types contain character data and elements only.
   e. All of the above.
4. True or false? If you will be validating an XML document with more than one schema document, make sure that all target namespaces are included in the XML document.
5. What three purposes are served by adding the namespace declaration xmlns:xs="http://www.w3.org/2001/XMLSchema" to an <xs:schema ...> start tag?
6. If the parser encounters the target namespace "http://www.SpaceGems.com/2047/gemdata" in an XML document, what will it also be on the lookout for?
7. As an alternative to the combination of targetNamespace and xsi:schemaLocation attributes, we could use element types containing which element and attribute combination?
   a. <xs:include xsi:schemaLocation= .... >
   b. <xs:import xsi:namespace= ... >
   c. <xs:schema xsi:noNamespaceSchemaLocation= ... >
   d. None of the above
   e. Any of the above
8. Fill in the blank. ________________ elements or attributes are those that are declared within the extent of the <schema> element type.

9. Which of the following is *not* an example of a compositor element type?
   a. <group>
   b. <sequence>
   c. <list>
   d. <choice>
   e. <pattern>
   f. <all>
10. Which of the two basic approaches to schema structures is composed predominately of local elements?
11. Fill in the blanks. When you need to declare character reference entities, consider using a combination of ________________ and _________.

Answers to Review Questions

1. **a.** Working with DTDs requires the mastering of their specific coding language, complete with vocabulary and structure. XML schemas, by comparison, use XML syntax.
2. True, but our use of "schema" refers only to those validating documents that are created according to XML Schema 1.0.
3. **c.** Simple and complex data types were defined in the text, in the section titled *The XML Schema Abstract Model.*
4. False. You only need to target one schema document. It can call the support schema documents.
5. The three purposes are as follows:
   a. They tell the parser that the elements that have the xs: prefix will use the standard XML Schema 1.0 definitions.
   b. They add uniqueness to the names.
   c. They help the schema document developer keep track of standard versus his or her own arbitrary element type names.
6. The parser will look for a schema document whose targetNamespace attribute has that same URL as its value. Once it finds that document, it will use it to validate the XML document.
7. **c.** As we discussed in the section titled *Target Namespaces*, the xsi:noNamespaceSchemaLocation ... attribute provides the parser with a URI for an appropriate schema document, but indicates to the parser that that document will not contain a targetNamespace attribute.
8. Global elements or attributes are those declared within the extent of the <schema> element type.
9. **a.**, **c.**, and **e.** The types of compositor element types are listed in the text, in the section titled *Compositors*.
10. The nesting structure.
11. When you need to declare character reference entities, consider using a combination of a schema and a DTD.

XHTML

In this chapter, we introduce the Extensible HyperText Markup Language (XHTML), which started out as an XML version of the HyperText Markup Language (HTML), but quickly developed into what the W3C calls "a family of current and future document types and modules that reproduce, subset, and extend HTML."

XHTML is the largest of the XML-derived languages developed so far. It resembles HTML 4 but contains structures and features that make it compatible with XML, especially its strict adherence to XML syntax. Where XML was developed to complement HTML, XHTML is designed to eventually replace HTML.

This chapter begins with a brief review of HTML, including a quick summary of its history. During the latter stages of which its history becomes interwoven with that of XHTML. Following the XHTML history lesson will be a definition of XHTML and an introduction to its major features and advantages. The chapter also includes a discussion of the process of converting existing HTML documents to XHTML, as well as the creation of XHTML documents from scratch. A discussion of some free utilities that can facilitate those activities is also included.

By the end of this chapter, you will be familiar with basic XHTML concepts and will be able to use two XHTML-related applications: HTML Tidy to convert HTML documents to XHTML, and HTML-Kit to create XHTML documents from scratch.

HTML Review

HTML is a derivative of SGML. HTML was revolutionary when it was first introduced. It was nonproprietary, easy to learn and implement, and with its hyperlinking capabilities, contributed to the success of the World Wide Web as the fastest-growing communication medium we've likely ever seen. As it developed and proliferated, HTML provided the capability for developers everywhere to display billions of documents on millions of terminal screens.

A Brief History of HTML and XHTML

The time line in Figure 6.1 lists most of the milestones reached during the development of HTML—and, later, XHTML—since the late 1980s.

Since its beginnings at the Conseil Européen pour la Recherche Nucléaire (CERN, the European Organization for Nuclear Research) in the late 1980s, when Tim Berners-Lee and Robert Caillaux began developing it as an SGML-related markup language combined with hyperlinking technology, HTML has achieved several significant distinctions, including the following:

- The development of several international HTML standards, as HTML became more universally popular.
- The "Strict," "Transitional," and "Frameset" DTDs contained in the final version of the HTML 4.0 Recommendation.
- HTML 4.0's adoption of the ISO/IEC:10646 standard document character set, the world's most inclusive standard for the representation of international languages.
- A constant drive by HTML standard developers to interoperate with other programming-related utilities and features (scripting, frames, embedded objects, tables, forms, accessibility by those with disabilities) and to reach consensus among those in the HTML industry.
- The constant movement to "internationalize" HTML, with more languages, better document indexing, better text-to-speech conversion, and other advancements.
- The adherence to the principle that all types of devices should be able to use information on the Web (for example, cellular phones, handheld devices, appliances, speech-related devices).

	Pre-1990	Early developments and experiments with markup languages (incl. SGML), electronic documents, hyperlinking, etc.
CERN's Berners-Lee and Caillau begin work on HTML as an application of SGML.	1990	
CERN launches the World Wide Web.	1991	A specification for HTML was released on the Internet.
	1992	
Draft HTML definition released.	1993	HTML+ discussion document circulated. Although it was not to be, it led the way to HTML 3.0.
	1994	
HTML 3.0 published, but dies in Sept.	1995	W3C's HTML Working Group was formed.
HTML 2.0 (RFC 1866) becomes an IETF Proposed Standard.	1996	First edition of the Cougar DTD model for HTML.
HTML 3.2 approved as a W3C Recommendation.	1997	HTML 4.0 approved as W3C Recommendation. Contains three DTD variants.
HTML 4.0 revised.	1998	
	1999	HTML 4.01 approved as W3C Recommendation.
XHTML 1.0 approved as W3C Recommendation. IETF RFC 2854 obsoletes original RFC 1866.	2000	First ISO/IEC International HTML Standard (15445:2000/COR 1:2002(E)).
XHTML 1.1— Module-based XHTML (w/ Ruby Annotation) approved as hybrid W3C Recommendation.	2001	Modularization of XHTML approved as W3C Recommendation.
August — First public Working Draft of HTML 2.0 released.	2002	August — XHTML 1.0 Second Edition approved as a W3C Recommendation. September — XHTML 1.0 in XML Schema published as a W3C Note. Provides informative XML Schemas for XHTML 1.0.

Figure 6.1 HTML/XHTML history time line.

HTML Shortcomings

HTML is the most popular publishing language on the World Wide Web. It uses over 100 tags and even more attributes to structure text into headings, paragraphs, lists, hypertext links, and other features. But HTML's predefined elements focus mostly on the display of data, with rudimentary structuring and formatting, and not on what the data really is. The same set of markups must be used in all HTML documents, and their meanings cannot be altered. HTML has served an important purpose, but as the Web focuses increasingly on commerce and data interchange, the restrictions of its element set are being felt (and criticized) everywhere.

One major complaint about HTML is that most Web page designers focused only on how their documents look. This overwhelming concern for display quality seemed to slow the progress toward extensibility, especially with respect to data semantics.

Further, the limited and strictly predefined set of HTML components (that is, its elements and attributes), resulted in something of a limited and restricted—and nonarbitrary from a developer's standpoint—set of document structure options. Developers in various fields tried to manipulate their data to fit it into HTML document models. Often there was no fit, or the fit was difficult and clumsy.

Over the years, the W3C has also tried to incorporate some extensibility into HTML. Revised versions of HTML have been released periodically since 1994. But the inconsistent implementation of the new features from browser to browser has disappointed many designers: They're unsure at times whether their extensible HTML coding will be supported.

Some browser manufacturers have supplemented HTML by adding proprietary extensions to their browsers. A reasonable stopgap approach, perhaps, but the supplemental code tends to violate the Open Source aspects that most developers expect of SGML-related languages.

Classroom Q & A

Q: Sorry to interrupt, but I've often seen this Open Source designation and don't know what it means. What is it?

A: Open Source Software certification is a standard developed by the Open Source Initiative (OSI) that indicates that the source code of a computer program is made available free of charge to the general public. The OSI is a nonprofit corporation dedicated to managing and promoting their Open Source Definition for the good of the computing community, specifically through the aforementioned certification program. For a discussion of the OSI's rationale, methods, and certification criteria, please consult their Web site at www.opensource.org/.

Since the mid-1990s, Web browser manufacturers have included in their applications a kind of "forgiving nature" flexibility, to accommodate the sloppy, proprietary, or otherwise convoluted HTML Web sites, documents, and scripts that appear more and more frequently on the World Wide Web. A lot of bad HTML results from being developed with applications that do not validate the HTML code. Meanwhile, the forgiving nature flexibility has actually manifested itself in larger and larger (some call them bloated) browser applications that include algorithms to "guess" what the sloppy Web sites are trying to express. Consequently, many Web developers and users began to forecast that the likelihood of further explosive Web expansion—especially if it was to remain responsive and robust—was beginning to diminish. One remedy to that dim prospect has been the adoption and growth of XML and its related languages and documents.

Realizing that the fundamental components of HTML would not scale up to meet future needs, most developers felt that nothing except an SGML-based solution would work in the long run.

XHTML Definition and Background

XHTML is, in the W3C's own words, "a Reformulation of HTML 4 in XML 1.0." Thus, XHTML is HTML that has been refined into an XML application. It consists of all the element types in HTML 4.01 combined with the syntax of XML. Thus, XHTML closely resembles HTML 4.01 but is a stricter and cleaner version of it. It follows that if every XHTML page is a complete XML document that also conforms to the XML Recommendation, then it will be compatible with all general-purpose XML tools and processors, including most HTML browsers.

XHTML is the largest of the XML-derived languages developed so far. It is the designated successor to HTML as the primary tool for designing Web sites. Development and expansion of XHTML continues at a rapid pace, while HTML development has essentially stopped.

XHTML documents look much like those created using HTML 4, with a few notable exceptions, which we will discuss as the chapter progresses. If you are familiar with HTML 4 design, XHTML should be easy to learn and use. Since it is a reformulation of HTML 4 as an application of XML, XHTML is the first step toward a modular and extensible Web based on XML. XHTML is a bridge for Web page designers: It can prepare them for the Web of the future, while maintaining compatibility with today's HTML 4-based browsers.

As indicated in Figure 6.1, the XHTML 1.0 Recommendation was endorsed by the W3C in January 2000, and XHTML development has continued nonstop. The W3C Recommendation titled XHTML 1.1–Module-based XHTML, along with Ruby Annotation (typically inserted in documents to indicate pronunciation or annotation), were released as a hybrid Recommendation on May 31, 2001. Together, the two XHTML 1.0 components are also referred to as

"XHTML Modularization." XHTML 1.1 is a reformulation of "XHTML 1.0–Strict"—one of three variants of XHTML 1.0.

The two XHTML 1.1 components represent a new generation of XHTML, developed because of the proliferation of the diverse computing platforms mentioned previously (for example, handheld computers, cell phones, and smart appliances). Each has its own requirements and capabilities with respect to the Web-related languages available. To get them to interact, a modularized XHTML can be used to build blocks of elements that can be understood and manipulated by all. Further discussion of a modularized XHTML and Ruby is beyond the scope of this introductory text. If you would like further information regarding the XHTML 1.1–Module-based XHTML Recommendation and the Ruby Annotation Recommendation, please consult www.w3.org/TR/2001/REC-xhtml11-20010531/Overview.html#toc and www.w3.org/TR/ruby/, respectively.

In August 2002, XHTML 1.0 Second Edition was published as an official W3C Recommendation. This second edition is not a new version of XHTML 1.0. The changes evident in the second edition reflect input from the XHTML and Web community and the work of the HTML Working Group. Also, in August 2002, the W3C published the first public Working Draft of XHTML 2.0. This version is intended for portable Web-based applications. During the same month, the W3C published the third public Working Draft of Modularization of XHTML in XML Schema. In September 2002, the W3C published XHTML 1.0 in XML Schema as a W3C Note. It contains XML Schemas for XHTML 1.0; these are still works in progress, and the W3C is still asking for comments on them.

The lower portion of the Figure 6.1 time line (the most recent part) shows that XHTML development activity is actually accelerating. This is borne out by a visit to the W3C's HTML/XHTML Web site at www.w3.org/MarkUp/, which indicates that XHTML development is taking place on a number of fronts, including the following:

- Further modularization
- Integration of Scalable Vector Graphics (SVG)
- Integration of mathematical and scientific expressions (MathML) and multimedia components (SMIL)
- Advances in linking (HLink) and XFrames (which are intended to eventually replace HTML frames)

Indeed, so that they may finish the various initiatives, the W3C HTML Working Group was rechartered by the W3C in August 2002 for an additional two years.

XHTML's developers acknowledge that it may not be the answer to every markup issue. Its element types may not be detailed enough for all purposes, and the lack of a capability to create nested section structure (all data element types must fall within the <body> or <frameset> element) is a hindrance to creating large, complex documents. But as a general-purpose, compact language for developing Web sites, it is proving very capable. And development of the W3C's XHTML family of standards is progressing rapidly.

Advantages of XHTML

With the introduction of more and more alternative Web-connected computing devices such as handheld computers, portable telephones (cellular and satellite), global positioning systems, "smart" home appliances, and automobile tracking systems, the need has grown for a more efficient method of Web programming because these resource-constrained (as the W3C refers to them) devices are usually not as powerful as a typical desktop computer and are not designed to accommodate bad HTML nor the bloated browser applications that have to contend with that bad HTML. And more of these alternate ways of accessing the Internet are constantly being introduced.

Meanwhile, on many other fronts, document and application developers, as well as user agent designers, continue to introduce new methods for describing data, expressing new ideas, and marketing products and services. A lot of that activity results in new markup.

Loosely defined, a user agent is an implementation that retrieves, parses, and evaluates an XHTML document according to the nine conformance criteria and related specifications in Section 3.2 of the XHTML 1.0 Recommendation. If the user agent claims to be a validating user agent, it must also validate documents against their referenced DTDs.

These situations present compelling reasons to migrate from HTML to XHTML and its XML-related descendants.

XHTML Is Related to XML

XML is a simplified subset of SGML, and it has stricter rules than HTML. Documents that follow XML's stricter rules are cleaner, more predictable, and better behaved than HTML when manipulated by browsers and other XML-related software. But HTML is found everywhere, and millions of developers are already familiar with its principles. So, combining the features, especially the strengths, of HTML and XML, yields a robust markup language that is useful immediately and will remain useful for the foreseeable future. Thus, because XHTML is an XML-conforming standard, XHTML documents can be used with any general-purpose XML editor, validator, browser, or other program designed to work on XML languages or documents.

Another benefit derived from separating document style settings from data description markup, as the stricter XHTML version tries to do, is that it forces authors to use style sheets. This reliance on style sheets means the faster development of style support, and richer and more flexible presentation. (Style sheets are the subject of the next chapter, "XML and Cascading Style Sheets.")

As XHTML becomes more widely known and utilized, and as more Web sites, Web languages, and Web-related documents meet XML standards, XHTML documents and style sheets will also be compliant with more browsers and other XML tools. It is generally hoped that browsers eventually may be pared down, sped up, and given new browsing features, since they will no longer have to include the same "forgiving" logic to accommodate sloppy markup.

XHTML Is Extensible

Under HTML, which is an SGML application, but not an XML application, the addition of any new group of elements requires alteration of the entire language specification DTD: not impossible, but potentially confusing and inconvenient. XHTML, on the other hand, is XML-related, so it is easier to extend by introducing new element types or additional attributes.

For example, the W3C is developing an XHTML+MathML+SVG profile as a work in progress (at this writing), which uses namespaces to facilitate the combining of XHTML 1.1, MathML 2.0, and SVG 1.1 code in the same document. Figure 6.2 is a simple example of a MathML namespace and MathML elements introduced to an XHTML document.

If you need further information on the XHTML+MathML+SVG profile (including its DTD), check its dedicated Web site at www.w3.org/TR/2002/WD-XHTMLplusMathMLplusSVG-20020809/#howto.

Another method for extending XHTML is to copy one of the variant DTDs or schemas, customize it, and then refer to the new customized DTD instead of the original DTD—although this is cumbersome to do and potentially confusing to implement, especially if other individuals or organizations will be using the new DTD or schema document.

The XHTML family has recently evolved to better accommodate extensions by the development of XHTML modules and techniques for developing newer XHTML-conforming modules.

```
<?xml version="1.0" encoding="UTF-8"?>
<!DOCTYPE html PUBLIC
        "-//W3C//DTD XHTML 1.1 plus MathML 2.0 plus SVG 1.1//EN"
        "http://www.w3.org/2002/04/xhtml-math-svg/xhtml-math-svg.dtd">
<!-- filename: gem_equation_01.xml - ->
<html xmlns="http://www.w3.org/1999/xhtml" lang="en">
  <head>
    <title>Gem Cost Equation</title>
  </head>
  <body>
    <p>MathML and XHTML Example</p>
    <mml:math xmlns:mml="http://www.w3.org/1998/Math/MathML">
      <mml:apply>
        <mml:eq />
          <mml:ci>Cost</mml:ci>
        <mml:apply>
          <mml:times />
            <mml:ci>costPerCarat</mml:ci>
        </mml:apply>
      </mml:apply>
    </mml:math>
  </body>
</html>
```

Figure 6.2 Using namespaces to extend XHTML.

XHTML Is Modular

XHTML is constantly moving toward increased modularity. In Figure 6.1, we saw that XHTML 1.1–Module-based XHTML (with Ruby Annotation) was approved as a hybrid W3C Recommendation in May 2001. DTDs and schemas are already being developed that are composed of interchangeable parts called *modules*. As this modularity continues, HTML languages and documents—and their descendants, too—will be able to mix, match, and otherwise integrate element sets more frequently and easily. This will facilitate the justification for and development of new collections of elements.

These modules also permit the combination of other existing and new feature sets for developing content and for designing new user agent implementations. Ultimately, the modular system will allow documents and languages to serve almost any Internet or intranet purpose, and it will contribute significantly to meeting the needs of diverse Internet appliances.

According to their document titled "XHTML Modularization–An Overview," dated February 2, 2000, and revised in April 2001 (see http://www.w3.org/MarkUp/modularization), the W3C states that several of their Working Groups are using the modularization methods and that OASIS, Project Gutenberg, WAP Forum (WAP stands for Wireless Application Protocol), and the Advanced Television Systems Committee (ATSC) are using or contemplating the use of various XHTML modularization recommendations to create new markup languages.

XHTML Is Portable

Today's Internet market consists of different browser technologies. Some conduct Web-related business and recreation from "normal" computers, and some communicate, buy, and sell over the Web through alternative technologies. Also, many new Web-attached alternative appliances currently do not have sufficient resources or power to constantly surf easily through the many sites and documents that contain sloppy HTML markup.

The W3C's XHTML family is designed with accessibility, device independence, and user agent interoperability in mind. Eventually, it will be possible to develop XHTML-conforming content that is searchable, usable, and transformable by any XHTML-conforming user agent on any device. While writing this book, we were impressed to see that more applications, especially Web browsers, have recently been developed to conform (more or less, depending on the developer and version) to XML.

Properly constructed XHTML documents are compatible with most HTML browsers in use today. It is the intent of XHTML developers that their documents be compatible with existing and future XML-related browsers and applications. So XHTML documents are future- and backward-compatible!

XHTML 1.0's Three Variants, DTDs, and Schemas

The XHTML 1.0 Recommendation defines XHTML and describes its Strict, Transitional, and Frameset variants. Those variants are successors to variants defined earlier for HTML 4. Until recently, each XHTML variant had its own specific DTD, named for the variant, which specified the vocabulary of the document or language (that is, element types, attributes, notations, entities), as well as the structure of grammar of the language (in other words, the content model for each element type).

The W3C has recently published XHTML 1.0 in XML Schema as a W3C Note. That document contains XML schemas for the respective XHTML 1.0 variants. Now, each XHTML variant has an official DTD and an informative schema.

At this writing, the W3C advises us that the schema documents are still works in progress and are subject to change unless and until the document becomes a W3C Recommendation, or until its status changes otherwise.

Notes are published by the W3C, but they are not nearly the same as W3C Recommendations. W3C Notes are published at the W3C director's discretion and do not represent any endorsement of the W3C or any commitment by the W3C to pursue work related to the topic of the Note. Notes are usually informative only and are often published to acknowledge the work that has gone into a technical submission by one or more W3C members. They may also be a method by which the W3C seeks additional input on a topic, which is apparently the motivation behind publishing the XHTML 1.0 in XML Schema Note. For further information regarding W3C Notes, check the W3C Web site (www.w3.org/). For further information regarding the XHTML 1.0 in XML Schema Note, go to www.w3.org/TR/xhtml1-schema/.

Meanwhile, the decision faced by each XHTML developer is this: Which variant should I use? The next few sections may shed some light on the decision process.

The XHTML 1.0 Strict Variant

Of the three variants of XHTML 1.0, the Strict variant should be used when we want really clean structural markup, free of any tags associated with layout. The Strict variant and its associated DTD or schema are used with W3C's Cascading Style Sheet (CSS) language to generate the fonts, colors, and layout effects desired (CSS is discussed in Chapter 7, "XML and Cascading Style Sheets"). If a developer chooses the Strict variant, then the name must be specified somewhere near the beginning of the document. If the developer wants to use a DTD, then the specification goes in the DOCTYPE definition statement, like this:

```
<!DOCTYPE html PUBLIC "-//W3C//DTD XHTML 1.0 Strict//EN"
     "http://www.w3.org/TR/xhtml1/DTD/xhtml1-strict.dtd">
```

Note that this statement tells the parser that the DTD is to use the Strict variant and that the DTD is found within the directory structure at the (public) W3C Web site. Incidentally, the W3C maintains and updates all DTDs and other informational resources there. The Strict DTD contains elements, attributes, and other components that have not been deprecated or that do not appear in framesets.

If the developer chooses to use a schema, then he or she must provide the appropriate schemalike namespaces and attributes in the start tag of the <html> element:

```
<html xmlns="http://www.w3.org/1999/xhtml" lang="en" xml:lang="en"
     xmlns:xsi="http://www.w3.org/2001/XMLSchema-instance"
     xsi:schemaLocation="http://www.w3.org/1999/xhtml
               http://www.w3.org/2002/08/xhtml/xhtml1-strict.xsd">
```

Once the parser reads these declarations, it will know which variant is being used and will validate the document against the specified DTD and schema.

As discussed in Chapter 5, "XML Schemas," we can change the namespace prefix xsi: to whatever we prefer, as long we maintain internal consistency. The value for the xsi:schemaLocation attribute is a pair of URI references, one for the target namespace and one for the location of an XML schema document.

If you want to have a look at the current DTD for the Strict variant, you can find it at www.w3.org/TR/2000/REC-xhtml1-20000126/DTD/xhtml1-strict.dtd or by going to the XHTML 1.0 Recommendation, scrolling to Appendix A, and selecting the appropriate XHTML-1.0-Strict link.

Similarly, if you want to look at the actual schema for the Strict variant, you can find it by going to the XHTML in XML Schema 1.0 Web site at www.w3.org/TR/xhtml1-schema/#schemas, scrolling down to Section 2, titled "XHTML 1.0 Schemas," and selecting the appropriate www.w3.org/2002/08/xhtml/xhtml1-strict.xsd link.

The XML schema does not support entities like &euro, the symbol for the Euro currency. If you will be using entities, then you have to either use a DTD mechanism or combine schemas with DTDs, as we discussed in Chapter 5.

The XHTML 1.0 Transitional Variant

The Transitional variant is the most commonly used XHTML variant. It's used by developers who are writing Web pages for the general public to access. Although developers can take advantage of XHTML features like style sheets, they may also want to make small adjustments to their markup so that those who surf to their Web sites with older browsers—ones that can't understand style sheets—can still see the displays and text. Thus, the DTD and documents may use the <body> element with deprecated attributes such as bgcolor, text, and link.

The DOCTYPE declaration statement for the Transitional variant is similar to that for the Strict variant. Here is an example of what it looks like:

```
<!DOCTYPE html PUBLIC "-//W3C//DTD XHTML 1.0 Transitional//EN"
          "http://www.w3.org/TR/xhtml1/DTD/xhtml1-transitional.dtd">
```

The Transitional DTD includes everything in the Strict DTD, plus deprecated elements and attributes. If we will be developing XHTML documents that will call upon a Transitional DTD, then we have to remember to include both the <lang> and <xml:lang> elements. Some browsers will not recognize <xml:lang>, so they will use <lang>. However, those that recognize <xml:lang> will give it precedence over the <lang> element.

If a developer chooses to use a Transitional schema, he or she must provide the appropriate schemalike namespaces and attributes in the start tag of the <html> element:

```
<html xmlns="http://www.w3.org/1999/xhtml" lang="en" xml:lang="en"
     xmlns:xsi="http://www.w3.org/2001/XMLSchema-instance"
     xsi:schemaLocation="http://www.w3.org/1999/xhtml
             http://www.w3.org/2002/08/xhtml/xhtml1-transitional.xsd">
```

If you want to have a look at the current DTD for the Transitional variant, you can find it at /www.w3.org/TR/2000/REC-xhtml1-20000126/DTD/xhtml1-transitional.dtd or by going to the XHTML 1.0 Recommendation, scrolling to Appendix A, and selecting the appropriate "XHTML-1.0-Transitional" link.

Similarly, if you want to look at the actual schema for the Transitional variant, you can find it by going to the XHTML in XML Schema 1.0 Web site at /www.w3.org/TR/xhtml1-schema/#schemas, scrolling down to its Section 2, titled "XHTML 1.0 Schemas," and selecting the appropriate www.w3.org/2002/08/xhtml/xhtml1-transitional.xsd link.

The XHTML 1.0 Frameset Variant

The Frameset variant is used when we want to partition the browser window using frames. The Frameset DTD includes everything in the transitional DTD, plus frames. Here is the Frameset DOCTYPE declaration statement:

```
<!DOCTYPE html PUBLIC "-//W3C//DTD XHTML 1.0 Frameset//EN"
     "http://www.w3.org/TR/xhtml1/DTD/xhtml1-frameset.dtd">
```

This DTD is almost identical to the Transitional DTD. The only difference is that, in frameset XHTML documents, the content portion of the <html> element is not called the <body> element; it is called the <frameset> element instead.

If you want to have a look at the actual DTD for the Frameset variant, you can find it at www.w3.org/TR/2000/REC-xhtml1-20000126/DTD/xhtml1-frameset.dtd or by going to the XHTML 1.0 Recommendation, scrolling to Appendix A, and selecting the appropriate XHTML-1.0-Frameset link.

Similarly, if you want to look at the current schema for the Frameset variant, you can find it by going to the XHTML in XML Schema 1.0 Web site at www.w3.org/TR/xhtml1-schema/#schemas, scrolling down to its Section 2, titled "XHTML 1.0 Schemas," and selecting the appropriate www.w3.org/2002/08/xhtml/xhtml1-frameset.xsd link.

As before, if a developer chooses to use a Frameset schema, the appropriate schemalike namespaces and attributes must appear in the start tag of the <html> element:

```
<html xmlns="http://www.w3.org/1999/xhtml" lang="en" xml:lang="en"
     xmlns:xsi="http://www.w3.org/2001/XMLSchema-instance"
     xsi:schemaLocation="http://www.w3.org/1999/xhtml
               http://www.w3.org/2002/08/xhtml/xhtml1-frameset.xsd">
```

If it is convenient and secure, consider installing the three variants of the DTDs and schema-related .xsd documents locally—on your local system or network. If you do so, you will have to change the system identifier (SYSTEM, plus a URI must be included) in the respective declarations in the XHTML documents. Using a local copy of the DTD can considerably speed the loading of your documents. Of course, it will be up to you to keep track of any changes to the respective DTDs and standards, too.

XHTML Syntax

Now that we have defined XHTML and listed its advantages, we will shift the discussion to more nuts-and-bolts topics. It is important to reemphasize that XHTML is an application of XML, and so, like XML, XHTML requires strict adherence to clean and structured syntax.

The Logical Structure of an XHTML Document

Because XHTML is an XML application, an XHTML document consists of two main parts:

- A prolog
- A data instance, which consists of an <html> element type that, in turn, contains <head> and <body> element types or, alternatively according to the designer's intentions, <head> and <frameset> element types.

The Prolog

An XHTML document has a prolog, like all other XML-related documents. In Figure 6.3, we see that the prolog consists of an XML declaration, a DOCTYPE definition, and a comment containing a filename.

The DOCTYPE definition is mandatory, since it indicates the type of XHTML document this is and which DTD the document is to be validated against. Remember, the DOCTYPE definition is not considered a part of the XHTML document. It is not an XHTML element, so it does not need to have an end tag. Declaring the default namespace is also required. For all flavors of XHTML, the default namespace is http://www.w3.org/1999/xhtml.

The Data Instance

In XHTML documents, all elements must be nested within the root <html> element type. The start tag of the <html> element also contains a default namespace declaration. Other elements may have child elements of their own or may simply contain text or attributes. Unless they declared empty element types, the child element tags must be in pairs, and the elements must be correctly nested within their respective parent element. The proper basic document structure resembles the following:

```
<html xmlns=" default namespace declaration" xml:lang="en" lang="en" >
     <head> <title>... </title></head>
     <body> ... </body>
</html>
```

In the XHTML document, the <head> element contains the <title> element. Further, the <title> element must be properly nested within the <head> element. The <body> element of the document consists of all elements and other content down to the </body> end tag, just before the </html> end tag. All other elements and content must be contained within the <body> element. The <body> element is a sibling to the <head> element; both are child elements of the <html> element.

If a developer chooses to use a Frameset DTD and/or schema document, the content portion of the <html> element is called a <frameset> element type, not a <body> element type. In other words, <html> will contain a <head> and a <frameset> element type.

```
<?xml version="1.0" encoding="UTF-8"?>
<!DOCTYPE html PUBLIC
            "-//W3C//DTD XHTML 1.1 plus MathML 2.0 plus SVG 1.1//EN"
            "http://www.w3.org/2002/04/xhtml-math-svg/xhtml-math-svg.dtd">
<!-- filename: gem_equation_01.xml - ->
<html xmlns="http://www.w3.org/1999/xhtml" lang="en">
   <head>
      <title>Gem Cost Equation</title>
   </head>
   <body>

...
```

Figure 6.3 XHTML document prolog.

We can see here the similarities between XHTML and HTML documents. Both have "HTML" elements, which are considered the root elements of their respective documents. In both cases, the root element must be named "HTML." The difference lies in the fact that in the HTML language, it doesn't matter whether "HTML" is lowercase or uppercase or a combination of the two, but in XHTML it does matter: In XML, the <html> element name must be the lowercase "html" only. This is a departure from XML: Generally, there are no case constrictions on element type names.

XHTML Follows XML's Strict Syntax Rules

All XHTML documents must be well formed and valid. Therefore, all XHTML documents, including DTDs and schemas, must follow XML's stricter syntax. Plus, additional constraints are placed upon XHTML documents, compared to other XML-related documents.

XHTML Element Types Must Be Properly Nested

HTML documents are often forgiven for being improperly nested. Look at the left side of Figure 6.4, where the end tag of the first (parent) element </b> is encountered before the end tag of the second (child) element </i>.

```
<head>
      <title>Gem Cost Equation</head>
      </title>
```

Improperly Nested Elements

```
<head>
      <title>Gem Cost Equation</title>
</head>
```

Properly Nested Elements

Figure 6.4 Improper and proper nesting.

While improper nesting may be allowed in HTML, it is never allowed in XHTML. In XHTML, as in all XML-related documents, all element types must be properly nested or they will incur fatal errors. This is a significant departure from the way HTML has been allowed to evolve. Therefore, the proper syntax for the example is illustrated by the right-hand side of Figure 6.4.

In addition to proper nesting in general, the <html> root element type must contain all other element types in the data instance portion of the document.

All HTML-Related Tag Names Must Be Lowercase

To be recognized as XHTML, the tags for all element types that have been inherited from HTML must be lowercase. The code on the left of Figure 6.5 is not considered XHTML. However, the code on the right side of Figure 6.5 could be interpreted as XHTML.

XHTML, like all XML-related documents or languages, is case-sensitive. If we are extending an XHTML document with namespaces and non-HTML tags like <xxx:gem>, <xxx:Gem>, or <xxx:name> (where xxx: is a generic namespace prefix), then we have to remember that, to XHTML and its user agents, those examples will all signify different elements.

All XHTML Elements Must Be Closed

Elements have been separated into nonempty (those that are declared able to contain data and must have start and end tags) and those that are declared empty (having only a start tag, but one which will contain an ending forward slash).

Figure 6.6 illustrates improperly closed elements on the left side and the remedied properly closed elements on the right side.

The improperly closed Sapphires <li> element is fairly obvious and can be easily remedied. But the improperly closed Rubies <li> element is not so obvious. In fact, it is a very common oversight in such nested lists to forget that an enclosed child element list type must be enclosed within proper <li> and </li> tags. This is another significant departure from the older-style HTML, where it was occasionally forgivable to leave end tags out.

```
<HEAD>
      <Title>Gem Cost Equation</Title>
<HEAD>
```

Improper XHTML Tags

```
<head>
      <title>Gem Cost Equation</title>
</head>
```

Proper XHTML Tags

Figure 6.5 XHTML tags must be lowercase.

```
<ul>
  <li>Sapphires
  <li>Rubies
    <ul>
      <li>Miss Scarlet</li>
      <li>Secretariat</li>
      <li>Jacques</li>
    </ul>
  <li>Emeralds
</ul>
```

Improperly Closed Elements

```
<ul>
  <li>Sapphires</li>
  <li>Rubies
    <ul>
      <li>Miss Scarlet</li>
      <li>Secretariat</li>
      <li>Jacques</li>
    </ul>
  </li>
  <li>Emeralds</li>
</ul>
```

Properly Closed Elements

Figure 6.6 Improperly versus properly closed elements.

In XHTML, all element types capable of holding content must have end tags. Whether the element types themselves eventually hold content depends on the intentions of the designer.

In XML, any element can be treated as an empty element, as long as it is declared empty in the DTD or schema. However, several HTML-related element types are commonly expected to be empty and so are treated automatically as empty. Among these are line break <br>, horizontal rule <hr>, image <img>, and metainformation <meta>. In XHTML documents, the start tags of all declared empty elements must end with />. Table 6.1 lists two common examples where both techniques have been used for elements presumed to have been declared empty in the DTD.

For each of the Table 6.1 examples, a second method could also be used. Instead of using a /> at the end of the respective start tags (
 or <hr />), we could use a pair of tags, like
</br> and <hr></hr>, respectively. We do not recommend this alternative because occasional unpredictable results can occur. It is best to stick to the method indicated in the table: using a /> at the end of the tag.

Table 6.1 XHTML Syntax for Common Declared Empty Elements

DEFINITION /INTENT	INCORRECT SYNTAX	CORRECT SYNTAX
Introduce a line break at the right-most end of a line of poetry.	"On Mars lives a handsome young miner" 	"On Mars lives a handsome young miner "
Introduce a horizontal rule (a horizontal line) after some text.	"Planet UMa 47 F is highlighted on the attached star chart." <hr>	"Planet UMa 47 F is highlighted on the attached star chart." <hr />

To ensure that the declared empty element's tag is recognized by most browsers, consider adding an extra white space before the "/" symbol like this:

```
<br  />
```

and this:

```
<hr  />
```

Attribute Names Must Be Lowercase; Attribute Values Must Be Quoted

HTML does not differentiate between uppercase or lowercase characters. However, XML-related languages and documents are case-sensitive and attribute names and values (where applicable) must also be lowercase, like HTML-inherited element type names. As with other XML-related documents, the values of XHTML attributes must be placed between quotation marks. Figure 6.7 depicts a table of several expressions, only one of which is correct.

Attribute Minimization Is Forbidden

In HTML, several attributes—the boolean true or false attributes—could be minimized. That is, if their name appeared in the start tag of an element, it meant that the value of the attribute was considered to be true. If their name didn't appear, then it implied that their value was false. This created a breed of standalone attributes whose names were synonymous with the value of the attribute and that, admittedly, saved some coding time and convenience.

Example Attribute=Value	Decision	Rationale
<li align="left">	**Correct**	Element name and attribute name are lowercase; quotes around value.
<li align=left>	Incorrect	No quotes around attribute value.
<li ALIGN="left">	Incorrect	Attribute name is uppercase.
<li ALIGN=left>	Incorrect	Attribute name is uppercase; no quotes around value.
<LI align="left">	Incorrect	Attribute name is lowercase; quotes around value; but element name is uppercase!
<li align="LEFT">	Incorrect	Attribute value is uppercase.

Figure 6.7 Proper versus improper attribute syntax.

With the adoption of XML syntax, these standalone attributes are no longer allowed. Table 6.2 illustrates the new expanded treatment of these specific XHTML attributes.

The name *Attribute Has Been Replaced by the* id *Attribute*

In HTML, for the elements <A>, <APPLET>, <FRAME>, <IFRAME>, <IMG>, and <MAP>, we could specify a name attribute and prescribe a value for it. In XHTML, the name attribute has been deprecated, and the id attribute should be used instead. All former name attribute values can be used for id. For example:

```
<img src="SpaceGems_29.gif" id="diamond_16" />
```

has replaced

```
<img src="SpaceGems_29.gif" name="diamond_16" />
```

To continue interoperating with older browsers for a while, consider using both the name and id attributes with identical values, like this:

```
<img src="SpaceGems_29.gif" id="diamond_16" name="diamond_16" />
```

To ensure that our XHTML document will remain compatible with today's browsers, we should add an extra space before the slash symbol (/) in the declared empty <img ... /> element type.

In addition to the rules listed in the preceding text, please consult and observe Appendix B, "Element Prohibitions," and Appendix C, "HTML Compatibility Guidelines," in the XHTML 1.0 Recommendation.

Table 6.2 XHTML Treatment of HTML Minimized Attributes

HTML MINIMIZED ATTRIBUTES	XHTML EQUIVALENTS	PARSER INSTRUCTION
<DL compact>	<dl compact="compact">	Display the definition in compact form.
<INPUT checked>	<input checked="checked">	Define this input element as *checked.*
<OBJECT declare>	<object declare="declare">	Declare this object, but don't do anything with it.
<INPUT readonly>	<input readonly="readonly">	This input text cannot be altered.

Table 6.2 *(continued)*

HTML MINIMIZED ATTRIBUTES	XHTML EQUIVALENTS	PARSER INSTRUCTION
<INPUT disabled>	<input disabled="disabled">	This input item is unavailable.
<OPTION selected>	<option selected="selected">	This option is predefined as selected.
<SCRIPT defer>	<script defer="defer">	Defer the execution of this script.
<IMG ismap>	<img ismap="ismap">	Use a server-side image map.
<AREA nohref>	<area nohref="nohref">	No action in this area.
<HR noshade>	<hr noshade="noshade">	Alter the appearance of the horizontal rule.
<TD nowrap>	<td nowrap="nowrap">	Suppress word-wrapping here.
<SELECT multiple>	<select multiple="multiple">	Multiple selections are possible from this listing.

Start Moving to XHTML Soon!

Because XHTML is the designated successor to HTML, it's in your best interest to begin creating documents in XHTML as soon as possible. Learning XHTML is not really that different from learning previous versions of HTML; it takes study, practice, and syntactic discipline. It will be worth it, though: Meeting XHTML standards from this point on is a good start. Keeping up with XHTML progress is a good strategy, too.

Converting Web Sites to XHTML

It is not recommended that you convert a Web site from HTML to XHTML manually, especially when several utilities are readily available to help you. (Several are discussed in the next couple of sections.) However, if you decide to convert manually, then prior to converting your Web site, you should become familiar with XHTML's XML-related syntax rules. Use a procedure similar to the following, which has been drafted from several smaller-scale conversions:

1. Create a prolog for every applicable document. In it, the most important addition will be the DOCTYPE definition. If this is to be a Web site conversion requiring some backward compatibility with older browser versions, the transitional DOCTYPE definition is recommended. Although the browsers themselves won't process the statement, it will be used when your XHTML files are validated.
2. Change tag and attribute names to lowercase. XHTML is case-sensitive and only accepts lowercase HTML-equivalent tags and attribute names. Specialized conversion and creation utilities can do a search and replace to insert lowercase tags and attribute names (we discuss a couple of examples of such utilities in the next section). If you have generated the HTML code, this may go smoothly. However, if outsiders have been hired in the past, or if you have copied code from out on the Internet at one time or another, this could be a very complex task.
3. Insert quotation marks around all attribute values. This may be a time-consuming job. If anything convinces you to use a specialized utility, this step probably will.
4. Repair empty element tags. If problems may be anticipated with some browsers, consider inserting a space just before (that is, to the left of) the forward slashes (" / ").
5. Validate the new XHTML document against the Document Type Definition specified in Step 1. It is suggested that you use the W3C DTD validator at http://validator.w3.org/.

XHTML Utilities and Services Provided by W3C

To facilitate the transition from older HTML versions to XHTML and to convert sites automatically, the W3C provides compatibility guidelines (these are located in Appendix C of the XHTML 1.0 Recommendation) and access to some conversion utilities and other services.

W3C's HTML Validation Service

The W3C provides a free validation service that checks HTML and XHTML documents for conformance to W3C Recommendations and other standards. At http://validator.w3.org/, we can validate documents by providing a URI for the document and then choosing validation parameters from a selection of 33 character encoding schemes and a selection of eight document type specifications (HTML 2.0; HTML 3.2; the Strict, Transitional, and Frameset variants of HTML 4.01; and the Strict, Transitional, and Frameset variants of XHTML 1.0).

Alternatively, by using the W3C's related form at http://validator.w3.org/file-upload.html, we can even validate documents on our computer by uploading them. Either way, the same validation parameter choices are available to us.

New features are being added to the W3C validation site constantly. Prior to using the validation service, you should check the most recent changes to it by going to http://validator.w3.org/ and clicking the What's New link.

Amaya, W3C's Editor and Browser

Amaya is an open source software project hosted by the W3C. Amaya is a complete Web browsing and authoring environment using a WYSIWYG interface. Using this interface, users can generate HTML and XHTML pages and cascading style sheets, without needing to know the HTML or CSS languages. At this writing, the Amaya supports HTML 4.01, XHTML 1.0, XHTML Basic, XHTML 1.1, HTTP 1.1, MathML 2.0, many CSS 2 features, and SVG.

Amaya focuses on integrating Web technologies, so an important benefit of Amaya is that it implements W3C specifications very carefully. This allows Web authors to make sure they are producing correct markup. It also lets authors mix W3C technologies and edit them in a uniform way. It is even used by several W3C groups to experiment with and demonstrate their work.

Amaya is covered by the free software W3C copyright statement. Its features include the following:

- The capability to let us create Web pages and upload them onto a server (even a remote server).
- The ability to create documents from scratch or browse the Web (from within Amaya), find the needed information, and copy and paste it to pages. We can also create and test hyperlinks to other Web sites.
- The representation of the document internally in a structured way consistent with Document Type Definitions. A properly structured document enables other tools to further process the data safely.
- The ability to work on several documents—including (X)HTML, MathML (.mml), and SVG (.svg) documents—at a time. Plus, it allows us to display the document structure at the same time as the formatted view.
- An annotation application named Annotea—based on Resource Description Framework (RDF), XLink, and XPointer—to create annotations, which are external comments, notes, and remarks that can be

attached to any Web document or a selected part of the document. If you want to know more about Annotea, visit its home page at www.w3.org/2001/Annotea/.

- Internationalization, so that users can select a dialog language from among several choices (English, French, German, Spanish, Portuguese, Italian, and Finnish). Other languages based on the Latin script may be added. Amaya also supports a large set of document encodings (UTF-8, ISO-8859, Windows, JIS, and others).
- Support for client/server architectures. Generally, both a client and a server are needed to experiment and demonstrate new Web specifications. Amaya works on the client side, and a counterpart product called Jigsaw plays the same role on the server side. Amaya allows us to publish documents on remote Web servers.
- The ability to download, edit, and publish CSS style sheets as well as HTML pages.
- Easy extensibility through several application programming interfaces and other mechanisms that are available to change and extend its functionality with the least modification to its source code. Amaya uses namespaces to integrate SVG and MathML math and scientific expressions into XHTML documents (we discuss these languages in Chapter 11, "VML," and Chapter 16, "MathML").
- The ability to display images in several formats (including PNG format images, which are more powerful than GIF format and increasing in Web popularity).
- Specialized printing functions, like printing tables of contents for the document, tables of hyperlinks, and document URIs. Amaya also makes use of CSS style sheets for printing.
- A profiles feature to customize Amaya according to your level of HTML expertise. Its templates can help you if you frequently create the same kinds of pages.

If you are interested, you can find a more detailed description of Amaya and its features in the W3C Note, "An Introduction to Amaya" (www.w3.org/TR/NOTE-amaya-970220.html), on the Amaya home page at www.w3.org/Amaya/, on its Overview page at www.w3.org/Amaya/Amaya.html, and on its Activity page at www.w3.org/Amaya/Activity.html. You can also download any of several different versions of Amaya from the www.w3.org/Amaya/ home page. Amaya is available as source code, ready to use, for Windows, Unix, and Mac OS X platforms.

Other XHTML Utilities and Services

In addition to the W3C, other utilities are available to help with XHTML creation and conversion.

HTML Tidy

In 1998, Dave Raggett created HTML Tidy (also called simply "Tidy," which is how we refer to it), which is a free downloadable utility for editing HTML. Tidy is available as open source software and also offers a means to convert existing HTML content into well-formed XML for delivery as XHTML.

Tidy is able to fix many problems by itself automatically. For example, sloppy HTML editing is "tidied up" into more easily understood markup. But it won't generate a cleaned up version of a document if it encounters problems that it can't handle confidently and unambiguously. In those cases, Tidy will bring those issues to our attention by logging them as "errors." Tidy can also help us determine how and where to make our pages more accessible to people with disabilities. Tidy has many features, is available for most platforms, and has been integrated into numerous authoring environments.

Recently, responsibility for future development and maintenance of HTML Tidy has been transferred from Mr. Raggett and the W3C to a group of developers at Source Forge (http://tidy.sourceforge.net/). Source Forge claims to have two major goals regarding Tidy: to provide a home for all of Tidy's patches and fixes, and to provide a library form of Tidy so that it can be incorporated into other software (for example, into HTML-Kit). You will be using Tidy in the first lab exercise in this chapter.

HTML-Kit

As stated on the Feature Tour page of its Web site, "HTML-Kit is a full-featured editor designed to help HTML, XHTML, and XML authors to edit, format, look up help, validate, preview, and publish Web pages."

You will be using HTML-Kit in the second lab of this chapter. You can find information about HTML-Kit, and even download a copy of it, at the Chami.com Web site (www.chami.com/html-kit/). To ensure that you can find the site and take advantage of all its features, make sure you use the most recent possible version of your browser to surf there.

Developed by Chami Wickremasinghe, HTML-Kit has many standard functions (for example, a built-in previewer, an FTP client, and even a repository for frequently used code and scripts) and can be extended by adding plug-ins. Plus, HTML-Kit is integrated with HTML Tidy to facilitate error detection and correction and for converting HTML documents to XHTML or XML with as little as a single mouse click. Although other applications may boast more functionality, HTML-Kit still has almost everything that users at all skill levels will require.

Classroom Q & A

Q: You explained Open Source earlier, but what is the W3C copyright statement you mentioned?

A: It is a statement issued by the W3C regarding titles, rights, permissions, and indemnifications. The copyright statement accompanies software developed under the auspices of the W3C. For further information, please consult www.w3.org/Consortium/Legal/copyright-software-19980720).

Chapter 6 Labs: Creating XHTML Documents

The two lab exercises in this chapter show you how to create XHTML documents and convert existing HTML documents to XHTML. The labs are interesting because the simple index.html file used here was generated with Microsoft's FrontPage application, with no modifications. As you will see, FrontPage didn't do too bad a job, but missed three small issues. However, in FrontPage's defense, it could be argued that those issues are the responsibility of the HTML programmer and that the programmer should have adequate knowledge of best practices.

By now, most modern page design programs are XHTML-compliant and require little modification. Files that require more work are those that were coded or modified by hand before the XHTML standards were developed and before the latest programs were developed.

Lab 6.1 Validate a Simple HTML File Using HTML-Tidy

As discussed in this chapter, HTML Tidy is a free utility that you can use to clean up HTML codes. It will actually fix the code in the file when it can figure out the logic. For those items that it can't determine a solution for, it logs errors to a file for you to ponder and research. If you have a good HTML editor, you will probably not have to use Tidy, but if you must clean up a site coded by someone else, Tidy can come in handy. Tidy can be found at several Web sites, or you can download it from the *XML in 60 Minutes a Day* Web site as noted in the book's introduction.

1. Create a working directory called C:\XMLIN60\TIDY.
2. Download Tidy from this book's Web site (again, the URL for the Web site is provided in the book's introduction).

3. Unzip the contents of tidy.zip into the C:\XMLIN60\TIDY folder.
4. Copy the C:\WWW\SpaceGems\index.html file into the C:\XMLIN60\TIDY folder.
5. Change to the C:\XMLIN60\TIDY folder.
6. Execute Tidy on the index.html file, using the following command:

```
tidy -output-xhtml  -f index-errs.txt  -in index.html
```

7. Open the resulting index-errs.txt file and review the comments. If you have downloaded the *XML in 60 Minutes a Day* version of Tidy and used our index.html file, then you will have zero errors and three warnings. The warnings will be as follows:

```
HTML Tidy for Windows (vers 1st August 2002; built on Aug 8 2002,
at 15:41:13)
Parsing "index.html"
line 18 column 3 - Warning: <table> lacks "summary" attribute
line 21 column 27 - Warning: <img> lacks "alt" attribute
line 29 column 27 - Warning: <img> lacks "alt" attribute
index.html: Document content looks like HTML 4.01 Transitional
3 warnings, 0 errors were found!
```

8. Apply some fixes to the code. The suggested fixes are listed in Table 6.3. The fixes you apply will depend on the feedback found inside the index-errs.txt file.

Table 6.3 Changes to Be Made to the index.html File

CODE CHANGES	
FROM	**TO**
<table border="0" cellpadding="20" cellspacing="0" width="71%">	<table summary="Table used to format images and text" border="0" cellpadding="20" cellspacing="0" width="71%">
<img border="0" src="images/secret_s.jpg" width="170" height="120" />	<img alt="secret_s.jpg" border="0" src="images/secret_s.jpg" width="170" height="120" />
<img border="0" src="images/C4D3_s.jpg" width="170" height="128" />	<img alt="C4D3_s.jpg" border="0" src="images/C4D3_s.jpg" width="170" height="128" />

9. Rerun Tidy on the modified file:

```
tidy -output xhtml -f index-fixed.txt  -im index.html
```

10. Open the resulting index-fixed.txt. The file should show a clean bill of health:

```
HTML Tidy for Windows (vers 1st August 2002; built on Aug  8
2002, at 15:41:13)
Parsing "index.html"
index.html: Doctype given is "-//W3C//DTD XHTML 1.0
Transitional//EN"
index.html: Document content looks like XHTML 1.0 Transitional
No warnings or errors were found.
```

11. Move the new index.html file from C:\XMLIN60\TIDY to the C:\WWW\SpaceGems folder.
12. Test the new file using the browser www.spacegems.com.
13. Confirm the updates using View, Source.

Lab 6.2: Using the HTML-Kit GUI Tool to Create XHTML Files

You may find the HTML-Kit easier to use. Here you'll use this GUI tool to fix some more HTML code that we have given you. The scope of this lab is to install the HTML-Kit tool, debug our HTML code using both the Transitional and Strict DTDs, then add the page to the SpaceGems Web site via a link on the index.html page. You are going to do this to keep all code XHTML-compliant.

1. Download a file called galaxys_largest_diamonds_problem.txt, and place the file in the C:\XMLIN60\TIDY folder.
2. Download HTML-Kit from this book's Web site as noted in the book's introduction.
3. Install HTML-Kit. Double-click HKSetup.exe and accept all defaults for the installation.
4. Start HTML-Kit by selecting Start, Programs, HTML-Kit, HTML-Kit. Accept all defaults to initiate the editor.
5. Create a blank file by selecting File, New. Click the All tab. Click the Blank HTML Page object. Click OK.
6. Replace the Transitional DTD with a Strict DTD. Highlight the entire DOCTYPE declaration, and click Actions, Document, Doctype–HTML 4.01 Transitional, Doctype–HTML 4.01 Strict.

7. Copy the contents of the galaxys_largest_diamonds_problem.txt into the HTML-Kit editor. Make sure that you replace all the appropriate code between the <html> and </html> tags only. Don't replace the document type declaration.
8. Click the Preview tab at the bottom of the editor to see the file. The images will be missing at this time because they point to images/thefile.jpg. These will work when the file is placed inside the C:\WWW\SpaceGems folder. Just leave it for now.
9. Click the Editor tab at the bottom of the editor to return to the code.
10. Validate this code using Tidy: Go to Tools, Check Code Using TIDY.

In the future, most HTML editors will have a code-validating feature like this.

11. You should now have two versions of the file inside your editor: the original on the left and the new file on the right. Work with the one on the left.
12. Click the error inside the feedback frame at the bottom of the editor. The editor will take you to the incorrect line of code inside the left pane. You can review the corresponding Tidy code inside the right pane. If you agree with the changes that Tidy has made, you can cut and paste the code into the left pane.

When you eventually do a Save As, it will save the code inside the left-side pane.

13. Make all the appropriate changes, and save the finished file as galaxys_largest_diamonds.htm to the C:\WWW\SpaceGems folder.
14. Click Preview to make sure that the file is still formatted correctly.
15. Add a link to the index.html for the new galaxys_largest_diamonds .htm file:
    a. Open the C:\WWW\SpaceGems index.html file with HTML-Kit.
    b. Open a line at the bottom of the index.html file between the </center> and </div> tags. Place the cursor between these lines.
    c. On the top menu bar go to Tags, Make Link.
    d. Click on the galaxys_largest_diamonds.htm file.
    e. Place the cursor inside the Content area and type "See the Galaxy's Largest Diamonds".
    f. Make sure that your view looks like Figure 6.8, and click OK.

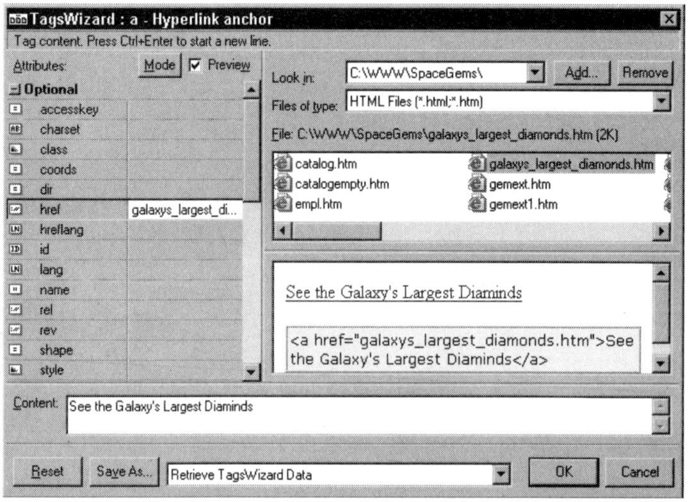

Figure 6.8 Using HTML-Kit to add a link to the index.html file.

16. Click Preview to view the file and test the new link.
17. Save the index.html file back to the C:\WWW\SpaceGems folder.
18. Test the file using IIS. Open Internet Explorer and enter http://localhost.spacegems/.

Summary

Here are some important facts to keep in mind about XHTML:

- With over 100 tags and even more attributes, hypertext linking capability, and other features, HTML is the most popular publishing language on the Web. But HTML proved to have several shortcomings: It focuses on data display more than data description and structure; its element types are limited and predefined; and a lot of sloppy HTML has spawned bloated applications.
- The W3C and other organizations have tried to extend HTML, but results have been disappointing and inconsistent.
- XML was developed to overcome HTML shortcomings and was meant to complement it. XHTML was developed as a successor to HTML.
- XHTML is a refinement of HTML, but it is also an XML application. It resembles HTML 4.01, but it is syntactically stricter and thus cleaner. Development of the XHTML family of standards is progressing rapidly.

- XHTML's advantages include that it's an application of XML and it is extensible, modular, portable, and applicable today and in the future.
- XHTML has three variants: Strict, Transitional, and Frameset. Respective DTDs exist for each, and schema documents are in the first stage of development and publication.
- The logical structure of an XHTML document includes a prolog (which must include an XML declaration and a DOCTYPE definition) and a data instance (containing a root <html> element type which, in turn, consists of a <head> element type plus a <body> or <frameset> element type).
- XHTML has strict syntax rules: element types must be properly nested, HTML-related tags are lowercase only, all element types must be closed, attributes are lowercase, attribute values must be quoted, and more.
- Converting Web site documents to XHTML involves meeting all the XHTML syntax rules. The documents must be well formed and valid.
- Several valuable utilities and services are available from the W3C and other organizations. Some are open source software. Their respective URLs are provided in this chapter.

Review Questions

1. Fill in the blank: "Faced with a lack of HTML scalability and the mixed results that resulted from the extensibility efforts of the W3C and other organizations, most developers realized that only a(n) _______________ solution could work."
2. What is the concept behind the "forgiving nature" built into Web browsers and other HTML-related applications?
3. Which of the following defines XHTML?
   a. A reformulation of HTML in XML
   b. HTML refined into an XML application
   c. A stricter and cleaner version of HTML
   d. The largest of the XML-related languages developed so far
   e. All of the above
4. List three advantages of XHTML over HTML.
5. Fill in the blank: "XHTML can be extended with arbitrary element types by using _______________."
6. Match the following:

a. Transitional	i. structural markup; no layout tags
b. Frameset	ii. allows for deprecated attributes
c. Strict	iii. partitions the browser view

7. True or false? "With XHTML, all tags and attributes must be lowercase."
8. Which is recommended?
   a. Came home one night with a big shiner
 </br>
   b. Came home one night with a big shiner
   c. Came home one night with a big shiner
   d. Came home one night with a big shiner
   e. All of the above

9. Which is recommended? (Tricky question!)
   a. <img src="SpaceGems01.jpg" name="SG01"/>
   b. <img src="SpaceGems01.jpg" id="SG01"/>
   c. <img src="SpaceGems01.jpg" id="SG01" />
   d. <img src="SpaceGems01.jpg" id="SG01" name= "SG01" />
   e. All of the above
10. Fill in the blank. "With HTML standalone attributes, if the name did not appear in the start tag of an element, it meant that the value of the attribute was considered to be ______________."

Answers to Review Questions

1. Faced with a lack of HTML scalability and the mixed results that resulted from the extensibility efforts of the W3C and other organizations, most developers realized that only an SGML-based solution could work.
2. Algorithms and other logic that "guess" the meaning of documents that contain sloppy HTML. They lead to the development of bloated applications.
3. **e.** The answers are found throughout the chapter, but mostly in the section titled *XHTML Definition and Background*.
4. Here are five to choose from:
   - XHTML is an application of XML.
   - XHTML is extensible by various means.
   - XHTML is modular and becoming more modular all the time.
   - XHTML is portable and development is geared toward device independence and user agent interoperability.
   - XHTML can be used with today's and tomorrow's browsers.
5. XHTML can be extended with arbitrary element types by using namespaces.
6. **a.** and **ii.**; **b.** and **iii.**; **c.** and **i**.
7. Strictly speaking, false. All HTML-related tags must be lowercase. Others are simply case-sensitive.
8. **b.** The answer follows the instruction and examples in the section titled *All XHTML Elements Must Be Closed*.
9. **d.** This is most likely to be displayed by all browsers; c. might be OK, with latest-version browsers.
10. With HTML standalone attributes, if the name did not appear in the start tag of an element, it meant that the value of the attribute was considered to be false.

XML and Cascading Style Sheets

Throughout this book, we have stated that it is good practice to separate document style settings from the actual data description markup. Thus, we believe, as many do, that the development of the Cascading Style Sheet (CSS) language for HTML and, later, XML-related languages and documents, has been beneficial, especially when external style sheet documents are used to prescribe the eventual appearance of the document components. Added benefits from CSS are the ability for document designers to maintain their control over data description and structure, while acquiring more control over the eventual appearance of the data. So their data will display the way they intend it to.

In this chapter, we introduce cascading style sheets and discuss the style controls they bring to HTML, XHTML, and other XML-related languages. CSS grammar and syntax differs from that of XML and HTML, and its constructs are sophisticated and complex. But its concepts are not difficult to grasp. By the end of this chapter, you will be able to create and combine simple style control rules. You will also learn how to create separate style sheet documents containing sets of style rules and then to affiliate HTML and XML-related documents with their respective style sheet documents. You will see how easy it is to get the style results you want, but you will also see how important it is to plan carefully and pay strict attention to CSS and XML coding. Finally, you will learn why CSS style rules are referred to as *cascading* and how to use cascading principles to your benefit.

Overview of Cascading Style Sheets

The Cascading Style Sheet language describes how to format HTML and XML-related element types. That is, it describes how to add style controls (also called presentation controls) that include fonts, colors, images, white space, and other display features to HTML and XML-related data, within the data documents themselves or in separate css documents that are consulted when needed. Those style control specifications can also be combined and coordinated from various sources. Not only can document designers attach their preferred style controls, end users can apply their own personal controls to adjust displays to compensate for human disabilities or to compensate for equipment that has different capabilities from that of the document developers. This overview explains the history of Cascading Style Sheets, the role of the W3C in CSS development, the levels of CSS that have been developed, and where you can find CSS-compatible editors, utilities, browsers, and other applications.

CSS and the World Wide Web Consortium

The W3C's CSS Working Group began developing the Cascading Style Sheet language in 1995 to add style to HTML documents. Over its comparatively short life, CSS achieved its HTML objectives and is being supported by more and more application developers all the time. Recently, the Working Group has expanded CSS to complement documents pertaining to XML-related languages (such as XHTML, SVG, SMIL, and others), as well as the numerous alternative, particularly modular, computing platforms.

CSS has so far been developed in three basic phases:

- Cascading Style Sheets, Level 1 became a W3C Recommendation in December 1996 (it was revised in January 1999). The CSS1 language provided for the development of simple style sheets that enabled designers to affiliate simple style controls (for example, colors, fonts, alignment and spacing, background images, and others) to HTML documents.
- Cascading Style Sheets, Level 2 was endorsed as a W3C Recommendation in May 1998. It included more sophisticated style control features, such as page-based layout, support for downloadable fonts, the definition of rectangular regions for displaying different parts of documents, and others. It provided developers the capability to develop style controls for additional media, not only for visual browsers, but also for printers, handheld devices, aural devices, Braille devices, and others.
- At this writing, a Cascading Style Sheets, Level 3 (CSS3) specification is still in development. CSS3 builds on the previous two Recommendations and includes new features suited to an international and multimedia

Internet. CSS3 consists of several separate module specifications, which enable developers to incorporate one or more modules at a time into new languages, documents, Web sites, and other facilities (examples: a more sophisticated color specification model, a mobile device profile module, and a specific element selector module).

As CSS development continues, the W3C's CSS Working Group coordinates its activities with the W3C's XSL Working Group, SVG Working Group, SYMM Working Group, MathML Working Group, XForms Working Group, and others. Meanwhile, the W3C CSS Web site at www.w3.org/Style/CSS/ is informative and useful. It provides the latest CSS news and updates regarding CSS development. Plus, it links to several authoring tools, browser applications, and other software developed by the W3C and other organizations. There are also links to tutorials, discussion groups, and other information sources.

If you are experienced with CSS1, you may feel that some of the changes introduced with CSS2 are confusing and even contradictory. If this happens, check Appendix B of CSS2 at www.w3.org/TR/REC-CSS2/changes.html#changes-from-css1, where you will find a summary of all CSS1-to-CSS2 changes, grouped according to three categories: new functionality, updated descriptions, and semantic changes from CSS1.

Dave Raggett's Adding a Touch of Style Web Site

Dave Raggett's Adding a Touch of Style Web site (www.w3.org/MarkUp/Guide/Style.html) helps users add style to Web pages with CSS and HTML. That Web site is linked to the HTML-Tidy Web site (http://tidy.sourceforge.net), which we discussed in Chapter 6, "XHTML." Tidy is useful for fixing HTML markup errors, converting HTML to XHTML, and checking CSS in data and style sheet documents. Tidy is often contained in other CSS-related applications, such as HTML-Kit, which you use in this chapter's lab exercises.

W3C's CSS Validation Service

The W3C also provides a CSS Validation Service at http://jigsaw.w3.org/css-validator/. The validator checks your CSS specifications in one of four ways:

- You can download the validator and use it on your system.
- You can validate a CSS by providing a URI at the Jigsaw site.
- You can validate a CSS by typing your style control text.
- You can validate a CSS source file by uploading it to the Jigsaw site.

Coping with CSS Issues

The only issue surrounding CSS style controls is that most applications, such as Web browsers, implement CSS support inconsistently, particularly CSS's cascading behavior. Some information sources, such as the W3C's CSS Web (www.w3.org/Style/CSS/) or Webmonkey's Browser Chart (http://hotwired.lycos.com/webmonkey/reference/browser_chart/), tell which applications support which levels of CSS.

Designers often test their Web pages repeatedly during development, much like we do during our lab exercises. They test their pages with several browsers on several computing platforms. They sometimes have to create more than one version of their site to accommodate the latest browser versions as well as legacy browser versions.

Specifying Styles for HTML and XML Documents

We can use three methods to specify styles for HTML and XML documents:

- Inserting style controls (also called inline style specifications) into the start tags of the respective elements in the data documents
- Inserting style rules into the data documents themselves—a process referred to as creating internal style sheets or embedded style sheets
- Affiliating HTML/XML documents with one or more external style sheet documents that contain lists of style rules by including specific references or declarations to the external sheet documents in the HTML/XML data documents

Inline Style Specifications

We can insert a STYLE attribute into the start tag of individual elements, to add style controls to those elements inline (that is, within the XML document, without having to resort to the external style sheet file). The generic syntax is:

```
<elementName STYLE="propertyname: value" >content  ... </elementName>
```

As an example of such an inline display style specification and using the original gems1.xml file, consider nesting an element called <uline> (an abbreviation for underline) within the <link> element, like this:

```
<link xml:type="simple" href="http://localhost/SpaceGems"
            OnClick="location.href='http://localhost/SpaceGems' ">
    <uline STYLE="text-decoration: underline" >
```

```
            Home
        <uline>
    </link>
```

The <uline> element type in the code sample ensures that the hyperlink is underlined when printed or displayed. At this point, to ensure that the gems1.xml document remains valid, the following declarations must also be added to the diamonds1.dtd DTD file:

```
<!ELEMENT uline (PCDATA)* >
<!ATTLIST uline STYLE PCDATA #IMPLIED >
```

We provide another example of an inline style control later in this chapter, in the *Absolute and Relative Positioning* section.

We recommend avoiding the use of inline controls if possible. Many of the advantages of CSS are lost if we rely on inline controls. However, they are handy for providing individual customized style specifications and are given a priority in processing.

Internal Style Sheet Specifications

Style rules can be collected into groups and included—embedded—in the data document. For simple documents or Web sites, this might be the preferred method, because it eliminates the need for external CSS document files. The methods for creating internal style sheet HTML and XHTML documents are similar. For other types of XML-related languages and their documents, though, the method differs. We will discuss both approaches.

Internal Style Sheet Specifications for HTML and XHTML

In HTML documents, the <STYLE> element provides the capability to embed style rules in the data document; in XHTML documents, it's the <style> element. Sometimes, this strategy is preferred, because it allows for style rules that are specific to the document. A simplified XHTML-version example appears following this paragraph. Notice that several generic style rules are represented within a <style> element, which is nested within the <head> element. These style rules have been simplified for this illustration:

```
<?xml version="1.0"?>
<!DOCTYPE html PUBLIC "-//W3C//DTD XHTML 1.0 Transitional//EN"
    "http://www.w3.org/TR/xhtml1-transitional.dtd">
<html xmlns="http://www.w3.org/1999/xhtml">
    <head>
        <title> Welcome to Space Gems Online Catalog!</title>
        <style type="text/css">
```

```
                    ...first style rule ...
                    ...
                    ...nth style rule ...
               </style>
          </head>
          <body>
          ...
          </body>
     </html>
```

This approach is practical for small-scale XHTML projects; but for larger scale development, we recommend the use of external CSS files, which is discussed very soon.

Internal Style Sheet Specifications for Other XML-Related Language Documents

Except for XHTML, most XML-related languages are unlikely to use a <style> element for style control, as illustrated in the previous example. However, they can use a reference link in a processing instruction. Instead of linking to an external style sheet file, they link to an embedded (internal) style sheet in the XML document as follows:

```
<?xml-stylesheet type="text/css" href="#sgStyles"?>
<diamonds id="sgStyles">
     ...first style rule ...
     ...
     ...nth style rule ...
     <gem>
     ...
</diamonds>
```

The *type*="text/css" pseudo-attribute must appear in the processing instruction, so that the parser knows which style sheet language is being used. The href pseudo-attribute does not point to an external file but to the internal style sheet within the XML document, inside an element type that contains a target id attribute whose value will be *sgStyles*. In this example, the <diamonds> element contains the appropriate id attribute.

In this and the previous examples, the style rules have been deliberately simplified to the representative phrase "...style rule ...". Actual style rules, including syntax and examples, are discussed later in this chapter, in the *Creating CSS Style Rules* section.

Affiliating Documents with External Style Sheets

The two previous strategies are acceptable for smaller projects. However, we recommend that you incorporate as many style control specifications as possible in external style sheet documents. Following are the major advantages to using these external style sheets:

- Style information for a collection of Web pages, even an entire Web site, can be stored in one place.
- Storing style sheets separately and centrally allows them to be used by several different documents at once and to be reused repeatedly, simplifying authoring and making better use of network data caching.
- Style additions or modifications can be quickly incorporated. Without having to access and modify all the relevant data documents, a designer can change the style of a single element type, a whole document, or a whole Web site.
- Less coding needs to be done, because the style rules have to be created only once.
- CSS doesn't alter the logical structure of your document. It is compatible with HTML- and XML-related markup.
- If style rules are moved to external style sheets, the remaining data instance documents are clearer to read, comprehend, and modify.
- Browsers that don't understand CSS still recognize the logical structure of a document and display it in a way that makes sense. It might not look like you want, but it will be legible and accessible.
- If jurisdiction over the data and style documents goes to another party at the production end, the transition will go more smoothly.
- At the user's end, the user can apply a local external style sheet to data that originates remotely to compensate for handicaps or to provide other preferred features.

The syntax for affiliating HTML/XHTML documents to their external style sheets differs slightly from the syntax for affiliating other XML-related documents to style sheets. We devote a section to each approach.

Affiliating HTML and XHTML Documents with External Style Sheets

HTML and XHTML have a <link> element (<LINK>, in HTML, of course), situated in the <head> (or <HEAD>) element, to affiliate, or link, the document to one or more external CSS style sheets.

The following code sample illustrates three methods for specifying style rules in an HTML document:

```
<html>
     <head>
          <title>Welcome to Space Gems</title>
          <link type="text/css" rel="stylesheet"
                 href="http://localhost/SpaceGems.com/styles/"
                 title="2047_01" />
          <style type="text/css">
                 @import url(http://SpaceGems.com/styles);
                 h1 { color: maroon }
          </style>
     </head>
     <body>
          <h1>Space Gems</h1>
          <p>2047 Catalog!</p>
     </body>
</html>
```

The preceding example uses the following three methods:

- Using the <link> element to link a specific external style sheet
- Using a <style> element inside the <head> element
- Importing a style sheet using the CSS language's @import notation

The <link> element references alternative style sheets that the user can select, whereas imported style sheets are automatically merged with the style sheet.

Affiliating Other Types of XML Documents with External Style Sheets

We've seen how the <link> or <LINK> elements provide a link between XHTML and HTML documents, respectively, and their CSS files.

Other XML-related languages, however, may not have that element type or structure. In those cases, we can still affiliate one or more external CSSs by using the <? xml-stylesheet ... > processing instruction in the document's prolog, as follows:

```
<?xml-stylesheet type="text/css" href="cssFilename.css" ?>
```

This processing instruction is displayed several times in this book but, until now, it hasn't been properly explained. The first part of the processing instruction informs the parser that an external style sheet is to be accessed. The media type specification type="text/css" follows next. Whenever external style sheets are being used, this specification must appear. It tells the parser what type of media is to be specified in the HTTP data headers when the external style sheet is retrieved. "text/css" means that the primary media type, also called the general media type, is text. The media subtype, also called the specific format, is css. If the parser doesn't support CSS, it won't process this instruction any further.

For further information regarding the text/css Media Type, refer to the Request for Comments RFC 2318 at the Internet Society's Web site at www.ietf.org/rfc/rfc2318.txt.

The value of the href pseudo-attribute is a URI. In this example, the URI is cssFilename.css, which is a generic filename that we are inserting here for illustration. We can give a style sheet file any name, but must specify the type and location of the file in the processing instruction or other link. As in previous examples in this book, because no directory path has been added to the style sheet's filename, we presume that the parser will look for the style sheet file in the same directory as the XML document.

CSS and the Parsing Process

Now that we have a basic idea of style controls, let's quickly review the parsing process. Our example uses a typical XHTML-compatible browser with a built-in validating parser, as depicted in Figure 7.1, which is processing the Space Gems home page document named index.html.

When the Web browser application is told that it must process an XHTML document, it activates the XML parser and provides it with the name of the XHTML home page document (in this case, index.html). The XML parser reads the data document and looks for inline style specifications, any internal style sheet, and references to any external style sheet documents. If there is a reference to an external style document, the parser retrieves that specified document and reads the specifications.

The parser also recognizes that the home page is written in XHTML and validates all declarations according to the specified version of the XHTML DTD, which is specified in the index.html file. After the document is validated, the parser processes and structures the data in index.html accordingly. It then structures the index.html data and passes it to the browser, which displays the results.

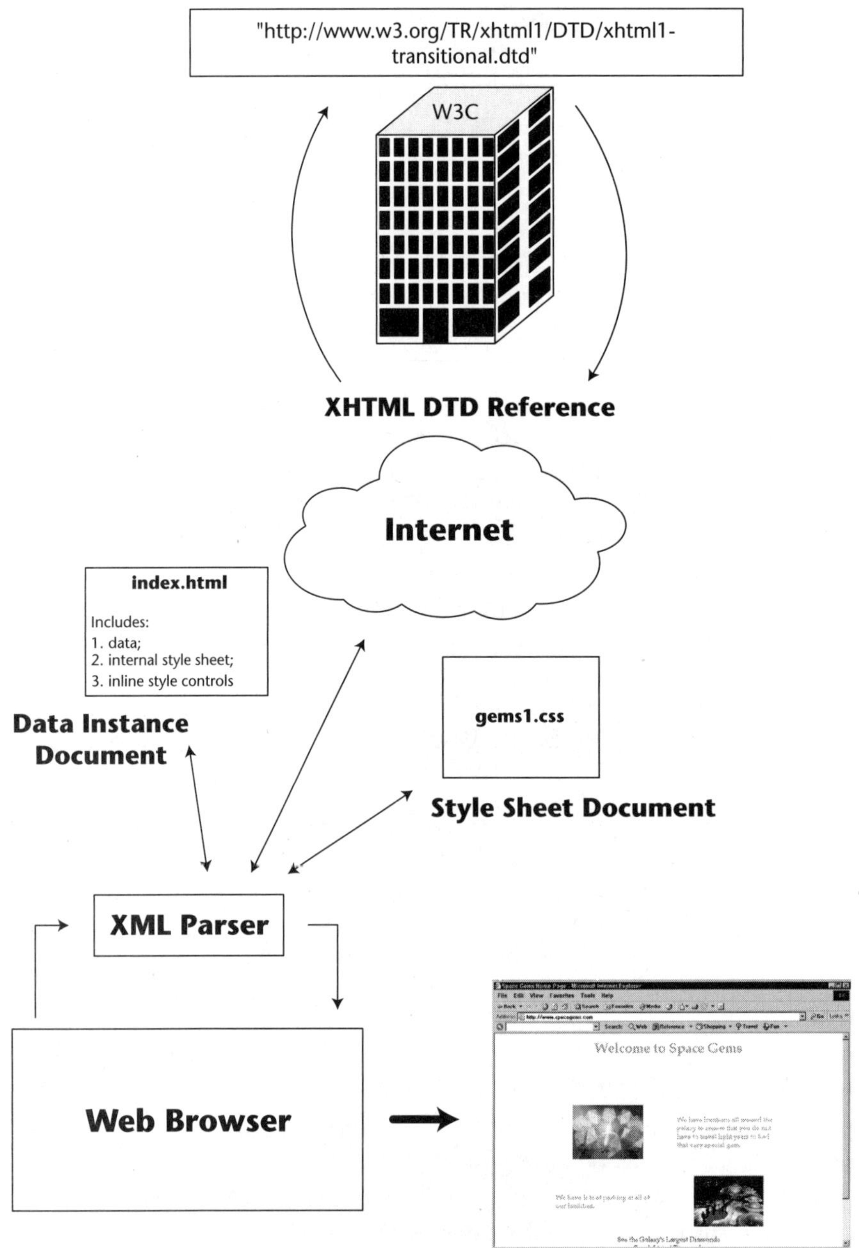

Figure 7.1 A browser processes the Space Gems XHTML home page.

Creating CSS Style Rules

Before applying styles to the elements in an XML document, it is important that we review some style rule design concepts. We will use three simple documents, depicted in Figure 7.2, to introduce and illustrate the style rules in this chapter:

- An XML document file named gems1.xml
- A DTD document named diamonds1.dtd
- An external CSS document named gems1.css

In this chapter, when each new style concept or technique is introduced, it is always applied to the *original* data and style sheet files to minimize the risk of confusion that might result if we started to combine the various techniques. However, after you are familiar with them, feel free to combine them to meet your needs.

Basic Style Rule Syntax

From the CSS file in Figure 7.2, you can see that CSS documents differ from XML documents. Comment lines at the beginning of the document use /*...*/ format, followed by, in this case, five CSS style rules. From their syntax, you can surmise that style rules require special but consistent notation. Here is an example, which illustrates typical style rule syntax:

```
gem {display: block; text-align: left}
```

A style rule has two major components: the selector (in this example, the element name *gem*) and the declaration (that is, the {display: ... left} component). Each declaration is made up of one or more properties, which are composed of name:value pairs. For example, in the first pair, display is the name of the property being specified and block is the value specified for display.

Selectors

The style rule selector lists one or more elements for which the properties in the declaration are specified. Any element names in an XML document can be used as selectors individually or as part of a selector group. For example, the elements <carat>, <color>, <clarity>, <cut>, and <cost> form a selector group in this next example:

```
carat,color,clarity,cut,cost {display: list-item; list-style: disc inside;
            font-size: 10pt; list-style-type: disc; text-indent: 50 }
```

```xml
<?xml version = "1.0" encoding = "UTF-8"?>
<!DOCTYPE diamonds SYSTEM "http://localhost/spacegems/diamonds1.dtd">
<?xml-stylesheet type ="text/css" href ="http://localhost/SpaceGems/gems1.css" ?>
<!-- filename:gems1.xml -->
<diamonds>
        <info>
                Space Gems, Inc.
                <link type="simple" href="http://localhost/SpaceGems"
                        OnClick="location.href='http://localhost/SpaceGems' ">
                        Home
                </link>
        </info>
        <gem>
                <name>Cullinan</name>
                <carat>3106</carat>
                <color>H</color>
                <clarity>VS1,VS2-Very Slightly Imperfect</clarity>
                <cut>Rough</cut>
                <cost>2174200</cost>
        </gem>
        <gem>
                <name>Dark</name>
                <carat>500</carat>
                <color>J</color>
                <clarity>SL1,SL2-Slightly Imperfect</clarity>
                <cut>Rough</cut>
                <cost>450000</cost>
        </gem>
</diamonds>
```

gems1.xml

```css
/* Chapter 7, XML & Cascading Style Sheets - Example Style Sheet */
/* filename:gems1.css */
diamonds        {font-family: Arial,Helvetica,Sans-serif; font-size: 12pt; }
gem             {display: block; text-align: left;}
name            {display: block; font-weight: bold;}
carat,color,clarity,cut,cost
                {display: list-item; list-style: disc inside; font-size: 10pt;
                                list-style-type: disc; text-indent: 50; }
link            {display: inline; color: #0000FF; text-decoration: underline;
                                cursor: hand; }
```

gems1.css

```
<?xml version='1.0' encoding='UTF-8' ?>
<!-- filename:diamonds1.dtd -->
<!ELEMENT    diamonds    (info?,gem+)>
<!ELEMENT    info        (#PCDATA | link)*>
<!ELEMENT    link         (#PCDATA)>
<!ATTLIST    link
            type          CDATA    #REQUIRED
            href          CDATA    #REQUIRED
            OnClick       CDATA    #REQUIRED >
<!ELEMENT    gem         (name , carat , color , clarity , cut , cost)>
<!ELEMENT    name         (#PCDATA)>
<!ELEMENT    carat        (#PCDATA)>
<!ELEMENT    color        (#PCDATA)>
<!ELEMENT    clarity      (#PCDATA)>
<!ELEMENT    cut          (#PCDATA)>
<!ELEMENT    cost         (#PCDATA)>
```

diamonds1.dtd

Figure 7.2 Sample XML, DTD, and CSS documents.

If a selector group is specified, the element type names within it must be delimited by commas. If we reexamine Figure 7.2, we see that the combination of all the selectors provides style rules for most if not all of the element types in the gems1.xml XML document.

Classroom Q & A

Q: In Figure 7.2, the <info> element is missing. Is this an oversight, or a typo?

A: Every element name does not have to be explicitly listed, but the name of the missing element's parent element probably appears. In the case of Figure 7.2, for example, the <diamonds> element, parent to the <info> element, *is* listed. Thus, style rules observe *inheritance*: a child element inherits the style rules specified for its parent elements unless a specific rule is created for the child.

Declarations

A declaration is the second major component of a style rule and contains at least one property. Each property, in turn, consists of one name:value pair. If there are two or more properties in a declaration, we use semi-colons to delimit them.

Presently over 100 properties are available for use with the CSS language. As CSS continues to develop, more properties are periodically added to the list, which appears as Appendix F of the CSS2 Recommendation. The properties that are available at this writing are listed in Table 7.1. Table 7.1 does not provide descriptions of each property; doing so would make it prohibitively long, although you can probably guess many of the meanings. Because the list of properties changes fairly frequently, if you are creating or modifying style sheets, we suggest that you visit the W3C's CSS Web site at www.w3.org/TR/REC-CSS2/propidx.html to find the latest information on all the properties that are currently available. Meanwhile, several of the more prominent properties are discussed in this chapter.

Displaying Inline versus Block Elements

In Table 7.1, under the Classification properties, there is a property called *display*. When creating style rules, we need to understand display and its two values, block and inline.

Table 7.1 Cascading Style Sheet Properties

CATEGORY	PROPERTY NAME		
Aural presentation properties	azimuth	cue	cue-after
	cue-before	elevation	pause
	pause-after	pause-before	pitch
	pitch-range	play-during	richness
	speak	speak-numeral	speak-punctuation
	speech-rate	stress	volume
Background properties	background	background-attachment	background-color
	background-image	background-position	background-repeat
Box properties	border	border-bottom	border-bottom-color
	border-bottom-style	border-bottom-width	border-color
	border-left	border-left-color	border-left-style
	border-left-width	border-right	border-right-color
	border-right-style	border-right-width	border-style
	border-top	border-top-color	border-top-style
	border-top-width	border-width	margin
	margin-bottom	margin-left	margin-right
	margin-top	padding	padding-bottom
	padding-left	padding-right	padding-top
Classification properties	clear	display	float
Element dimension properties	height	line-height	max-height
	max-width	min-height	min-width
	width		
Element shape and position properties	bottom	left	position
	right	top	vertical-align
	z-index		
Font properties	font	font-family	font-size
	font-size-adjust	font-stretch	font-style
	font-variant	font-weight	
Generated content, numbering and list properties	content	counter-increment	counter-reset
	list-style	list-style-image	list-style-position
	list-style-type	marker-offset	quotes
Paged media properties	marks	orphans	page
	page-break-after	page-break-before	page-break-inside
	size	widows	
Table properties	border-collapse	border-spacing	caption-side
	empty-cells	speak-header	table-layout

Table 7.1 *(continued)*

CATEGORY	PROPERTY NAME		
Text properties	color line-height text-indent unicode-bidi word-spacing	direction text-align text-shadow vertical-align	letter-spacing text-decoration text-transform white-space
User interface properties	cursor outline-style	outline outline-width	outline-color
Visual effects properties	clip	overflow	visibility

In the gems1.css document in Figure 7.2, the style rule for the element <name> states that the value for the element's display property is block. That means that the <name> element does not start on the same line as the previous element; it starts on a new line. After the <name> element is finished, the next element (<carat>) starts on its own new line. Thus, the element <name> has its own display block. Elements such as <name> are referred to as *block-level elements*.

By contrast, the display value for the element <link> is inline. That means that there is no line break before the <link> is encountered. If we examine Figure 7.2 again, we see that <link> is nested within the <info> element and is actually included within the phrase Space Gems, Inc. Home.

The <link> element, and any others that do not have their own display blocks and have style rules that say inline, are called *inline-level elements*. These block-versus-inline display values are for XML, especially. HTML has default display property values for predefined HTML elements. (For example, the HTML element <H1> is automatically deemed to be a display: block). But there can't be default values prescribed for many XML elements, because those elements are usually given unique and arbitrary names and declarations by the language or document authors. Thus, for all XML-related languages, including XHTML, the parser must be explicitly told how to display the elements, right down to block versus inline. And the style rules are the places for that information.

Selectors with Pseudo-Elements

So far, we have based our style selectors on individual elements or groups of elements. Most of the time, that approach is fine. But sometimes we like to add special style features that an element type-based selector doesn't have the flexibility for. For example, there isn't an element that refers to the first line of text in an element type, or to its first letter. So there is no simple CSS selector we can use to single those out for special treatment.

That's why the CSS developers introduced pseudo-elements and pseudo-classes. They permit style controls based on information that lies outside the document tree—that is, on information other than element names, attributes, or content. As we'll see in the upcoming example, the :before and :after pseudo-elements give access to generated content that doesn't exist in the source document.

First, let's look at pseudo-elements. Pseudo-elements are added to style sheets to add specific effects to selectors or parts of selectors. Here is the generic syntax for defining pseudo-elements:

```
selectorname:pseudo-elementname
            {propertyname1: value ... propertynamen: value}
```

Several pseudo-elements can be combined in one style rule. Table 7.2 lists the pseudo-elements presently available in the CSS language. Pseudo-elements and pseudo-class names are case-insensitive. An example follows.

1. In the original gems1.css style sheet document, no style rules were explicitly specified for the <info> element. To modify the appearance of the text in that element, insert the following code into that style sheet file:

   ```
   info {font-size: 12pt}
   info:first-line {color: #00FF00}
   info:first-letter {color: #FF0000; font-size: 300%}
   info:before { content: open-quote; color: black }
   info:after { content: close-quote; color: black }
   ```

2. Now the normal font size of the text in the <info> element will be 12 points. The first-line pseudo-element specifies that the first line is green, but the first-letter pseudo-element specifies that the first letter of that first line is red and three times the size of the normal 12-point font.

3. The last two rules, which contain the before and after pseudo-elements, instruct the parser to place black quotation marks around the text in the <info> element.

4. Figure 7.3 illustrates what gems1.css might look like after this code is inserted.

Table 7.2 Available Pseudo-Elements

PSEUDO-ELEMENT NAME	EXPLANATION
first-line	Adds a special style to the first line of text in a selector. The size of the browser window determines the extent of the first line. Used with block-level elements only.
first-letter	Adds a special style to the first letter of the text in a selector. Used with block-level elements only.

Table 7.2 *(continued)*

PSEUDO-ELEMENT NAME	EXPLANATION
before	Specifies the location of specific display-related content that is to be displayed before an element's actual data-related content. Must be used with the content property, whose value will be the content to be inserted.
after	Specifies the location of specific, display-related content that is to be displayed after an element's actual data-related content. Must also be used with the content property, whose value will be the content to be inserted.

```
/* Chapter 7, XML & Cascading Style Sheets - Example Style Sheet */
/* filename:gems1.css */
diamonds        {font-family: Arial,Helvetica,Sans-serif; font-size: 12pt }
gem             {display: block; text-align: left}
name            {display: block; font-weight: bold}
carat,color,clarity,cut,cost
                {display: list-item; list-style: disc inside; font-size: 10pt;
                                        list-style-type: disc; text-indent: 50 }
link            {display: inline; color: #0000FF; text-decoration: underline;
                                        cursor: hand }
```

```
/* Chapter 7, XML & Cascading Style Sheets - Example Style Sheet */
/* filename:gems1.css */
diamonds            {font-family: Arial,Helvetica,Sans-serif; font-size: 12pt }
gem                 {display: block; text-align: left}
name                {display: block; font-weight: bold}
carat,color,clarity,cut,cost
                    {display: list-item; list-style: disc inside; font-size:
                              10pt; list-style-type: disc; text-indent: 50 }
link                {display: inline; color: #0000FF;
                              text-decoration: underline; cursor: hand }
info                { font-size: 12pt}
info:first-line     { color: #00FF00}
info:first-letter   { color: #FF0000; font-size: 300%}
info:before         { content: open-quote; color: black }
info:after          { content: close-quote; color: black }
```

Figure 7.3 Pseudo-elements: gems1.css before and after.

Grouping Selectors by Classes

The original gems1.css style sheet document had the following selector group:

```
carat,color,clarity,cut,cost {display: list-item;
            list-style: disc inside; font-size: 10pt;
            list-style-type: disc; text-indent: 50 }
```

The selector group indicates that we have several elements to display with the same property name:value pairs. As an alternative to the selector group, we can create a selector class within the style sheet file that contains the specified property name:value pairs. Then, in the gems1.xml document, we can assign the individual elements to the class by inserting the appropriate attribute specification into the element's start tag. Here is the generic syntax for defining the selector class:

```
.nameOfClass {nameOfProperty_01: value ... nameOfProperty_n: value}
```

Then, in the actual XML document, we have to assign the element types to the class we just created, by inserting the appropriate CLASS="..." attribute specification, which must be called CLASS, into the respective element's start tag. The value for the CLASS attribute will be the name of the class we created in the CSS document.

It is important to include the period (.) at the beginning of the name of the selector class.

This example treats the 5C's in a consistent manner. Here are the basic steps for creating and using a selector class:

1. Start within the style sheet document gems1.css. Remove the carat, color,clarity,cut,cost group selector and replace it with the following class definition:

   ```
   five_Cs {{display: list-item; list-style: disc inside;
           font-size: 10pt; list-style-type: disc; text-indent: 50; }}
   ```

   The gems1.css document should resemble the modified document in Figure 7.4.

2. Apply the new class definition to the selected elements, by going to their XML documents and inserting the attribute that refers to the class definition. Following the example, go to the gems1.xml document and modify several elements as follows:

   ```
   <carat CLASS="five_Cs">3106</carat>
   <color CLASS="five_Cs">H</color>
   <clarity CLASS="five_Cs">VS1,VS2-Very Slightly Imperfect</clarity>
   <cut CLASS="five_Cs">Rough</cut>
   <cost CLASS="five_Cs">2174200</cost>
   ```

and

```
<carat CLASS="five_Cs">500</carat>
<color CLASS="five_Cs">J</color>
<clarity CLASS="five_Cs">SL1,SL2-Slightly Imperfect</clarity>
<cut CLASS="five_Cs">Rough</cut>
<cost CLASS="five_Cs">450000</cost>
```

3. Finally, to ensure that the gems1.document file is valid, we have to declare the new CLASS attribute in the appropriate DTD or schema. For this example, we go to the diamonds1.dtd file and insert the following declarations:

```
<!ATTLIST carat     CLASS CDATA #IMPLIED >
<!ATTLIST color     CLASS CDATA #IMPLIED >
<!ATTLIST clarity   CLASS CDATA #IMPLIED >
<!ATTLIST cut       CLASS CDATA #IMPLIED >
<!ATTLIST cost      CLASS CDATA #IMPLIED >
```

```
/* Chapter 7, XML & Cascading Style Sheets - Example Style Sheet */
/* filename:gems1.css */
diamonds        {font-family: Arial,Helvetica,Sans-serif; font-size: 12pt }
gem             {display: block; text-align: left}
name            {display: block; font-weight: bold}
carat,color,clarity,cut,cost
                {display: list-item; list-style: disc inside; font-size: 10pt;
                                        list-style-type: disc; text-indent: 50 }
link            {display: inline; color: #0000FF; text-decoration: underline;
                                        cursor: hand }
```

```
/* Chapter 7, XML & Cascading Style Sheets - Example Style Sheet */
/* filename:gems1.css */
diamonds        {font-family: Arial,Helvetica,Sans-serif; font-size: 12pt }
gem             {display: block; text-align: left}
name            {display: block; font-weight: bold}
.five_Cs        {display: list-item; list-style: disc inside;
                        font-size: 10pt; list-style-type: disc;
                                text-indent: 50 }
link            {display: inline; color: #0000FF; text-decoration: underline;
                                        cursor: hand }
```

Figure 7.4 Selector class: gems1.css before and after.

So far, the five_Cs class selector we created in the gems1.css style sheet document could be applied to any element in the gems1.xml document. All we have to do is select an element and insert the CLASS="..." attribute specification in its start tag. As a variation on class selectors, we could create a class that applies to only specified elements. Here is the generic syntax that we would insert into the CSS file:

```
elementname.classname {propertyname1: value ... propertynamen: value}
```

Previously, placing the period (.) at the beginning of the name of the selector class made it possible to apply the class to all elements. Here, placing a period between a specific element name and the class name ensures that the class will apply to only that element.

Let's look at an example. In the small Space Gems diamond list, let's say that we want to modify the appearance of the names of the gems (that is, Cullinan and Dark) so that, even though they keep their existing display style, they appear gold on a magenta background. Follow these steps:

1. Start with the original gems1.css style sheet document. In addition to the existing <name> element selector, add another selector with the following class definition:

   ```
   name.royal_emph {display: block; font-weight: bold;
           text-align: center; color: gold; background-color: magenta}
   ```

   The resulting style sheet document should resemble the modified gems1.css document in Figure 7.5.

2. To apply the class definition to the names of the diamonds, go to the gems1.xml file and modify the name elements as follows:

   ```
   <name CLASS="royal.emph">Cullinan</name>
   <name CLASS="royal.emph">Dark</name>
   ```

3. Finally, to ensure that the gems1.xml document is valid, declare the new CLASS attribute in the diamonds1.dtd DTD document. Insert the following attribute declaration into that document:

   ```
   <!ATTLIST name CLASS CDATA #IMPLIED >
   ```

Grouping Selectors by Pseudo-Classes

Like pseudo-elements, pseudo-classes classify elements on characteristics that cannot be deduced from the document tree; pseudo-classes, like pseudo-elements, don't appear in the logical data structure of a document. The exception is :first-child, which can be deduced from the document tree. As we demonstrate in this section, pseudo-classes can be dynamic; they can acquire or lose a style even as a user interacts with the data.

Pseudo-classes enable us to customize selectors. Following is the generic syntax for defining pseudo-classes. (Note that pseudo-class names are *not* case-sensitive.)

```
selectorname:pseudo-classname
            {propertyname1: value ... propertynamen: value}
```

Pseudo-classes are allowed anywhere in selectors, whereas pseudo-elements may only appear after the subject of the selector. Table 7.3 lists and explains the pseudo-classes available with the CSS language. Like pseudo-elements, pseudo-classes are case-insensitive.

```
/* Chapter 7, XML & Cascading Style Sheets - Example Style Sheet */
/* filename:gems1.css */
diamonds        {font-family: Arial,Helvetica,Sans-serif; font-size: 12pt }
gem             {display: block; text-align: left}
name            {display: block; font-weight: bold}
carat,color,clarity,cut,cost
                {display: list-item; list-style: disc inside; font-size: 10pt;
                              list-style-type: disc; text-indent: 50 }
link            {display: inline; color: #0000FF; text-decoration: underline;
                              cursor: hand }
```

```
/* Chapter 7, XML & Cascading Style Sheets - Example Style Sheet */
/* filename:gems1.css */
diamonds        {font-family: Arial,Helvetica,Sans-serif; font-size: 12pt }
gem             {display: block; text-align: left}
name            {display: block; font-weight: bold}
name.royal_emph
                {display: block; font-weight: bold; text-align: center;
                        color: gold; background-color: magenta}
carat,color,clarity,cut,cost
                {display: list-item; list-style: disc inside; font-size:
                        10pt; list-style-type: disc; text-indent: 50 }
link            {display: inline; color: #0000FF; text-decoration: underline;
                              cursor: hand }
```

Figure 7.5 Selector class: gems1.css before and after.

Table 7.3 Available Pseudo-Classes

PSEUDO-CLASS	EXPLANATION
active	Adds a specified style to a selected hyperlink.
hover	Adds a specified style to a hyperlink when the mouse pointer is placed over it.
focus	Adds a specified style while an element has the focus (that is, while it is accepting keyboard or other forms of text input).
link	Adds a specified style to an unvisited hyperlink.
visited	Adds a specified style to an already visited hyperlink.
first-child	Adds a specified style to an element that is the first child element of a specified parent element.
lang	Enables the author to specify a language to be used in a specified element.

A common use for pseudo-classes is changing the hyperlink color depending on its status, for example, after it has been clicked. The list of gems in gems1.xml includes a link to the Space Gems home page on the Web. The following procedure demonstrates how we can change its color:

1. Modify the gems1.css style sheet document by altering the <link> element style rule declaration to

   ```
   link {display: inline; text-decoration: underline; cursor: hand}
   ```

2. Beneath the declaration, insert

   ```
   link:link {color: #00FF00}    /* hyperlink is green until selected */
   link:hover {color: #FF0000}   /* hyperlink turns red when the mouse
                                  pointer is moved over it */
   LINK:visited {color: #FFFFFF}  /* visited hyperlink turns black */
   ```

   These changes are illustrated in the modified document in Figure 7.6.

Combining Pseudo-Classes with Other CSS Classes

We can combine pseudo-classes with other CSS classes. The generic syntax is as follows:

```
elementname.classname:pseudo-class {propertynames: values ... }
```

Placing a period between the element name and the class name ensures that the combination class/pseudo-class applies to only that element.

```
/* Chapter 7, XML & Cascading Style Sheets - Example Style Sheet */
/* filename:gems1.css */
diamonds        {font-family: Arial,Helvetica,Sans-serif; font-size: 12pt }
gem             {display: block; text-align: left}
name            {display: block; font-weight: bold}
carat,color,clarity,cut,cost
                {display: list-item; list-style: disc inside; font-size: 10pt;
                                list-style-type: disc; text-indent: 50 }
link            {display: inline; color: #0000FF; text-decoration: underline;
                                cursor: hand }
```

↓

```
/* Chapter 7, XML & Cascading Style Sheets - Example Style Sheet */
/* filename:gems1.css */
diamonds        {font-family: Arial,Helvetica,Sans-serif; font-size: 12pt }
gem             {display: block; text-align: left}
name            {display: block; font-weight: bold}
carat,color,clarity,cut,cost
                {display: list-item; list-style: disc inside; font-size: 10pt;
                        list-style-type: disc; text-indent: 50 }
link            {display: inline; text-decoration: underline; cursor: hand}
link:link       {color: #00FF00}  /* hyperlink is green until selected */
link:hover      {color: #FF0000}  /* hyperlink turns red when the mouse
                                     pointer is moved over it */
link:visited    {color: #FFFFFF}  /* visited hyperlink turns black */
```

Figure 7.6 Pseudo-classes: gems1.css before and after.

Combining classes and pseudo-classes can save steps. Consider, for example, a document with many links. We can design the document so that we change the visited status property for all the links at one time without having to access individual data documents.

Let's create a pseudo-class called VISITED in the style sheet document and specify an appropriate attribute in each hyperlink element start tag in the data document. That attribute ensures that the <link> element observes the modified VISITED display behavior:

1. In the gems1.css file, in addition to the existing link selector, add another selector with the following combined pseudo-class/class definition:

   ```
   link.VISITED:visited {color: #FFD700; background-color: black}
   ```

   The modified gems1.css document in Figure 7.7 illustrates this addition.

```
/* Chapter 7, XML & Cascading Style Sheets - Example Style Sheet */
/* filename:gems1.css */
diamonds          {font-family: Arial,Helvetica,Sans-serif; font-size: 12pt }
gem               {display: block; text-align: left}
name              {display: block; font-weight: bold}
carat,color,clarity,cut,cost
                  {display: list-item; list-style: disc inside; font-size: 10pt;
                                    list-style-type: disc; text-indent: 50 }
link              {display: inline; color: #0000FF; text-decoration: underline;
                                    cursor: hand }
```

↓

```
/* Chapter 7, XML & Cascading Style Sheets - Example Style Sheet */
/* filename:gems1.css */
diamonds          {font-family: Arial,Helvetica,Sans-serif; font-size: 12pt }
gem               {display: block; text-align: left}
name              {display: block; font-weight: bold}
carat,color,clarity,cut,cost
                  {display: list-item; list-style: disc inside; font-size: 10pt;
                          list-style-type: disc; text-indent: 50 }
link              {display: inline; color: #0000FF; text-decoration: underline;
                                          cursor: hand }
link.VISITED:visited {color: #FFD700; background-color: black}
```

Figure 7.7 Classes combined with pseudo-classes: gems1.css before and after.

Here, the class name is VISITED and the pseudo-class name used is also visited. After the hyperlink has been used, its color turns gold (#FFD7000).

2. Now let's apply the new class definition to the hyperlink. In the gems1.xml document, we'll modify the <link> element to read as follows:

```
<link CLASS="VISITED" xml:type="simple"
        href="http://localhost/SpaceGems"
        onClick="location.href='http://localhost/SpaceGems'">
        home page
</link>
```

3. Finally, to ensure that the gems1.xml document will still be valid, we declare the new CLASS attribute for the element <link> in the diamonds1.dtd DTD document. Insert the following into that document:

```
<!ATTLIST link CLASS CDATA #IMPLIED >
```

After making this change, if we want to change the visited status color on any element with the CLASS=VISITED attribute in its start tag again, we have to alter only the color code in the gems1.css document. We won't have to visit the individual documents, as long as they remain affiliated with the gems1.css document.

Grouping Selectors by the ID Attribute

You may have seen the ID (or the XHTML/XML version referred to as id) attribute before. Properly used, id can be helpful to XML developers in many situations. Following is the general syntax for changing the display style for a specific element:

```
elementname#IDvalue {propertyname1: value ... propertynamen: value}
```

Let's change the color of the font and the background for the name of the first diamond (Cullinan) in the gems1.xml document. Here is how to do it:

1. In the original gems1.css document, alter the existing <name> element style rule to:

   ```
   name {display: block; text-align: center}
   ```

2. Then add the following new rule:

   ```
   name#first {color: black; background-color: yellow}
   ```

   The change and addition are shown in the modified gems1.css document in Figure 7.8.

3. Apply the new id attribute to the first diamond. Go to the original gems1.xml document and modify the first <name> element to read as follows:

   ```
   <diamonds>
           <name id="first">Cullinan</name>
           ...
   ```

4. To ensure that the gems1.xml document will still be valid, we declare the new CLASS attribute for the element <name> in the diamonds.dtd DTD document. Insert the following into that document:

   ```
   <!ATTLIST name id CDATA #IMPLIED >
   ```

```
/* Chapter 7, XML & Cascading Style Sheets - Example Style Sheet */
/* filename:gems1.css */
diamonds        {font-family: Arial,Helvetica,Sans-serif; font-size: 12pt }
gem             {display: block; text-align: left}
name            {display: block; font-weight: bold}
carat,color,clarity,cut,cost
                {display: list-item; list-style: disc inside; font-size: 10pt;
                              list-style-type: disc; text-indent: 50 }
link            {display: inline; color: #0000FF; text-decoration: underline;
                              cursor: hand }
```

```
/* Chapter 7, XML & Cascading Style Sheets - Example Style Sheet */
/* filename:gems1.css */
diamonds        {font-family: Arial,Helvetica,Sans-serif; font-size: 12pt }
gem             {display: block; text-align: left}
name            {display: block; text-align: center}
name#first      {color: black; background-color: yellow}
carat,color,clarity,cut,cost
                {display: list-item; list-style: disc inside; font-size: 10pt;
                        list-style-type: disc; text-indent: 50 }
link            {display: inline; color: #0000FF; text-decoration: underline;
                              cursor: hand }
```

Figure 7.8 id attribute selector: gems1.css before and after.

Inserting Images as Backgrounds

Page developers sometimes insert images as backgrounds to text and other elements, or as discrete elements on their own. We'll look at both techniques here.

Here is the generic syntax for inserting a background image style rule into a CSS style document:

```
nameOfElement {imagePropertyName_01: value ... imagePropertyName_n:
value }
```

We can specify that the image appear behind the root element or behind individual elements. Table 7.4 lists the available image property names and their values; their names alone were listed previously in Table 7.1.

Table 7.4 Available Image Property Names

IMAGE PROPERTY NAME	EXPLANATION
background	A shorthand property for setting the individual background properties (background-color, background-image, background-repeat, background-attachment and/or background-position) in the same declaration in the style sheet.
background-attachment	Values may be fixed or scroll. The background image stays in the same place, or scrolls as the end user scrolls through the document.
background-color	Sets the background color of an element. Values are a color value or the keyword transparent, which lets the underlying colors shine through.
background-image	Specifies the background image of an element. Value is the URI of the image or none. When specifying a background image, specify a background color that will be used if and when the image is unavailable. When the image is available, it is rendered on top of the background color. The color is visible in the transparent parts of the image.
background-position	Specifies the initial position of the image, if it is used. Values are x and y coordinates in percentages (0 %, 100 %, and so on) to specify the location of the image's upper left corner.
background-repeat	Specifies whether an image, if specified, is repeated (also called tiled), and how. Values are repeat, no-repeat, repeat-x (repeat in the horizontal direction), or repeat-y (repeat in the vertical direction).

If we want to insert a background logo indicating that the Web page is in compliance with CSS1 and CSS2 standards, in the gems1.xml page, we add the following to the gems1.css style sheet document:

```
diamonds {font-family: Arial,Helvetica,sans-serif;
          font-size: 12pt; background-image: url (diam_logo_02.tif);
          background-repeat: no-repeat; background-position: 0% 0% }
```

The modified gems1.css document in Figure 7.9 illustrates these modifications.

```
/* Chapter 7, XML & Cascading Style Sheets - Example Style Sheet */
/* filename:gems1.css */
diamonds        {font-family: Arial,Helvetica,Sans-serif; font-size: 12pt }
gem             {display: block; text-align: left}
name            {display: block; font-weight: bold}
carat,color,clarity,cut,cost
                {display: list-item; list-style: disc inside; font-size: 10pt;
                                     list-style-type: disc; text-indent: 50 }
link            {display: inline; color: #0000FF; text-decoration: underline;
                                     cursor: hand }
```

```
/* Chapter 7, XML & Cascading Style Sheets - Example Style Sheet */
/* filename:gems1.css */
diamonds        {font-family: Arial,Helvetica,sans-serif; font-size: 12pt;
                      background-image: url(diam_logo_02.tif);
                           background-repeat: no-repeat;
                                background-position: 0% 0% }
gem             {display: block; text-align: left}
name            {display: block; font-weight: bold}
carat,color,clarity,cut,cost
                {display: list-item; list-style: disc inside; font-size: 10pt;
                         list-style-type: disc; text-indent: 50 }
link            {display: inline; color: #0000FF;
                         text-decoration: underline; cursor: hand }
```

Figure 7.9 Images as background: gems1.css before and after.

Inserting Images as Discrete Elements

If we want to insert an image by itself, we create a dedicated element for it in the XML document. In the style sheet document, we specify the image as the background to that dedicated element. Because we are building another background image, the syntax we use in the style sheet document is the same as in the previous example. Here is an example of the procedure:

1. To add a discrete image to the list of diamonds, begin by nesting a <diam_pix01> element within the <diamonds> element in the gems1.xml document:

```
<diamonds>
     <diam_pix01> </diam_pix01>
     <gem>
```

```
            <name>Cullinan</name>
            ....
        </gem>
    </diamonds>
```

2. We alter the gems1.css document by adding the following style rule:

```
diam_pix01 {background: url (diam_logo_01.tif) no-repeat 0% 0%;
            height: 50 px; width: 100 px; float: left}
```

This change is illustrated in the modified gems1.css document in Figure 7.10.

We deliberately changed the image syntax in the discrete element example. The syntax is a shorthand treatment that is permissible, provided the values are entered in that order only.

```
/* Chapter 7, XML & Cascading Style Sheets - Example Style Sheet */
/* filename:gems1.css */
diamonds        {font-family: Arial,Helvetica,Sans-serif; font-size: 12pt }
gem             {display: block; text-align: left}
name            {display: block; font-weight: bold}
carat,color,clarity,cut,cost
                {display: list-item; list-style: disc inside; font-size: 10pt;
                                list-style-type: disc; text-indent: 50 }
link            {display: inline; color: #0000FF; text-decoration: underline;
                                cursor: hand }
```

↓

```
/* Chapter 7, XML & Cascading Style Sheets - Example Style Sheet */
/* filename:gems1.css */
diamonds        {font-family: Arial,Helvetica,sans-serif; font-size: 12pt}
diam_pix01      {background: url (diam_logo_01.tif) no-repeat 0% 0%;
                        height: 50 px; width: 100 px; float: left}
gem             {display: block; text-align: left}
name            {display: block; font-weight: bold}
carat,color,clarity,cut,cost
                {display: list-item; list-style: disc inside; font-size: 10pt;
                        list-style-type: disc; text-indent: 50 }
link            {display: inline; color: #0000FF;
                        text-decoration: underline; cursor: hand }
```

Figure 7.10 Images as elements: gems1.css before and after.

Drawing Borders around Elements

To draw borders around elements, we simply add one or more of the border-related properties listed under the Box properties category in Table 7.1. To see descriptions for the Box properties in Table 7.1, check the W3C's latest descriptions and syntax for all CSS properties by going to www.w3.org/TR/REC-CSS2/ and clicking the Properties link.

Let's draw a red border (horizontal lines will be solid; vertical lines will be dashed) with varying thickness around each of the <cost> elements in the gems1.xml document. The only coding necessary is the modification of the cost style rule in the gems1.css file:

```
cost {display: block; font-weight: bold; text-align: left;
        border-color: red; border-style: solid dashed;
        border-top-width: 10 px; border-bottom-width: 15 px;
        border-left-width: 5 px; border-right-width: 5 px }
```

These additions are depicted in the modified gems1.css file in Figure 7.11.

```
/* Chapter 7, XML & Cascading Style Sheets - Example Style Sheet */
/* filename:gems1.css */
diamonds        {font-family: Arial,Helvetica,Sans-serif; font-size: 12pt }
gem             {display: block; text-align: left}
name            {display: block; font-weight: bold}
carat,color,clarity,cut,cost
                {display: list-item; list-style: disc inside; font-size: 10pt;
                                list-style-type: disc; text-indent: 50 }
link            {display: inline; color: #0000FF; text-decoration: underline;
                                cursor: hand }
```

↓

```
/* Chapter 7, XML & Cascading Style Sheets - Example Style Sheet */
/* filename:gems1.css */
diamonds        {font-family: Arial,Helvetica,sans-serif; font-size: 12pt}
gem             {display: block; text-align: left}
name            {display: block; font-weight: bold}
carat,color,clarity,cut
                {display: list-item; list-style: disc inside; font-size: 10pt;
                        list-style-type: disc; text-indent: 50 }
cost            {display: block; font-weight: bold; text-align: left;
                        border-color: red; border-style: solid dashed;
                        border-top-width: 10 px; border-bottom-width: 5 px;
                        border-left-width: 15 px; border-right-width: 15 px }
link            {display: inline; color: #0000FF;
                        text-decoration: underline; cursor: hand }
```

Figure 7.11 Drawing borders: gems1.css before and after.

Text Alignment, Margins, and Indentations

Text alignment, margins, and indents are common specifications to Web designers. They involve the properties listed under the Text Properties and Box Properties categories in Table 7.1. We've already seen them in the gems1.css style sheet document. Note the following example:

1. The <name> elements are already center-aligned. Make them align to the left margin by modifying the name style rule in gems1.css:

   ```
   name {display: block; font-weight: bold; text-align: left}
   ```

2. Now increase the margins for the <carat>, <color>, <clarity>, <cut>, and <cost> elements to 0.5 centimeter by making the following modification to their original selector group style rule:

   ```
   carat,color,clarity,cut,cost {display: list-item;
             list-style: disc inside; font-size: 10pt;
             list-style-type: disc; margin: 0.5cm }
   ```

3. Finally, we insert a 25-pixel indentation to the Space Gems home page link by modifying the original link style rule to look like this:

   ```
   link {display: inline; color: #0000FF; text-decoration: underline;
             text-indent: 25px; cursor: hand}
   ```

   These changes are all shown in the modified gems1.css file in Figure 7.12.

Absolute and Relative Positioning

Absolute positioning means telling the parser to place an element type at a specific location within the browser window display. *Relative positioning* tells the parser to place element types relative to their normal position in the flow of elements and/or text. We can use the Element shape and position properties from Table 7.1 to position element types.

Example: Absolute Positioning

To illustrate absolute positioning, let's revisit the previous image display example.

1. Again, start with the original gems1.xml document and insert the <diam_pix01> image element:

   ```
   <diamonds>
        <diam_pix01> </diam_pix01>
        <gem>
             <name>Cullinan
             ....
        </gem>
   </diamonds>
   ```

```
/* Chapter 7, XML & Cascading Style Sheets - Example Style Sheet */
/* filename:gems1.css */
diamonds        {font-family: Arial,Helvetica,Sans-serif; font-size: 12pt }
gem             {display: block; text-align: left}
name            {display: block; font-weight: bold}
carat,color,clarity,cut,cost
                {display: list-item; list-style: disc inside; font-size: 10pt;
                                list-style-type: disc; text-indent: 50 }
link            {display: inline; color: #0000FF; text-decoration: underline;
                                cursor: hand }
```

↓

```
/* Chapter 7, XML & Cascading Style Sheets - Example Style Sheet */
/* filename:gems1.css */
diamonds        {font-family: Arial,Helvetica,Sans-serif; font-size: 12pt }
gem             {display: block; text-align: left}
name            {display: block; font-weight: bold; text-align: left}
carat,color,clarity,cut,cost
                {display: list-item; list-style: disc inside;
                        font-size: 10pt; list-style-type: disc;
                                margin: 0.5cm }
link            {display: inline; color: #0000FF;
                        text-decoration: underline; text-indent: 25px;
                                cursor: hand}
```

Figure 7.12 Alignment, margins, and indentations: gems1.css before and after.

2. Modify the gems1.css style sheet to provide an absolute location within the browser window display for the diamond logo image. To do so, add the following style rule:

```
diam_pix01 {background: url (diam_logo_01.tif) no-repeat 0% 0%;
            height: 75 px; width: 75 px; position: absolute;
            left: 100; top: 125}
```

The *left* property specifies how far the element type box's left edge is offset to the right from the left edge of the containing block. The *top* property specifies how far the element type box's top edge is offset below the top edge of the containing block. For further information regarding these concepts, visit Appendix F (that is, the property index) of CSS2 at www.w3.org/TR/REC-CSS2/propidx.html and follow the appropriate links. With a little practice, you will develop a feel for these and the other related concepts. Meanwhile, these changes are shown in the modified gems1.css document in Figure 7.13.

```
/* Chapter 7, XML & Cascading Style Sheets - Example Style Sheet */
/* filename:gems1.css */
diamonds        {font-family: Arial,Helvetica,Sans-serif; font-size: 12pt }
gem             {display: block; text-align: left}
name            {display: block; font-weight: bold}
carat,color,clarity,cut,cost
                {display: list-item; list-style: disc inside; font-size: 10pt;
                        list-style-type: disc; text-indent: 50 }
link            {display: inline; color: #0000FF; text-decoration: underline;
                                cursor: hand }
```

```
/* Chapter 7, XML & Cascading Style Sheets - Example Style Sheet */
/* filename:gems1.css */
diamonds        {font-family: Arial,Helvetica,Sans-serif; font-size: 12pt }
diam_pix01      {background: url (diam_logo_01.tif) no-repeat 0% 0%;
                      height: 75 px; width: 75 px;
                          position: absolute; left: 100; top: 125}
gem             {display: block; text-align: left}
name            {display: block; font-weight: bold}
carat,color,clarity,cut,cost
                {display: list-item; list-style: disc inside; font-size: 10pt;
                      list-style-type: disc; text-indent: 50 }
link            {display: inline; color: #0000FF; text-decoration: underline;
                      cursor: hand }
```

Figure 7.13 Absolute positioning: gems1.css before and after.

Example: Relative Positioning

Relative positioning is used to move elements one way or another relative to their normal position in the flow of elements and text. Relative positioning is often used inline for superscripting and subscripting.

Let's use relative positioning to make the price of the Cullinan diamond a little fancier by adding a superscript dollar sign ($) at the beginning of the price and two superscript, underlined zeros at the end of the price. The Cullinan diamond's price will be $^{\$}$2,174,200$^{\underline{00}}$. Here is the code to add to <cost> in the gems1.xml document:

```
<gem>
     ...
     <cost>
          <super_scpt STYLE="font-size: 10pt;
               position: relative; top: -5" >
          $
          </super_scpt>
```

```
            2,174,200
            <super_scpt STYLE="font-size: 10pt;
                 position: relative; top: -5;
                 text-decoration: underline">
            00
            </super_scpt>
      </cost>
      ...
</gem>
```

The Cascading Nature of Cascading Style Sheets

Style controls can be specified in one or more external style sheet files, inside internal style sheets, or inline within the start tags of elements. But when a document or individual element has access to more than one style control source, how does the parser determine which style specifications should take precedence over its competitors?

The answer lies with the concept of *cascading*, which is defined by the W3C as the capability provided by some style sheet languages to allow style information from several sources to be blended in an ordered sequence, so that some rules have precedence over others—for example, to reflect personal preferences or corporate guidelines. With cascading, all specifications can be combined into a virtual style sheet.

Here is the sequence in which style controls are applied, with the highest priority first:

1. Inline specifications within element start tags.
2. Specifications in internal style sheets.
3. Specifications in external style sheets. If there is more than one and there is a contradiction or overlap with respect to selectors, the most recent style sheet specification prevails.
4. Styles inherited from parent elements.
5. Browser default styles.

In addition to those general rules, there are additional considerations:

- Specifications applied by the ID attribute prevail over those specified by class.
- Class specifications prevail over group selectors.
- General author rules prevail over general reader rules, which are advanced concepts beyond the scope of this text.

- With CSS2, the end user's !Important rules prevail over the document author's Important rules. These, too, are advanced concepts that we will not be discussing in this introductory book. But this relationship is still worth noting because in CSS1 the reverse was true.

The final appearance of a document in a browser display or in hard copy results from the interaction of the original XML document and its style specifications, plus the behavior of the browser or other application. And specific rules generally prevail over more general rules.

Chapter 7 Labs: Applying CSS

In these lab exercises, we will use cascading style sheets to determine the styles for the contents of:

- an XHTML file (Lab 7.1)
- an XML file (Lab 7.2)
- a hyperlink within an XML file that is, in turn, validated by a DTD (Lab 7.3)

Cascading style sheet concepts are fairly easy to grasp, but the style sheet specification files themselves take a little time to plan and create. For this lab, we thought it would be more productive to supply you with some draft style sheet files to examine and modify, rather than have you create them from scratch. This way, you can focus on the higher-level details, such as how to use style sheets in conjunction with XHTML and XML data instance files.

If you are already an HTML or CSS guru, please feel free to modify these or create your own, because the basic look and feel of any Web site is a personal or organizational choice. For example, we may be good at coding, but the art department staff is likely to be better at creating design and visuals. So we will not make any artistic demands upon you here, although, if you have the skill set already, then feel free to indulge yourself.

Lab 7.1: Combining CSS with XHMTL

In this first lab exercise, you will add a cascading style sheet reference to an XHTML file, the Space Gems index.html document.

1. If you have not already done so, download the master.css style sheet file from the *XML in 60 Minutes a Day* Web site, as described in the book's introduction, and save the file to the C:\WWW\SpaceGems directory.

2. Open the HTML-Kit editor.
3. Click Open Existing File when prompted, and browse to open the C:\WWW\SpaceGems\index.html file.
4. Before proceeding, check the file with HTML Tidy. To do this, choose Tools from the top menu bar, and then select Check Code Using TIDY F9. Any issues should have been resolved from the previous chapter. If not, fix them now.
5. In the index.html document, add a link to the external master.css style sheet. To do so, add the following code to index.html:

```
<link rel="stylesheet" type="text/css"  href="master.css" />
```

Alternatively, you can go to the HTML-Kit top menu bar and click Actions, Style, StyleSheet Link to create the code.

6. Click the Preview tab inside HTML-Kit to view the results. If the style sheet link is correct, the file should have a different look and feel.
7. Feel free to adjust the style coding as you see fit using the chapter material as a reference. You can also test the view using your browser.
8. Save the changes to the index.html and master.css files.
9. Using the preceding instructions, add an external link to the galaxys_largest_diamonds.htm to the master.css style sheet as well.

Lab 7.2: Combining CSS with XML

In this exercise, you will add a hyperlink from the Space Gems index.html page to the Space Gems Quick List of Diamonds, defined in the gems1.xml document. Then, in that XML document, you will add a cascading style sheet reference.

1. Open the HTML-Kit editor.
2. Click Open Existing File when prompted, and browse for the C:\WWW\SpaceGems\index.html file.
3. Add a new link called Quick List of Diamonds that points to gems1.xml to the bottom of the index.html document. To do so, add the following code directly under the existing link to the Galaxy's Largest Diamonds.

```
<br />
<a href="gems1.xml">Quick List of Diamonds</a>
```

4. Save the changes to the index.html file.
5. Click Preview to verify that the link is visible at the bottom of the index.html page. If you click the Quick List of Diamonds link at this time, it should show a raw XML instance document.
6. If you have not already done so, download gems1.css and save it to the C:\WWW\SpaceGems directory.
7. Open the C:\WWW\SpaceGems\gems1.xml file.
8. In the gems1.xml document, add a link to the external gems1.css style sheet:

```
<?xml-stylesheet href = 'gems1.css' type = 'text/css'?>
```

9. Save gems1.xml back to C:\WWW\SpaceGems.
10. Test the file inside the browser. Type "http://localhost/spacegems" into the browser's locator bar, and press Enter. When the page is displayed, click Quick List of Diamonds.
11. Feel free to adjust the style coding as you see fit using the chapter material as a reference.
12. Save any subsequent changes to the gems1.xml file.

Lab 7.3: Inserting a Link into an XML File That Has a DTD

In this lab, you will add a hyperlink to the gems1.xml file, and use a cascading style sheet to format the link. However, since the XML file must eventually be validated, this process will involve three steps:

1. Modify the respective DTD or schema file to declare the necessary elements within the structure (our example will use a DTD).
2. Add the link information to the XML instance document.
3. Format the link inside the CSS file so that the link is fully functional on the rendered page.

Step 1: Declare the Necessary Components in the DTD File

1. Using either TurboXML or the HTML-Kit editor, modify the diamonds1.dtd file for gems1.xml and add the following:
   - Two elements named <info> and <link>
   - Three attributes named xml:type, href, and OnClick

2. Now adjust the code in diamonds1.dtd by inserting the highlighted code in this sample:

```
<?xml version='1.0' encoding='UTF-8' ?>
<!ELEMENT diamonds (info?,gem+)>
<!ELEMENT info (#PCDATA | link)*>
<!ELEMENT link (#PCDATA)>
<!ATTLIST link  xml:type CDATA  #REQUIRED
                  href      CDATA  #REQUIRED
                  OnClick   CDATA  #REQUIRED>
<!ELEMENT gem (name , carat , color , clarity , cut , cost)>
<!ELEMENT name (#PCDATA)>
<!ELEMENT carat (#PCDATA)>
<!ELEMENT color (#PCDATA)>
<!ELEMENT clarity (#PCDATA)>
<!ELEMENT cut (#PCDATA)>
<!ELEMENT cost (#PCDATA)>
```

3. Check for errors and save the diamonds1.dtd file to C:\WWW\SpaceGems.

Step 2: Add the Link and Other Components to the XML File

1. Using TurboXML or the HTML-Kit editor, add the two new <info> and <link> elements to the gems1.xml file. To do so, adjust your code to the following:

```
<?xml version = "1.0" encoding = "UTF-8"?>
<!DOCTYPE diamonds SYSTEM "diamonds1.dtd">
<?xml-stylesheet href = 'gems1.css' type = 'text/css'?>
<diamonds>
     <info>Home Page,
          <link xml:type = "simple" href =
"http://localhost/SpaceGems"
               OnClick =
"location.href='http://localhost/SpaceGems' ">
                click here.
          </link>
     </info>
     <gem>
          <name>Cullinan</name>
          <carat>3106</carat>
          <color>H</color>
          <clarity>VS1,VS2-Very Slightly Imperfect</clarity>
          <cut>Rough</cut>
          <cost>2174200</cost>
     </gem>
     <gem>
```

```
            <name>Dark</name>
            <carat>500</carat>
            <color>J</color>
            <clarity>SL1,SL2-Slightly Imperfect</clarity>
            <cut>Rough</cut>
            <cost>450000</cost>
        </gem>
        <gem>
            <name>Sparkler</name>
            <carat>105</carat>
            <color>F</color>
            <clarity>IF-Internally Flawless</clarity>
            <cut>Super Ideal</cut>
            <cost>126000</cost>
        </gem>
        <gem>
            <name>Merlin</name>
            <carat>41</carat>
            <color>D</color>
            <clarity>FL-Flawless</clarity>
            <cut>Ideal</cut>
            <cost>82000</cost>
        </gem>
    </diamonds>
```

2. Check for errors and save the gems1.xml file to C:\WWW\SpaceGems.

Step 3: Format the Link by Modifying the CSS File

1. Using HTML-Kit editor, add a style element to the gems1.css file, as follows:

```
/* Chapter 7 - Cascading Style Sheet to format gems1.xml with
link */
diamonds {font-family: Arial,Helvetica,Sans-serif; font-size:
12pt; }
gem      {display: block; text-align: left;}
name     {display: block; font-weight: bold;}
carat,color,clarity,cut,cost
         {display: list-item; list-style: disc inside;
              font-size: 10pt; list-style-type: disc;
              text-indent: 50;}
link     {display: inline; color: #0000FF;
              text-decoration: underline; cursor: hand; }
```

2. Save the gems1.css file to the C:\WWW\SpageGems directory.

3. Test the link using Internet Explorer:
   a. Enter "http://localhost/spacegems" into the locator bar of the browser.
   b. Click the Quick List of Diamonds link on the bottom of the index.html page.
   c. Click the Click here link on the gems1.xml page.
   d. If the links work, you are done.

Summary

Following are some important facts about cascading style sheets and the Cascading Style Sheet language:

- The Cascading Style Sheet (CSS) language describes how to add style controls (also called presentation controls) to HTML- and XML-related data, either within the data files themselves or in separate files that are summoned when needed.
- The W3C's CSS Working Group began developing the Cascading Style Sheet language for HTML style control in 1995. Two levels of CSS have reached Recommendation status; development continues on CSS3. The W3C CSS home page has links to CSS-compatible applications, authoring tools, tutorials, and other services.
- There are three methods we can use to specify styles for HTML and XML documents: inline style specifications, internal (also called embedded) style sheets, and affiliating HTML/XML documents with one or more external style sheet documents. The syntax for HTML varies from that for most XML-related languages.
- Whenever possible, designers should incorporate as many style controls as possible in external style sheet documents. There are several advantages to doing so.
- CSS style rules have two major components: a selector (which can take various forms) and a declaration (which contains one or more property:value).
- Over 100 properties are available; more are added periodically. If you design style rules, it pays to check the W3C list of properties occasionally to stay current with what is available.

- Elements that have their own display blocks are called block-level elements; those that don't are called inline level.
- Pseudo-elements and pseudo-classes were developed to apply style specifications based on content that is not evident from a data document's logical tree structure.
- When documents have more than one style control source, CSS observes cascading, which is the capability to allow style information from several sources to be blended together in an ordered sequence to create a single virtual style sheet. The CSS cascading sequence is contained near the end of this chapter. Among competing style rules, precedence is generally given to more specific rules over more general rules and to most recent rules over older rules.

Review Questions

1. The Cascading Style Sheet language was originally developed for:
   a. Desktop publishing applications
   b. XML
   c. SGML
   d. XHTML
   e. HTML
2. At what level of CSS were style controls introduced for aural device presentation?
   a. CSS1
   b. CSS2
   c. CSS3
   d. CSS Modular
   e. None of the above
3. What is the major issue pertaining to CSS development so far?
4. What are the three methods for incorporating style control rules?
5. Which style control method uses the STYLE attribute?
6. Which of the following is not an advantage to using external style sheets?
   a. Style changes can be incorporated more quickly.
   b. Ultimately, especially for larger projects, less coding has to be done.
   c. Better use of network data caching.
   d. Data instance documents remain cleaner.
   e. None of the above.
7. True or false. Because CSS is its own language with its own grammar and syntax, when style controls are incorporated by the inline or internal style sheet methods, there is no need to modify schema documents (that is, DTDs or XML schemas) to ensure that data instance documents remain valid.
8. What are the two major components of any style rule?
9. According to the text, how do style rules observe inheritance?
10. Fill in the blank. Element types that are not given their own display blocks are called ______________________________.
11. How are pseudo-elements and pseudo-classes similar?

12. The following is an example of which kind of syntax?

```
link.VISITED:visited {color: #FFD700; background-color: black}
```

    a. Pseudo-class
    b. Class combined with pseudo-class
    c. Grouping by class
    d. Pseudo-element
    e. Class combined with pseudo-element

13. True or false. The background-attachment property determines whether an image stays in one place or scrolls.
14. Which type of positioning tells the parser to place an element's data content at a specific location?
15. What is the proper sequence in which the following style rules will be applied?
    a. Specifications in external style sheets
    b. Browser default styles
    c. Specifications in internal style sheets
    d. Styles inherited from parent elements
    e. Inline specifications within element start tags

Answers to Review Questions

1. **e.** CSS1 was developed for use with HTML.
2. **b.** This answer is found in the section titled *CSS and the World Wide Web Consortium*.
3. Available applications have implemented CSS inconsistently: Some are fully compatible with CSS1 and CSS2; some are fully compatible with CSS1 and only partially with CSS2; and other variations.
4. The three basic methods are inline, in the start tags of respective elements; within internal style sheets; and in external style sheet documents.
5. The inline method.
6. **e.** These are all advantages to using external style sheets. We hope you weren't fooled by the intentional use of a double-negative-like question.
7. False. Incorporating style controls with the inline and internal style sheet methods always impacts data instance document components. So schema documents (including DTDs and XML schema documents) must always be adjusted to allow the data documents to remain valid.
8. The two major components are the selector and the declaration.
9. A child element inherits the style controls specified for its parent element unless a specific style rule is created for the child element.
10. Element types that are not given their own display blocks are called inline-level elements.
11. They both apply style rules based on characteristics that are not evident from the document's logical tree structure.
12. **b.** This syntax is found in the section with the same name.
13. True. You only need to specify the value as fixed or scroll.
14. Absolute positioning.
15. **e., c., a., d., b.** This information is found in the section titled *The Cascading Nature of Cascading Style Sheets* near the end of the chapter.

XLinks

The World Wide Web owes a lot of its utility and popularity to its resource-linking capability. But the overwhelming number of links are relatively simple HTML hyperlinks, and they are proving inadequate for XML documents and languages.

This chapter explains a linking solution in the form of several different XML-related languages. By the end of this chapter, you should be able to create these links and integrate them with your existing projects. But please be aware of two things: two of these new XML-related languages (XPath and XPointer) have their own syntax style, and the respective W3C specifications are pretty far ahead of the related application developers. The common Web browsers are only slowly catching up to these linking standards. You will see, through this chapter's lab exercises, that browser applications—from manufacturer to manufacturer and version to version—implement XML linking inconsistently. If you are interested in using XML links in your documents, you should monitor the progress of these languages and their respective applications and standards. However, if you are successful integrating them, they will serve you well.

XLink: The XML Linking Language

XLink provides us with the capability to create links in XML documents using XML syntax (which can't be said for the other languages—XPath and XPointer—we discuss in this chapter). You can use all three, though, to create simple HTML-like unidirectional links (links with one source and one destination, activated by a user's mouse click) or sophisticated (even automatic) links among several sources and destinations.

The W3C and XLink

XLink uses XML syntax to define explicit relationships between addressable units of information or other resources. The W3C's XLink Working Group began developing XLink in late 1996. The XML Linking language (XLink) Version 1.0 Recommendation was endorsed by the W3C in June 2001. XLink was created to do the following:

- Expand hyperlinking capability by creating linking element types with unique names that can be specified by the document developer, while still remaining compatible with and complementary to HTML.
- Link documents with multiple sources and destinations (a departure from the HTML "one source/one destination" model).
- Introduce different link actuation methods (in addition to the HTML method of moving the mouse over an element and clicking it).
- Use standard XML constructs (concepts, syntax, and formats), complying with XML's rules for well-formedness and validity, and providing other XML-related functionality, including human legibility.
- Indicate to the user/developer something about the nature and behavior of the link (title, destination, traversal rules, and the like).
- Locate link definitions in separate locations (for example, link databases), so that a write permission does not have to be given to as many individuals. (A discussion of link databases is beyond the introductory level of this book. If you are interested in that subject, consult the W3C Web site and other information sources.)

To realize its full linking potential, XLink relies on concepts and constructs found in these other XML-related standards:

- XML Path Language (XPath) 1.0, W3C, 1999.
- The XML Pointer Language family of Working Drafts, which is based on the original W3C XML Pointer Language (XPointer) Version 1.0 Candidate Recommendation of September 2001:

  - The XML XPointer Language Framework
  - The XPointer Element() Scheme
  - The XPointer xmlns() Scheme
  - The XPointer xpointer() Scheme
- XML Base (XBase), W3C, 1999

The XML Base Recommendation specifies how base URIs can be applied to XML documents; it is discussed to some extent in Chapter 9, "XML Transformations."

XLink and XPointer Implementations

Many XML developers, programmers, and authors are concerned that the IT industry is lagging behind the W3C in "XLinking" and "XPointing," and that implementations—especially browsers—have so far been slow to adopt the concepts and practices mentioned in the W3C Recommendations and Working Drafts. That said, however, lists of XLink, XPath, and XPointer implementations can be obtained from the W3C's XML Pointer, XML Base, and XML Linking home page at www.w3.org/XML/Linking.

Basic XLink Concepts

An XLink link defines explicit relationships between addressable resources or portions of resources. As we discuss XLinks, we will encounter additional fundamental definitions and concepts. We'll quickly define a few very basic concepts here, to facilitate your understanding of subsequent sections.

Resources

Resources is a common term used during the discussion of XLinks. Applications, text files, images, documents, programs, and other entities—or portions thereof—may serve as resources. Table 8.1 describes four resource types as XLink defines them. As we progress through this chapter, we'll notice that, occasionally, these categories may seem to overlap.

Table 8.1 Types of XLink Resources

RESOURCE TYPE	EXPLANATION/DEFINITION
Starting resource	The resource from which a traversal is begun.
Ending resource	The destination resource (or resource portion) for a traversal.

(continued)

Table 8.1 *(continued)*

RESOURCE TYPE	EXPLANATION/DEFINITION
Local resource	An XML element that participates in a link by being a linking element or a child to a linking element. It, or its parent, is the linking element.
Remote resource	A resource, or portion of a resource, that participates in a link addressed with a URI reference. It may even be in the same XML document or inside the same linking element, as long as it is addressed by a URI.

Link Traversal, Arcs, and Link Direction

In Table 8.1, the first two terms are defined in terms of the concept of traversal, which simply means to follow a link from where it starts to where it ends. In its strictest sense, the process of traversal involves a single pair of participating resources or portions of resources: a source and a destination.

All information about how to traverse a pair of resources, including the direction of traversal and any subsequent action prescribed for the application once the link has been traversed, is called an *arc*. More than one arc can be defined for an XLink.

If two resources participate in a link, but there is only one arc—one source and one destination—then the link is unidirectional. However, if two arcs are defined, and both arcs connect the same pair of resources, but the resources switch places as starting and ending resources in each arc definition, then the link is multidirectional. But please don't confuse a multidirectional link with pressing the browser's back button after traversing a link: The back button is a convenient browser function that accesses the browser's history list to insert an address into the locator bar without having to type it in. It is a function of the browser application, but it is not related to the links themselves.

An arc that has a local starting resource and a remote ending resource is called an *outbound arc*. Conversely, if the ending resource is local but the starting resource is remote, then the arc is an *inbound arc*. The third variation is an arc where neither the starting resource nor the ending resource is local. This is a *third-party arc*. If we are trying to link resources that we do not have write access to (or we choose not to exercise our write access at that time for security or other purposes), then we must use either an inbound or third-party arc.

XLink Logical Structures

There are no XLink documents as such. XLinks result from specific features that are incorporated into other XML-related documents. We discuss those features next.

Declare an XLink Namespace

Before we can create linking elements, we have to insert a declaration of the specific XLink namespace. Minimally, the XLink namespace declaration must be within the designated linking element's start tag. However, we suggest that the namespace declaration be included in the root data instance element of the document. Here is an example of such a declaration:

```
<elementName xmlns:xlink="http://www.w3.org/1999/xlink" .... >
```

Later in the document—within the extent of the element in whose start tag the namespace was declared—all XLink elements will have an xlink prefix. Although the xlink prefix is used by convention, it is not absolutely necessary to use xlink as a prefix; as with all namespaces, it is the developer's choice which prefix he or she wants to use. Using xlink allows a user to quickly recognize the linking elements, attributes, and other related resources when examining the document's source code.

Thereafter, for validity, the chosen namespace attribute must also be declared in a DTD or schema document. Please refer to Chapter 4, "Document Type Definitions," or Chapter 5, "XML Schemas," for the appropriate namespace declaration syntax.

Naming XLink Links

In XML, as in HTML, resource links are defined in elements. But HTML specifies that only the <A> and <IMG> elements are to be used for linking. XLink elements, by contrast, can be given any name the developer chooses. Whether or not elements are to be links is determined by specific attributes that are inserted into their start tags.

XLink's Global Attributes

XLink linking elements (also called XLink links or simply XLinks) are defined (the W3C uses the term asserted) by the global (meaning link-related) attributes inserted in their start tags. The global attributes indicate which elements are linking elements. They also allow document developers to specify other properties about the links and their resources, such as when to load the linked resources or how they should appear once they are loaded.

The global attributes provided by XLink are grouped according to their functions in Table 8.2.

Table 8.2 XLink Global Attributes

CATEGORY	ATTRIBUTE NAME AND DEFINITION
XLink definition/assertion attribute	type—Indicates the XLink element type (); a value for this attribute is mandatory and must be one of *simple, extended, locator, arc, resource, title,* or *none.*
Locator attribute—Allows an XLink application to find a remote resource (or resource fragment)	href—May be used on simple-type elements; must be used on locator-type elements; value must be a URI reference or must result in a URI reference after a specific escaping procedure described in XLink 1.0.
Semantic attributes—Describe the meaning of resources within the context of a link	role—May be used on extended-, simple-, locator-, and resource-type elements; value must be a URI reference, with some constraints as found in XLink 1.0.; the URI reference identifies some resource that describes the intended property. arcrole—May be used on arc- and simple-type elements; value must be a URI reference, with constraints as described in XLink 1.0; the URI reference identifies some resource that describes the intended property; if no value is supplied, no particular role value is to be inferred. title—May be used on extended-, simple-, locator-, resource-, arc-, and simple-type elements; used to describe the meaning of a link or resource in human-readable form; a value is optional (if one is supplied, it should contain a string that describes the resource); this information is highly dependent on the type of processing being done.
Behavior attributes—Signal behavior intentions for traversal to a link's remote ending resources	show—May be used on simple- and arc-type elements to communicate the desired presentation of the ending resource on traversal from the starting resource; when used on arc-type elements, it signals behavior intentions for traversal to whatever ending resources are specified. actuate—May be used on simple- and arc-type elements; similar to "show"; used to communicate the desired timing of traversal from the starting resource to the ending resource.

Table 8.2 *(continued)*

CATEGORY	ATTRIBUTE NAME AND DEFINITION
Traversal attributes	label—May be used on resource- and locator-type elements; value must be an NCName (i.e., any name that begins with a letter or underscore and has no space or colon in it, because its author may add a namespace prefix to it).
	from—May be used on the arc-type element; value must be an NCName; if a value is supplied, it must correspond to the same value for some label attribute on a locator- or resource-type element that appears as a direct child inside the same extended-type element as does the arc-type element.
	to—May be used on the arc-type element; the value must also be an NCName. As with "from," if a value is supplied, it must correspond to the same value for some label attribute on a locator- or resource-type element that appears as a direct child inside the same extended-type element as does the arc-type element.

A Linking Element Needs a type Attribute

XLink elements must have an attribute named type, which is one of the 10 global XLink attributes listed in Table 8.1. Possible values for this attribute are as follows:

simple. Provides syntax for a common outbound link with only two participating resources; less functionality than extended.

extended. Provides full functionality (examples: inbound arcs, third-party arcs, links with multiple participating resources); can be fairly complex; can be used to find linkbases (thus, can help an XLink application process other links).

locator. Addresses the remote resources participating in an extended link.

arc. Provides traversal rules among an extended link's participating resources.

resource. Supplies local resources that participate in an extended link.

title. Describes the meaning of an extended link or resource in human-readable terms; provides a human-readable label for the link.

none. Provides its element with no XLink-specified meaning; any XLink-related content or attributes have no XLink-specified relationship to its element. For example, "none" is useful occasionally in helping XLink applications to avoid checking for the presence of an href.

XLink convention states that when a linking element containing the type attribute has a value of *xxx*, it is called an *xxx-type linking element*. Thus, in this element:

```
<gem xlink:type="locator" ...
```

<gem> is a locator-type linking element or a locator-type element. Thereafter, the linking element type dictates certain XLink-related functions and constraints that, in turn, influence the behavior of applications when they encounter that kind of linking element.

Two types of XLink links—simple and extended—can be configured to allow human intervention or to provide automatic instructions to the system.

A simple link (also called a simple-type link) associates exactly two participating resources, one local and one remote, with an outbound arc (an arc traversing from the local resource to the remote resource). Thus, HTML's <A> and <IMG> links are simple links. An example of a simple link is provided in the section titled *Example: Simple-Type XLink.*

Extended links offer full XLink functionality, including inbound and third-party arcs (arcs between remote resources), as well as arcs that can simultaneously connect a local resource to several remote resources. As a result, the structure of an extended link can be fairly complex and may include elements for pointing to remote resources, elements for containing local resources, elements for specifying arc traversal rules, and elements for specifying human-readable resource and arc titles. A fairly typical extended link example occurs later in this chapter, in the section titled *Example: Extended-Type XLink.*

If you are a newcomer to XLinks, it may be convenient to think of simple links, conceptually, as a subset of extended links. However, bear in mind that simple and extended links differ syntactically and in purpose. The purpose of a simple link is to provide, when applicable, a convenient shorthand version of an equivalent extended link. You could convert a simple link back into extended link format, but several structural changes would be needed, since a properly constructed simple link is capable of combining all the basic functions of a combined extended-type element, a locator-type element, an arc-type element, and a resource-type element. Figure 8.1 shows a comparison of XML code in a simple link and an equivalent extended link. Please note that the coding of the simple link could be made even shorter if, for example, default behavior for XLink attributes like xlink:type and xlink:show were declared within the affiliated DTD or schemas.

```
<simple_link
        xlink:type="simple"
        xlink:href="..."
        xlink:show="..."
        ... />
```

Simple Link

```
<gem_ext_link
        xlink:type="extended">
   <gem_ext_res_01
        xlink:type="resource"
        xlink:label="local"
     ... />
   <gem_ext_res_02
        xlink:type="locator"
        xlink:label="remote"
        xlink:href="..."
     ... />
   <gem_arc
        xlink:type="arc"
        xlink:from="local"
        xlink:to="remote"
        xlink:show="..."
     ... />
</gem_ext_link>
```

Equivalent Extended Link

Figure 8.1 Comparison of simple link and equivalent extended link.

Despite the impression given by Figure 8.1, simple-type links are not always superior to extended-type links. Simple-type links are only used as shorthand for otherwise extended links and are only appropriate for certain simple one resource/one locator, outbound arc situations. Otherwise, extended links—although they may appear complex at first—are far more flexible and powerful.

Other Important Attributes: show and actuate

The show and actuate attributes are very important and, next to the type attribute, probably the most commonly used. As indicated in Table 8.2, the show attribute is used with simple- or arc-type elements and tells the application how to display the data in the ending resource after the link has been traversed. The show attribute is not absolutely required but is especially important when used with Web browser applications. Possible values for show are as follows:

new. Opens a new window and displays the data in the resource.

replace. Replaces the existing window and displays the data.

embed. Embeds the ending resource data inside the extent of the linking element.

other. Indicates that the XLink-oriented application's behavior is unconstrained, but that the application should look for direction from other attributes in the linking element.

none. Indicates that the application's behavior is unconstrained, but no other attribute is present to help the application determine the appropriate behavior.

The actuate attribute (see Table 8.2) is also used on simple- and arc-type elements. Actuate dictates the timing of the link's traversal, or at what point the link is activated. Possible values for actuate are as follows:

onLoad. The application should traverse to the ending resource immediately on loading the starting resource. However, if a single resource contains multiple arcs whose behavior is set to show="replace" and actuate="onLoad", then application behavior is unconstrained.

onRequest. The application should traverse from the starting resource to the ending resource only on a post-loading event (that is, when a user clicks on the linking element, or after a specified countdown is completed).

other. Similar to the show attribute, indicates that application behavior is unconstrained, and the application should look to other markup to determine the appropriate behavior.

none. Indicates that application behavior is unconstrained, but no other markup is present to help the application determine the appropriate behavior.

Combining XLink Type Elements and Attributes: Two Restrictions

As linking elements are developed and defined, two restrictions apply: Only certain XLink elements can be combined, and only certain XLink attributes can be combined. Once you are familiar with these constraints, you can create XLinks that connect your designated resources in the manner you expect.

One of the attractions of XLink is that links can be nested within one another. However, only certain XLink type elements can be combined. Table 8.3 summarizes the first restriction: It indicates those relationships that are permitted among linking elements.

Simple elements only require an href locator attribute and, as Table 8.3 indicates, no child XLink elements of any kind. So, beyond the row that addresses the simple-type element, Table 8.3 also applies to extended-type elements.

Table 8.3 Combining XLink Element Types

XLINK ELEMENT TYPE	PERMITTED CHILD ELEMENT TYPES
simple	None
extended	locator, arc, resource, title
locator	title
arc	title
resource	None
title	None

The second restriction is that, given a particular value specified for the type attribute in a linking element's start tag, only certain other XLink attributes can be combined in the same start tag. Table 8.4 is a variation of one found in the W3C Recommendation and indicates restrictions to the combinations of global attributes and type attribute values that are permitted when one defines a linking element. Each R (required) indicates that one or more of the global attribute values must be supplied before the linking element will function. Each O (optional) indicates which global attribute values may be used. If a table entry is blank, that global attribute must not be used in combination with the type attribute.

Table 8.4 Combining XLink Element Types and Global Attributes

TYPE ATTRIBUTE VALUE	GLOBAL ATTRIBUTES									
	type	href	role	arcrole	title	show	actuate	label	from	to
simple	R	O	O	O	O	O	O			
extended	R		O		O					
locator	R	R	O		O			O		
arc	R			O	O	O	O		O	O
resource	R		O		O			O		
title	R									

Example: Simple-Type XLink

Here we present <gem>, a simple example of a simple-type linking element. In it, we can see that the element type is declared empty, that it applies the restrictions found in the previous two tables, and that it includes a declaration of the XLink namespace:

```
<gem xmlns:xlink="http://www.w3.org/1999/xlink
          xlink:type="simple"
          xlink:href="2047diaprice.xml"
          xlink:show="new"
          xlink:title="Diamond Prices"
          xlink:actuate="onRequest" />
```

All the XLink-related attributes of this simple link are contained in one element. Simple-type linking elements can be considered a subset of extended links. They can exist as a linking notation for those occasions when you don't require the power and flexibility—and resource overhead—of an entire extended-type link. XLink doesn't care about the child elements of a simple-type link, only about the linking element itself and its attributes. This linking element uses the optional attribute *show* to instruct the application to open a new window to display the results of the link, and it uses *actuate* to indicate when the link is to be traversed. This <gem> linking element is equivalent to a basic HTML link.

To review, the valid XLink attributes for a simple-type link are *href*, *title*, *role*, *arcrole*, *show*, and *actuate*. For a simple-type linking element to function correctly and reliably, the document it's in and its referenced XML document must both be well formed and valid. The following is an example of DTD code for our simple-type <gem> linking element:

```
<!ELEMENT gem EMPTY>
<!ATTLIST gem
     xmlns:xlink    CDATA  #FIXED  "http://www.w3.org/1999/xlink"
     xlink:type     (simple | extended | locator | arc | resource | title)
                           #IMPLIED
     xlink:href     CDATA  #IMPLIED
     xlink:show     (new | replace | embed | other | none)  #IMPLIED
     xlink:title    CDATA  #IMPLIED
     xlink:actuate  (onLoad | onRequest | other | none)  #IMPLIED>
```

Notice that all the options have been listed for the various attributes, except the namespace declaration. If you intend to create simple links with consistent properties, then consider declaring a number of defaults in the DTD or schema. For example, if the <gem> element link types are all going to be simple, and will all be traversed on request and open up in new windows, consider declaring those as defaults in the DTD as follows:

```
<!ELEMENT gem EMPTY>
<!ATTLIST gem
     xmlns:xlink     CDATA         #FIXED  "http://www.w3.org/1999/xlink"
     xlink:type      (simple)      #FIXED  "simple"
     xlink:href      CDATA         #IMPLIED
     xlink:show      (new)         #FIXED  "new"
     xlink:title     CDATA         #IMPLIED
     xlink:actuate   (onRequest)   #FIXED  "onRequest" >
```

Later, when inserting the links, the coding for each could be simplified to the following:

```
<gem xmlns:xlink="http://www.w3.org/1999/xlink
       xlink:href="2047diaprice.xml" xlink:title="Diamond Prices" />
```

If the namespace declaration has already occurred in a common parent element, the coding for each link would be even simpler, rivaling HTML syntax.

Example: Extended-Type XLink

Extended-type links can be used to create a dynamic online product catalog. For example, Space Gems' various database files may contain all sorts of varied information about all of their gemstones, but only a certain combination of information might be published in a catalog of gems that are actually available for sale. Table 8.5 lists some information we might expect Space Gems to carry about the Smokey diamond. Let's presume that the data is stored in separate files at various locations throughout the Space Gems network.

Table 8.5 contains plenty of Smokey diamond-related information, but we wouldn't expect a catalog to contain all that information just to provide a quick description of one gemstone. Further, creating the appropriate catalog files to dynamically relate Smokey and other gemstones to their respective data sources, especially if those sources are in separate locations, presents issues beyond the capabilities of simple HTML-like <A> or <IMG> element links.

Table 8.5 Smokey Diamond Information

PROPERTY	VALUE	PROPERTY	VALUE
Name	Smokey	**Weight, carats**	1003.29
Color	F-gray	**Clarity**	IF
Cut	Ideal	**Cost, USD**	2,250,000
Taxes	2% Sol, 5% Earth, 10% Cayman	**Reserved?**	No
System	47 Ursae Majoris	**Planet name, formal**	47 Uma F
Planet name, common	Capitan	**Region**	Montis Glacialis
Mine Name	Capitan Uno	**Depth, m GL**	1257
Formation	Trebozoic	**Discovery Date**	2035.10.10.53 Sol
Publish in catalog?	Yes	**Image filename**	smokey_img01.tif

Extended-type links are capable of three functions:

- They can contain data.
- They point to local and remote resources.
- They use arc-type elements to describe the relationships among the resources.

Let's say we work in Space Gems' Retail Sales department, which has jurisdiction over catalog preparation. Before we begin building catalog-related links, chances are that several of the relevant data documents will be stored remotely and within the jurisdiction of departments other than ours (for example, Exploration, Operations, Finance, and others). So, the respective data documents will be beyond our control (in other words, we will not have write access to those documents). Therefore, we wouldn't be able to impose our own scheme of catalog-related element names on the remote element types in their original files. But we can still create such names in our own catalog-related files and then use the type="locator" attribute to link or refer to the originals.

As we build one or more extended-type links, the first step will be not to copy data into our own elements, but to specify link (data) resources.

In the following example, we provide a root element type named <catalog>, whose start tag will contain the XLink namespace declaration. Then, because the catalog will contain information about individual gemstones, <catalog>'s child elements will be several <gem>s. However, we provide only one <gem> example, which will describe Space Gems' Smokey diamond. In this example, the <gem> elements will be used as container elements for all of the data, resource description, and arc-type elements:

```
<?xml version="1.0" ... ?>
...
<catalog xmlns:xlink="http://www.w3.org/1999/xlink" >
     <gem xlink:type="extended">
          <name    xlink:type="resource" xlink:label="gemstone" >
          Smokey
          </name>
          <carats xlink:type="locator" xlink:label="info"
                   xlink:href="smokey_weight.xml" />
               <color xlink:type="locator" xlink:label="info"
                        xlink:href="smokey_color.xml" />
               <clarity xlink:type="locator" xlink:label="info"
                        xlink:href="smokey_clarity.xml" />
               <cut xlink:type="locator" xlink:label="info"
                        xlink:href="smokey_cut.xml" />
               <cost xlink:type="locator" xlink:label="info"
                        xlink:href="smokey_price.xml" />
               <taxes xlink:type="locator" xlink:label="info"
                        xlink:href="smokey_tax_reg.xml" />
               <pix xlink:type="locator" xlink:label="smokey_img"
                        xlink:href="smokey_img01.xml" />
...
     </gem>
...
```

The <name> element is specified as a resource element, indicating that it is the local resource participating in the links (we could almost consider it to be the target of the link). The value of the resource-type element's xlink:label attribute must differ from that specified for the locator-type elements to ensure that there will be no confusion with the remote resources when the arc-type elements are defined. The locator-type <pix> element has a different xlink:label value from the other locator-type elements, since it will participate in a different arc than the other locator-type elements.

Since the various resources are already identified, all we have to do is define the relationships among them. To do so, we provide one or more inbound arc elements, so that the information will be provided when a potential customer accesses the Smokey diamond. Arc-type elements use additional child to and from attributes to designate the start and end points of the specified arc. Those attributes help to determine whether the arcs are inbound, outbound, or third-party. Arcs often include the show, title, actuate, and arcrole attributes. The example that follows contains most of those attributes.

In our example, then, we'll add two arc elements, named <smokey_info> and <smokey_pix>, immediately after the <taxes> element, to create two inbound arcs (we've highlighted the two arc-type elements for emphasis here):

```
<?xml version="1.0" ... ?>
...
          <taxes xlink:type="locator" xlink:label="info"
                    xlink:href="smokey_tax_reg.xml" />
          <smokey_info xlink:type="arc" xlink:from="info"
                    xlink:to="gemstone" xlink:actuate="onLoad"
                    xlink:show="embed" />
          <smokey_pix xlink:type="arc" xlink:from="smokey_img"
                    xlink:to="gemstone" xlink:actuate="onRequest"
                    xlink:show="new" xlink:title="The Smokey Diamond" />
     </gem>
...
```

We can see that the locator-type linking elements (those with xlink:type= "locator" attributes) are used to point to remote resources. The xlink:label attributes are traversal attributes, used to identify the elements when arc elements are built. Remember that locator-type elements can have the same title, role, and label attributes as resource-type elements. However, they also require an href semantic attribute, which ultimately does the pointing to the remote resource.

Notice that the single <smokey-info> arc will initiate action among seven resources: one local resource-type element and six remote locator-type elements. This one-to-many link is not possible with HTML. The one-to-one <smokey_pix> arc, on the other hand, is more like HTML. The word Smokey, contained within the resource-type <name> element, will act as the visible presence for the <gem> element. In other words, Smokey will be the hyperlink.

When the catalog application (presumably a Web browser) eventually encounters the Smokey <gem> element, it will automatically search for, retrieve, and display the "info" data. If the user wants to see a picture of Smokey, he or she can click the word *Smokey,* and the picture is displayed in a new window.

For extended-type XLink elements to function correctly and reliably, their respective DTD or schema declarations must also be correct. You might expect to find the following declarations in a DTD for the example linking elements <catalog>, <gem>, <name>, and others. Please note that the declarations for the elements named <color>, <clarity>, <cut>, <cost>, and <taxes> have been omitted, since they would be identical to the declaration for <carats>:

```
<!ELEMENT     catalog      (gem)*>
<!ATTLIST     catalog
     xlink:xmlns      CDATA      #FIXED "http://www.w3.org/1999/xlink"
```

```
<!ELEMENT     gem (name, carats, color, clarity, cut, cost, taxes, pix)*
<!ATTLIST     gem
     xlink:type   (simple | extended | locator | arc | resource | title)
                  #IMPLIED
     xlink:label    CDATA    #IMPLIED
<!ELEMENT     name (#PCDATA)
<!ATTLIST     name
     xlink:type   (simple | extended | locator | arc | resource | title)
                  #IMPLIED
     xlink:label    NMTOKEN    #IMPLIED
     xlink:href    CDATA    #IMPLIED
<!ELEMENT     carats (#PCDATA)
<!ATTLIST     carats
     xlink:type   (simple | extended | locator | arc | resource | title)
                  #IMPLIED
     xlink:label    NMTOKEN    #IMPLIED
     xlink:href    CDATA    #IMPLIED
...
<!ELEMENT     pix (#PCDATA)
<!ATTLIST     pix
     xlink:type   (simple | extended | locator | arc | resource | title)
                  #IMPLIED
     xlink:label    NMTOKEN    #IMPLIED
     xlink:href    CDATA    #IMPLIED
     xlink:title    CDATA    #IMPLIED
<!ELEMENT     smokey_info (#PCDATA)
<!ATTLIST     smokey_info
     xlink:type   (simple | extended | locator | arc | resource | title)
                  #IMPLIED
     xlink:from    CDATA    #IMPLIED
     xlink:to    CDATA    #IMPLIED
     xlink:actuate    (onLoad | onRequest | other | none)    #IMPLIED
     xlink:show    (replace | new | embed)    #IMPLIED
<!ELEMENT     smokey_pix (#PCDATA)
<!ATTLIST     smokey_pix
     xlink:type   (simple | extended | locator | arc | resource | title)
                  #IMPLIED
     xlink:from    NMTOKEN    #IMPLIED
     xlink:to    NMTOKEN    #IMPLIED
     xlink:actuate    (onLoad | onRequest | other | none)    #IMPLIED
     xlink:show    (replace | new | embed)    #IMPLIED
     xlink:title    CDATA    #IMPLIED
```

Combining XLink, XPath, and XPointer to Access Subresources

In the extended-type link example in the previous sections, several different documents were accessed and each contributed specific information about the Smokey diamond. However, all links were to whole documents—that is, to whole resources.

Although the example helped us visualize resources and arcs, it was not totally realistic. Often, the information we want to access will comprise only a part of a document, not the whole document. On other occasions, we want to select more than one piece of information, but not all of the information, from a single document. Going back to our catalog example, do we really think that a whole document would be dedicated to just listing the weight (in carats) specification of a single diamond? Or, alternatively, if we are simply searching for a diamond's weight specification, would we really want to link to and embed all the information from a document that contains the weight, clarity, cut, origin, and other information? A mechanism that provides access to just one portion of a document—in this case, to just the clarity specification within a document that contains other technical information—would therefore be appreciated. Combining XLink with various aspects of the XML Path language (XPath) and the XML Pointer language (XPointer) provides such a mechanism. Here's an example of a linking element that contains a combined XPath/ XPointer expression:

```
<smokeyPrice xmlns:xlink="http://www.w3.org/1999/xlink"
        xlink:type="simple" xlink:show="new"
        xlink:href="http://www.SpaceGems.com/2047prices.xml#xpointer
            (/diamonds/child::gem[position()=3]/cost) />
```

The XPath/XPointer expression in this case is part of the value specified for the xlink:href attribute and consists of a location path introduced by the keyword xpointer. Technically, it is an XPath expression inside an XPointer pointer, since it is introduced by XPointer's keyword xpointer. However, beyond that keyword, the rest of this particular example is an XPath expression, and XPath predates XPointer. The XPointer family all support and extend XPath expression constructs.

The XML Path Language (XPath)

XML Path Language (XPath) Version 1.0 was endorsed as a W3C Recommendation in November 1999. XPath allows us to address parts of an XML document. XPath's method of addressing document components, with its basic facilities for text string, number, and boolean (true-false) manipulations, allows for document searches down to the node level. Thus, it provides more precision in targeting and retrieving data than XLink alone.

XPath treats the target XML documents as logical tree structures consisting of nodes of various types: root, element, attribute, text, comment, and processing instruction nodes. However, nodes are not simply equivalent to element types. For example, the root node is not the same as the document root element in an XML document. Although there is such a thing as a document root element node, it is a subnode of the root node. The root node contains processing instruction and comment nodes, as well as the root element node.

Any element node may consist of one or more attribute nodes, a text node that represents the data in the element, or even other child element nodes.

XPath Expressions, Location Paths, and Location Steps

Like certain other XML-compatible languages (DTDs and Cascading Style Sheets), XPath has its own specific non-XML syntax. But, thankfully, its syntax is fairly straightforward and provides several abbreviations to make life a little easier. In this section, we look at three important XPath concepts.

XPath Expressions and Location Paths

XPath's instructions to the parser are called *expressions*. XPath expressions take several different forms, the most important of which are location paths and function calls. XPath expressions instruct the parser to go to an initial context node in a document and search from that starting point through specified parts of the document's nodal structure. However, when the parser is through searching, it doesn't return to the application with actual data; it returns to the application with pointers to the data.

XPath expressions often occur as specified values for certain XML attributes. Let's look again at the example linking the element named <smokeyPrice>, which contains an XPointer pointer that, in turn, consists of an XPath expression. It is the same example that we introduced in the previous section:

```
<smokeyPrice xmlns:xlink="http://www.w3.org/1999/xlink"
         xlink:type="simple" xlink:show="new"
         xlink:href="http://www.SpaceGems.com/2047diaprice.xml#xpointer
              (/diamonds/child::gem[position()=3]/cost) />
```

In the example, the XPath expression comprises the latter part of the value specified for the xlink:href attribute. It follows the keyword xpointer and consists of a location path.

As we can see from the URI, the parser evaluates the XPath expression to find what context to search through in the target XML document

2047diaprice.xml, located at the Space Gems Web site. The expression also tells the parser something about the nature of the information objects it is to select: In this case, because the expression is solely XPath, the parser will look for nodes.

Before we go on, let's look at the 2047diaprice.xml file, which is the price list for Space Gems' diamonds. Knowing what 2047diaprice.xml contains makes it easier to understand the expressions we will be creating. The top portion of the file is depicted in Figure 8.2.

Since our example expression is primarily composed of an XPath location path, let's now look at the generic syntax for an XPath location path:

```
axis1::node-test1[predicate1]/.../axisn::node-testn[predicaten]
```

The location path is made up of one or more location steps. The number of location steps in the path dictates how many stages of traversal the parser will negotiate. If more than one location step exists in the path, then the location steps are separated by forward slash (/) characters. Here is the location path found in our <smokeyPrice> linking element:

```
/diamonds/child::gem[position()=3]/cost
```

```
<?xml version="1.0" encoding="UTF-8" standalone="no"?>
<!DOCTYPE diamonds SYSTEM "http://localhost/SpaceGems/diamonds1.dtd" >
<?xml-stylesheet type="text/css" href="http://localhost/SpaceGems/gems1.css" ?>
<!-- filename: 2047diaprice.xml - ->
<diamonds>
        <gem id="cullinan">
                <cost >2174000</cost> <system>Sol</system>
        </gem>
        <gem id="dark">
                <cost >450000</cost> <system>Sol</system>
        </gem>
        <gem id="smokey">
                <cost>2250000</cost> <system>47 Ursae Majoris</system>
        </gem>
        <gem id="inukshuk">
                <cost>1950000</cost> <system>Sol</system>
        </gem>
        <gem id="ares">
                <cost>1500000</cost> <system>Sol</system>
                <reserved />
        </gem>
...
```

Figure 8.2 2047diaprice.xml: The XML document containing Space Gems' diamonds price list.

In the location path, we see three forward slashes, so we presume that this location path contains three location steps. When a location path contains more than one location step, the parser evaluates the steps from left to right, starting with the context defined in the far left location step. If the whole location path is prefixed with a forward slash (/), as it is in the example, then the parser must begin its search with the document's root node as its initial evaluation context. Thus, according to the example location path, the parser is told that its initial context node is the root node of the 2047diaprice.xml document.

XPath searches do not always have to start at the root node, as is the case here. However, since this path is part of an XPointer pointer, and XPointer requires starting at the root node, our example path will begin at the root node.

Eventually, whatever node-set results from the right-hand step must also have passed the evaluation tests of the step at the left end and all the steps in between.

Classroom Q & A

Q: That location path syntax, with the two colons, looks familiar. It's used in the XML Recommendations and other places. What is it and how do you interpret it?

A: The formal grammar for XPath is Extended Backus-Naur Form (EBNF) notation, which is described in W3C XML Recommendation 1.0 and elsewhere. EBNF has been around since the early 1960s and is usually used to describe programming grammar and syntax. So playing an active programming role, as it does in XPath, is rare for EBNF. To interpret EBNF: the expression *::=* means "the expression on the left is defined by the expression on the right."

Location Steps

Once again, here is the generic syntax for a location path:

```
axis1::node-test1[predicate1]/... axisn::node-testn[predicaten]
```

In location paths, each axis*n*::node-test1[predicate*n*] portion is called a *location step*. Location steps contain components such as:

- XPath-related nodes, axes, node tests, and zero or more predicates
- XPointer-related features, such as points and ranges (not shown in the preceding generic example for simplicity)

Whatever node-sets result from evaluating a location step (that is, whatever nodes are selected as a result of the step's predicate filter, a concept discussed later) must have answered "yes/true" to the conditions imposed by the step.

Let's look again at the <smokeyPrice> linking element:

```
http://www.SpaceGems.com/2047prices.xml#xpointer
                                   (/diamonds/child::gem[position()=3]/cost)
```

We've already stated that the latter part of the element—(/diamonds/child::gem[position()=3]/cost)—is an XPath location path and contains three location steps. The first location step is /diamonds. The instruction to the parser is "start at the initial context (the document's root node) and look for a child node named diamonds. When you find it, go there and make diamonds the current context." The single forward slash not only tells the parser where to start, but it also serves as an abbreviation for (the default) child node traversal. If only one child node is named diamonds (and in this case, 2047diaprice.xml has just one <diamonds> element), then a developer can get away with the simple forward slash followed by the name of the (single) child node. If there had been two <diamonds> child nodes to choose from, then the step would have had to contain additional qualifiers, as the second step does.

Once the parser has traversed to the <diamonds> element node, it reads the second location step /child::gem[position()=3]. This step's syntax better resembles the generic location step syntax axis*n*::node-test1[predicate*n*]. In the expression /child::gem[position()=3], *child* is the name of the axis, *gem* is the node test, and *[position ()=3]* is the predicate.

Here, the parser is told to check the child element nodes of the current context node (which has passed from the document's root node to the <diamonds> element node) and select, from those element nodes that share the name <gem>, the third <gem> element node. (Don't worry; you aren't expected to be able to read this example expression yet. The next few sections will tell you how to do that.)

The third location step is another shorthand step. The instruction to the parser is this: "Once you have found the third <gem> child element node under <diamonds>, look for a child element node called <cost> within the <gem> element node."

That concludes the XPath traversal instructions to the parser. Now let's examine the components named axis, node test, and predicate, which we mentioned in our examination of the second location step.

Axes

Here again is the syntax for a generic location step:

```
axis::node-test[predicate]
```

An axis provides navigational instructions to the parser so that it can traverse across the nodal structure in the quickest and least ambiguous way. Thus, axes point the parser to one or more nodes, within which the subresource will be found, or from which the parser moves on to another node.

In our <smokeyPrice> path, the parser is always told to move "down" through the nodal structure to its destinations, using explicit or default child-oriented navigation steps. Other XPath axes could direct the parser to move down, up, across to the right, and across to the left to look for an element node, to look for an attribute node, or to perform other maneuvers to reach the appropriate node. All XPath axes and their respective instructions are listed in Table 8.6.

Table 8.6 XPath Axes

AXIS NAME	INSTRUCTION TO PARSER
child	Examine the child nodes of the context node. Because this is the default axis, the term "child::" is considered optional. Abbreviation: /.
descendant	Examine all descendant nodes (the child nodes, the children of the child nodes, and their children, and so on). Abbreviation: //.
parent	Examine the parent node of the context node. If the parser is starting at the root node, then the returned node set will be empty. Abbreviation: ..
ancestor	Examine all ancestor nodes, from the parent node back to and including the root node.
following-sibling	Examine all the sibling nodes "to the right" of the context node; in other words, examine all the nodes, on the same level as the context node, that follow the context node in the XML document.
preceding-sibling	Examine all the sibling nodes "to the left" of the context node; in other words, examine all the nodes, on the same level as the context node, that precede the context node in the XML document.
following	Examine all the nodes in the document that follow the context node, but exclude descendant nodes, attribute nodes, and namespace nodes.
preceding	Examine all preceding nodes in the document, excluding ancestor nodes, attribute nodes, and namespace nodes.
attribute	Examine all the attributes in the context node. Abbreviation: @.

(continued)

Table 8.6 *(continued)*

AXIS NAME	INSTRUCTION TO PARSER
namespace	Examine all the namespace declarations in the context node.
self	Examine only the context node.
descendant-or-self	Examine the union set of the context node and its descendant nodes.
ancestor-or-self	Examine the union set of the context node and its ancestor nodes.

Notice that some of the axes refer to attribute and namespace nodes that cannot contain other nodes, only data values. However, most other axes refer to nodes that can actually contain other nodes (for example, element nodes can contain data, attributes, or other element nodes). These axes are called *content axes*, and the nodes they refer to are called *content nodes*.

Node Tests

Once again, back to the generic location step syntax:

```
axis1::node-test1[predicate1]
```

The node test is a preliminary filtering test, based on element names or a type of processing instruction or something similar. Although XPointer uses the same axes as XPath, XPointer uses some node tests that XPath doesn't. Table 8.7 lists the node tests you can use with XPath and XPointer, and what they match. We've listed the XPath and XPointer node tests together for convenience and to prevent confusion. The concept of node tests, similar to axes, will be clearer after you practice with the node tests from Table 8.7.

Table 8.7 Node Tests for XPath and XPointer

NODE TEST	EXPLANATION
*	Any element, attribute, or namespace node. Use for all types of axes.
node()	Any type of node. Use for all types of axes.
text()	Any text node. Use for content axes only.
comment()	Any comment node. Use for content axes only.
processing-instruction()	Any processing instruction node. Use for content axes only.

Table 8.7 *(continued)*

NODE TEST	EXPLANATION
processing-instruction(*string)*	A processing instruction node containing the specified text string. Use for content axes only.
elementName	All nodes created from an element node with the name elementName (elementName is used here as a generic name to represent an actual element type name).
point()	A point in a resource. This is an XPointer node test used to extend XPath.
range()	A range in a resource. This is an XPointer node test used to extend XPath.

To extend XPath to include points and ranges, the XPointer language contains a concept called a *location*, which can be an XPath node, a point, or a range. However, even in XPointer, node tests are still referred to as node tests, not location tests, even though they will function correctly with the points and ranges.

In the second location step, child::gem[position()=3] of the <smokeyPrice> example, gem serves as a node test, since it tells the parser to search for an element node named <gem>, which is a child of the <diamonds> element node. The terms diamonds and cost serve as node tests in their respective first and third locations steps.

Predicates

The location step's generic syntax is probably familiar by now, but here it is again:

```
axis1::node-test1[[predicate1]...[predicaten]]
```

At some point, a parser will select a set of nodes that meet the criteria in the axes and node tests. At that point, predicates can be used as the final filter to select a designated node from the set. Notice that we've altered the generic syntax to show that a developer can specify more than one predicate per location step. The nodes that survive the predicate filter are those that have answered a booleanlike *true* to the predicate conditions.

Table 8.8 lists examples of the types of expressions you can use in predicates.

Table 8.8 Predicate Expression Examples

PREDICATE TYPE	EXPLANATION AND EXAMPLE
Node set	Uses an expression resembling a location path. Example: *//gem[./reserved]*, which means select all gems that have a child element node named <reserved> .
Strings	These require a match to a sequence of zero or more Unicode characters. Example: *gem[system=Ursae]* calls for any gem element node where the value of the cost element node contains the text string "Ursae".
Position within the context	Within a given context, other nodes may exist. We can specify that the node at a certain position in the current context is the one to be selected. Example: *gem[position()=3]* calls for the third element node named <gem>.

Boolean expressions like AND or OR can also be used as part of the predicates. The XPointer family of languages supports the same predicate types as XPath.

XPath Expressions Can Contain Functions

We mentioned that XPath expressions can contain location paths, functions, or a combination of both. Now that we have discussed location paths, let's look at functions. Previously, we saw a generic expression that consisted of a location path, which, in turn, consisted of one or more location steps:

```
axis1::node-test1[predicate1]/... axisn::node-testn[predicaten]
```

This is the generic syntax for an expression that contains a function:

```
function1 (argument1-1...argument1-n)/...
                              /functionn (argumentn-1...argumentn-n)
```

XPath has a core function library that consists of over two dozen functions in four categories. XPointer supports those functions and adds another eight functions to provide additional precision. Each function takes zero or more arguments and returns a single selection result.

Table 8.9 lists all the XPath and XPointer functions, so that you can find them in one location. An XPath-compatible parser only uses the XPath functions to evaluate XPath expressions; an XPointer parser can use all the functions.

For explanations, syntax, and other details regarding the XPath functions, please refer to the W3C Web site www.w3.org/TR/xpath#corelib. For similar information regarding the XPointer functions, please refer to www.w3.org/TR/2001/CR-xptr-20010911/#xptr-functions.

Table 8.9 XPath and XPointer Functions

XPATH FUNCTION GROUP	FUNCTION NAME
Node-set functions	last()
	position()
	count(node-set)
	id(object)
	local-name(node-set?)
	namespace-uri(node-set?)
	name(node-set?)
String functions	string(object?)
	concat(string, string, string*)
	starts-with(string, string)
	contains(string, string)
	substring-before(string, string)
	substring-after(string, string)
	substring(string, number, number?)
	string-length(string?)
	normalize-space(string?)
	translate(string, string, string)
Boolean functions	boolean(object)
	not(boolean)
	true()
	false()
	lang(string)

(continued)

Table 8.9 *(continued)*

XPATH FUNCTION GROUP	FUNCTION NAME
Number functions	number(object?)
	sum(node-set)
	floor(number)
	ceiling(number)
	round(number)
XPOINTER FUNCTIONS	**FUNCTION NAME**
	string-range
	range-to
	here
	origin
	start-point
	end-point
	range
	range-inside

Example: id() Function

The id() function is well known and can be used to return locations whose ID attribute values are a match to that specified in the location part of the extension. The simplest example of an XPointer id() function refers to an id attribute in the element you want to point to. For example, the Space Gems price list in 2047diaprice.xml contains the element <gem id="smokey">, which uniquely identifies the <gem> element containing information about the Smokey diamond.

Using an id() function, we could point specifically to the Smokey diamond element with the fragment identifier #id("smokey"). The full URI would be as follows:

```
http://www.SpaceGems.com/2047diaprice.xml#xpointer(id("smokey"))
```

Using XPath and XPointer, you can also use a concept called a *bare name*, which is a syntactic abbreviation for the name specified with id(). Here is the shorthand bare name equivalent of the previous id() function example:

```
http://www.SpaceGems.com/2047diaprice.xml#smokey
```

We can see now that XPath expressions can contain paths or functions. In a full path, the function is contained in a predicate. In an abbreviated path, the function follows the connector symbol #.

Example: position() Function

We have already introduced the position() function in our <smokeyPrice> linking element example. Here it is again, in the second location step of the location path:

```
#xpointer(/diamonds/child::gem[position()=3]/cost)
```

The position() function acts as a counter for the various nodes the parser might encounter in a given context. In this example, the parser is told to look among the child nodes of the context node (at this point in the evaluation, the current context would be the <diamonds> element node) and select the third <gem> element node found there.

The XML Pointer Language Extends XPath

XPath expressions allow the parser to select document subresources down to the node level. In Chapter 9, when we work with Extensible Stylesheet Language (XSL) transformations, we will find XPath to be adequate, since we will only be working to the node level. However, for various reasons, we may find that node-level selections are not always adequate for selecting subresources. In this section, we discuss how the XPointer family of languages can extend XPath expressions to bring more precision to link traversal.

In the words of the W3C, "[XML Pointer Language], which is based on the XML Path Language (XPath), supports addressing into the internal structures of XML documents and external parsed entities. It allows for examination of a hierarchical document structure and choice of its internal parts based on various properties, such as element types, attribute values, character content, and relative position."

XML Pointer Language (XPointer) Version 1.0 became a Candidate Recommendation of the World Wide Web Consortium in September 2001. At that point, the document was considered stable by the XML Linking Working Group and was available for public review. In July 2002, however, XPointer 1.0 was superseded by the W3C's Working Drafts of:

- XML XPointer Language Framework (XPointer Framework, at www.w3.org/TR/xptr-framework)
- XPointer Element() Scheme at www.w3.org/TR/xptr-element/, for addressing elements by their position in the document tree

- XPointer xmlns() Scheme at www.w3.org/TR/xptr-xmlns/, for binding namespace prefixes to namespace name
- XPointer xpointer() Scheme at www.w3.org/TR/xptr-xpointer/, for full XPath-based addressing

These four XPointer documents are essentially subsets of the original September 2001 XPointer Candidate Recommendation. The W3C advises that all four documents are works in progress and "it is inappropriate to use W3C Working Drafts as reference material or to cite them as other than 'work in progress.'"

The twofold advantage of the XPointer family lies in its combined abilities to reach more precise locations in a document and to ultimately save network bandwidth, since it allows us to download only the data we need. The level of search and retrieval precision provided by XPath with XPointer fragment identifier features could not be achieved by HTML or by XLink/XPath combinations.

XPointer also does not require the addition of extra elements, attributes, or other components to target documents. However, if we have write access to those documents, we could add markup to them (for example, unique id attributes to element tags) that would enhance subresource selection.

Pointers Address a Document's Internal Structure

In the XPointer community, the name given to the latter part of the value specified for the locator attribute xlink:href is called a *pointer* (or extension or fragment identifier). The pointer consists of the xpointer keyword, followed by the path to the subresource location. Here, we focus mainly on full pointer specifications, since they make it easier to introduce basic XPointer concepts.

Earlier, we introduced an example linking element named <smokeyPrice> that contains an XPointer pointer:

```
<smokeyPrice xmlns:xlink="http://www.w3.org/1999/xlink"
     xlink:type="simple" xlink:show="new"
     xlink:href="http://www.SpaceGems.com/2047prices.xml#xpointer
          (/diamonds/child::gem[position()=3]/cost) />
```

The pointer is reproduced in the following:

```
#xpointer(/diamonds/child::gem[position()=3]/cost)
```

The pointer follows the target document name and is connected to that name by a connector symbol (in this case, it's #, which we call a hash symbol, pound sign, or number sign). It tells the parser to search for a portion of a resource within the 2047prices.xml document found in the document root directory at the Space Gems Web site.

For now, the pointer is essentially just an XPath expression, but we can add XPointer extensions to tell the parser to traverse to more precise locations within a target XML document to select subresources.

XPointer Basics: Points, Ranges, and Locations

To introduce more precision into the subresource selection process, we can use XPointer points and ranges. A *point* is a specific location in a document, whether between nodes or between characters within a node. A *range* is made up of all the XML content between two points, which can include parts of elements and text strings. To support points and ranges, XPointer also defines a concept called a *location*, which is either a point, range, or XPath node. Therefore, XPath's concept of a node set has expanded into a location set with the XPointer Working Drafts. Thus, location results returned by XPointer-compatible parsers can include nodes, points, and ranges, while those generated by XPath-compatible parsers consist only of nodes.

XPointer Points

XPointer allows us to select a specific point within a document. An XPointer point is defined in terms of two concepts: a node and an index consisting of a zero or positive integer. The node identifies the point's origin; the index indicates how far away a referenced point is from that origin.

Two different types of points exist—node-points and character-points. Node-points correspond to the gaps between nodes, whereas character-points correspond to positions within a single node. Thus, their index values are expressed using different units. We discuss node-points first, since the concept of child nodes is important to both but is better introduced with a discussion of node-points.

Node-points

Any container node may contain child nodes. If it does, then a point selected inside the node is called a *node-point*. When a developer specifies an index for a node-point, it is measured in child nodes. Thus, when a developer specifies an index number for a node-point inside a node, that index number must be equal to or less than the number of child nodes in the container node. If we specify an index of zero in the pointer, the parser will select a node-point just inside the container node, immediately before any child nodes. Any nonzero index *n* indicates the point immediately after the *nth* child node. Thus, an index of 3 selects a node-point immediately after the third child node and before the fourth.

To create a node-point, use the start-point() function:

```
xpointer(location path/node-test/start-point()[position()=position-
number]
```

Referring to the Space Gems price list, if we want to select a reference node-point just before the <system> element node in the fifth <gem> element node, we should code the pointer as follows:

```
xpointer(/diamonds/gem[5]/node()/start-point()[position()=1])
```

Character-points

If the origin node can contain only text and no child nodes, then the index is measured in characters. These are called *character-points*. The index of a character-point must be a positive integer or zero, and less than or equal to the length of the text string in the node. An index of zero indicates that the point selected by the parser will be immediately before the first character. If the index is 4, for example, then the point is immediately after the fourth character. Character-points cannot have preceding or following siblings or children in the location path/pointer. Note that XPointer collapses all consecutive white spaces into a single white space. Also, since the characters referred to are strictly within the data, we cannot place points inside markup tags.

To create our example character-point, we use the same start-point() function syntax as illustrated in the previous node-point section. Please refer to 2047diaprice.xml in Figure 8.2. If we want to place a reference character-point just before the "U" in Ursae, in the third <gem> element, then we should create the following pointer:

```
xpointer(/diamonds/gem[3]/system/text()/start-point()[position()=3])
```

XPointer Ranges

A range consists of all the XML structure between a start point and an end point. However, both points must be in the same document, and the start point cannot occur after the end point. If the start point and the end point coincide at the same location, then the range is said to be *collapsed*.

A range does not have to be completely contained within one subtree of a document. It can extend from one subtree to another. All you need are a valid start and end point, both situated within the same document.

To select a range, you can use the following functions:

- Start-point and end-point functions
- Range-oriented XPointer functions listed in Table 8.9 (range, range-inside, range-to, and string-range)

Example: XPointer Range

Here are a few examples of the use of XPointer range functions. (If you would like to learn about the many options available to you, please consult the XPointer Web site at www.w3.org/TR/xptr-xpointer/#datatypes.)

If we want to select the entire Smokey diamond <gem> element, including its tags, we can create a range with the start-point and end-point functions:

```
#xpointer start-point(/diamonds/gem[3]) to end-point(/diamonds/gem[3])
```

The range function also selects all content and tags. If we want to create the same selection with range, we use:

```
#xpointer (range/diamonds/gem[3])
```

If we just want to select the price of the Smokey diamond, and we don't want the start and end tags, we use the range-inside function:

```
#xpointer (range-inside/diamonds/gem[3]/cost)
```

If we want to select the nodes that pertain to all the diamonds that originated in the Sol system, we use string-range:

```
#xpointer (string-range/diamonds/gem/system, "Sol")
```

Finally, if we want to select the first two diamonds based on their unique id attribute values, we use range-to:

```
#xpointer (id ("cullinan")/range-to (id ("dark")))
```

Browser Display of XLink Links and Syntax

Figure 8.3 represents a typical Web page that includes our example <smokeyPrice> link. When the mouse pointer is placed over the Smokey link, the whole URI appears in the status bar at the bottom of the window. When the URI is clicked, link traversal is initiated, and Smokey's price displays according to the Web page document's link and style sheet specifications.

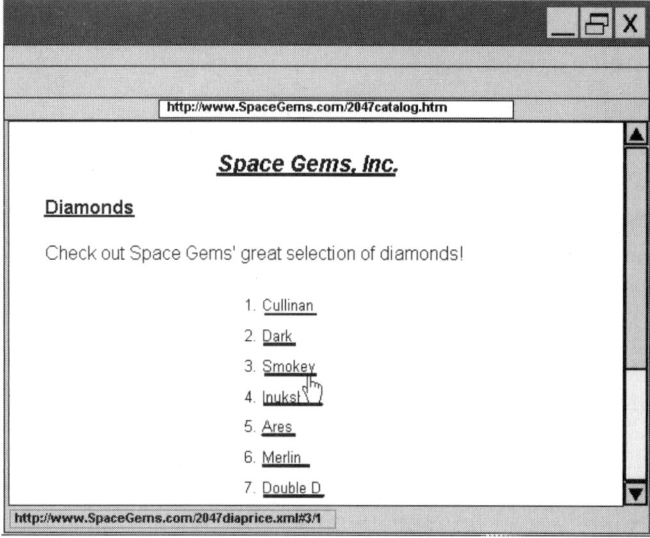

Figure 8.3 Web page with XPointer links.

If you are interested in seeing links like this in action, go to the W3C Web site at www.w3.org, which contains many examples.

Chapter 8 Labs: Using XLink, XPath, and XPointer

These are basic lab exercises. Many of these techniques are difficult to demonstrate using a set of basic tools such as XML editors and browsers. XLink, XPath, and XPointer devices are more often used in more sophisticated environments such as Java programming, application development, and transformations. Using such tools requires time and money. Without them, we can only create rudimentary labs.

The XLink and XPath Recommendations, as well as the XPointer family of Working Drafts, are not entirely supported by all browsers yet, and support is inconsistent from browser to browser. So, for these labs, we will use both Internet Explorer and Netscape Navigator to demonstrate that some features will only work in one while some will work in the other. This is still a young and rapidly evolving technology, and it may be a while yet before these techniques should be implemented on production Web sites. For these exercises, we provide the capability to deploy some basic working examples that should save you from having to generate all of the content yourself.

Lab 8.1: A Simple XLink

As you work through this lab, remember that the first link you create may work with Internet Explorer but not with Netscape. Meanwhile, the second link may work with Netscape but not with Internet Explorer.

1. Download the latest version of the Netscape Navigator browser. You can find it by following the Download Netscape links at www .netscape.com. When installing Netscape, accept all the default settings.
2. If you have not already done so, download the master.css, magicgems.xml, and research.xsd files from the lab exercises portion of the Chapter 8 page of this book's Web site (see the introduction for details). Save them to the C:\WWW\SpaceGems directory.
3. Using TurboXML or another XML editor, open gems1.xml.
4. Modify the existing XLink slightly and add a new simple XLink to the file that will point to magicgems.xml. When you are done, the modified code should look like this:

```
<!-- This link can be seen with both Netscape and
     Internet Explorer but only works with Internet Explorer -->
<info>Home Page,
     <link type="simple"
           href="http://localhost/SpaceGems"
           OnClick="location.href='http://localhost/SpaceGems' ">
           click here.
     </link>
</info>
<!-- This link can be seen with both browsers but will not work
with either; the specification is too new -->
<info>To see our Magical Gems,
     <link type="simple"
           xlink:href="magicgems.xml"
           xlink:actuate="onRequest"
           xlink:show="new"
           xlink:title="To Magical Gems and Spells">
           Magic Gems
     </link>
</info>
```

5. If you are using TurboXML as your editor, check for errors. You may have to remove any reference to any DTD or schema in order to make this document work.
6. Save the file.

7. Test the new links using both browsers.
   a. In each browser, type http://localhost/SpaceGems in the browser's location bar.
   b. When the home page appears, click the Quick List of Diamonds link to display gems1.xml.
   c. When the page displays, click the Magic Gems link following the phrase, To see our Magical Gems.
   d. Also, try to click the Click Here link following the phrase, To go back to the Home Page.

Some versions of Netscape may return a blank page. To fix this, change Netscape's caching preferences: On the toolbar, click Edit, Preferences, Advanced, Cache. Click Never, OK.

If the links work in one browser and not the other, do not worry. This is exactly what we are trying to demonstrate to you. We can't say exactly what will work and what will not work, because of the many different versions of browsers available. Hopefully, when the various specifications are more mature, these will likely all work.

8. This is an optional step. In the Chapter 7 lab exercises, you created cascading style sheets to format the display of XML files. At that point, to check the display results, you had to type "http://localhost/SpaceGems/magicgems.xml" in the locator bar of your browser.
9. Now create an HTML link in the Space Gems home page index.html document. Open index.html in Notepad and add the following code after the Quick List of Diamonds link but before the </div> tag:

```
<a href="magicgems.xml>The Magic of Gems</a>
```

10. As you can tell, this is not an XLink, just a normal HTML anchor link. Since this document is an HTML file, an XLink would not function.

Lab 8.2: Simple XLinking: Multiple Links Inside XML File

In this second lab, you will download another version of magicgems.xml and test its links. In Netscape, the page will display and the links will work. In Internet Explorer, the page will display, but the links won't work. Lab 8.3 takes this same file and implements XLinks in a more efficient fashion.

1. Download into the C:\WWW\SpaceGems directory a new version of magicgems.xml from the lab exercises portion of the Chapter 8 page on this book's Web site. (See the book's introduction for the URL and more information on this site.) This version contains several simple links to images of the magic gems.
2. Test the new links using both browsers.
   a. Start the browser applications in turn, and in each, type "http://localhost/SpaceGems" in the locator bar.
   b. When the home page displays, click the Quick List of Diamonds link, and when that page displays, click Magic Gems.
   c. From that page, click the title/links of the gems to display the images.
3. Internet Explorer should fail, but Netscape should work. Again, the images are linked to the gem names in the magicgems.xml file.
4. Click View (Page) Source on the toolbar inside one or both of the browsers to examine the modified code inside the magicgems.xml file. This shows you how the links were coded.

Lab 8.3: Outbound XLinks

This lab exercise may give you a better idea of how XLinks should function. Unfortunately, you will not be able to test it using either browser. Instead, you will install two new tools:

Fujitsu XLink Processor(XLiP). Developed by Fujitsu Limited, this implementation of XLink and XPointer is based on Fujitsu's Interstage XLiP product, which contains an XLink Processor. It can be used on platforms that support the Java Runtime Environment.

Java 2 Platform, Standard Edition (J2SETM) software, Version 1.4.1. From Sun Microsystems, Inc., this provides essential applications and utilities for developing applets and applications in the Java programming language.

Fujitsu's XLiP is a simple, straightforward, and very handy tool that allows you to test your XLink and XPointer code. We supply a couple of files for you to play with. As you will see in this lab, Fujitsu also provides some files that will help you understand the fundamental differences between simple and extended linking.

Downloading and Installing the Java J2SE Software

1. The Java platform software must be downloaded and installed first. Go directly to http://java.sun.com/j2se/1.4/, or use the link we have provided on the book's Web site provided in the introduction. Download the Java J2SE 1.4 software, and follow installation instructions. During the installation, accept all default settings.
2. Modify your computer system's PATH environment variable. If you are working on a Windows 2000 platform, follow steps similar to these:
   a. On your desktop, right-click the My Computer shortcut icon, and on its menu, click Properties.
   b. When the System Properties dialog window appears, click the Advanced tab.
   c. Click the Environment Variables button, and under System Variables, scroll down through the list of variables to the Path variable and highlight it.
   d. Click Edit, and in the Variable Value field of the resulting dialog window, add *;C:/jdk1.4.0_01/bin* to the end of the PATH (you should add the actual path to where the J2SE software was installed; you may have to check the directory locations with Windows Explorer). Once you have modified the Path variable, click OK to close all the dialog windows.
3. Test to ensure that the Java SDK is installed. Click Start, Programs, Accessories, Command Prompt to open a Command Prompt window. At the prompt, type in the following and then press Enter:

   ```
   java  -fullversion
   ```

4. The system responds with something similar to "java full version 1.4.x_0y", where major and minor revision numbers will appear instead of the x and y.
5. At this point, it is a best practice to reboot the computer system before downloading and installing the Fujitsu XLiP software. Rebooting ensures that the operating system internalizes the modified PATH environment on startup.

Downloading and Installing the Fujitsu XLiP Software

1. To download the Fujitsu XLiP software, go directly to the Fujitsu Web site at www.labs.fujitsu.com/free/xlip/en/. Read the messages there, and then click the [DOWNLOAD] link at the bottom of the page.

2. You will link to the first of two Fujitsu XLink Processor(XLiP)-Download pages. If you accept their conditions, click the [I ACCEPT] link.
3. At the next Fujitsu XLink Processor(XLiP)-Download page, select the link reflecting the appropriate executable file to download the file.
4. When prompted, choose to install (with some applications, you will use the Run button) the software, and while doing so, accept all default settings.
5. Eventually, you will see a page called XLink Tree Demo Application. This is the one. Move down to the "Let's get started!" section and follow the instructions.
6. Whenever you want to start the Fujitsu XLiP software, locate and double-click the XLinkDemo.jar file. You might find it handy to install a shortcut to that file on your Windows desktop.

Testing XLink Functionality of magicgems.xml

1. Download into the C:\WWW\SpaceGems directory another new version of magicgems.xml from the lab exercise portion of the Chapter 8 page of the book's Web site (see the introduction for its URL). Download the magicgems.dtd file, too.
2. If you haven't already done so, start the Fujitsu XLiP software by double-clicking the xlinkdemo.jar file.
3. In the XLiP software window, click Open File, and browse to find the C:\WWW\Spacegems\magicgems.xml file. Highlight that file and click Open.
4. Click the bullets to expand the items until you see the red TXT marker, as shown in Figure 8.4. The red marker denotes the location of the starting resource.
5. Click the object named Go to Spells, which has a red TXT mark next to it, and click Start Traversal.
6. Click the Outbound Link example, then click OK.
7. Click Malachite, then click Traverse.
8. The application will highlight a magic gem element. Click the bullets to the left of the (E) to expand the items until you see the actual text. That will confirm that you have traversed to the Malachite element.

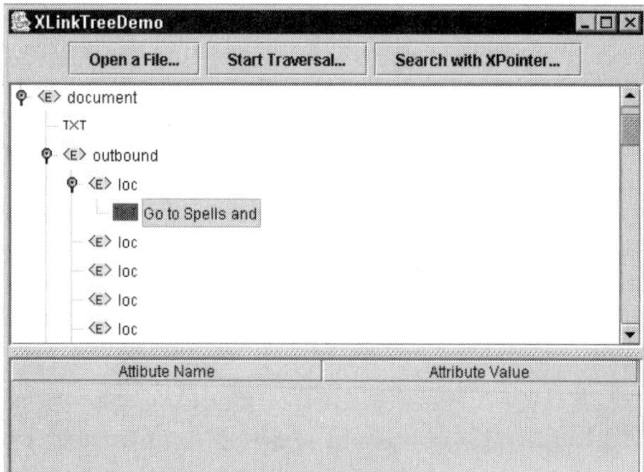

Figure 8.4 The red TXT marker denotes the starting resource for the traversal.

9. You can repeat the last two steps using the other two Outbound Link example choices. When traversing the various elements, try clicking the three options new, replace, and embed to observe their different behavior (none and other don't work). Choosing these options overrides the option that might have been coded directly in the magicgems.xml file.
10. Without exiting from XLiP, open either HTML-Kit or TurboXML, and view the source code for magicgems.xml. Notice how the elements have been reorganized and how id attributes have been inserted, compared to the version of the magicgems.xml file used in the second lab exercise.
11. Go back to XLiP, and click Search with XPointer. Deliberately enter an incorrect ID attribute value (for example, O110 for obsidian, instead of its correct O101 value). You will get an error message.
12. Now enter a correct ID attribute value for the Search with XPointer prompt.
13. Continue to play with the file until you understand the coding and functionality of the links.
14. Close all open files.

Lab 8.4: Comparing XLink Types

Fujitsu Limited's XLiP comes with several different sample files that illustrate the correct coding and use of XLinks. These files are installed on your system and located in the \extended and \simple subdirectories within a parent directory called xlinkdemo-1.4\examples. Within these subdirectories are a series of working examples of both simple and extended XLinks. Under the \extended directory, for example, four subdirectories are named:

- Inbound
- Multidirectional
- Outbound
- Third-party

View the source code for these files using HTML-Kit or TurboXML as you work with these files so that you can see the subtle differences in coding between the files as you work.

Inbound Links

1. Activate the XLiP application, then open the hub.xml file under the inbound directory.
2. Locate the red marker near the bottom of the file by expanding the <body> element.
3. Highlight the red marker on the <chapter> element, and click Start Traversal.
4. When XLiP prompts you, highlight Inbound link example and click OK.
5. The XLink should return you to the top of the file, where the code for the XLink resides. Thus, the term inbound. You are traversed inbound from the <body> of the file back into the XLink or into the defined xlink:type=resource.

Outbound Links

1. Now, with XLiP, open the hub.xml file under the outbound directory.
2. Locate the red marker near the top of the file by expanding the <loc> and <outbound> elements.
3. When XLiP prompts you, click Outbound link example and click OK. When prompted, highlight Chap. 1 and click Traverse.
4. Highlight the red marker on the TXT "From here" object, and click Start Traversal.

5. The XLink should take you to the chapter 1 <chapter> element where the Chap 1 id attribute resides. Thus, the term outbound. You are traversed outbound from the XLink into the data of the file, or away from the defined xlink:type=resource.

Multidirectional Links

1. Using XliP, open the hub.xml file under the multidirectional directory.
2. Locate the red marker near the top of the file by expanding the <doc> element and then expanding the <item> element.
3. Highlight the red marker on the <item> element, and click Start Traversal.
4. When XLiP prompts you, highlight Traversal to content page and click OK.
5. When prompted, click Chap. 1 cont and click Traverse.
6. XLiP should take you to the content of chapter 1. There should be another red marker on your target. Neither the term inbound nor outbound is used here because no resource is defined, only locators and arcs.
7. Use Notepad to examine the content of the hub.xml file. Notice that the Chap. 1 toc <loc> element is labeled *boo*, whereas the Chap.1 cont and Chap. 2 cont <loc> elements are labeled *hoge*. The arcs say that you can traverse from boo to hoge and then from hoge back to boo. Thus, you can travel from the Table of Contents to the chapters and back.
8. Continue to test the file and confirm that you can traverse back and forth.

Third-Party Links

1. Using XLiP, open the hub.xml file under the third-party directory.
2. Locate the red marker near the top of the file by expanding the <doc> element and then expanding the <item> element.
3. Highlight the red marker on the <item> element and click Start Traversal.
4. When prompted, click Third-Party Traversal, then click OK.
5. When prompted again, click Chap. 1 cont and click Traverse.

6. The XLink should take you to the content of chapter 1 in the file where the data resides. This time no additional red markers appear on the elements beneath that target. Again, neither the term inbound nor outbound is used here because no resource is defined, only two locators and one arc.
7. Examine the hub.xml file with Notepad. This time, the arc says that you can traverse from boo to hoge only, as opposed to the previous multidirectional demonstration, where you could traverse in both directions. Note that the top locator is labeled boo and the next locator is labeled hoge. The arc says boo to hoge, and that is it!
8. Continue to test the file and confirm that you can traverse back and forth.

Summary

Following are a few key concepts about XLink and XPath to review before proceeding to Chapter 9:

- HTML hyperlinks have proved inadequate for some XML-related situations. The solution has been to combine several XML-related languages: XLink, which is used for linking among documents; XPath, used for addressing nodes within XML documents; and XML Pointer, which extends XPath concepts and utilities to point to specific locations and ranges within documents.
- XLink provides the capability to create links in XML documents: simple HTML-like unidirectional links or sophisticated, even automatic, links among several sources and destinations.
- Generally speaking, XLink links are explicitly defined relationships between addressable resources or portions of resources. Simple-type links are those that associate exactly two participating resources, one local and one remote, with an outbound arc (that is, an arc traversing from the local resource to the remote resource).
- Extended links offer full XLink functionality, including outbound, inbound, and third-party arcs, plus arcs that can simultaneously connect a local resource to several remote resources. The structure of extended links can be fairly complex. XLink links can be nested within one another. However, only certain XLink elements can be combined and only certain attributes can be combined with certain type attributes.

- XPath addresses documents down to the node levels, so XPath treats its target XML documents as logical tree structures consisting of nodes. There are several types of nodes: root, element, attribute, text, comment, and processing instruction nodes. Nodes are not equivalent to element types.
- XPath's instructions to the parser are called expressions, which can be of several different forms. The most important are location paths and function calls. Location paths are composed of location steps that, in turn, are composed of axes, node tests, and predicates. They instruct the parser regarding navigation through the target document's structure.
- The XML Pointer family of languages is based on the XPath and allows addressing into the internal structures of XML documents and external parsed entities. Common XPointer concepts are locations, points, and ranges. They provide more precise location selection and reduced bandwidth usage.
- Browsers and other XLink/XPath/XPointer applications implement XML linking inconsistently. Various features may work with one but not with another. If you are interested in using XLink, XPath, and XPointer, check which implementations support them, and to what level.

Review Questions

1. Which of the following are considered resources from a linking standpoint?
   a. Programs
   b. Image documents
   c. Text files
   d. Applications
   e. All of the above
2. Match the following:

a. XPointer	i. Node selection
b. XPath	ii. Document selection
c. XLink	iii. Range selection

3. Which of the following are mandatory in XLink? (Choose all that apply.)
   a. A role="value" attribute in the start tag of the linking element
   b. A title="value" attribute in the start tag of the linking element
   c. A namespace declaration
   d. A type="value" attribute in the start tag of the linking element
4. Fill in the blank. "A simple link associates two resources, one termed ___________ and one termed ___________, with an arc traversing from the former to the latter."
5. In general terms (that is, without going into specifics), what are the two restrictions we discussed regarding XLink type elements and attributes?
6. True or false? "If you intend to create several simple links with consistent properties, then consider declaring a number of defaults in the DTD or schema to save time and effort while coding the linking elements."
7. Which is not a feature of extended-type links?
   a. They can contain data.
   b. They use arc-type elements to describe relationships among the resource.
   c. They don't have to be declared in DTDs or schemas.
   d. They point to local and remote resources.
   e. None of the above.
8. What two general groups of components do XPath/XPointer location steps contain?

9. If you want to select siblings "to the right" of the context node, which do you specify?
   a. child
   b. following
   c. attribute
   d. preceding-sibling
   e. None of the above
10. True or false? "Each location step consists of one axis, one node-step, and one predicate."
11. Briefly define the XPointer concept of a "location"; that is, what does it consist of?
12. Which of the following can you not use to define a range in XPointer?
   a. range-inside
   b. string-range
   c. start-point
   d. end-point
   e. None of the above

Answers to Review Questions

1. **e.** They are all resources that can be designated in XLinks. This information is found in the text, in the *Resources* section.
2. **a.** and **iii.**; **b.** and **i.**; **c.** and **ii**.
3. **c.** and **d.** This information is found in the text, in the *XLink Logical Structures* section.
4. A simple link associates two resources, one local and one remote, with an arc traversing from the former to the latter.
5. The two general restrictions are:
   a. Only certain XLink elements can be combined (or nested).
   b. Only certain attributes can be combined with each type attribute.
6. True. Details are in the text, in the section titled *Example: Simple-Type XLink*.
7. **c.** This information is found in the text, within the *Example: Extended-Type XLink* section.
8. Location steps contain components like the following:
   a. XPath-related nodes, axes, node tests, and zero or more predicates.
   b. XPointer-related features, such as points and ranges.
9. **e.** The answer should be "following-sibling," but it isn't one of the choices provided.
10. False. Generally, each step has one axis and one node-step. But they can have one or more predicates.
11. XPointer defines a location as either a point, a range, or an XPath node. So XPath's concept of a node set has expanded into a location set.
12. **e.** This information is found in the *XPointer Basics: Points, Ranges, and Locations* section.

XML Transformations

This chapter focuses on transforming XML documents for output, but not the same way as Chapter 7, "XML and Cascading Style Sheets," did. While cascading style sheets pertain to adding visual style to an XML document for its eventual display, these Chapter 9 transformations prepare XML data for further processing. These transformations will utilize the Extensible Stylesheet Language Transformation (XSLT) language, which is one component of the Extensible Stylesheet Language (XSL) family—XSL, XSLT, and XPath.

Unfortunately, in a single introductory-level chapter like this, we can only scratch the surface of XML transformations. But we'll show you the basics by discussing why transformations are necessary and explaining the operational model of a transformation—that is, how a transformation parser operates on a source XML document, according to instructions in a specific style sheet, to create a target document. We take you step-by-step through a simple transformation to introduce you to some of the considerations, concepts, components, and syntax involved. In the lab exercises, you will install and configure TIBCO Software, Inc.'s transformation software application called XMLTransform and then use it to do similar transformations.

Why Transform XML Data?

More and more XML vocabularies and documents are being developed by organizations within common industries, by individual organizations, and by individuals themselves. They are drawn to XML by its capability to represent data with unique and arbitrary element type names, its structuring capabilities, and its human-readable nature. But because several data standards were already in existence when XML came along, and several XML-related data standards have been developed since XML appeared, two general data compatibility problems have arisen: how to get XML to fit in with the existing non-XML standards and how to develop some level of compatibility among the XML-related vocabularies and data.

Although XML may present an effective format for structuring data, by itself it isn't a data-related panacea. It still has to get along with various databases, provide data for publishing tools, and cooperate with voice and video applications. At times, its documents must be expanded, reduced, reordered, and otherwise modified to meet many data challenges. Thus, wherever it comes from and whatever standards it meets when it's created, XML data can't always be used in its original form. It has to be transformed into another XML or non-XML format first. This is especially true as XML strives to meet the demands of the world of commerce and e-commerce. As more businesses link to their customers, clients, and other partners—or as departments within individual organizations are linked—the need arises to exchange information and conduct transactions online. These businesses create even more demands for data conversion. Take, for example, invoices. Invoices can be presented on a screen or printed, but they can also be used to "feed" applications pertaining to inventory, shipping, accounting, and even tax preparation. All or part of the data from a single XML invoice document might wind up as comma-delimited values in a database file, as part of an SQL script or HTTP message, or combined with a sequence of calls on a particular programming interface.

Converting the data involves several related and important activities: finding the raw data, extracting what is needed, converting it to a form that is useful to another party, and transmitting it to that party so that they can further manipulate it (add to it, subtract from it, add it to databases, distribute it further, or display it).

Just as increasing pressures exist to easily share and transmit information among organizations, pressures also arise to do so without having to create or purchase proprietary or otherwise-customized software. The XML development community has responded to some extent by creating the Extensible Stylesheet Language family of languages, and especially the XSL Transformation language, the primary subject of this chapter. These languages provide mechanisms for other XML developers to mine their XML data and modify it so that it can be used to the benefit of the rest of the connected world.

Converting XML to HTML for display is very common. At present, it may be the most common application of XML transformation. Consequently, this aspect of XML transformation is discussed in the text and lab exercises here. We show you how to perform transformations, and how to display the transformed data with your browser.

The W3C and Transformations

We will focus primarily on XML document transformations using XSLT, which is one component of a trio of XML-related languages:

- Extensible Stylesheet Language (XSL)
- XSL Transformations (XSLT)
- XML Path language (XPath)

Let's briefly discuss the development history of XSL, XSLT, and XPath.

The Extensible Stylesheet Language (XSL)

Because of its influence on the languages we will be using, it's important to know something of the origins of the Extensible Stylesheet Language. XSL hasn't always been the XSL it started out to be. The original XSL proposal was drafted and submitted to W3C in 1997, and a W3C XSL Working Group was formed just prior to the February 1998 endorsement of the first edition of the XML Recommendation.

XSL's developers originally thought XSL would be a platform- and media-independent formatting language composed of two parts: a formatting language and a transformation language. The formatting language would be a set of descriptive XML elements called *formatting objects* that would describe the various parts of page media as tables, headers, footnotes, and so on. The transformation language, in turn, would convert the structure and components (elements, attributes, and so on) found in one source XML document into a new structure (a result tree), consisting of those formatting objects, perhaps even in new and different target documents.

However, during XSL's development, the original XSL concept evolved, and three separate XML-related programming languages developed:

XSL Formatting Objects (XSL or XSL-FO). The XML vocabulary for specifying formatting semantics.

XSL Transformation (XSLT). The language for transforming XML documents.

XML Path language (XPath). An expression language used to access or refer to parts of an XML document.

XSLT 1.0 and XPath 1.0 became W3C Recommendations in November 1999; but for technical and nontechnical reasons, the (modern) Extensible Stylesheet Language (XSL) 1.0 Recommendation wasn't fully developed and endorsed as a W3C Recommendation until October 2001. XSL shares functionality and is compatible with the latest versions of CSS, although it uses a different syntax. But XSL also adds advanced styling features in the areas of pagination and scrolling, result tree construction, page layout, display areas, internationalization, and linking. The XSL-FO vocabulary was designed so that data could be displayed with a wide variety of media—on-screen, hard copy, or voice.

For further information on XSL, start at the W3C's XSL Web site at www.w3.org/Style/XSL/WhatIsXSL.html

XSL Parsers

An XSL/XSLT parser (their functions are often combined in a single application) takes an XML document and an XSL style sheet and produces a rendering of the document. XSL and XSLT processors are readily available. Some processors are standalone; others can be integrated with other integrated development environments. You can find several by checking these Web sites:

- The W3C Web site at www.w3.org/Style/XSL/
- The XSL Implementations page at the Open Directory Project Web site at http://dmoz.org/Computers/Data_Formats/Markup_Languages/XML/Style_Sheets/XSL/Implementations/
- The software library Web page of "The XML Cover Pages–Extensible Stylesheet Language (XSL)" at http://xml.coverpages.org/xslSoftware.html

In the lab exercises, you will download and install TIBCO Software Inc.'s application named XMLTransform, which is part of their TIBCO Extensibility platform. It is an individual XSL processor that doesn't require an integrated development environment.

The XSL Transformation Language (XSLT)

XSLT is the language we'll use for the actual XML document transformations in this chapter. XSLT is designed for transforming one XML document into another (or into HTML), and it uses its own kind of style sheet to do so. But don't confuse XSLT style sheets with cascading style sheets. Cascading style sheets concentrate on how data is displayed. XSLT style sheets actually change the structure and type of XML data. They can add, subtract, duplicate, and sort nodes (elements, attributes, text, processing instructions, namespaces, comments, and other components). XSLT style sheets, therefore, have a vocabulary and structure different from CSS. XSL and XSLT use XML notation, whereas, as we saw in Chapter 7, CSS uses its own vocabulary. XSLT style sheets can transform one XML document into another XML document, one using an XML vocabulary different from the original. XSLT is often used as a general-purpose XML processing language, independent of XSL, to create HTML Web pages, other text formats, audio and video presentations, and database input from XML data.

Although they are quite different, and CSS is more appropriate for some tasks, XSL, XSLT, and CSS can also be used together. For example, XSL/XSLT can be used to transform XML data from a source document to a target document, and then CSS can be used to style the resulting target document data.

Like CSS, XSLT is different from conventional programming languages because it is a declarative language that uses template rules to specify how XML documents should be processed. Unlike conventional programming languages, which are sequential, these declarative template rules can occur in any order.

Like XPath, XSLT considers documents to be composed of nodes in a treelike structure. Its style sheets declare what output should be produced when the parser matches a pattern in a given source XML document.

At this writing, the XSL Working Group has generated Working Draft documents for the XSLT 2.0 and XPath 2.0 Recommendations. For information regarding the new proposals, check them out at www.w3.org/TR/xslt20/ and www.w3.org/TR/xpath20/, respectively.

XML Path Language (XPath)

As we discussed in Chapter 8, "XLinks," the XML Path language (XPath) is used to find the information in an XML document. XPath considers documents to be composed of nodes of various types in a treelike logical structure and, so, allows us to address parts of an XML document.

In Chapter 8, we used XPath to create links. But XPath is an important component of XML style sheet transformations because it enables us to specify the parts of a document that we want to transform. Using XPath we can specify the locations of structures or data in an XML document and then process the information in them with XSLT.

In practice, we'll see that—just as when we applied XPath with XPointer and XLink—it can be difficult to determine where XSLT stops and XPath starts. But with practice, using the two together will become almost second nature.

Sample XML Transformation: Tabulating a List of Diamonds

The best way to discuss XML transformations at an introductory level is to actually do a sample transformation. Throughout the remainder of this chapter, a sample transformation will be examined to illustrate some XSLT transformation concepts, syntax, and structure. The transformation extracts a portion of a list of diamonds currently stored in an XML document called gems1_source.xml. It then displays the extracted portion in a browser in HTML format. You will do the same transformation exercise in Lab 9.3.

Our approach here is to briefly describe the overall process, then examine the source document. After that, we'll examine the XSLT style sheet in some detail, since that is where the transformation is defined and shaped.

There are two basic phases to a transformation:

Structural transformation. The data is converted from the structure of the incoming source XML document to the structure of the target output.

Formatting. The new structure is output in the required format (examples: markup appropriate for HTML, PDF, DB2, Oracle, or other formats).

Figure 9.1 illustrates a basic XSLT transformation process inside an XSL/XSLT compatible application. The tornado in the lower portion of the figure represents the two-phase transformation, as defined in the XSLT style sheet. The documents and other terms in the figure will be clarified as the chapter progresses.

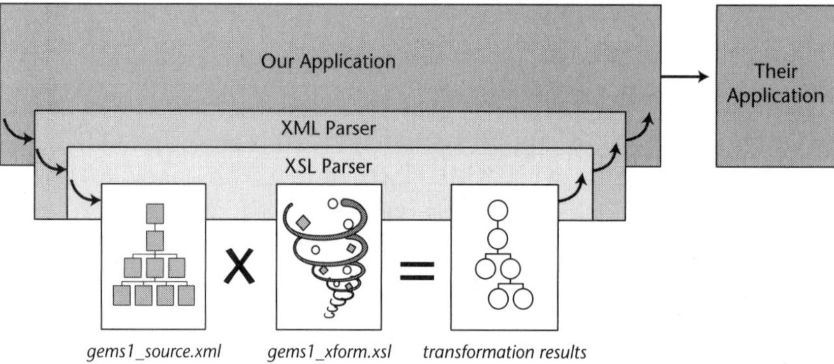

Figure 9.1 Basic XSLT transformation process.

Briefly summarized, that overall process is as follows:

1. An application activates an XML parser and passes it the name of a source XML document, which contains the source nodes in a treelike structure. The application could be an integrated development environment, an industry- or organization-specific application, or some commercial application. In Figure 9.1, the application is called "our application," and the source document is represented by gems1_source.xml.
2. From references within the source document, the XML parser locates a validating DTD or schema and an XSLT style sheet (represented in the figure by gems1_xform.xsl).
3. The XML parser validates the various documents and passes control to an XSL parser. The XSL parser, using the XSLT style sheet as its guide, performs the specified transformation according to the style template rules in the style sheet and generates the appropriate structure containing the transformation results (also called the results tree). The results may, depending on "our application," become an actual target file. Regardless, the results will, in turn, be used as a data source by another application (represented by "their application"). It is likely that any subsequent formatting of the data for display, if applicable, will be done by "their application" using cascading style sheets.

The XML Source Document

Have a look at the gems1_source.xml source document in Figure 9.2. It is a well formed and, we presume, valid XML document. In the figure, we have numbered all the nodes. Attributes and pseudo-attributes have been numbered according to their corresponding prolog statements or element nodes. The root node contains three prolog statement nodes and the root element node named <diamonds>. The root element, in turn, contains several more nested element nodes, some of which have attribute nodes.

By now, you should recognize most of the statements, element types, and attributes in the gems1_source.xml document. The third node (second line) of the XML document contains a style sheet processing instruction statement with a type="text/xsl" pseudo-attribute. Here, the parser is told to find and apply an XSL type of style sheet (if the value of the type had been specified as text/css, then the processor would have to apply a cascading style sheet). The href="gems1_xform.xsl" pseudo-attribute tells the processor where to look for the style sheet file. The interpretation of this instruction is "look in the same directory in which you found this XML document for an XSLT style sheet document named gems1_xform.xsl."

```
[1]                              [2A]    [3A]    [2B]
[2] <?xml version = "1.0" encoding = "UTF-8"?>   [3B]
[3] <?xml-stylesheet href = 'gems1_xform.xsl' type = 'text/xsl'?>
[4] <! DOCTYPE DIAMONDS SYSTEM "gems1.dtd" >
[5] <diamonds>
[6]         <info>To go back to the Home Page,  [7B]
[7]                 <link type = "simple" href = "http://localhost/SpaceGems"
                [7A]  OnClick = "location.href='http://localhost/SpaceGems' ">
                [7C]  click here. </link>
        </info>
                                                          [9D]   [9B]
[8]         <info>To see our Magical Gems,
[9]                 <link xmlns:xlink = "http://www.w3.org/1999/xlink" xlink:type = "simple"
                [9A]  xlink:href = "magicgems.xml" xlink:actuate = "onRequest"
                [9C]  xlink:show = "new" xlink:title = "To Magical Gems and Spells">
                [9E]  Magic Gems</link>
        </info>
[10]        <gem>                                  [9F]
[11]                <name>Cullinan</name>
[12]                <carat>3106</carat>
[13]                <color>H</color>
[14]                <clarity>VS1,VS2-Very Slightly Imperfect</clarity>
[15]                <cut>Rough</cut>
[16]                <cost>2174200</cost>
        </gem>
[17]        <gem>
[18]                <name>Dark</name>
[19]                <carat>500</carat>
[20]                <color>J</color>
[21]                <clarity>SL1,SL2-Slightly Imperfect</clarity>
[22]                <cut>Rough</cut>
[23]                <cost>450000</cost>
        </gem>
[24]        <gem>
[25]                <name>Sparkler</name>
[26]                <carat>105</carat>
[27]                <color>F</color>
[28]                <clarity>IF-Internally Flawless</clarity>
[29]                <cut>Super Ideal</cut>
[30]                <cost>126000</cost>
        </gem>
[31]        <gem>
[32]                <name>Merlin</name>
[33]                <carat>41</carat>
[34]                <color>D</color>
[35]                <clarity>FL-Flawless</clarity>
[36]                <cut>Ideal</cut>
[37]                <cost>82000</cost>
        </gem>
    </diamonds>
```

Figure 9.2 The XML source document.

Table 9.1 lists six pseudo-attributes that may appear in style sheet processing instructions.

Table 9.1 Pseudo-Attributes Used in <?xml-stylesheet ?> Processing Instructions

PSEUDO-ATTRIBUTE	EXPLANATION
alternate	"Yes" or "no"; default is "no"
charset	Optional; the character set pertaining to the style sheet
href	Required; indicates the location of the style sheet; format is URI
media	Optional; indicates the type of target medium/media
title	Optional; names the style sheet
type	Required; indicates the kind of style sheet (for example, text/xsl indicates an XSL style sheet; text/css indicates a cascading style sheet)

An XSLT style sheet can also be embedded in an XML source document. If it is, then the style sheet declaration in the source document is similar to:

```
<?xml-stylesheet type="text/xml" href="#stylesheetIdName" ... ?>
```

The following element should appear later in the document, and the style sheet components would follow:

```
<xsl:stylesheet id="stylesheetIdName" .... >
```

Figure 9.3 depicts the nodal structure of the gems1_source.xml document. The source tree is presented here so that, once we've reviewed the transformation, you can compare the source tree with the result tree. Source and target trees are valuable design tools for planning transformations and valuable result-checking tools. This source tree is not just an element tree; it shows not only the elements in gems1.xml but other types of nodes as well: elements, attributes, and declarations. We suggest creating nodal structure diagrams for all documents you want to transform. You can make them as simple or as complex as you want. For example, empty elements (there aren't any in this case) might be in different types of containers, or we could have indicated which elements contain text and which have other entities (to keep things simple here, we stayed with text only). In Figure 9.3, we included node numbers in the diagram that correspond to the numbers in the source document; attribute and pseudo-attribute numbers have been grayed.

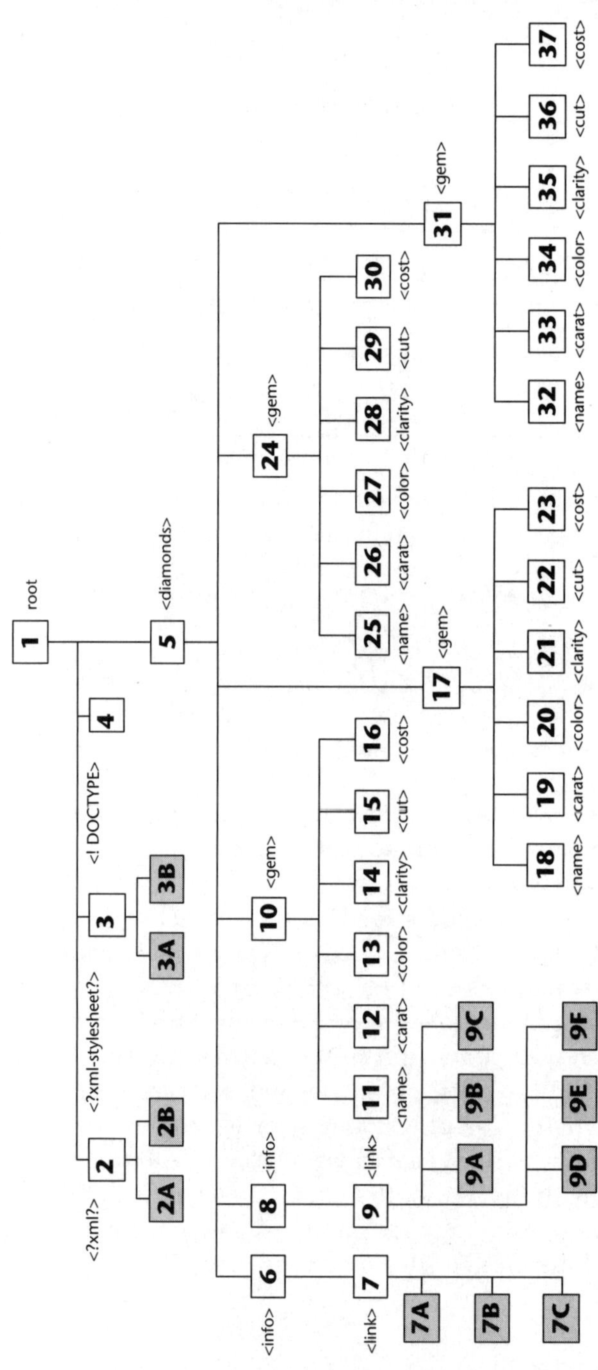

Figure 9.3 Nodal structure of the XML source document.

The document's root node is at the top of the source tree structure. Beneath it is the document node <diamonds> with its prolog statements. Beneath them, from left to right, are the child nodes from gems1_source.xml. The order matches the order presented in gems1_source.xml.

The XSLT Style Sheet

The following step-by-step explanation provides an overview of the considerations, concepts, components, options, and syntax involved in the design and construction of a simple transformation. This explanation will come in handy when you conduct the labs at the end of the chapter.

XSLT style sheets can occur:

- As XML documents of their own, with an <xsl:stylesheet> element as the root element.
- Within XSLT style sheets embedded in non-XML resources.
- Within <xsl:stylesheet> elements in XML documents (we provided the syntax earlier, when we discussed the XML source document).

For our example, the XSLT style sheet is a well-formed, separate XML document. Figure 9.4 illustrates our XSLT style sheet, named gems1_xform.xsl.

The first node of the style sheet is its root node, which contains both the prolog and the data instance portions of the document. The second node (the first line of text) is the now-familiar XML declaration or header. It is the only mandatory prolog statement.

The third node is the style sheet element <xsl:stylesheet>. Not surprisingly, this tag tells the parser that this is a style sheet document. The tag <xsl:transform> could be used instead of <xsl:stylesheet>; they are synonymous. The <xsl:transform> tag also uses the same attributes as <xsl:stylesheet>: id, extension-element-prefixes, exclude-result-prefixes, and version.

We include the namespace declaration xmlns:xsl="http://www.w3.org/1999/XSL/Transform" in the start tag for the <xsl:stylesheet> element. Every conventional XSLT element tag in this style sheet begins with the prefix xsl: to indicate that the tag conforms to the W3C XSLT Recommendation and to make it easier for any other reader to pick out the style sheet components. Remember, you can always specify your own unique prefix, but generally, we suggest going along with this convention.

The xsl:stylesheet tag is followed by a version attribute, indicating the version of XSLT to which the style sheet conforms. In this case, the version is XSLT 1.0. (At this writing, XSLT 2.0 has reached Working Draft status with the W3C, so version numbers may have changed by the time you read this. Check the status at the XSLT 2.0 Web site at www.w3.org/ TR/xslt20/.)

```
1
2  <?xml version = "1.0" encoding = "UTF-8"?>
3  <xsl:stylesheet xmlns:xsl = "http://www.w3.org/1999/XSL/Transform" version = "1.0">
4    <xsl:output method = "xml" indent="yes" version="1.0" />
5    <xsl:template match = "/diamonds">
6      <xsl:element name = "html">
7        <xsl:element name = "head">
8          <xsl:element name = "title">
9            <xsl:text>Space Gems Quick List of Diamonds</xsl:text>
           </xsl:element>
         </xsl:element>
10       <xsl:element name = "body">
11         <xsl:element name = "h1">
12           <xsl:text>Space Gems Quick List of Diamonds</xsl:text>
           </xsl:element>
   <!-- This is where we create an HTML table to display the information in our gems1_source.xml document -->
                               <!-- Begin the HTML table -->
13                                         <xsl:element name = "table">
14                                          <xsl:apply-templates select = "gem"/>
                                             </xsl:element>
                               <!--End of the HTML table-->
         </xsl:element>
       </xsl:element>
     </xsl:template>
15   <xsl:template match = "gem">
16     <xsl:element name = "tr">
17       <xsl:apply-templates select = "name"/>
18       <xsl:apply-templates select = "carat"/>
19       <xsl:apply-templates select = "color"/>
20       <xsl:apply-templates select = "clarity"/>
21       <xsl:apply-templates select = "cut"/>
22       <xsl:apply-templates select = "cost"/>
       </xsl:element>
     </xsl:template>
23   <xsl:template match = "name">
24     <xsl:element name = "td">
25       <xsl:value-of select = "."/>
       </xsl:element>
     </xsl:template>
26   <xsl:template match = "carat">
27     <xsl:element name = "td">
28       <xsl:value-of select = "."/>
       </xsl:element>
     </xsl:template>
29   <xsl:template match = "color">
30     <xsl:element name = "td">
31       <xsl:value-of select = "."/>
       </xsl:element>
     </xsl:template>
32   <xsl:template match = "clarity">
33     <xsl:element name = "td">
34       <xsl:value-of select = "."/>
       </xsl:element>
     </xsl:template>
35   <xsl:template match = "cut">
36     <xsl:element name = "td">
37       <xsl:value-of select = "."/>
       </xsl:element>
     </xsl:template>
38   <xsl:template match = "cost">
39     <xsl:element name = "td">
40       <xsl:value-of select = "."/>
       </xsl:element>
     </xsl:template>
   </xsl:stylesheet>
```

Figure 9.4 An XSLT style sheet.

The <xsl:stylesheet> element may contain any of several types of element types as direct children or top-level elements; these are listed in Table 9.2. They provide additional specifications to the style sheet. We discuss some of them in more detail later in this section. If we miss one you are interested in, or if you just need more information about them, check the W3C XSLT Recommendation at www.w3.org/TR/xslt.

Table 9.2 Top-Level Elements

ELEMENT NAME	EXPLANATION
xsl:output	Specifies how to output the result tree.
xsl:template	Indicates a template rule, which tells the parser how to transform a node.
xsl:include	Includes an additional XSLT style sheet; uses an href attribute with a URI value to indicate the location of the style sheet to be included.
xsl:import	Imports a style sheet. Importing is the same as including, except that the definitions and template rules in the *importing* style sheet will take precedence over those in the *imported* style sheet.
xsl:strip-space	If an element name matches a name test in an xsl:strip-space element, then it is removed from the set of white space-preserving element names.
xsl:preserve-space	If an element name matches a specific name test in an xsl:preserve-space element, then it is added to the set of white space-preserving element names.
xsl:key	Declares a set of keys for each document using this element. A key is a generalized identifier.
xsl:decimal-format	Declares a decimal-format, which controls the interpretation of a format pattern used by the format-number function. A name attribute specifies a particular format. If there is no name attribute, then the element declares the default decimal-format.
xsl:namespace-alias	Declares that a namespace URI is an alias for another namespace URI.
xsl:attribute-set	Defines a named set of attributes. A following *name* attribute specifies the name of the attribute set.

(continued)

Table 9.2 *(continued)*

ELEMENT NAME	EXPLANATION
xsl:variable	One of two elements used to bind variables (the other is xsl:param). Adds a *name* attribute and specifies a parsed character data-related name as a value for it. That specified value becomes a variable name that can thereafter be combined with other specifications (for example, element names) to search for data or to create display specifications. For more details and examples, refer to www.w3.org/TR/xslt. For the difference, see xsl:param, below.
xsl:param	Binds variables (the other is xsl:variable, above). Also uses a *name* attribute. The difference between xsl:param and xsl:variable is that the value specified on the xsl:param variable is only a default value for the binding. For more details and examples, refer to www.w3.org/TR/xslt.

The top-level elements may occur in any order except for the <xsl:import> element or its alternate, <xsl:include>; these must occur first when they're used.

The <xsl:stylesheet> element may contain elements that do not originate in the XSLT namespace, as long as the expanded names of those elements have non-null URIs. Thus, you can't specify a null namespace like xmlns:xyz= " " and then attempt to use xyz: as a prefix for an element name.

In the fourth node, with the <xsl:output> element, the style sheet tells the parser what output should be produced when a pattern in the XML document is matched. The <xsl:output> element allows style sheet authors to specify how they wish the result tree to be output. The <xsl:output> element is only allowed as a top-level element, since the specification it provides is fundamental to the transformation.

Ten possible attributes are allowed within the <xsl:output> element. These are listed in Table 9.3.

Table 9.3 List of Available xsl:output Attributes

ATTRIBUTE NAME	EXPLANATION
method	The format of the output; optional. Values = xml, html, text, "qualifiedName."
version	The version of the output format version specified; optional. Value = version number (decimal).
encoding	The character set used for encoding; optional. Value = text specification (for example, UTF-8, UTF-16); case-insensitive.

Table 9.3 *(continued)*

ATTRIBUTE NAME	EXPLANATION
omit-xml-declaration	Optional; values = yes, no. "Yes" indicates that the XML declaration (i.e., <?xml...?>) should be omitted in the output. "No" indicates otherwise.
standalone	Optional; values = yes, no. "Yes" indicates that the result should be a standalone document. "No" indicates otherwise.
doctype-public	Optional; value = text. Indicates the public identifier to be used in the <!doctype> declaration in the output.
doctype-system	Optional; value = text. The system identifier to be used in the <!doctype> declaration in the output.
cdata-section-elements	Optional; value = list of names. A list (separated by white space) of elements whose content is to be output in CDATA sections.
indent	Values = yes, no; optional. "Yes" indicates that output should be indented to indicate the hierarchic structure (for readability). "No" indicates that output should not be indented.
media-type	Value = mimetype (the media type of the output); optional.

Of the 10 attributes available, only three are specified in our <xsl:output> element: method, indent, and version.

The method attribute specifies the method that the developer wants to use to output the result tree. The value must be a qualified name (that is, it must contain a prefix, a colon, and a local name portion, as discussed in Chapter 3, "Anatomy of an XML File"). If there is no prefix, then only three options are available for the values specified for the method attribute: xml, html, or text. Under certain circumstances, the default value may be html (for further information, check the XSLT Web site); usually, the default value is xml (a well-formed XML document). In this case, the result tree is actually specified as xml.

Although XML is specified as the output method, nodes 6 through 12 seem to stipulate HTML as the output method. XML information is provided, but the HTML tags prevail. This will be explained when the <xsl:template ... > element types are discussed later in this chapter.

The version attribute specifies the version of the output method. In our example, we've specified XML Version 1.0 as the output method for the result tree. In the future, things are likely to change, so if the XSLT parser does not support a specified version of XML, it should use a version of XML that it does support. The XML version specified in the style sheet's XML declaration should correspond to the version of XML that the XSLT processor uses to output the result tree. The default value is Version 1.0.

The indent attribute specifies whether the XSLT processor should add white space when outputting the result tree. Possible values are yes or no. A yes value means the xml output method may add white space to the result tree output to create the familiar hierarchical structure, which makes the output more readable. A no value means no additional white space is required. The default value is no. If you are using XML documents that contain mixed content elements, then we suggest you not specify indent = "yes".

Node 5: Begin Transformation Using Query Contexts and First Template Rule

To this point, the transformation process hasn't quite begun. For processing to begin, we must specify the relevant query context portion within the source tree's nodes—the portion of the gems1_source.xml that contains the information that we want the XSL parser to access, manipulate, and copy to the output. This process is also called setting the context or matching the context. Setting the query context for the parser and keeping track of the context in which the parser is operating at any given moment during the transformation is crucial to planning, execution, and troubleshooting.

In node 5, we see the first significant XSLT programming feature: a mapping construct called a *template rule*. XSLT is different from conventional programming languages because it is based on template rules that specify how XML documents should be processed. In this case, node 5 is the preeminent template rule of this transformation.

A template rule is specified with the <xsl:template...> element type and consists of two parts: the pattern and the template. The pattern identifies the query context portion—the source nodes to be manipulated. The template, in turn, describes the structure to generate. The pattern is indicated by specifying a match attribute and its respective value in the <xsl:template ... > start tag.

The value specified for the match attribute sets the context for the new template rule. In other words, it identifies the source node or nodes to which the new template rule applies. That value is an XPath expression. In node 5, we specify the /diamonds node; thus, the node named diamonds is a child of the root node in the source document. The literal translation is "I want to replace the whole /diamonds node with what is found in this template rule, between the <xsl:template> start and end tags in node 5 here." Stated another way, the content listed within node 5—that is, between the <xsl:template ... > start tag and its corresponding </xsl:template> end tag—will appear in the output. This is a pretty far-reaching rule, in this case, because what falls between those node 5 tags is an entire HTML document!

Classroom Q & A

Q: In the W3C XSLT 1.0 Recommendation and in other XML books, I've seen that template rule <xsl:template> start tags can contain name attributes, but the explanations aren't very good. When do we use name="value" in the <xsl:template> start tag?

A: Template rules themselves can be given names of their own, then later be invoked by their names. For those template rules, the respective <xsl:template> elements are given name attributes that specify the name of the template. The value specified for the name attribute is a qualified name. If such a template rule's <xsl:template> tag contains a name attribute, it may also, but not necessarily, contain a match="value" attribute to indicate that it should only apply to certain nodes.

So far, we have set the context to an element node—the document element node named <diamonds>. If you need to match to other types of nodes, Table 9.4 will help by providing syntax for setting the context of other node types.

Table 9.4 Syntax for Matching to Nodes

NODE TYPE	SYNTAX	EXPLANATION
Document root	<xsl:template match="/">	The source document's root node
Element	<xsl:template match= "nodeName">	A specific node
	<xsl:template match= "nodeName1/nodeName2">	A specific child of another specific node
	<xsl:template match= "nodeName1//nodeName">	Specific grandchild(ren) of a specified element node
	<xsl:template match= "docnodename/*/ nodename">	Specific descendants of a specified element node
Namespace	<xsl:template match= "nodeName"> <xsl:value-of select= "@prefix:nameSpaceName"/>	Specific element node and select the namespace value
Comment	<xsl:template match= "comment()">	Specific comment (used to convert a comment from XML's <!–comment --> form to another form)

(continued)

Table 9.4 *(continued)*

NODE TYPE	SYNTAX	EXPLANATION
Processing instruction	<xsl:template match="/ processing instruction()">	All the processing instructions in the document root
	<xsl:template match="/ processing instruction (piName)">	A specific processing instruction named piName
Text	<xsl:template match= "text()">	All text
Attribute	<xsl:value-of select= "@attributename">	A specific attribute
	<xsl:value-of select= "nodeName/@*">	All the attributes of a specific node

Nodes 6 through 12: Creating Elements Using <xsl:element>

Although we could insert element nodes with their original names, XSLT provides us with the capability to create customized elements. The name of the new element is specified as the value for the name attribute within the <xsl:element> start tag. We could even provide a namespace attribute in the start tag, but in the case of nodes 6 through 12—and others in this transformation document—that isn't necessary.

In a similar vein, we could use XSLT's <xsl:attribute> element to add attributes to elements created with <xsl:element>. We could create whole attribute sets independent of the element with XSLT's <xsl:attribute-set name="attributeSetName"> element and call the attribute sets in with the use-attribute-sets="attributeSetName" attribute. However, that won't be necessary for these nodes.

In node 6, we only want to create a basic HTML document structure: the root element <html>, which contains <head> and <body> elements. Nodes 7 through 12 create the basic HTML document structure element types.

Node 13: Building an HTML Table with XSLT Element Types

Node 13 marks the beginning of the creation of an HTML table within the body of the HTML document. However, instead of containing a number of <tr> elements that, in turn, would contain <td> elements, the <xsl:element name="table"> element only contains one child of its own: the <xsl:apply-templates> element. What does that mean? We can explain as we go along.

Node 14: Processing Continues on the Source <gem> Node

The <xsl:apply-templates> element in node 14 instructs the parser to apply at least one template rule for the source document nodes; the names of those nodes are specified with its select attribute. In this case, courtesy of node 5, the parser is already in the <diamonds> node query context, so select="gem" means to look for a child node named <gem> in that context.

From the source document, we see that the parser will find four <gem> nodes nested in the <diamonds> node. Which <gem> should it choose? Actually, the <xsl:apply-templates> instruction is recursive: It tells the parser to apply the new template rule once for each <gem> node that it encounters. So the parser is told, in effect, to apply the new template rule four times. Its recursive nature makes <xsl:apply templates> another fairly powerful instruction.

Now that the parser knows where it is (in <diamonds>) and what it is to look for (the four <gem>s), how will it know what template rule to apply? The answer follows.

Node 15: The Current Template Rule and a Template Rule for <gem>

Now that the parser is aware that it needs a template rule to apply to the four <gem> nodes, it will look for a template rule introduced by an <xsl:template match="gem"> start tag. It finds one immediately, in node 15. Node 15 effectively says "make the <gem> node your query context now, and replace the <gem> node with the template rule pattern to follow, between the <xsl:template> start and end tags."

Here we have invoked something called the *current template rule*. At any point in the processing of an XSLT style sheet, if another template rule is activated by matching a pattern like "nodeName"—here the node name is gem—then the "gem" template rule suspends the current "/diamonds" template rule for the extent of the instantiation of "gem." When the "gem" template rule is finished, control passes back to the "/diamonds" template rule.

We don't use the term *instantiation* very often in this book, though we could. It means the creation of a data structure with its own set of subroutines.

Node 16: Creating the First Row in the HTML Table

Node 16 begins with the <xsl:element name="tr"> start tag, which tells the parser to create an HTML row element. From our knowledge of HTML/XHTML, we know that the contents of the row will be found between the row element's start and end tags. So the parser looks at nodes 17 through 22.

Node 17: More Template Patterns Fill Out the Table Row

When the parser reaches node 17, it encounters another <xsl:apply-templates> element. It is told by that element that the query context is now the <name> node within the <gem> node. It now must find a template rule that begins with an <xsl:template match="name"> start tag and apply it to every <name> node within this <gem> node (there is only one <name> node per <gem> node so, wherever the new template rule is, it will only be applied once at this point).

Nodes 23 through 25: Filling Out the Individual Name Table Cell

Node 23 contains the template rule that meets the parser's requirements at this time. It begins with <xsl:template match="name">. This template rule tells the parser to make the <name> node the query context and to replace <name> with what is found between this <xsl:template> element's start and end tags.

Node 23 contains node 24, which tells the parser to create an HTML/XHTML table data element named <td> that, we know, will contain the data to insert in an individual cell in the table. Those contents are found in node 25's <xsl:value-of> element. The <xsl:value-of> element is used to create a text node at this location (in the first <td> element, in the first <tr> row of the HTML table). But what is the parser supposed to insert here? The clue is in the value specified for the select attribute. The period (.) is an XPath expression or abbreviation (discussed in Chapter 8, "XLinks") that tells the parser to "insert the contents of the query context node." The query context is the <name> node of the first <gem> node in the source document: the word Cullinan, found in node 11 of the gems1_source.xml document.

So the parser inserts Cullinan into the first cell in the first row and fulfills the requirements of this template rule.

Nodes 18 through 22: Filling Out the Other Cells in the Table Row

Once the parser has inserted the diamond's name into the first cell in the row, it returns to the most recent template rule that it left—the node 15 template rule. The parser makes this the current template rule. It has already accomplished the task set forth in <xsl:apply-templates select="name">, so it moves to the next template rule, namely, <xsl:apply-templates select="carat">. Then it proceeds to nodes 26 through 28, the result of which will be the inserting of the weight of the diamond into the second cell in the same (first) table row.

The parser continues through the template rules contained within node 15 until it has completed the insertion of the diamond's cost in the last cell of the row (nodes 38 through 40, which were called by node 22). At that point, the parser has completed its tasks for the first gem.

Filling In the Other Rows in the Table

After inserting the cost of the diamond into the last cell in the first row, the parser will have accomplished the tasks set forth by the template rules found in nodes 38 and 15. It will then go back to node 14 and select the next gem (Dark) from the source document and repeat nodes 15 and on for that gem (that is, it will build a table row for Dark). Upon completion of the second row, it will return to node 14 and select the third gem (Sparkler) and build its row. With that done, it will return to node 14 and build a row for the diamond named Merlin.

Once the row for Merlin has been built, the parser has accomplished all the tasks for all the template rules in gems1_xform.xsl. It will continue past node 40 to the end of the file. The last </xsl:template> end tag signals the end of the first template rule—the one that replaced the <diamonds> node—and the last </xsl:stylesheet> end tag signals the end of the XSLT transformation.

Figure 9.5 depicts the nodal structure of the results tree. Notice that not all the information from all the nodes in the gems1_source.xml document is displayed (for example, the <info> and <link> element types are not represented). We can see, then, that the output data—represented by the results tree in Figure 9.5—is not identical to the source tree depicted in Figure 9.3.

In Lab 9.3, Figure 9.12 displays the output from the XSL parser after the results from a similar transformation have been passed to a browser. The results are tabulated on the Web page just as we prescribed in the XSLT style sheet.

Chapter 9 Labs: Using XML Transformation Software

As you can see from the text, XML transformation can be a complex process. If you can construct one from scratch using a simple text editor like Notepad, many would regard you as some sort of real-life XML hero. However, in the best interest of efficiency, accuracy, and, yes, sanity, we are going to show you how to use another specialized tool. TIBCO Software, Inc. has a specialized XML tool called XMLTransform, which is part of their TIBCO Extensibility platform. Here, you'll learn how to obtain a trial version of the tool and how to use it to perform two basic types of transformation: XML to XML and XML to HTML.

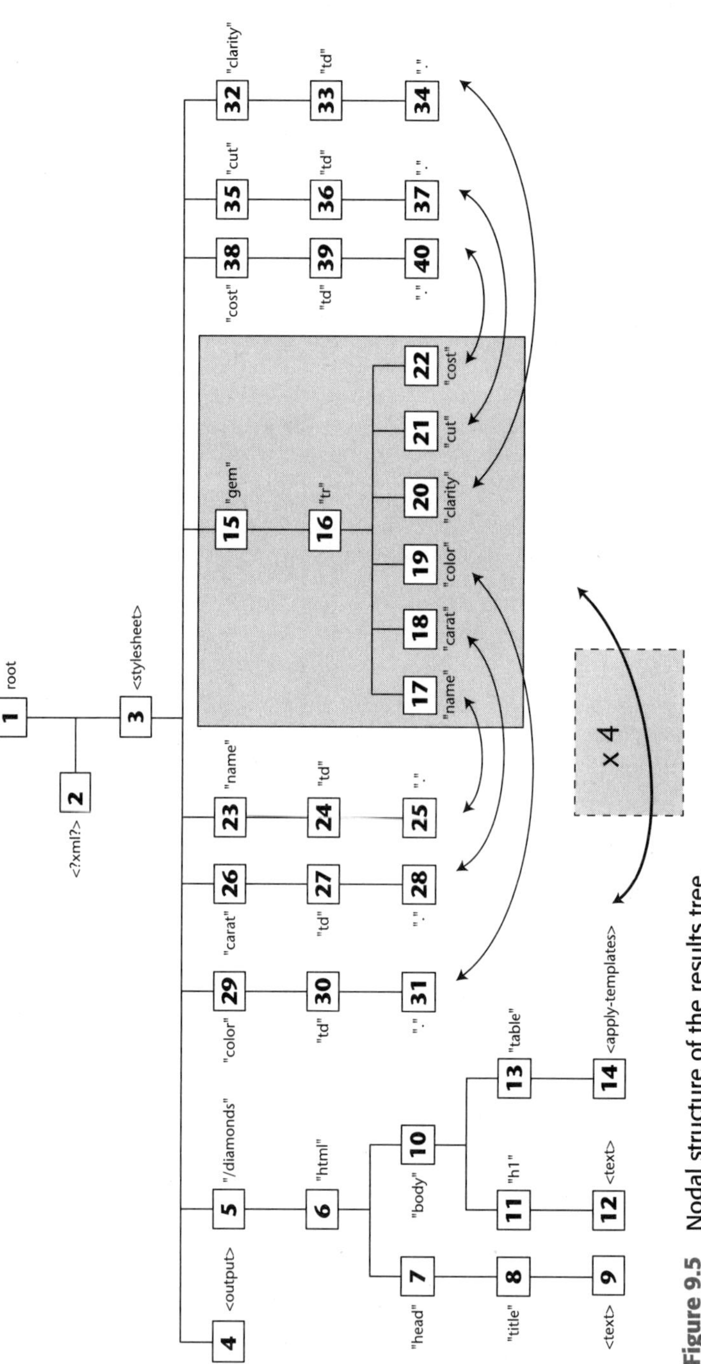

Figure 9.5 Nodal structure of the results tree.

Lab 9.1: Installing TIBCO's XMLTransform Software

To find, download, install, and initialize TIBCO's XMLTransform software, perform these steps:

1. Download the newest version of XMLTransform available from the TIBCO Web site at www.tibco.com. The following steps will guide you through the process.
   a. Click the Solutions link on the TIBCO home page.
   b. Click the XML link under the Technology Solutions heading.
   c. Click the TIBCO Extensibility link under the heading that says "The Products Behind TIBCO's XML Solutions."
   d. On the right-hand side of the Web page is a column with a heading that says "Free Trial Downloads." Click the XMLTransform XML Mapping and Transformation Solution link.
   e. Click Try on the top of the page.
   f. Fill out the required information on the form and click Submit. After you click the Submit button, TIBCO will send you an email with all the necessary information for you to install and initialize their XMLTransform software.
2. Retrieve the TIBCO email message and follow the software downloading instructions in it.
3. Install the software; accept all the suggested defaults.
4. Start the TIBCO XMLTransform tool:
   a. Click Start, Programs, XMLTransform 1.1.0.
   b. To initialize the product, enter the information TIBCO sent you in the email message.
   c. If the image shown in Figure 9.6 appears, you are ready to move on to Lab 9.2.

Figure 9.6 Splash screen for XMLTransform.

Lab 9.2: XML-to-XML Transformation

Using TIBCO's XMLTransform software, you will transform data from one XML format to another. This lab simulates a very typical scenario, where an XML data instance needs to be transformed into a different format. This is common when systems or vendors have to exchange information, as when Vendor A has the necessary data in XML format, but its data element types and associated attributes are different from those for Vendor B's system. For example, Vendor A's <first.name> element might correspond to Vendor B's <ship.to.first.name>. In a situation like this, especially where you have a significant amount of data, it would be appropriate to perform a transformation similar to the one we are about to do. To reduce the time required to perform this lab, we have provided both XML instance files. All you have to do is perform the transformation using XMLTransform.

1. Create a directory called C:\SpaceGems\work.
2. Download both the vendorA.xml and vendorB.xml files from the lab exercise portion of the Chapter 9 page of this book's Web site into your new C:\SpaceGems\work directory.
3. Using Notepad, open the vendorA.xml file. This is the source file. Note that this file has some data inside its elements.

4. Without making any changes, exit the file.
5. Using Notepad again, open the vendorB.xml file. This file has no data inside the elements. This is the target file for the reformatted data.
6. Without making any changes, exit this file, too.
7. Start XMLTransform. Click Start, Programs, XMLTransform 1.1.0.
8. Click Continue Trial, if necessary.
9. Click Create Transform. A workspace similar to Figure 9.7 should appear.
10. At this point, prior to opening any files, review the XMLTransform workspace. Familiarize yourself with the workspace by observing the following objects within it:
    a. Note that there are three panes in the top frame called Input, Graph, and Output. Most of the work takes place here.
    b. Note that both the Input and Output panes allow either a schema or instance file as an option. The Input pane is for the source file, and the Output pane is for the target file. When you start the mapping process, the Graph pane will start to build itself.

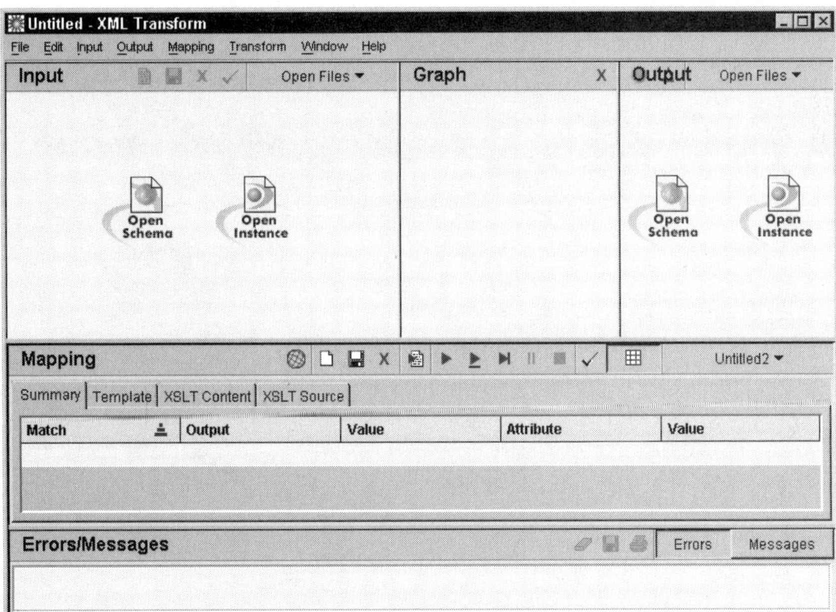

Figure 9.7 XMLTransform workspace.

c. Note that the middle frame, called Mapping, has four views: Summary, Template, XSLT Content, and XSLT Source. As you work in the top frame, this middle frame will display the generated code for the transformation.

d. The bottom frame is called Errors/Messages. As you can tell from its name, this is where any errors and messages will display. Use this frame for problem determination and troubleshooting as you work.

11. Click Open Instance inside the Input pane, and open the vendorA.xml source file from the C:\SpaceGems\work directory.

12. Click Open Instance inside the Output pane, and open the vendorB .xml target file from the C:\spacegems\work directory.

13. Before proceeding, ensure that your view looks like Figure 9.8.

14. Start mapping elements back and forth:

a. Click the <general_description> element inside the Input pane (left side). It turns dark gray.

b. Holding your left mouse button down, drag the <general_description> element from the Input pane to the <general_description> element in the Output pane, and release. A line should appear in the middle Graph pane indicating a relationship.

c. Move down to the middle Mapping frame, and click the XSLT Source tab. You should see the newly generated code for the transformation. Don't touch or edit this code at this time.

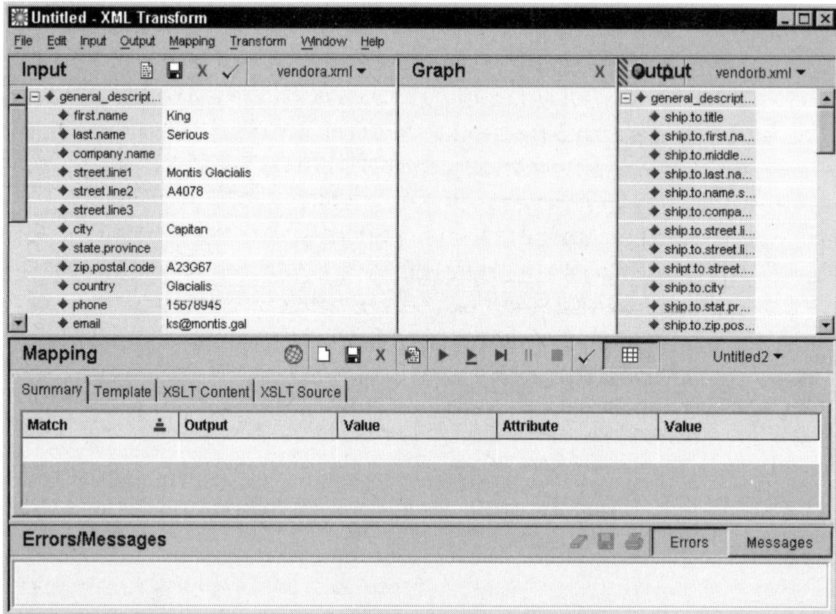

Figure 9.8 XMLTransform with both source and target files loaded (prior to mapping).

15. Check your view with Figure 9.9 to make sure that you are on track.
16. Using the same technique as described in Step 14, drag and drop the <first.name> element from the Input pane onto the <ship.to.first.name> element in the Output pane.
17. Notice that two new indicators appear inside the Graph: one pink stub next to the <ship.to.title> element, which indicates that there is no mapping and another indicator showing the relationship between <first.name> and <ship.to.first.name>.
18. Review the newly generated code for the new element mapping inside the Mapping/XSLT Source pane. So far, so good. . . .
19. Note that there is no code inside the XSLT Source code to represent the pink stub. The stub is just an indicator that confirms that no mapping is required here and, subsequently, no element will be created inside the resulting transformation. Don't worry about this.
20. Our vendorA.xml source file doesn't have a <middle name> element to map over to the target file. Here's how to perform a different kind of "stub out" on an element.

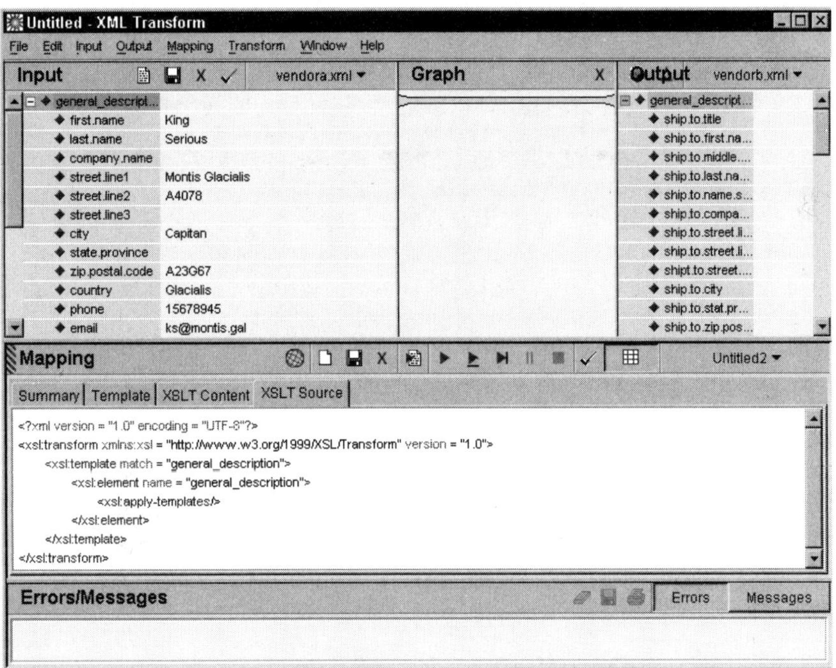

Figure 9.9 Showing the code generated for the first element mapping.

a. This time, highlight the <ship.to.middle.name> element inside the Output pane.

b. Holding down the left mouse button, drag <ship.to.middle.name> into the white space inside the Graph area and release. You should end up with a blue stub like the one in Figure 9.10. Now code is added to the XSLT Source. Hang in there; there is a difference.

21. Before we get too far, run the transformation. To do this, use the F5 key or use the top menu bar and go to Transform, Run. The result should look like Figure 9.11.

22. Let's review the results:

a. Notice that the data has been copied from the source file into the target file—the data appears to the right of the element names—but that the target file element names have been retained.

b. Also notice that the element that had the pink stub (the <ship .to.title> element) is missing entirely, but the element that had the blue stub (the <ship.to.middle.name> element) has been retained. Thus, the subtle difference between the two stub types is this: The pink stub means "won't need it"; the blue stub means "may need it, please retain." So the treatment of the element depends on what you're trying to achieve and what your future intentions for the element are.

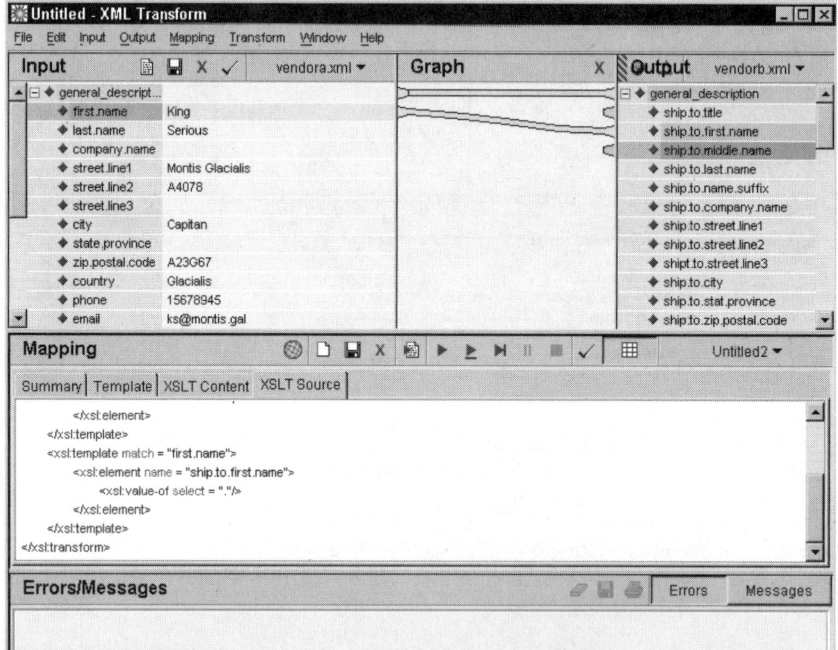

Figure 9.10 XMLTransform workspace with two connectors and two stubs.

   c. Finally, please note that we didn't have to create a mapping for every element to run a successful transform.

23. Save all the files using the following instructions:

   a. Inside the Input page, click the leftmost icon (it looks like a white page with printing on it). This is the Toggle Source View; it will switch your view to a source code. This small step makes sure that you know what you are saving here. Click the Save icon (floppy disk icon) next to the Toggle Source View icon to save the file.

   b. Inside the Output page, using the same icons, switch your view to Toggle Source View and save the file. This time a Save As window will appear. Avoid overwriting your existing vendorB.xml file, and save the new file as vendorB_T1.xml to remind you that this is transform test 1.

   c. Inside the Mapping frame, make sure that the XSLT Source view is active, and using the save icon, save the file as VendorB_T1.xsl to remind you that this is the transformation code that was used to transform VendorA.xml into VendorB_T1.xml.

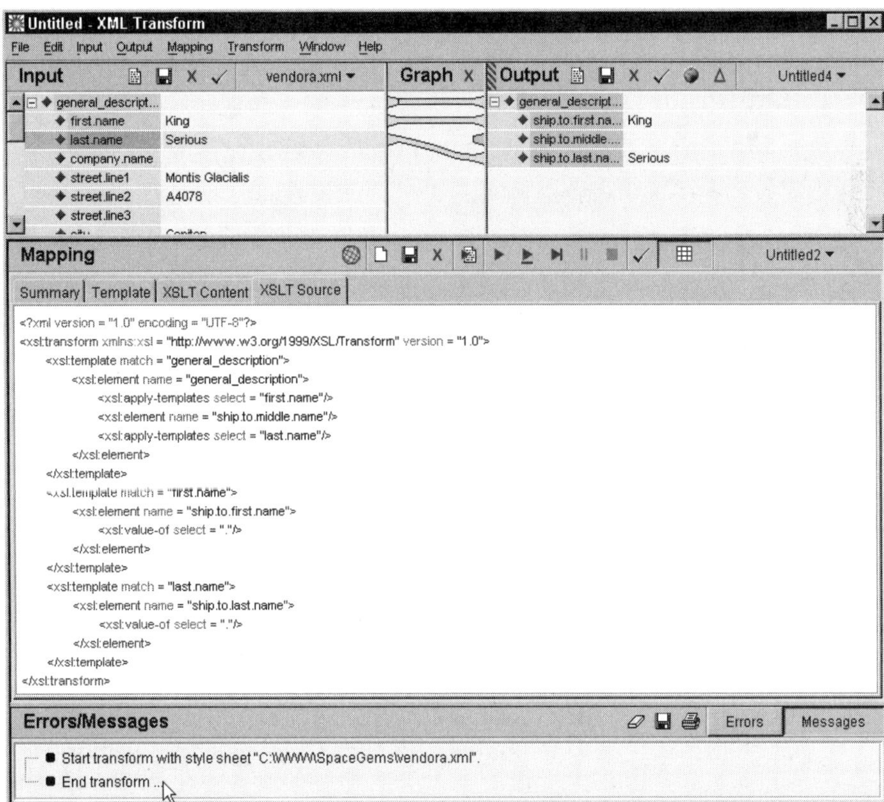

Figure 9.11 Completed XML-to-XML transformation.

Just to review: The resulting vendorB_T1.xml is the file that you would provide to vendorB to process. You would retain the VendorB_T1.xsl file in the event that you have to run another identical transformation in the future (for example, next month).

24. Continue to practice with the XML Transform to become more familiar with its capabilities. Like we said earlier, you could create all this transformation code manually but, hey, your time may be better spent on other activities.

Close all the files. Close and reopen the XMLTransform application if you have to. Redo all the steps from the beginning, but this time map all the elements from the vendorA.xml source file to the vendorB.xml file and call the resulting file vendorB_T2.xml.

Lab 9.3: Simple XML-to-HTML Transformation

In this lab, you will take information from inside the elements of the XML instance file, arrange it inside an HTML table, and display it in a browser. Unlike the previous lab, you will be required to do some manual coding.

Perform these steps:

1. Open XMLTransform, Start, All Programs, XMLTransform 1.1.0.
2. Click Continue Trial if necessary.
3. Click Create Transform.
4. Inside the Input pane, click Open Instance. Navigate to C:\WWW\SpaceGems, and open the gems1.xml file.
5. Go to the Mapping pane and click the XSLT Source tab. Modify the code to read as follows. Don't forget to close the <xsl:stylesheet> element.

```
<?xml version = "1.0" encoding = "UTF-8"?>
<xsl:stylesheet
 xmlns:xsl = "http://www.w3.org/1999/XSL/Transform" version =
"1.0">
</xsl:stylesheet>
```

6. The next few lines of code set the output method and template match criteria. Remember that the <xsl:output> element is a top-level element that must appear as a child node of the <XSL:transform> element—it is mandatory. The template match "/diamonds"

sets the rule to be the diamonds node. Note that the <xsl:output> element is coded as empty, but don't forget to close the template element. The new code—the code you are to add—is highlighted.

```
<?xml version = "1.0" encoding = "UTF-8"?>
<xsl:stylesheet
 xmlns:xsl = "http://www.w3.org/1999/XSL/Transform" version =
"1.0">
      <xsl:output method = "xml"/>
      <xsl:template match = "/diamonds">
      </xsl:template>
</xsl:stylesheet>
```

7. The next few lines of code create some of the HTML tags necessary to display the information inside the browser. We also have to ensure that we have nested the elements correctly before we add too much code. Add the following lines of code (highlighted code indicates the new code and the proper nesting):

```
<?xml version = "1.0" encoding = "UTF-8"?>
<xsl:stylesheet
 xmlns:xsl = "http://www.w3.org/1999/XSL/Transform" version =
"1.0">
<xsl:output method = "xml"/>
<xsl:template match = "/diamonds">
<xsl:element name = "html">
      <xsl:element name = "head">
            <xsl:element name = "title">
                  <xsl:text>Space Gems Quick List of
Diamonds</xsl:text>
            </xsl:element>
      </xsl:element>
      <xsl:element name = "body">
            <xsl:element name = "h1">
                  <xsl:text>Space Gems Quick List of
Diamonds</xsl:text>
            </xsl:element>
<!-- This is where we are going to further develop the HTML
      tables to display the information from the gems1.xml file -->
      </xsl:element>
</xsl:element>
</xsl:template>
</xsl:stylesheet>
```

8. Inside the Mapping pane, click the Save icon. Save the file as gems1.xsl (the program adds the xsl extension to the filename).

9. Return to the Mapping pane and click the XSLT Content tab. Any errors will be displayed now. You will have to fix the errors

before proceeding. The errors will probably be typos or nested </xsl:element> closings. Check your code very carefully.

10. When all the errors are fixed, run the Transform. To do this, go to the top menu bar and click Transform, Run. Or just use the F5 key.
11. If you are successful, you will now have entries inside the Output pane that look like those in Figure 9.12.
12. Inside the Output pane, click the Toggle Source View icon to view the newly generated HTML tags.
13. Inside the Output pane, click the Preview in Browser icon that looks like a small planet Earth (between the check mark and the triangle). Your browser will open, and you should see that both the title bar in the browser and the <h1> heading read Space Gems Quick List of Diamonds. This indicates that the transformation is working so far.

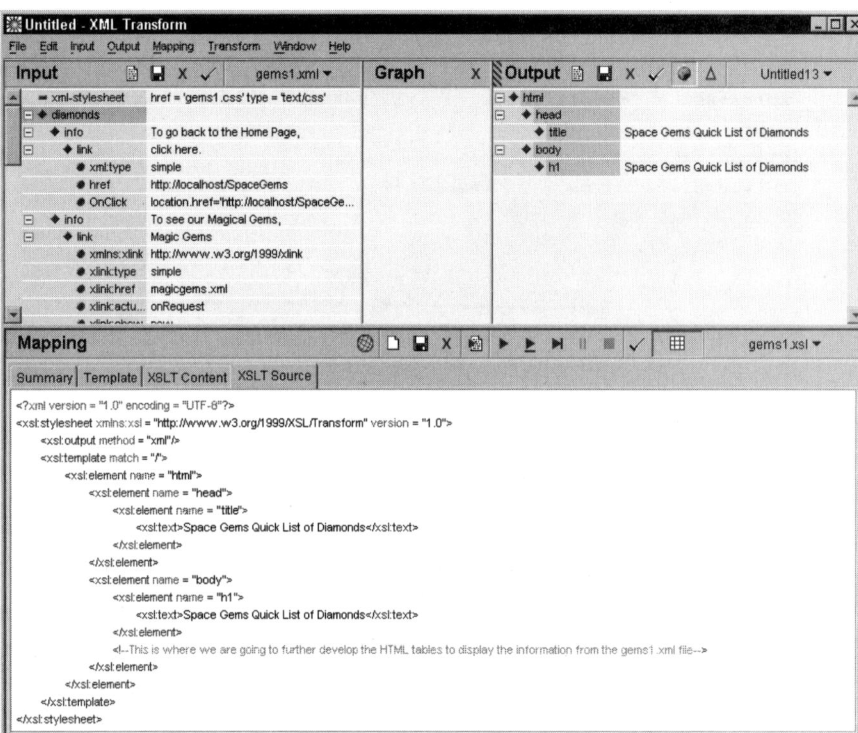

Figure 9.12 View after a successful transformation.

14. Now add the HTML table code. One <tr> tag represents the single table row. The six <td> cell tags represent each child element inside the <gem> element. The code you are to add appears highlighted in the following:

```
<xsl:stylesheet
 xmlns:xsl = "http://www.w3.org/1999/XSL/Transform" version =
"1.0">
   <xsl:output method = "xml"/>
   <xsl:template match = "/diamonds">
      <xsl:element name = "html">
         <xsl:element name = "head">
            <xsl:element name = "title">
               <xsl:text>Space Gems Quick List of
Diamonds</xsl:text>
            </xsl:element>
         </xsl:element>
         <xsl:element name = "body">
            <xsl:element name = "h1">
               <xsl:text>Space Gems Quick List of
Diamonds</xsl:text>
            </xsl:element>
<!-- This is where we are going to further develop the HTML
tables to display the information from the gems1.xml file -->
<!-- Begin HTML table -->
            <xsl:element name = "table">
               <xsl:element name = "tr">
                  <xsl:element name = "td"/>
                  <xsl:element name = "td"/>
                  <xsl:element name = "td"/>
                  <xsl:element name = "td"/>
                  <xsl:element name = "td"/>
                  <xsl:element name = "td"/>
               </xsl:element>
            </xsl:element>
<!--End HTML table-->
         </xsl:element>
      </xsl:element>
   </xsl:template>
</xsl:stylesheet>
```

15. Inside the Mapping pane, click the Save icon. Save the file as gems1.xsl.

16. Rerun the transformation. Use the F5 key. Your view should now look like Figure 9.13.

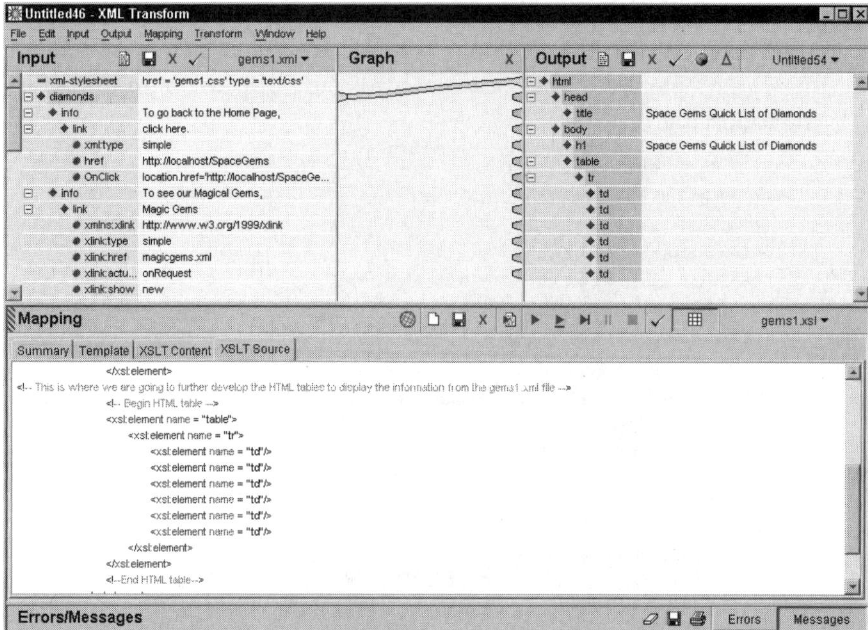

Figure 9.13 XMLTransform's Output view with table tags added.

17. Now we save you about a hundred lines of coding by using the mapping feature inside the XMLTransform tool. Adjust the positions of both your Input and Output panes so that that <gem>'s subelements are visible across from the HTML code, as shown in Figure 9.14.

18. Using the same technique as that described in the previous lab, drag and drop the <gem> element on the <tr> HTML tag. Drag the <name> element to the first <td> HTML tag. Drag the <carat> element to the second <td> HTML tag. Continue until all six subelements are mapped to their corresponding <td>s, and compare your mapping with Figure 9.15.

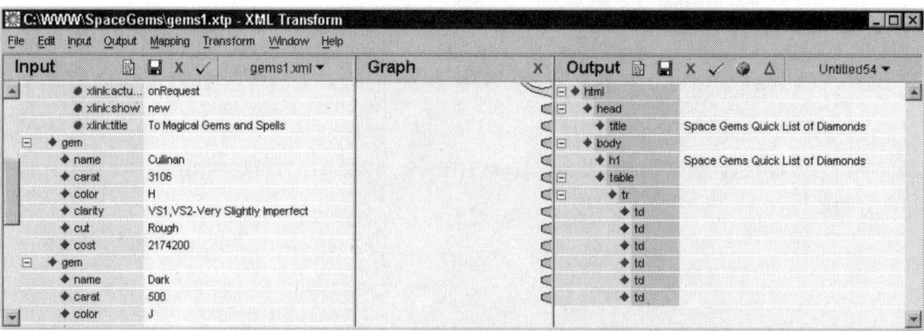

Figure 9.14 XMLTransform with both the gem subelements and HTML code visible.

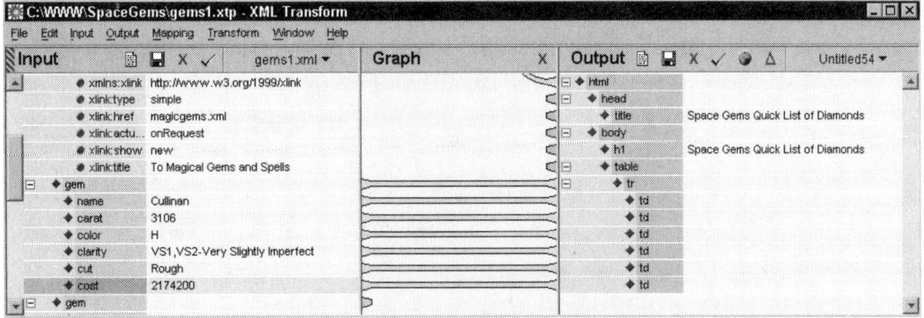

Figure 9.15 View of XMLTransform after mapping XML elements to HTML tags.

19. Just before we run the new transformation, review the autogenerated code inside the XSLT Source (with all due modesty, it's pretty impressive). Notice that the value of each subelement of <xsl:value-of select = “.”/> has been specified to be “.” (which we call “dot,” not surprisingly), meaning “the current node.” (You saw this type of shorthand coding previously in Chapter 8, “XLinks.”) This is because we set the <xsl:apply-templates select ="gem" /> value to the gem node after the <xsl:template match = “/diamonds”> node. There are a couple of ways this could have been handled.
20. Inside the Mapping pane, click the Save icon. Save the file as gems1.xsl.
21. Now rerun the transformation, using the F5 key. XMLTransform should create a row of information for each gem element it found inside the XML file.
22. Click the Preview in Browser icon to view the results inside the browser. You should now have a roughly formatted table similar to that depicted in Figure 9.16.

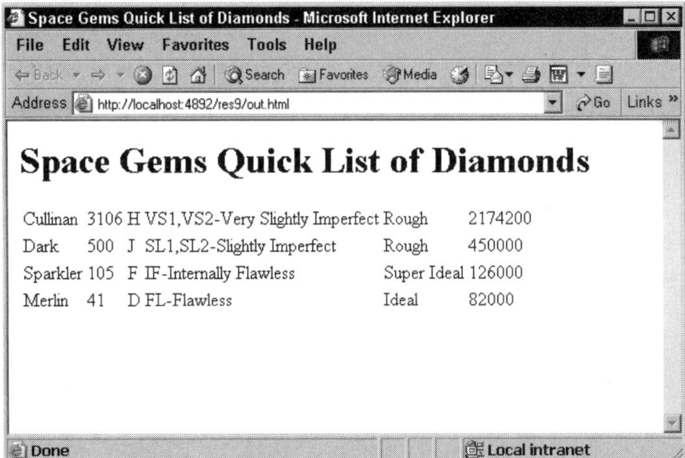

Figure 9.16 Result of XML-to-HTML transformation, displayed in Internet Explorer.

You can use this transformation in a couple of ways. You could just save the transformed HTML code and deploy it to the Web server as a static HTML page (not recommended, but sometimes done). Or you could add a link from the gems1.xml file to the new style sheet called gems1.xsl.

23. Open the gems1.xml file inside the C:\WWW\SpaceGems directory in any editor and update the existing processing instruction so that the reference to the cascading style sheet is changed to a reference to the new transformation style sheet. Change the existing

```
<?xml-stylesheet href = 'gems1.css' type = 'text/css'?>
```

    to the new:

```
<?xml-stylesheet href = 'gems1.xsl' type = 'text/xsl'?>
```

24. Copy the new gems1.xsl file into the C:\WWW\SpaceGems directory (if it is not already there), and test your work in both browsers. You can access gems1.xml by using the Quick List of Diamonds link on the Space Gems index.html page or by entering the following URL directly into the locator bar:

```
http://localhost/SpaceGems/gems1.xml
```

    This URL will work in Internet Explorer but will not work in Netscape.

You may have to close and reopen the browser to force it to process the new style sheet directive inside the gems1.xml file.

Lab 9.4: Transforming XML to HTML with Images

Next, you will replace the cascading style sheet for magicgems.xml with an XSL style sheet and test to make sure it works, then add data to the XML file and retest the file to ensure that the new data displays. This lab exercise is a little more advanced. It shows how to use attributes to enhance the HTML document, to give that document a more sophisticated look and feel. The sky is the limit here, really. Setting up the HTML document is somewhat painful, but once it is done, it can display any information found inside the XML file. This enhances the separation of data from display and demonstrates the organizational flexibility of a scenario like this. Using such a strategy, Developer A could be responsible for maintaining the data inside an XML file while Developer B could be responsible for the final look and feel of the displayed data.

Replace the Cascading Style Sheet with an XSL Style Sheet

Perform these steps:

1. Download the magicgems.xsl file from the lab exercise portion of the Chapter 9 page of the *XML in 60 Minutes a Day* Web site. Place it into the C:\WWW\SpaceGems directory.
2. Using the TurboXML editor, replace the style sheet directive inside the C:\WWW\SpaceGems\magicgems.xml file from the existing

   ```
   <?xml-stylesheet href = 'master1,css' type = 'text/css'?>
   ```

   to

   ```
   <?xml-stylesheet href = 'magicgems.xsl' type = 'text/xsl'?>
   ```

3. Save the file back to C:\WWW\SpaceGems with the same name.
4. Test the magicgems.xml file to make sure that the style sheet works. You can access magicgems.xml by using The Magic of Gems link on the Space Gems index.html page or by entering the following URL directly into the locator bar of the browser:

   ```
   http://localhost/SpaceGems/magicgems.xml
   ```

   This will work in Internet Explorer but will not work in Netscape.

You may have to close and reopen the browser to force it to process the new style sheet directive inside the magicgems.xml file.

Add a New <magicgem> Data Element to magicgem.xml

Perform these steps:

1. Using the TurboXML editor, open the magicgems.xml file.
2. Add a new <magicgem> element to the bottom of the file just before the </document> tag:

   ```
   <magicgem id = "Z101">
      <name>Zirconia</name>
      <image href="images/zirconia.gif"/>
      <para> Zirconia is responsible for all sorts of delays or very
   late
               fulfillment of ambitions. It also increases appetite,
               vitality, confers good health, wealth and happiness
   and all
               round prosperity.
               It is said to be the best gem to avert stomach
   ailments,
               disaster, insanity, and evil spirits.
   ```

```
                It should be used in silver on Saturday on 2nd finger
of
                right hand. The weight should be 6, 11, 13 grams.
    </para>
</magicgem>
```

3. Save the file back to C:\WWW\SpaceGems with the same name.
4. Test the magicgems.xml file to make sure that the new Zirconia element appears as new data. You can access magicgems.xml by clicking The Magic of Gems link on the Space Gems index.html page or by entering this URL directly into the browser's location bar:

   ```
   http://localhost/SpaceGems/magicgems.xml
   ```

   This procedure will work in Internet Explorer but will not work in Netscape.

You may have to close and reopen the browser to force it to process the new style sheet directive inside the magicgems.xml file.

Summary

We have only scratched the surface of the topic of XML transformations. If you need to convert XML data documents, please consult the W3C's Web site or any other XML transformation sources online or in your local technical bookstore.

Following are a few key facts to keep in mind about XML transformations:

- XML transformations prepare XML data for further processing using the XSLT, which is one component of the XSL family. These transformations differ considerably from the visual style transformation concepts learned in Chapter 7, "XML and Cascading Style Sheets."
- As more and more individuals and businesses link—and especially conduct business—they create more demands for data conversion. But because of pressures to avoid proprietary formats and applications, the XML community has responded in part by creating the XSL family of languages: XSL, XSLT, and XPath.
- Don't confuse XSLT style sheets with cascading style sheets (CSS). Cascading style sheets concentrate on how data is displayed. XSLT style sheets can actually change the structure and type of XML data. XSLT uses XML-like structure and vocabulary, while CSS use their own structure and vocabulary.

- XSLT uses XPath's node and tree structure approach to XML documents, to address those parts of an XML document that it will transform.
- The two basic phases to a transformation are structural change and formatting. Three steps perform a transformation within an XSL-/XSLT-compatible application: The application activates an XML parser; the XML parser finds and validates the various relevant documents and then passes the documents to an XSL/XSLT parser; and the XSL parser conducts the transformation and creates the result node tree.
- XSLT style sheets can occur as separate XML documents within non-XML resources and between <xsl:stylesheet> tags in XML data documents.
- When you include the namespace declaration in the start tag for the <xsl:stylesheet> element, although you can always specify your own unique prefix, we suggest that you follow the xsl: prefix convention.
- When creating XSLT style sheets, ensure that you set the query context for the parser and constantly keep track of the context the parser is operating in. It is crucial for planning, execution, and troubleshooting. Plus, be mindful of the current template rule. If a new template rule is instantiated while another is already running, the original template rule will be suspended until the new one finishes. Control then reverts to the original template rule.

Review Questions

1. Fill in the blanks. ________________ style sheets pertain to adding visual style to an XML document, and ______________ style sheets prepare XML data for further processing.
2. Which of the following did not evolve from XSL development?
   a. XPointer
   b. XPath
   c. XSL-FO
   d. XSLT
   e. None of the above
3. What are the two basic phases of a transformation?
4. True or false? XPath considers documents to be composed of elements of various types in a treelike logical structure.
5. True or false? Since the source document will be undergoing transformation, it doesn't have to be well formed or valid as long as the results are.
6. Where can XSLT style sheets be located (Choose all that apply.)?
   a. Within non-XML resources
   b. In separate documents of their own
   c. Within appropriate style sheets in XML source documents
   d. a. or c., but not b.
   e. a., b., and c.
7. Which of the following is not a top-level XSLT style sheet element?
   a. <xsl:template>
   b. <xsl:method>
   c. <xsl:include>
   d. <xsl:import>.
   e. None of the above
8. Which of the following is not an attribute for <xsl:output>?
   a. version
   b. indent
   c. key
   d. omit-xml-declaration
   e. None of the above

9. Which of the following <xsl:template> attributes below would set the query context?
   a. context="value"
   b. match="value"
   c. node="value"
   d. template="value"
   e. query="value"
   f. None of the above
10. When the XSL/XSLT parser sees <xsl:apply-templates select="gem">, what will it look for?
    a. <xsl:template match="gem">
    b. <xsl:template gem="context">
    c. <xsl:template rule="gem">
    d. <xsl:template context="gem">
    e. None of the above
11. True or false? As it turned out, there was no effective difference between the two "stub-outs" (that is, the pink and the blue) in Lab 9.2.
12. What was the motivation behind the "Warnings" in Labs 9.3 and 9.4?

Answers to Review Questions

1. Cascading style sheets pertain to adding visual style to an XML document, and XSLT style sheets prepare XML data for further processing.
2. **a.** XPointer. All others evolved from the evolution of the original XSL concepts.
3. Structural transformation (data is converted from the structure of the source document to a new result structure) and formatting (node types are changed to be acceptable to the target application).
4. False. XPath considers documents to be composed of nodes of various types in a treelike logical structure.
5. False. The documents involved have to be well formed. Almost all XML parsers require that source documents be well formed and valid.
6. **e.** They can occur in all three locations.
7. **b.** There is no such element. Method is an attribute in <xsl: output>.
8. **c.** The <xsl:key> is a top-level element.
9. **b.** The value would be the node name you want the parser to set as the context.
10. **a.** When the parser sees an <xsl:apply-templates select="gem"> element, it will look for an <xsl:template ...> element with a match attribute in it whose value is identical to the value of the select attribute in the <xsl:templates ...> element. In other words, it will search for an <xsl:templates match="gem"> element.
11. False. Elements that had pink stubs were not to be transformed. Those with blue stubs were retained, even if they were given no initial mapping.
12. The browser may have saved a previous version of the Web page in its cache. After you've made modifications to the source or transformation documents and you want to test them, the browser may return the previous version of the Web page. Thus, you may not see the updated results of your activity. Closing and reopening the browser application forces it to reprocess your data and display the new results.

CHAPTER 10

XML Data Binding

As more individuals and organizations are adopting or developing their own XML-related languages and documents, they are also developing applications that benefit from retrieving and processing data as XML data, and then storing the results as XML data, too. This so-called native XML data is expected to eventually play a significant role with respect to database management systems, thus creating an apparent advantage for XML data in the future. But the growing movement toward native XML-oriented databases likely won't bring about a wholesale revolution to the relational database (RDB) world, which is expected to remain the dominant data storage technology. And there are problems when XML data must be combined with other corporate data, such as that stored in relational tables.

Nevertheless, the industry generally agrees that XML and relational data will eventually become interchangeable, although converting XML to and from relational data will pose some difficulties. So far, no one has created a solution that can cover all aspects of XML integration (there is no "magic bullet"). Automatic conversion utilities have fallen short with respect to the complex conversions required (especially with respect to DTDs or XML schemas). Interactive GUI applications have been developed, but they can slow the conversion process while consuming excessive resources. But progress continues to be made: Some vendors have released native XML database products, and some RDB vendors are incorporating XML-related extensions—either proprietary or nonproprietary—so that their products will coexist with native XML database technology. Meanwhile, XML mapping technology, including XPath, XSLT, and other XML-related languages, may help to bridge the gap so that XML data may be properly retrieved from and returned to relational databases. However, given the existing prevalence of already-installed relational databases, unless the existing RDB vendors and manufacturers, or the middleware industry, can one day seamlessly integrate native XML database and relational database technologies, the future of native XML databases may not be as bright as XML proponents once thought.

In this chapter, we define some basic data binding concepts and illustrate how XML-related documents can be used as data sources and as data retrieval—in other words, Web page—documents. We focus on Microsoft's Internet Explorer browser as our data display and manipulation application, simply because Microsoft has done a lot of (albeit somewhat proprietary) data binding development on IE. We examine the logical components and structures for data binding, discuss the nature of and access to XML data islands, review the agent utilities that retrieve and synchronize data with Web pages, and demonstrate some basic local data manipulation with JavaScript.

By the end of this chapter, you will be familiar enough with XML data binding to understand some of its strengths and weaknesses, and you will know enough about the basic concepts to discuss and compare data binding technologies with respect to other data formats.

What Is Data Binding?

The basic, generic definition of data binding is "the process of mapping and synchronizing the data in a local or remote data source to a designated (usually local) placeholder for the data." Although these terms will be clarified as we progress through this chapter, quick definitions include the following:

Mapping. The process of defining a relationship between data in a data source and the data placeholder.

Data placeholder. Also called data consumers, these could be elements on an HTML page that are designated to receive and render data.

Synchronization. A process by which linked systems exchange data so that both systems contain the same data; this may involve additions, deletions, or modifications of the data at a regular or irregular interval.

Data binding also involves moving data from a (usually remote) Web server to an XHTML/HTML Web page on a local system. Once the data is rendered on the Web page, an end user can locally search, sort, filter, or perform other simple manipulations on the data. Binding data in this manner means that the Web server does not have to be called upon time and again to perform every single data manipulation, no matter how minor, and then retransmit the manipulated data. The end user can request and receive the data once and then manipulate it—to some limited extent—on his or her own system.

We bind data to data consumers to reduce traffic on the network, to reduce the load on the Web server, and to use the resources on the local client system more efficiently. Binding data also plays a role in separating the task of maintaining data from the tasks of developing and maintaining binding and presentation programs. Thus, the database administrator and the Web page designer can work independently, especially on large projects.

With data binding, the data source provides the data, and the appropriate server and client applications synchronize the data and present it on the terminal screen. If the data changes, these applications contain utilities that can update the presentation to reflect those changes. Figure 10.1 depicts a simplified database architecture diagram and introduces more basic data binding terms.

You are probably familiar with the concepts of a data source, represented by the server icons on the left side of Figure 10.1, and data presentation, represented by the terminal screen on the right side. Those other unfamiliar concepts listed in the figure will be explained as the chapter progresses.

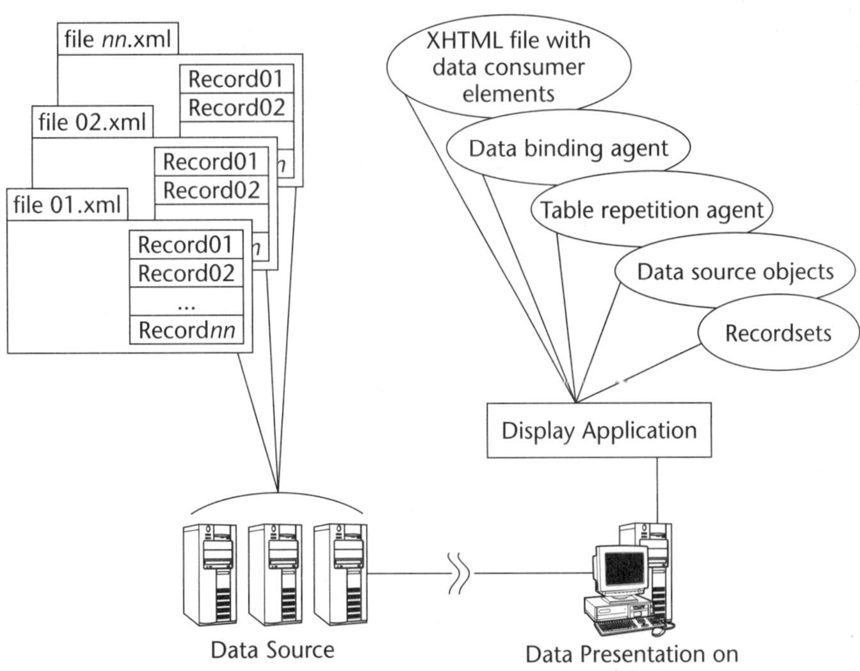

Figure 10.1 Simplified database architecture diagram.

Performing Data Binding

You can bind XML data components (for example, elements and attributes) to presentation models (combinations of software and hardware used for data display and manipulation) using Java, C++, JavaScript, and XHTML/HTML. In this chapter, we illustrate how to use XHTML to bind data and JavaScript to manipulate the data locally. We start by discussing the logical components of the Web page documents, then address those that perform data binding operations.

The discussion may occasionally seem a little loopy. By that, we mean that it will not be quite linear as we move from concept to concept. For example, when we discuss data consumer elements, as we do in the next section, we'll mention the datasrc and datafld attributes, without having discussed them in detail yet. Later, when we discuss those attributes, we'll mention data source objects without having discussed them yet, and so on. Fear not: By the end of the chapter, you will be familiar with all of the basic data binding concepts. You might consider reviewing them at your leisure to better develop a certain comfort level with them.

Data Placeholders: Data Consumer Elements

During the planning stages for a Web site, its designers must decide what information and data they will present to the end users on their local systems. After the designers acquire or develop the data, they design the documents that will appear as Web pages. Because this is an XML book, the Web page documents will be XHTML documents, but you could use HTML documents.

In addition to text, graphics, and formatting elements, the Web page document can also contain elements that function as data placeholders. These elements are commonly called *data consumer elements* or *data bindable elements*. These data consumer elements are predefined to display the results of data queries, as occurs when a user accesses a Web page and searches for information about a particular product. In other words, these elements can receive and render data.

Table 10.1 lists those XHTML/HTML elements that can function as data consumers. They are shown in lowercase, which is correct for XHTML; in HTML files, they could be uppercase (although HTML is not case-sensitive).

Figure 10.2 depicts a document that can be used to display some Space Gems diamond data in an XHTML/HTML table. The ellipse (...) in the seventh line represents the actual data. Space constraints prevent us from inserting all the data in the figure. The <table> and <div> elements, shown in bold text, are the document's data consumer elements. Along with the <span> element, these are discussed in more detail later in this chapter. Information on the other data consumer elements is available at Microsoft's Developer Network (MSDN) Web site at http://msdn.microsoft.com/library/default.asp?url=/library/en-us/xmlsdk30/htm/xmcondataislands.asp, or go to the MSDN home page at http://msdn.microsoft.com/library/ and search the contents with the phrase "XML data islands."

```
<?xml version="1.0" encoding="UTF-8" ?>
<!-- filename - gems_IDI_01.htm -->
<html>
  <head>
    <xml id="gemdata">
      <diamonds>
          ...
      </diamonds>
    </xml>
    <title>Space Gems Details - Abridged</title>
  </head>
  <body text="9999CC" >
    <h1>Welcome to Space Gems</h1>
    <h2>Space Gems Details - Abridged</h2>
    < table datasrc="#gemdata" border="1" width="100%"
           summary="Space Gems Detail List - Abridged" >
      <thead style="background-color: #ffcc33;">
        <tr>
          <th>Name</th>
          <th>Carat, ct</th>
          <th>Cost, $</th>
        </tr>
      </thead>
      <tbody>
        <tr>
          <td align="left" >< div  datafld="name" /></td>
          <td align="center">< div  datafld="carat" /></td>
          <td align="right">< div  datafld="cost" /></td>
        </tr>
      </tbody>
    </ table>
  </body>
</html>
```

Figure 10.2 Data consumer elements.

Table 10.1 XHTML Data Consumer Elements

<a>	<legend>
<applet>	<marquee>
<button>	<object>
<div>	<param>
<frame>	<select>
<iframe>	<span>
<img>	<table>
<input type="button | checkbox | hidden | password | radio | text > <textarea>	<textarea>
<label>	

Data consumer elements are used to bind two types of data:

Single-valued data consumer elements. These elements bind with only a single value from the records found in the data source. For example, the <span> element is a single-valued data consumer.

Tabular data consumer elements. These elements allow you to insert more than one value—in fact, a whole structured set of records—from the data source. Inserting more than one value at once is a practice called *data set binding*. The <table> element is an example of such an element.

The <div> Element

The <div> and <span> elements are called *grouping elements*. They provide mechanisms that keep elements together and add structure to Web page documents. The <div> element is used to provide blocks of text by acting as a paragraph start or end, thus helping to define the Web page's logical divisions. Although you can have paragraphs within a <div>, you can't have a <div> inside a paragraph and expect to keep the paragraph together. The <div> element will break it up.

You can also use <div> with its align attribute to specify the alignment of a section of data on a page. If you use <div> with style sheet specifications, you can customize the HTML tags and, therefore, the appearance of the resulting Web page.

Although HTML is not as extensible as XML, you can use the <div> and <span> elements to achieve the effect of creating unique element names. To illustrate, a <div> element provides the name of a specific emerald here:

```
<xml id="gemdata_e02" src="emeralds02.xml" />
<p> </p>
<h1>Space Gems' Emeralds</h1>
<p>Name of Gem</p>
<p>
   <div datasrc="gemdata_e02" datafld="name" />
</p>
```

Attributes used with <div> include the following:

style Specifies style information (color, font size) for the element content.

datasrc Specifies the location of the data source.

datafld Specifies the data to look for within the data source.

id A unique identifier for the element (as discussed in previous chapters, for reference from the XML-related application).

align Specifies the horizontal alignment of the <div> element with respect to its surrounding context (left, center, right, and justify); although deprecated with HTML 4.01, align is still commonly used because it just makes sense.

name Assigns a control name, similar to an id; although deprecated with HTML 4.01—use the id attribute instead—name is still occasionally used.

The attributes in the preceding list aren't the only ones you can use with <div>. They're just those that are most often used for data binding. Check your HTML sources for other <div> attributes.

The <div> element is used inside HTML tables, within individual table data cells—that is, within <td> elements—because you can bind data to <div>'s but not to <td>'s. Here's an example:

```
<xml id="gemdata_e02" src="emeralds02.xml" />
<p> </p>
<h1>Space Gems' Emeralds</h1>
<table datasrc="#PList" cellspacing="1" cellpadding="1"
       width="75%" border="1">
  <tbody>
     <tr bgcolor="purple">
            <td>Name:</td>
            <td>
                   <div datafld="name" />
            </td>
      </tr>
     ...
```

To bind with a <div> element within a <td> element, we provide a datafld attribute, the value of which is named within the <div> element's start tag. Using <div> means that the name will appear on a new line following the Name: line.

The <span> Element

Similar to the <div> element, <span> allows you to specify the content and style of the text it prescribes. However, unlike the <div> tag—which is a block-level element—<span> is used inline with the designated text. Thus, it doesn't have any default formatting features. Therefore, although <div> can act as a break between paragraphs and affect a document's logical structure, <span> can only tell the browser to apply content or style to the data within the <span> element's extent.

For data binding, we usually use the same attributes as listed for the <div> element. If you would like to know about the additional <span> element attributes, please check your HTML or XHTML information sources.

You can use <span> when you want to change the style of an element without naming it in a separate division within the document. For example, if you want a Level 2 heading (<h2>) to read "Free Delivery in the Sol System Ends June 30!" and you want the word "Sol" to be gold-colored and the phrase "June 30" to be red, and you also want Sol and June 30 to be selected from data fields in a specific data source document, you could use <span> twice, as follows:

```
 <h2>Free Delivery in the
     <span datasrc="gem_sale_notice" datafld="sys_name"
              style="color:gold"> </span>
     System Ends
     <span datasrc="gem_sale_notice" datafld="freedel_exp"
             style="color:red"> </span>!
</h2>
```

When using <span> to display text data from a data source, make sure that, in the data source, the text data does not include any block-level elements of its own, such as <h1>. This could lead to unpredictable and undesirable results. If you can, try to keep the data in your data sources just data, with no styling.

The <table> Element

Data consumer elements support the binding of two types of data: single-valued or tabular. The data retrieved from a data source often is displayed in a

```
<html>
  <!-- filename: sapphires_02.html -->
  <head>
    <title>Space Gems Sapphires</title>
  </head>
  <body>
    <xml id="gemdata_sap01" src="gemdata_sapphires01.xml" />
    <p> </p>
    <h1>Space Gems Sapphires</h1>
     <p>
      <table datasrc="#gemdata_sap01" cellspacing="1" cellpadding="1" width="75%" border="1">
        <tbody>
          <tr bgcolor="silver">
            <td>Name:</td>
            <td>
              <div datafld="name" />
            </td>
          </tr>
  ...
```

Figure 10.3 The <table> element.

table. The <table> element provides retrieval and display functionality as a tabular data consumer, allowing us to insert whole sets of records at once. As mentioned, this practice is called data set binding.

To achieve data set binding, you must insert a datasrc="value" attribute in the start tag of the <table> element. Then, each child element in the extent of the <table> element will inherit the value of the datasrc attribute, although each must still specify its own datafld="value" attribute to display the actual data values. For example, in Figure 10.3, <table> specifies that its data comes from the source it calls gemdata01 (defined in the <xml> element as an external document named gemdata_sap01.xml). Note that the <td> element—a child element of <table>—includes a <div> element to facilitate data binding to the <td> element.

If you want one or more <table> child elements to obtain their data from independent data sources, you must insert the specific appropriate datasrc and datafld attributes. For example, if the <div> element in Figure 10.3 is supposed to get its data from a data source in the gemdata_sapphires03.xml document (whose id is gemdata_sap03), then the respective syntax would resemble the following:

```
<p>
    <table datasrc="#gemdata_sap01" cellspacing="1"
        cellpadding="1" width="75%" border="1" >
          <tbody>
              <tr bgcolor="silver">
                  <td>Name:</td>
                  <td>
                      <div datasrc="#gemdata_sap03" datafld="name" />
                  </td>
              </tr>
...
```

Sizing the Web Page Using the dataPageSize Attribute

Once you bind data consumer elements to a data source, by default the Web page displays all the records you specify. If this recordset is large, the dynamic table behavior might cause a Web page to grow beyond what is practical to display. You might get an overwhelming and confusing display of data. If you suspect that this is going to happen, consider including a datapagesize= "value" attribute in the start tag of your data consumer element, to specify the maximum number of records that should be displayed at any one time. Use syntax similar to this:

```
<table id="SapphireData" dataSrc="#gemdata_sap01" dataPageSize="10"
          border="1" >
```

To enable the user to move to the next and previous pages of records viewed in the table, code nextPage( ) and previousPage( ) methods in the HTML document, in a manner similar to the navigation code we demonstrate later in this chapter.

Single-Valued Elements Avoid Overrestrictive Data

Occasionally, the <table> element and its child elements can be too restrictive or exacting for displaying data. If this is the case, but you still want to display data in a table, you can still use one or more single-valued consumer elements (those listed in Table 10.1) to create a sort of quasi table. One method is to bind the data to <span> or <div> elements, thus creating a logical structure with those elements anywhere on a Web page. Two methods are used. The first uses <div> elements:

```
<html>
   <head>
       <link rel="stylesheet"
           href="http://localhost/SpaceGems/styles/specials.css"
                   type="text/css" />
           <title>Space Gems Emeralds</title>
   </head>
   <body>
       <xml id="gemdata_eme02" src="gemdata_emeralds02.xml" />
       <p> </p>
       <h1>Space Gems, Inc.</h1>
       <h2>Specials on Emeralds!</h2>
       <br />Name:
           <div datasrc="#gemdata_eme02" datafld="name" ></div>
       <br />Color:
           <div datasrc="#gemdata_eme02" datafld="color" ></div>
       <br />Weight, carats:
           <div datasrc="#gemdata_eme02" datafld="carats" ></div>
       <br />Shape:
```

```
                <div datasrc="#gemdata_eme02" datafld="shape" ></div>
            <br />Size:
                <div datasrc="#gemdata_eme02" datafld="LxW" ></div>
            <br />Price:
                <div datasrc="#gemdata_eme02" datafld="cost_ret_disc"
></div>
            <br />Origin:
                <div datasrc="#gemdata_eme02" datafld="origin" ></div>
        </body>
</html>
```

The second method uses <span> elements:

```
<html>
    <head>
        <link rel="stylesheet"
            href="http://localhost/SpaceGems/styles/specials.css"
                    type="text/css" />
            <title>Space Gems Emeralds</title>
    </head>
    <body>
        <xml id="gemdata_eme02" src="gemdata_emeralds02.xml" />
        <p> </p>
        <h1>Space Gems, Inc.</h1>
        <h2>Specials on Emeralds!</h2>
        <br />Name:
            <span datasrc="#gemdata_eme02" datafld="name" ></span>
        <br />Color:
            <span datasrc="#gemdata_eme02" datafld="color" ></span>
        <br />Weight, carats:
            <span datasrc="#gemdata_eme02" datafld="carats" ></span>
        <br />Shape:
            <span datasrc="#gemdata_eme02" datafld="shape" ></span>
        <br />Size:
            <span datasrc="#gemdata_eme02" datafld="LxW" ></span>
        <br />Price:
            <span datasrc="#gemdata_eme02" datafld="cost_ret_disc"
></span>
        <br />Origin:
            <span datasrc="#gemdata_eme02" datafld="origin" ></span>
    </body>
</html>
```

The results resemble a simple table and are identical for either method, as illustrated in Figure 10.4.

As Figure 10.4 indicates, when using these solutions, you may only be able to see a partial view of your data. To navigate to the next line or page of data, you will have to add scripting code to your XHTML document to help users navigate the pages. A demonstration of such code can be found later in this chapter.

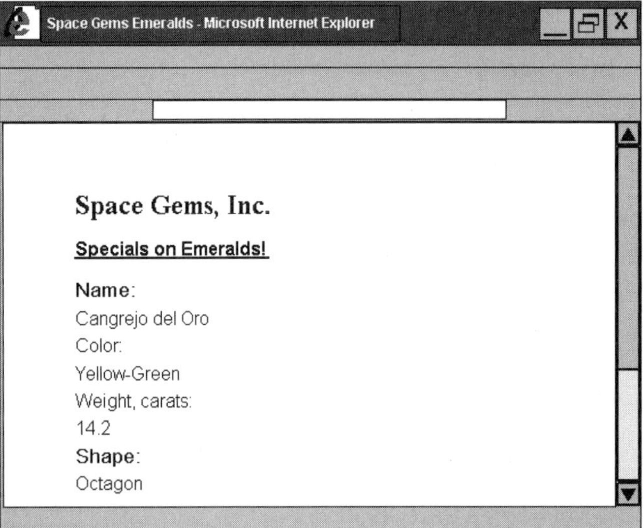

Figure 10.4 Result of using alternatives to <table> elements.

To quickly display the data from all the fields in an entire XML data source, use "$text" as the value for your datafld attribute, as follows:

```
<html>
    <head>
        <link rel="stylesheet"
            href="http://localhost/SpaceGems/styles/specials.css"
                type="text/css" />
            <title>Space Gems Emeralds</title>
    </head>
    <body>
        <xml id="gemdata_eme02" src="gemdata_emeralds02.xml" />
        <p> </p>
        <h1>Space Gems, Inc.</h1>
        <h2>Specials on Emeralds!</h2>
        <br />Description:
            <div datasrc="#gemdata_eme02" datafld="$text" ></div>
    </body>
</html>
```

The results resemble Figure 10.5, except that where the information for only one emerald appears in Figure 10.5, all the data for all the emeralds would be displayed. Adding the appropriate JavaScript code to the Web page document would help to control this behavior.

This example used the <div> element, but you could substitute a <span> element or rely on a <table> element with child elements.

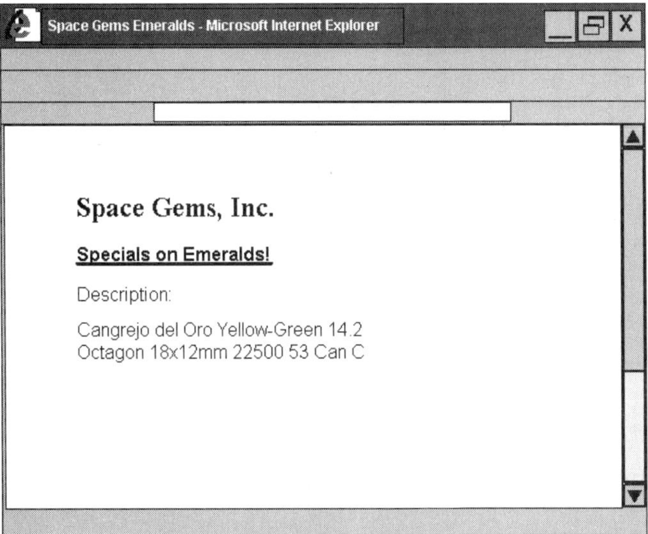

Figure 10.5 Using $text to display data.

Data Source/Data Fields: The datasrc and datafld Attributes

When you have decided which data consumer elements you want to use for data binding, to actually insert data on a Web page, you must insert the appropriate parser instructions in your Web page document. This tells the parser where to go to locate the data and exactly what data to display. When using the bindable <div>, <span>, and <table> data consumer elements, you know that their start tags must contain specific attributes to initiate data binding. At some point, in proper order, one or more datasrc="value" attributes must be specified in the start tags, and corresponding datafld="value" attributes must follow in the same or subsequent element tags.

The datasrc attribute indicates the name of a data source (also called the data source object), which, in turn, is tied to the location of the data. The datafld attribute indicates what to query for and retrieve from the data source once it has been located. These are examples of HTML extended attributes, developed with Microsoft's Dynamic HTML, beginning with Internet Explorer 4. As effective as they are, these attributes are not officially recognized in the W3C's HTML Recommendations, nor in the XHTML Recommendation. So be careful if you use them in other than Microsoft environments.

The datasrc and datafld attributes usually occur in close proximity to one another. In fact, it's not unusual to find them in the same element start tag. For example, to bind a single-valued element to a data consumer, you use both the datasrc and datafld attributes to pinpoint the data. Both attributes are mandatory in these cases. They are demonstrated in this example:

```
Price: <span datasrc="#gemdata_sap3" datafld="cost" > </span>
```

This code tells the parser (a data source object parser, discussed later in this chapter), "Immediately after displaying the text string 'Price:,' insert the value you obtained from the <cost> element in the data source in an element whose unique identifier is gemdata. Insert the value on the same line as 'Price:'; do not start a new line."

Notice that datasrc's value includes a pound sign (#), preceding the reference to the data source. This symbol indicates that the data source is identified by a unique identifier attribute like *id*, and it is mandatory.

The datasrc attribute can be used with both internal and external data islands. In both cases, the value of the datasrc attribute identifies the value specified by the unique identifier in the appropriate <xml> element, either that which surrounds an internal data island or contains a reference to an external data document. Thus, the datasrc attribute points to the <xml> element that contains an attribute that further points to the data, whether the data appears in the Web page document or in a separate document external to the Web page document. Remember that data binding involves two tasks—locating a data source and displaying the data. You use the datasrc attribute to execute the initial step of identifying the data source.

When the browser (in this case, Internet Explorer) loads a Web page, it scours the Web page document, looking for data consumer elements. The browser (actually the data binding agent within the browser) looks for datafld="value" attributes in the start tags of any data consumer elements. The datafld="value" attribute is also known as the *data field key*. The value specified for the datafld attribute is the name of the node (usually an element) in the data source that contains the data. In database terms, the value specified for datafld is the name of the field that contains the data. Adding this data field key completes the second step in the data binding task—it binds the XML element data to a position within the Web page document.

After finding datafld attributes, the browser searches for any datasrc attributes also affiliated with the elements containing the datafld attribute. Based on what datasrc points to, the browser executes additional programs, such as the appropriate data source object. Once it has identified the data source, the browser endeavors to retrieve and display the appropriate data from that data source, using the data field values it has observed in the data consumer elements.

Looking at Figure 10.3, the datafld attribute in the <div> element (itself within a <td> element) names a *name* component. The application then looks for a datasrc attribute in the same or a parent element start tag. In the <table> element, it sees a datasrc attribute whose value identifies a data source named gemdata_sap01. Now the application looks for an element containing an id attribute whose value is gemdata_sap01. In the <xml> element, it finds such an attribute, so it activates the XML Data Source Object for further parsing. The data source object (DSO) parser sees that the actual data source is a local file named gemdata_sapphires01.xml. It will query that file, looking for the values attributed to a *name* component. When it finds that component, it will return with the data affiliated with it.

Don't forget that when you use XML namespaces in XML-related data source files, you must declare the whole universal name as the value for the datafld binding. For example, if you name a targeted field <d:clarity> instead of <clarity>, the specified datafld value would be "d:clarity", and not just the unqualified "clarity".

Data Nesting and the Two-Level Rule

So far, your various data source files have been fairly flat—the elements and other components have not been nested too deeply below their respective root elements or nodes. You can nest XML data elements many layers deep; however, when binding data, if the data is nested any deeper than two levels from the root element, you must extend the datafld="value" attributes in the consumer element's start tags by adding a specific type of path specifications to them. This is where the Two-Level Rule comes in.

Examine Figure 10.6. In the upper left corner, the designer is creating an XHTML nested table structure; whole tables are being constructed within individual cells of a larger table. In the bottom left corner, you can see how the designer wants the tables and their respective data to be rendered. The right-hand side of the figure shows the XML data file named gemdata_03.xml and below it, the element structure of the data file.

In the Web page document, the designer wants to specify retail and wholesale prices of the Aries diamond. In the data file, that data is found on the third level down from the root element. Therefore, the datafld attributes for the respective <div> elements require full path descriptions to enable the DSO to access the data all the way down to the <retail> and <wholesale> element level. So, while the attributes that require data found in the second level only need simple "location", "carat", or "clarity" value specifications, the price-related attributes need values like "cost retail" and "cost wholesale". The parser can get down to the second level <cost> element, but needs help to go deeper. That's why, when creating the extended path, we started at the second level (that is, the <cost> element level). Notice, in the value specification, that a period delimiter is used between the deeper element levels. This is standard syntax for an extended path specification.

If you want to be absolutely precise about references to first- and second-level element data, too, you can also use extended path references with their value specifications. For example, "clarity" could be "diamonds.gem.clarity".

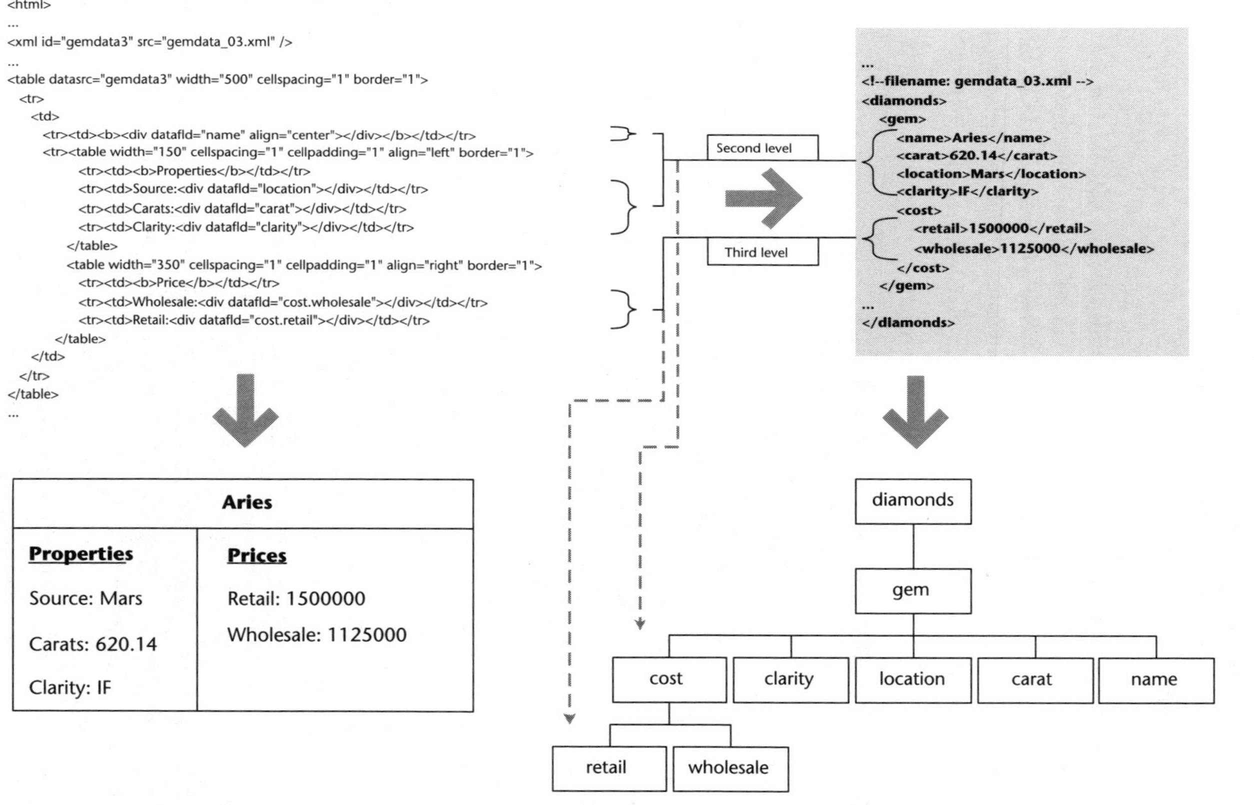

Figure 10.6 Data nesting and the Two-Level Rule.

Data Island Storage of XML Data

To display data on a Web page, your browser must access the source of the data. This data source can be a simple ASCII delimited data file, an HTML file, another XML-related file (such as an XHTML file), or a more complex relational database table. Here, we concentrate on XML-related document files. For very simple Web sites, the data might be stored in the corresponding Web page document file. For any larger-scale Web site, however, the data will likely be stored separately (even remotely). When users begin to issue requests through their respective remote browsers, this data is accessed and transmitted across a network. However you bind XML data, it must be stored in the form of a well-formed XML document. That statement may seem straightforward when you think of external XML documents, but it may not seem so straightforward when you consider internal XML data.

When XML documents are used for data storage, the data is stored in specific elements, thus giving rise to the term XML data islands. If you choose not to employ separate XML documents, you can include the XML data, in a very specific structure, within the Web page (XHTML or HTML) documents. XML data elements contained in a Web page document are called *internal data islands*. If the XML data elements are included in a separate document, the document is called an *external data island*. The following sections explain how Internet Explorer binds data from internal and external XML data islands.

External Data Islands

In Chapter 1, "XML Backgrounder," we mentioned that individual software manufacturers have supplemented HTML through proprietary extensions. Beginning with Version 5, Microsoft's Internet Explorer began to support an <xml> element, born earlier with their version of dynamic HTML (DHTML), which is used to introduce XML data to HTML documents. Previous to Version 5, Web page developers could only introduce XML data by inserting a specific Java-related <applet> element or an ActiveX-related <object> element into the Web page document. When detected, those elements activated their respective XML DSOs in the browser. The DSO read the instructions in the <applet> or <object> elements and then accessed external XML documents—early versions of external XML data islands. The XML DSO retrieved the XML data from that document, parsed it, and passed it to the binding agent (or table repetition agent, if appropriate) in the browser. In turn, the browser bound the data to the appropriate data consumer elements on the Web page. We discuss the DSO, table repetition agent, and data binding agent with their processes in more detail later in this chapter.

Beginning with IE 5.0, the DSO was written in C++ instead of Java (although the Java DSO is still supported), and activating the XML DSO became more automatic. Now the Web page developer has only to add an <xml> element, containing either the XML data itself (the internal data island) or a reference to external XML data islands, to a Web page document. When the data binding or table repetition agents within the browser encounter that element, the XML DSO is activated. The <xml> element thus is used to introduce the islands of XML data into the Web page document. Depending on the configuration of the <xml> element, the browser will be informed whether the XML data is internal or external. (The <xml> element is sometimes called an "unofficial" HTML element because it is not listed within the W3C's HTML Recommendations.)

As a Web designer, you can employ external data islands by doing one of the following:

- Storing XML data in an XML document file that is separate from the Web page document
- Inserting a src="value" attribute in the <xml /> element tag, then specifying the identity (as a URI) of the external document as the value for that attribute

Notice that, for external data islands, <xml> must be declared an empty element type.

As stated in Chapter 1, although features like the <xml> element or the datasrc and datafld attributes may be important for execution, extensibility, and flexibility, because they are not strictly classic XHTML/HTML features, they tend to "stretch" the open source aspect of SGML-related languages.

Figure 10.7 shows an XHTML Web page document named gems_EDI_01.htm that references an external data island in an XML file named gemsB.xml. The #gemdata value of a datasrc attribute inserted in the <table> element points to the id attribute in the <xml /> element, thus identifying it as the data island. Two facts—that the <xml /> element is declared empty and that it contains a src="value" attribute—inform the DSO parser that the data island is external and can be found at the URL value gemsB.xml, a document file apparently located on a local system.

Creating an external data island demonstrates the recommended best practice of separating data from presentation. The data is kept in one file—an XML document—and the data consumers are kept in another file—an XHTML Web page file. Using this strategy and file structure, Web page designers and database administrators can work on separate tasks, a particular advantage when working on large projects.

Do not use any elements named <xml> in the external data island. The <xml ... /> element that appears in the Web page document is the only one the parser should encounter. If it encounters another <xml> element in the data file, an error will result.

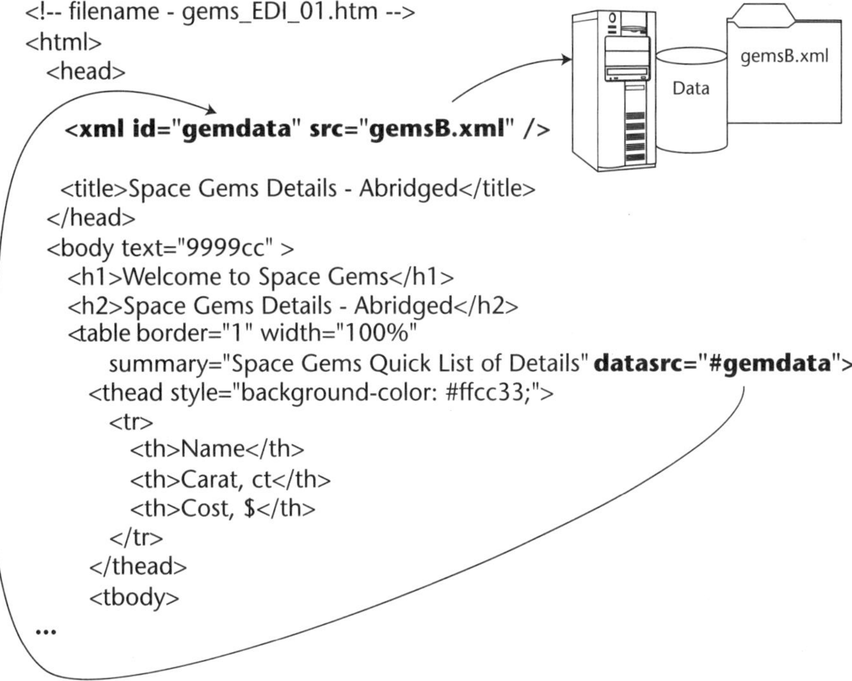
<!-- filename - gems_EDI_01.htm -->
<html>
<head>
<xml id="gemdata" src="gemsB.xml" />
<title>Space Gems Details - Abridged</title>
</head>
<body text="9999cc" >
<h1>Welcome to Space Gems</h1>
<h2>Space Gems Details - Abridged</h2>
<table border="1" width="100%"
summary="Space Gems Quick List of Details" datasrc="#gemdata">
<thead style="background-color: #ffcc33;">
<tr>
<th>Name</th>
<th>Carat, ct</th>
<th>Cost, $</th>
</tr>
</thead>
<tbody>
...
Data
gemsB.xml

Figure 10.7 Reference to an external data island.

Internal XML Data Islands

Figure 10.8 depicts a Web page document named gems_IDI_01.htm that contains another kind of <xml> element, one that is not a declared empty element type. This <xml> element contains an internal data island consisting of a list of two diamonds whose features are specified by attributes within their respective <gem> element start tags.

As in the external data island example, the #gemdata value specified for the datasrc attribute inserted in the <table> element points to the id attribute in the <xml > element, thus identifying it as the data island. This time, the <xml> element's start tag includes id="gemdata", but no src="value" attribute. The DSO parser recognizes this and looks for the XML data nested within the extent of the <xml> element. It will not seek any data in separate external documents.

Earlier, we mentioned that the XML data islands must be well formed, thus making processing more straightforward for external data islands than internal data islands. The Figure 10.8 document is well formed and written in XHTML. However, if the document in Figure 10.8 had been written in HTML, the XML declaration would have had to be moved to a position immediately following the <xml> element start tag—that is, to a position within the extent of the <xml> element.

```
<!-- filename - gems_IDI_01.htm -->
<html>
  <head>

    <xml id="gemdata">
     <?xml version="1.0" encoding="UTF-8" ?>
      <diamonds>
        <gem id="Sparkler" carat="105" cost="126000"/>
        <gem id="Merlin" carat="41" cost="82000"/>
      </diamonds>
    </xml>

   <title>Space Gems Details - Abridged</title>
  </head>
  <body text="9999cc" >
    <h1>Welcome to Space Gems</h1>
    <h2>Space Gems Details - Abridged</h2>
    <table border="1" width="100%"
        summary="Space Gems Quick List of Details" datasrc="#gemdata">
      <thead style="background-color: #ffcc33;">
        <tr>
          <th>Name</th>
          <th>Carat, ct</th>
          <th>Cost, $</th>
        </tr>
      </thead>
      <tbody>
...
```


Figure 10.8 Internal XML data island.

Meanwhile, the XML data elements are properly nested within the <xml> element. This is an inline data binding structure, because the child elements fall between the <XML> element's start tag and end tag within the Web page document. This is not the same kind of inline concept we mentioned earlier. With the <span> element, inline only meant that the data and style information was to be inserted on the same line of XHTML/HTML code as the parent element.

Internal data islands are most appropriate for small amounts of data. We suggest that if you want to introduce larger amounts of data to Web page documents, you use external data islands.

Data Binding and Table Repetition Agents

The data binding agent and table repetition agent utilities establish and maintain the synchronization of data values with the data consumer elements in the Web page document. These agents are implemented by respective dynamic link libraries in Internet Explorer, and they operate as background processes. When a Web page is loaded, these agents search through it, looking for single value elements (data binding agent) and tabular data consumer elements (table repetition agent). If they encounter them, they interpret the element/attribute combination to determine which DSO to activate to retrieve the appropriate data and then maintain data synchronization. For example, when the DSO obtains more data from its data source, the binding agent is the process that actually transmits the new data to the consumers. These data-related agents can also follow a script to alert a developer or administrator to changes in the state of the data.

As the Web page receives data from the data source, the table repetition agent in the browser works with the XHTML <table> data consumer elements (for example, the <tbody> element) to expand the table rows. Thus, the page designer does not need to continually recode (add to, subtract from, or otherwise modify) the Web page table as data is added or removed. This dynamic table behavior is represented in Figure 10.9.

The diamond list on the left indicates that at the time the page was originally displayed, its XML data source file only contained one set of diamond records, for the Black Orlov diamond. The list on the right represents the same Web page after another recordset, for the Blue Magic diamond, has been added and the displayed page updated. The table repetition agent in the browser expanded the table in the Web page document to accommodate the second diamond. If you added a third diamond to the XML data file, the browser table would again expand automatically.

Because the browser expands the table on the client system, network bandwidth use can be optimized. The remote Web server is only used to provide the data, not to reformat it on the page, because the end user's system did so.

Data Source Objects (DSOs)

Internet Explorer uses data source objects to facilitate data binding. Developed along with Dynamic HTML (DHTML), DSOs search for and return with the data and work with the data binding agent and/or table repetition agents to update data automatically. (Please refer back to the *External Data Islands* section for additional XML DSO background.) If the data within the XML data elements changes, the changes are automatically updated the next time the browser refreshes the Web page. This adds extra end-user system-based data manipulation functionality that is not typically offered when a Web server has to perform all manipulations and then send whole static pages back across the Web. This ability is particularly useful when you want to display current information in forms, tables, fields, or other compatible objects on your Web site (as in the operation of frequently updated news, weather, sports, or business Web sites).

The XML data source object triggers events when the source XML data changes. Internet Explorer contains several data source objects for use with various kinds of data, including:

- Tabular data control
- Remote data service

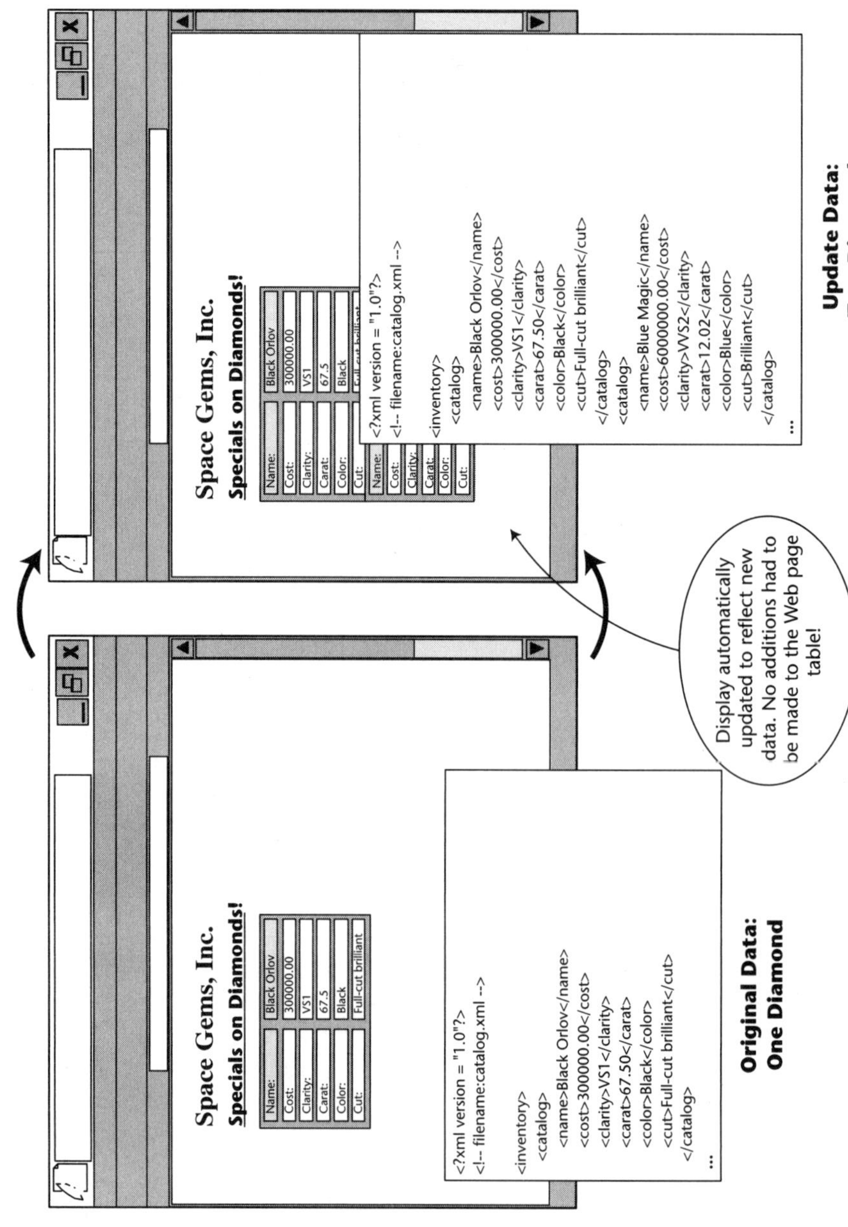
Space Gems, Inc.
Specials on Diamonds!
Name: Black Orlov
Cost: 300000.00
Clarity: VS1
Carat: 67.5
Color: Black
Cut: Full-cut brilliant
<?xml version = "1.0"?>
<!-- filename:catalog.xml -->
<inventory>
<catalog>
<name>Black Orlov</name>
<cost>300000.00</cost>
<clarity>VS1</clarity>
<carat>67.50</carat>
<color>Black</color>
<cut>Full-cut brilliant</cut>
</catalog>
...
Original Data:
One Diamond
Space Gems, Inc.
Specials on Diamonds!
<?xml version = "1.0"?>
<!-- filename:catalog.xml -->
<inventory>
<catalog>
<name>Black Orlov</name>
<cost>300000.00</cost>
<clarity>VS1</clarity>
<carat>67.50</carat>
<color>Black</color>
<cut>Full-cut brilliant</cut>
</catalog>
<catalog>
<name>Blue Magic</name>
<cost>6000000.00</cost>
<clarity>VVS2</clarity>
<carat>12.02</carat>
<color>Blue</color>
<cut>Brilliant</cut>
</catalog>
...
Update Data:
Two Diamonds
Display automatically updated to reflect new data. No additions had to be made to the Web page table!

Figure 10.9 Dynamic table behavior.

- Java Database Connectivity (JDBC) DataSource applet
- Custom data source objects
- MSHTML data source object
- XML data source object

Each DSO gathers data from different sources and has unique methods for manipulating the data. DSOs access the respective data sources, query for specific data, and then return with that data to provide it to the data consumer elements in the XHTML file. If you wish to learn more about these DSOs, check with the Microsoft Developer Network library at http://msdn.microsoft.com/library/default.asp.

After you create and identify your data, you specify in the Web page document the DSO that you want to use to retrieve and provide the data. For XML data, as of IE 5, you need use only one form or another of the <xml> element, with id or src attributes (or both), to implicitly add the XML DSO specification to your Web page document file. When you use an internal XML data island, you specify the XML DSO by using the <xml> element with the attribute:value pair id="value". When you use an external data island, you add a src="value" attribute to a declared empty <xml /> tag. The data binding or table repetition agent will pick up on those clues and activate the XML DSO.

To understand how the DSO acts during data retrieval and conveyance, start by reviewing the XML data source file in Figure 10.10.

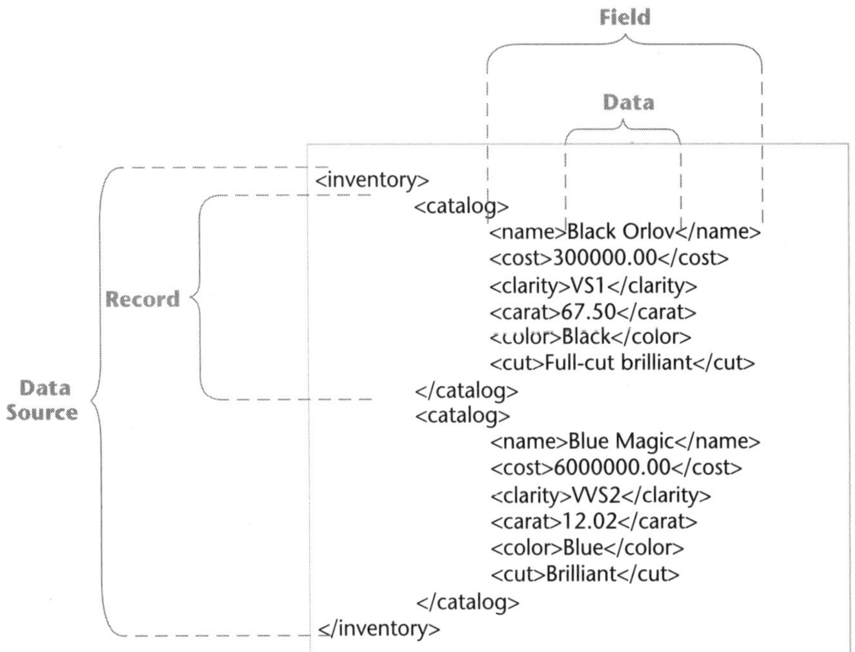
Field
Data
Record
Data Source
<inventory>
<catalog>
<name>Black Orlov</name>
<cost>300000.00</cost>
<clarity>VS1</clarity>
<carat>67.50</carat>
<color>Black</color>
<cut>Full-cut brilliant</cut>
</catalog>
<catalog>
<name>Blue Magic</name>
<cost>6000000.00</cost>
<clarity>VVS2</clarity>
<carat>12.02</carat>
<color>Blue</color>
<cut>Brilliant</cut>
</catalog>
</inventory>

Figure 10.10 Data source file components.

The whole data source is contained within the <inventory> element. It contains two records, each defined within a <catalog> element. Each record contains six fields: the <name>, <cost>, <clarity>, <carat>, <color>, and <cut> elements. Each field contains data. To be well formed and valid, the file itself must meet the W3C's well-formedness constraints and conform to its DTD or schema.

During data retrieval, when the DSO builds its recordsets in preparation to hand them to the two agent utilities, it may or may not retrieve data from all the fields in any given data source record. The recordsets constructed by the DSO are usually subsets of the data source records, because the fields that the DSO queries are those specified by the various datafld attributes from which the DSO gets its instructions.

Each time the DSO obtains the data from its designated fields within a data source record, it constructs one record. Thus, a single record can be defined as one tabular row of data (these concepts are illustrated in Figure 10.10). The records that the DSO builds are actually data objects; therefore, they can be manipulated by the browser application when they return to the end user's system. The data is transmitted to the end user system's RAM record-by-record, and the DSO combines them into recordsets there. The recordsets are then passed to the binding agent and/or table repetition agent. If more data source records have been added, the DSO retrieves the new extra information and passes it to the data binding agent or the table repetition agent for further processing.

Navigating Recordsets

Recordsets returned by the DSO parser are separate objects unto themselves, so they can be navigated or manipulated by any utility or program that understands data binding. This allows Web page users to process and manipulate the records in the recordsets at their own computers, resulting in a more flexible and informative presentation. Because users don't have to keep sending minor requests back to the Web server, they save bandwidth.

However, the Web page developer must always be aware of the information contained in recordsets. Having a handle on that information enhances security and further Web service development.

A comparatively simple way to navigate recordsets is with simple JavaScript techniques. Figure 10.11 demonstrates a Web page file named catalog.htm. Notice the four major sections:

JavaScript code. Located within a <script> element, which is in turn nested in the <head> element. That code defines basic JavaScript functions that are explained later in this section and uses the keyword *data* as the first extension in its recordset navigation instructions. *Data* points to the unique identifier in the XML data island.

```
<!DOCTYPE xhtml PUBLIC "-//W3C//DTD XHTML 1.0 Strict//EN" "DTD/xhtml1-strict.dtd">
<!-- filename:catalog.htm - Solution -->
<html xmlns="http://www.w3.org/1999/xhtml" xml:lang="en" lang="en">
  <head>
    <title>Space Gems Catalog</title>
```

JavaScript Section

```
        <script language="JavaScript">
          function first(){data.recordset.moveFirst();}
          function previous(){ if(data.recordset.absoluteposition>1)
                                    data.recordset.movePrevious();}
          function next(){ if(data.recordset.absoluteposition
                                <data.recordset.recordcount)
                                data.recordset.moveNext();}
          function last(){ data.recordset.moveLast();}
        </script>
  </head>
  <body text="#9999cc">
```

Data Island Section

```
    <xml id="data" src="catalog.xml"></xml>
    <h2>Space Gems Catalog</h2>
```

Table Definition Section

```
    <table border="0" style="font: 10pt Verdana,sans-serif;cellpadding="5">
      <tr>
        <td><img dataSrc="#data" dataFld="image" /></td>
      </tr>
    </table>
    <table border="0" style="font: 10pt Verdana,sans-serif;" cellpadding="5">
      <tr>
        <td>Name</td>
        <td><span style="background: white; width:150; border: inset;
             border-width:1" dataSrc="#data" dataFld="name"></span></td>
        <td>Carat</td>
        <td><span style="background: white; width:150; border: inset;
             border-width:1" dataSrc="#data" dataFld="carat"></span></td>
      </tr>
      <tr>
        <td>Origin </td>
        <td><span style="background: white; width:150; border: inset;
             border-width:1" dataSrc="#data" dataFld="origin"></span></td>
        <td>Shape</td>
        <td><span style="background: white; width:150; border: inset;
             border-width:1" dataSrc="#data" dataFld="shape"></span></td>
      </tr>
      <tr>
        <td>Cost $</td>
        <td><span style="background: white; width:150; border: inset;
             border-width:1" dataSrc="#data" dataFld="cost"></span></td>
      </tr>
    </table>
    <hr />
```

Navigation Button Code

```
    <input type="button" style="width:70px" value="|<" onClick="first()"></input>
    <input type="button" style="width:70px" value="<" onClick="previous()"></input>
    <input type="button" style="width:70px" value=">" onClick="next()"></input>
    <input type="button" style="width:70px" value=">|" onClick="last()"></input>
  </body>
</html>
```

Figure 10.11 Navigating recordsets with JavaScript.

The <xml> element. Constitutes the reference to the external XML data island. That reference points to the separate catalog.xml document, which contains the diamond data to be displayed and manipulated.

XHTML table definition. Contains several elements, most of which we are familiar with.

Button descriptions. Defines a set of navigation buttons that will be used to execute the JavaScript functions defined previously. This code is tied to the JavaScript code section by the function names first(), previous(), next(), and last().

Classroom Q & A

Q: Whoa! Sorry to interrupt, but that's at least the second time you've mentioned JavaScript. I'm not familiar with it. Is it "Java scripts," so it's the same as Java?

A: No, JavaScript is not the same as Java. Although it shares some Java concepts and features–and an unfortunate similarity in name–JavaScript was developed independently. JavaScript is an open source scripting language (similar in function and capability to Microsoft's Visual Basic, IBM's REX, or Sun's Tcl) that anyone can use without purchasing a license. Because it's a scripting language, it's easier and faster to code with than compiled languages, but it generally takes longer to process, so it's useful for shorter programs like those we're creating here. JavaScript was originally developed by Netscape to enable Web authors to design dynamic sites. It interacts with HTML/XHTML and is supported by Netscape and Microsoft Internet Explorer (however, IE only supports a subset of JavaScript). It can also be run at the server (such as Microsoft's Active Server Pages) before a page is sent to a requester.

Figure 10.12 depicts an excerpt from the data file named catalog.xml, which is the external data island for the Web page document. We only show data for two of the 11 diamonds listed in catalog.xml.

The Web page document instructs the parser to query the records in catalog.xml and then return the information from five fields in each record in a recordset. Figure 10.13 lists all 11 records in the recordset. The figure also indicates the BOF (beginning of file) and EOF (end of file) positions. When navigating through a recordset, the JavaScript navigation functions always refer to these positions.

The JavaScript function code in the catalog.htm file in Figure 10.13 defines these four functions: moveFirst, movePrevious, moveNext, and moveLast. Those who browse the Web page can use these built-in behaviors to navigate through the recordset. They see a rendered display similar to the Web page on the lower right side of Figure 10.14.

```
<?xml version = "1.0"?>
<!-- filename:catalog.xml -->

<inventory>
  <catalog>
    <name>Black Orlov</name>
    <image>images/orlov.jpg</image>
    <origin>Earth</origin>
    <shape>Baguette</shape>
    <cost>300000.00</cost>
    <clarity>VS1</clarity>
    <carat>67.50</carat>
    <color>Black</color>
    <cut>Full-cut brilliant</cut>
  </catalog>
  <catalog>
    <name>Blue Magic</name>
    <image>images/bluemagic.jpg</image>
    <origin>Earth</origin>
    <shape>Pear</shape>
    <cost>6000000.00</cost>
    <clarity>VVS2</clarity>
    <carat>12.02</carat>
    <color>Blue</color>
    <cut>Brilliant</cut>
  </catalog>
...
```

Figure 10.12 Catalog data to be navigated.

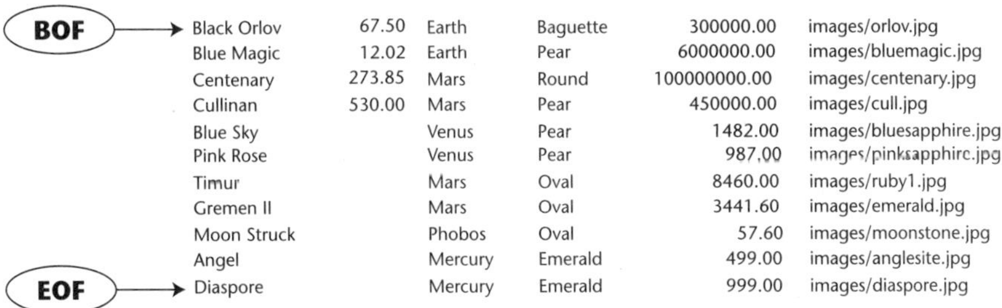

BOF →	Black Orlov	67.50	Earth	Baguette	300000.00	images/orlov.jpg
	Blue Magic	12.02	Earth	Pear	6000000.00	images/bluemagic.jpg
	Centenary	273.85	Mars	Round	100000000.00	images/centenary.jpg
	Cullinan	530.00	Mars	Pear	450000.00	images/cull.jpg
	Blue Sky		Venus	Pear	1482.00	images/bluesapphire.jpg
	Pink Rose		Venus	Pear	987.00	images/pinksapphire.jpg
	Timur		Mars	Oval	8460.00	images/ruby1.jpg
	Gremen II		Mars	Oval	3441.60	images/emerald.jpg
	Moon Struck		Phobos	Oval	57.60	images/moonstone.jpg
	Angel		Mercury	Emerald	499.00	images/anglesite.jpg
EOF →	Diaspore		Mercury	Emerald	999.00	images/diaspore.jpg

Figure 10.13 Recordset returned by the DSO parser.

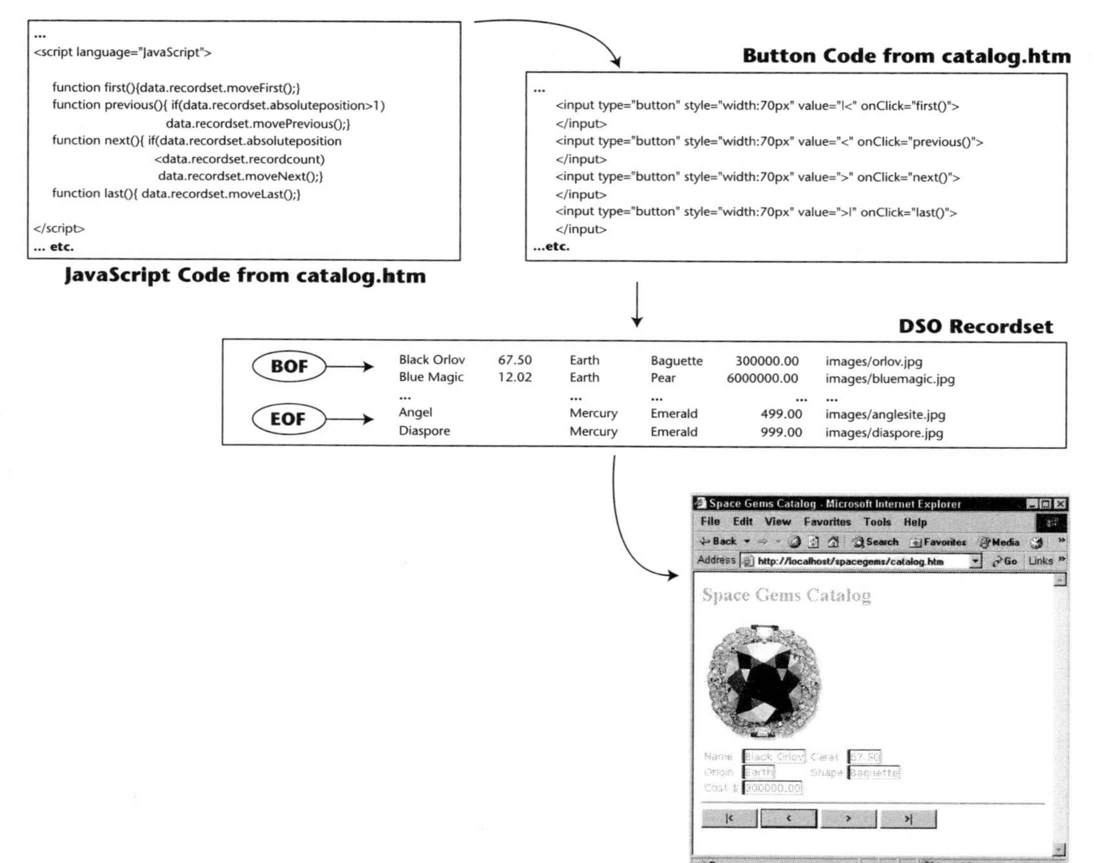

Figure 10.14 Navigating the diamonds in catalog.xml.

The JavaScript and XHTML code features work together to allow an end user to navigate through the recordset as follows:

- When a user clicks the moveFirst (<<) button, the moveFirst() function backs the user up to the very first record in the recordset and the XHTML code retrieves information for that record—the information for the Black Orlov diamond—and displays it.
- When a user click the Back (<) button, the movePrevious() function points to the previous record unless it is already at the top (the BOF position). If it is at BOF, the moveLast() function is executed and points to the last record in the recordset (the user is "fast-forwarded" to the last record).
- When a user clicks the Next (>) button, the moveNext() function points to the next record unless it is already at the bottom (EOF position). If it is at EOF, the moveFirst() function is executed and points to the first record in the recordset.
- When a user clicks the moveLast (>>) button, the moveLast() function points to the last record in the recordset.

Chapter 10 Labs: Data Binding with XML

In practice (and, certainly, *with* practice), XML data binding with XHTML or HTML is fairly easy to accomplish. We need only to remember a few rules and there aren't too many tough decisions to make. The main idea is to separate the maintenance of data from the display or rendering of the data.

The first two lab exercises are fairly basic. In the first, you will learn how to work with an XHTML document file that contains its own internal data island. The second exercise teaches you how to modify the XHTML document to refer to an external data island, which we'll provide. The third lab exercise is a little more advanced. In it, you will perform four basic steps as you create a catalog data island, bind its data fields, insert your own JavaScript data navigation mechanism on a Web page, and then test your new navigation functionality.

Lab 10.1: XHTML File Containing a Simple Internal XML Data Island

The best way to discover how an internal data island is used is to work with one. In this lab, we supply you with an XHTML display file containing an internal XML data island, and we explain how it works. This exercise is simple and fast, and you won't have to do a lot of typing. Once you see how it works and that it works, you will actually own a functioning example of this kind of data file. You can copy and modify this file to create more of them.

1. Download the file called gemsB_IDI.htm from the Chapter 10 page of the *XML in 60 Minutes a Day* Web site, as described in this book's introduction, and put the file in the C:\WWW\SpaceGems directory. The _IDI has been inserted into the filename to remind you that it contains an internal XML data island.
2. Test the gemsB_IDI.htm file in the browser to make sure that it works. There is no link to this particular file yet, so you must enter the filename as part of the URL (don't forget the underscore between the B and the IDI). In the browser's locator bar, type:

   ```
   http://localhost/spacegems/gemsB_IDI.htm
   ```

3. When the file is displayed, it should look like Figure 10.15.
4. Using HTML-Kit, open the gemsB_IDI.htm file.
5. Using the following steps as a guide, examine the content of the gemsB_IDI.xml file:
   a. Note that the actual XML data instance is situated between the HTML <head> tags.
   b. Look closely at the <xml id="gemdata"> opening and </xml> closing tags. This element type can only be named <xml>. It indicates to the browser's parser that the information between the start and end tags is the data island. If you were to change the element name from <xml> to <xmla>, for example, it would not work.
   c. The id attribute defined inside the <xml id="gemdata"> start tag is also mandatory. The value *gemdata* provides the subsequent data island with a data source reference that will be used later in the file.
   d. Now examine the HTML <table> element start tag in the following:

      ```
      <table border="1" width="100%"
      summary="Space Gems Quick List of Details"
      datasrc="#gemdata">
      ```

   e. The datasrc="#gemdata" attribute binds the data source (specified by the id attribute mentioned in Step c.) to the HTML table. This attribute therefore designates the HTML table as a data consumer.

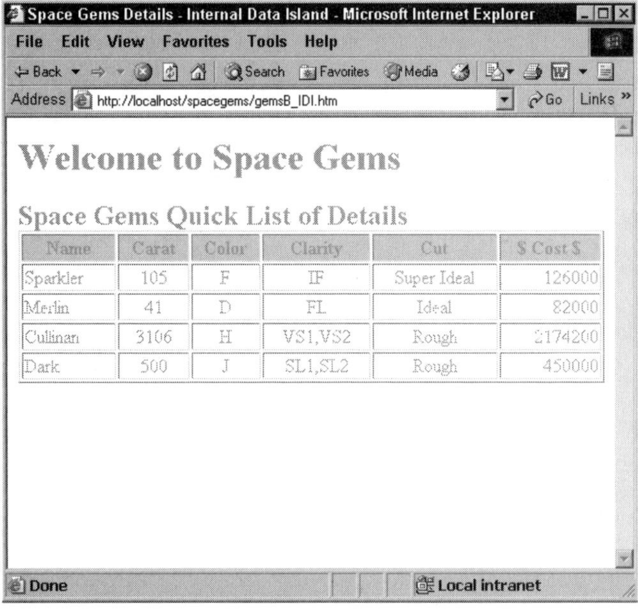

Figure 10.15 Displaying the gemsB_IDI.htm file.

f. You must include a pound sign (#) as the first character of the value specified for the datasrc attribute.

g. Every table must have table data <td> tags that define the individual cells where data is to be displayed.

h. You must define the <div> tag. Refer to the chapter notes for alternatives. The datafld="name" attribute inside the <div datafld="name" /> element tag (which is nested within the <td align="left" > </td> tags) binds the value of name= attribute to that table cell.

i. The rest of the code is similar and binds more table cells to respective <gem> elements and the values of their attributes. Beyond that, several regular HTML tags specify display formats for the various elements.

Lab 10.2: XHTML File Containing a Reference to an External Data Island

With two quick changes, you can morph the internal data island in the first example data file into a reference to an external data source or external data island. After you make the changes to your XHTML file, we'll provide an already created data file named gemsB.xml as the data source.

In a situation where you have a small Web site without a lot of data, you may not need a sophisticated database. Keeping your data inside external XML files like gemsB.xml is sufficient. (Incidentally, it is no coincidence that the data in that file is identical to the data found in the internal data island example.)

1. If you do not already have a fully functional gemsB.xml data file, you can download a new copy from the Chapter 10 page of the *XML in 60 Minutes a Day* Web site.
2. Using HTML-Kit, open the gemsB_IDI.htm file.
3. Before you begin modifying this file, save it as gemsB_EDI.htm to the C:\WWW\SpaceGems directory. The EDI in the filename is intended to remind you that this document will contain the reference to the external data island.
4. Delete all the code nested within the <xml id="gemdata"> and </xml> tags, including the <xml id="gemdata"> and </xml> tags themselves.
5. Replace the deleted code with the following new <xml> tag, which contains the reference to the external data island file named gemsB.xml:

   ```
   <xml id="gemdata" src="gemsB.xml" />
   ```

6. Check to make sure that this new <xml> tag is situated between the <head> and <title> elements.
7. Replace the word Internal with External inside the <title> tag.
8. Save the modified file.
9. Test the gemsB_EDI.htm file in the browser to make sure that it works. Because there is no link to this particular file yet, you must enter the filename as part of the URL in the browser's locator bar. (Don't forget to include the underscore between the B and the EDI in the filename.)

   ```
   http://localhost/SpaceGems/gemsB_EDI.htm
   ```

   When displayed, the file should once again look like Figure 10.15.
10. So that you won't have to keep entering the filename as part of the URL, modify the existing Quick List of Diamonds hyperlink on the index.html file. To do this:
    a. Using HTML-Kit, open the index.html file.
    b. Change the code for the link from.

```
<a href="gems1.xml">Quick List of Diamonds</a>
```

to

```
<a href="gemsB_EDI.htm">Quick List of Diamonds</a>.
```

11. Save the file back as index.html.
12. Test the link on the index.html file in the browser to make sure that it works. Type the following into the browser's locator bar:

```
http://localhost/SpaceGems/
```

13. When the index/home page appears, click the Quick List of Diamonds hyperlink. The successful display should look like Figure 10.15.

Lab 10.3: JavaScript Using Internet Explorer's DSO Binding Technology

This is a slightly more advanced lab, but we won't let it get too far beyond you. Whether or not you understand and use JavaScript regularly, this lab should interest you and perhaps stimulate your creativity. In it, we show you how to create and bind data, then how to navigate it on your local system, without having to enlist the original Web server to recast and retransmit the data. In a situation where you have a small Web site with little data, you may not need a database at all. Keeping your data inside an external XML file is just fine. This data may even be exported from a larger database, in which the XML file is just a temporary store.

Four basic steps make up this JavaScript lab exercise:

- Creating the data island
- Binding the data fields
- Creating a JavaScript navigation mechanism
- Testing the catalog.htm Web page

Please note that this lab is a Microsoft-specific solution.

1. Download both the catalog.xml and catalogempty.htm files from the Chapter 10 page of the *XML in 60 Minutes a Day* Web site into the C:\WWW\SpaceGems directory.

2. Open the catalogempty.htm file using HTML-Kit. You should see a partial HTML file solution with comments inside it, similar to this code:

```
<!DOCTYPE html PUBLIC "-//W3C//DTD XHTML 1.0 Strict//EN"
"DTD/xhtml1-strict.dtd">
<html xmlns="http://www.w3.org/1999/xhtml" xml:lang="en" >
   <head>
      <title>Space Gems Catalog</title>
      <!-- JavaScript start -->
      <!-- JavaScript end -->
   </head>
   <body text="#9999cc">
      <!-- Data island start -->
      <!-- Data island end   -->
      <h2 font-family:Verdana,sans-serif">
         Space Gems Catalog
      </h2>
      <!-- HTML table start -->
      <!-- HTML table end -->
      <!-- Navigation buttons start-->
      <!-- Navigation buttons end -->
   </body>
</html>
```

3. Rename the file catalog.htm and save it.
4. Open the catalog.xml file using HTML-Kit. This is the data source for this exercise. Review the document but do not make any changes to it. When you are familiar with the file's structure and contents, you can close it.
5. Open the catalog.htm file again and create a reference to an external data island inside it by adding the appropriate code between the data island comment lines. When done, the lines should look like this:

```
<!-- Insert the XML data island -->
<xml id="data" src="catalog.xml"></xml>
<!-- Insert the HTML table code after this line -->
```

6. Note that the value specified for the id attribute—the data source id—is *data*.
7. Add the following HTML table code to the catalog.htm Web page between the appropriate comment lines:

```
<!-- HTML table start -->
<table border="0" style="font: 10pt Verdana,sans-serif;"
     cellpadding="5">
   <tr>
      <td>
         <img dataSrc="#data" dataFld="image" />
      </td>
   </tr>
```

```
</table>
<table border="0" style="font: 10pt Verdana,sans-serif;"
     cellpadding="5">
   <tr>
      <td>Name</td>
      <td>
         <span style="background: white;
            width:150; border: inset;
            border-width:1" dataSrc="#data"
            dataFld="name">
         </span>
      </td>
      <td>Carat</td>
      <td>
         <span style="background: white;
            width:150; border: inset;
            border-width:1" dataSrc="#data"
            dataFld="carat">
         </span>
      </td>
   </tr>
   <tr>
      <td>Origin </td>
      <td>
         <span style="background: white;
            width:150; border: inset;
            border-width:1" dataSrc="#data"
            dataFld="origin">
         </span>
      </td>
      <td>Shape </td>
      <td>
         <span style="background: white;
            width:150; border: inset;
            border-width:1" dataSrc="#data"
            dataFld="shape">
         </span>
      </td>
   </tr>
   <tr>
      <td>Cost $</td>
      <td>
         <span style="background: white;
            width:150; border: inset;
            border-width:1" dataSrc="#data"
            dataFld="cost">
         </span>
      </td>
   </tr>
</table>
<!-- HTML table end -->
```

8. Anytime you want to see the progress, click the Preview tab within HTML-Kit. Feel free to change the HTML look and feel if you think this file is too ugly for words.

9. Add the following JavaScript code to the catalog.htm Web page between the appropriate comment lines, as indicated:

```
<!-- JavaScript start -->
   <script language="JavaScript">
      function first(){
      data.recordset.moveFirst();
   }
   function previous(){
   if(data.recordset.absoluteposition>1)
      data.recordset.movePrevious();
   }
   function next(){
      if(data.recordset.absoluteposition <
         data.recordset.recordcount)
         data.recordset.moveNext();
   }
   function last(){
      data.recordset.moveLast();
   }
   </script>
<!-- JavaScript end -->
```

10. This code uses some standard predefined JavaScript functions that will navigate the recordset. Here the recordset is defined as the data island, which in our case is everything inside the catalog.xml file.

11. Create the navigation buttons that will invoke the functions defined previously. Add the following code to the catalog.htm file between the appropriate comment lines:

```
<!-- Navigation buttons start-->
<hr />
           <input type="button" style="width:70px"
               value="|<" onClick="first()">
        </input>
        <input type="button" style="width:70px"
               value="<" onClick="previous()">
        </input>
        <input type="button" style="width:70px"
               value=">" onClick="next()">
        </input>
        <input type="button" style="width:70px"
               value=">|" onClick="last()">
        </input>
<!-- Navigation buttons end -->
```

12. View the file inside HTML-Kit Preview, and save the file.
13. Using Internet Explorer, enter http://localhost/SpaceGems/catalog.htm into the locator bar. If successful, the display should resemble Figure 10.16. Check the functionality by clicking the navigation buttons.
14. For optional practice, you can add another link to the index.html page, one that will give you instant access to this page. The code is as follows. Just follow the procedure indicated in the earlier exercises.

    ```
    <a href="catalog.htm">Space Gems Catalog</a>
    ```

15. When you are done, don't forget to test the new link.

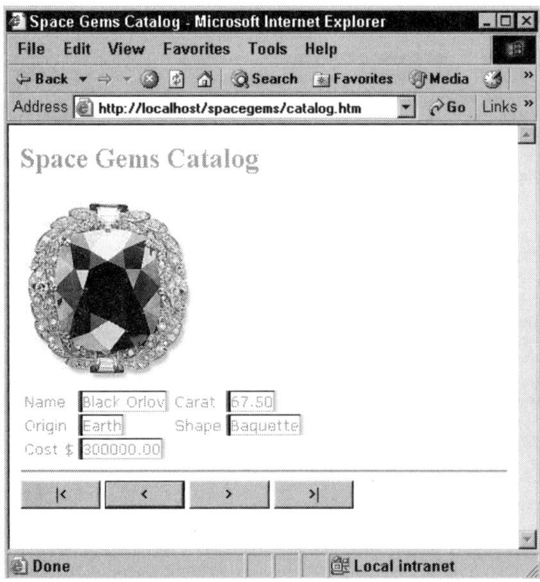

Figure 10.16 Space Gems Catalog including JavaScript navigation functions.

Summary

Several concepts discussed in this chapter serve us well with respect to native XML data and to discussions of other database technologies, especially when they are applied in the Internet world:

- More and more individuals and organizations are adopting XML technologies and standards, and native XML databases are expected to play a larger role in the future. However, they are not expected to unseat relational database technology. The challenge will be to increase their interchangeability.
- Data binding is the process of mapping and synchronizing data in a data source to designated (usually local) data placeholders. In this chapter, data consumer elements, also called bindable elements, are the placeholders. Data binding also involves moving and synchronizing data from a remote server to a local system and manipulating it on the local system.
- The advantages to data binding are reduced network traffic, lighter loading on servers, and more efficient use of local resources.
- Data consumer elements bind two types of data: single-valued and tabular. Inserting more than one value at once is called data set binding.
- HTML extended attributes, such as datasrc and datafld, allow us to point to data sources and to the data fields within those sources, respectively.
- XML data is stored in internal or external data islands. Internal data islands are located within the Web page documents that display and manipulate the data. External data islands are located in separate documents that are referred to by the Web page documents.
- XML data retrieval and synchronization are performed by the XML data source object plus the data binding agent or the table repetition agent. XML DSO activation is easier and more automatic since the release of Internet Explorer 5.
- The DSO is activated by the data binding agent or the table repetition agent. The DSO retrieves data and assembles it in recordsets in the local browser.
- Basic XML recordset navigation can be facilitated quite easily with JavaScript coding in the Web page documents themselves.

Review Questions

1. Which of the following is not an aspect of data binding?
   a. Mapping and synchronizing data
   b. Interchangeability with relational databases
   c. Transmitting data from sources to data placeholders
   d. Local data manipulation
   e. None of the above
2. Which of the following are data bindable elements? (There may be more than one correct answer.)
   a. <div>
   b. <table>
   c. <span>
   d. <td>
   e. All of the above
3. True or false? The <div> element is a grouping element, but the <span> element is only an inline element.
4. True or false? Single valued elements can be used to build tablelike structures.
5. To display data from a data source without worrying about the format of the data, which of the following attributes would you use?
   a. datasrc="$text"
   b. datafld="$text"
   c. datasrc="$table"
   d. datafld="table"
   e. None of the above
6. Which of the following attributes points to an external XML data island?
   a. datasrc
   b. datafld
   c. src
   d. id
   e. None of the above

7. The standard syntax for specifying data located below the second nesting level resembles which of the following?
   a. cost.retail
   b. cost/retail
   c. cost;retail
   d. cost:retail
   e. cost_retail
8. Which of the following is the proper syntax for an external data island?
   a. <xml id="gemdata" src="gems.xml" />
   b. <xml id="gemdata" datasrc="gems.xml" />
   c. <xml id="gemdata" src="gems.xml" >
   d. <xml datasrc="gemdata" datafld="data" />
   e. None of the above
9. True or false? The DSO searches a Web page document for bindable elements, then activates the data binding agent or the table repetition agent.
10. Which of the following atttributes could tie navigation buttons to JavaScript functions?
   a. input="value"
   b. function="value"
   c. recordset="value"
   d. onClick="value"
   e. None of the above

Answers to Review Questions

1. **b.** The interchangeability of native XML data and relational databases is an objective of developers and vendors of both technologies. But interchangeability is not an aspect of XML data binding.
2. **a.**, **b.**, and **c.** The <td> element can only be used if a <div> element is nested within it.
3. False. In fact, the statement is a little nonsensical. Both the <div> and <span> elements are grouping elements. However, <div> is block level while <span> is inline level.
4. True. In fact, two examples are provided in the text, in the section titled *The <table> Element*.
5. **b.** This is discussed in the *Single-Valued Elements Avoid Overrestrictive Data* section.
6. **c.** This is discussed in the *External Data Island* section.
7. **a.** Remember, the first term is the name affiliated with the second level. The delimiter is a period.
8. **a.** The <xml /> element has to be declared an empty element type, and the two relevant attributes are id and src.
9. False. Actually, the reverse is true: The data binding and table repetition agents search a Web page document for bindable elements; if they find any, they activate the appropriate DSO.
10. **d.** This is discussed in the *Navigating Recordsets* section.

VML

Even though it has only been about 10 years, the World Wide Web seems to have moved worlds away from its initial "text-only" days. During the past decade, graphics have become so important that—let's face it—a Web site without graphics isn't even considered a proper Web site. Research demands graphics, e-commerce demands graphics, and those who just want to have fun really demand graphics. In light of these ever-increasing demands, it is imperative to deliver graphic images (diagrams, still pictures, movies) while simultaneously optimizing the consumption of system and network resources.

In this chapter, we introduce the Vector Markup Language (VML), presently the most widespread of the XML-related graphic languages. We start by reviewing some basic graphic technology concepts, then provide a quick definition and background for VML itself. Finally, we show you how to create VML documents and figures. By the end of the chapter, you will be able to create your own VML objects, manipulate them, and display them in your browser.

A word of caution, though: As a graphics standard, Scalable Vector Graphics (SVG) is gaining acceptance in the IT world. Within the next few years, it may eclipse VML.

Basic Digital Imaging Technologies

Two basic digital imaging technologies exist: those using bitmap graphics and those using vector graphics. Although VML involves vector graphics, each is discussed in turn.

Bitmap Graphics

A *bitmap* graphic file (also known as a *raster* graphic file) is one in which each bit of data in the file corresponds to a specific location on a raster—which is the viewing area of a terminal screen—or to a specific ink dot on a printed page. Actually, the converse of that statement may be easier to understand: The data value for each picture element (usually called a *pixel*) is stored in a data file. Pixels are easily seen on terminal screens (and television screens) by looking at the screen through a magnifying glass. They are similar in nature to the combinations of black and white or colored ink dots that are still used to create newspaper and magazine photographs. The resolution (Windows calls it the screen image) that you specify for your terminal is measured in pixels. For example, 800 by 600 (also indicated by 800x600) means that there are 800 columns and 600 rows of pixels in your viewing area. The higher the numbers, the sharper the image that can be displayed. However, if you have higher numbers in your resolution setting, you will generally need larger data files to store the image data.

A bitmap is also characterized by its color density, which is the number of data bits required to display each pixel. The bits per pixel may vary from four to 32, depending on the number of shades of gray, or the combination of red, green, and blue colors per pixel. For example:

- If we want 16 colors, each pixel requires four bits of data.
- If we want 256 colors, each pixel requires eight bits.
- If we want 65,536 colors (high color), each pixel requires 16 bits.
- If we want 16.78 million colors (true color), each pixel requires 24 bits.

We can readily see that if we want a higher color density in an image, we need a larger data file.

Classroom Q & A

Q: What's with all those bitmap formats: GIFs, TIFFs, JPEGs, and the others? What's the difference?

A: Bitmap files do indeed occur in various formats, depending on the features of the various algorithms used to compress the data within them. If the files weren't compressed, they would take up

> much more storage space and take much longer to transmit and display. These formats are referred to by their acronyms (BMP, TIFF, GIF, PNG, or JPEG) and are also reflected in the extensions added to the respective data filenames. The various formats allow graphic files to be exchanged between several different platforms and applications.

The header of a bitmap file specifies the file format, the dimensions of the display in pixels, and information about color density. Following the header are the data bytes that create the image. Output devices, such as printers and monitors, contain rasterizers, which are combinations of hardware and software that translate all graphic objects into bitmaps. Thus, with some output devices, all graphic objects (including vector graphic objects, which are discussed in the next section) must be translated into bitmaps before being produced.

The advantages to bitmap graphics include the following:

- Because the composition of each individual display pixel or printed dot is controlled, bitmapped images do not need on-time calculation, which lessens their consumption of CPU cycles.
- Bitmaps are found just about everywhere on the Web and on private networks.
- Bitmaps allow us to enhance image details; we can literally modify each pixel in an image using applications that are commonly called paint programs or photo suites.

But bitmap graphics have several disadvantages, too. Among them:

- They may require a larger amount of RAM on motherboards, video adapter cards, or within printers.
- Bitmap images still require fast processors, since video terminals may require a wholesale image change (also called a refresh) between 50 and 200 times per second, depending on monitor characteristics.
- The generally larger file sizes cause them to download slowly (especially frustrating when subject to slow Web connections).
- The files are usually stored externally with respect to the rest of the Web page or other containing documents, which causes processors to work harder, makes the images more difficult to distribute, and causes extra system administration issues.
- They do not provide real overall flexibility: Once the image has been created, significant changes cannot be easily made. Even minor changes cannot be made without using the appropriate paint or photo software (which likely includes software to uncompress and then recompress the

files) on a system that must meet certain minimum requirements. Thus, you cannot access a bitmap, make quick (and, especially, significant) changes, and redraw it quickly.

- Bitmap graphic images become jagged looking beyond a certain magnification level.

Vector Graphics

Vector graphic images are objects created by drawing a series of lines, polygons, and text, while providing only the starting positions and directions for each line. Vector graphic images are also called *object-oriented* graphics, but they are not related to object-oriented programming.

The drawing activity is actually the activation of mathematical expressions and descriptions in an application, which, in turn, will use attributes provided in the respective Web document to create representations of the vector images. Vector graphics always use one or more algorithms in real time to create a shape and then draw that image on the screen or send it to a printer. Vector graphic files create bitstreams that describe their images as display lists that contain a mathematical description of every object in a shape (imagine a jewel being composed of triangles, octagons, and other individual objects grouped together), including their respective locations and dimensions, as well as other attributes like fill colors, line stroke widths, and layers.

Vector graphics are widely used in word processing, graphics editing, publishing, and presentation applications. Almost all sophisticated graphics systems, including computer-aided design and drafting (CADD or CAD) systems and animation software, use vector graphics. Applications used to create and manipulate vector graphics are generally called drawing programs (as opposed to the paint programs used to manipulate bitmap graphics). In everyday word processing, fonts are often created using vectors. These are called vector fonts, scalable fonts, object-oriented fonts, and outline fonts. Some vector graphic-enabled output devices contain built-in interpreters that execute the instructions (as opposed to rasterizing into bitmaps).

Vector graphics have several advantages:

- Vector graphics files use smaller amounts of memory to represent a respective object no matter what the intended actual size. If the graphics files are altered to create bigger or smaller images, almost no difference occurs in the size of their already smaller definition files, thus saving RAM and hard disk drive storage.
- The smaller files also transmit (download) faster.

- Vector graphics are more scalable. Their representations can potentially be output on any device, with any resolution, and at any size, with no loss of clarity and no distortion. In fact, they look better when displayed at higher resolutions and at higher magnifications. By contrast, bitmapped images become jagged at higher magnification and look no better on higher-resolution devices than on lower-resolution devices.
- Overlapping shapes can be manipulated independently without using different layers for each.
- Once vector graphic files are created, the objects within them can be selected, resized, moved, and reordered at any time; significant changes can be made, more quickly than the "pixel detailing" of bitmap manipulation.
- Vector graphic files are searchable for data and attributes.
- Users can interact easily with the created image files using a simple computer system and text editor. Vector files are actually text files.

The disadvantages of vector graphics are as follows:

- As vector graphics become more sophisticated (possibly containing scores, hundreds, or even thousands of mathematical expressions that define many finer details), more powerful processors may be needed to handle them. It may take significant time to redraw or output (that is, recalculate, pass the information to a rasterizer, store the data in RAM, and quickly transfer and refresh it to a screen) all the objects, not only all at once, but at perhaps hundreds of times a second as a monitor screen refreshes. This may result in flicker as you move an image to a new location on a page.
- The very fine image details might be better handled by bitmaps.

As a workaround for these bottlenecks and to save processing time, some programmers develop software that includes strategically placed bitmapped fonts or other images in otherwise vector graphic files. They still allow the use of vector fonts and images to produce fine results in hard copy.

VML Development

VML was designed to help developers address the problems and disadvantages of bitmap technology and to provide a textual method for prescribing vector graphics. Those prescriptions can be easily transferred to a wide variety of authoring tools, from the simple to the sophisticated, by simple cut-and-paste methods. Further, VML is written so that it can be integrated into existing HTML 4.0 Web-related documents.

The initial VML draft specification was authored jointly by Autodesk Inc., Hewlett-Packard Company, Macromedia Inc., Visio Corporation, and Microsoft Corporation, and it was submitted to the W3C in May 1998. The VML specification never attained W3C Recommendation status, despite the support of Microsoft and other developers. This support included the incorporation of VML graphic-rendering functionality into recent versions (since Version 5.0) of Microsoft's Internet Explorer browser. The VML specification document survives as a W3C Note. (As mentioned in Chapter 6, a W3C Note is a dated, public record of an idea, comment, or document. Publication as a Note does not represent any commitment by the W3C to pursue work related to it. Neither does its Note status indicate any endorsement of its content, nor any present or future allocation of resources to the issues addressed by it.)

Thus, no further VML development is likely to take place. In fact, both the VML Note and the (rival) Precision Graphics Markup Language Note (also submitted in 1998) were overtaken and passed by the development of the Scalable Vector Graphics specification, which became a W3C Recommendation in mid-2001. We discuss these documents in the last sections of this chapter.

What Is VML? A Definition

The W3C (at www.w3.org/TR/NOTE-VML) describes VML as follows: "VML is an application of the Extensible Markup Language (XML) 1.0, which defines a format for the encoding of vector information together with additional markup to describe how that information may be displayed and edited."

VML is fully compliant with other W3C standards such as Cascading Style Sheets, HTML, XHTML, and others. For example, all top-level VML elements support the <style> element and its related attributes, in the same manner that all HTML elements support it. Further, since VML also supports CSS, shapes can be styled and positioned as required by a Web document developer.

True to its vector graphics heritage, VML uses mathematical descriptions to prescribe its shapes. VML's vector graphics definitions can be included within XHTML-/HTML-compliant documents (integrated with the Web page coding). Unlike bitmaps, VML definitions are not relegated to external files. True to its Microsoft heritage, VML also contains a few MS Office-related features that allow it to cooperate with VML generated by Microsoft 2000 and XP technologies.

Images can be generated using nothing but VML. However, bitmap data is still considered important to VML and can be combined with vector data by including appropriate references. Furthermore, VML provides (admittedly limited) transformation attributes (such as chromakey, gamma, picture, and black level adjustments) that can be applied to the bitmap data from within the VML/Web document.

Some of VML's advantages stem from its vector graphics heritage; some from its Microsoft Internet Explorer affiliation:

- VML's vector graphic files are generally smaller, so they transmit faster than bitmap images.
- VML documents are easily and quickly created, updated, and published to servers. Editing activities can be done using text editors or other office environment applications. The files can be republished directly and quickly after that.
- VML is both open and standards-based. It is compliant with other W3C standards such as HTML, XHTML, and others, including, as mentioned previously, Cascading Style Sheets.
- Because it is a text-based encoding system, developers are able to search, cut, and paste vector graphics from one document to another, and scale VML graphics to interact with other page elements and objects. When a page is displayed in a browser window, the source code can also be viewed.
- VML has become the most widespread graphics-related XML application (although the Scalable Vector Graphics Recommendation is closing the gap) and comes incorporated with recent versions of Microsoft's Internet Explorer browser. Thus, it is accessible to a wide audience and requires no additional downloads or plug-ins to be functional.
- VML does not always require the implementation of a rasterizer. Existing operating system facilities can be used, such as those found in the Win32 Graphical Device Interface (GDI, the Windows standard for representing graphical objects and transmitting them to output devices) or Macintosh QuickDraw (the underlying graphics display system for Apple Macintosh computers).
- Although images can be generated using nothing but VML, bitmap data can also be combined with vector graphics data. VML also provides some bitmap transformation attributes.

These advantages all contribute to faster Web site design and have allowed VML to contribute to geographic information system technologies, where VML's map-making and drawing strengths can be quickly and easily employed alongside XML-related spatial databases.

Creating VML Documents

Now that we know something about VML's background and basic vector graphic technology, it's time to introduce its structure and other features.

Because VML is an application of XML, if it is used in an XML/XHTML environment, its syntax must be strictly adhered to. If VML is used in an HTML environment, however, not all XML-like features need be included.

Logical Structure: A Prolog and an <html> Element

VML document structures are very similar to XHTML/HTML documents. A VML document consists of two main parts: a prolog and an <html> element.

The prolog resembles other XHTML-related documents. It consists of an XML declaration and a DOCTYPE declaration indicating the DTD variant. However, a prolog is not necessary when VML is used with HTML.

The <html> element consists of the <head> element and the <body> element. In a VML/XHTML document, the <head> element contains a <title> element followed by a <style> element. The <style> element also contains a behavior declaration, which is discussed later.

Namespace Declarations

For VML to render properly, we must pay attention to the namespace declarations. Two namespace declarations are necessary: a VML namespace and a default namespace for the HTML or XHTML tags. Both declarations must appear in the <html> element's start tag.

Here is the VML namespace declaration that should appear in the <html> start tag:

```
<html xmlns:v="urn:schemas-microsoft-com:vml">
```

When we are declaring a VML namespace, convention prescribes the prefix *v:*. Later in the document, needless to say, the v: prefix precedes each VML-related element tag.

If we omit the VML declaration, the VML figures will not be displayed. If you ever have trouble producing VML output, start debugging by looking for this declaration in your documents.

The default namespace is inserted next, in the same <html> element start tag. If our document is XHTML-compliant, the default declaration must reflect that. In that case, add the following as the default namespace declaration to the <html> start tag:

```
xmlns="http://www.w3.org/1999/xhtml">
```

If our document is not XHTML-compliant (that is, if it is only HTML-compliant), then we have to add the following default namespace declaration to the <html> start tag, instead of the previous declaration:

```
xmlns="http://www.w3.org/TR/REC-html40">
```

The code used tells Internet Explorer that all tags without prefixes are part of the XHTML or HTML namespaces, respectively.

Because of VML's Microsoft heritage, it is supported by Microsoft Office 2000/XP applications: Microsoft Word, PowerPoint, and Excel. We can use those applications to draw VML objects, but you must add a third namespace declaration to the <html> start tag, since those applications will add the prefix o: to their VML elements. The third declaration follows:

```
xmlns:o="urn:schemas-microsoft-com:office:office"
```

Please remember that if we are not creating VML objects with Microsoft Office applications, we can omit that third namespace declaration.

Behavior Declarations

VML is supported as a default behavior in Microsoft Internet Explorer Version 5.0 and later. Introduced in Microsoft IE 5, behaviors are complete and encapsulated subroutines that, when called, extend MS IE browser functionality. If the IE browser does not include a VML behavior, we may need to add it as an option. Look for the VGX.DLL in the C:\Program Files\Common Files\Microsoft Shared\VGX folder on the Windows system.

Since they are complete in themselves, we can declare behaviors at the beginning of an XHTML/HTML document and then apply (or "call") them to any element in our document. Thus, behaviors provide the ability to reuse blocks of code and to keep our content separated from that actual code.

To activate IE's VML behavior, insert the following code into the <style> element within the <head> element:

```
<style>
   v\:* { behavior: url(#default#VML); }
</style>
```

This instructs the browser to pass all tags beginning with v: to its VML rendering subroutine.

Like the VML namespace declaration, if you omit the behavior, your VML images will not be displayed. So, if you have trouble producing VML output, consider looking for this code once you have examined your namespace declarations.

Once again, because VML is supported in several recent Microsoft Office applications, if we create VML objects with those programs, we must add this behavior declaration to the <style> element:

```
o\:* {behavior:url(#default#VML);}
```

Later, you will learn how to create primitive graphic objects (objects created by setting a path for a virtual pen to traverse). When adding such objects to a VML document, we must add a shape behavior declaration to the <style> element:

```
.shape {behavior:url(#default#VML);}
```

The *.shape* referred to here is like an object-oriented programming class name. In embedded-style behaviors like this, the class name is used as a selector and begins with the period (.). This causes every element assigned the class name of *shape* to be rendered according to the specifications in this IE behavior.

VML Elements in the <body> Element

The VML elements that we use to create shapes will appear within the <body> element of the XHTML/HTML Web page document. Those elements are categorized according to their function within a VML-related hierarchy of categories. Some elements are members of more than one category. The main categories, along with examples from each, are listed in Table 11.1. (Several of the elements listed in Table 11.1 are discussed in this chapter; for details on these and other elements, please refer to the W3C VML Note at www.w3.org/TR/NOTE-VML.)

VML applies to each element a default template consisting of the full set of attributes that may apply to that particular element. In the following section, for example, we discuss the <shape> element and Table 11.2 lists the default VML template for that element. However, when we specify a particular element type, we can override the default values for any of its attributes by specifying the attribute name and a new value.

Table 11.1 VML Element Categories

CATEGORY	MEMBERSHIP (EXAMPLES)
Top-level	<group>, <shape>, <shapetype>, and <background>
Primary	<group>, <shape>
Subelements	Several. Examples include <fill>, <formulas>, <strokeweight>, <handles>, <image>, <imagedata>
Predefined	Several. Examples include <rect>, <roundrect>, <line>, <oval>, <polyline>, <curve>, <arc>

The <shape> Element

Creating a <shape> element is the first step toward defining our own vector graphic figure. But <shape> really only defines the containing box for the actual figure we want to create. When this *block-level box* is created, we use the <shape> element's coordsize and coordorigin attributes to define a local coordinate system for any subelement figures that may be created within the box. Thus, any subsequent positioning information specified for subelement figures is expressed in terms of the box's local coordinate space. As a result, position attributes like left, top, width, height, and others are not expressed in commonly recognized measures like inches, millimeters, or the like; they are expressed as coordinate divisions, as you have defined them, within the box.

To clarify, the coordsize attribute defines how many divisions exist along the base of the containing box, across its width. The coordorigin attribute specifies the coordinates of the top left corner of the containing box. This strategy allows the vectors defining a figure inside the block-level box to be specified with respect to its local coordinate system. Later, if the dimensions of the containing box are changed, the outline of the figure will be automatically scaled to the new dimensions.

To create a figure inside the block-level box, specify a path within <shape>. The path may take the form of a path attribute or a <path> element. Both are discussed in the next section.

Table 11.2 lists the attributes, complete with their default values, that make up the <shape> element's default VML template. Notice that some values use quotes, while others do not. Those with quotes are standalone attributes; those without, appear within a style="..." attribute. To override any of <shape>'s default attribute values, insert the attribute name and specify a new value in the <shape> element's start tag.

Table 11.2 Default Template for the <shape> Element

ATTRIBUTE=VALUE	ATTRIBUTE=VALUE
flip=null	chromakey=null
height=100	coordorigin="0, 0"
left=0, margin-left=0, center-x=0, etc.	strokecolor="black"
position="static"	opacity="100%"
rotation=0	fillcolor="white"
top=0, margin-top=0, center-y=0, etc.	coordsize="1000, 1000"
style='visibility=visible'	strokeweight= "0.75pt"

(continued)

Table 11.2 *(continued)*

ATTRIBUTE=VALUE	ATTRIBUTE=VALUE
width=100	type=null
z-index=0	adj=null
stroke=true	path=null
wrapcoords=null	alt=null
href=null	id=null
title=null	class=null
v=null	print=true
fill=true	target=null

As a simple example of <shape> element usage, the following code is just about the minimum needed to produce a shape. Don't worry about the path attribute yet; after reading the next few sections, you will be able to interpret it easily.

```
<shape fillcolor="gray"
          style="position:relative;top:1;left:1;width:400;height:300"
          path="m 1,1 l 1,300, 400,300, 400,1 x e">
</shape>
```

From the example, you can see that we must define, at a minimum, a <shape>'s position, top, left, width, height, and path attributes. The fillcolor attribute was included because the path is an attribute. If instead we had used a <path> element, the fill color would have been specified within the <path> element's start tag.

Although the most basic of VML's graphic elements, <shape> is not used as frequently as we would expect. Most developers prefer to use predefined shapes like <rect>, <oval>, <line>, and others. These are discussed later, in the section titled *VML's Predefined Shapes*.

Creating Graphic Objects Using the path Attribute or <path> Element

To define what are called primitive graphic objects (which we refer to as *shapes* or *figures*) within the <shape> element, we either use a nested <path> element within the <shape> element, or specify a path attribute within the start tag of the <shape> element.

As stated earlier, if we are going to add primitive graphic objects to our VML documents using a path attribute or a <path> element, then we have to add a shape behavior declaration to the <style> element. For details, refer back to the *Behavior Declarations* section.

The path Attribute

Within the <shape> element, we can specify the figure we wish to draw by using the attribute named path and specifying, as a value for that attribute, an expression that includes a string of x,y coordinates plus one or more virtual pen commands. The path attribute thus defines the outline of a shape by prescribing a path consisting of a sequence of straight lines, Bézier curves, or both (technically, these represent a list of vector-based drawing operations).

Classroom Q & A

Q: Sorry to interrupt again, but what kind of curves?

A: Bézier curves (pronounced "bez-ee-ay" and named after the French mathematician Pierre Bézier) are curved lines defined by at least three specified points. Mathematical formulas are used to plot the rest of the points (see the c command in Table 11.3).

Once prescribed, the outline of the shape may then be stroked, filled, or otherwise modified according to the values you specify for other attributes. The basic syntax for a path attribute within a shape element is as follows:

```
<shape path="expression" ... >
```

Nineteen pen commands are available: m, l (the letter "ell"), c, x, e, t, r, v, nf, ns, ae, al, ar, at, wa, wr, qx, qy, and qb. The most commonly used commands are described briefly in Table 11.3.

Table 11.3 Path Attribute Pen Commands

COMMAND	FULL NAME	INSTRUCTION
m	moveto	Start a new subpath at the given (x,y) coordinate.
l	lineto	Draw a line from the current point to the given (x,y) coordinate, which becomes the new current point. To form a polyline, specify a number of coordinate pairs.

(continued)

Table 11.3 *(continued)*

COMMAND	FULL NAME	INSTRUCTION
c	curveto	Draw a Bézier curve from the current point to the coordinate given by the final two parameters (the control points are given by the first four parameters following the c).
x	close	Close the current subpath by drawing a straight line from the current point to the original moveto point.
e	end	End the current set of subpaths.
t	rmoveto	Start a new subpath at the (relative) coordinates specified.
r	rlineto	Draw a line from the current point to the given relative coordinate.
v	rcurveto	Draw a Bézier curve from the current point, using the given coordinate relative.

Here is an example that draws a simple diamond shape:

```
<shape id="diamond01"
     fillcolor="gray" strokecolor="blue"
     coordorigin="0 0" coordsize="200 200"
     style="position:relative;top:1;left:1;width:20;height:20"
     path="m 0,100 l 100,200, 200,100, 100,0 x e">
   </shape>
```

The square is prescribed in the expression that serves as the value for the path attribute. The starting point occurs at coordinates 0,100 (halfway along the left-hand side of a 200-by-200 rectangle) as defined by the moveto command (m). Next, a line is drawn, using the lineto command (l), from the starting point to the other three points, in the order listed (to 100,200; then to 200,100; and finally to 100,0). We close the figure—that is, we draw a line from the last point specified back to the starting point—using the close (x) command. The path is ended with the end (e) command. Note that, according to the style-position attribute, the given coordinates are in *relative coordinate* space (the space is prescribed by the coordorigin and coordsize attributes); the true size will be determined by the width and height specifications. The points specified are just x,y values in the units of the coordsize attribute of the shape element.

Spaces, as well as commas, may be used as delimiters when specifying point coordinates. For example, path="m 0 100 l 100 200 200 100 100 0 x e" is equivalent to path="m 0,100 l 100,200, 200,100, 100,0 x e."

Furthermore, if we are using zeros in our path description while using commas as delimiters, we should consider leaving the zeros out. Thus, path="m 0,100 l 100,200,200,100,100,0 x e" is equivalent to path="m ,100 l 100,200,200,100,100, x e."

The <path> Element

As an alternative to the path attribute, a <path> element can be nested within a <shape> element—or even within a <shapetype> element, which we discuss later in a section titled *The <shapetype> Element for Frequently Used Custom Figures,* to prescribe an outline for a figure.

Within the <path> element (notice that it is a declared empty element), prescribe your figure by inserting the attribute named *v* and specifying as values for that attribute an expression that includes a string of x,y coordinates plus one or more virtual pen commands. Thus, the procedure is similar to that of the path attribute within <shape>.

Although the activation syntax differs, ultimately the pen commands are the same as those listed for the path attribute: m, l (the letter "ell"), c, x, e, t, r, v, nf, ns, ae, al, ar, at, wa, wr, qx, qy, and qb. The most common of those commands are described in Table 11.3.

Using the simple diamond example again, the <shape> syntax, including the nested <path> element with its v attribute, is as follows:

```
<shape strokecolor="black" fillcolor="gray" coordorigin="0 0"
   coordsize="200 200" style="top:1;left:1;width:20;height:20" >
       <path v="m 0,100 l 100,200, 200,100, 100,0 x e" />
</shape>
```

Besides the v attribute, other attributes we can use with the <path> element include id, limo, fillok, strokeok, shadowok, arrowok, gradientshapeok, textpathok, and textboxrect. Using these attributes gives us more control and more features than if we had just used the path attribute in the <shape> element to draw our figure. For example, although the limo attribute is not discussed in detail in this introductory-level text, it and the <formulas> element provide greater control of figure scaling.

Classroom Q & A

Q: What if a <shape> element contains both a path attribute and a <path> element with a v attribute, and the paths contradict? Which will prevail?

A: If that happens, the specifications within the <path> element will prevail over any values specified for the path attribute in the <shape> element.

Q: So, which should we use? A <shape> element containing a path attribute? Or a <path> element?

A: If we are not prescribing a complex shape, we are more likely to conserve resources by using the path attribute strategy. Otherwise, for more sophisticated shapes, it would be better to use the <path> element and its attributes.

The same use of spaces as delimiters and the omission of zeros when commas are used as delimiters also apply to the use of the <path> element.

VML's Predefined Shapes

If we create graphic figures with <shape> and <path> elements, we could be faced with a lot of work. To save a great deal of effort, especially with respect to common shapes that are used frequently, VML provides several predefined shape elements.

Table 11.4 lists VML's predefined shapes and provides an example of each. The examples are illustrated in Figure 11.1. As you look at Figure 11.1, note that, in VML graphics, positive numbers are arrayed to the right of the left margin and downward from the top margin.

Table 11.4 VML's Predefined Shapes

ELEMENT NAME	EXPLANATION

<arc>	Creates an arc. Example:
	
	`<arc style='width:200pt;height:200pt'`
	`startangle="0"`
	`endangle="-90" coordorigin="200 500"`
	`strokecolor="black" strokeweight="2pt"/>`

<curve>	Draws a curved line. Example:
	
	`<curve from="300pt,350pt"`
	`control1="400pt,350pt"`
	`control2="600pt,500pt" to="670pt,600pt"`
	`strokecolor="black" strokeweight="2pt"/>`

Table 11.4 *(continued)*

ELEMENT NAME	EXPLANATION

<image>	Inserts a specified image into a shape. An implied rectangle is created that is the same size as the image. Example:
	
	<image style="width:300pt;height:200pt"
	   coordorigin="300pt, 550pt"
	   src="c:\SpaceGems\images\diamond.gif" />

<line>	Creates a straight line. Horizontal line example:
	
	<line from="700pt,100pt" to="950pt,100pt"
	   strokecolor="black" strokeweight="4pt">
	
	Vertical line example:
	
	<line from="150pt,50pt" to="150pt,250pt"
	   strokecolor="black" strokeweight="4pt">

<oval>	Creates an oval (or a circle, depending on the width and height property values). Oval example:
	
	<oval style='width:100pt;height:200pt'
	   fillcolor="gray"
	   coordorigin= "850pt, 500pt"
	   strokecolor="black" strokeweight="1pt"/>
	
	Circle example:
	
	<oval style='width:100pt;height:100pt'
	   fillcolor="white"
	   coordorigin="650, 350" strokecolor="black"
	   strokeweight="4pt"/>

<polyline>	Creates any number of lines specified, connected to one another "head-to-toe." Example:
	
	<polyline
	   points="550pt,200pt,650pt,200pt,750pt,
	   300pt,850pt, 300pt,950pt,400pt,950pt, 500pt"
	   strokecolor="black" strokeweight="3pt"/>

<rect>	Creates a rectangle. Example:
	
	<rect style='width:150pt;height:100pt'
	   fillcolor="gray"
	   coordorigin="400, 50" strokecolor="black"
	   strokeweight="1pt"/>

(continued)

Table 11.4 *(continued)*

ELEMENT NAME	EXPLANATION
<roundrect>	Creates a rectangle with rounded corners. Note the addition of the arcsize attribute, which accepts values between 0 (square corners) and 1.0 (semicircular). Example: `<roundrect style='width:250pt;height:100pt' arcsize="0.25" fillcolor="white" strokecolor="black" strokeweight="2pt"/>`

Predefined shapes provide a method for quickly drawing frequently used figures. The shapes are easily edited, since they have a more natural-sounding syntax. For example, instead of drawing a rectangle using a combination of the <shape> and <path> elements, we only have to use the <rect> element.

Table 11.5 lists the default templates for VML's predefined shapes. Notice that both common and specific attributes are listed for each element type.

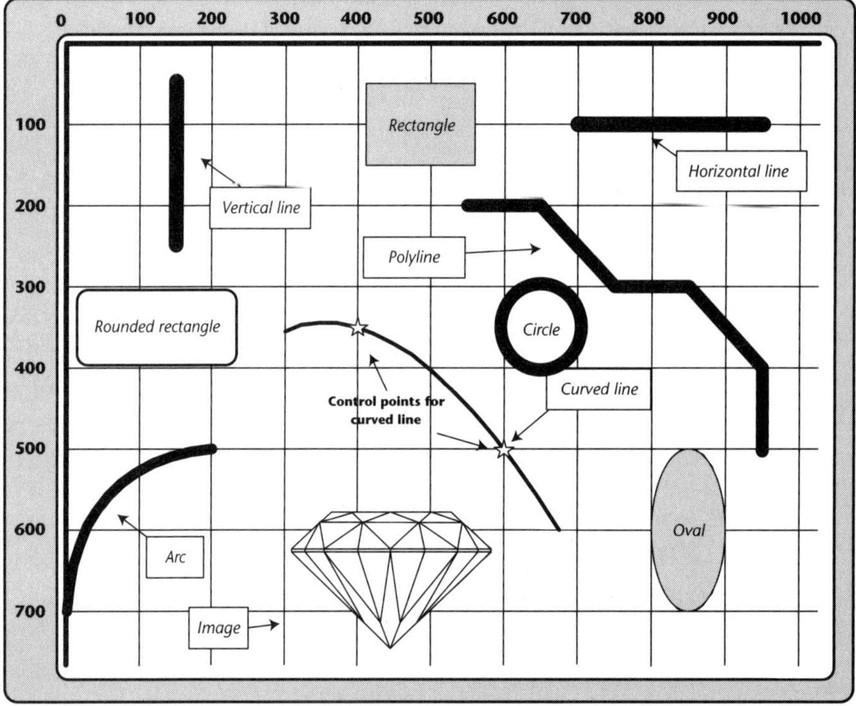

Figure 11.1 Predefined shapes in VML.

Table 11.5 Default Templates for VML's Predefined Shapes

ATTRIBUTE	DEFAULT VALUES						
	<RECT>	<ROUNDRECT>	<LINE>	<OVAL>	<POLYLINE>	<CURVE>	<ARC>
id	null	null	null	null	null	null	null
href	null	null	null	null	null	null	null
target	null	null	null	null	null	null	null
class	null	null	null	null	null	null	null
title	null	null	null	null	null	null	null
alt	null	null	null	null	null	null	null
style	'visibility: visible'	'visibility: visible'	'visibility: visible'	'visibility: visible'	'visibility: visible'	'visibility: visible'	'visibility: visible'
opacity	"1.0"	"1.0"	"1.0"	"1.0"	"1.0"	"1.0"	"1.0"
chromakey	"null"	"null"	"null"	"null"	"null"	"null"	"null"
stroke	"true"	"true"	"true"	"true"	"true"	"true"	"true"
strokecolor	"black"	"black"	"black"	"black"	"black"	"black"	"black"
strokeweight	"1"	"0.75pt"	"1"	"0.75pt"	"1"	"1"	"0.75pt"
fill	"true"	"true"	"true"	"true"	"true"	"true"	"true"
fillcolor	"white"	"white"	"white"	"white"	"white"	"white"	"white"
print	"true"	"true"	"true"	"true"	"true"	"true"	"true"

(continued)

Table 11.5 *(continued)*

ATTRIBUTE	DEFAULT VALUES						
	<RECT>	<ROUNDRECT>	<LINE>	<OVAL>	<POLYLINE>	<CURVE>	<ARC>
coordsize	"1000, 1000"	"1000, 1000"	"1000, 1000"	"1000, 1000"	"1000, 1000"	"1000, 1000"	"1000, 1000"
coordorigin	"0 0"	"0 0"	"0 0"	"0 0"	"0 0"	"0 0"	"0 0"
arcsize		"0.2"					
from			"0 0"			"0 0"	
to			"10 10"			"10 10"	
position				"0 0"			
size				"100 100"			
points					"0 0 10 10 20 0"		
control1						"10 10"	
control2						"20 0"	
startangle							"0"
endangle							"90"

The <shapetype> Element for Frequently Used Custom Figures

Although predefined shapes are very handy for defining commonly used shapes and are convenient alternatives to using <shape> elements with path attributes or nested <path> elements, there are times when we want to create a custom-designed figure and use it repeatedly. At these times, when predefined shape elements can't help us, the <shapetype> element can be used.

The <shapetype> element allows us to predefine a customized figure that can be used repeatedly later. Thus, we can create a prototype shape, provide it with a unique identifier, and refer to it when needed. The following example of a customized <shapetype> element defines a simple envelope shape:

```
<shapetype id="envelope" coordsize="10 10" >
     <path v="m 1,1 1 1,5,4,8,7,5,1,5,7,1,7,5,7,1, x e"
         textboxrect="0,2,8,4" fillcolor="red" strokecolor="blue".../>
</shapetype>
```

See the unique id attribute in the start tag? The value of the id attribute (in this case, envelope) is the attribute name we can use later, in conjunction with a <shape> element, to draw a copy of this figure wherever we want it. Note that the <shapetype> element definition must appear before the figure is drawn.

When we want to insert the customized figure, we use syntax resembling the following at each designated location:

```
<shape type="envelope" fillcolor="white" strokecolor="black"...>
</shape>
```

Thus, the <shape> element references a specific <shapetype> element by using a type attribute.

Please note that the <shapetype> element by itself does not cause the figure to be inserted. It only contains the specifications for the figure. Only when we insert the subsequent and corresponding <shape> elements will the figure be drawn. Please note, too, that in the sample <shape> element syntax, the fillcolor and strokecolor attributes were specified as white and black, respectively. Specifying different values in the <shape> element will override the values originally specified in the <shapetype> element. We can also alter other aspects of the figure by setting or changing other property attributes within the <shape> element.

Figure Placement

A discussion of figure placement involves one or more of three aspects:

- Deliberate positioning
- Figure overlap (accidental or deliberate)
- Flipping or rotating

If a designer intends to control any or all three aspects, the VML style attribute will play a major role. This section discusses all three aspects.

Static Positioning

VML's default position style is static positioning, which instructs the parser to place a figure at the current point in the text flow and to ignore any top or left settings that might appear in the style attribute.

As a simple example, say that we want to place a blue circle immediately after the text "This is our blue circle" but before the word "See?".

```
<body>
    This is our blue circle.
        <v:oval style='width:100pt;height:100pt' fillcolor="gray"
            strokecolor="blue" strokeweight="2pt" />
    See?
</body>
```

The circle will appear immediately after the first statement, just like an inline image. Static positioning isn't the usual design strategy, because designers normally want to place their images in specific locations.

Absolute Positioning

If we insert the position property into the style attribute of a figure's start tag and then set the value of the position property to absolute, the application looks for subsequent properties as a prescription for where to place the figure's containing box. The subsequent properties specify the distance from the top left corner (the base point) of its parent element (presumably, another positioned element that is intended to contain the figure).

To clarify, let's look at an example. Note that in the static positioning example, the blue circle is contained within the <body> element (that is, within the entire Web page). Its base point, then, is the top left corner of the Web page. Now we alter the code with the position:absolute property so that the circle's block-level display box is exactly 20 points to the right of and 10 points down from the top left corner of the Web page:

```
<body>
There is our blue circle.
    <oval style='position:absolute;left:20pt;top:10pt;
       width:100pt;height:100pt' fillcolor="gray" strokecolor="blue"
       strokeweight="2pt" />
See?
</body>
```

Now that we have positioned the figure with the absolute designation, it will not be considered part of the text flow and will not appear between the two statements. That's why we changed the first statement to "There is our blue circle" from "Here is our blue circle."

Relative Positioning

Relative positioning allows us to place (that is, offset) a figure's block-level display box in a precise position relative to the current (or base) point in the text flow. Relative positioning is activated by the use of the value *relative* for the position property within the style attribute. The offset distance is prescribed by the values specified for the top and left properties in the style attribute. The containing box will once again, as in VML's default static positioning, take up space in the text flow.

Let's create another blue circle example that places the blue circle 100 points to the left and 25 points lower than the current point in the text flow:

```
<body>
There is our blue circle.
    <oval style='position:relative;left:100pt;top:25pt;width:100pt;
       height:100pt' fillcolor="gray" strokecolor="blue"
       strokeweight="2pt" />
See?
</body>
```

Overlapping Figures: The z-index

Occasionally, figures overlap, whether by accident or by design. VML's default behavior is to display the most recently prescribed figure on top of those prescribed earlier. However, by specifying z-index properties in the style attribute of the respective figures' start tags, a designer can create a layering hierarchy. The value of the z-index specification can be a negative integer (for example, –2), zero, or a positive integer (like +3). The figure with the most positive z-index value will be displayed on top of figures with less positive z-index values. Meanwhile, if two or more figures have the same z-index value, the layering reverts to default behavior. Z-indexes can also be applied to <shapetype> and <group> elements.

In the following example of respective z-indexes, our blue circle with gray fill will be displayed on top of another figure, a green rectangle:

```
<body>
    <oval style='position:relative;left:50pt;top:15pt;width:100pt;
       height:100pt;z-index:3' fillcolor="gray" strokecolor="blue"
       strokeweight="2pt" />
   <rect style='position:relative;left:50pt;top:15pt;width:100pt;
       height:160pt; z-index:0' fillcolor="green" strokecolor="green"
       strokeweight="1pt" />
</body>
```

Z-indexes can be used to insert a background graphic. If Space Gems wants their diamond logo to appear as a backdrop on their Web page and make it independent from the text flow, it requires a negative z-index value and absolute positioning, like this:

```
<body>
    <image style='position:absolute;left:20pt;top:10pt;width:400pt;
      height:400pt; z-index:-3' src="c:\SpaceGems\images\diamond.gif" />
</body>
```

Rotating Images

Sometimes, for design or other reasons, we may want to rotate an object or a figure on a Web page. We can insert a property named rotation into the style attribute and then specify a value for the rotation. The values specified for a figure rotation are clockwise or counterclockwise degrees about the figure's center (that is, about the figure's axis). The number specified indicates the degrees and direction of rotation. If the number is positive, the rotation will be clockwise; if negative, counterclockwise.

Suppose, for example, Space Gems wants to use an image of one of its transport ships as a background graphic. Instead of the craft appearing horizontal, however, they want to create the impression that it is gaining altitude from left to right. The following code could achieve that:

```
<body>
    Free Delivery in the Sol System!
       <image style='position:absolute;left:20pt;top:10pt; width:400pt;
            height:400pt; z-index:-3;rotation:-45'
            src="c:\SpaceGems\images\sgi-37x.gif" />
</body>
```

Flipping Images

Occasionally, for design or esthetic reasons, an image may fit better with the text or the posture of someone in a picture may look more dynamic if they are oriented differently. At these times, you can use the flip property specification within the style attribute. The value you specify for flip dictates whether the figure rotates about its x-axis or its y-axis. The values are listed in Table 11.6.

Table 11.6 flip Property Values

VALUE	DESCRIPTION
x	Invert the figure's x ordinates (that is, flip the figure about its y-axis)
y	Invert the figure's y ordinates (flip the figure about its x-axis)

Let's say Space Gems wants use the SE-SGI-37X transport vehicle image again, but they want to flip it around. Here's its basic nonflipped descriptive code (some details have intentionally been omitted):

```
<body>
    <image style='.....width:400pt;height:200pt; z-index:-3;
        src="c:\SpaceGems\images\sgi-37x.gif"/>
</body>
```

Here is the code used to perform a horizontal flip:

```
<body>
    <image style='.....width:400pt;height:200pt; z-index:-3; flip:x'
        src="c:\ SpaceGems\images\sgi-37x.gif "/>
</body>
```

And here is the code used to perform a vertical flip:

```
<body>
    <image style='.....width:400pt;height:200pt; z-index:-3; flip:y'
        src="c:\ SpaceGems\images\sgi-37x.gif "/>
</body>
```

Figure 11.2 illustrates these flip maneuvers.

We are not restricted to flipping horizontally *or* vertically. We can also specify both x *and* y flips.

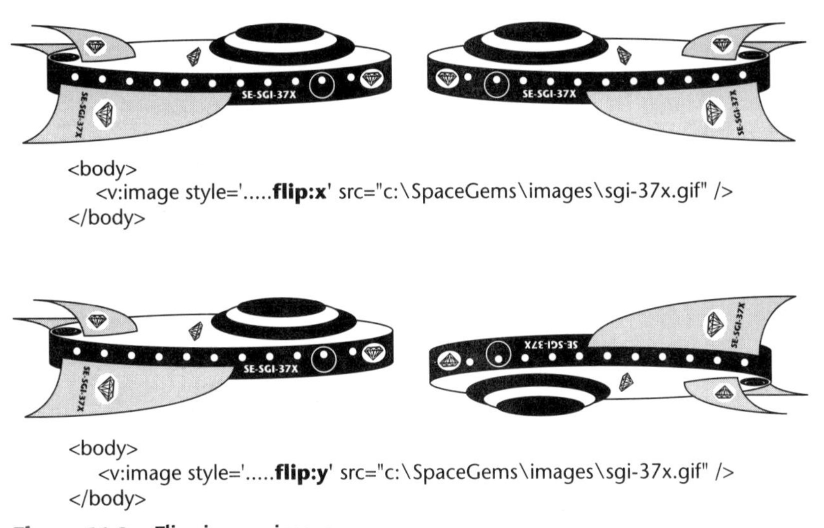

Figure 11.2 Flipping an image.

Altering the Appearance of VML Figures

Several approaches can be used to alter the appearance of figures drawn with VML: adding color, changing fill aspects, and altering scale (increasing or decreasing their size). To add color and alter scale, use the style attribute. To change fill aspects, use a nested <fill> element.

Adding Color to Shapes

Colors are specified three ways in VML:

- Using predefined color names (VML observes HTML 4.0 predefined color names)
- Specifying the hexadecimal value
- Specifying the RGB function

Table 11.7 lists HTML 4.0's named colors along with their respective hexadecimal values and RGB functions.

Table 11.7 HTML 4.0 Named Colors

NO.	NAME OF COLOR	HEXADECIMAL VALUE	RGB FUNCTION
1	Aqua	#00FFFF	0 255 255
2	Black	#000000	0 0 0
3	Blue	#0000FF	0 0 255
4	Fuchsia	#FF00FF	255 0 255
5	Gray	#808080	128 128 128
6	Green	#008000	0 128 0
7	Lime	#00FF00	0 255 0
8	Maroon	#800000	128 0 0
9	Navy	#000080	0 0 128
10	Olive	#808000	128 128 0
11	Purple	#800080	128 0 128
12	Red	#FF0000	255 0 0
13	Silver	#C0C0C0	192 192 192
14	Teal	#008080	0 128 128
15	White	#FFFFFF	255 255 255
16	Yellow	#FFFF00	255 255 0

Table 11.8 Example Color Specifications

METHOD	EXAMPLE CIRCLE SYNTAX
Named color	<oval style='width:100pt;height:100pt' fillcolor="gray" coordorigin="-300 100" strokecolor="blue" strokeweight="2pt" />
Hexadecimal value	<oval style='width:100pt;height:100pt' fillcolor="#808080" coordorigin="-300 100" strokecolor="#0000FF" strokeweight="2pt" />
RGB function	<oval style='width:100pt;height:100pt' fillcolor="rgb(128,128,128)" coordorigin="-300 100" strokecolor="rgb(0,0,255)" strokeweight="2pt" />

Table 11.8 lists examples of all three methods, using identical specifications for a predefined circle (that is, an oval whose width and height are the same dimension). Note the variations in syntax, according to the specification approach.

Changing Fill Characteristics using the <fill> Element

We've seen how the fillcolor attribute can be used to specify the color of various figures. But when we want to alter figure colors in other ways, and the fillcolor, strokecolor, strokeweight, and other attributes do not provide the options we want, we can nest a separate element <fill> in the extent of the figure element. In these sections, we illustrate how <fill> can be used to create three effects: gradient fills, pattern fills, and picture fills. The <fill> element has 19 attributes: alignshapes, angle, aspect, color, color2, colors, focus, focusposition, focussize, id, method, on, opacity, opacity2, origin, position, size, src, and type. Table 11.9 describes 12 that are commonly used at an introductory level.

Table 11.9 Basic <fill> Attributes

ATTRIBUTE	EXPLANATION
angle	The angle along which a fill gradient is directed (default value is "0")
color, color2, colors	*color* sets the fill color (default value is "white"); *color2* sets a secondary fill color, for patterns (default value is "white"); *colors* sets intermediate colors in a gradient (default value is null)
focusposition, focussize	For radial gradients. *focusposition* sets the position of the innermost rectangle (default value is "0,0"). *focussize* sets the size of the innermost rectangle (default value is "0,0")

(continued)

Table 11.9 *(continued)*

ATTRIBUTE	EXPLANATION
id	Specifies a unique identifier for the figure (default value is "null")
method	Sets the fill method. Options are "none", "linear", "sigma", or "any" (default value is "sigma")
origin	Specifies the origin, relative to the upper left of the image (default value is "auto", the center of the image)
size	Specifies the size of the image (default value is "auto")
src	Provides the URI of an image to insert for image and pattern fills (default value is null)
type	Specifies the fill type. Options are "solid", "gradient", "gradientradial", "tile", "pattern", or "frame" (default value is "solid")

Creating a Gradient Fill

Gradient fills are a progression from one color to another across a figure. There are two types of gradient fills: normal and radial. To create gradient-filled figures, we use a type attribute in the start tag of a <fill> element, which, in turn, is nested within the element that prescribes the figure. We can also specify additional attributes like *method*, *color2*, *focus*, and *angle*. Consider this example:

```
<body>
    <oval style='position:relative;left:50pt;top:15pt;width:100pt;
       height:100pt; z-index:0' fillcolor="gray" strokecolor="blue"
       strokeweight="2pt" >
         <fill type="gradient" method=" linear sigma" angle="30" />
    </oval>
</body>
```

Here we've prescribed a blue circle with a gradient ranging from white (the default color2) to blue (the circle's fillcolor), moving across it at an angle of 30 degrees.

A radial gradient fill employs a figure that, at its outer regions, is one color but also contains a small rectangle of another color. The gradient occurs as the fill changes color, beginning at the small rectangle, out to the color of the outer regions. In this next example, a small white rectangle will be placed in the circle, creating a highlight spot. The focusposition attribute specifies the center of the small rectangle.

```
<body>
    <oval style='position:relative;left:50pt;top:15pt;width:100pt;
       height:100pt;z-index:0' fillcolor="blue" strokecolor="blue"
       strokeweight="1pt" >
       <fill type="gradientradial" method="sigma" angle="45"
           focus="100%" focusposition=".25, .75" focussize="0,0" />
    </oval>
</body>
```

Filling a Shape with a Pattern

To create a pattern fill, we must first have created a pattern and stored it in an image file. Then, in the <fill> element start tag, we insert a type attribute and specify its value as "pattern". Then we insert the source location attribute src and, for its value, specify the URI that describes the location of the image file.

In this example, a circle is filled with a pattern:

```
<body>
    <oval style='position:relative;left:50pt;top:15pt;width:100pt;
       height:100pt;z-index:0' fillcolor="gray" strokecolor="blue"
       strokeweight="2pt" >
     <fill type="pattern" src="c:\SpaceGems\images\diamonds.gif"/>
    </oval>
</body>
```

When using pattern fills, we can also specify custom fill colors by specifying a different value for the fillcolor or color2 attributes.

Filling a Shape with a Picture

If we want to fill a shape with a picture, we first store the picture in an image file. Then, in the <fill> element, we specify a value of "frame" for the type attribute. Like the pattern fill, we then insert an src attribute whose value specifies the URI location of the picture file.

Here, a picture is inserted into a circle:

```
<body>
   <oval style='position:relative;left:50pt;top:15pt;width:100pt;
       height:100pt;z-index:0' fillcolor="gray" strokecolor="blue"
       strokeweight="2pt" >
      <fill type="frame" src="c:\SpaceGems\images\diamond04.gif"/>
    </oval>
</body>
```

Altering the Size of a Shape

To alter the scale of a shape, we must respecify the size of the figure's containing box. To do that, we change the values of the width and height in the style attribute, within the figure's element start tag. The figure can then be redrawn within the newly specified containing box. For example, let's change the size of our blue circle with the gray fill. Its original specifications are similar to the following:

```
<oval style='width:100pt;height:100pt' fillcolor="gray"
   coordorigin="-300 75" strokecolor="blue" strokeweight="2pt"/>
```

To make the circle twice as big, we do some simple arithmetic and come up with the appropriate multipliers. We then substitute them as follows:

```
<oval style='width:141pt;height:141pt' fillcolor="gray"
   coordorigin="-300 75" strokecolor="blue" strokeweight="2pt"/>
```

Grouping Shapes Together

If we are manipulating several figures but want them to maintain their relative sizes, shapes, and positions with respect to one another, it is tedious to respecify their attributes individually. It is easier to just group them together and then specify new attributes for the entire group at once. With most drawing applications, this process is called *grouping*. We can group figures using VML. VML allows us to use the top-level <group> element to group more than one shape together so that they can all be manipulated as one image.

The <group> element supports the same attributes as the <shape> element, with some exceptions. For example, <group> only works with four child elements: <group>, <shapetype>, <shape>, and <lock>.

We can create a <group> element by nesting any number of other <shape> elements and <group> elements. There are no limits on the levels of nesting or on the number of elements nested within a group.

When elements are grouped, they use the local coordinate space of the group. The new group is then referenced by a single ID. These features allow the figure elements within the group to be scaled and moved together. For example, Figure 11.3 depicts the components of a two-level nested group named *miner*, in which:

- The drill, pick, and shovel shapes are combined to form the tools group.
- The hardhat and body shapes are combined to form the worker group.
- The tools and worker groups, combined with the buggy shape, form the miner group.

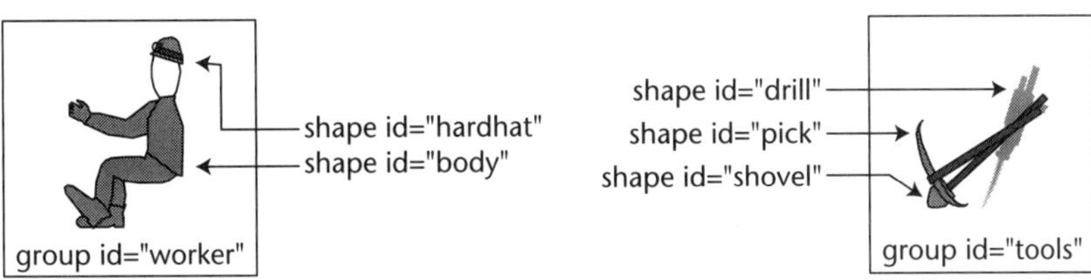

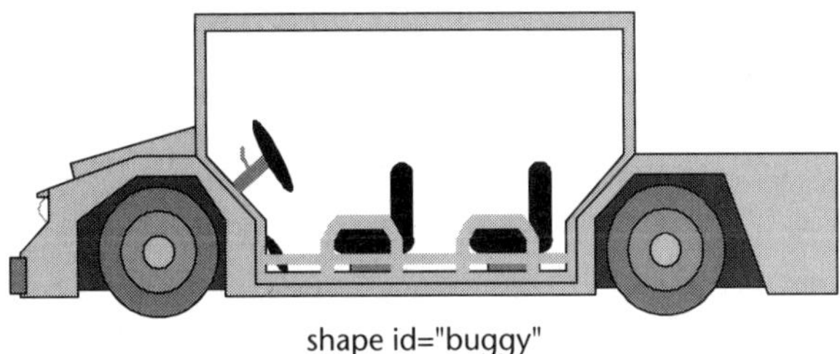

Figure 11.3 Grouping shapes.

The following code forms the basic structure of the miner group. We've left out the details to save time and preserve the clarity of the structure.

```
<body>
   <group id="miner"...>
      <group id="worker"...>
         <shape id="hardhat" ...> </shape>
         <shape id="body" ...> </shape>
      </group>
      <group id="tools"...>
         <shape id="drill" ... > </shape>
         <shape id="pick" ...> </shape>
         <shape id="shovel" ...> </shape>
      </group>
```

```
        <shape id="buggy" ...> </shape>
    </group>
</body>
```

Scalable Vector Graphics (SVG)

In addition to VML, three other vector graphic-related submissions were received by the W3C in 1998:

- The Precision Graphics Markup Language (March 1998).
- Web Schematics on the World Wide Web, a proposal submitted by representatives of the Council for the Central Laboratory of the Research Councils in March 1998 (also given Note status by the W3C).
- The DrawML Specification, submitted by Håkan Lothigius of Excosoft AB, a Swedish IT consulting company (December 1998). DrawML resembles Web Schematics, but relies on Java functionality.

All proposals were submitted to initiate and facilitate discussion and consultation. As a result of the proposals, in early 1999, the W3C created their Scalable Vector Graphics (SVG) Working Group. It consisted of representatives from Adobe; Apple; Autodesk; BitFlash; Canon; CSIRO; Corel; Excosoft; HP; IBM; ILOG; Intranet Solutions, Inc.; Kodak; Lexica; Macromedia; Microsoft; Netscape; Opera Software; Oxford Brookes University; OASIS; Quark; RAL (CCLRC); Sun; Visio; Xerox; and the W3C itself. Many other members of industry, academia, chat and email groups, and the general public also contributed.

In September 2001, after almost three years of drafting, discussion, consultation, and development, the SVG group's proposal was endorsed by the W3C as the Scalable Vector Graphics (SVG) 1.0 Specification. Since then, development has continued. Two proposed W3C Recommendations were released in late 2002: a Scalable Vector Graphics (SVG) 1.1 Specification and the combined Mobile SVG Profiles, SVG Tiny and SVG Basic. A Working Draft proposal for the XHTML +MathML +SVG Profile was released in August 2002.

Thus, SVG is a very stable XML-based standard that many companies have worked to implement. If you check the SVG Web site at www.w3.org/Graphics/SVG/overview.htm8 you can link to a page that lists dozens of new SVG implementations for viewers, editors, conversion tools, and server-side applications. We expect that SVG will eventually replace VML as the prevailing graphics-related XML application.

Chapter 11 Labs: Creating VML Documents

VML graphics can be very complex and impressive, but if they are complex, they can also be resource-hungry. In these exercises, we show you how to spice up the Space Gems Web page using a keep-it-simple approach. Then we show you just how far you can take VML. Because the second example is complex, and because deriving code of this nature requires a lot of practice, skill, and time, we provide it for you.

Lab 11.1: A Simple but Impressive VML Example

With just a few lines of code, you can create some pretty interesting effects. Granted, we could have created another JPEG or GIF graphic here, but we think you'll agree that it is simpler and more convenient to create and then play with the few lines of text in the Web page document presented in this lab exercise.

1. Download the file called SPFeature.htm from the Chapter 11 page of this book's Web site as noted in the book's introduction, and put the file in the C:\WWW\SpaceGems directory.
2. Open the SPFeature.htm file using HTML-Kit.
3. Click the Preview tab to confirm that the existing HTML tags in the file are correct. You should see something like Figure 11.4.
4. Click the Editor tab to return to the code view of the file.

Figure 11.4 Initial view of Special Feature page.

5. Add the *v* XML namespace to the <html> tag at the top of the file. To do this, change the <html> tag from

```
<html xmlns="http://www.w3c.org/TR/REC-html40">
```

to

```
<html xmlns:v="urn:schemas-microsoft-com:vml"
      xmlns="http://www.w3c.org/TR/REC-html40">.
```

6. Now declare your intentions to use VML by inserting the following code between a set of <style> tags. Insert the following code inside the file under the appropriate comment tag. This sets up the environment within the browser so that the browser can invoke and interpret the VML type tags correctly.

```
<style>
     v\:* {behavior:url(#default#VML);}
/style>
```

7. Now let's have some fun. Place the next two lines of code inside the file under the appropriate comment tag. These two lines of code will display an image of a Citrine gem inside the file. Note the use of the *v* namespace here inside the code.

```
<v:image style="width:150;height:150" src="images/citrine.gif">
</v:image>
```

8. Click the Preview tab and confirm that the Citrine gem image is displayed.
9. Click the Editor tab to return to the code.
10. Now draw a circle (or oval). Enter these two lines of code directly underneath the <v:image> code.

```
<v:oval style="width:350;height:150" fillcolor="#ffcc66"
          strokecolor="#ffcc66">
</v:oval>
```

11. Click the Preview tab and confirm that the oval shape is displayed. If you prefer to create a circle, make the oval's width equal to its height. Both the fill color and stroke color have been set to the same value so that a black line doesn't appear in the oval.
12. Click the Editor tab to return to the code.
13. Next, to fancy up the fill inside the oval shape a bit, enter the following line of code directly beneath the <v:oval> code.

```
<v:fill method="linear" angle="45" type="gradient" />
```

14. Click the Preview tab and confirm that the fill inside the oval shape has a gradient applied. Cool, huh?

15. Click Editor tab to return to the code.
16. Next, place some text inside the oval shape. To do this, declare a textbox and place text inside it. Be careful where you place the following code. These lines of code must be placed inside the oval so that it knows where to display the text. Modify your existing code to look like the code shown here. The new code is highlighted.

```
<v:image style="width:150;height:150" src="images/citrine.gif">
</v:image>
<v:oval style="width:350;height:150" fillcolor="#ffcc66"
strokecolor="#ffcc66">
<v:fill method="linear" angle="45" type="gradient" />
<v:textbox style="font-size:20pt;font-color:white;
text-align:center">
<p>Feature of the Month<br>
20% off<br>
Expires: 2048</p>
</v:textbox>
</v:oval>
```

17. Click on the Preview tab. Your display should now look like Figure 11.5.
18. Once you are satisfied that the page displays properly, test the view inside the browser. Enter the following into the browser's locator bar:

```
http://localhost/SpaceGems/SPFeature.htm
```

19. Optionally, you can place a link to this page from the index page for easy access:

```
<a href="SPFeature.htm">Space Gems Special Features</a>
```

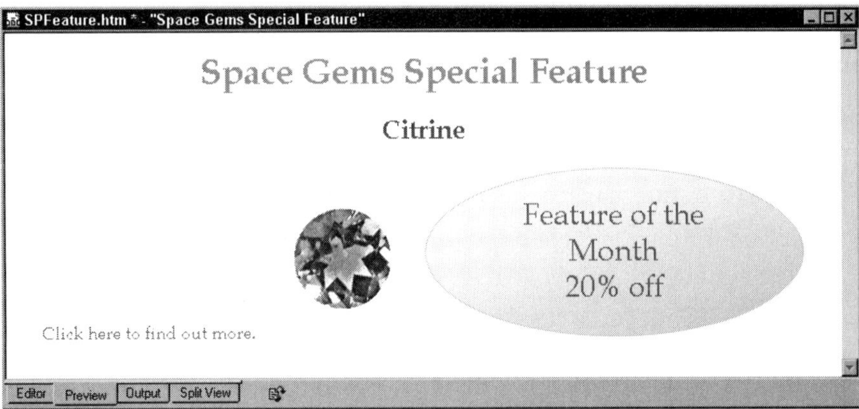

Figure 11.5. Final view of Special Feature page.

Lab 11.2: A Truly Impressive VML Example

The following example is set up as a surprise. You don't actually have to do any work! Just download the file and take a look at the various roving VML shapes. (To see other great examples of VML, go to www.p-richards.demon.co.uk.)

1. Download the file called SPFeature_Starts.htm from this book's Web site, as discussed in the introduction, and put the file in the C:\WWW\SpaceGems directory.
2. View the file inside your browser.

   ```
   http://localhost/SpaceGems/SPFeature_Starts.htm
   ```

3. You should see many stars roving all over your new page. Cool!
4. Take the time to view the source for the roving VML objects. To do this, right-click the page and select View Source. Not so trivial!
5. Before closing the browser, notice how many resources this process uses. To do this, right-click the bottom Windows tool bar and bring up the Task Manager. Click on the Performance tab and look at the CPU Usage. Yikes! Did we say "hungry"?

Summary

Several concepts discussed in this chapter are shared with other XML-related graphics applications, although the names of element types, attributes, and properties, and the applicable values assigned to them, may vary from application to application:

- The ever-increasing demand for graphics must be met while optimizing the use of system and network resources.
- Two basic digital imaging technologies exist: bitmap graphics and vector graphics. VML is an example of vector graphics technology.
- Over the past few years, VML rose to prominence as the premier graphics-related XML application. It will likely be eclipsed by Scalable Vector Graphics, but it remains prominent today because of support provided by the Internet Explorer browser application.
- The VML specification reached W3C Note status but will not reach Recommendation status. SVG has overtaken it.

- In VML documents, designers must insert up to three namespace declarations and up to three behavior declarations in the <style> element within the <head> element. Behaviors are subroutines that extend Internet Explorer functionality.
- VML shape-related elements appear nested within the <body> element. Primitive graphic objects are created with the <shape> or <shapetype> elements. However, most VML objects are created with VML's predefined shapes.
- VML graphic objects are placed using static, absolute, or relative positioning. Overlap is controlled by assigning a z-index value to each shape. VML shapes can also be flipped, rotated, filled, resized, colored, and grouped. There is no limit to the number of shapes that can be grouped together, nor to the levels of such grouping.

Review Questions

1. The differences between the various bitmap formats arises from:
   a. Differing bits per pixel
   b. Differing compression algorithms
   c. Differing image creation hardware and software
   d. Differing associations that promote each format specification
   e. None of the above
2. True or false? A rasterizer is a combination of hardware and software that translates graphic objects into bitmaps.
3. True or false? Vector graphic "drawings" result from mathematical expressions and descriptions inside an application that utilize the attribute and property values provided by the data documents.
4. True or false? Vector graphics are tougher on system RAM, and bitmap graphics are tougher on CPU resources.
5. True or false? A W3C Note represents one stage along the way to the development of a W3C Recommendation.
6. If your VML objects don't display, what VML document statements should you check first?
7. Which of the following is not a top-level VML element?
   a. <image>
   b. <group>
   c. <shape>
   d. <background>
   e. None of the above
8. Which of the following pen commands closes the current subpath?
   a. c
   b. x
   c. e
   d. m
   e. None of the above
9. True or false? There is no real difference between using a path attribute in the <shape> element as opposed to a nested <path> element when creating customized shapes.

10. To control the overlapping of VML shapes, which attribute should we use?
    a. rotation
    b. z-index
    c. flip
    d. position
    e. None of the above
11. To alter the size of a VML shape, which style attribute property should we use? (There may be more than one answer.)
    a. dimension
    b. width
    c. size
    d. height
    e. Any of the above
12. True or false? There is no limit to the number of shapes that can be grouped in VML.

Answers to Review Questions

1. **a.** Several different compression algorithms exist, each with its own features.
2. True. Rasterizers were discussed in the *Bitmap Graphics* section.
3. True. This was discussed in the *Vector Graphics* section.
4. False. The reverse is true: Vector graphics are capable of using a lot of CPU resources, whereas bitmap graphics can use up a lot of RAM and hard disk storage.
5. False. A W3C Note represents no commitment to further development. In fact, Notes are often a dead-end street for proposals, in that no development will likely ever take place.
6. Check to see if the correct namespace declarations have been included. If that fails to correct the display problem, then check to see if the correct behavior declarations have been inserted.
7. **a.** The answer can be verified by looking at Table 11.1.
8. **b.** x is the close command. This can be verified by looking at Table 11.3.
9. False. For simple shapes, there may be no, or very little, difference (some might argue, however, that attributes are easier on resources). However, for more complex shapes, it is better to use the flexibility of the <path> element and its attributes.
10. **b.** The answer can be found in the text.
11. **b.** and **d.** The answer for this can also be found in the text.
12. True. This was stated in the *Grouping Shapes Together* section.

SMIL

In this chapter, we introduce the Synchronized Multimedia Integration Language (SMIL), an XML application that developers can use to create multimedia presentations. The multimedia includes text, still images, and streaming audio and video. You're already pretty familiar with text and graphics. But because not all of you may be so familiar with streaming media, we'll discuss it first. The rest of the chapter delves into the W3C SMIL Recommendations, the creation of SMIL documents (in other words, the creation of SMIL multimedia presentations), and where to find SMIL implementations.

By the end of this chapter, you will be able to create a SMIL-related multimedia presentation and incorporate it into the Space Gems Web site.

What Is Streaming Media?

Streaming media is a technology for transferring and displaying audio, video, and other multimedia data in real time over the Internet or even over private networks. Streaming media's objective is to process and display the media objects seamlessly, as a steady and continuous stream, when the Web page that contains it is downloaded to a user's system. However, that system must have an appropriate *player* application (that is, a viewer or plug-in) installed on it to display the media data objects.

Streaming results in little or no initial delay between the download action and the display and no delay as additional data is downloaded. The recipient's viewer application actually displays the data before the file transmission is completed.

Streaming is especially beneficial when users cannot download large multimedia files quickly. Prior to streaming, users had to download one or more files to their hard disk drives and then, after the files were completely downloaded, they could play them. With streaming, almost any user can enjoy a Web page's contents immediately after selecting it.

Here are the three common methods for delivering streaming media:

True streaming. This is the latest trend. It requires a separate server for the streaming media and a media viewer application that is specific to the format of the requested media.

HTTP streaming. Also called progressive download streaming, or serverless streaming, HyperText Transfer Protocol streaming was the first popular form. It uses a standard Web server—not a separate, dedicated streaming server—but it also needs a specific media player application.

Clientless streaming. For this technology, the viewer application is provided during the streaming process.

As streaming media has become almost commonplace, it has created a demand for better media creation tools. Consequently, a number of competing streaming technologies and standards have been developed.

What Is the Synchronized Multimedia Integrated Language?

The Synchronized Multimedia Integration Language (SMIL, pronounced "smile") is an XML application that enables you to create multimedia data presentations and integrate them with the text and graphics on Web sites. It was developed specifically to integrate multimedia presentations while optimizing bandwidth.

SMIL provides several capabilities, including the following:

- The integration of text, image, audio, and video media.
- Control of visual media layout.
- Control of synchronization (also called the temporal behavior) of the various media.
- The creation of hyperlinks to include additional media (for example, to jump to another part of the presentation, initiate a new presentation, or open another Web page).

- Local or remote storage of the media content.
- The ability to search SMIL files for component names or text strings. SMIL files are really just text files.
- The division of multimedia content into separate streams for individual transmission, without sacrificing the integrated display aspect.
- The ability to adapt media streams to match the recipient system characteristics. For example, media objects can be created and stored in multiple versions to facilitate transmission or display, or to accommodate different language soundtracks.
- Reuse of any or all media objects in multiple presentations, because each object is accessed with a unique URI.

SMIL differs from Java, which, we acknowledge, has had multimedia capability for a long time. But SMIL's human-legibility makes it easier for non-Java programmers to use. Meanwhile, SMIL documents can still be assembled on the fly by Java servlets or CGI scripts.

In this chapter, we focus on the W3C's SMIL 1.0 Recommendation. Recently, the W3C endorsed the more powerful, more sophisticated, and much larger SMIL 2.0 Recommendation; but because this is an introductory level discussion, SMIL 1.0's principles are sufficient to provide a basic understanding of the technology.

The W3C and SMIL

The W3C's SMIL Recommendations have been prepared by the Synchronized Multimedia Working Group (SYMM-WG), which over the years has included representatives from the following organizations: Alcatel, Apple, CNET/DSM, Canon, Compaq, CSELT, CWI, DAISY Consortium, DEC, Ericsson, France Telecom, Gateway, Glocomm, GMD, Havas, IBM, INRIA, Intel, Lucent/Bell Labs, Macromedia, Microsoft, Netscape/AOL, NIST, Nokia, Oratrix, Panasonic, Philips, The Productivity Works, RealNetworks, WGBH, and the W3C. The first Working Group was assembled in January 1997. It published a public draft of SMIL 1.0 in November 1997. Development has continued since then.

SMIL 1.0

The full specification of SMIL 1.0, Synchronized Multimedia Integration Language (SMIL) 1.0 Specification, was endorsed as a W3C Recommendation in June 1998.

Microsoft contributed to SMIL 1.0 development up until the last draft, but it did not embrace the SMIL 1.0 Recommendation. Microsoft said that SMIL 1.0 overlapped with several existing standards, for example, CSS2, HTML, and the XML Document Object Model (DOM), and was unnecessary. Macromedia did not embrace SMIL because it claimed that SMIL's features were not sophisticated enough. Macromedia also believed that SMIL overlapped and potentially conflicted with existing standards, most notably the XML DOM.

SMIL 2.0

The SYMM Working Group also produced Synchronized Multimedia Integration Language (SMIL) 2.0, which was endorsed as a W3C Recommendation in August 2001. It is approximately 10 times larger than SMIL 1.0 and, unlike SMIL 1.0, consists of sets of markup modules. Each module defines the semantics and syntax for nine types of SMIL functionality: animation, content control, layout, linking, media objects, metainformation, structure, timing, and transition effects. Several of these functions are new, compared to SMIL 1.0, and were provided in response to developer requests. The modules can be used alone or in combination (for example, event-based interaction and transition effects can be combined). As you can see in Figure 12.1, SMIL 2.0 has nine DTDs, one for each module type, and/or 11 schemas that govern the same functionality. By comparison, the older and less sophisticated SMIL 1.0 uses only one DTD. The references to the appropriate validation documents (DTDs or schemas) are specified in the DOCTYPE definitions of the respective documents.

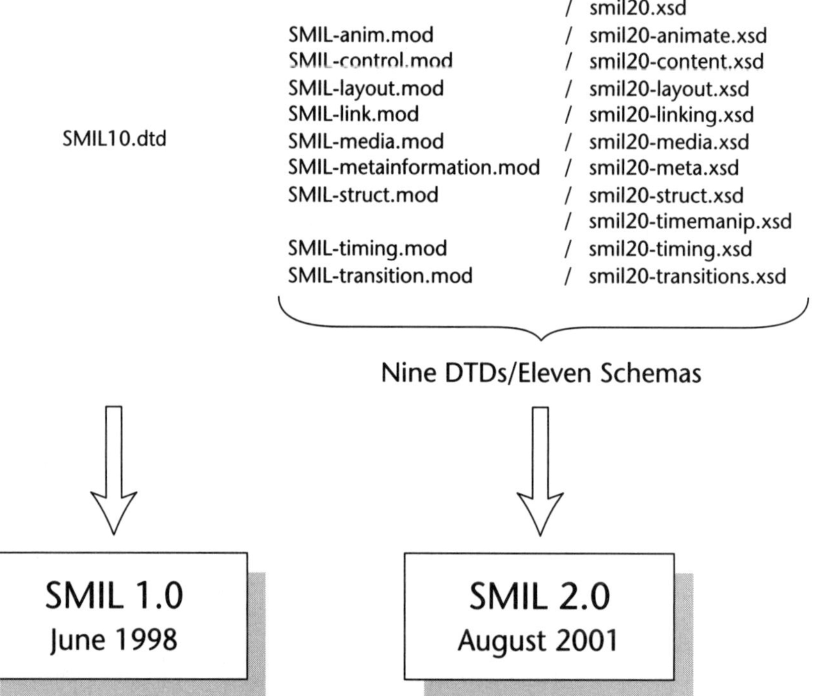

Figure 12.1 SMIL 1.0 and SMIL 2.0 validation documents.

XHTML+SMIL Profile

This profile, published as a W3C Note, describes the SMIL modules that are added to XHTML to add timing, animation, and multimedia functionality to XHTML elements. The profile supports all of the modules defined in the April 2001 W3C Recommendation titled Modularization of XHTML.

The Note was produced by the SYMM Working Group and published by the W3C in late January 2002. It is made available for discussion only, and its publication indicates no endorsement by W3C, the SYMM Working Group, or any W3C members. Comments are welcome, but there is no guarantee of any action stemming from the comments, or even a reply.

Meanwhile, as a specification, the Note revises a previous Working Draft of the same title previously available in, but now removed from, SMIL 2.0. The profile includes several XHTML modules and SMIL 2.0 modules governing the following functionality: animation, content control, media objects, timing and synchronization, time manipulation, and transition effects. It also integrates these features with XHTML and CSS and describes how SMIL can be used to manipulate XHTML and CSS features. It also explains why the SMIL 2.0 layout, linking, structure, and metainformation modules were not included.

SMIL 1.0 can be viewed at www.w3.org/TR/REC-smil/; SMIL 2.0 at www.w3.org/TR/smil20/; and the XHTML+SMIL profile at www.w3.org/TR/XHTMLplusSMIL/.

Viewing and Creating SMIL Documents

We suggest visiting the W3C's Synchronized Multimedia Web site at www.w3.org/AudioVideo/ for links to SMIL-related features, including the following:

- SMIL definitions and specifications
- Recent and past news articles
- Tutorials and other information sources
- Players, listed according to the two SMIL versions
- SMIL authoring tools
- Demonstrations

Creating SMIL Documents

As we create SMIL documents, we have to remember that we are creating a SMIL presentation. So we should keep the following basic process in mind:

1. First, we create one or more display regions, into which we are going to place media objects, within the viewer application's display area.
2. Then we specify the media objects to be used and assign them to their respective regions.
3. Finally, we determine the order in which to display the media objects. They can be displayed consecutively (in sequence or one following another), concurrently (in parallel or one alongside another), or in some combination of those two.

The structure and syntax of SMIL documents will be familiar. They are similar to HTML/XHTML syntax. Like XML, SMIL is case-sensitive. Like XHTML, component names and tags must be lowercase.

A SMIL document, like other XML-related documents, consists of two main parts: the prolog and the <smil> element, which, in turn, consists of a <head> element and a <body> element. We can give SMIL documents any name we want, as long as we add an .smi extension to the name.

The Prolog

SMIL documents have prologs similar to all other XML-related documents. That prolog consists of an XML declaration and a DOCTYPE definition indicating the location of the SMIL DTD. After that, their prologs can contain any other statements the developer wants to include. Often, comment statements are included.

The SMIL 1.0 DTD

A SMIL 1.0 document usually contains a document type declaration, which names the DTD in use for the document. For SMIL, the document type declaration should look like the following:

```
<!DOCTYPE smil PUBLIC "-//W3C//DTD SMIL 1.0//EN"
              "http://www.w3.org/TR/REC-smil/SMIL10.dtd">
```

As discussed in Chapter 4, this form of declaration facilitates accessing an external DTD that is intended for public use. Furthermore, the declaration indicates that the DTD is located at a different Web site from the one at which the XML document is located.

In Chapter 4, we mentioned that you can add or update declarations found in external DTDs by including them within an internal DOCTYPE definition in the prolog of the data document. Do not use this technique with SMIL, because many SMIL applications will not support it.

If you want to view the SMIL 1.0 DTD, go to www.w3.org/TR/REC-smil/#smil-dtd. To view the SMIL 2.0 DTDs, go to www.w3.org/TR/smil20/smil-DTD.html, and if you want to see the SMIL 2.0 schemas, visit www.w3.org/ TR/smil20/smil-SCHEMA.html.

The Root Element: <smil>

The root data element in a SMIL document is named <smil>, as indicated by the simplified SMIL document in Figure 12.2. The direct child elements of the <smil> element are <head> and <body>.

The Synchronized Multimedia Working Group anticipated that SMIL 1.0 elements and attributes would be used in other XML-based documents besides the SMIL documents. For those cases, the Recommendation states that the following XML namespace declaration should be added to the root element start tag of those other XML language-based documents, so that they may include the SMIL 1.0 elements and attributes:

```
<rootelementname xmlns:t="http://www.w3.org/TR/REC-smil" ... >
```

However, in the SMIL 1.0 documents, namespace declarations are not necessary. Furthermore, things did not work out quite the way the W3C anticipated in the SMIL 1.0 Recommendation: SMIL 1.0 components are generally not included in other XML-related documents in the classic namespace-related way.

As you will see in the Chapter 12 labs, HTML or XHTML documents often link to SMIL 1.0 documents. When those links are activated, SMIL 1.0 player applications (for example, those manufactured by RealNetworks, Inc.) are usually activated automatically. It is those applications that use the SMIL 1.0 documents.

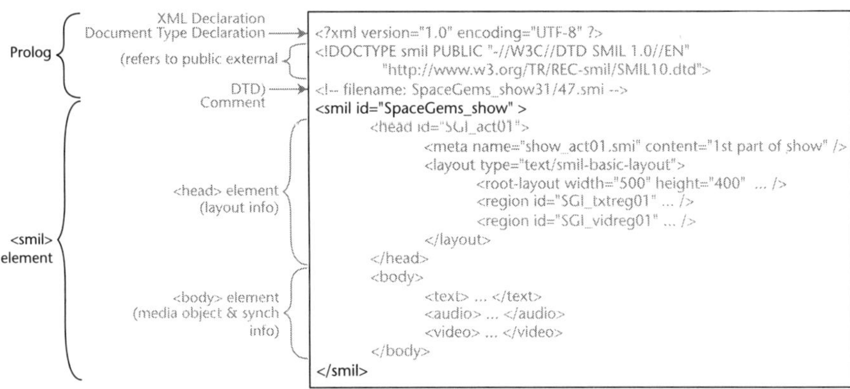

Figure 12.2 Simplified SMIL 1.0 document.

So it is not necessary to include the namespace declaration in the XML documents in the browser in the classic manner. Microsoft Internet Explorer, for example, uses HTML+TIME behaviors in its HTML or XHTML documents to accommodate linking to SMIL 1.0 documents and invoking the SMIL 1.0 players.

In the meantime, the start tag of the <smil> element can, although it is not required, contain the attribute ID to identify the element within the document, so applications can find it. Not all applications are written so that they can search for ID values, but it is possible to do so.

The <head> Element

As we mentioned earlier, the <smil> element contains a <head> element and a <body>element. The <head> element has to contain a <layout> element or a <switch> element and can also contain any number of <meta> elements, a <title> element, and even a <style> element. The <head> element can also have an id attribute.

As indicated in Figure 12.2, the <head> element contains the SMIL document's layout information. That is, the spatial relationships among the media objects are defined within the <head> element, even though the media objects and their timing and synchronization are defined elsewhere. Those aspects are defined later in this chapter, in the section titled *The <body> Element: Content, Temporal, and Linking Information*.

The <layout> Element

The spatial positioning of the media objects in the viewport—that is, in the application's viewing window, where the SMIL presentation is displayed—is defined within the <layout> element, which must be properly nested within the <head> element and nowhere else. Generally, you should follow a <layout> element strategy similar to that shown in Figure 12.2: The root-layout region size is specified and regions are defined for any text and video objects that will appear. If you don't specify a <layout>, the spacing is left up to the application that is activated to present the media objects.

Two attributes can appear in a <layout> element start tag: id and type. As with many element types, an id attribute can be used to assign a unique identifier to the <layout> element. The type attribute specifies which layout language you are going to use in the layout element. The default value is text/smil-basic-layout, which is the language we will discuss as the chapter proceeds. However, other values, such as text/css, can also be used. If another value is used, the layout definitions within <layout> appear in that language, using its semantics and syntax. However, if the player application does not understand the language specified, it must skip all content it encounters up until the </layout> end tag.

In this chapter, we will use the default SMIL basic layout language for all our media object elements. To do so, we can either leave out the type attribute or use the following syntax:

```
<layout type="text/smil-basic-layout"> ... </layout>
```

The SMIL basic layout is consistent with the W3C's Cascading Style Sheets, Level 2 Specification Recommendation (CSS2). Now we have two choices:

- Leave the <layout> element empty, which activates the default CSS2 property values for the media objects (for example, all absolutely positioned elements will be contained within the single containing block defined by the <smil> element) and otherwise rely on the player application's other defaults.
- Specify the layout, using the <layout> element and its appropriate child elements. This is the approach we recommend using, because it provides the developer with the most control over media object layout.

There are two child elements that may be used within the <layout> element: <root-layout> and <region>.

The <root-layout> Element

You use the <root-layout> element to specify the size and other features of the area within the player application's viewport in which you want to display the media objects. Occasionally, the viewport itself is referred to as the root-layout region, but that is not always correct. The viewport is created by the player application and automatically adjusted to accommodate the root-layout region. However, if one or more of the viewport's dimensions cannot be expanded sufficiently, the player application begins to adjust (that is, reduce) the SMIL document's dimensions accordingly.

Figure 12.3 illustrates a typical SMIL 1.0 player display, indicating the viewport, the root-layout region, and three sample regions. We have shown three regions, but the number, size, and positioning of regions is left to each SMIL document developer's requirements. Meanwhile, most player applications have more than one view; the user can generally select a view that shows the player application portion with or without the browser portion.

Classroom Q & A

Q: So you're saying that the root-layout region is not the same as the viewport?

A: That's right. With earlier player applications, certain views gave us the impression that the viewport and the root layout regions were synonymous. It's not so. We have some control over the root-layout region and the regions within it, but the application governs the viewport.

A SMIL document cannot have more than one <root-layout> element. The <root-layout> element is a declared empty element that can contain the following attributes: background-color, height, width, id, skip-content, and title.

The following example code creates a root-layout region 600 pixels wide and 450 pixels high with a white background. The color can be specified using the color name, a hexadecimal function, or the RGB function:

```
<root-layout width="600" height="450" background-color="white" />
```

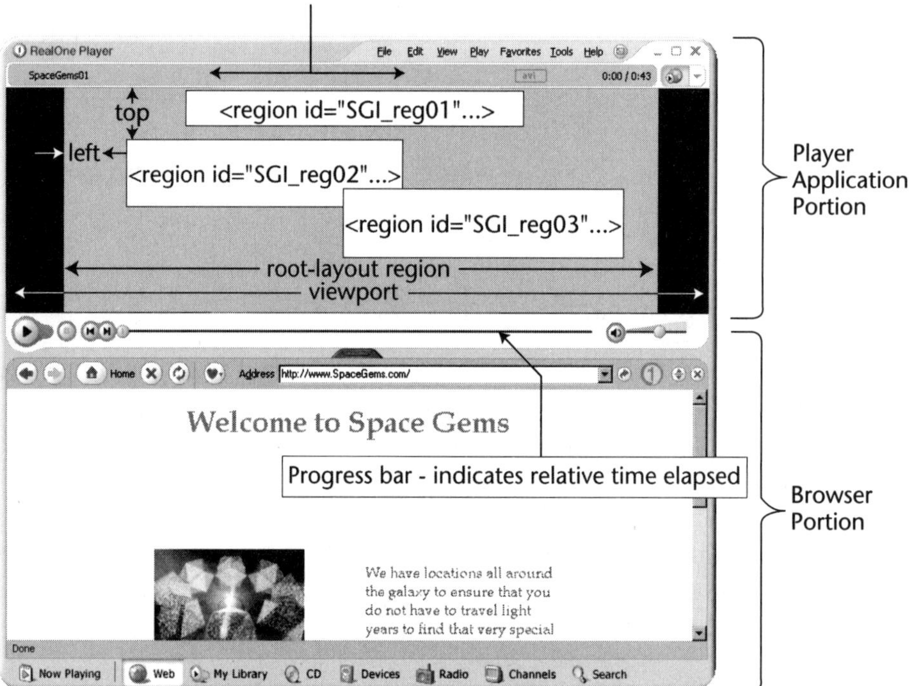

Figure 12.3 Player application display.

If there is no <root-layout> specification, the player application's default value is used.

The <region> Element

By specifying positions, dimensions, and unique identifiers, we can divide the root-layout region into smaller regions. Any region should be treated as a sort of container in which we can display one or more visual media objects, such as text, graphic images, or streaming video. Thus, each media object is associated with a specific region through the use of a URI reference, and the regions are identified, positioned, and sized according to the specifications found in their respective <region> elements. As developers create SMIL documents, they can use any region to host more than one visual media objects. Furthermore, regions can be created, used in a limited fashion, and then discarded—that is, overwritten—as different regions are created.

Each region's identity, position, and dimensions are controlled by the values specified for the id, left, right, width, height, and z-index attributes in the respective <region> element start tag.

Here are two examples. We'll use two <region> elements to define two regions in the same display. Figure 12.3, which appears in the previous section titled *The <root-layout> Element*, illustrates the two regions defined in the examples.

```
<region id="SGI_reg01" left="40" top="5" width="95" height="10"
     z-index="1" />
<region id="SGI_reg02" left="15" top="20" width="70" height="20"
     z-index="0" />
```

In both examples, id attributes are specified for each region. We assign unique IDs to each region so that later, when we define the image, text, or streaming video in the <body> element, we can refer to the regions individually by the ID values.

The positioning and sizing (that is, left, top, width, and height) values provided are expressed in pixels and indicate that we're using an absolute positioning technique. Although the width and height attributes seem straightforward, the left and top attributes may seem confusing. They are absolute references from the top left corner of the region to the top left corner of the <root-layout> region. Using SGI_reg01 as an example, left="40" and top="5" specify that to get from the top left corner of the SGI_reg01 region to the top left corner of the <root-layout> region, you move 40 pixels to the left and 5 pixels toward the top.

We can also specify the positions of regions relative to the <root-layout> region's dimensions. For example, if we want to display an image with its right border at a point that is 25 percent of the distance from the <root-layout> region's left border to the right, and its top at a point that is 33 percent of the distance down from the top of the <root-layout> region, we modify the previous example code to read like the following:

```
<region id="SGI_reg04 left="25%" top="33%" width="100" height="30"
        z-index="1" />
```

Meanwhile, the height and width of the region are still specified in pixels.

In Figure 12.3, the SGI_reg02 and SGI_reg03 regions overlap. If we want to prevent overlap, we have to be careful with the positions and dimensions we specify. On the other hand, if we want multiple regions to overlap (for example, to create a background pattern), we can use the z-index attribute with the <region> element the same way you used it with VML: The region with the most positive z-index will be rendered on top. If neither region has a z-index specified or if their z-index values are identical, the most recent elements lay over the earlier ones.

When Media Object Dimensions Don't Match Region Dimensions

Developers generally strive to create <region> elements so that the respective media objects will fill their container areas. And occasionally, they're successful, which isn't very encouraging. Unfortunately, because of differences in video settings or browser applications, visual media objects do not turn out to be the same size as the regions originally defined for them. In this section, we discuss four situations where they don't and provide suggestions for mitigating them by doing the following:

- Stretching a small visual object to fit the region, with no care about any resulting distortion
- Expanding a small visual object until its larger dimension matches a region boundary
- Expanding a small visual object until its smaller dimension matches a region boundary
- Displaying a larger visual object without reducing its dimensions

All the remedies involve adding a fit attribute with appropriate values to the <region> start tag.

Fill the Region: Distortion Is Not an Issue

Look at Figure 12.4. On the left, the original object, when displayed, is smaller than the defined sg_reg1 region. In this case, we want to expand the object to completely fill the region, even if the image becomes distorted, as shown on the right of the figure. Let's presume that because of the nature of the image, distortion in one direction or another will not be an issue.

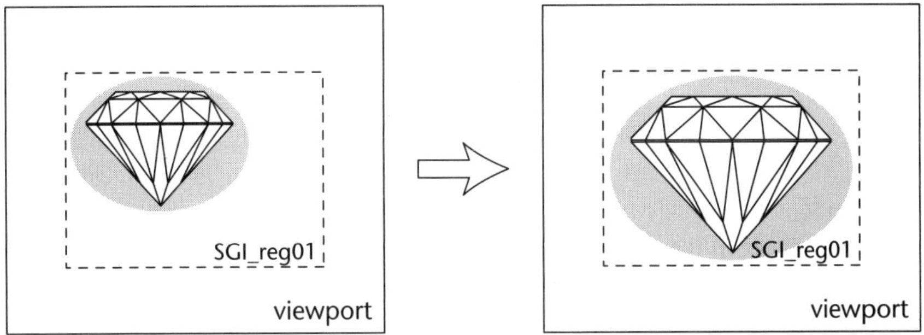

Figure 12.4 Fill: Distortion.

To accomplish this expansion, we use syntax similar to the following:

```
<region id="sg_reg1" left="10" top="10" width="150" height="100"
     background-color="black" fit="fill" />
```

Expand the Object until There's a First-Dimension Match: No Distortion

Now look at Figure 12.5. As in the first example, the object, when displayed, would be smaller than the sg_reg1 region. This time we want to expand the object until the first of the object's dimensions matches one of the region's dimensions. But we do not want any distortion.

Use syntax similar to the following to achieve this result:

```
<region id="sg_reg1" left="10" top="10" width="150" height="100"
     background-color="black" fit="meet" />
```

Figure 12.5 shows that the object expands until the bottom of the object touches the bottom of the region. A gap, represented in the figure by a black band (no such band would really appear; we've only included it here for emphasis), still remains on the right side of the object, between the right edge of the object and the right edge of the defined region, indicating the part of the region that does not contain any of the image.

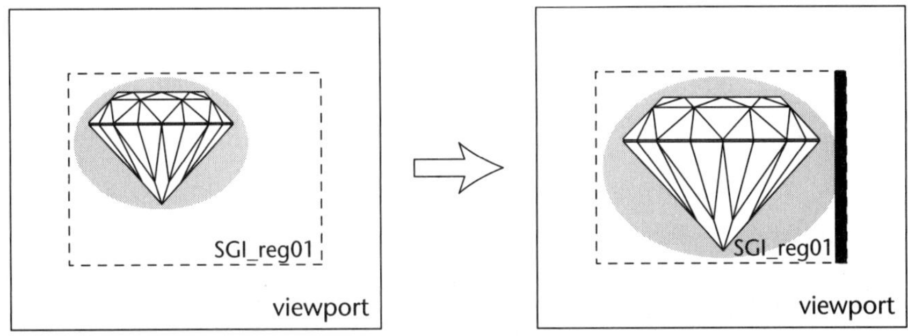

Figure 12.5 Meet: No distortion.

Expand the Object Until the Second Dimensions Match: No Distortion

This situation is depicted in Figure 12.6. Again, the original displayed object is smaller than its designated region. This time, however, we want to expand the object to fill the region, until the second of the object's dimensions matches the corresponding region dimension. Figure 12.6 shows that this creates the impression that the region crops (or slices off) the bottom of the media object. Let's presume then that because of the nature of the image, we would rather sacrifice some of the image than create distortion.

To accomplish this objective, we use syntax similar to the following:

```
<region id="sg_reg1" left="10" top="10" width="150" height="100"
     background-color="black" fit="slice" />
```

Don't Alter the Media Object's Dimensions: No Distortion

Now look at Figure 12.7, where the original object, when displayed, will be larger than its region. This time we do not want to reduce the size of the object, nor do we want any distortion. Instead, we prefer to let end users scroll if they really want to see the entire image.

To do this, use syntax similar to the following:

```
<region id="img_reg1" left="10" top="10" width="150" height="100"
     background-color="black" fit="scroll" />
```

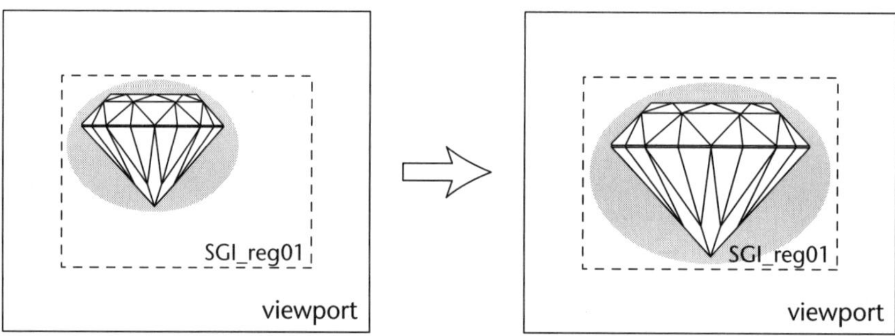

Figure 12.6 Fill: No distortion.

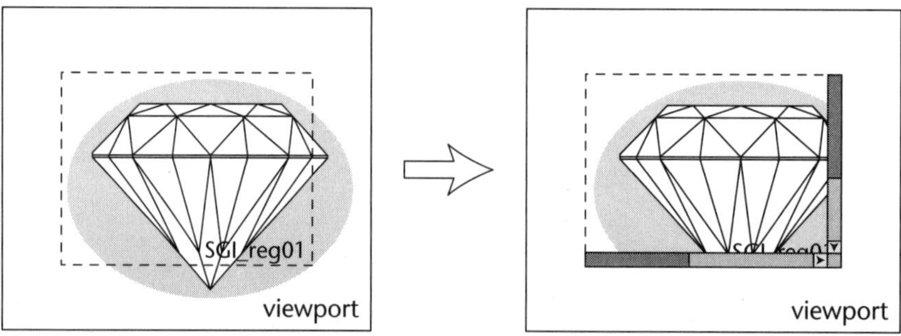

Figure 12.7 Scroll: No distortion.

Table 12.1 <meta> Element Attributes

ATTRIBUTE NAME	EXPLANATION
content	Required for <meta> elements. Specifies the value of the property defined in the meta element.
id	Uniquely identifies the element within the document, in case it is being searched for by an application.
name	Required for <meta> elements. Identifies the property defined in the meta element.
skip-content	Introduced in SMIL 1.0 for future extensibility. Possible values are true (ignore the content of this element) or false (parse the content of this element).
base	The value of this property determines the base URI for all relative URIs used in the document.
title	The title of the presentation.

The <meta> Element

The declared empty <meta> element can be used to provide additional information, for example, a unique identifier, the author's name, keywords, and base URIs from which to create relative location paths, about a SMIL document. There is no restriction on the number of <meta> elements you can include. However, the <meta> element can only be included in the <head> element of a SMIL 1.0 document. Table 12.1 lists the attributes we can use with the <meta> element.

To illustrate, here are two examples of some metainformation we could add to our SMIL presentation:

```
<meta name="title" content="Space Gems Catalog, Fall/Winter 2047"/>
<meta name="base" content="http://www.SpaceGems.com/images/" />
```

The <switch> Element

With the <switch> element, SMIL provides the capability to adapt our presentations according to the properties of our end users' systems. The <switch> element contains a number of child elements that, in turn, contain attributes against which to conduct boolean true/false tests. The first child under <switch>, whose attribute tests all prove to be true when tested against the user's system, prevails over the others and is executed. By default, any child element that contains no test attributes is automatically considered to be true.

Using this strategy, then, different sets of elements, and thus, a different-looking or -sounding Web presentation (for example, in a different language, at a different video resolution, or with video instead of stills), might be activated automatically depending on the user's system.

The <switch> element can be placed in the <head> or <body> element. Because it is more likely to be placed in the <body> element to be used in conjunction with the media object elements and the synchronization elements nested there, we have placed a more detailed discussion of <switch> in its own section under *The <body> Element* section, coming up next.

The <body> Element: Content, Temporal, and Linking Information

You've seen how the <head> element of the SMIL document contains appearance and layout information. The <body> element, by comparison, contains all the actual media content and timing information. Some call the contents of the <body> element the "content, temporal, and linking" behavior information.

The <body> element contains child elements that specify to the SMIL parser and the application what to render in the regions defined within the <head> element. In other words, the region's visual characteristics are defined in the <head> section, and the audio and visual contents are defined in the <body> section.

The <body> element's start tag can also contain an id attribute. The <body> element can contain the following child elements: <a>, <animation>, <audio>, <img>, <par>, <ref>, <seq>, <switch>, <text>, <textstream>, and <video>.

Synchronizing Media Objects with the <par> and <seq> Elements

Regions can have the same content all the way through a presentation or different contents at different times. The rendering of different components (that is, different media objects) can occur either consecutively (sequentially) or concurrently (in parallel). Sequential operations are governed by the use of <seq> elements inserted as child elements within the <body> element; concurrent operations by <par> elements. Because of their time-oriented functions, the <seq> and <par> elements are called *synchronization elements*.

The <body> element itself is similar to a <seq> element. In fact, it is considered to be a special type of <seq> element, because its child elements are displayed one after another. However, <body> lacks the time attributes provided with <par> and <seq>, and that, basically, is why <par> and <seq> are used.

The <seq> elements may contain one or more child elements, and the contents referenced by those elements are displayed in sequence, one after another, according to the order they appear in the SMIL document. That is, the children of a <seq> element form a temporal sequence.

The <seq> element can contain these child elements: other <par> or <seq> synchronization elements; hyperlink elements, such as <a>; media object elements, such as <animation>, <audio>, <img>, <ref>, <text>, <textstream>, and <video>; and other elements, such as <switch>.

The children of the <par> and <seq> elements have attributes used to define the media object life cycle. Table 12.2 lists the attributes that you can use with the <seq> element (with the <par> element, too, as you'll soon see).

Table 12.2 <seq> and <par> Element Attributes

ATTRIBUTE NAME	EXPLANATION
abstract	Brief content description.
author	Content author's name.
begin	The time for the explicit beginning of an element (seconds). Two types, both clock-based: delay-value; event-value.
copyright	Content's copyright notice.
dur	The explicit duration of an element (seconds).
end	The explicit end of an element (seconds).
endsync	Attribute that influences the implicit duration of the <par> element.
id	Unique identifier.
region	Specifies the abstract rendering surface defined within the <layout> elements.
repeat	Number of times the object should be repeated. Value can be an integer (default value is 1), or the text string "indefinite".
system-bitrate	Specifies the approximate bandwidth.
system-captions	Determines whether closed captioning will be "on" or "off".
system-language	Value is a comma-separated list of language names. (Consult RFC 1766). Determines whether there is a match between end-user system and objects.
system-overdub or caption	Users prefer overdubbing or captioning when those features are available.
system-required	Specifies the name of an extension (for example, namespaces).

(continued)

Table 12.2 *(continued)*

ATTRIBUTE NAME	EXPLANATION
system-screen-size	"True" if the player is capable of displaying a resolution of the given size ("width × height" in pixels).
system-screen-depth	Specifies the depth of the screen color palette in bits per pixel.
title	The developer's preferred title. All <seq> elements should contain a title attribute with a meaningful value.

The begin and end attributes are the most obvious of the life-cycle controls. The begin attribute tells the SMIL player application when to begin displaying the elements contained in the <seq> element. The end attribute indicates when the display should finish.

Figure 12.8 illustrates a simplified example of the use of the <seq> element. In the example, three logo images, representing a diamond ring, necklace, and bracelet, are presented in sequence. Each is displayed for five seconds with one second in between. We suggest that if you are planning sequences, you create a time line similar to the one shown in Figure 12.8, to maintain better life-cycle control of your media objects.

Just as we use <seq> elements to govern consecutive operations, we can indicate and govern concurrent (parallel) operations by using the <par> element within the <body> element. The <par> elements also contain child elements. But in contrast to the sequential nature of the <seq> element children, the contents of <par> children are displayed at the same time. However, the children of a <par> element can still appear to overlap in time, or to be spaced apart in time, by using specific life-cycle control attributes.

You can see these life-cycle controls at work in Figure 12.9, which presents a simplified example of the use of the <par> element. Again, it is recommended that a time line, such as that shown in Figure 12.9, be used during the planning stages.

The <par> element can contain the same child elements as the <seq> element. That attributes that are applicable to the <par> element are identical to the <seq> attributes listed in Table 12.2.

The SMIL Media Object Elements

SMIL's media object elements enable us to include media objects in a SMIL presentation. There are several SMIL media object elements:

<animation> An animated graphic (example: AVI or QuickTime files).

<audio> An audio clip (examples: MP3, WAVE, or RealAudio files).

<img> A still image (examples: PNG, JPEG, GIF, or TIFF files).

<text> A text reference (examples: text or HTML files).

<textstream> Streaming text (example: ASP TextStream files).

<video> A video clip (examples: ASX, RealVideo, AVI, or MPEG files).

<ref> A generic media reference (suggested when a developer is in doubt about the category that a media object belongs to).

```
<body>
   <seq>
      <img src="dia_ring_sm_logo.gif"
         alt="New Diamond Rings"
         region="SGI_reg01"
         dur="5s" />
      <img src="dia_neck_sm_logo.gif"
         alt="New Diamond Necklaces"
         region="SGI_reg01"
         dur="5s" begin="1s" />
      <img src="dia_brace_sm_logo.gif"
         alt="New Diamond Bracelets"
         region="SGI_reg01"
         dur="5s" begin="1s" />
   </seq>
</body>
```

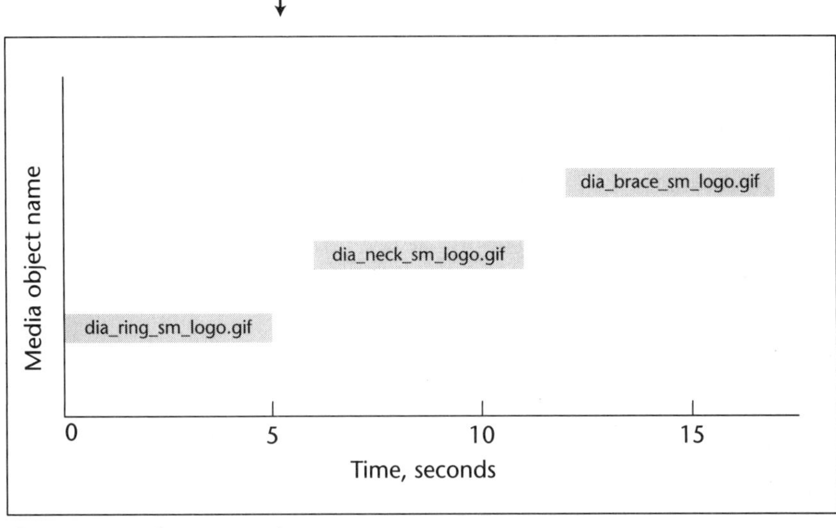

Figure 12.8 The <seq> element.

```
<body>
   <par>
      <img src="SpaceGems_sm_logo.gif"
         alt="Space Gems, Inc."
         region="SGI_reg05"
         dur="20s" />
      <audio src="SpaceGemsTheme.wav"
         begin="2s" repeat="3"
         end="30s" />
      <text src="SG_sales.txt"
         alt="Welcome to Space Gems!"
         region="SGI_text_reg01"
         begin="1s" dur="10s" />
   </par>
</body>
```

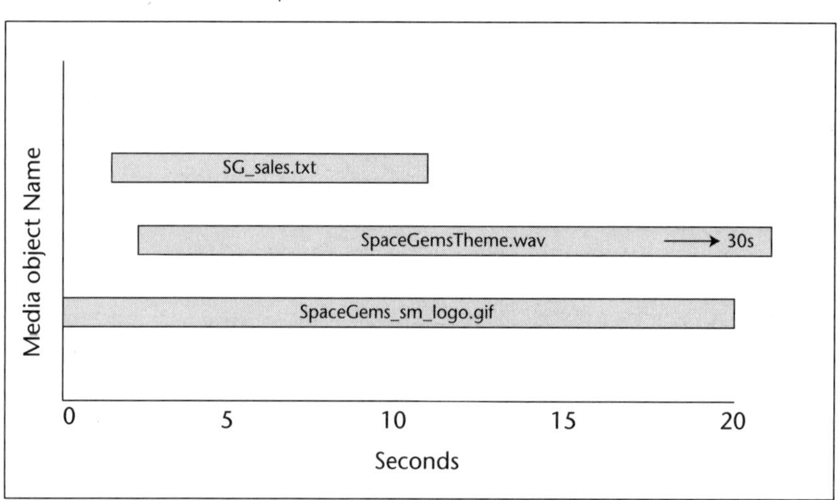

Figure 12.9 The <par> element.

The W3C groups media objects as follows:

- Those with an intrinsic (that is, built-in) duration; also called continuous media. Examples are videos and audio files.
- Those without intrinsic duration; also called discrete media. Examples are text files and still images.

Each visual media object, for example, a video image, is displayed by the SMIL player in an individual region within the root-layout region, or the viewport, if those two areas coincide. The regions are treated as containers.

The media objects are associated with them by URI references used as values for the src attribute within the start tag for the media object element.

For example, if we want to insert an actual visual image (in this case, let's say it's a GIF graphic image), we can insert an <img> element within the <body> element and use code similar to the following:

```
<img src="dia_ring_sm_logo.gif" alt="Space Gems Rings!"
          region="SGI_reg01" ... />
```

Notice that the value of the region attribute in the <img> element start tag is identical to the value given to the id attribute inside the start tag of the respective <region> element inside the <layout> element. Thus, the value is a pointer to the respective region and links the two components together.

Try to ensure that the category into which a media object is placed is appropriately reflected in the element name. This facilitates readability and searchability of the SMIL document. For example, it would be confusing to create a series of elements with image-related names if some actually contained audio or animation references. If there is doubt about how to categorize a media object (for example, some animation objects are considered to be video), rely on the more generic element name <ref>.

Table 12.3 lists the attributes that are applicable to all media object elements. Most are probably familiar; they've been mentioned and defined in tables pertaining to other elements.

Table 12.3 Media Object Elements Attributes

ATTRIBUTE NAME	EXPLANATION
abstract	Brief content description.
alt	For viewers/players that cannot display a particular object; specifies alternate message. Strongly recommended for all object elements.
author	Content author's name.
begin	The time for the explicit beginning of an element (seconds). Two types: clock-based delay-value and event-value.
clip-begin	Specifies the beginning of a subclip of a continuous object as offset from the object's start. Various formats, syntaxes.

(continued)

Table 12.3 *(continued)*

ATTRIBUTE NAME	EXPLANATION
clip-end	Specifies the end of a subclip of a continuous object that should be played. Same syntax as clip-begin.
copyright	Content's copyright notice.
dur	The explicit duration of an element (seconds).
end	The explicit end of an element (seconds).
fill	Attribute that determines the effective end of the child element and the parent.
id	Unique identifier.
longdesc	Specifies a URI link to a longer object description. Should supplement the description provided by alt.
region	Specifies the abstract rendering surface defined within the <layout> elements.
src	URI of the media object.
system-bitrate	Specifies the approximate bandwidth.
system-captions	Determines whether closed captioning will be on or off.
system-language	Value is a comma-separated list of language names (RFC 1766). Determines whether there is a match between end-user system and objects.
system-overdub-or-caption	Determines whether end users prefer overdubbing or captioning when they are available.
system-required	Specifies the name of an extension (for example, namespaces).
system-screen-size	True if the SMIL viewer is capable of displaying a resolution of the given size ("width x height" in pixels).
system-screen-depth	Specifies the depth of the screen color palette in bits per pixel.
title	All <seq> elements should have a title attribute with a meaningful description.
type	Type of media object referenced by src.

It is important to consider including the alt attribute in the start tag for all media objects. There is a two-fold reason for including alt:

- If the object fails to play or display, the author still has an opportunity to send some message to the end user.
- If the alt message appears, it signals the author or end user that there are malfunctions in the document, the browser, or other SMIL-related applications.

Finally, anchors and links can be attached to visual media objects, too. One way to do so is to include an <anchor> element within the extent of a media object element.

The <switch> Element

The <switch> element was mentioned just prior to the <body> element section, earlier in this chapter. As we discussed briefly there, we are listing it twice because it can be nested within the <head> or <body> element.

The <switch> element provides SMIL with the ability to adapt a presentation according to the capabilities and other properties of the end user's system. The adaptability is provided through specific child elements, whose attributes allow the execution of one or more boolean true/false tests against the system settings. The first set of child elements whose attribute tests all prove to be true is executed. Any child element that contains no test attributes is, by default, automatically considered to be true.

The <switch> element syntax resembles the following code:

```
<switch>
     <!-- Test 1 -->
               <elementname test-attribute="value" ... />
     <!-- Test 2 -->
               <elementname test-attribute="value" ... />
...
</switch>
```

Here are the elements that are used as children of <switch>:

- The media object elements <animation>, <audio>, <img>, <ref>, <text>, <textstream>, and <video>
- The synchronization elements <par> and <seq>
- <a>, <anchor>, and <switch>

Table 12.4 lists the test attributes that can appear in those child elements.

Table 12.4 <switch> Test Attributes

TEST ATTRIBUTE NAME	EXPLANATION
<elementname system language= "langcode" />	End user's system language. Values are a list of two character language codes (examples: en, fr, es, de; see RFC 1766), delimited by commas
<elementname system bitrate= "integer value" />	Approximate bandwidth. Value is a single integer value (examples: 9600, 14400, 28800, 56000).
<elementname system screen size= "integerxinteger" />	Monitors screen resolution. Value is composed of two integers indicating the width and the height in pixels, in that order, and separated by an *x* (example: "800x600").
<elementname system screen depth= "integer" />	Color definition expressed in the number of bits per pixel. The value is an integer. Choices are 4 (indicating 16 colors), 8 (256 colors), 16 (65,536 colors), or 24 (16.78 million colors, also called true color).
<elementname system-captions= "on | off" />	True if closed captioning has been activated; false if closed captioning is not activated.
<elementname system-overdub-or-caption= "caption | overdub" />	Determines whether end users prefer overdubbing or captioning when the option is available. Evaluates to true if the end-user preference matches this attribute value; to false if there is no match.
<elementname system-required= "namespace | *others*"	Specifies the name of an extension (for example, a namespace supporting additional element types). Evaluates to true if the extension is supported by the implementation. Otherwise, evaluates to false.

For example, what if you are aware that some of your end users prefer to communicate in Spanish, or that others have monitors that are capable of 800x600-pixel resolution only? How do you code your SMIL document to anticipate communicating with those users? Here is one possible solution:

```
<body>
   <switch>
      <!- - English Language - ->
      <par system-language="en">
         <text src="SGI_english.doc" region="SGI_reg_07" />
```

```
            <switch>
               <!- - English Language Screen Rez - ->
               <text src="800x600_SGI_eng.doc" region="SGI_reg07"
                   system-screen-size="800x600" />
               <text src="1024x768_SGI_eng.doc" region="SGI_reg07"
                   system-screen-size="1024x768" />
               <text src="other_SGI_eng.doc" region="SGI_reg07" />
            </switch>
      </par>
      <!- - Spanish Language - ->
      <par system-language="es">
         <text src="SGI_espanol.doc" region="SGI_reg07" />
            <switch>
               <!- - Spanish Language Screen Rez - ->
               <text src="800x600_SGI_esp.doc" region="SGI_reg07"
                   system-screen-size="800x600" />
               <text src="1024x768_SGI_esp.doc" region="SGI_reg07"
                   system-screen-size="1024x768" />
               <text src="other_SGI_esp.doc" region="SGI_reg07" />
            </switch>
      </par>
   </switch>
</body>
```

There are other solutions besides this one. If you have the time, we invite you to create your own.

SMIL's Hyperlinking Elements

Occasionally, you may want to link SMIL with other SMIL or non-SMIL applications or plug-ins:

- A SMIL browser may use an HTML plug-in to display an embedded HTML page.
- An HTML browser may use a SMIL plug-in to display a SMIL document embedded in an HTML page.

To create access points, you can use the SMIL link elements: <a> or <anchor>. Both enable you to describe inline navigational links between objects.

The SMIL 1.0 Recommendation lists several linking rules. Meanwhile, here are a few worth remembering:

- SMIL provides for unidirectional, single-headed (that is, one source/one destination) inline links only.
- SMIL supports the locators currently used in HTML, including name fragment identifiers and the # connector. So, for example, SMIL parsers should understand and use fragmented object locators, such as http://SpaceGems.com/cat_files/catalog2047#diam_img29.

The fragment part is an ID value that identifies one of the elements within the referenced SMIL document. If a link containing a fragment part is followed, the presentation should start as though the end user had fast-forwarded through a remote destination document to the beginning of the element designated by the fragment.

- If the object addressed by the link has a repeat attribute with a value of more than 1 or indefinite, all of the specified repetitions of the object will be played. Furthermore, if the object addressed by the link is contained within a parent element that contains its own repeat attribute, those repetitions are played, too.
- It is forbidden to link to elements that are the content of <switch> elements.

Although we present introductory lessons and simple examples of SMIL links, we recommend that if you are going to use links in your SMIL documents, you study the SMIL Recommendation in detail (www.w3.org/TR/REC-smil/; SMIL 2.0, at www.w3.org/TR/smil20/).

The <a> Element

The <a> element is used to link with a complete media object, as opposed to the <anchor> element, which facilitates linking to parts of other media objects. The <a> element can contain the following child elements: <animation>, <audio>, <img>, <par>, <ref >, <seq>, <switch>, <text>, <textstream>, and <video>. The <a> element does not influence the synchronization (that is, the ordering or timing) of its child elements. However, <a> elements may not be nested within one another.

Table 12.5 lists the attributes that are applicable to the <a> element.

Although the functionality of the <a> element is similar to the functionality of the <A> element in HTML, SMIL includes the show attribute in an <a> element, which controls the temporal behavior of the source document after the link on that document has been followed.

Here is an example of an <a> element link that starts up a new video presentation in a new window:

```
<a href="http://www.SpaceGems.com/cat_2047_spring.smi"
        title= "Sale Items - Spring 2047" show="new" >
    <video id="import_sgi_vid47q2" region= "SGI_vidreg01" />
</a>
```

Table 12.5 <a> Element Attributes

ATTRIBUTE NAME	EXPLANATION
href	Specifies the URI of the link's destination. This attribute is required for <a> elements.
id	Unique identifier.
show	Controls the behavior of the source document containing the link when the link is followed. Possible values: replace (current presentation is paused and replaced by the destination resource; default value); new (presentation of the destination resource starts in a new context, not affecting the source resource); pause (source presentation is paused, and the destination resource starts in a new context).
title	All <anchor> elements should have a title attribute. The value for title should include a meaningful description of the linked media object.

The following is a link that activates a replacement presentation, instead of the original presentation that contained the link. It allows a SMIL player to spawn from an HTML browser:

```
<a href="budget_guide_2047.smil" show="new" region="SGI_adminreg04">
     Click here for 2047 exploration budget preparation guidelines.
     Please submit your regional plans and estimates by 2047-02-28!
</a>
```

The <anchor> Element

As mentioned in the <a> element section, the <a> element enables you to create a link with another complete media object. On other occasions, though, it might be useful to create links to (just) spatial or temporal subparts of another media object. SMIL's <anchor> element enables you to do that. Using its id and href attributes, you can identify the target media object. Then, using its coords attribute, you can break the media object into spatial subparts. Alternatively, using its begin and end attributes, you can break it into temporal subparts.

Table 12.6 lists all the attributes applicable to the <anchor> element. This element, however, does not allow for child elements. The explanation of the coords attribute contains a reference to Figure 12.10.

Table 12.6 <anchor> Element Attributes

ATTRIBUTE NAME	EXPLANATION
begin	The time for the explicit beginning of an element (seconds). Two types: clock-based delay-value and an event-value. The value is relative to the beginning of the destination media object.
coords	Specifies a rectangle within the display area of a visual media object. Coordinates are relative to the top-left corner of the visual media object (see Figure 12.10). Values are left-x,top-y,right-x,bottom-y (for example, coords="50,10,200,110"). If specified as percentages (that is, coords= "10%,10%,55%,40%"), the values are relative to the total width or height of the media object display area.
end	The explicit end of an element (seconds). Value is relative to the beginning of the destination media object.
href	Contains the URI of the link's destination.
id	Unique identifier.
show	Controls the behavior of the source document containing the link when the link is followed. Possible values: replace (current presentation is paused and replaced by the destination resource; default value); new (presentation of the destination resource starts in a new context, not affecting the source resource); pause (source presentation is paused, and the destination resource starts in a new context).
skip-content	Introduced for future extensibility. Possible values are true (ignore the content of this element) or false (process the content of this element).
title	Like <a>, all <anchor> elements should have a title attribute. The title should include a meaningful description of the linked media object.

Following is a link that is associated with a video concerning Space Gems exploration techniques on the Patella Regina planet in the 51 Pegasi system. The <video> element automatically links to a portion of a tour presentation made by the Patella Regina mine manager:

```
<video id= "pat_reg_mgr_tour29" region="SGI_vid_reg08">
      <anchor show="pause"
               href="http://www.SpaceGems.com/pat_reg_tour_2047.mpg"
               begin="20s" end="81s" />
</video
```

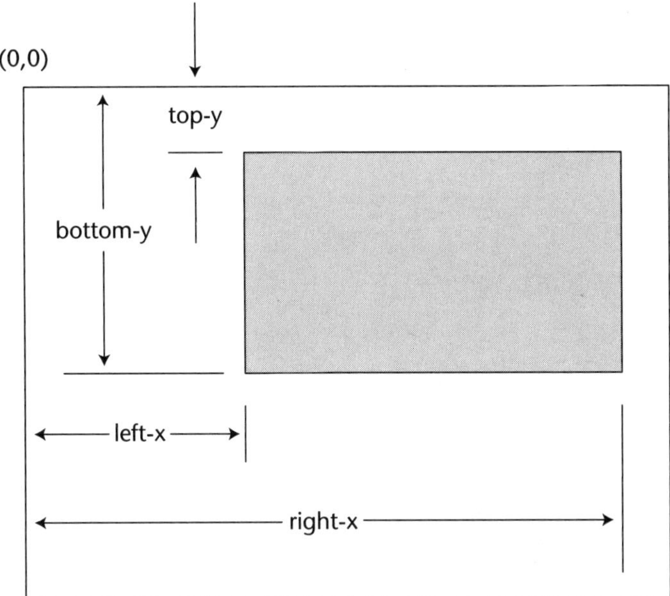

Figure 12.10 <anchor> element; coords attribute schematic (see Table 12.6).

The following example shows how to navigate to Patella Regina. The <img> element automatically links to a specific portion of a star map graphic stored locally:

```
<img id= "Peg51_map" region="SGI_navreg29">
      <anchor show="new"
               href="\exploration\maps\Pegasi51\route_direct03.jpg"
               coords="60,30,270,90" />
</img
```

Chapter 12 Labs: Getting Started with SMIL

In these labs, you work with some very basic SMIL 1.0 media objects. For this lab to work properly, though, you have to install a RealPlayer display application on your system. After that, you create a SMIL file and then add some display (for example, image, text and video) information, plus some synchronization code, to make the Space Gems site more interesting. You will recognize how Internet Explorer displays an XHTML file and how that file calls your SMIL file.

Lab 12.1: Install RealOne Media Player

A free RealOne Player is available from the RealNetworks, Inc. Web site at www.real.com. If you already have a copy of RealOne Player, go to Lab 12.2: Internet Explorer's Media Environment. Otherwise, follow these steps:

1. Activate a browser and go to www.real.com.
2. Locate the small link to the Free RealOne Player software in the top right corner of the home Web page.

We are not talking about the Free 14-Day Trial, or the 14-day trial SuperPass. Those offers ask you for a credit card number. The Free RealOne Player does not. For these labs, the basic RealOne Player is sufficient.

3. Click the Free RealOne Player link.
4. Locate the link for the basic player, not Player Plus. Click the Download the Free RealOne Player Only link.
5. Click Yes to allow it to update your browser and proceed to download the code using the following options:
   a. Choose Express Install, and click Next.
   b. Click Accept.
   c. Click the appropriate radio button to specify your Internet connection speed.
   d. If asked for Basic or Plus, choose Basic, and click Next.
   e. Click Finish.
   f. Reboot.
6. Start RealOne to test the installation. If the installation does not automatically install a shortcut on your Desktop, click Start, All Programs, Real, RealOnePlayer, RealOne Player. It should connect to the http://home.real.com site and launch an ad campaign.

Lab 12.2: Internet Explorer's Media Environment

We felt that it was necessary to show you how Microsoft's media environment differs from SMIL. The file that you install or create in this lab exploits Internet Explorer's media behavior. This environment is not SMIL-compliant yet, and neither is Windows Media Player. So we decided to create an Internet Explorer file that has similar timing, synchronization, and display features as a SMIL file. In Lab 12.3, you launch a real SMIL file using the RealOne Player that you just installed.

1. Download the following files from the Chapter 12 page of the *XML in 60 Minutes a Day* Web site, described in the book's introduction, and save them to the \WWW\SpaceGems\images directory: emerald.jpg, ruby.jpg, and diamond.jpg.
2. Download the promo1.html file from the same Web site and save it to the C:\WWW\SpaceGems directory.
3. View the file inside your browser. Type the following in the locator bar:

   ```
   http://localhost/SpaceGems/promo1.html
   ```

   You should see a page that says "Space Gems Out of this World Sale!"
4. At this time, take a look at some of the Internet Explorer specific code that sets up the timing and synchronization of the file:

   ```
   <smil>
      <body>
         <h1 class="slide">SpaceGems Out of this World Sale!</h1>
         <XML:NAMESPACE PREFIX="t" />
         <style>
            /* This is still IE 5 specific! */
            .time  { behavior: url(#DEFAULT#TIME); }
            t\:seq { behavior: url(#DEFAULT#TIME); }
         </style>
         <t:par>
            <h2 class="time" id="h11" t:timeaction="display"
   t:dur="2">
         Something for everybody.
            </h2>
   ```

```
            <h2 class="time" t:beginevent="h11.onend"
t:timaction="display">
            Participating locations.....
            </h2>
            <ul>
               <li style="color:red;font-size:12pt" CLASS="time"
t:BEGIN="4">
               Sol - Earth
               </li>
               <li style="color:blue;font-size:20pt" CLASS="time"
t:BEGIN="6">
               Pegasi
               </li>
               <li style="color:yellow;font-size:24pt" CLASS="time"
                  t:BEGIN="7">
               Sol - Mars
               </li>
               <li style="color:lime;font-size:20pt" CLASS="time"
t:BEGIN="8">
               Auriga.
               </li>
            </ul>
            <h2 CLASS="time" t:BEGIN="11" t:TIMEACTION="display">
            Each gem is different!
            </h2>
            <!-- sequence of logos -->
            <t:SEQ t:BEGIN="12" t:TIMEACTION="display">
            <img CLASS="time" alt="1st example map" ID="img1"
               t:TIMEACTION="display" SRC="images/emerald.jpg"
t:DUR="4" />
            <img CLASS="time" alt="2nd example map" ID="img2"
               t:TIMEACTION="display" SRC="images/ruby.jpg"
t:DUR="4" />
            <img CLASS="time" alt="3rd example map" ID="img3"
               t:TIMEACTION="display" SRC="images/diamond.jpg"
               t:DUR="indefinite" />
            </t:SEQ>
         </t:par>
      </body>
</smil>
```

Lab 12.3: SMIL's Media Environment

You are now going to code the equivalent functionality using SMIL 1.0 tags. For this lab, we have supplied the content only, and you have to code the file. When you are finished, you can observe and compare the differences in how the timing and synchronization are handled.

1. Download the following files from this book's Web site at the URL provided in the introduction and save them to the C:\WWW\SpaceGems\images directory: directions.avi and directions.jpg.
2. Open HTML-Kit (from the Windows desktop, click Start and then click, in turn, Programs, HTML-Kit, HTML-Kit).
3. Open promo1.html and add a link to an XML file called directions.smi under the comment line that says Create Link to Directions.

```
<a href="directions.smi">Click here for flying directions!</a>
```

4. Click the Preview button at the bottom of the window to view the rendered version of the file.
5. If the rendering of the document is acceptable, save the file to the C:\WWW\SpaceGems folder.
6. Close HTML-Kit.
7. From the Windows desktop, open the Turbo XML editor by clicking Start, Programs, Turbo XML 2.3.1, Turbo XML Version 2.3.1.
8. With Turbo XML activated, start a new XML file by clicking File on the menu bar and then clicking, in turn, New, New (XML Document). In the new XML Instance window that appears, type in the following code:

```
<?xml version = "1.0" encoding = "UTF-8"?>
<!DOCTYPE smil PUBLIC "-//W3C//DTD SMIL 1.0//EN"
    "http://www.w3.org/TR/REC-smil/SMIL10.dtd">
```

9. Call the new file directions.smi. To do this, click File, Save As, and when the Save as dialog box appears, save the file as C:\WWW\SpaceGems\directions.smi.
10. Add a set of <smil> tags:

```
<?xml version = "1.0" encoding = "UTF-8"?>
<!DOCTYPE smil PUBLIC "-//W3C//DTD SMIL 1.0//EN"
"http://www.w3.org/TR/REC-smil/SMIL10.dtd">
<smil>

</smil>
```

11. Add a set of <head> and <body> tags:

```
<?xml version = "1.0" encoding = "UTF-8"?>
<!DOCTYPE smil PUBLIC "-//W3C//DTD SMIL 1.0//EN"
"http://www.w3.org/TR/REC-smil/SMIL10.dtd">
<smil>
   <head>
   </head>
```

```
    <body>
    </body>
  </smil
```

12. Add the highlighted lines from the following code to create a root-layout window in which to display the media objects. We calculated the width and height required, based on the size of window required to simultaneously display the contents of the two large objects, whose contents are defined in the documents named directions.jpg and directions.avi:

```
<?xml version = "1.0" encoding = "UTF-8"?>
<!DOCTYPE smil PUBLIC "-//W3C//DTD SMIL 1.0//EN"
     "http://www.w3.org/TR/REC-smil/SMIL10.dtd">
   <smil>
      <head>
         <layout>
            <root-layout width = "400" height = "450"/>
         </layout>
      </head>
      <body>
      </body>
</smil>
```

13. Create two regions inside the root-layout window called image and video. Again, we calculated the size required for each region. The directions.jpg file is 399x281 and the video requires a size of 50x50. Therefore, if you position the large JPEG on top, you can't start the video region until at least 300:

Failure to calculate the regions in Step 13 of the accompanying procedure correctly causes the media player to display errors.

```
<?xml version = "1.0" encoding = "UTF-8"?>
<!DOCTYPE smil PUBLIC "-//W3C//DTD SMIL 1.0//EN"
"http://www.w3.org/TR/REC-smil/SMIL10.dtd">
<smil>
   <head>
      <layout>
         <root-layout width = "400" height = "450"/>
         <region id = "image" top = "0" left = "0"/>
         <region id = "video" top = "300" left = "120"/>
      </layout>
   </head>
   <body>
   </body>
  </smil>
```

14. Add a set of <par> and <seq> tags to the <body> element. This declares intentions to display these files in parallel, and you are going to define a specific timing sequence:

```
<?xml version = "1.0" encoding = "UTF-8"?>
<!DOCTYPE smil PUBLIC "-//W3C//DTD SMIL 1.0//EN"
     "http://www.w3.org/TR/REC-smil/SMIL10.dtd">
<smil>
   <head>
      <layout>
         <root-layout width = "400" height = "450"/>
            <region id = "image" top = "0" left = "0"/>
            <region id = "video" top = "300" left = "120"/>
      </layout>
   </head>
   <body>
      <par>
         <seq>
         </seq>
      </par>
   </body>
  </smil>
```

15. Now you add the actual content to display the timing mechanisms. The following code instructs the application to display the contents of the directions.jpg file inside the previously defined region called image for two seconds, and then remove (that is, make it disappear) the last static image in the region. The directions.avi file displays inside the previously defined file called video.

```
<?xml version = "1.0" encoding = "UTF-8"?>
<!DOCTYPE smil PUBLIC "-//W3C//DTD SMIL 1.0//EN"
     "http://www.w3.org/TR/REC-smil/SMIL10.dtd">
<smil>
   <head>
      <layout>
         <root-layout width = "400" height = "450"/>
            <region id = "image" top = "0" left = "0"/>
            <region id = "video" top = "300" left = "120"/>
      </layout>
   </head>
   <body>
      <par>
         <seq>
            <img region = "image" src = "images/directions.jpg"
               dur = "2s" fill = "freeze"/>
            <video region = "video" src =
"images/directions.avi"/>
```

```
            </seq>
         </par>
      </body>
   </smil>
```

16. Save the directions.smi file to the C:\WWW\SpageGems directory.
17. Test the file inside the browser. Type the following into the locator bar:

    ```
    http://localhost/SpaceGems/promo1.html
    ```

    Then click the Click Here for Flying Directions! link.
18. Optionally, you can add a link to the SPFeature.htm page for this file from magicgems.xml to promo1.html. To do so, modify the code until it looks like the following:

```
<html xmlns:v="urn:schemas-microsoft-com:vml"
      xmlns="http://www.w3c.org/TR/REC-html40">
   <head>
      <title>Space Gems Special Feature</title>
      <link rel="stylesheet" type="text/css" href="master.css" />
      <style>
         v\:* {behavior:url(#default#VML);}
      </style>
   </head>
   <body>
      <center>
         <h1>Space Gems Special Feature</h1>
         <h2>Citrine</h2>
    <!-- <a href="magicgems.xml">Click here to find out more.
</a> -->
         <a href="promo1.html">Click here to find out more.</a>
         <v:image style="width:150;height:150"
src="images/citrine.gif">
         </v:image>
         <v:oval style="width:350;height:150" fillcolor="#ffcc66"
            strokecolor="#ffcc66">
            <v:fill method="linear" angle="45" type="gradient" />
            <v:textbox style="font-size:20pt;font-color:white;
               text-align:center">
               <p>Feature of the Month<br>
                  $20% off<br>
                  Expires: 2010
               </p>
            </v:textbox>
         </v:oval>
      </center>
   </body>
</html>
```

Summary

SMIL media objects are often the most attention grabbing of the XML-related features that you can incorporate into your Web documents. However, coding them and synchronizing them can be a challenge. Here are some facts to remember when you consider using SMIL-related media objects:

- Streaming media is a technology for transferring and displaying audio, video, and other multimedia data in real time over a network (including the Internet) and displaying the media objects as a steady and continuous stream. However, an appropriate player is needed on the user's system.
- There are three types of streaming media: HTTP streaming (the earliest), clientless streaming, and true streaming (the latest).
- SMIL provides several media-related capabilities, the most notable of which are integration of text, graphics, video, and audio; control of visual layout; and control of synchronization.
- Development of SMIL specifications continues at a rapid pace. SMIL 2.0 is modular in nature and over 10 times larger than SMIL 1.0. SMIL 2.0 uses up to 11 schemas and 9 DTDs; SMIL 1.0 used only one DTD.
- The basic process of creating SMIL presentations is to create and specify characteristics of the display regions, specify the media objects and assign them to their respective regions, determine the order of presentation, and create the synchronization components.
- The SMIL document's root data element is named <smil>. Its child <head> element contains all the layout information, the <body> element, the media object, and synchronization information.
- In this chapter, we discussed the features of the SMIL Basic Layout Language. It dictates that in the <head> element, the <layout>, <root-layout>, and <region> elements are most important. Although a document can have several <regions> defined, it can have only one <root-layout> region. The application's viewport is, on occasion, confused with the root-layout region, but the viewport is usually larger. The <region> elements must have id attributes with unique values, so that the media objects can be specifically assigned to their respective display regions.
- The fit attribute, with its fill, meet, slice, and scroll values, is used to make media objects fit their display regions. Meanwhile, <meta> elements are often used to provide additional information about the SMIL document and its features.

- The <par> and <seq> elements found in the <body> element control the operation of concurrent and consecutive media objects, respectively.
- The names of the elements that we associate media objects with should reflect the type of media object. Otherwise, creation and searching operations can be hampered. If in doubt, place a media object in the <ref> element.
- The <switch> element enables you to adapt, to a limited extent, a SMIL presentation to the capabilities of your end users' systems.
- The <a> element enables you to link to other whole media objects; the <anchor> element to parts of media objects.

Review Questions

1. Which of the following is not a type of media streaming? (Choose all that apply.)
   a. Seamless
   b. Clientless
   c. True
   d. HTTP
   e. TCP/IP
2. True or false? One of the drawbacks to SMIL is that its presentations can't be adjusted to match any capabilities of an end user's system.
3. True or false? The basic SMIL presentation design is identify and assign media objects, create display regions for them, and then provide synchronization controls.
4. The <head> element contains (choose all that apply):
   a. Titles
   b. Synchronization information
   c. Layout information
   d. Media object information
   e. Metainformation
5. True or false? Another name for the root-layout region is the viewport.
6. True or false? For <region> elements, the id attribute is optional.
7. True or false? After a region is assigned to one media object, it can't be used by any other media object.
8. Which <region> attribute is used to adjust media object size?
   a. fill
   b. fit
   c. layout
   d. width
   e. None of the above

9. True or false? The <seq> element is used to control consecutive operations, and the <par> element is used to control concurrent operations.
10. True or false? The <seq> element and the <par> have the same attributes.
11. Which <anchor> attribute is used to extract a chunk out of a visual media object?
    a. fill
    b. begin, end
    c. trace
    d. coords
    e. None of the above

Answers to Review Questions

1. **a.** and **e.** These are defined in the *What Is Streaming Media?* section.
2. False. The <switch> element helps build at least some potential adjustments into the presentations.
3. False. The steps are correct but out of order. The answer is create the regions, identify assign the media objects, then build the synchronization controls.
4. **a.**, **c.**, and **e.** These are listed in the section titled *The <head> Element*.
5. False. A common misconception. The viewport is governed by the application; the root-layout region is governed by the SMIL developer. The viewport can be the same size, but it is usually bigger than the root-layout region.
6. False. If we don't insert id attributes, we can't assign media objects to the display regions.
7. False. Display regions can be used repeatedly. You need to control the synchronization and z-index overlapping, though.
8. **b.** This is discussed in the subsections within the section titled *When Media Object Dimensions Don't Match Region Dimensions*.
9. True. These are discussed in the section titled *Synchronizing Media Objects with the <par> and <seq> Elements*.
10. True. Attributes for both are listed in Table 12.2.
11. **d.** The coords attribute is defined in Table 12.6.

CHAPTER 13

RDF

In this chapter, we introduce the Resource Description Framework language (RDF), an XML application that is still under development but allows us to use metadata to provide descriptive information about the information we include in our Web page documents. RDF grew out of the need to organize and search through the billions of Web page documents available over the World Wide Web. RDF resolves metadata ambiguity, thus creating what the W3C calls the Semantic Web, a smarter Web in which systems themselves can learn about the data they search for and store. Chapter 13 reviews some issues facing those who have historically developed and categorized Web information, and those who have to search for the information they need. Then we review some early metadata developments that led to RDF development. After that, we have a look at RDF document constructs: the elements, attributes, and other components that facilitate information management. The lab exercises introduce simple RDF implementations to create and check our sample RDF documents.

By the end of this chapter, you should be aware of the major Web information management and search issues, understand the development of the Semantic Web and RDF, and be able to create RDF documents or introduce RDF components into Web page documents. However, in this introductory-level chapter, we can show you only the tip of the RDF iceberg. As it continues to develop, it could very well revolutionize the way we publish to and access information from the World Wide Web.

Web Search and Publication Issues

Today's Internet holds billions of Web pages of information. Some are useful, some are not quite so useful, and some you will want to avoid for various reasons. More information, good and bad, is added every day. And every day, more of us become concerned with categorizing, accessing, and using the information in a meaningful way.

The Web was originally built for human legibility and interpretation, and although the information on it is machine-readable (we are able to access it with our various computer systems, after all), it is not as machine-understandable as we want or need it to be. Humans perform most access and management functions more or less manually. Because of the sheer volume of information out there to search through and the difficulty involved in building "smart" search processes to determine the nature and quality of the information, automating access and management activities is difficult.

The primary Web searching technology available today consists of simple word- or phrase-matching provided by search services, such as Google, AltaVista, Yahoo, HotBot, or others. The process hasn't fundamentally changed: We access the service, type some keywords, initiate the search activity, and then sit back and wait for hundreds or even thousand of matches, which we call hits, to be listed on our screens. Even then, we are faced with having to do a lot of manual information screening. (Weeding is probably a better term.) And if that isn't daunting enough, if the keywords we used were not the most appropriate, or they didn't appear on the best Web page documents, or if some Web page documents mislead us with respect to their content, we might never find what we're looking for. We might even face embarrassment or other sanctions at home or in the workplace if our search words or phrases resemble those used by less reputable Web-based industries.

By way of example, here is a true story. A couple of years ago, our visiting nephew was eating some Washington State cherries and asked if we knew how to germinate the pits, so that he might try starting his own trees. Not knowing the answer but thinking that might be a good way to keep him out of trouble, we suggested that he check the Internet for cherry-related information and advice. He did that, and when we heard him murmur "who-o-o-a" under his breath, we raced over to check his search result listing. Needless to say, when he saw his initial "unprotected" search results, he was distracted from his original search topic. After that, we vowed to monitor his Web surfing activities. (We also made him promise *not* to tell his folks or his grandmother about his first orchard-related Web search endeavor.)

Nephew X's experiences lead us to another Web information issue: the lack of a complete and standard way to describe Web site content. Even if we are working for Space Gems and we initiate a search for *diamonds*, we might encounter baseball rules or rules for card games; or a search for *drills* might result in dentistry, hardware stores, and military exercise, along with (the intended) mining exploration and production technology. And these are simple semantic problems. What if we were faced with linguistic or cultural variables? We might never find what we need.

On the flip side, if we are publishing information on the Web, we would want to ensure that our information is available to those looking for jewelry or gemstones, not to those searching with other terms that are potentially ambiguous or offensive. (We are intentionally avoiding examples here, but the aforementioned Nephew X/cherry tree episode ought to provide enough of a word to the wise.) We do not want to risk confusing and perhaps even offending those whose business, information, or other cooperation we would otherwise invite.

Another issue that arises is that there is no standard or uniform query capability for discovering Web-based resources. For example, nonuniform or nonstandard proprietary Webmaster or database systems exist. Further, we also face varying rules for more sophisticated/advanced searches from the various search engines. Each uses its own individual symbols or combinations. Between plus signs, dashes, boolean terms such as AND or NOT, and other tips and tricks, it's difficult to keep track of all of them. The development of standard search and retrieval tools, then, could give searchers and publishers more information without the risk of dead-end streets on one hand, or information overload on the other.

Metadata Is the Key to the Solution

The key to many of our searches, successful and unsuccessful, has been the introduction of metadata into Web documents. Metadata is referred to by many similar-sounding phrases: *data about data, information about information*, or, specific to our current context, *data describing Web resources*. In addition to all those descriptions, metadata should be understood as *machine understandable information about Web resources*.

In Chapter 1, "XML Backgrounder," we mentioned the concept of metamarkup, which, as one of the six basic types of markup, provides the ability to control the definition and interpretation of markup tags and helps us extend the vocabulary of markup languages. Metadata, the concept of information about information (to use just one of the catchy phrases listed previously), is related to metamarkup.

Metadata, when added to a Web document by its developers, describes how, when, and by whom a particular set of data has been collected, and how the data is formatted. Metadata has become essential for understanding information stored in databases everywhere. It is not a new concept, not even to the Web. In fact, from a Web standpoint, it has been around since the earliest versions of HTML. Witness the use of <meta> elements (also called *meta tags*), within the <head> element of Web documents. The data provided within the <meta> elements is examined by search engines and thus becomes valuable because it helps them understand the content found in Web page documents so that they can find documents that match their search criteria. However, <meta> elements are not the only indicators search engines use. Their automated crawlers also use other keyword-related algorithms as they attempt to determine the nature and quality of the data.

Aside from our discussions of HTML and XHTML, the only significant exposure we have had to metadata so far in this book has been through the use of DTDs, beginning with Chapter 4, and schemas, beginning with Chapter 5. We will discuss metadata in this chapter and again in our discussion of the Channel Definition Format in Chapter 14, "CDF."

As we'll see throughout the rest of this chapter, metadata in a proper and standard framework plays a major role in RDF and its related standards.

The W3C, PICS, and RDF

In 1995, several members of the Internet community began developing technical specifications that would enable Web users to find appropriate Web content easily, while avoiding inappropriate or unwanted Web content. They understood the global nature of the Web and the fact that it serves communities with diverse values. But they also understood that there was appropriate and inappropriate information on it too, and that national or international laws restricting certain kinds of text-, audio-, or video-based expression would probably not be desirable, let alone effective or enforceable for the Web. Their specifications, called the Platform for Internet Content Selection (PICS), were intended to facilitate the creation of compact, computer-readable metadata labeling schemes, along with content-selection and filtering mechanisms implemented by individuals or organizations. The specifications were not intended to restrict only offensive content. The developers hoped that the PICS would be used for other purposes, such as self-rating of content and third-party ratings, and would be easy to implement and use.

The PICS specifications reached W3C Recommendation status in 1996. Thereafter, they were incorporated into a number of products, and a variety of PICS-based rating services have been developed for the Web. Several standalone content-filtering tools are also available. PICS gives users a measure of personal control over the content they receive without requiring the imposition of additional restrictions or sanctions on content providers.

In 1997, the W3C chartered the Metadata Activity to acknowledge that metadata development was common not only to PICS and Digital Signature Initiative (Dsig) at W3C, but also to HTTP and WebDAV work at the Internet Engineering Task Force (IETF), the Dublin Core, and other projects. The primary work of the W3C's Metadata Activity was the development of the

Resource Description Framework (RDF), although it also worked on PICS, the Digital Signature Initiative, which, along with RDF, will be instrumental to the building of the "Web of Trust" for electronic commerce, collaboration, and other applications, the Platform for Privacy Preferences (P3P) Project, and the Composite Capability/Preference Profiles (CC/PP). Thus, the W3C Metadata Activity would address the combined needs of several groups for a common framework to describe information on the Web.

As a result of many communities coming together and agreeing on basic principles of metadata representation and transport, RDF development was influenced by several different sources. The main influences came from the following:

- The Web standardization community, most notably, those who developed HTML metadata and PICS.
- The library community.
- The structured document community, for example, SGML and XML proponents.
- The knowledge representation (KR) community (object-oriented programming and modeling languages).
- Recent submissions to the W3C by Microsoft (XML Web Collections), Netscape (XML/MCF), and Microsoft XML-Data and Site Map. In addition, those involved with the W3C's Metadata Activity knew of other initiatives, such as the Dublin Core/Warwick Frameworks.
- The database community.

Classroom Q & A

Q: **When you mention the knowledge representation community, are you implying that artificial intelligence of some sort will be facilitated by RDF or similar specifications?**

A: No. Although RDF draws from the KR community, RDF has no reasoning mechanism specifications. RDF is simply helping the W3C pursue its goal of a "Semantic Web," which we define and discuss in the section titled *The Semantic Web and Recent RDF Developments* later in this chapter.

In early to mid-1997, the W3C also received several Internet-related push technology proposals. Push technology involves the use of metadata to a limited extent, and the proposals are discussed in more detail in Chapter 14, "CDF." As a result of those proposals, metadata related to content distribution was the theme of the W3C-sponsored September 1997 Workshop on Push

Technology. None of the content distribution vocabularies outlined in the proposals garnered enough support to warrant further W3C-sponsored development. Meanwhile, the W3C continued its work on a generalized, vendor-neutral, operating system-independent metadata infrastructure.

The RDF Working Group was one of the earliest components of the W3C's generalized metadata initiative. The collaborative design effort surrounding RDF originated as an extension of the earlier PICS content-description technology. RDF design was also influenced by XML components and requirements.

The W3C published the first public draft of the Resource Description Framework (RDF) in October 1997. The W3C Recommendation, titled Resource Description Framework (RDF) Model and Syntax Specification, was eventually endorsed in February 1999.

RDF Defined

RDF is a declarative language and provides a standard way for using XML to represent metadata in the form of statements about properties and relationships of any Web resource. Examples include the title, author, and modification date of a Web page; copyright and licensing information about a Web document; or other descriptive information.

RDF provides a model for representing metadata that is even more general than the PICS metadata model, with more expressive power, and it uses XML syntax. RDF does not specify a vocabulary (that is, it doesn't impose element types for every kind of data description) for describing resources. Rather, it provides a metadata framework, within which the vocabulary authors can create descriptions about their own specific resources. In other words, RDF allows the developers within different application communities to define their own specific metadata property sets—those that best serve their own individual needs or the needs of their application community.

Although RDF development was influenced by PICS experience, it deviated from the narrower PICS model by providing a generalized model for describing resources. Plus, a goal of RDF was to permit the mechanical translation of PICS metadata into RDF form.

RDF complements XML by layering on top of XML. It provides some relief for Web information search problems and for the proliferation of automated crawlers or agents that roam the Web searching for information. Given a mechanism that allows more precise descriptions of data or information, Web documents rise from machine-readable to something more akin to machine-understandable or, at least, machine-processible. So, with RDF, we attempt to assign meaning to resources in such a way that a machine or, more properly, a code engine can actually understand something about the nature of the data. That way, RDF provides a measure of interoperability.

RDF can be used in a variety of application areas:

- Resource discovery, by providing better search engine capabilities.
- Cataloging, by allowing a developer to describe the content and content relationships available at a particular Web site or digital library, so that software agents can facilitate knowledge sharing and exchange.
- Content rating.
- The description of collections of pages such that they can represent a single logical document.
- The description of intellectual property rights for Web pages.
- The expression of privacy preferences of a user and the privacy policies of a Web site.

In RDF documents, Web and other resources are defined as anything that can be designated by a URI. The URI can no longer be thought of as just an address to provide access to someone's Web page. The URI is going to be the key to defining resources on the new RDF-oriented Web. Essentially, those resources could be anything that can be identified on the Web, even when they can't be directly retrieved from the Web.

This new reliance on URIs implies that, because they will be used to identify a resource, they should be properly constructed and should not change. As URIs change—for example, as businesses change or go out of business—information will become disassociated. Furthermore, changing file or directory/folder names or suffixes would have a similar and devastating effect. Last year, for example, a file might have been called spacegems.com/4cs/data.html. Perhaps, as a result of a filesystem or Web site makeover, the filename and path designation later became spacegems.com/4cs/data.asp, and, finally, spacegems.com/4cs/data.jsp.

Here is a possible solution. Remember that most tools and Web services can be configured to display a URI or URL without file extensions. If this resource had a URI of spacegems.com/4cs/data, it would not have suffered the loss of association. File extensions are not necessary or mandatory, and leaving them out breathes a longer life into a resource. For today's search engines, this is not a serious issue. An issue might arise, however, if someone somewhere has already created links to our information. Those links will eventually have to be modified.

The responsibility of maintaining stable URIs or changing references within documents resides with the resource owner or administrator. Meanwhile, in the future, more attention and thought is going to have to be given to creating and maintaining URIs if this is going to work.

If we can create documents that adhere to the RDF data model, a marketplace of more advanced services will eventually be developed to accommodate us. Here are some examples:

- Document viewers and editors.
- Data storage.
- Data query devices.
- Inferential services, such as type checking and inheritance.
- Compositors (in other words, applications that provide merged views of multiple RDF graphs; RDF graphs are discussed later in this chapter).
- Serialization and transmission services that use RDF-XML format.

As the Web fills with richer RDF-based metadata, searching will become easier, faster, and better focused because search engines will have more and better search information available. Better and faster automated software agents will roam the Web, looking for information or transacting business on our behalf. Information could be accessed, analyzed, extracted, sorted, styled, and otherwise manipulated to create customized documents for people or machines. Thus, data publishing and searching will become "smarter." Web pages will become true Web services, and the Web itself will progress toward being a truly Semantic Web, one of the W3C's major goals. We'll discuss the nature of the Semantic Web next.

The Semantic Web and Recent RDF Developments

The W3C Metadata Activity was officially replaced with the W3C Semantic Web Activity when that Semantic Activity was chartered in February 2001. The establishment of Semantic Activity reflected a commitment by the W3C to pursue their Semantic Web objective. Needless to say, Semantic Web Activity succeeded Metadata Activity. A single RDF Core Working Group was created. Composed of 19 members from over a dozen organizations, plus 5 invited experts, it inherited RDF development.

Semantic is defined as "of or relating to meaning in language," or "of or relating to semantics." In turn, the term semantics is defined as "the study of meanings." The Semantic Web is a vision and a goal shared by the W3C and many Web-oriented organizations. Its major objective is the defining and linking of Web data so that it can be used by systems not just for display purposes, but also for automation, integration, and reuse across various applications.

The Semantic Web is an abstract representation of data on the World Wide Web that is based on the RDF standards and other future standards. Chapter 1, "XML Backgrounder," stated that the Semantic Web will be part of an extension of the current Web but will differ somewhat. Information on the Semantic

Web will be given well-defined descriptions within a standard framework to enable computers and people to work cooperatively. Its developers expect that a new generation of applications will soon be developed: applications that will offer enhanced navigation and precise, accurate information retrieval. Thus, the Semantic Web will achieve its goal of being what the W3C calls ". . . a software environment that permits each user to make the best use of the resources available on the Web." Computer "ignorance" will be reduced as systems begin to emulate a kind of rudimentary understanding of the data they share.

According to the W3C's Semantic Activity statement, their work will involve the following:

- Continuing the work of the existing RDF Interest Group—that is, coordinating the implementation and deployment of RDF and providing liaison with new work in the W3C and the wider community on matters relating to RDF.
- Undertaking revisions to the RDF Model and Syntax specification.
- Completing the RDF Schema Recommendation.
- Coordinating with the W3C and external activities focused on Semantic Web technologies.
- Developing advanced XML and RDF technologies to increase the level of automation of the W3C Web site and to develop open source RDF infrastructure support modules.

As of this writing, the RDF Core Working Group has just released six Last Call Working Drafts to facilitate the development and deployment of the Semantic Web:

- RDF Primer
- RDF Test Cases
- RDF/XML Syntax Specification (Revised)
- RDF Vocabulary Description Language 1.0: RDF Schema
- RDF Semantics
- Resource Description Framework (RDF): Concepts and Abstract Syntax

Some of these are new standards, and some are updates of existing standards. The W3C has also just published a W3C Note titled LBase: Semantics for Languages of the Semantic Web. It's a framework for specifying Semantic Web languages in a uniform and coherent way.

To link to these RDF-related documents and more, go to the W3C Semantic Web News and Events Archive Web site at www.w3.org/2001/sw/news#x20030124b.

RDF Implementations

Here are four suggested RDF implementations. The first two, in fact, will be used in the lab exercises at the end of this chapter:

- The W3C has an online RDF Validation Service that supports the Last Call Working Draft specifications issued by the RDF Core Working Group. It is located at www.w3.org/RDF/Validator/. However, the site explains that deprecated elements and attributes of the standard RDF Model and Syntax Specification are no longer supported. All we need to do there is enter a URI or paste an RDF/XML document into a text field, and a 3-tuple (triple) representation of the corresponding data model, as well as a graphical visualization of the data model, will be displayed. Other input and output options exist as well.

At one time, the W3C provided the Simple RDF Parser and Compiler (SiRPAC). However, Janne Saarela, the original author of SiRPAC, no longer works with the W3C. All the same, if you would like to participate in further development and maintenance of SiRPAC, some SiRPAC links are still available at the W3C RDF Validator Web site at www.w3.org/RDF/Validator/.

- To help you test and write your RDF, you should check out RDFedt, a piece of Windows freeware by Jan Winkler, available from www.jan-winkler.de/dev/e_rdfe.htm.
- Mozilla.org uses RDF to develop applications with the intention of integrating and aggregating Internet resources. RDF is used to support Aurora—a single-user interface program for managing bookmarks, history, search results, filesystems, and other resources that can be reflected in an RDF data model—and Mozilla's SmartBrowsing metadata services. For information regarding Mozilla and RDF, visit Mozilla's Web site at www.mozilla.org/rdf/doc/.
- Microsoft has an RDF Viewer available at http://msdn.microsoft.com/downloads/samples/internet/default.asp?url=/downloads/samples/internet/xml/xml_rdf_viewer/default.asp. If that link is out-of-date, go to the Microsoft Developer Network at http://msdn.microsoft.com and search "All of MSDN" for "RDF Viewer" with the MSDN search engine. Be aware, though, that to use the RDF Viewer, you must have Internet Explorer 5.0, Visual Basic 6.0, and Windows 98, Windows NT 4.0, or Windows 2000 installed already.

For comprehensive listings of RDF implementations, applications, and other RDF resources, check the W3C's RDF home page at www.w3.org/RDF/ or Dave Beckett's Resource Description Framework (RDF) Resource Guide at www.ilrt.bris.ac.uk/discovery/rdf/resources/.

RDF Concepts and Syntax

Like other XML-related applications we've seen, RDF has its own concepts and terms. In the case of RDF, though, it has been our experience that its concepts and terms (including the aliases for those terms) cause the concepts to sound more complex than they really are. We discuss the concepts here and within the framework of our customary logical structure approach. Between the two approaches, we hope we can clarify the most basic concepts.

Following is a simple example of an RDF document. It refers to the 2047 Space Gems catalog and provides the name of the vendor. Again, because RDF is advancing and expanding rapidly, we can only introduce you to basic RDF concepts. We won't go into any detail here, but we will use the following Space Gems–oriented example, as we go along, to illustrate the first basic concepts. Later, we'll use the same example document to discuss the logical structure of an RDF document.

```
<?xml version="1.0" encoding="UTF-8" ?>
<rdf:RDF xmlns:rdf="http://www.w3.org/1999/02/22-rdf-syntax-ns#"
            xmlns:sgs="http://www.spacegems.com/sales/" >
    <rdf:Description rdf:about="http://www.spacegems.com/2047/catalog/" >
        <sgs:vendor>Space Gems, Inc.</sgs:vendor>
    </rdf:Description>
</rdf:RDF>
```

Statements

As its name indicates, Resource Description Framework provides a framework for describing a resource. It uses statements to provide the descriptions. The statements are built similarly, but not identically, to the way statements in English or any other language are built: They are considered to have subjects, predicates, and objects. The difference is that, with RDF, other components fill those roles. For example, documents of all sorts (electronic and even nonelectronic), XML element types, attributes, and data are used, instead of the nouns, pronouns, verbs, adjectives, and other components we would expect to find in English grammar.

RDF statements are also called RDF assertions and RDF triples. In fact, the term triple is more or less the official term used for an RDF statement. They are called triples because they contain and define the relationship between the subject, its predicate, and its object.

Resources

If we are going to describe a resource, we must first decide which resource to describe and then indicate the name of that resource in our statement. Resources can be almost anything, such as Web pages, email accounts, graphics, audio files, video clips, or other data sources in electronic or nonelectronic formats, as long as they have Universal Resource Identifier as a form of identification. For example, a URI, such as www.spacegems.com/4cs/data, can be a resource.

URIs are defined according to the IETF Network Working Group's Request for Comments (RFC) 2396 titled Uniform Resource Identifiers (URI): Generic Syntax at www.isi.edu/in-notes/rfc2396.txt.

After we have chosen a specific resource to describe with our RDF statement, the URI for that resource becomes the subject in our descriptive statement.

In our example, the <rdf:Description> element start tag contains the following attribute code:

```
rdf:about="http://www.spacegems.com/2047/catalog/"
```

The value of the attribute identifies the resource about which we will create descriptive statements; namely, the Space Gems 2047 Catalog.

Properties

After we have chosen a resource to describe, we have to decide two things:

- Which resource characteristics we want to describe
- Which resource characteristics other people or systems might be interested in

Those characteristics are called the resource's *properties*. (They're also called named properties.)

In our simple example, the <sgs:vendor> element type is a property and appears as follows:

```
<sgs:vendor>Space Gems, Inc.</sgs:vendor>
```

Each property has its own name and is used to help distinguish or define a specific characteristic among similar resources. Other properties that might be used to describe the Space Gems catalog, for example, could be <publisher>, <publication date>, and <no_of_pages>. Because of our URI naming conventions, properties can become resources, too.

The property is considered to be the predicate in the descriptive statement.

Values

Now that we have chosen a resource to describe (the 2047 Space Gems catalog) and the property of the resource we are going to describe (the vendor), we can provide a value for the property. In our example, the data within the <sgs:vendor> element type—Space Gems, Inc.—is that value.

The full descriptive statement says, "The subject is the Space Gems 2047 catalog, which has a property named vendor and a value of Space Gems, Inc." It's a simple statement with expected components. For example, a property value *other* than Space Gems, Inc. would be unexpected.

The value of the property is called the *object* of the statement.

RDF Graphs

To help us design and translate RDF triples, RDF provides a standard graphical data model. The basics are simple, although occasionally the diagrams and RDF constructs can be complex. Take a look at the simple RDF graph in Figure 13.1.

The subjects and objects are shown within their respective nodes and are connected by arcs, which is why RDF graphs are also called node-and-arc diagrams. By convention, subjects are within ovals and objects within rectangles. The predicates are arrows that connect the two; their tails are always connected to the subject and their heads to the object. The arc is always the equivalent of a logical AND.

Later in this chapter, in the *Property Elements* section, we use a slightly more complex node-and-arc diagram to help us design and illustrate a more complex set of descriptive statements.

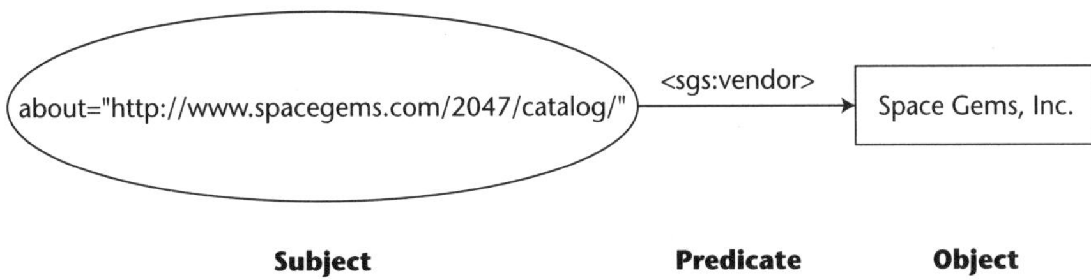

Figure 13.1 RDF graph (aka a node-and-arc diagram) showing a simple triple.

In Figure 13.1, the predicate is indicated by its element type tag. We've done this here for simplicity. Actually, the same element is given a URI, which drills down to its element name. In the lab exercises, you will work with the W3C RDF Validator. It creates similar diagrams automatically and labels the predicate with its full URI.

The Logical Structure of an RDF Document

It is possible for an RDF document to be part of a larger overall XML document. However, in this chapter, we construct and analyze RDF documents as separate documents.

As with other XML-related languages, an RDF document consists of a prolog and a data instance. The following is a simple (separate) RDF document example:

```
<?xml version="1.0" encoding="UTF-8" ?>
<rdf:RDF xmlns:rdf="http://www.w3.org/1999/02/22-rdf-syntax-ns#"
             xmlns:sgs="http://www.spacegems.com/sales/" >
     <rdf:Description
             rdf:about="http://www.spacegems.com/2047/catalog/" >
          <sgs:vendor>Space Gems, Inc.</sgs:vendor>
     </rdf:Description>
</rdf:RDF>
```

The Prolog

In an RDF document, the only mandatory prolog statement is the XML declaration. The first line of our example RDF document is typical and looks like all the others we've encountered so far in *XML in 60 Minutes a Day*.

In the next section, we briefly discuss several different RDF-related content models. If we were to incorporate any of the elements from those models, we would need to tell the parser to check DTDs or schemas. For our example, however, we won't include one.

The <RDF> Root Element, Namespaces, and Content Models

An RDF data instance consists of a root element and any elements contained within the root element. The root element in an RDF data instance is named <RDF>. Because the RDF namespace is generally used, the root element often looks like <rdf:RDF>. Nested within the <RDF> element are other element types that, in turn, contain the RDF document's statements.

As in other XML-related languages, we can insert namespaces in the start tag of the root element, which is usually most convenient, or in the start tags of child elements, depending on our intentions. For our example document, we have inserted the namespaces in the <RDF> element start tag, like so:

```
<rdf:RDF xmlns:rdf="http://www.w3.org/1999/02/22-rdf-syntax-ns#"
         xmlns:sgs="http://www.spacegems.com/sales/" >
```

The namespace declaration, xmlns:rdf="http://www.w3.org/1999/02/22-rdf-syntax-ns#", is the official one for RDF. The prefix rdf is RDF convention, so we recommend that you always use it. The number sign on the end must be included. After the namespace is declared, any element types with tags that include the rdf prefix are those from the RDF element set.

Other namespace declarations are unique to the developer of the RDF document or refer to other content models. In our example document, element types that begin with sgs are not members of the RDF set but are unique to the developer, Space Gems. The Dublin Core Metadata Initiative (DCMI, or the Dublin Core), which is an organization dedicated to promoting the development of specialized metadata vocabularies and the adoption of interoperable metadata standards, has developed a content model. DCMI's most notable initiative was the development of several elements pertaining to the description of documents. The initiative has been adopted by government agencies, libraries, educational institutions, museums, and other industries. DCMI has also developed its own DTD and XML schema, which means if we use them, we must remember to inform the parser appropriately. For further information regarding the DCMI, visit its Web site at www.dublincore.org.

Other metadata initiatives are as follows:

Publishing Requirements for Industry Standard Metadata (PRISM). Developed by the PRISM Working Group for the publishing industry. See www.prismstandard.org for details.

XML Package Specification (XPackage). Metadata that provides a framework for structured groupings of resources and their associations that are, or may be, used as a unit. Developed by the Publication Structure Working Group of the Open eBook Forum. See www.xpackage.org/specification/index.html for details.

RDF Site Summary (RSS). A lightweight, multipurpose, extensible metadata description and syndication format. Developed by the RSS-DEV Working Group. See http://web.resource.org/rss/1.0/for details.

CIM/XML. An RDF application that supports the electronic exchange CIM models (common semantics for power system resources, attributes, and relationships). Developed by the power industry. See www.langdale.com.au/CIMXML/ for details.

GO. This Gene Ontology project provides controlled yet dynamic vocabularies for the description of the molecular function, biological process, and cellular component of gene products. Developed by the Gene Ontology Consortium. For details see www.geneontology.org/doc/GO.doc .html.

Composite Capabilities/Preferences Profile Specification (CC/PP). Defines a generic framework for describing delivery contexts for mobile computing and communication devices. Developed by the W3C's CC/PP Working Group as part of the W3C Device Independence activity. For details see www.w3.org/TR/2001/WD-CCPP-struct-vocab-20010315/.

To use any of the aforementioned models, consult the listed Web sites, especially with respect to incorporating their various namespaces, DTDs, and schemas.

Resource Descriptions Are Nested within <Description> Elements

Element types that contain the RDF document's descriptive statements are nested within the <RDF> element. Statements for any single subject resource are *usually* contained within one element named <Description>. The start tag of the <Description> element introduces the resource. Here is the <Description> element from our simple example:

```
<rdf:Description rdf:about="http://www.spacegems.com/2047/catalog/" >
     <sgs:vendor>Space Gems, Inc.</sgs:vendor>
</rdf:Description>
```

The attribute rdf:about="...", which has a URI value, indicates the resource being described. Thus, it also indicates that the URI is the subject of this set of statements. From our previous discussions of subjects, predicates, and objects, we can tell that our example contains only the three basic parts. The <Description> element contains the subject, and the <sgs:vendor> element, called a *property element*, identifies the property (vendor) and contains the value data (Space Gems, Inc.).

If the resource does not yet exist (in other words, if the resource does not yet have a resource identifier), the <Description> element's start tag can actually use an id="value" attribute to supply an identifier. Here is our original example, slightly reworked to include the id attribute:

```
<rdf:Description rdf:id="http://www.spacegems.com/2047/catalog/" >
     <sgs:vendor>Space Gems, Inc.</sgs:vendor>
</rdf:Description>
```

Table 13.1 contains descriptions of the <Description> element attributes. Notice that the prefix rdf is included with their names. We suggest that the RDF namespace and rdf prefix be included at all times. Otherwise, you may find that only some RDF implementations will support the attributes without the prefix; others will not.

Property Elements

Each property element contains the predicate (in its tags) and object (within its data) pertaining to its respective subject. Although the basic RDF framework elements and attributes are located within the RDF specification, it contains no property elements. At this point, we as developers can create our own property elements, with our own namespace declarations, and prefixes, or, if they are suitable, we can incorporate property elements from the content models we discussed in the previous section, *The <RDF> Root Element, Namespaces, and Content Models*.

Table 13.1 <Description> Element Attributes

ATTRIBUTE NAME	EXPLANATION
rdf:about	The value would be the URI of the resource to be described.
rdf:aboutEach	To describe a child element. The value would be the name of the element.
rdf:aboutEachPrefix	To describe an RDF container item. The value would specify the prefix of the container item.
rdf:bagID	To describe a bag container. The value should specify the id of the bag container.
rdf:id	To provide a new resource description. The value will be a URI and specify a name for the resource.
rdf:type	The value is arbitrary and left to the developer to specify. Will then indicate the type of description being provided.

Each <Description> element usually contains the description statements for a single resource. But it is not an error if more than one <Description> element is used to describe one subject resource, as long as the descriptive statements are not contradictory. Thus, the following is permitted:

```
<?xml version="1.0" encoding="UTF-8" ?>
<rdf:RDF xmlns:rdf="http://www.w3.org/1999/02/22-rdf-syntax-ns#"
              xmlns:sgs="http://www.spacegems.com/sales/" >
     <rdf:Description
              rdf:about="http://www.spacegems.com/2047/catalog/" >
          <sgs:vendor>Space Gems, Inc.</sgs:vendor>
     </rdf:Description>
     <rdf:Description
              rdf:about="http://www.spacegems.com/2047/catalog/" >
          <sgs:publ_date>Spring 2047</sgs:publ_date>
     </rdf:Description>
</rdf:RDF>
```

In addition to providing more than one <Description> element for a single resource, we can combine statements within a single <Description> element, like this:

```
<?xml version="1.0" encoding="UTF-8" ?>
<rdf:RDF xmlns:rdf="http://www.w3.org/1999/02/22-rdf-syntax-ns#"
              xmlns:sgs="http://www.spacegems.com/sales/" >
     <rdf:Description
              rdf:about="http://www.spacegems.com/2047/catalog/" >
          <sgs:vendor>Space Gems, Inc.</sgs:vendor>
          <sgs:publ_date>Spring 2047</sgs:publ_date>
     </rdf:Description>
</rdf:RDF>
```

This example is equivalent to the previous example: the one that contained two <Description> elements. Its node-and-arc diagram looks like Figure 13.2.

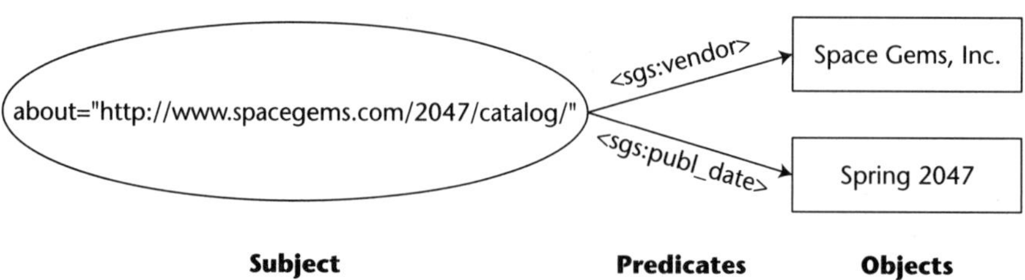

Figure 13.2 RDF graph showing a more complex triple.

Abbreviating RDF

RDF provides the capability to abbreviate its syntax, by changing property elements to <Description> element attributes. Here is an example:

```
<?xml version="1.0" encoding="UTF-8" ?>
<rdf:RDF xmlns:rdf="http://www.w3.org/1999/02/22-rdf-syntax-ns#"
              xmlns:sgs="http://www.spacegems.com/sales/" >
    <rdf:Description
              rdf:about="http://www.spacegems.com/2047/catalog/" >
          <sgs:vendor>Space Gems, Inc.</sgs:vendor>
          <sgs:publ_date>Spring 2047</sgs:publ_date>
    </rdf:Description>
</rdf:RDF>
```

We can abbreviate the preceding code to the following:

```
<?xml version="1.0" encoding="UTF-8" ?>
<rdf:RDF xmlns:rdf="http://www.w3.org/1999/02/22-rdf-syntax-ns#"
              xmlns:sgs="http://www.spacegems.com/sales/" >
    <rdf:Description rdf:about="http://www.spacegems.com/2047/catalog/"
          sgs:vendor="Space Gems, Inc."
          sgs:publ_date="Spring 2047">
    </rdf:Description>
</rdf:RDF>
```

We've highlighted the corresponding text for clarity. Such abbreviation provides two benefits:

- It's easier and faster to type.
- We can embed RDF into Web page documents more easily. There is less risk that HTML, for example, will ignore element types that it doesn't understand. If we convert them to attributes, the data will be preserved.

Substituting Our Own XML Data into Others' Data Content Models

If we intend to use another party's content model and elements, but we want to treat their element types a little differently, we can use a substitution technique similar to the following RDF code example, which describes the creator of the 2047 Space Gems catalog. Highlighting has been added for clarification.

```
<?xml version="1.0" encoding="UTF-8" ?>
<rdf:RDF xmlns:rdf="http://www.w3.org/1999/02/22-rdf-syntax-ns#"
              xmlns:dc="http://purl.org/dc/elements/1.1/"
              xmlns:sgt="http://www.spacegems.com/cutting/" >
```

```
    <rdf:Description
            rdf:about="http://www.spacegems.com/2047/catalog/">
        <dc:creator rdf:parseType="Literal" >
            <sgt:author>Glitterlich, Carley</sgt:author>
            <sgt:dept>Cutting and Polishing</sgt:dept>
            <sgt:email>glitter@spacegems.com</sgt:email>
           <sgt:publ_date>Spring 2047</sgt:publ_date>
        </dc:creator>
    </rdf:Description>
</rdf:RDF>
```

Instead of adding a name as the value for the property <Creator>, as the Dublin Core model requires, we can add our own elements, which contain the name and a little more information. However, earlier we had to add the appropriate namespace declaration.

Using the resource Attribute

In the previous section, we substituted our own information to identify the creator/author of the Space Gems catalog. What if Carley has her own Web page that contains all her information? We could provide a pointer to her Web page as a resource, using the resource attribute. The following example illustrates this. Highlighting has been added for clarity.

```
<?xml version="1.0" encoding="UTF-8" ?>
<rdf:RDF xmlns:rdf="http://www.w3.org/1999/02/22-rdf-syntax-ns#"
               xmlns:dc="http://purl.org/dc/elements/1.1/"
    <rdf:Description rdf:about="http://www.spacegems.com/2047/catalog/"
      <dc:Creator
        rdf:resource="http://www.spacegems.com/tekstaff/glittec.html >
      </dc:Creator>
    </rdf:Description>
</rdf:RDF>
```

Chapter 13 Labs: Creating and Validating RDF

RDF is a rather new, but rapidly developing XML language, so there are not many tools and utilities in the marketplace to use with it at this time. Meanwhile, RDF files are easy to code, but issues arise when we try to get an agent or engine to use the information in them. However, this is often the case with new technology and specifications, so it shouldn't cause extraordinary worries. In this lab exercise, we will start by having you validate some existing code. Later, you will re-create some code using an RDF editor.

Lab 13.1: Validating RDF Code

In this exercise, we show you where to go to find a validator and how to validate your RDF code.

1. Go to the W3C's online RDF Validation Service at www.w3.org/RDF/Validator.
2. Enter the following example code in the text field of the validation service.

```
<?xml version="1.0" encoding="UTF-8" ?>
<rdf:RDF xmlns:rdf="http://www.w3.org/1999/02/22-rdf-syntax-ns#"
               xmlns:sgs="http://www.spacegems.com/sales/" >
     <rdf:Description
             rdf:about="http://www.spacegems.com/2047/catalog/" >
          <sgs:vendor>Space Gems, Inc.</sgs:vendor>
     </rdf:Description>
</rdf:RDF>
```

3. Click the gray Parse RDF button located under all the options, but just above the Notes.

It is our experience that this validator provides good error messages, so read them carefully. Also, if you choose to cut and paste the code rather than type it, the quotes used in the first line of code may not be the correct ones. You may have to change them and try again.

4. The completed results of the validation should provide the following information:
   a. The original RDF/XML document
   b. Triples of the data model
   c. Validation results
   d. An RDF graph (also called a node-and-arc diagram) that resembles Figure 13.3
   e. Feedback

Figure 13.3 Resulting RDF graph showing logic of RDF/XML code.

5. You can now trust the logic and syntax of this piece of code for use inside any XML document.

6. Now try adding some more information to the RDF file. Add another element named <publ_date> and rerun the validator. To do so, modify the existing RDF code to resemble the following code. The new code is shown in highlight for clarity.

```
<?xml version="1.0" encoding="UTF-8" ?>
<rdf:RDF xmlns:rdf="http://www.w3.org/1999/02/22-rdf-syntax-ns#"
            xmlns:sgs="http://www.spacegems.com/sales/" >
    <rdf:Description
            rdf:about="http://www.spacegems.com/2047/catalog/" >
        <sgs:vendor>Space Gems, Inc.</sgs:vendor>
    </rdf:Description>
    <rdf:Description
            rdf:about="http://www.spacegems.com/2047/catalog/" >
        <sgs:publ_date>Spring 2047</sgs:publ_date>
    </rdf:Description>
</rdf:RDF>
```

7. Click the Parse RDF button again.

8. You should see a much different RDF graph of the data model; compare your new results to Figure 13.4.

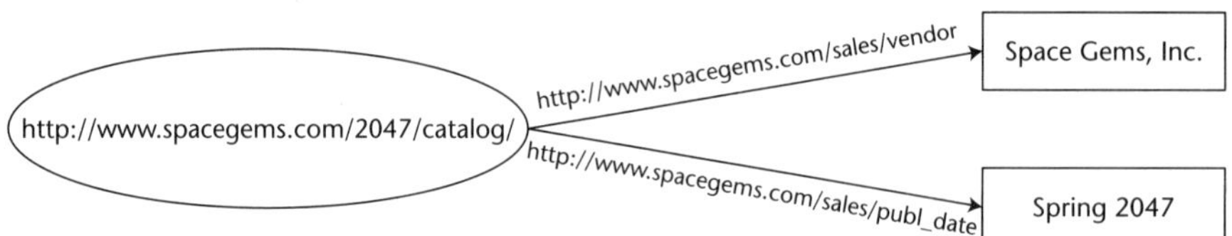

Figure 13.4 RDF graph showing multiple predicates and objects.

9. Now modify the information in the file, nesting the <vendor> and <publ_date> property elements into the same <Description> element. The new code is shown in the following. The main changes are highlighted for clarity.

```
<?xml version="1.0" encoding="UTF-8" ?>
<rdf:RDF xmlns:rdf="http://www.w3.org/1999/02/22-rdf-syntax-ns#"
            xmlns:sgs="http://www.spacegems.com/sales/" >
    <rdf:Description
            rdf:about="http://www.spacegems.com/2047/catalog/" >
        <sgs:vendor>Space Gems, Inc.</sgs:vendor>
        <sgs:publ_date>Spring 2047</sgs:publ_date>
    </rdf:Description>
</rdf:RDF>
```

10. Click the Parse RDF button again.

11. The results of the validation should still look identical to Figure 13.4.
12. Test one more final scenario. This time, convert the combined code from Step 9 into abbreviated vendor and publ_date attributes within <Description>, as shown in the following code. The main changes are highlighted.

```
<?xml version="1.0" encoding="UTF-8" ?>
<rdf:RDF xmlns:rdf="http://www.w3.org/1999/02/22-rdf-syntax-ns#"
               xmlns:sgs="http://www.spacegems.com/sales/" >
    <rdf:Description
rdf:about="http://www.spacegems.com/2047/catalog/"
          sgs:vendor="Space Gems, Inc."
          sgs:publ_date="Spring 2047">
    </rdf:Description>
</rdf:RDF>
```

13. Click the Parse RDF button again. The results of the validation should be identical to Figure 13.4.

Lab 13.2: Using RDFedt to Create a Basic RDF File

In this exercise, we introduce you to a free RDF editor named RDFedt, available from Jan Winkler at www.jan-winkler.de. This easy-to-use editor will help you write and test your own RDF/XML code.

1. Activate a browser and surf to Jan Winkler's Web site at www.jan-winkler.de/dev/e_rdfe.htm. Download the editor by clicking the http://www.jan-winkler.de ...(1) hyperlink.
2. Double-click the resulting rdfedt_10.exe file to initiate the installation process.
3. Accept all defaults while installing the editor.
4. Double-click the RDFedt icon that was placed on the Windows desktop to open the editor.
5. Expand the only element shown at the top of the work area to expose the two namespace attributes. Both are required.
6. Note that you have access to the <rdf:Model&Syntax>, <rdfs:Schema>, <dc:Dublin Core>, and <rss:RSS 1.0> elements from the top menu bar. This is convenient, because the editor will guide you and will not allow you to use any illegal elements that are not recognized by the W3C's RDF standards and specifications. These are exactly the kinds of features we expect from an editor.

7. Add two new namespace declaration attributes to the new file. To do this, place the cursor directly on the <rdf:RDF> element at the top of the workspace, click the right-mouse button to open the context menu, and then click Add Attribute.

8. Place the cursor just to the right of the empty green box that represents the new attribute. Click the Edit tab on the right-hand side of the editor.

9. Enter the following namespace information into the Name field inside the Objects window:

```
xmlns:dc="http://purl.org/dc/elements/1.1/"
```

Your editor view should look like Figure 13.5.

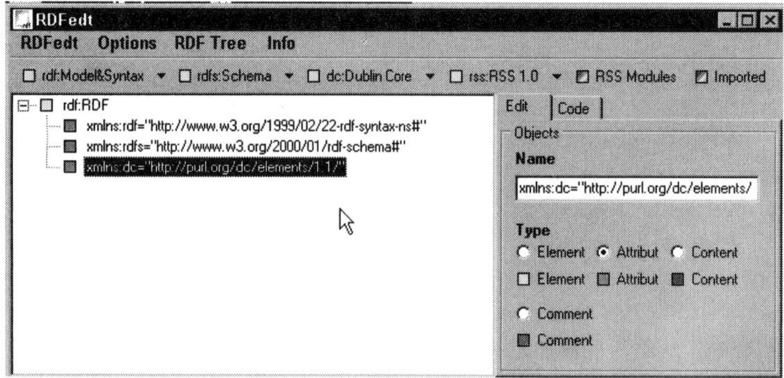

Figure 13.5 RDFedt editor showing the first user-created namespace attribute.

10. At any time, you can click on the Code tab on the right-hand side of the editor to view the resulting code. However, you can't edit the code directly; you have to return to the Edit window to do code edits.

11. Add the second new namespace attributes to the new file. To do this, place the cursor directly on the <rdf:RDF> element at the top of the workspace, right-click to open the context menu, and click Add Attribute.

12. Place the cursor to the right of the empty green box that represents the new attribute. Click the Edit tab on the right side of the editor.

13. Enter the following namespace information into the Name field inside the Objects window:

```
xmlns:sgt="http://www.spacegems.com/cutting/"
```

Here, sgt is an abbreviation for Space Gems Technology. The Cutting and Polishing group is found within that part of the company.

14. Next, add an <rdf:Description> element to the file. To do this, place the cursor directly on the <rdf:RDF> element at the top of the workspace, right-click to open the context menu, and click Add Element.
15. Place the cursor to the right of the empty yellow box that represents the new element. Click the Edit tab on the right side of the editor.
16. Enter the following information all on one line in the Name field inside the Objects window.

    ```
    rdf:Description
    ```

    Notice this is a user-defined element named <rdf:Description>, which will have an rdf:about="..." attribute inside of it.
17. Now add the rdf:about attribute to the <rdf:Description> element. To do this, place the cursor directly on the <rdf:Description> element, right-click to open the context menu, and click Add Attribute.
18. Place the cursor to the right of the empty green box that represents the new attribute. Click the Edit tab on the right side of the editor.
19. Enter the following information, all on one line, into the Name field inside the Objects window:

    ```
    rdf:about="http://www.spacegems.com/2047/catalog/"
    ```

20. Add a <dc:creator> element with an rdf:parseElement attribute to handle literals. To do this, place the cursor directly on the <rdf:Description> element at the top of the workspace, right-click to open the context menu, and click Add Element.
21. Place the cursor to the right of the empty yellow box that represents the new element. Click the Edit tab on the right side of the editor.
22. Enter the following namespace information, all on one line, into the Name field inside the Objects window:

    ```
    dc:creator
    ```

23. Add an rdf:parseElement attribute to handle literals. To do this, place the cursor directly on the <dc:creator> element, right-click to open the context menu, and click Add Attribute.
24. Place the cursor to the right of the empty green box that represents the new attribute. Click the Edit tab on the right side of the editor.
25. Enter the following information into the Name field inside the Objects window:

    ```
    rdf:parseType="Literal"
    ```

26. Define four new user-defined elements named <sgt:author>, <sgt:dept>, <sgt:email>, and <sgt:publ_date> to hold predicate and object data. These new elements will belong to the sgt user-defined namespace. To do this, place the cursor on the new <rdf:creator> element, right-click to open the context menu, and click Add Element.

27. Place the cursor to the right of the empty yellow box that represents the new element. Click the Edit tab on the right side of the editor.

28. Enter the following namespace:element information into the Name field inside the Objects window:

```
sgt:author
```

29. Using the technique described in Steps 26 through 28, add the next three namespace:elements information:

```
sgt:dept
sgt:email
sgt:publ_date
```

30. Add the literal string information to the four new elements. To do this, place the cursor directly on the <sgt:author> element, right-click to open the context menu, and click Add Content.

31. Place the cursor to the right of the empty red box that represents the new content. Click the Edit tab on the right side of the editor.

32. Enter the following literal into the Name field inside the Objects window:

```
Glitterlich, Carley
```

33. Using the technique described in Steps 30 through 32, add the next three literals to their respective elements:

    a. Enter "Cutting and Polishing" inside <sgt:dept>.

    b. Enter "glittec@spacegems.com" inside <sgt:email>.

    c. Enter "Spring 2047" inside <sgt:publ_date>.

34. Save the file. Click RDFedt on the top menu bar. Click Save as RDF File. Type "sg_rdf," and click Save. Compare your RDFedt file to Figure 13.6.

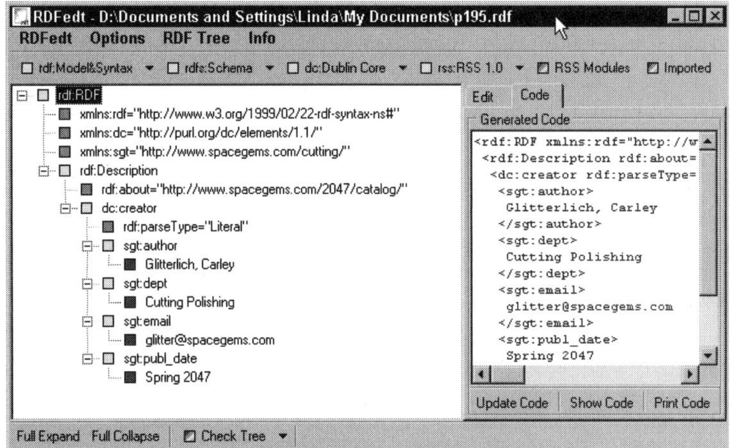

Figure 13.6 RDFedt file with all elements and attributes added.

35. Click the Check Tree menu. Click Check All to check the RDF/XML code. There should be 0 errors found in all categories. If there are errors, fix them now.

36. If you would like to check this RDF file code, copy and paste this information into the W3C's online RDF Validation Service at www.w3.org/RDF/Validator. The results should validate and show an interesting RDF graph that points to all user-defined elements and literal data.

Summary

RDF is a rapidly expanding technology. In this chapter, we introduced the issues behind its development and indicated how it may help shape the Web of the future. There are several key concepts to remember. Here are a few to keep in mind:

- More information is added to the Internet and the World Wide Web every day. More and more, we are faced with issues regarding access and management of that information. The Web was originally developed for human legibility and interpretation, but if we could automate our access and management activities, our interactions with the Web would become and remain more meaningful.

- Web searchers and publishers face ambiguity, content screening, information overload, nonstandard technologies, and other issues listed in this chapter. The introduction of standard metadata (machine understandable data about Web resources) to our Web documents would alleviate or, at least, mitigate some of the issues. Metadata is not a new concept; it has been around for years. However, a standard framework for using it would be beneficial.
- Predecessors to RDF were the metadata-related PICS specifications, the first of which were approved in 1996. In 1997, the W3C chartered its Metadata Activity after it recognized that metadata development was common to PICS and other Web-related initiatives. The primary work of the W3C's Metadata Activity became the development of the RDF.
- RDF development was influenced by several events, such as PICS, metadata and push technology proposals to the W3C and others, and communities of Web-oriented individuals and organizations. A first public draft of RDF appeared in October 1997. The W3C Recommendation was endorsed in February 1999.
- RDF is a declarative language that provides a standard method for using XML-related components and syntax to represent metadata in the form of statements that describe Web resources. RDF is more generalized than PICS, with more potential for developing expressions. As a mechanism that allows precise descriptions of data or information, RDF lets Web documents rise from machine-readable to machine-processable, if not machine-understandable.
- RDF can be used in many application areas. As RDF continues to develop, and as more Web-oriented organizations adopt it, they will realize an expanded and more efficient information highway and marketplace.
- RDF has caused many to rethink the role of URIs. They can no longer be considered only Web page addresses. They will be a key to defining resources on the Web, even when the resources may not be directly retrieved on the Web. So URIs will need to be properly constructed and should remain stable longer than they have in the past. The responsibility for creating and maintaining stable URIs falls to the resource owner or administrator.
- As more Web proponents adopt the RDF metadata framework, the Web will more closely resemble the Semantic Web envisioned by the W3C. Data structures and Web search agents will become smarter as Web pages evolve into Web services.

- RDF uses its statements (also called assertions and triples) to describe resources. The statements are enclosed within <Description> elements, which are nested within the root <RDF> data instance element. The statements are called triples, because they contain and define relationships among a resource's subject, predicate, and object. The subject is identified in the start tag of the <Description> element. The predicate and object appear in each property element.
- RDF graphs (also called node-and-arc diagrams) are handy for RDF document design, analysis, and troubleshooting. However, they have strict syntax and conventions. There are several implementations that can create them from RDF code.
- Several metadata initiatives can make RDF coding easier and help us to create standard documents that can be accessed and understood by search agents.
- In the latter part of the chapter, we introduced some shortcuts and workarounds. More are located at the W3C RDF Recommendation Web site at www.w3.org/TR/REC-rdf-syntax/.

Review Questions

1. Ultimately, we want Web data to be
   a. Machine-accessible
   b. Machine-processible
   c. Machine-understandable
   d. All of the above
   e. None of the above
2. Which of the following are issues faced by Web publishers and Web searchers?
   a. Ambiguity
   b. Cultural semantic problems
   c. Nonstandard query technologies
   d. Nonstandard metadata
   e. All of the above
3. True or false? RDF introduced metadata as the solution to the issues faced by Web publishers and searchers.
4. Which of the following was a precursor to RDF?
   a. CDF
   b. PICS
   c. DSig
   d. P3P
   e. PPCLI
   f. None of the above
5. The <Description> element start tag identifies
   a. Subject
   b. Object
   c. Predicate
   d. Named property
   e. Statement

6. The predicate and object of a statement are found in which element?
   a. <propertyelementname>
   b. <RDF>
   c. <Description>
   d. <Object>
   e. <Resource>
7. Which metadata initiative is used by the publishing industry?
   a. XPackage
   b. PRISM
   c. Dublin Core
   d. PICS
   e. None of the above
8. Which <Description> attribute provides the identity of the subject resource?
   a. rdf:aboutEach
   b. rdf:RDF
   c. rdf:type
   d. rdf:resource
   e. None of the above
9. True or false? All statements describing a resource do not have to be contained within the same <Description> element.
10. To abbreviate RDF syntax, we change property elements into
   a. <Description> elements
   b. <Description> attributes
   c. <RDF> attributes
   d. <Resource> attributes
   e. None of the above

Answers to Review Questions

1. **c.** The others are lesser in status. Our Web search results are already machine-accessible.
2. **e.** All of these are common issues.
3. False. RDF introduces a standard metadata framework.
4. **b.** PICS was also an influence on RDF development.
5. **a.** This is mentioned in the section titled *Resource Descriptions Are Nested within <Description> Elements*.
6. **a.** The predicate is identified in the tags of the property elements, whose names are arbitrarily chosen by the Web page document designer.
7. **b.** The metadata initiatives are described in the section titled *The <RDF> Root Element, Namespaces, and Content Models*.
8. **e.** None of the above. The actual answer is rdf: about.
9. True. It is not an error to describe a resource with more than one <Description> element. The number of such elements are left to the developer's discretion.
10. **b.** This is discussed in the *Abbreviating RDF* section.

CHAPTER 14 CDF

This chapter introduces the Channel Definition Format language (CDF). In its March 1997 (specification) Submission request to the W3C, Microsoft defined CDF as "an open specification that permits a Web publisher to offer frequently updated collections of information. . .for automatic delivery to compatible receiver programs on PCs or other information appliances."

CDF gives a Web site owner the ability to provide information, usually updated information, to end-user subscribers on a periodic basis. Web site developers can create CDF documents that manipulate, combine, or condense their information, and then deliver that information on request or, preferably, on a regular schedule. The CDF documents are then affiliated with Web page documents.

After introducing some basic broadcasting and webcasting concepts, this chapter takes two approaches to CDF:

- It shows you the end user's side of CDF services. You'll see that channels of information function like TV or radio channels. After you tune in and download information, you can read or manipulate it immediately in real time or even later, when you're offline.

- Then the chapter shows you the CDF/XML developer's side of CDF the same way other chapters introduce XML-related applications: by explaining and demonstrating the use of its main components. You'll see how it's similar and different from the other languages described so far in this book.

By the end of this chapter, you'll know the following:

- How, as a user, to determine which channels your browser was configured, by default, to subscribe to.
- How to subscribe to new channels.
- How, as Web publishers, we can create CDF documents that allow others to subscribe to our Web sites.

After CDF first appeared in 1997, it became popular quickly. However, its popularity among Web publishers has tapered off. In fact, few Web sites provide CDF-related push subscriptions anymore. Yet the push capability is still there, and the CDF-related user pull functions (we explain push and pull technologies in the next section) in the Internet Explorer browser are still available and valuable, and have actually been imitated by other browsers.

Basic Communication Concepts

We start off by listing a few basic communication concepts, to show you the context that channels and CDF work in and adjacent to.

We are surrounded by mass-communication media; most have become second nature to us. So the applications of the following terms should be familiar even if, at first, the terms themselves are not:

Push technology. Data and information are broadcast without particular regard to whether anyone is connected to the medium, although the broadcaster presumes that someone is. Push technology is the basis of radio and television broadcasting. In the IT world, email is similar. Messages are sent to individuals whether or not they are online, with the presumption that, at some point, the intended receivers will connect and download their messages. But the sender still recognizes that the message may not be received immediately, if at all.

Pull technology. A receiver sends a request for specific data or information to a specific address. The classic example is a telephone call: A code is sent, requesting a reply from the other end. The reply is likely to include the requested information. In the IT world, Web surfing is a common example of pull technology: An end user activates a Web browser application and sends a request to a specific location by inserting that location's URI/URL.

Webcasting. This IT-related concept, developed in the mid-1990s, is an example of push technology. Webcasting is an expansion of email concepts. Web-oriented organizations can use push technology for mass delivery of information, services, and advertising. Its enticement to end users is that, with webcasting, they can avoid much of the effort required to search for content. Users can subscribe to their favorite information suppliers, who, in turn, distribute Web site content to them directly and automatically on a regular schedule. The nature of the subscriptions differs from supplier to supplier. Some Web sites provide their products (that is, merchandise, services, or information) for free. Other Web sites charge for them. Some Web sites do both: They provide some products for free and charge for others.

Basic Webcasting and Managed Webcasting

Over the past few years, more and more end users and suppliers have come to depend on Internet webcasting to receive or deliver information, respectively. To them, webcasting has been a good development. If you have configured your browser's home page—the page that first displays when you start your browser—to msn.com, yahoo.com, a stock ticker, your favorite sports or entertainment Web site, a weather channel, or any of the millions of similar Web sites available to you, to some extent, you are depending on webcasting, too.

Basic webcasting uses a sitecrawler, which is a configurable set of dynamic link libraries that the browser accesses and then uses to:

- Examine information on Web pages to which the user subscribed
- Compare that information to similar information already stored on the end user's system for that Web site
- Decide whether to import the data from the Web site

Although this type of webcasting demonstrated progress compared to services that had been available before—that is, searching and comparing by the end users themselves—it still had several drawbacks:

- Configuration, although simple in concept, was complex and confusing for the average user.
- Users could not specify the actual types of information they wanted; the sitecrawler grabbed all the new and updated information. So, a lot of extra information, sometimes all the Web site's information, had to be downloaded to ensure that the users got what they wanted. Downloading too much information wasted resources and bandwidth.
- The Web site owner had no way to offer organized groups of information to users.

- The Web site could not instruct the user's system when to schedule updates, so users always struggled to stay current and could never be confident that they were current at any given time. To increase confidence, update schedules were (rarely) advertised on the Web site, and end users had to download manually at those times.
- Some Web sites disabled sitecrawling, because it caused excessive loading on their Web servers.
- Web site owners had limited control over site subscriptions and updating, because the end users were subscribing and doing the scheduling. Thus, the organizations had difficulty scheduling maintenance or optimizing their own intranet performance.

To address these issues, in 1997 Microsoft introduced, with Internet Explorer 4, concepts called Active Channels and the Active Desktop. The objective was to refine its webcasting technology by creating managed webcasting. To incorporate these concepts into IE 4, Microsoft developed the specification for the XML-related application and Channel Definition Format (CDF). The new managed webcasting, using CDF configuration documents that are affiliated with Web page documents, provides the following improvements over basic webcasting:

- Web site owners can specify which documents on their Web site are available for a user to subscribe to, which reduces network traffic. Plus, because this specification process determines the number of pages downloaded and stored on the subscriber's system for offline viewing, if the subscriber selects the offline viewing feature (discussed later in this chapter, in the section titled *Viewing a Channel Offline*), it also minimizes the hard disk space required at the subscriber's end.
- The owner can also provide a structured view of its Web site content to make navigation easier and faster.
- Subscriber update schedules can be restricted to coincide with Web site content updates, or to take place during times of lower network loading.
- Web site owners can convert an existing Web site to managed webcasting without having to overhaul the Web site completely. The only new requirement is the addition of a CDF file.

What Are Channels?

To paraphrase the Microsoft definition, channels are prescribed collections of information that Web publishers broadcast from their standard Web servers to compatible receiving applications on end-user systems or other information-processing appliances. Those information collections can contain anything from individual pieces of data to the content of the whole Web site. Web servers are defined in Chapter 2, "Setting Up Your XML Working Environment," but a standard Web server is commonly defined as any Web server that uses the HTTP 1.0 or later protocol to broadcast its messages.

Channels usually involve the automatic delivery of frequently updated collections, according to a schedule prescribed by the end user or the Web site publisher/administrator, after the end user has visited the Web site at least once and, while there, has chosen to receive updates. Thereafter, the users don't need to return to the source Web sites and initiate update requests. In other words, the end user chooses to become a subscriber to the Web site, whether the subscription is provided free of charge or for a fee. As a subscriber, the user automatically receives periodic updates of the Web site's collections of materials or other services.

In the case of CDF, a compatible program is any program that implements processing and retrieving content as specified by the CDF specification.

Classroom Q & A

Q: In later versions of Internet Explorer, for example, Version 6, I don't see a reference to channels under Favorites in the menu bar. And Netscape doesn't mention channels. So are channels just another word for favorites, or bookmarks?

A: Some users get confused with respect to channels versus favorites or bookmarks, which are similar but not identical concepts. There is a difference, even though IE appears to treat them similarly. When you add a favorite or bookmark, you are simply adding an Internet shortcut containing a Web page's URL to a file accessed by the browser, to save on user's memories and keystrokes. Favorites make it easy to access individual Web pages repeatedly.

When we add channels, however, we generally add a reference to more than one page at the same Web site, because we are creating a reference to a collection of information. We can enable your system to display the information while we are online, or we can download and store it so we can examine it (including links) when our system is offline. With IE we can also create a schedule for updating our copies of the Web site pages. Many channel definitions and prescriptions are facilitated, controlled, or restricted by CDF-related options configured by us or by Web site developers. Furthermore, we can configure Internet Explorer to notify us if and when updates are available. So channels are definitely different from the more ordinary favorites or bookmarks.

From a user's standpoint, the benefits of managed webcasting through the use of channels include the following:

- The ability to keep better track of sites they subscribe to
- The ability to receive notification when their channels or favorites have been updated
- The ability to review content on their systems on- or offline

At one time, Netscape offered only a primitive manual Web site/ bookmark checking utility. To be fair, it has recently begun to offer automatic, scheduled update searches. However, the Netscape utilities are still not as sophisticated as Microsoft channels.

The User's Side of CDF: Accessing Channels

As a quick and practical introduction to channels, we will perform two simple procedures: investigate which channels are currently available to us in Microsoft Internet Explorer and add a channel to that list.

The procedures provided in this chapter are applicable to Microsoft Internet Explorer Version 6 equipped with Service Pack 1. IE 5 referred to channels as channels, but IE 6 , for administrative purposes, doesn't. Version 6.0 still supports channels and CDF, but groups channels in with favorites, despite the differences between channels and favorites. With IE 6, administration and manipulation has been split between Favorites, Organize Favorites on the main tool bar, and the Favorites button on the toolbar beneath it. If you upgrade to IE 6, IE 6 will still respect any channels you created with earlier versions of IE. In fact, IE 6 will actually create a folder called Channels and install in that folder any channels created with previous IE versions. To create and administer channels with IE 6, use the procedures provided in this chapter. If you need further assistance, consult the instructions displayed in IE 6's Help, Contents and Index directory; you can find instructions by searching the index with the terms *channel* and *offline Web browsing*.

Investigating Available Channels

To see which channels are already available to you, you can use one of three methods:

- Click the Favorites button on the Internet Explorer menu bar. As demonstrated in the top of Figure 14.1, the drop-down menu displays any favorites. (Those favorites will be a mix of references to channel-related Web sites and bookmarklike Web sites.)
- Click the Favorites button on the button bar, which, as demonstrated in the bottom of Figure 14.1, opens the Favorites menu on the left side of the browser window. The Favorites menu is also called a Favorites bar or a Favorites Explorer bar. (In previous versions of IE, the word Channel was used instead of Favorites in these names.)
- Click the View button, scroll to the Explorer bar, and click Favorites, which results in the same view you see when you click the Favorites button.

With either display, if you want to surf to any favorites, all you have to do is scroll to the reference and click it. If at any time you don't want to see the Favorites bar in the browser window, click the Close button in its upper right corner.

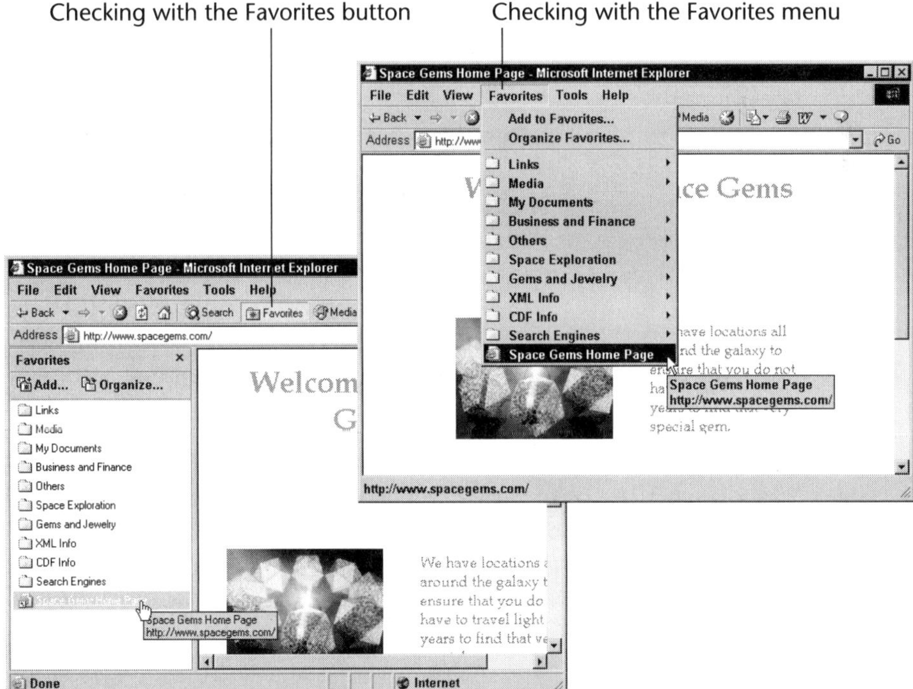

Figure 14.1 Investigating available channels.

These displays are typical of an installation of the full version of Internet Explorer 6. If you are using IE 4 or 5, or the upgrade version of IE 6, one of the folders displayed might actually be named Channels. Versions 4 and 5 provided access to specifically identified channels that came with the software and honored any existing channels that the user created with previous versions. The upgrade version of IE 6 also honors channels that were created with previous versions. The full version of IE6 does not honor previously created channels, although it allows you to create new ones. If you are using IE6 and you want to keep your channels in a separate folder from your Favorites, you can easily do so with the Organize Favorites function.

Remember that a channel, as displayed in Figure 14.1, can represent a single page, multiple pages, or the content of a whole Web site.

Adding a Web Site Channel to Your Favorites List

There are two ways to add a channel to your Favorites list: the hard way and the easy way. The hard way has to be used when a Web site publisher doesn't facilitate the process by creating the appropriate CDF documents. Use the easy way when the CDF documents are in place and a proper channel creation button is provided. First, let's look at the hard way.

Adding a Channel from a Web Site That Does Not Provide a CDF Subscription

Adding a new channel to your Favorites list when the Web site publisher doesn't use CDF is a little more involved than when CDF is used. Suppose you want to create a channel for the Space Gems Web site, which has no CDF installation. First, you surf to the Space Gems site. Now, as illustrated in Figure 14.2, with the Space Gems Web site displayed in the IE browser, follow these steps:

1. Click the Favorites button on the menu bar.
2. Scroll down, and click Add to Favorites.
3. When the Add Favorite dialog box opens, you can choose the following options:

   Make available offline. You select this check box because you want to make the channel available offline—that is, when your system is not connected to the Internet. This strategy can facilitate entertainment or research and can reduce the amount of time and expense involved in telephone line access, if applicable. The Web site synchronizes with your system and downloads its pages to the system cache. (Synchronizing is the process by which the latest version of the Web site's information is downloaded to your system, so that your information remains current.)

Name. Here you accept the Web site publisher's default name, Space Gems Home Page, as the name for your channel.

Create in. Here you select the folder named Gems and Jewelry to house your new Space Gems channel.

4. Click the Customize button to start the Offline Favorite Wizard.
5. The wizard prompts you to tell it whether you want to download Web site content to your system and if so, how much. This step makes the content available to you offline, and you can specify a schedule for synchronizing those offline pages with the pages on the Web site. Figure 14.3 illustrates the next three steps of the process.

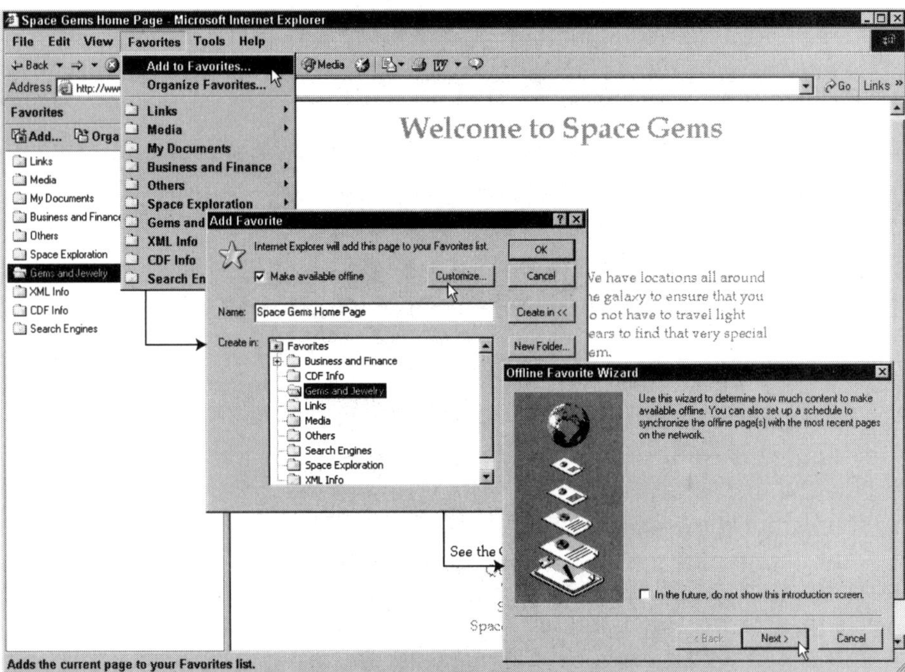

Figure 14.2 Adding a channel: The first two steps.

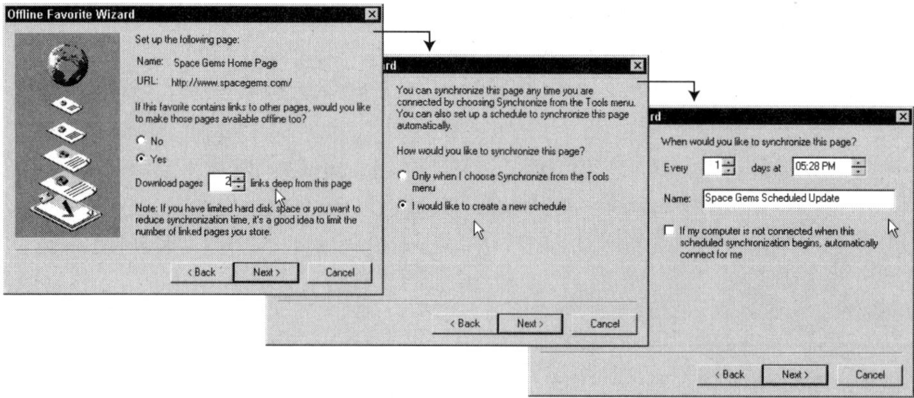

Figure 14.3 Adding a channel: Using the Offline Wizard.

6. In the next dialog box, you specify that, if the home page links to other pages, you want to download/synchronize them too. You specify that you only want to go two links deep into the Web site. This setting depends on the actual depth of the Web site, where the information you're interested in is located, and the size of your hard disk drive. Click Next.
7. Indicate that you want to specify a synchronization schedule, and click Next again. Then you state that that you want synchronization to occur every day at 5:28 P.M. and that this schedule is to be named Space Gems Synchronization Schedule.
8. Then click Next again. Figure 14.4 illustrates what happens next.

The last wizard dialog box asks whether you want to add some minimal authentication requirements. It's up to you, of course, but we selected the No option for simplicity and then clicked Finish to complete this configuration and return to the Add Favorite procedure. At this point, you verify where you want the channel to be installed and click OK. Then the browser begins its first synchronization procedure. (Watch closely; it usually happens quickly.) The application provides a synchronization status box and a Synchronization Complete notification. When everything is done, you are returned to your browser view of the Web site.

If you want to delete the channel, highlight the name of the channel in the Web browser's Favorites bar, right-click, and select Delete.

If you have used or added channels with a previous version of Internet Explorer on the same system, in the upgraded IE version, those channels are still listed in a Channels folder in the Favorites bar and menu.

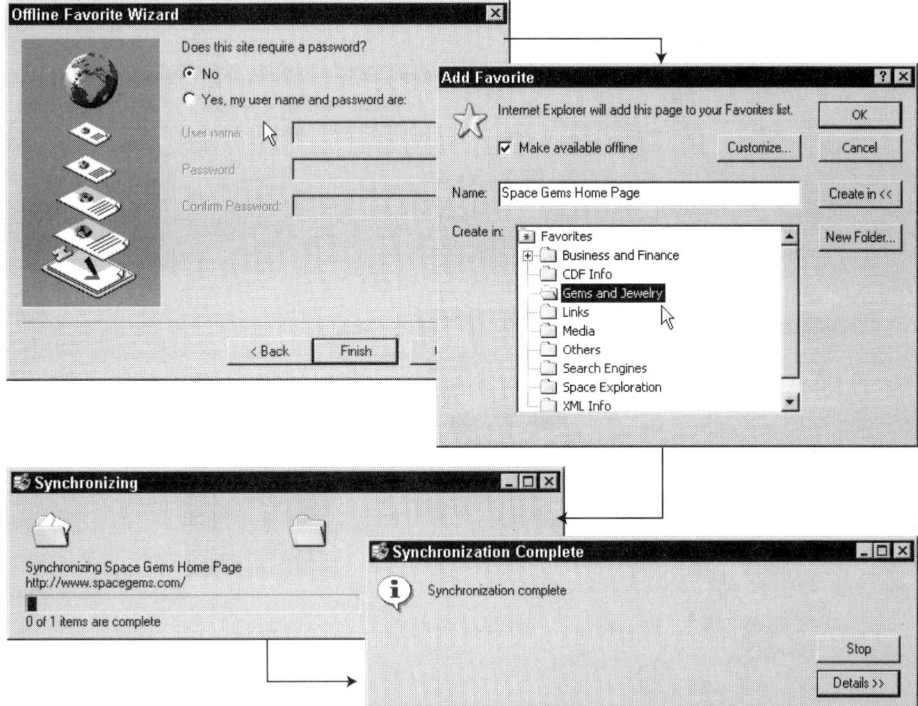

Figure 14.4 Adding a channel: Last steps.

Adding a Channel from a Web Site that Offers CDF Subscription

Adding a new channel when the Web site owner provides a CDF subscription process is less complicated than when the owner does not provide one.

There are two basic ways to make a channel available:

- Convert the main or primary link to the Web page into a CDF subscription file, so that the subscription is created automatically when a user clicks the link simply to visit the Web site.
- The alternative strategy is preferable, because it is more transparent and enables the end user to make a conscious choice: Place a Microsoft channel marker on the Web page so that the user can subscribe voluntarily.

Here's an example: Suppose you want to create a channel after you travel to the Space Gems Web site. Figure 14.5 illustrates the Space Gems home page and the IE Favorites bar prior to creating a channel for Space Gems.

Button that indicates creation of a channel

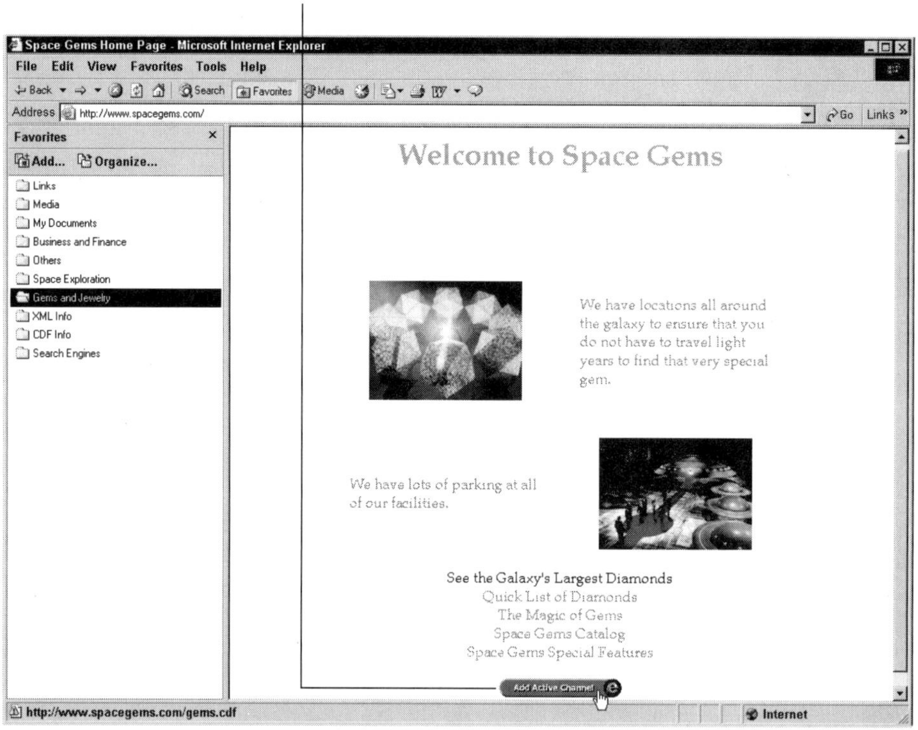

Figure 14.5 Channel creation button on Space Gems home page.

The Add Active Channel channel subscription link appears at the bottom of the page. On other sites, you may not see small logos. You might see a hyperlink, such as Subscribe to Our Channel. Either way, the link is located in an <A> tag in the Web page document that refers to the appropriate CDF file. Just by clicking the link, you accomplish what it took several channel wizard boxes to do in the previous section. Look at Figure 14.6, which illustrates what happens after the Add Active Channel button has been clicked. You are presented with the Add Favorites dialog box. If you don't select any options, the process and results are simplified to exactly what is shown in Figure 14.6. Notice that all the designated Space Gems Web pages have now been added to the Favorites bar.

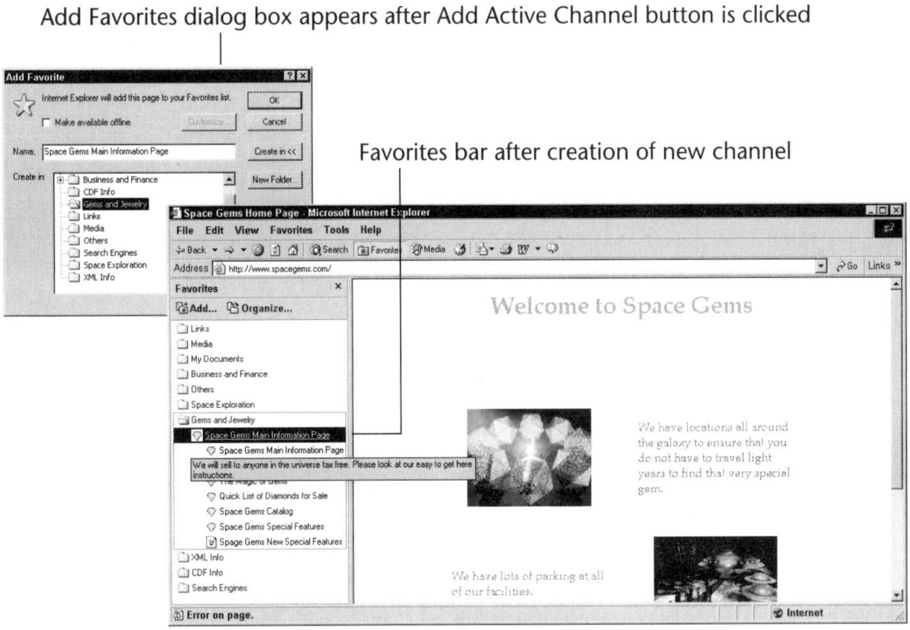

Add Favorites dialog box appears after Add Active Channel button is clicked

Favorites bar after creation of new channel

Figure 14.6 Space Gems channel has been added to Favorites bar.

If you don't want the Favorites bar to appear, click the Close button in its upper right corner.

Besides the Space Gems Web site at www.spacegems.com, you can surf to several other CDF-related Web sites that offer channel subscriptions:

- The Wired Channel at http://hotwired.lycos.com/livewired/intro/index.html
- CNN Interactive at http://channels.cnn.com/intro/index.htm
- ZDNet, the Computing Channel at www1.zdnet.com/datafeed/ie4/channels/zdnet/cached/index.htm
- National Geographic at www.nationalgeographic.com/connection/cdrom/INDEX.HTM
- Epicurious Food and Travel at www.epicurious.com/channels/intro/page/intro.htm
- MSNBC at www.msnbc.com/tools/channel/guide/intro.asp

To investigate the push aspects of these Web sites, we suggest you hurry. Web publishers are altering them constantly. However, from a pull standpoint, you can experiment with almost any Web site.

Channel Synchronization: Setup and Activation

The previous sections discussed how to select and install channels on your Favorites bar. You also learned about making your channels available for offline viewing and specifying synchronization schedules. This section discusses setting up and activating manual synchronization and other forms of automatic synchronization. If you intend to view channel material offline, it is a best practice to synchronize the channel manually prior to actually going offline. The synchronization procedure is depicted in Figure 14.7.

If you have already configured the synchronization setup, the synchronization procedure is easy: Click Tools on the Internet Explorer browser's menu bar; then scroll down and click Synchronize. When the Items to Synchronize dialog box appears, you need to check that your chosen channel is selected and if it is, click Synchronize. You then see the Synchronization (status) and Synchronization Complete boxes.

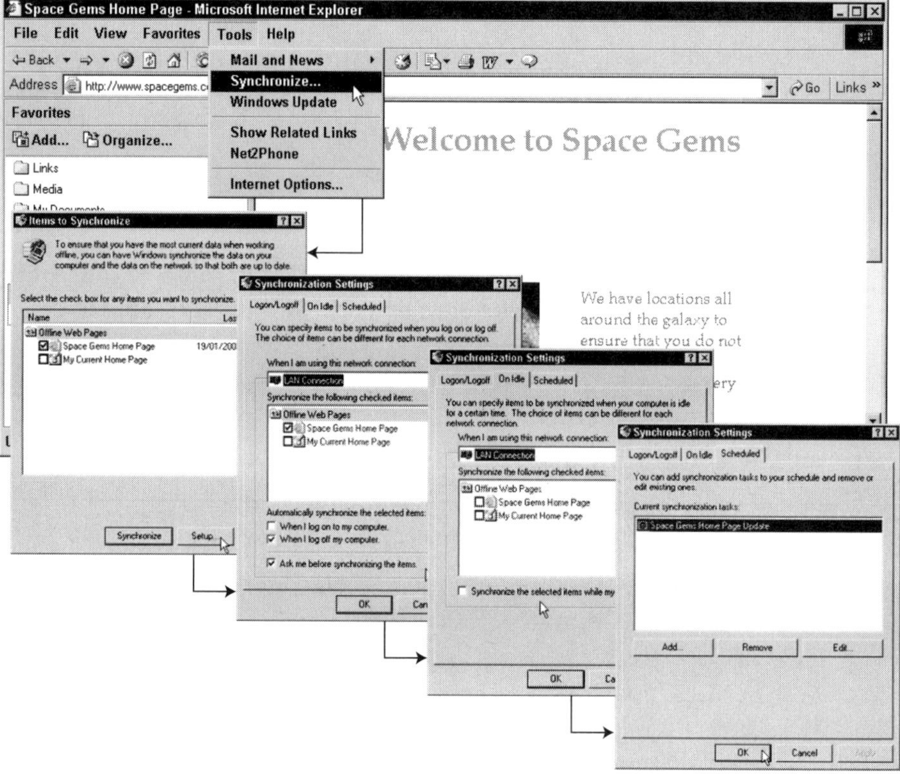

Figure 14.7 Making a channel available for offline viewing later.

If your synchronization has not yet been set up, the procedure is slightly more involved. Click Tools on the menu bar, and then click Synchronize. The Items to Synchronize dialog box appears. You select the Web channels you want to synchronize and click the Setup button. You then see the Synchronization Settings box, which contains three tabs:

Logon/Logoff. You can choose the channels on which network connections and synchronization are to occur, and whether they should occur when you log on to your system, log off from it, or both. You can also select whether the application should prompt you before synchronization begins.

On Idle. Again, you can select which channels to synchronize and whether synchronization should occur when the system is idle for any length of time.

Scheduled. On this tab, you make adjustments (including deletions) to the channels whose synchronization schedules you've already created, or you can create new ones.

After you finish the setup, you are returned to the Items to Synchronize dialog box. Now, for example, you could select one or more channels to synchronize, and then click Synchronize. You are then free to shut down the browser. Later, you can activate the browser offline and still examine the version of the channel to which you synchronized.

Viewing a Channel Offline

To read an offline version of one of your channels, start Internet Explorer, click File, and scroll down and click Work Offline. None of the normal hyperlinks will function. If you try them, you get a dialog box that states that the Web page you requested is not available offline. To view this page, click Connect. After the message, you can click Connect or Stay Offline.

To read the offline version of a channel, use one of the methods mentioned earlier to list the favorites. Scroll to the name of the channel you want and click it. The channel appears in the browser window just like it would if you were surfing online, except that its content might be restricted depending on the configuration you selected, or the configuration created by the Web site publisher, which would override your preferences. For example, you may have all or just a little of the original linking functionality.

If you select the Work Offline feature in your browser, you remain offline when you activate the browser until you click File, Work Offline to remove the check mark next to that selection. If you don't do so, the browser keeps that setting. If you try to surf, you are confronted with the message mentioned in this section that the site you are requesting is not available.

Development of the CDF Specification

Earlier in this chapter, we listed several issues that led to the development of new types of push webcasting technologies. Microsoft submitted its proposal for the Channel Definition Format specification to the W3C in March 1997. The CDF specification defined CDF as an XML-related push webcasting language and then specified definitions for CDF's elements and attributes, as well as DTD declarations for those components. Its proponents believed that the CDF specification document would be reviewed, discussed, and further developed by W3C members, and then it would become the Internet standard. However, in the same year, the W3C received two other push technology proposals: the Open Software Description Format (OSD) and the HTTP Distribution and Replication Protocol (DRP). They shared several common themes: the use of channels, the use of meta data, and multicasting over the IP protocol, among others. As a result of the three proposals and a Push Technology Workshop the W3C conducted in September 1997, all the proposals were given W3C Note status.

The W3C then stated that any subsequent W3C Metadata Activity would focus on a common framework approach to address the combined needs of all proponent groups and to create a single format that might enhance push technology. Ultimately, the W3C Metadata Activity produced the Resource Description Framework Model and Syntax Specification (RDF), which provides a more general treatment of metadata and achieved W3C Recommendation status in February 1999. (An RDF schema specification became a W3C Recommendation later, in March 2000.) These were discussed in Chapter 13.

Meanwhile, true to its policy regarding Notes, the W3C did not pursue further development of the CDF or the other similar proposals. However, Microsoft continued to develop CDF by adding more elements and attributes, so that it would provide additional functionality and work with newer versions of the Internet Explorer browser.

CDF Resources

Among all the good CDF resources found on the World Wide Web, including some good tutorials, we think the following provide the most comprehensive information:

- The Microsoft Note submitted to the W3C, containing the CDF Specification, at www.w3.org/TR/NOTE-CDFsubmit.html. This is the site that also contains the DTD declarations for the significant elements and attributes.
- The W3C site, www.w3.org/submission/1997/2/Overview.html, contains a copy of the Microsoft submission of CDF to the W3C, as well as its request that the submission be adopted as a W3C standard.

- CDF Version 0.4, which is Microsoft's suggested revision to Channel Definition Format (CDF), is located at http://msdn.microsoft.com/library/default.asp?url=/workshop/delivery/cdf/reference/channels.asp. This Web site has a comprehensive list of elements for the various Microsoft CDF applications: Microsoft Active Channel, Microsoft Active Desktop items, and Software Update Channels.
- A downloadable automatic CDF generator is available at http://msdn.microsoft.com/downloads/samples/internet/default.asp?url=/Downloads/samples/Internet/browsertools/cdfgen/default.asp. The Microsoft CDF Generator is an easy-to-use tool for creating CDF files. It has a graphical interface that does not require previous knowledge of channels. It supports all CDF tags and UTF-8 encoding and can also be used for testing, because it parses the CDF files and detects the errors. Also, there is a tutorial and reference for the CDF generator at http://msdn.microsoft.com/library/default.asp?url=/workshop/delivery/cdf/reference/CDF.asp.

Channel Definition Format: A Definition

We have already discussed the end user's experience with channels and the development of the Channel Definition Format (CDF) as one solution to the issues posed by early webcasting technology. In this section, we look a little more closely at the specification itself and its functionality.

The Channel Definition Format (CDF) is an XML-related language that provides Web site publishers with the capability to deliver all or part of a Web site's information automatically to subscribing end users. The ability of a Web publisher to provide specific collections of information regularly and automatically in the form of channels reflects the smart-push aspect of managed webcasting with CDF. The ability of an end user to subscribe to, synchronize, and review the information online or offline reflects the smart-pull aspects.

A Web site publisher uses specialized CDF elements and attributes to define information groupings into channels, subchannels, and other constituent items. Other specialized elements enable subscribers to configure the scheduling for updating/synchronizing the channels. A channel can be designed as a single page, multiple pages, or the content of a whole Web site and can be distributed from any Web server that supports the HTTP protocol. In a way, channels are similar in nature to specialized TV or radio channels, or specialized magazines and newspapers. After channels are created, we need only click a link to subscribe to the owner's Web site. We can then download the information prescribed in the CDF file that defines the channel. We have only to select and configure a channel once. After that, information is delivered, according to the specified schedule without any more intervention, unless we choose to intervene, cancel, or otherwise modify the nature of the information to be delivered or the delivery schedule.

CDF differs from most XML-related languages in two major ways:

- There is no universal DTD for it, so its documents need only be well formed and not necessarily valid. However, individual Web publishers can create their own validity documents to test against for validity.
- The CDF specification is presently (only) a W3C Note, with no realistic prospect of ever becoming a W3C Recommendation. Nevertheless, Microsoft continues to develop and refine CDF, just as it continues to develop successive versions of IE.

Additionally, CDF enables automatic user notification when Web site content changes. It has what are called "other data operations" too: the ability to search, index, profile, filter, and personalize content.

When downloaded to an end user's browser, CDF channels resemble local links to and indexes of remote resources. They are links that, if you are online (in other words, if you are connected to the Web), can take you directly to the Web site source. If you are not online but are using the offline browser options, you can configure your channels to display their content whenever you want to, even if you are not connected to the Web, as long as your system was given an opportunity to go on online and download the information to your hard disk.

The Publisher's Side of CDF: Creating CDF Channels

So far, we have examined channels from a user's standpoint. Now let's examine CDF from the Web publisher's side to see how channels are created and added to Web sites.

We stated earlier that a channel is a collection of information, commonly considered to be specific Web pages within one Web site. We can put the specifications for any single channel in one CDF document, which is an XML-related document, or we can create hierarchies of channels and subchannels within one CDF document. In fact, you may have noticed that in your list of example (surviving) Web sites that provide the opportunity to create channels by using the Add Active Channel buttons, the CDF files are often the files that appear in the Web site URL. The CDF document is separate from other Web pages but is usually linked to one of the Web pages.

The CDF files also provide means for Web publishers to specify Web page document titles, URLs, content, description, browser and desktop icons, user traffic logging, the creation of a schedule for updating and synchronization, and additional functionality. They also provide the capability for end users to subscribe to a channel, as well as other features, such as authentication and other personalization features, that are beyond the introductory level of this book.

If you intend to create channels, here is the general strategy:

1. Design the channel.
2. If you will be using customized logo images instead of the default images, you have to create the logo images first.
3. Create the actual CDF file, reflecting your design.
4. Post the CDF file so that it will be publicly accessible when end users choose to subscribe to the corresponding channel.
5. Create some means to make the channel available for subscription by the user community.

In the next few sections, we discuss the steps in more detail.

Designing the Channel

Our first and arguably most important step is determining the structure of the channel(s) and the hierarchy of subchannels, items, and other functions within it. The design could, but doesn't have to, reflect the structure of an existing Web site. The design may even consist of just a sample of the Web site's content and can also have a different hierarchy. Figure 14.8 illustrates the relationship between a Web site, a channel definition document, and the view that appears in the browser of an end user who subscribes to the channel.

The Web site structure is indicated in the diagram at the top. (The connecting lines indicate various hyperlinks among the documents.) The corresponding channel definition document, named gems.cdf, is shown on the lower left. Its top-level channel calls for one document—in this case, the home page document—and its seven subchannels call for various pages located at various link levels in the Web site. The documents referenced in the gems.cdf channel definition document are shaded for illustration. Notice that, after the relevant documents have been specified in the CDF file, other documents that are not referenced remain in the Web site. They are displayed when you surf to the Web site online but do not form part of the channel definition. So they will not appear if you download the channel and examine it offline. On the bottom right side of the figure is a depiction of a browser window belonging to an end user who has subscribed to the channel. In the browser's Favorites bar, on the left of the window, you can see how the channel and the items are referenced.

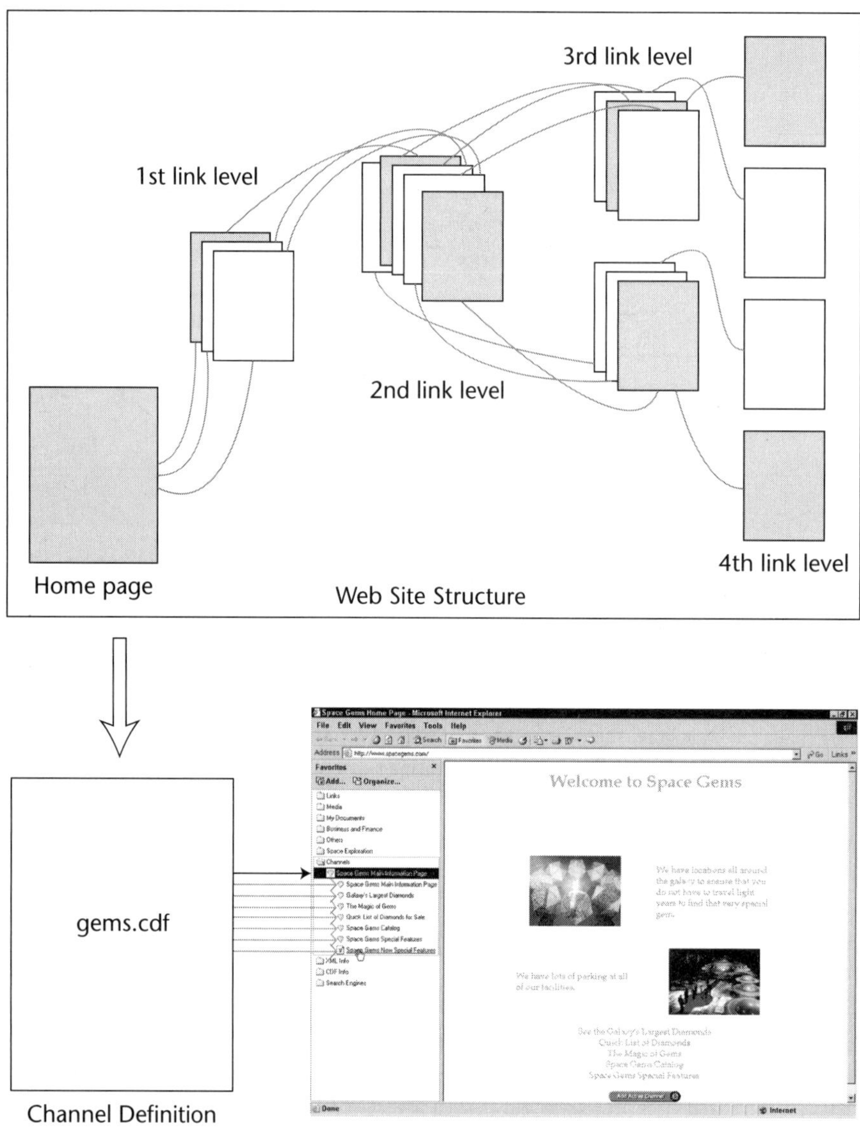

Figure 14.8 Simplified channel development schematic.

The structure of the channel is created in the CDF file using one or more <channel> elements that represent the major segments—that is, the top-level channel and other subchannels, if you choose to use subchannels—and usually more <item> elements. All these components form the hierarchy within the <channel>. When designing channels, observe the following best practices:

- Microsoft recommends that a channel should have no more than eight total subitems in the first level. We agree. If you follow these suggestions, you prevent subscribers from being overwhelmed with information and images, provide a uniform look and feel among your channels, and conserve bandwidth while minimizing download delays.
- You should create and use your own unique logo images with channels and items. Early versions of IE didn't provide any default logos, but later versions do. But the default logos should be replaced by logos more appropriate to your Web site and channels.
- Consider inserting a <schedule> element in the file, so that as the Web site owner, you maintain control over updates and synchronization.

Creating Logo Images

Web publishers should create and use appropriate images for their channel and item logos. However, Internet Explorer 4.0 and later provides default images wherever necessary.

You can place various types and sizes of logo images in several locations in a channel's user interface, for example, in the Favorites bar in the browser, in the Favorites menu, and on the Active Desktop. To do so, we recommend observing Microsoft's logo dimension and other requirements. These requirements are listed in the discussion of the <logo> element, later in this chapter.

The Logical Structure of a CDF Document

After we design our channel and create logo images, we can create the channel definition document, which we'll also refer to as the CDF document or CDF file. Because CDF is an XML-related application, it is important to remember that the CDF document must observe XML's stringent vocabulary and structural rules as discussed throughout the earlier chapters of this book.

CDF files contain a prolog and a root element called <channel>. The other elements that make up the CDF file are nested within the top-level <channel> element. We discuss the logical structure requirements in the next few sections.

The Prolog

It is mandatory to include a prolog in a CDF document. The prolog could be as simple as a one-line XML declaration, or it could contain the XML declaration, a document type declaration, and one or more comments.

A document type declaration, if included, contains a reference to an XML DTD that you develop on your own. There is no official publicly posted DTD or schema for CDF, as there is for other XML-related languages. Therefore, integrated development environment applications and other editors are not likely to be able to validate CDF files automatically without having been provided with DOCTYPE declarations and URIs that point to those validation documents.

If you intend to create your own validation documents, you can get a head start by examining the declarations for the early-version CDF elements and attributes in the original specification submission to the W3C at www.w3.org/TR/NOTE-CDFsubmit.html. You can adopt or adapt those declarations into your own DTD (or schema, if you want to do the converting) file and add declarations for your unique custom elements or attributes.

The <channel> Element

The <channel> element performs two functions:

- A <channel> element is used as the top-level (or root) element.
- Each channel or subchannel definition must be contained within its own <channel> element. In other words, the full definition of the channel (its title, description, schedule information, and other associated items) must fall between the corresponding <channel> tags.

A CDF document can contain one or more channel definitions. If it contains more than one channel definition, each must be enclosed within its own <channel> element. Channels can thus be nested within other channels. The child channels are called subchannels and are subordinate to the parent channel in which they are nested. The top-level <channel> element in a document has no parent element, but subchannel <channel> elements have a <channel> element as a parent.

Table 14.1 lists the attributes we can use with the <channel> element. Remember that all attribute values must be enclosed in quotation marks, even if the value is a number.

If we use more than one mechanism (for example, BASE and HREF) to specify a URL for a channel and the URLs contradict one another, IE applies the following precedence:

1. The HREF attribute found in the start tag of the <channel> element.
2. The HREF attribute specified in the start tag of an <A> (anchor) element that has been inserted as an immediate child of the <channel> element, if one has been inserted.

Thus, CDF document developers must be aware of their options. They must be precise in the selection of the location of the HREF attribute. If we want one to appear in an <A> element, the HREF specification should not appear in any parent <channel> element of the <A> element.

Table 14.1 <Channel> Element Attributes

ATTRIBUTE NAME	EXPLANATION
BASE	Optional. Specifies the base URL for the channel and is used to resolve the relative URLs specified in <item> and <channel> elements contained within the same channel or subchannel. Inheritance is downward only, not across to other sibling subchannels nor upward. BASE attributes in a subchannel supersede those in parent channels from that point downward. When specifying, ensure that it ends with a trailing / to avoid confused pathing.
HREF	Optional. Value is also a URL. Specifies which Web page will be displayed in the browser when the channel is selected. Optional because the same URL could also be specified in a child <A> element. If a BASE attribute specification has been specified in a parent element, BASE is inherited, and then the HREF only has to be a relative path. If no BASE has been specified, the HREF URL must be an absolute address.
LASTMOD	Optional. Provides the date and time, in terms of Greenwich Mean Time, when the page referenced by the HREF attribute was last modified. Allows the channel's end user to determine whether the content has changed since the last download. Updates are downloaded only if the date associated with the cached information is older than the LASTMOD value in the CDF file. The date format is yyyy-mm-ddThh:mm. The capital T must appear between the date and the time.
LEVEL	Optional. Specifies the number of levels (or links, if you prefer) deep that the client should site crawl and precaches the Web page content from the URL specified in the HREF attribute. Default is 0 (zero), meaning that the end user can only precache the data found at the URL specified in the <channel>, along with any images it uses. If the URL page contains frames, all content inside the frames is retrieved. The maximum number is three. Remember the structure of the target Web site. If there are many links, even low numbers can create excessive traffic and long download times.
PRECACHE	Optional. Specifies whether content is downloaded. Values: No (content will not be downloaded into the cache; value of the LEVEL attribute is subsequently ignored); Yes (default value; content will be downloaded only if the user has specified that it should be); Default (whatever the end user has specified is acceptable).
SELF	Optional. Added to the top-level channel, to indicate the location of the CDF file used for creating a channel subscription. This attribute is unnecessary and is deprecated. Only supported by newer versions for backward compatibility.

Other CDF Elements

There are two basic varieties of child elements within <channel> elements:

- Those that can occur only once per <channel> element. Examples: <A>, <abstract>, <log>, <login>, <logo>, <logtarget>, <schedule>, and <title>.
- Those that can occur one or more times. Examples: <channel>, <item>, and <softpkg>.

Figure 14.9 illustrates the hierarchical structure and syntax for a sample CDF document.

This CDF document contains one top-level channel that contains three subchannels. The third subchannel contains three <item> elements.

Figure 14.10 demonstrates what we see in the Favorites bar inside an IE browser window if we created a channel structured similar to the document in Figure 14.9.

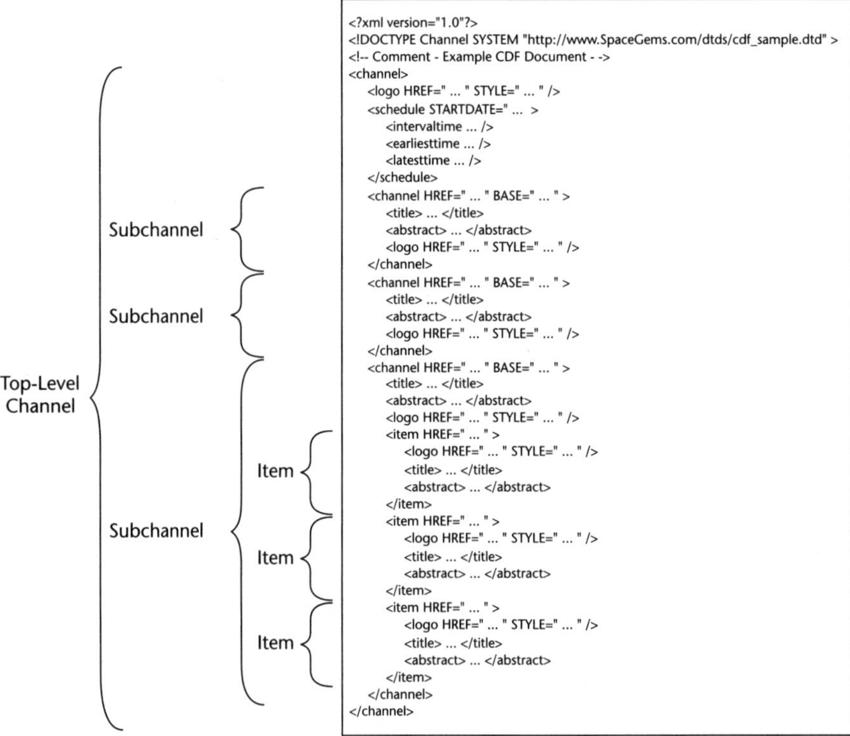


```
<?xml version="1.0"?>
<!DOCTYPE Channel SYSTEM "http://www.SpaceGems.com/dtds/cdf_sample.dtd" >
<!-- Comment - Example CDF Document - ->
<channel>
  <logo HREF=" ... " STYLE=" ... " />
  <schedule STARTDATE=" ... >
    <intervaltime ... />
    <earliesttime ... />
    <latesttime ... />
  </schedule>
  <channel HREF=" ... " BASE=" ... " >
    <title> ... </title>
    <abstract> ... </abstract>
    <logo HREF=" ... " STYLE=" ... " />
  </channel>
  <channel HREF=" ... " BASE=" ... " >
    <title> ... </title>
    <abstract> ... </abstract>
    <logo HREF=" ... " STYLE=" ... " />
  </channel>
  <channel HREF=" ... " BASE=" ... " >
    <title> ... </title>
    <abstract> ... </abstract>
    <logo HREF=" ... " STYLE=" ... " />
    <item HREF=" ... " >
      <logo HREF=" ... " STYLE=" ... " />
      <title> ... </title>
      <abstract> ... </abstract>
    </item>
    <item HREF=" ... " >
      <logo HREF=" ... " STYLE=" ... " />
      <title> ... </title>
      <abstract> ... </abstract>
    </item>
    <item HREF=" ... " >
      <logo HREF=" ... " STYLE=" ... " />
      <title> ... </title>
      <abstract> ... </abstract>
    </item>
  </channel>
</channel>
```

Figure 14.9 A simplified CDF document.

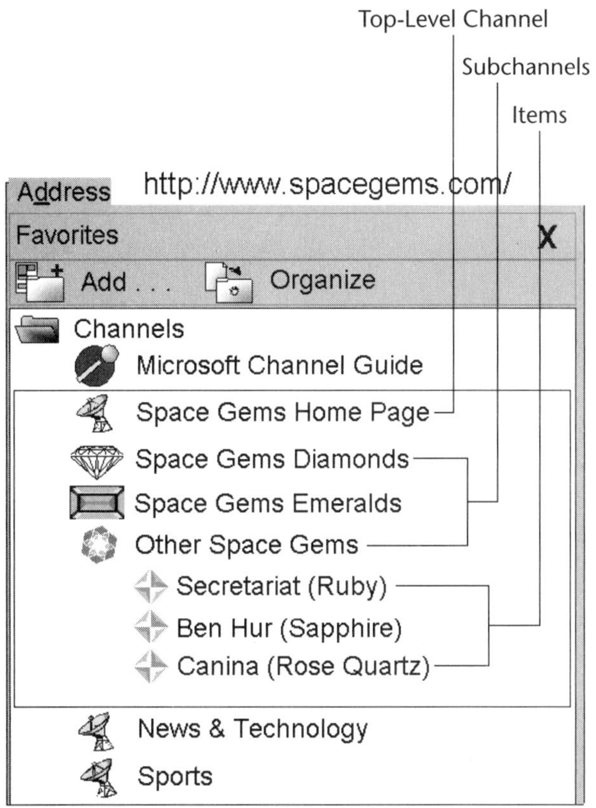

Figure 14.10 Favorites bar version of channel defined in previous CDF file.

From Figure 14.10, we would presume that the top-level channel is called Space Gems Home Page. The three subchannels would be called Space Gems Diamonds, Space Gems Emeralds, and Other Space Gems. The three items that would be displayed if you clicked the Other Space Gems subchannel, as apparently someone has done in Figure 14.10, are called Secretariat (Ruby), Ben Hur (Sapphire), and Canina (Rose Quartz).

Now we'll discuss the other elements and attributes that are valuable to the creation of CDF files. Depending on your ultimate intentions for your channels and the associated CDF files, you will include some and exclude others. Some CDF files, for example, may be intended for Microsoft-related webcasting, such as Active Desktop channels or software update channels, which we will not discuss in this introductory-level chapter. The elements you use depend on the values you specify for the <usage> element.

<A>

The <A> element defines a hyperlink. Its only attribute is the mandatory HREF, whose value is the URL to be associated with the parent element, which can be a <channel> or <item> element. <A> has no child elements. We discuss other <A> element implications in the section pertaining to the <item> element.

The <A> element is also important to the Web page document that contains the CDF file. In the <body> element of the Web page document, the CDF file is specified as the value of an HREF attribute in the document's <A> element.

<abstract>

When a mouse pointer pauses over a <channel> or <item> title, Internet Explorer displays the content specified within the <abstract> element in the respective <channel> element. On-screen, in the browser window, the content appears in a shaded box called a ToolTip (some call it a ScreenTip) that appears briefly and then disappears. Figure 14.11 shows us an example of a ToolTip that appears as the mouse pointer hovers over the Space Gems Main Information Channel in the Favorites bar.

The <abstract> element can be used as a child element of the <channel>, <implementation>, <item>, and <softpkg> elements. <abstract> has no child elements of its own. At one time, <abstract> was an attribute of <channel>, but it became its own element with CDF Version 0.4. The only attribute for <abstract> is the optional XML-SPACE, whose value specifies how white space is to be treated in the ToolTip. Possible values for XML-SPACE are Default, which permits white space to be filtered out during file processing, and Preserve, which ensures all white-space characters are retained.

Figure 14.11 ToolTip example.

<schedule>

The <schedule> element, with the help of other related elements, allows us to define an update/synchronization schedule—that is, how often, and during what time period, the channel should be updated. The parent element of <schedule> is <channel>. Child elements of <schedule> are <start>, <end>, <intervaltime>, <earliesttime>, and <latesttime>.

<schedule> has three optional attributes:

STARTDATE. The date on which the schedule is to take effect; specified in yyyy-mm-dd.

STOPDATE. The date on which the schedule is no longer in effect; also specified in yyyy-mm-dd.

TIMEZONE. Values are expressed as +/- *zzzz*, where the *z*'s specify a time offset from GMT in hhmm. The plus or minus signs indicate whether the time specified is ahead (+) or behind (-) GMT. Values for TIMEZONE impact the child elements <earliesttime> and <latesttime>.

<intervaltime>

<intervaltime> specifies the length of time between channel updates. Its parent element is <schedule> and it has no child elements, although it is commonly coordinated with the sibling elements <earliesttime> and <latesttime>.

Its attributes are all optional:

DAY. The value is a nonzero number specifying the days between updates.

HOUR. Value is a nonzero number based on a 24-hour clock, specifying the number of hours, in addition to the value of DAY, that you have to wait before updating is allowed.

MIN. Value is a nonzero number specifying additional minutes that you have to wait before updating is allowed.

As indicated by the attributes and their values, the interval effects of the attributes are additive. Here is an example that specifies that the interval between updates will be 7 days, 12 hours, and 15 minutes:

```
<INTERVALTIME DAY="7" HOUR="12" MIN="15" />
```

<earliesttime>

The <earliesttime> element specifies the beginning of a valid range of time within which channel updates are allowed. Its parent element is also <schedule>, and it has no child elements. Its attributes are optional and include the following:

DAY. The value is a nonzero number specifying the day within the specified <intervaltime> that updates are allowed.

HOUR. The value is a nonzero number, based on the 24-hour clock, specifying the first hour within the <intervaltime> that updates can take place.

MIN. The value is a nonzero number specifying the first minute within the <intervaltime> that updates can take place.

<latesttime>

<latesttime> is similar to <earliesttime>. It specifies the end of a valid range of time during which channel updates are allowed. Its parent element is also <schedule>, and it also has no child elements.

Its attributes are identical in name and definition to those listed for <earliesttime>.

<item>

<item> defines a channel item, which is an additional, likely supplementary, information Web page document within the channel or subchannel. <item> elements enable you to build and fill a hierarchical structure of information within a channel. By structuring <channel> elements with <item> elements, a balance can be achieved between information provided and network traffic generated.

Information channels and their items will be listed in the end users' Favorites bars and Favorites menus in order according to the Web site publisher's designed hierarchy.

<item> has only one parent element: <channel>. But it has the following child elements: <A>, <abstract>, <channel>, <log>, <logo>, <title>, and <usage>. However, in any single <item> element, each child element can occur only once.

The <item> element has four attributes:

HREF. Specifies the URL—the Web page document—activated when the user clicks the channel item. This attribute is mandatory, with the following exception: When a child <A> element is nested within the <item> element, the <A> element will specify the URL. If traffic logging is desired, the URL cannot contain more than 255 characters. If and when this limitation threatens to cause a problem, consider adjusting the <channel> element's BASE attribute.

LASTMOD. This attribute is optional and, similar to its role with <channel>, specifies the last date and time, in terms of GMT, that the page specified by the HREF attribute was modified. The value for LASTMOD affects whether the URL referenced by the HREF attribute is downloaded. Again, the format for the LASTMOD specification is yyyy-mm-ddThh-mm. Again, don't forget the capital T between the date and the time.

LEVEL. This attribute is optional and specifies the number of levels (or links) deep within the channel URL that an end user's browser should site crawl to obtain and precache content. The default value is 0 (zero), specifying that the client browser can precache only on the page specified by the URL and the images it references, but not linked documents. However, if the URL contains frames, the client may also retrieve the content in them.

PRECACHE. Another optional attribute, this one specifies whether content is downloaded. Like the <channel> element, the available values are No (content will not be downloaded into the cache, and the value of the LEVEL attribute is subsequently ignored); Yes (the default value, whereby content will be downloaded only if the user has also specified that channel content should be downloaded); and Default, which specifies that whatever the end user has specified is acceptable.

Items specified in the CDF document by the Web publisher supersede any created by the end users with their Offline Favorite Wizard, which we discussed earlier in this chapter. Thus, the Web publisher can optimize and control synchronizations by limiting the selections to specific information collections.

There are other aspects of items that the <usage> element can help with. Refer to the discussion of that element for further details.

<title>

The <title> element specifies a text string that will eventually appear as the title of the respective channels, subchannels, items, or within the <softpkg> element. Use of <title> is fairly straightforward; the only cautions are those against improper coding of special characters and the treatment of white space, such as spaces, tabs, blank lines, or special characters, as discussed in Chapter 3, "Anatomy of an XML Document."

<title>'s parent elements are <channel>, <item>, and <softpkg>; it does not have any child elements. It has one optional white-space-related attribute, XML-SPACE, whose candidate values are Default, which specifies to the parser that white space doesn't matter, and Preserve, which specifies that the white space should be preserved during processing and display.

When used as an attribute of any parent element, the value specified for the XML-SPACE attribute applies to all child elements unless it is specifically overridden with another XML-SPACE attribute in one of the child elements.

When applied to a top-level <channel> element, ensure that the <title> element appears near the beginning, prior to any <item> elements or nested <channel> elements.

<logo>

The <logo> element specifies the image used to represent the respective <channel>, <item>, and <softpkg> elements. Those are its parent elements; it does not have child elements.

As we mentioned in the best practices listed in the previous section, Web publishers should create and use appropriate images for their channel and item logos. However, Internet Explorer 4.0 and later provides default images wherever necessary.

You can place various types and sizes of logo images in several locations in a channel's user interface, for example, in the Favorites bar in the browser, in the Favorites menu, and on the Active Desktop. To do so, we recommend observing the Microsoft logo dimension and other requirements shown in the following list.

The <logo> element has two required attributes:

HREF. The value specified for HREF is the URI/URL of the image file.

STYLE. There are three possible values for the STYLE attribute:

- **icon.** When this value appears as a specification for the STYLE attribute within a <channel> element, the image specified by the HREF URL appears in the Favorites menus and is 16 pixels high by 16 pixels wide (16H x 16W).
- **image-wide.** If this value is specified for the STYLE attribute, the image appears in the Favorites bar in the link to the main channel page and is 32 pixels high by 194 pixels wide (32H x 194W).
- **image.** If this value is specified for the STYLE attribute, the image appears on the Active Desktop and is 32 pixels high by 80 pixels wide (32H x 80W).

See Figure 14.12, which demonstrates the syntax for the <logo> element and the placement of the respective logo images. Don't worry if the screen details in Figure 14.12 are illegible. The important aspects of Figure 14.12 are the syntax of the three different <logo> elements and the eventual on-screen location of the logo images.

If you want to investigate all the requirements, refer to the article "Creating Active Channel Logo Images" at http://msdn.microsoft.com/workshop/delivery/channel/tutorials/images.asp.

GIF, JPEG, and other standard graphic image formats are supported for logo images. Animated GIF documents are not supported with this element.

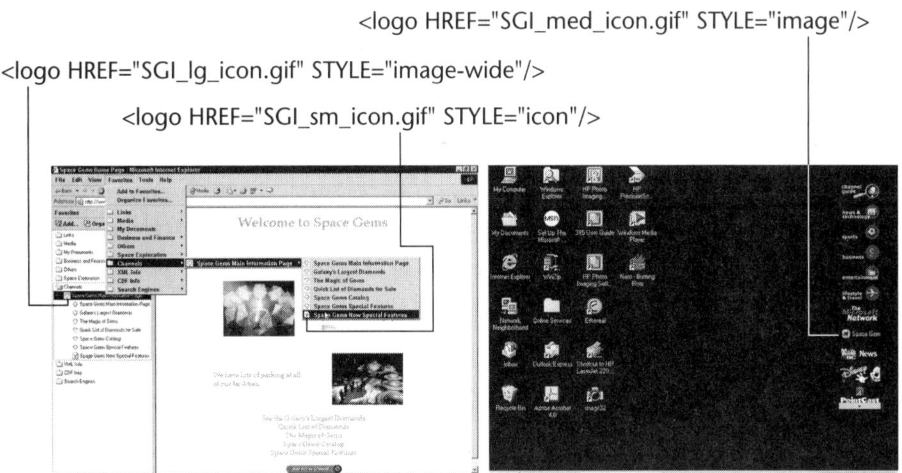

Figure 14.12 Icon image specifications.

As a best practice, the top-level <channel> element should include three <logo> child elements, one for each type of style attribute, like this:

```
<CHANNEL HREF="http://spacegems.com/mainpage.htm">
<!-- For the Favorites Bar -->
   <LOGO HREF="SGI_lg_icon.gif" STYLE="image-wide"/>
<!-- For the Active Desktop Bar -->
   <LOGO HREF="SGI_med_icon.gif" STYLE="image"/>
<!-- For the Favorites Menus -->
   <LOGO HREF="SGI_sm_icon.gif" STYLE="icon"/>
```

All other <channel> and <item> elements in the CDF file should include only one <logo> element, and the value specified for their respective STYLE attributes should be icon.

The Active Desktop is beyond the scope of this introductory-level CDF discussion, but it is instructional to see the effects of all three specifications. Plus, we suggest including the STYLE="icon" attribute in the top-level <channel> element. If an Active Desktop is eventually installed, in some future configuration, the channel appears on the desktop.

<log>

If we want to monitor Web page traffic, we can include a <log> element to log the information about online and offline hits to an item within a channel. Each time an end user views the URL of the <log> element's parent <item>, that URL is recorded in the Web page log file. If we want to monitor traffic to more than one URL in the channel, we must insert a <log> element into each respective <item> element.

If, as a Web site publisher, we log this information, large log files can be created quickly if the URL is popular. So we include <log> elements in only those <item> elements for which we really want to measure traffic.

The <log> element's only parent element is <item>, and it has no child elements. After you insert a <log> element, you must include a VALUE="document:view" attribute in its start tag.

<logtarget>

If we decide to log traffic to our URLs, we use the <logtarget> element to specify where we want the log information sent. <logtarget> specifies the URI of the log file in which the information should be recorded. Be aware that this activity can produce large log files quickly.

<logtarget>'s only parent is the <channel> element, but it can have two child elements: <http-equiv> and <purgetime>. These child elements can occur only once per channel. <logtarget> has three attributes:

HREF. The value for this mandatory option is a URI that specifies where the log information is to be sent.

METHOD. The values for this mandatory attribute are POST or PUT, the two HTTP-related methods of storing data. The value you choose depends on the additional processing that you expect the data to undergo. The usual value is POST. However, because this attribute requires more extensive knowledge of network protocols and database technology, further discussion is beyond the introductory level of this chapter. If you would like further information regarding this attribute, visit the Microsoft CDF Web site at http://msdn.microsoft.com/workshop/delivery/cdf/reference/logtarget.asp.

SCOPE. The values for this optional attribute are *offline*, meaning that the traffic to those pages that are downloaded to an end user's system during a synchronization is to be logged; *online*, which specifies offline work traffic is to be ignored, but online work traffic is to be logged; or *all*, which specifies that traffic during online and offline work is to be logged.

The traffic log file is stored in the end user's local cache in the %userprofile%\history\log folder. That file is cleared after it is successfully posted to the HTTP server during the Channel Definition Format (CDF) update/synchronization. That's why offline logging is possible and the traffic data can eventually be returned to the Web site. Again, the log information is in the form of a record of URLs.

In the CDF file, the <logtarget> element must occur before any <item> elements.

<http-equiv>

This element is fairly specialized; it supplies information to the parser using HTTP response headers as the transmission medium. As logging information is sent over the HTTP protocol according to the attributes in the <logtarget> element, its child <http-equiv> indicates that an HTTP header parameter should be added, based on the specifications in the <http-equiv> element's attributes.

<http-equiv>'s parent element is <logtarget>, and it has no child elements. <http-equiv> has two mandatory attributes:

NAME. A string value that names the HTTP protocol header parameter sent with the traffic log file.

VALUE. A string value of the corresponding parameter.

This is how the a Web publisher might specify the compression algorithm for a log file that is to be sent back to the Space Gems Web site's HTTP server:

```
<LOGTARGET HREF="http://www.spacegems.com/logs/" METHOD="POST">
     <HTTP-EQUIV NAME="encoding-type" VALUE="gzip" />
</LOGTARGET>
<purgetime>
```

This element specifies the maximum age of valid page hits when a traffic log file is being uploaded to the Web publisher's server(s). Like <http-equiv>, <purgetime> is nested within a <logtarget> element. Thus, <purgetime> is a child element of <logtarget> but has no child elements of its own. The only attribute for <purgetime> is HOUR, with a value that must be a positive integer.

The log file is stored in the end user's local cache in the %userprofile%\history\log folder. That file is cleared after its records are successfully posted to the Web publisher's HTTP server(s) during a CDF update/synchronization.

Here's an example:

```
<PURGETIME HOUR = "36" />
```

This code says that as the traffic information is uploaded, discard any information older than 36 hours.

<usage>

The <usage> element specifies how its parent elements, <item> or <softpkg>, should be used. <usage> has no child elements. It has one mandatory attribute, VALUE, which can have one of the following values:

Channel. The item will appear in the browser's Favorites bar. This is the default behavior when no <usage> element appears under an <item>.

DesktopComponent. The item will be displayed in a frame located on the Microsoft Active Desktop. Attributes assigned this value can only be used in the context of an Active Desktop item.

Email. Instructs the parser that its parent element is an email message that is sent when the channel content is updated. Only one of these can be inserted per CDF document.

NONE. Indicates that the item will not appear in the Favorites bar.

ScreenSaver. Indicates the item will be displayed in the special Microsoft Internet Explorer screen saver. Only one of these is allowed per CDF file.

SoftwareUpdate. Indicates that the CDF file is being used for an automatic Software Update channel. This value is only valid when used in the top-level channel.

The <usage> element deprecates an older attribute that used to appear in the start tag of a parent <item> element: the SHOW attribute. That is to say, some older implementations of CDF clients look for a SHOW attribute, instead of a <usage> element nested within the <item> element.

Here is an example of a <usage> element:

```
<item HREF="tlscrn01.htm">
    <usage VALUE="ScreenSaver"></usage>
```

This code is a designation of an <item> element as a screen saver for an Active Desktop. Further discussion of this topic is beyond the scope of this introductory-level material. However, if you want more information, consult the *CDF Resources* section earlier in this chapter.

If you want to prevent an item from appearing in a Favorites bar—for example, when you just want the item to be downloaded and used as a link from some other page in the channel—include a <usage> element as a child element of the <item> element, and then insert a VALUE="none" attribute in the <usage> element's start tag.

<login />

This declared empty element specifies that the channel requires authentication before permission is given to subscribe to it. This element is found within the top-level <channel> element, but it has no child elements nor any attributes.

A CDF file containing the <login /> element causes the end user to be prompted for a name and password during the channel-subscription process.

Then the actual authentication input information is checked against a separate third-party authentication, authorization, and accounting application.

Special Characters and Character Encoding

Although we've also discussed this topic in previous chapters, for example, in Chapter 3, "Anatomy of an XML Document," it is worth mentioning again here. When inserting data content in an element, you must remember to use specific codes, called *predefined entity references*, for certain reserved characters, to prevent CDF parsing errors. Table 14.2 lists the five reserved characters, along with their predefined entity references.

Here's an example of the ampersand in action:

```
<channel HREF="prods/othergems.htm" >
     <title>Other Space Gems</title>
     <item HREF="prods/corundum.htm" >
          <title>Rubies &amp; Sapphires</title>
     </item>
     <item HREF="prods/beryls.htm" >
          <title>Emeralds &amp; Beryls</title>
     </item>
     <item HREF="prods/quartz.htm" >
          <title>Rose, Peridot &amp; Clear</title>
     </item>
</channel>
```

The example demonstrates the coding we would use in three <title> elements so that the ampersands appear correctly and won't be misinterpreted by the parser.

For a complete list of other named character set entities, see Microsoft's HTML Character Set Web site (Charsets) and Named Entities at http://msdn.microsoft.com/library/default.asp?url=/workshop/delivery/cdf/reference/CDF.asp.

Table 14.2 Predefined Entity References for Reserved Characters

CHARACTER TO INSERT	PREDEFINED ENTITY REFERENCE
< (less than)	<
> (greater than)	>
' (an apostrophe)	'
" (a double quotation mark)	"
& (an ampersand, to mean "and")	&

The CDF specification also supports encoding for any ASCII character, which uses the format &#nnn. The ampersand characters in this example could also be encoded with the ASCII decimal value of 38; thus, we would encode the string & instead of & in a CDF document.

Test Your Comprehension with a Sample CDF File

Figure 14.13 illustrates a simple CDF document consisting of a top-level channel with two items and a subchannel with three items. To test your comprehension of the major CDF file creation concepts presented in this chapter and to prepare for the lab exercises at the end of this chapter, have a look at this sample file.

A description of the coding is posted on the Chapter 14 page of this book's Web site as noted in the book's introduction.

To help you along, we are providing a rendering of the resultant Favorites bar in Figure 14.14.

A related file directory diagram appears in Figure 14.15.

Posting the CDF File to the Web Server

After creating the CDF file, we handle it like any other Web entity and affiliate it with the appropriate Web site pages. We then place it in the publicly available and predefined document root directory on the Web site's HTTP server. That way, a user who clicks a Subscribe Here link gains access to the CDF document and, thus, the channel. If in doubt, consult your system and security administrator.

Providing Access to the Channel

Finally, as Web site publishers, we should consider how to allow our users to access the channel. For example, as you will see in a lab exercise at the end of this chapter, we can initiate the channel subscription process by inserting an HREF attribute that has the value of the URI of the CDF file in the start tag of an <A> element, which, in turn, is nested within the <BODY> element of a Web page document. Nesting the <A> element within the <BODY> element in the HTML document is preferred, although some suggest putting it in the <HEAD> element. Here's an example of such an <A> element:

```
<A HREF="http://www.spacegems.com/gems.cdf">
        Subscribe to Space Gems 2047 Catalog!
</A>
```

```
<?XML version="1.0" ?>
<!DOCTYPE Channels SYSTEM "http://www.spacegems.com/dtds/SGI_cdf.dtd" >
<!-- Top-level channel - Corporate Info - ->
<channel HREF="http://www.spacegems.com/channels/index.htm"
   BASE="http://www.spacegems.com/channels/"
   LASTMOD="2047-06-30T01:59:59" >
   <logo HREF="pix/SGI_corp_lg.gif" STYLE="image-wide"/>
   <logo HREF="pix/SGI_corp_med.gif" STYLE="image"/>
   <logo HREF="pix/SGI_corp_sm.gif" STYLE="icon"/>
   <title>Space Gems, Inc.</title>
   <abstract>Space Gems! Satisfaction Guaranteed!</abstract>
<!-- Update Schedule - ->
   <schedule  STARTDATE="2047-07-01" STOPDATE="2048-06-30">
      <intervaltime DAY="7" />
      <earliesttime HOUR="3" TIMEZONE="-0700" />
      <latesttime HOUR="5" TIMEZONE="-0700" />
   </schedule>
<!-- Logging End User Traffic - ->
   <logtarget HREF="http://www.spacegems.com/cgi-bin/traffic.cgi"
                                       METHOD="POST" SCOPE="All" />
   <purgetime HOUR="24" />
<!-- Item - Corporate Info - ->
   <item HREF="corp/spacegems.htm">
      <logo HREF="pix/SGI_sm.gif" STYLE="icon"/>
      <title>Company Info</title>
      <abstract>All you need to know!</abstract>
<!-- Logging End User Traffic to the Corporate Info Page - ->
      <log VALUE="document:view" />
   </item>
<!-- Item - Screensaver - ->
   <item HREF="SGI_screen_01.htm">
      <usage VALUE="ScreenSaver"></usage>
   </item>
<!-- Subchannel - Product Info - ->
   <channel HREF="prods/SGI_cat_2047.htm" >
      <title>Space Gems Catalog</title>
      <abstract>Best selection! Lowest prices!</abstract>
      <logo HREF="pix/SGI_cat_lg.gif" STYLE="image-wide"/>
      <logo HREF="pix/SGI_cat_med.gif" STYLE="image"/>
      <logo HREF="pix/SGI_cat_sm.gif" STYLE="icon"/>
<!-- Item - Diamonds - ->
      <item HREF="prods/diamonds.htm">
         <logo HREF="pix/diamond_sm.gif" STYLE="icon"/>
         <title>Space Gems Diamonds</title>
         <abstract>The most precious gems!</abstract>
```

Figure 14.13 A simple CDF document. *(continued)*

```
        </item>
<!-- Item - Emeralds - ->
        <item HREF="prods/emeralds.htm">
            <logo HREF="pix/emerald_sm.gif" STYLE="icon"/>
            <title>Space Gems Emeralds</title>
            <abstract>Green, blue and gold!</abstract>
        </item>
<!-- Item - Other Gems - ->
        <item HREF="prods/othergems.htm">
            <logo HREF="pix/citrine_sm.gif" STYLE="icon"/>
            <title>Other Space Gems</title>
            <abstract>Rubies, sapphires and more!</abstract>
        </item>
<!-- End of subchannel - ->
  </channel>
<!-- End of Top-level channel - ->
</channel>
```

Figure 14.13 *(continued)*

Figure 14.14 Rendering of the simple CDF document.

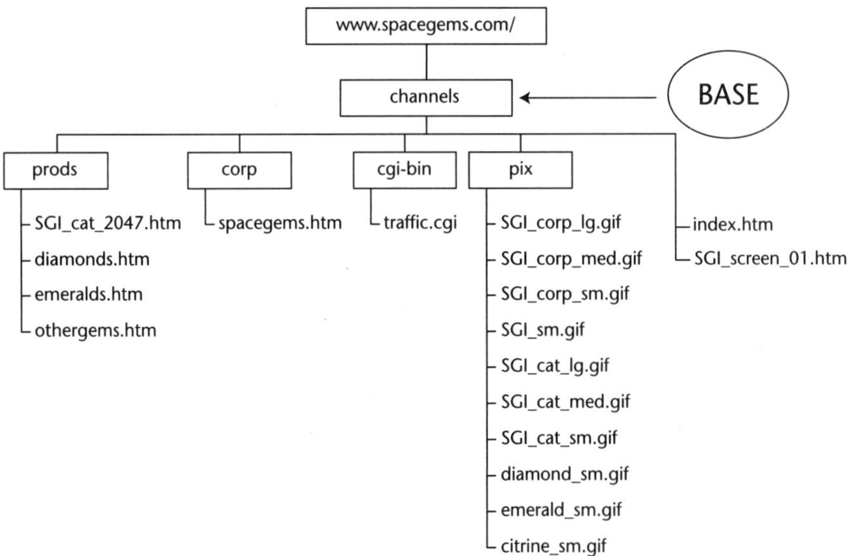

Figure 14.15 File directory structure for the simple CDF document.

Alternatively, Microsoft suggests for better functionality that your Web page include their Add Active Channel or Add to Active Desktop logo button. That means, of course, that you would also have to store the associated button logos with your other images and make them accessible to the pages. Using these buttons requires you to agree beforehand to the terms of the Active Channel Logo agreement. Then you have to place specific JavaScript elements in the <HEAD> element and add HTML coding in the <BODY> element. The benefits are that when end users click these buttons, they access a more visible, consistent, and easily recognizable method for adding Active Channel sites and Active Desktop items in any browser.

For further information regarding these buttons and the method of installation, go to http://msdn.microsoft.com/workshop/delivery/cdf/tutorials/generic.asp

Chapter 14 Labs: Getting Started with CDF

CDF is an established XML technology that has been around since the introduction of Internet Explorer 4.0. However, in recent years, Web publishers have tended not to advertise CDF's push technology-related features on their sites to the same extent that they did in the late 1990s. Also, there are few tools and utilities in the marketplace. However, the files are not that difficult to code, although assistance from a CDF editor certainly doesn't hurt.

Basic CDF File for Web Pages

In this multistage lab, we show you how to replace the basic navigational links on the bottom of the Space Gems start Web page, index.html, with active channel technology. Here are the four basic steps you will accomplish:

1. Install Microsoft's CDF Generator application.
2. Create a basic CDF File.
3. Modify the CDF File.
4. Make the CDF file available and verify that it works.

Lab 14.1: Installing Microsoft's CDF Generator

Here's the procedure to install the Microsoft CDF Generator application:

1. The URL for this file is too long to enter accurately here, so we ask you to use the MSN Search For engine. Go to http://www.microsoft.com. Type "CDF Generator" inside the Search For box, and click Go.
2. Click the link called Microsoft CDF Generator that was returned from the search.
3. Click the link that says "You can download CDF Generator from MSDN Online."
4. On the cdfgenerator Web page that appears, click the Download sample link.
5. The file (the name should be similar to sample.zip) is downloaded to the directory of your choice. After it has been downloaded, go to that directory and double-click the CDFGen.exe file to install the application. During the installation procedure, the application will suggest installing to the C:\Workshop or C:\Program Files\Microsoft CDF Generator directories. Either location is acceptable.

As of this writing, there was a problem with the link to the Microsoft CDF editor. If your download does not succeed—that is, if you get a license file only—visit the Chapter 14 page at the *XML in 60 Minutes a Day* Web site, which contains instructions for downloading the editor.

Lab 14.2: Creating a Basic CDF File

Here's the procedure to create a basic CDF file:

1. Download the 16x16-pixel image files named diamond.gif and red-star.gif from the *XML in 60 Minutes a Day* Web site and save them to your C:\WWW\SpaceGems\images directory.
2. Open the Microsoft CDF editor by double-clicking the cdfgen.exe file in the directory you selected for the installation in the previous section of this lab exercise. A blank editing area appears.
3. From the top menu click File, New.
4. Enter the following information inside the Channel window:
   a. HREF: Then click the Attribute radio button.
   b. Enter "http://localhost/spacegems/" in both the HREF and BASE input boxes. Leave the SELF input box empty. Click Next.
   c. Type "Space Gems Main Page" inside the Title input box.
   d. Type "We will sell to anyone in the universe tax-free! Please look at our easy-to-follow directions!" inside the Abstract input box. Click Next.
   e. Type "images/diamond.gif" inside the Icon input box. Click Next.
   f. In the Schedule box, enter today's date in the Start Date and at least five days from the current date inside the End Date. Click Interval Time and enter Day=1, Hour=1 and Min=2.
   g. Click Earliest Time and enter Day=1, Hour=0 and Min=2.
   h. Click Latest Time and leave 12 as the default (that is, Day and Min should remain blank while Hour=12). Click Next.
   i. Uncheck the Log Target box. Click Next.
   j. Several lines of code appear, reflecting the choices you made. Click Finish.
   k. Highlight the root Channel–Space Gems Main Page element and right-click. Choose New, Item from the context menu.
   l. Type "galaxys_largest_diamonds.htm" inside the HREF input box. Click Next.
   m. Type "The Galaxy's Largest Diamonds" in the Title input box.
   n. Type "Learn about the largest diamonds in the galaxy! Images of all diamonds are available!" in the Abstract input box. Click Next.

o. Select the Icon selection box by clicking it. Then type "images/diamond.gif" in the Icon input box. Click Next.

p. Several more lines of code appear, reflecting the choices you made. Click Finish.

5. Click the Save icon on the menu bar, and save the file as gems.cdf to the C:\WWW\SpaceGems directory. Leave the file and editor open.

If you experience trouble saving the gems.cdf file, don't despair. Simply download a copy of the final gems.cdf file from the book's Web site discussed in the book's introduction and save it to the C:\WWW\ SpaceGems directory.

6. Test the CDF file by activating Internet Explorer and entering "http://localhost/spacegems/gems.cdf" into its locator bar. An Add Favorites menu should appear. Click OK and proceed. Click the new Favorite entry in the sidebar to verify that the links work.

Lab 14.3: Modifying the CDF File

This next section checks your understanding of how the CDF components in the gems.cdf document work. However, rather than provide step-by-step instructions for using the Microsoft CDF generator/editor to add new code, we are just going to provide the new code, and you can add it using the methods we've already shown you.

1. With the Microsoft CDF editor still open and the gems.cdf file still on-screen, add the lines of code that are highlighted (the lines that are not highlighted are the existing lines of code that are already on-screen).

```
<?XML VERSION="1.0" ENCODING="UTF-8"?>
<CHANNEL HREF=http://localhost/spacegems/
        BASE="http://localhost/spacegems/">
    <TITLE>Space Gems Main Information Page</TITLE>
    <ABSTRACT>We will sell to anyone in the universe tax free.
            Please look at our easy-to-get-here directions.
    </ABSTRACT>
    <LOGO HREF="http://localhost/spacegems/images/diamond.gif"
            STYLE="ICON"/>
    <SCHEDULE STARTDATE="2003-01-14" ENDDATE="2004-11-14"
            TIMEZONE="-0700">
        <INTERVALTIME MIN="2"/>
        <EARLIESTTIME DAY="15" HOUR="1"/>
        <LATESTTIME DAY="31" HOUR="23"/>
```

```
</SCHEDULE>
<ITEM HREF="http://localhost/spacegems/galaxys_largest_
        diamonds.htm"
        PRECACHE="NO">
     <TITLE>Galaxy's Largest Diamonds</TITLE>
     <ABSTRACT>Find out where the largest diamonds in the
              universe are.
     </ABSTRACT>
     <LOGO HREF="http://localhost/spacegems/images/
           diamond.gif"
           STYLE="ICON"/>
</ITEM>
<ITEM HREF=http://localhost/spacegems/magicgems.xml
            PRECACHE="yes">
     <TITLE>The Magic of Gems</TITLE>
     <ABSTRACT>Buy, sell, trade and learn about precious
              gems.
     </ABSTRACT>
     <LOGO HREF="http://localhost/spacegems/images/
           diamond.gif"
           STYLE="ICON"/>
</ITEM>
<ITEM HREF="gemsB_EDI.htm" LASTMOD="2003-01-14T23:44"
PRECACHE="YES" LEVEL="0">
     <TITLE>Quick List of Diamonds for Sale</TITLE>
     <ABSTRACT>We pride ourselves in having the best quality
              diamonds in the universe. We also guarantee
              that we have the largest diamonds available!
              If you know where there is a larger one, let
              us know and we will actually try to buy it!
     </ABSTRACT>
     <LOGO HREF="images/diamond.gif" STYLE="ICON"/>
</ITEM>
<ITEM LASTMOD="2003-01-14T23:47" PRECACHE="YES" LEVEL="0">
     <A HREF="catalog.htm"></A>
     <TITLE>Space Gems Catalog</TITLE>
     <ABSTRACT>These diamonds are the best we have. Please
             find the time to visit us and see them in
             person. We simply can't capture the beauty of
             these gems in a holograph!
     </ABSTRACT>
     <LOGO HREF="images/diamond.gif" STYLE="ICON"/>
</ITEM>
<ITEM HREF="SPFeature.htm" LASTMOD="2003-01-14T23:51"
      PRECACHE="YES" LEVEL="0">
     <TITLE>Space Gems Special Features</TITLE>
     <ABSTRACT>These are limited time offers. So if you are
              interested please drop by soon.
     </ABSTRACT>
     <LOGO HREF="images/diamond.gif" STYLE="ICON"/>
     <LOG VALUE="document:view"/>
```

```
        </ITEM>
        <ITEM HREF="SPFeature_Starts.htm" LASTMOD="2003-01-15T22:03"
                PRECACHE="YES" LEVEL="0">
            <TITLE>Spage Gems New Special Features</TITLE>
            <ABSTRACT>This is a limited time offer and will only be
                    available for another 12 hours!
            </ABSTRACT>
            <LOGO HREF="images/redstar.gif" STYLE="ICON"/>
        </ITEM>
    </CHANNEL>
```

2. Save the file.
3. Retest the CDF file. Using Internet Explorer, enter "http://localhost/spacegems/gems.cdf". An Add Favorites menu appears. Click OK. Click the new Favorite entry in the sidebar to validate that the links work.

Lab 14.4: Making the Channel Available and Verifying that It Works

There are two basic ways to make a channel available. One is to make the main or primary link the CDF file itself so that it is automatically invoked. The second method is to place a Microsoft channel marker on the page so users can voluntarily add the channel. The following code snippet supports the second option:

1. Download the ch_chbtn.gif file from the Chapter 14 page of the *XML in 60 Minutes a Day* Web site, and save it to the C:\WWW\SpaceGems\images directory. This button image can also be obtained from many Microsoft sites.
2. Using HTML-Kit, add the following code to the bottom of the index.html file. The new code is shown in highlight.

```
<!DOCTYPE HTML PUBLIC "-//W3C//DTD HTML 4.01 Transitional//EN">
<html>
    <head>
        <title>Space Gems Home Page</title>
        <link rel="stylesheet" type="text/css"
                href="master.css"></link>
        <meta name="generator" content="HTML Tidy for Windows
                (vers 1st August 2002), see www.w3.org" />
        <meta http-equiv="Content-Language" content="en-us" />
        <meta http-equiv="Content-Type"
                content="text/html;charset=windows-1252" />
        <meta name="GENERATOR"
                content="Microsoft FrontPage 4.0" />
```

```
      <meta name="ProgId" content="FrontPage.Editor.
          Document" />
</head>
<body>
     <h1 align="center">Welcome to Space Gems</h1>
     <p align="center"> </p>
     <p align="center"> </p>
     <div align="center">
          <center>
               <table
                   summary="Table used to format images
                            and text"
                   border="0" cellpadding="20"
                   cellspacing="0" width="71%">
                    <tr>
                         <td width="50%">
                              <p align="center">
                                   <img alt="C4D3_s.jpg"
                                   border="0" src="images/
                                   C4D3_s.jpg"
                                   width="170" height="128"/>
                              </p>
                         </td>
                      <td width="50%">We have locations all
                                   around the galaxy to
                                   ensure that you do not
                                   have to travel light years
                                   to find that very special
                                   gem.
                         </td>
                    </tr>
                    <tr>
                         <td width="50%">
                              <p>We have lots of parking
                                 at all of
                                 our facilities!
                              </p>
                         </td>
                         <td width="50%">
                              <p align="center">
                                   <img alt="secret_s.jpg"
                                        border="0" src=
                                        "images/secret_s.jpg"
                                        width="170"
                                        height="120" />
                              </p>
                         </td>
                    </tr>
               </table>
               <a href="galaxys_largest_diamonds.htm">See the
```

```
                    Galaxy's Largest Diamonds
            </a>
            <br />
            <a href="gemsB_EDI.htm">Quick List of
                    Diamonds</a>
            <br />
            <a href="magicgems.xml">The Magic of
                    Gems</a>
            <br />
            <a href="catalog.htm">Space Gems Catalog</a>
            <br />
            <a href="SPFeature.htm">Space Gems Special
                    Features</a>
        </center>
    </div>
        <center>
            <p>
                <a name="chbut"
             href="http://localhost/spacegems/gems.cdf">
               <img srcC="images/ch_chbtn.gif" border=0
                         width=136 height=20>
                </a>
                <script language="JavaScript">
                 if ( isMsie4orGreater())
    { uniqueName.href="http://localhost/spacegems/gems.cdf"; }
                </script>
            </p>
        </center>
  </body>
</html>
```

3. Save the index.html file to the C:\WWW\SpaceGems directory.
4. Test the index.html file. Activate Internet Explorer and enter "http://localhost/spacegems/" in its locator bar.
5. Click the Microsoft channel image on the bottom of the page.
6. An Add Favorites menu should appear. Click OK and proceed. Click the new Favorite entry in the sidebar to verify that the links work.

Summary

Although CDF is falling out of favor from a push technology standpoint, it has thrived from a pull technology standpoint and has inspired imitators among competitor browsers.

Here are some key points we'd like you to take away from this chapter:

- The Channel Definition Format language (CDF) is, according to Microsoft, ". . . an open specification that permits a Web publisher to offer frequently updated collections of information . . . for automatic delivery to compatible receiver programs on PCs or other information appliances." It gives Web site publishers the capability of providing information, usually updated information (even software updates), to its end user subscribers on a periodic or regular basis. They create CDF documents that manipulate, combine, or condense their information. Then they deliver that information upon request, or preferably, on a regular schedule, and affiliate those documents with Web page documents.
- Microsoft introduced CDF in 1997 to overcome the existing shortcomings of webcasting by introducing managed webcasting. In the same year, CDF and two other push technology proposals—OSD and DRP—were submitted to the W3C. All the proposals were given W3C Note status. W3C metadata activity was initiated to develop a standard that created a common ground. RDF was developed and approved as a Recommendation in 1999. RDF, thus, surpassed its forebears. Microsoft, however, continued to develop CDF.
- A Web site publisher uses certain CDF specialized elements and attributes to define information groupings into channels, subchannels, and other constituent items. Other specialized elements allow publishers to configure the scheduling for updating/synchronizing the channels.
- A channel can be designed as a single page, multiple pages, or the content of a whole Web site and can be distributed from any Web server that supports the HTTP protocol.
- Because they have both push and pull aspects, including scheduling capability, channels are not the same as favorites or bookmarks.
- In this chapter, you learned three ways to investigate available channels, two ways to subscribe to channels, one method for synchronization, and one method for viewing channels offline.
- The general strategy for creating channels is to design the channel, create logo images, create the CDF document, post the CDF file so it will be accessible from its affiliated Web page documents, and provide a means for end users to subscribe to the channel.
- You learned about several elements and attributes for creating CDF documents. The most important of these is the <channel> element, which is the top-level element in the document and the container for other subchannels and information items, if applicable.

Review Questions

1. Television, email, and webcasting are samples of which kind of technology?
   a. Pull
   b. CDF
   c. Push
   d. Webcasting
   e. None of the above
2. Channels are ________________________ that a Web publisher broadcasts from standard Web servers to compatible receiving applications.
3. True or false? Because CDF was submitted to the W3C first, development was initiated, and that's why Microsoft continued to use it with Internet Explorer.
4. Which of the following are drawbacks to early webcasting? (Choose all that apply.)
   a. Configuration could be complex.
   b. Bandwidth usage could not be optimized.
   c. Web publishers could not specify the information to be sent to subscribers and, so, could not optimize their delivery.
   d. Updating often occurred at inopportune times.
   e. All of the above.
5. True or false? Favorites (or bookmarks) are the same as channels.
6. The general strategy for creating channels includes designing the channel, creating logo images, creating the CDF document, ____________________, and providing a means for end users to subscribe. Which step is missing?
   a. Creating an appropriate file structure
   b. Consulting with administrators and Internet Service Providers
   c. Creating synchronization schedules
   d. Posting the CDF file for public access
   e. Nothing is missing. All the steps are there.
7. True or false? The main channel page has to be the Web site's home page, and sub-channels and items come from lower positions in the Web site hierarchy, just as they are lower positions in the channel hierarchy.
8. True or false? A <channel> element must be used as the document root element, but <channel> elements can be nested.

9. If you want to create a message that appears when a mouse pointer hovers over a channel, subchannel, or item title, which element would you insert in the CDF file?

   a. <abstract>

   b. <title>

   c. <style>

   d. <item>

   e. None of the above

10. Which value for the style attribute creates an icon with the 32H x 194W dimensions?

    a. image

    b. image-wide

    c. icon

    d. icon-wide

    e. None of the above

Answers to Review Questions

1. **c.** They are both examples of push technology. They are actually forerunners of webcasting, which is an example of push technology.
2. "Channels are prescribed collections of information that Web publishers broadcast from standard Web servers to compatible receiving applications." Any phrase equivalent to "collections of information" will suffice.
3. False. CDF was given Note status and the W3C did not initiate any further development. Its Metadata Activity went off in a different direction. However, Microsoft continued development of CDF on its own.
4. **e.** They are all examples of drawbacks of early webcasting.
5. False. Channels are more sophisticated than bookmarks or Favorites, although Microsoft's smart-pull technology is being applied to old-style Favorites to make them more like channels. Old-style Favorites and bookmarks are URLs stored on an end user's system to save wear and tear on our own memories.
6. **d.** Some might choose c. However, creating those schedules are considered part of creating the CDF document.
7. False. Although this is a common misconception, you can design the channels, subchannels, and items in any order you want them to appear.
8. True. The question covers the two major functions of the <channel> element. Check the text for a further explanation.
9. **a.** This was discussed in the *Other CDF Elements* section, under <abstract>.
10. **b.** This was also discussed in the *Other CDF Elements* section, under <logo>.

SOAP

It seems like everyone wants to know about the Simple Object Access Protocol (SOAP): what is it and how is it used? Although a lot of attention has been focused on it, SOAP is just part of a larger solution: an Internet consisting of many Web services that rely on XML to enhance system and commerce integration. SOAP is becoming a popular, high-profile protocol used to carry XML messages to and from Web services. These Web services—which we call SOAP-aware or SOAP-capable—use SOAP as a message format protocol. But without the support of the Web Services Description Language (WSDL) and HTTP, SOAP wouldn't work. In fact, Web services don't even have to include SOAP, because the information and messages could be carried over HTTP only. So why do we want to discuss SOAP? Because it has become the most popular protocol for exchanging messages, especially machine-to-machine messages, in the Internet's distributed environment.

In this chapter, we demonstrate how SOAP fits into the Web services architecture and how you can use it. First, we define Web services and discuss where they are and how to find them, using the Universal Description, Discovery, and Integration service (UDDI). UDDI is a multifaceted concept that includes project, organization, specification, and business registries, all of which play an important role in the discovery of and integration with Web services. Our descriptions of Web services available through UDDI lead to a discussion of the Web Service Description Language (WSDL) and, finally, SOAP.

By the end of this chapter, you should have a better grasp of Web services, how to find them yourself, and SOAP's role in accessing them. You will even have created some simple SOAP messages to access existing services.

What Are Web Services?

The W3C formally defines a Web service as "a software system identified by a URI, whose public interfaces and bindings are defined and described using XML. Its definition can be discovered by other software systems. These systems may then interact with the Web service in a manner prescribed by its definition, using XML-based messages conveyed by Internet protocols." The UDDI.org defines Web services as "self-contained, modular business applications that have open, Internet-oriented, standards-based technologies. These standards-based communications allow Web services to be accessed by customers, suppliers, and partners independent of hardware, operating system, or even programming environment."

The W3C Web service definition is excerpted from the W3C's November 2002 Working Draft of their Web Services Architecture specification. That document can be found at www.w3.org/TR/2002/WD-ws-arch-20021114/#whatisws. The UDDI definition is excerpted from the "UDDI Executive White Paper," published by the UDDI.org in November 2001, and can be found at www.uddi.org/whitepapers.html.

A hierarchy of concepts is at work here. The first is Web-based services, which are any kind of service available over the Web. Web services, on the other hand, are considered Web-based services that are implemented with Web service technologies. Web service technologies, in turn, are defined as the Web Services Description Language and two XML-based protocols: SOAP and UDDI. These three mechanisms form the foundation of SOAP messaging. They allow different programs on different systems to communicate with each other, especially "automatically" (consider, for example, a customer system that can read inventory records, and if it perceives that certain supplies have fallen below their programmed thresholds, it can automatically order new supplies and authorize payment).

The UDDI: Organization, Project, Specification, and Registry

Before the UDDI project was developed, no industry-wide single-access approach existed that enabled businesses to provide their customers, suppliers, and partners with product and service information. The only technology available was Internet search engines, with all their inherent shortcomings: no ideal choice of search engine to register a business with, the question of "membership level" to purchase with each, the lack of clarity with respect to what metadata (that is, keywords and other information) to emphasize on a Web site, lack of knowledge with respect to formulating a proper search, and the limited information received from a search attempt (a hyperlink to a URL and, after traversing the link, some HTML pages).

Also, prior to the UDDI project, no universal method existed for integrating communication and commerce systems among business suppliers, customers, or partners. Many companies created proprietary approaches, content, and architectures, which aggravated the already-diverging nature of Internet e-commerce.

Before we define the UDDI project, be aware that you may eventually encounter the term *UDDI* in several contexts. It is a multifaceted term, and it refers to the following:

Sponsoring organization. UDDI.org now consists of 14 Working Group members—of which four (IBM, Microsoft, Hewlett-Packard, and SAP) are the UDDI operators—and approximately 200 advisory group members, which are software developers and e-business leaders.

Project. The UDDI project is a pan-industry project undertaken by platform providers, software developers, and business leaders to create a global, open approach to service provision computing. This approach allows participants to discover one another, to define their lines of business, to indicate how they will interact over the Internet (their applications, platforms, and policies), and to share information in a global registry. The UDDI project, originally developed by Ariba, Inc., IBM Corporation, and Microsoft Corporation, began in 2000. The project includes the specification and the business registry, described next.

Specification. The UDDI.org participants developed a standards-based specification for Web service descriptions, for discovery of those services, and for company-to-company integration. Integration involves making a network connection, discovering services, agreeing on a common data representation (XML is becoming the data representation of choice), and agreeing on a common communication protocol (SOAP is rising in popularity). The UDDI specification builds on XML, HTTP,

DNS, WSDL, and other common standards. The UDDI Version 1.0 draft specification was released in September 2000; Version 2.0 was released in June 2001; and Version 3.0 in July 2002.

Business registry. The UDDI Business Registry (UBR) is a master directory of available e-business services. The directory is installed on four highly available sets of server services (called UBR Nodes), each operated by IBM, Microsoft, SAP, and NTT-Com. Those UBR operators (also occasionally called discovery agencies) must maintain their services so that downtime never occurs. NTT-Com is the most recent addition to the roster of UBR operators; more are anticipated in the future.

A business registry is created to provide opportunities for those companies who wish to provide services and to create affordable solutions for those businesses who wish to consume or use those services, or to exchange data or information. One of the goals of UDDI is to create a model that companies can use to safely and conveniently register their Web services and, when they find suitable customers, suppliers, or partners, to integrate their systems.

Registries like this are expected to have a significant impact on global business-to-business transactions. But a UDDI-compliant registry is more than a resourceful public business directory. Besides simply sharing data, the UDDI model requires security and integrity components to be included in the registries.

Three types of business registries exist: private, shared, and public. Organizations build private UDDI registries to facilitate services between departments or locations within a common firewalled environment. Many Web services are private, to be shared among specific applications and never viewed by the general public. Shared registries are created to allow password-related or other authorized access to an organization's system by clients, suppliers, or other partners. Currently, only a few UDDI registries are maintained for public service, and these are kept by the UDDI Node operators.

However, even these public registries are exclusive to the companies that register with them—companies that offer Internet Web services of their own. Thus, real commerce is facilitated and conducted.

When a Web service provider registers its service with a UDDI UBR Node, it provides its identity; a description of the goods, services, or information it provides (the descriptions are kept within the WSDL document files that comprise the registry; we discuss WSDL in the next section); and its point of service for access purposes.

Classroom Q & A

Q: How do the UDDI Business Registries keep track of all the potentially millions of Web service providers?

A: A mechanism is used to ensure that each and every service registered with a UDDI service is uniquely classified. Once the registration is approved, the newly registered service provider is assigned a unique key that ensures the uniqueness of its identity. That unique key would be the only way to differentiate between similar services, like Credit Service A and Credit Service B, for example.

During the registration process, the provider must give precise instructions about how to access or use their Web service. Later, other end users will be responsible for establishing a connection to a Web service after discovering it. How is that done? First, the end user or programmer looks for a WSDL document that contains the descriptions of the service and the point of service access. Once the WSDL document has been located, the end user can construct a SOAP message with the appropriate body content—content that the Web service provider would expect to receive from a potential consumer.

At the risk of getting ahead of ourselves, the following code shows part of such a SOAP message. This code is a snippet only—it's the payload or actual request portion of the <Body> element of a SOAP request message:

```
<find_business generic='1.0' xnkbs='urn:uddiorg:api'>
     <name>SpaceGems</name>
</find_business>
```

The actual service or information being offered by a registered UBR provider is not kept on the UDDI registry servers (in other words, not kept on the UBR Nodes). Only information describing the service and how to access it are stored in the registry. The UDDI registries resemble Domain Name Services (DNS)—Internet services that translate domain names into IP addresses—since they perform name resolution only and don't contain any content.

Figure 15.1 illustrates the role of the UDDI Business Registry Nodes and their relationships with a client end user (a potential customer, supplier, or partner) and the Web service provider.

For further information about any aspect of UDDI, visit the UDDI.org Web site at www.uddi.org. There, you can register your own organization, find services, read the UDDI white papers, check the latest UDDI news, or contact UDDI.org. You can also access the UBR Nodes.

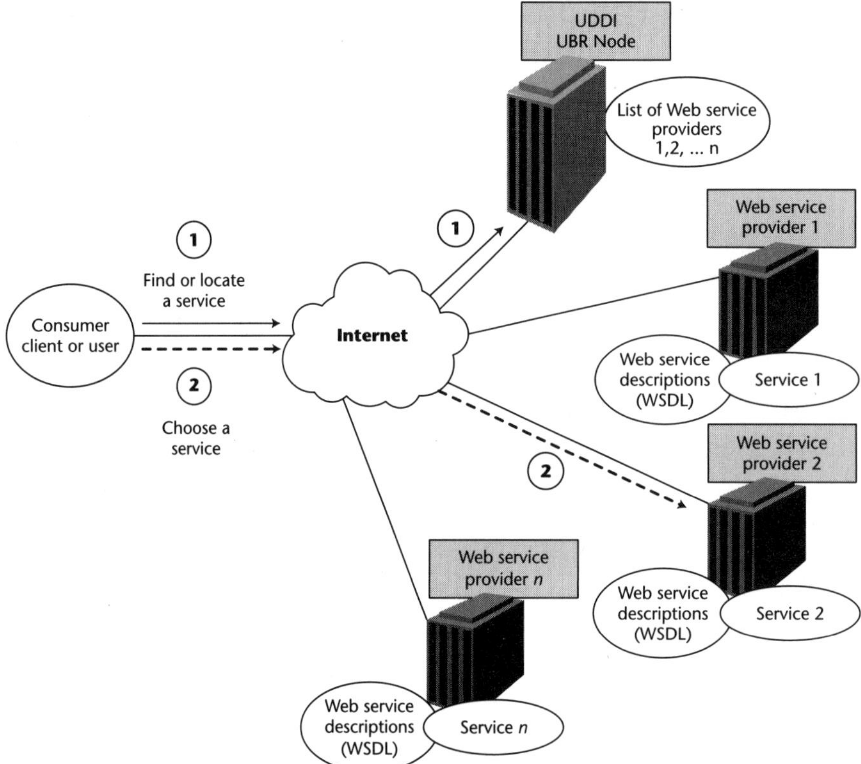

Figure 15.1 UDDI UBR Node operators maintain lists of available Web services.

OASIS sponsors a UDDI Technical Committee (TC) that continues to work on UDDI.org's Web service specifications. OASIS is a not-for-profit, global consortium that works to standardize e-business transactions. OASIS works in parallel with the W3C and continues to propose and develop XML interoperability specifications.

♦ Is Space Gems Registered on a UBR Node?

To see what SpaceGems has to offer, try the following:

1. Go to http://uddi.microsoft.com.
2. Click Search.
3. Click the Services tab.
4. Enter the word "space" into the search field, and click Search.

The results should appear on the left panel of the browser window. You will see SpaceGems as a provider. The SpaceGems Inventory Service should appear. Immediately under that you will see the SpaceGems URL with the *Access Point* defined.

The Web Service Description Language (WSDL)

The Web Service Description Language is an XML application used to describe the interface, protocol bindings, and deployment details of network services. In other words, WSDL describes how to connect to a Web service. In this section, we discuss the development of WSDL as a specification and show how WSDL document files play a role in the discovery and provision of access to a Web service. Later, we discuss WSDL document components using a real WSDL file as an example.

WSDL Development

WSDL was originally developed by IBM, Microsoft, and Ariba by merging three previous proposals: Microsoft's SOAP Contract Language (SCL), the Service Description Language (SDL), and IBM's Network Accessible Services Specification Language (NASSL). Version 1.0 of the WSDL specification was released by its developers in September 2000. In March 2001, those three developers, along with 17 other industry proponents, submitted the WSDL 1.0 specification to the W3C as a proposal for eventual development into a W3C Recommendation. It was immediately published as a W3C Note titled Web Services Description Language (WSDL) 1.1. As with all W3C Notes, publication by the W3C is not meant to indicate that they endorse the document as a specification and does not commit them to further development. However, in this case, the W3C did continue to work on the WSDL specification, publishing its own Working Drafts of Web Services Description Language (WSDL) Version 1.2 and Web Services Description Language (WSDL) Version 1.2: Bindings in July 2002.

The W3C also published a Working Draft of Web Services Internationalization Usage Scenarios in late December 2002, the goal of which is to examine the different ways that language, culture, and related issues affect Web service architecture and technology. The WSDL specification is used by numerous developers, most notably with the public UDDI Business Registry.

Once we use the Business Registry to locate a service, we must review the service's WSDL document file, which tells us how to use the Web service. It is the responsibility of the Web service provider to create the WSDL file when it registers, maintain it, and make it available. The service provider must do this because the WSDL document should describe in detail all the capabilities or methods the XML Web service exposes for use.

As a simple analogy, let's say we write a Visual Basic or Java class to add two numbers together. To use it, an external client user must supply the numbers he or she wants added together. Once we obtain the numbers, we can perform the operation and send back the answer. So, as a developer, how do we communicate that we need those two numbers, and how do we specify the format we expect the numbers to be in? Because we are the only ones who know these requirements, we have to express them in a WSDL document file and then allow potential clients to examine it.

Once a client has examined the WSDL document, he or she creates a SOAP request in the form of an XML SOAP message to supply the two numbers. This process is also referred to as *creating the client*. The actual class or business logic code can be written in almost any programming language that has the necessary APIs or foundation classes required to connect to a Web service (Java, C#, Visual Basic, C++, and Perl, to name a few). Figure 15.2 illustrates a simplified SOAP request/response Web service usage process.

Classroom Q & A

Q: Are there alternatives to creating SOAP requests to invoke a response from a Web service?

A: Yes. For example, a simple HTTP Get will work, but using something like that would defeat the purpose of implementing standard SOAP messaging.

Normally, we would not code WSDL files by hand. Many IDE tools, such as Microsoft Studio, WebSphere Studio Application Developer, and others have the necessary built-in tool set to allow us to easily create an XML-related WSDL document to describe a service. WSDL coding is highly standardized, resulting in very predictable behavior. That's why WSDL and these applications work as well as they do.

Meanwhile, development tools and editors, such as those listed in the preceding paragraph, can also connect to a Web service and create skeletal code for client users to use as they create service request code. Later, in the lab exercises, we'll show you how to take advantage of this capability.

A Real WSDL File at Work: The GetLocalTime Web Service

In this section, we demonstrate how WSDL files and client requests work without having to code up a storm (just yet, anyway). To do so, let's look at the GetLocalTime Web service. At this site, the development team has provided access to the code and the necessary service descriptions. (Actually, it's this transparency that influenced us to use it here for illustration. In fact, this time service site serves as a good example of best practices for those who may want to provide a Web service.)

As of this writing, the GetLocalTime Web site is operating with no problem. But we recognize that, as good as it is, it may not last forever. If it has disappeared by the time you read this, then visit the *XML in 60 Minutes a Day* Web site, where we provide a link to an alternate Web service.

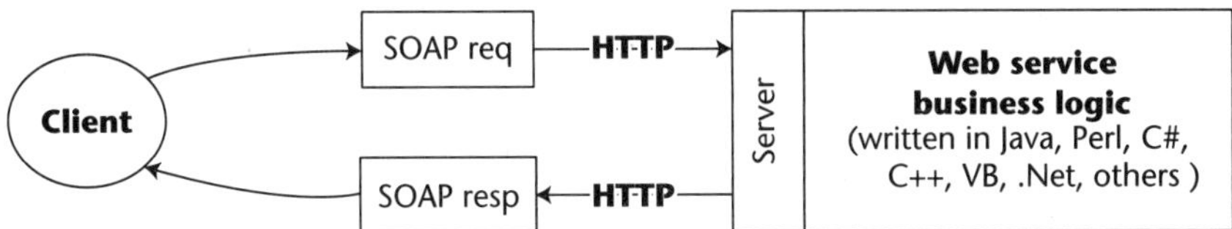

Figure 15.2 SOAP request/response process.

To see how the GetLocalTime Web service works:

1. Activate your browser.
2. Go to http://services.develop.co.za/GetLocalTime.asmx.
3. Click the GetTime link.
4. Click the Invoke button.

A response similar to Figure 15.3 should appear.

The Invoke button was supplied by Web service developers to allow you to see the results quickly. Clicking the Invoke button automatically creates and sends the client request. Client creation and transmission devices like this are used by a Web service provider to facilitate the use of its service.

The GetLocalTime Invoke button executes a GetLocalTimeHTTPGet, but the developers there have configured the Web service so that it can activate, send, and respond to SOAP-based requests as well. Please refer to Figure 15.4 and note the subtle differences between the SOAP/HTTP versus the HTTP Get communication paths.

How do we know that they first used an HTTPGet strategy? We already examined the WSDL file! The developers have also provided their WSDL file code for us, too.

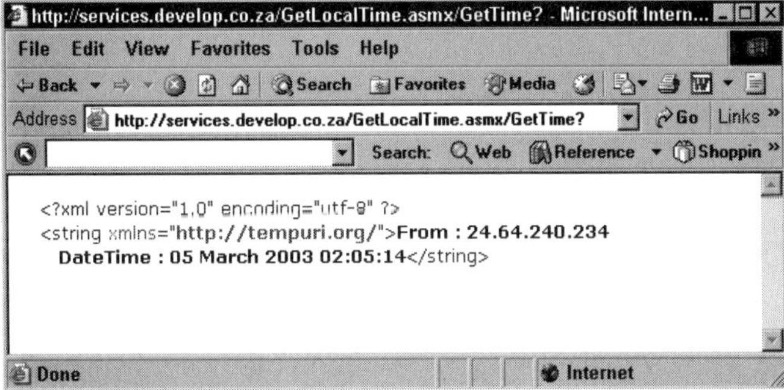

Figure 15.3 Message returned from the GetLocalTime service provider.

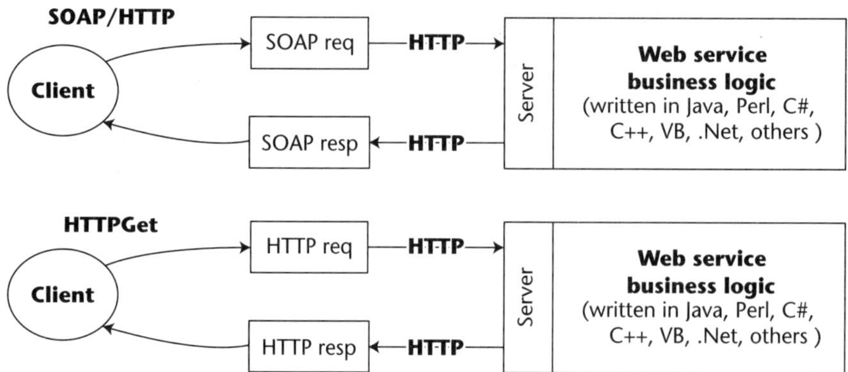

Figure 15.4 Clients invoking Web services. Top view: SOAP. Bottom view: HTTPGet.

WSDL File Structure

Every WSDL document has a specific structure that defines the Web service. WSDL files are not difficult to create; true to their name, they are documents that consist of definitions. The code and structure of a WSDL file is so standard that most coding tools will automatically generate the WSDL file from the class or business logic code. The major mandatory elements are as follows:

A prolog. The only mandatory prolog statement is the <? xml ... ?> XML declaration statement.

<definitions> element. The <definitions> element functions as the root data element. It is no surprise that, since WSDL is a definitions language, the root element should be named <definitions>.

Child elements. Within the <definitions> element, several child elements are required: <types>, <message>, <portType>, <binding>, <port>, and <service>.

We briefly describe the role of each element as we discuss our sample GetLocalTime WSDL file.

A Sample WSDL Document File: GetLocalTime

In this section, we explore the details of a sample WSDL file, top to bottom, a portion at a time. The sample WSDL file we use is available from the GetLocalTime Web service. To find it on the Web:

1. Activate a browser.
2. Go to http://services.develop.co.za/GetLocalTime.asmx.
3. Click the Service Description link.

The Prolog

The GetLocalTime document has only one prolog statement, its XML declaration:

```
<?xml version="1.0" encoding="utf-8" ?>
```

The <definitions> Root Data Element

The <definitions> element type is the root data element for a WSDL document file. Its start tag contains all the namespace declarations for GetLocalTime:

```
<definitions xmlns:http="http://schemas.xmlsoap.org/wsdl/http/"
    xmlns:soap="http://schemas.xmlsoap.org/wsdl/soap/"
    xmlns:s="http://www.w3.org/2001/XMLSchema"
    xmlns:s0="http://tempuri.org/"
    xmlns:soapenc="http://schemas.xmlsoap.org/soap/encoding/"
    xmlns:tm="http://microsoft.com/wsdl/mime/textMatching/"
    xmlns:mime="http://schemas.xmlsoap.org/wsdl/mime/"
      targetNamespace="http://tempuri.org/"
    xmlns="http://schemas.xmlsoap.org/wsdl/">
```

Notice that the service provider customizes the declarations for components whose names begin with the prefix s0. The default namespace is the WSDL namespace.

The end tag, as we'll eventually demonstrate, appears at the end of the WSDL document. From several declarations in this start tag, though, we can see that WSDL files use XML schemas exclusively to provide their component declarations. DTDs are not supported by WSDL.

The <types> Element

The <types> element defines the data types of the messages to be used in the service. XML schema concepts are used (complexTypes, simpleTypes). The values for the name attributes within the <s:element> elements are the pointers to the <part> elements within the respective <message> elements found further on in the WSDL document. As with the <definitions> element, this element provides a major clue that WSDL documents use XML schemas exclusively.

```
<types>
   <s:schema elementFormDefault="qualified"
      targetNamespace="http://tempuri.org/">
      <s:element name="GetTime">
         <s:complexType />
      </s:element>
      <s:element name="GetTimeResponse">
```

```
            <s:complexType>
               <s:sequence>
                  <s:element minOccurs="0" maxOccurs="1"
                     name="GetTimeResult" type="s:string" />
               </s:sequence>
            </s:complexType>
         </s:element>
         <s:element name="string" nillable="true" type="s:string" />
      </s:schema>
   </types>
```

GetTime and GetTimeResult are dealt with as simple string type data. The service provider has defined its own targetNamespace (a reminder, in addition to the <definitions> start tag, that it has created its own schema), so that it can define customized required elements named GetTime, GetTimeResponse, and GetTimeResult without running the risk of clobbering a previously declared element type. In addition, the GetTimeResult element imposes its own min and max specifications: GetTimeResult is actually optional, but if one appears, then only one can appear—the maximum number is one.

The <message> Element

The <message> element is the part or parameter required to access data or fields inside the WSDL <portTypes> (that is, inside the functions or classes).

```
<message name="GetTimeSoapIn">
   <part name="parameters" element="s0:GetTime" />
</message>
<message name="GetTimeSoapOut">
   <part name="parameters" element="s0:GetTimeResponse" />
</message>
<message name="GetTimeHttpGetIn" />
<message name="GetTimeHttpGetOut">
   <part name="Body" element="s0:string" />
</message>
<message name="GetTimeHttpPostIn" />
<message name="GetTimeHttpPostOut">
   <part name="Body" element="s0:string" />
</message>
```

Separate parameters support SOAP requests and HTTP requests. If we want to construct a SOAP request, we would be concerned with GetTimeSoapIn/GetTimeSoapOut, not the GetTimeHTTPGetIn/GetTimeHTTPGetOut pair or the GetTimeHTTPPostIn/GetTimeHTTPPostOut pair. The GetTimeSoapIn and GetTimeSoapOut messages both perform operations; together they form the <portType>.

At this point, we should have a good idea about the code that the service provider has created. This WSDL document almost constructs its own SOAP request; the SOAP request simply sends a string called GetTime. A slightly more complex example is used in the lab exercises, which requires a parameter inside the SOAP message.

The <portType> Element

This portion of the document defines the Web services available. In the GetTime example you should see three <portType> elements that define GetLocalTimeSoap, GetLocalTimeHTTPGet, and GetLocalTimeHTTPPost.

```
<portType name="GetLocalTimeSoap">
   <operation name="GetTime">
      <input message="s0:GetTimeSoapIn" />
      <output message="s0:GetTimeSoapOut" />
   </operation>
</portType>
<portType name="GetLocalTimeHttpGet">
   <operation name="GetTime">
      <input message="s0:GetTimeHttpGetIn" />
      <output message="s0:GetTimeHttpGetOut" />
   </operation>
</portType>
<portType name="GetLocalTimeHttpPost">
   <operation name="GetTime">
      <input message="s0:GetTimeHttpPostIn" />
      <output message="s0:GetTimeHttpPostOut" />
   </operation>
</portType>
```

The provider exposes three functions or methods that we can access to acquire the time. Think of these as interface classes that we can activate for the desired information. If we were going to perform this operation using a SOAP request, we would only be concerned with GetLocalTimeSoap.

This is the second indication that both SOAP and HTTP requests can be sent. At this point, we should make note of the name of the operation: GetTime. We will need this to call the code's interface, which may be one or more methods, functions, or similar items.

The fact that there are both <input> and <output> elements defined for all three <portType> elements indicates that this is a request-response operation. The values of the respective name attributes in the <operation> child elements within the <portType> elements specify the data type of the messages, since they point back to the name attributes of the <s:element> elements within the preceding <types> element.

The <binding> Element

The <binding> elements define both the message format and the protocol used for transporting the operations and messages. Three bindings are defined in this example. The value for the type attribute within the <binding> element start tag ties the binding back to the name attribute found within the respective <portType> elements.

```
<binding name="GetLocalTimeSoap" type="s0:GetLocalTimeSoap">
   <soap:binding transport=http://schemas.xmlsoap.org/soap/http
      style="document" />
   <operation name="GetTime">
      <soap:operation soapAction="http://tempuri.org/GetTime"
         style="document" />
      <input>
         <soap:body use="literal" />
      </input>
      <output>
         <soap:body use="literal" />
      </output>
   </operation>
</binding>
<binding name="GetLocalTimeHttpGet" type="s0:GetLocalTimeHttpGet">
   <http:binding verb="GET" />
   <operation name="GetTime">
      <http:operation location="/GetTime" />
      <input>
         <http:urlEncoded />
      </input>
      <output>
         <mime:mimeXml part="Body" />
      </output>
   </operation>
</binding>
<binding name="GetLocalTimeHttpPost" type="s0:GetLocalTimeHttpPost">
   <http:binding verb="POST" />
   <operation name="GetTime">
      <http:operation location="/GetTime" />
      <input>
         <mime:content type="application/x-www-form-urlencoded" />
      </input>
      <output>
         <mime:mimeXml part="Body" />
      </output>
   </operation>
</binding>
```

The binding for the SOAP-related request is defined in the first <binding> element, the one containing the name attribute whose value is GetLocalTimeSoap. This binding element tells us that the name of the service is GetLocalTimeSoap, GetLocalTimeSoap is defined as the port, and GetTime is the operation.

Within the <input> and <output> elements, there are <soap:body> elements whose start tags contain use attributes. The value specified for each use attribute is literal, indicating that the message that appears within the <Body> element of the SOAP request message will not be encoded. It will be identical to the messages specified previously in the <input> or <output> elements within the <operation> elements within the respective <portType> element. In other words, the input message will be s0:GetTimeSoapIn, and the output will be s0:GetTimeSoapOut.

From the attributes in the <soap:binding> element within the <binding> element, we see that we are using HTTP as the transport protocol, and the message styles are documents. The only other option for the value of the style attribute in the <binding> element is RPC (Remote Procedure Call).

The <service> and <port> Elements

The <port> element defines the end point by specifying a single address for a specific binding (that is, it defines the connection point or address of the service). In this example, the GetLocalTimeSoap port name points to the <binding> element of the same name, since the name of the binding is specified as the value for the binding attribute in <port>. The specific address http://services.develop.co.za/GetLocalTime.asmx is tied to the port by being specified as the value for the location attribute within the <soap:address> child element within <port>. We can specify only one address per port.

```
<service name="GetLocalTime">
   <port name="GetLocalTimeSoap" binding="s0:GetLocalTimeSoap">
      <soap:address
        location="http://services.develop.co.za/GetLocalTime.asmx" />
   </port>
   <port name="GetLocalTimeHttpGet" binding="s0:GetLocalTimeHttpGet">
      <http:address
        location="http://services.develop.co.za/GetLocalTime.asmx" />
   </port>
   <port name="GetLocalTimeHttpPost"
        binding="s0:GetLocalTimeHttpPost">
      <http:address
        location="http://services.develop.co.za/GetLocalTime.asmx" />
   </port>
</service>
```

The <service> element groups all the port information for the ports related to a single service—the one specified by the value for the name attribute in the <service> element start tag. Remember, a single WSDL document may define several services, bindings, and ports; this document only defines one, the GetLocalTime service. Two HTTP-binding ports also exist within the <service> element, since they, too, are related to the GetLocalTime service.

The Last Line

After the <service> element has been defined, one last line is inserted:

```
</definitions>
```

This last line closes the WSDL document file for the GetLocalTime service.

The Bottom Line

From this exploration of a sample WSDL document file, we see that the operation GetTime requires no input parameters and returns a time result as a string. Basically, to the service consumer, WSDL files are really quite simple. When looking at them, try not to get caught in the quagmire of code. Just keep in mind that, whether you are developing WSDL files or analyzing them, there are only so many services and only so many major elements, so many ports and so many bindings. It's like going to a grocery store: We won't be interested in buying everything in stock. We usually look for and select comparatively few items. The same is true in a WSDL file.

What Is SOAP?

When describing the four aspects of the UDDI, we mentioned that business integration needs a common communications protocol. The Simple Object Access Protocol is just such a protocol. SOAP is a standard, lightweight, platform- and language-neutral (but still specialized) machine-to-machine protocol that is used to format messages, information, and responses into a common format in a decentralized, distributed environment, so that any Web service that implements SOAP can read, process, and respond to them. Although our introductory-level approach to SOAP won't really reflect it, SOAP is a metaprotocol (in other words, a protocol that can also be used to create other protocols).

SOAP uses XML technologies to define a messaging framework and provide a specific message construct that can be exchanged over a variety of underlying protocols like HTTP or SMTP. The SOAP framework was designed to be simple, extensible, and independent of any particular programming model and other implementation-specific semantics.

To summarize, SOAP facilitates message exchanges in a distributed environment. It does so by creating an envelope to surround an XML-based message called its *payload*. That message must be delivered and processed. The overall premise is that if we can get everyone to conform to the new SOAP-aware XML Web services using SOAP as the primary protocol, then information and messages will flow freely and there will be a reduction in redundant development.

SOAP itself is not a transport-level protocol. In other words, a SOAP message still requires the help of a transport protocol such as HTTP on TCP/IP. And, by the way, HTTP on TCP/IP is not the only transport protocol that SOAP can bind to or use. Any protocol that is designed to support RPCs will work. But since HTTP has become so prevalent over the Web, it has become the most common protocol for transporting SOAP messages. Messages combining SOAP and HTTP are accepted and processed by servlets running on the Web service provider's servers. Such messages can be used to transfer information or to invoke remote services on other systems.

As an example, let's say the Space Gems site is looking for an economical way to perform credit card validation. It could locate an existing service, send a SOAP message request to that Web service to perform a credit card validation, and ship our product only after receiving a positive response. This alleviates Space Gems from having to purchase, maintain, and store all the database information on its own systems. What the world doesn't need is thousands of copies of the same consumer credit database information everywhere (unless, of course, your business is selling such databases).

The uses for these types of services and the business opportunities they breed are limitless.

Development of the SOAP Specification

The development of the SOAP specification took place in two major phases. The first SOAP specification was developed by DevelopMentor, Inc., Microsoft Corporation, and UserLand Software, Inc., beginning in 1998. Industry feedback on the first publicly announced SOAP 0.9 specification was solicited by Microsoft in September 1999. The SOAP/1.0 specification was published in December 1999. For various reasons, development slowed, and UserLand subsequently developed a separate protocol, XML-RPC.

SOAP development restarted with contributions from the original developers plus IBM and Lotus Development Corp. These industry proponents made some technical changes to make SOAP's modular nature more apparent. This resulted in SOAP/1.1, which some argue was not much better than SOAP/1.0. It was submitted as a proposal to the W3C in May 2001. Parallel developments in Java, specifically the J2EE specification, and the introduction of Microsoft's .NET technology further spurred SOAP development.

Upon receipt of the SOAP/1.0 submission, the W3C published it as a Note, titled Simple Object Access Protocol (SOAP) 1.1, in May 2001. Further SOAP development is being done by the XML Protocol Working Group, which is part of the W3C's Web Services Activity. Basic SOAP/1.1 messages have survived virtually intact, with only a few changes in document structure, syntax, HTTP binding, RPCs, and SOAP encodings.

Table 15.1 Components of the Three-Part SOAP 1.2 Specification

SOAP VERSION 1.2 PART	COMPONENTS
Part 1 – Messaging Framework	SOAP processing model SOAP extensibility model Framework for SOAP to underlying protocols SOAP message structure
Part 2 – Adjuncts	SOAP data model SOAP data encoding RPC calls and responses Features and binding Message exchange patterns WWW method controls Binding SOAP to HTTP
Part 0 – Primer	Tutorial describing SOAP 1.2 features

A last call for technical drafts for SOAP 1.2 was issued July 2, 2002. In December 2002, the W3C published three SOAP 1.2 Candidate Recommendations, each prescribing a part of the full SOAP 1.2 specification. Table 15.1 summarizes the components of the three-part SOAP 1.2 specification.

By the time you read this, we expect that the candidate recommendations will already have been endorsed as full W3C Recommendations. We also expect that the final version of the SOAP specifications may be called XP.

(If you need to know what implementations are available for SOAP 1.2, check the W3C's SOAP 1.2 Implementation Summary at www.w3.org/2000/xp/Group/2/03/soap1.2implementation.html.)

If you need further information regarding the three parts of the W3C SOAP specification, visit the following three Web sites:

Part 1: www.w3.org/TR/2002/CR-soap12-part1-20021219/

Part 2: www.w3.org/TR/2002/CR-soap12-part2-20021219/

Part 0: www.w3.org/TR/2002/CR-soap12-part0-20021219/

Meanwhile, for developers and providers who have already invested in SOAP/1.1, a complete list of enhancements and changes can be viewed by visiting the SOAP 1.2 Part 0 specification at www.w3c.org/TR/soap12-part0 and clicking the link titled "6. Changes between SOAP 1.1 and SOAP 1.2."

Basic SOAP Message Construct

The basic premises for SOAP messages have not changed substantially from SOAP 1.1 to 1.2. Referring back to Figures 15.2 and 15.4, consider those little request messages that are volleyed from the client to the XML Web service on the server, and those response messages that are volleyed back from the server to the client, both courtesy of HTTP as the transport protocol. Figure 15.5 represents a basic HTTP/SOAP message. Here, we focus on the SOAP coding, because various coding tools generally provide sufficient HTTP header coding.

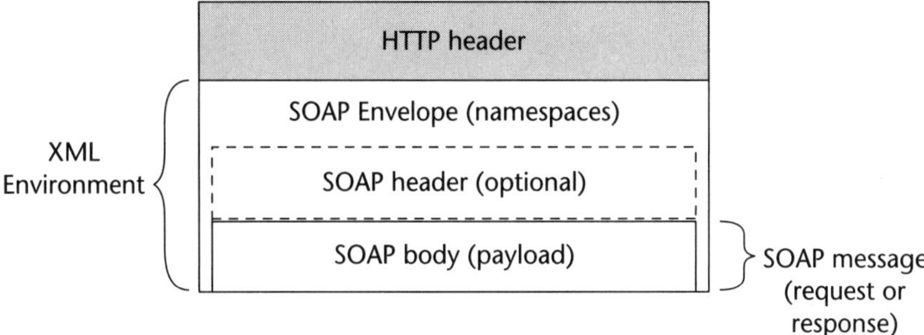

Figure 15.5 Graphical representation of a SOAP message.

The SOAP message itself is written with XML-related components in an XML-related structure. We'll examine the components in order, using the following code as an illustrative example. It is an actual, functional request message used to retrieve a daily quote from a Web service.

```
<?xml version="1.0" encoding="UTF-8" standalone="no"?>
<SOAP-ENV:Envelope
     xmlns:SOAP-ENV="http://schemas.xmlsoap.org/soap/envelope/"
     xmlns:wsdlns="http://tempuri.org/wsdl/"
     xmlns:typens="http://tempuri.org/type"
     xmlns:soap="http://schemas.xmlsoap.org/wsdl/soap/"
     xmlns:xsd="http://www.w3.org/2001/XMLSchema"
     xmlns:stk="http://schemas.microsoft.com/soap-toolkit/wsdl-extension"
     xmlns:SOAP-ENC="http://schemas.xmlsoap.org/soap/encoding/"
     xmlns:xsi="http://www.w3.org/2001/XMLSchema-instance" >
   <SOAP-ENV:Body>
     <mns:getTodaysQuote xmlns:mns="http://tempuri.org/message/"
        SOAP-ENV:encodingStyle="http://schemas.xmlsoap.org/
        soap/encoding/">
     </mns:getTodaysQuote>
   </SOAP-ENV:Body>
</SOAP-ENV:Envelope>
```

You can clearly see the XML elements that represent the Envelope and Body parts. Did you notice that there is no <Header> element (also referred to as a SOAP Header)?

Classroom Q & A

Q: What would the previous request message look like if it had a SOAP header?

A: The identical message, including a <Header> element, is shown below. The <Header> element code is highlighted for emphasis.

```
<?xml version="1.0" encoding="UTF-8" standalone="no"?>
   <SOAP-ENV:Envelope
        xmlns:SOAP-ENV="http://schemas.xmlsoap.org/soap/envelope/"
        xmlns:wsdlns="http://tempuri.org/wsdl/"
        xmlns:typens="http://tempuri.org/type"
        xmlns:soap="http://schemas.xmlsoap.org/wsdl/soap/"
        xmlns:xsd="http://www.w3.org/2001/XMLSchema"
        xmlns:stk="http://schemas.microsoft.com/
           soap-toolkit/wsdl-extension"
        xmlns:SOAP-ENC="http://schemas.xmlsoap.org/soap/encoding/"
        xmlns:xsi="http://www.w3.org/2001/XMLSchema-instance" >
      <SOAP-ENV:Header>
         <mn:alertcontrol xmlns:mn="http://tempuri.org/alertcontrol>
            <mn:priority>1</mn:priority>
            <mn:expires>2002-06-22T14:00:00-03:00</mn:expires>
         </mn:alertcontrol>
      </SOAP-ENV:Header>
      <SOAP-ENV:Body>
         <mns:getTodaysQuote xmlns:mns="http://tempuri.org/message/"
            SOAP-ENV:encodingStyle="http://schemas.xmlsoap.org/
            soap/encoding/">
         </mns:getTodaysQuote>
      </SOAP-ENV:Body>
</SOAP-ENV:Envelope>
```

The SOAP Envelope

The <Envelope> element is the SOAP message's root element. Each message is composed, at a minimum, of the SOAP <Envelope>, its optional child <Header> element, and its mandatory child <Body> element. Sometimes the <Envelope> element is mistakenly referred to as the environment because in its start tag, we declare all the namespaces—including any user-defined namespaces—and schema references. Notice that the start tag is actually <SOAP-ENV:Envelope>. The prefix SOAP-ENV stems from its namespace declaration, the value of which must be http://schemas.xmlsoap.org/soap/envelope/ to indicate that it is a SOAP-related envelope (as opposed to other kinds of envelopes). The namespace value reflects the current schema for the SOAP 1.1 envelope.

One of the frustrating issues about SOAP specifications in general is that in an overall SOAP version (SOAP 1.2), current versions for each SOAP part—that is, for the Envelope, Header, and Body—also exist. If you need further information regarding the SOAP Envelope schema, visit the W3C's Web site at www.w3.org/2001/06/soap-envelope.

Notice that the <Envelope> start tag contains a comprehensive list of namespace declarations. All the message's components must be accounted for, with respect to namespaces.

```
<?xml version="1.0" encoding="UTF-8" standalone="no"?>
<SOAP-ENV:Envelope
     xmlns:SOAP-ENV="http://schemas.xmlsoap.org/soap/envelope/"
     xmlns:http="http://schemas.xmlsoap.org/wsdl/http/"
     xmlns:soap="http://schemas.xmlsoap.org/wsdl/soap/"
     xmlns:s="http://www.w3.org/2001/XMLSchema"
     xmlns:s0="http://tempuri.org/"
     xmlns:soapenc="http://schemas.xmlsoap.org/soap/encoding/"
     xmlns:tm="http://microsoft.com/wsdl/mime/textMatching/"
     xmlns:mime="http://schemas.xmlsoap.org/wsdl/mime/"
     xmlns:xsi="http://www.w3.org/2001/XMLSchema-instance"
     xmlns:xsd="http://www.w3.org/2001/XMLSchema" >
   <soap:Header>
      <m:Trans xmlns:m="http://www.tampuri.org/transaction/"
         soap:mustUnderstand="1" soap:actor=http://tempuri.org/timeapp/>
 13:00:06
      </m:Trans>
   </soap:Header>
   <SOAP-ENV:Body>
      <s0:GetTime xmlns:s0="http://tempuri.org/"> </s0:GetTime>
   </SOAP-ENV:Body>
</SOAP-ENV:Envelope>
```

The SOAP Header

In any SOAP message, the <Header> element is optional, but when one appears, it must be nested within the <Envelope> element and must appear before the <Body> element. Meanwhile, SOAP is a clever protocol, but you can make it even more clever by adding metadata to the <Header> element. In theory, this metadata is processed prior to opening the actual message in the <Body> element. Thus, the metadata header is the place to give instructions to the parser regarding how the message should be processed before the message is actually read. The metadata in the <Header> element is user-defined and is based on priority setting, transaction-based requirements, alerts, expiration, authentication, or other coding or transmission requirements.

For example, let's consider a situation where there may be a queue full of SOAP messages. It would make sense to order the queued SOAP messages by priority before processing and to put such order or urgency-related information into the Header as metadata, so that the receiver doesn't have to process or read the actual message to determine its priority.

In the following example, we coded in the concept of priority, but this could also have been a transaction-based requirement (for example, a typical transaction-based requirement might state that if a network fault is encountered, a rollback or retry should occur).

Metadata information might also be handy if the SOAP messages are intended to be one-way, two-way, or multidirectional. A multidirectional message passes from A to B over a network, and also passes through one or more intermediary systems (that is, through intermediate nodes). Information in the header can be read and processed by the intermediary nodes as the message travels to its ultimate receiver (that is, its ultimate destination server). Thus, decisions in processing can be made en route.

The following three attributes, which can be used to enhance the header's meaning, do not appear inside our previous code example. A code example containing the three attributes is presented after the discussion of the attributes.

The role Attribute

The role attribute (which replaces the older actor attribute) can be used to address the message to a specific end point. It indicates the SOAP node to which the SOAP message block is targeted. The value is a URI. This attribute should only appear in SOAP headers. A SOAP receiver must ignore the role attribute if it appears on any descendant of a SOAP <Body> element. A SOAP-aware application is expected to process a header block if its URI is the one identified as the value of the role attribute.

The mustUnderstand Attribute

By default, if servers don't understand an element, they follow the rule "Ignore all elements you don't understand." To modify this default behavior with respect to SOAP headers, the mustUnderstand attribute was developed. The mustUnderstand attribute in the <Header> start tag, or in the start tag of a child element within <Header>, indicates whether the processing of a SOAP header block is mandatory (mustUnderstand="1" or mustUnderstand="true") or optional (mustUnderstand="0" or mustUnderstand="false"). A SOAP header block *may* carry this attribute information item; it's not mandatory.

When the value of the attribute is "true" or "1," the SOAP header block is said to be mandatory and the receiving system software must attempt to recognize the header element in which the attribute is inserted. If the receiving system cannot recognize the element, it must generate a SOAP fault message.

If there is no mustUnderstand attribute or if the value of the mustUnderstand attribute is "0" or "false," the system can ignore the element. Mandatory SOAP header blocks will thus modify the semantics of other SOAP header blocks or SOAP body elements. In summary, for every mandatory SOAP header block targeted to a node, that node must either process the header block or not process the SOAP message at all and instead generate a fault. SOAP fault messages are discussed later in this chapter, in the section titled *SOAP Faults*.

The encodingStyle Attribute

The encodingStyle attribute information item may appear:

- In the start tag of a SOAP header block or a descendant element
- In the start tag of a child element (or descendant) of the SOAP <Body> element, as long as that child element is not a SOAP <Fault> element
- In the start tag of a child element of the SOAP <Detail> element, or in any of its descendants

Otherwise, the attribute must not appear within any element other than those candidates in the preceding list. The attribute's value (in the form of a URI) identifies a set of serialization rules that can be used to deserialize the SOAP message. The possible values we can specify for the encodingStyle attribute are as follows:

www.w3.org/2002/12/soap-encoding. Indicating SOAP encoding.

www.w3.org/2002/12/soap-envelope/encoding/none. Indicating that there is no encoding.

http://example.org/encoding/. Here, we are using a generic URI to indicate that an organization (in this case, the fictitious Example Org) can create and specify its own custom encoding scheme.

Because in the example this attribute is not exclusive to the <Header> element, its namespace declaration is shown inside the <Envelope> start tag.

Here is the previous example, now supplemented to show you how we might use the three <Header> attributes (components containing the supplemental code are highlighted for emphasis):

```
<?xml version="1.0" encoding="UTF-8" standalone="no"?>
<SOAP-ENV:Envelope
    xmlns:SOAP-ENV="http://schemas.xmlsoap.org/soap/envelope/"
```

```
      xmlns:http="http://schemas.xmlsoap.org/wsdl/http/"
      xmlns:soap="http://schemas.xmlsoap.org/wsdl/soap/"
      xmlns:s="http://www.w3.org/2001/XMLSchema"
      xmlns:s0="http://tempuri.org/"
      xmlns:soapenc="http://www.w3.org/2002/12/soap-envelope"
      xmlns:tm="http://microsoft.com/wsdl/mime/textMatching/"
      xmlns:mime="http://schemas.xmlsoap.org/wsdl/mime/"
      xmlns:xsi="http://www.w3.org/2001/XMLSchema-instance"
      xmlns:xsd="http://www.w3.org/2001/XMLSchema" >
    <soap:Header>
      <m:Trans xmlns:m="http://www.tempuri.org/transaction/"
         soap:mustUnderstand="1" soap:role=http://tempuri.org/timeapp/
         soapenc:encodingStyle="http://www.w3.org/2002/12/
           soap-envelope/encoding/none >
    13:00:06
      </m:Trans>
    </soap:Header>
    <SOAP-ENV:Body>
      <s0:GetTime xmlns:s0="http://tempuri.org/">
      </s0:GetTime>
    </SOAP-ENV:Body>
</SOAP-ENV:Envelope>
```

The SOAP Body

The SOAP <Body> element is required. It contains the SOAP message or payload intended for the end point or ultimate receiver (that is, the SOAP-aware application to which the payload is addressed). Thus, the SOAP Body contains the actual SOAP request or SOAP response. The <Body> element is also where you find any returned fault or error messages. No elements are allowed after the <Body> element.

It is best practice to assign an explicit namespace to the element inside the SOAP Body—do not use or inherit the default namespace from the root element, if possible.

Although not shown in this example, any parameters required as arguments to the receiver are set in the <Body> element. Examples in the lab exercises demonstrate how parameters are passed. In *Lab 15.3: Email Verifier with Parameters*, for example, you must supply an email address as an argument for the Web service to validate.

SOAP Request Example

SOAP requests sent over an HTTP protocol are sent as an HTTP POST. Here is our small but typical GetTime SOAP request, not including the HTTP header:

```
<?xml version="1.0" encoding="UTF-8" standalone="no"?>
<SOAP-ENV:Envelope
     xmlns:SOAP-ENV="http://schemas.xmlsoap.org/soap/envelope/"
     xmlns:http="http://schemas.xmlsoap.org/wsdl/http/"
     xmlns:soap="http://schemas.xmlsoap.org/wsdl/soap/"
     xmlns:s="http://www.w3.org/2001/XMLSchema"
     xmlns:s0="http://tempuri.org/"
     xmlns:soapenc="http://www.w3.org/2002/12/soap-envelope"
     xmlns:tm="http://microsoft.com/wsdl/mime/textMatching/"
     xmlns:mime="http://schemas.xmlsoap.org/wsdl/mime/"
     xmlns:xsi="http://www.w3.org/2001/XMLSchema-instance"
     xmlns:xsd="http://www.w3.org/2001/XMLSchema" >
  <soap:Header>
    <m:Trans xmlns:m="http://www.tempuri.org/transaction/"
      soap:mustUnderstand="1" soap:role=http://tempuri.org/timeapp
      soapenc:encodingStyle="http://www.w3.org/2002/12/" />
      13:00:06
    </m:Trans>
  </soap:Header>
  <SOAP-ENV:Body>
    <s0:GetTime xmlns:s0="http://tempuri.org/"> </s0:GetTime>
  </SOAP-ENV:Body>
</SOAP-ENV:Envelope>
```

SOAP Response Example

Here is a typical GetTime SOAP response (not including the HTTP header):

```
<?xml version="1.0" encoding="utf-8" ?>
<soap:Envelope xmlns:soap="http://schemas.xmlsoap.org/soap/envelope/"
     xmlns:xsi="http://www.w3.org/2001/XMLSchema-instance"
     xmlns:xsd="http://www.w3.org/2001/XMLSchema">
  <soap:Body>
    <GetTimeResponse xmlns="http://tempuri.org/">
      <GetTimeResult>
        From : 63.75.203.6 DateTime : 29 December 2002 11:10:05
      </GetTimeResult>
    </GetTimeResponse>
  </soap:Body>
</soap:Envelope>
```

SOAP Faults

When an error or fault occurs, it results in the generation of a fault message. A SOAP <Fault> element exists exclusively for this purpose. To be recognized as carrying SOAP error information, a SOAP message must contain a single

<Fault> element as the only child element of the <Body> element. The subelements to the <Fault> element must appear in this order:

A mandatory <Code> element. <Code> contains a mandatory <Value> element and an optional <Subcode> element. We discuss the values for the <Value> element later.

A mandatory <Reason> element. <Reason> contains one or more <Text> elements, each of which should have a different value as its xml:lang attribute.

An optional <Node> element. The value of the <Node> element is the URI of the SOAP node that generated the fault. If it is not the ultimate receiver, the SOAP node must include this element. If it is the ultimate receiver, the node may include this element to indicate explicitly that it generated the fault.

An optional <Role> element. The value for this element must be one of the roles assumed by the node.

An optional <Detail> element. This element contains zero or more attributes or zero or more child elements. <Detail> might contain information message deficiencies. All child elements are called detail entries.

Values for the <Value> Element within the <Code> Element

The following possible values might be specified within the <Value> element nested within the <Code> element that, in turn, is nested within the <Fault> element:

VersionMismatch. Found an invalid namespace for the SOAP <Envelope> element.

MustUnderstand. An immediate child element of the <Header> element, with the mustUnderstand attribute set to "1," was not understood.

DataEncodingUnknown. A SOAP header block or SOAP body child element has data encoding that the "X" node does not support.

Sender. The message was incorrectly formed or did not contain the appropriate information (examples: lacks proper authentication or payment information). Generally, the message must not be re-sent without changes.

Receiver. Message could not be processed for reasons attributable to the server processes, not to the message contents (example: an upstream SOAP node, if applicable, might not have responded). The message might succeed if re-sent later.

SOAP's fault structure becomes quite involved. If you need further information, please visit the SOAP—Part 1 Candidate Recommendation Web page at www.w3.org/TR/soap12-part1/#soapfault.

Example SOAP Fault Message

This sample SOAP error message shows what SOAP faults look like:

```
<?xml version="1.0" encoding="utf-8" ?>
<soap:Envelope xmlns:soap="http://schemas.xmlsoap.org/soap/envelope/">
   <soap:Body>
      <soap:Fault>
         <soap:Code>
            <soap:Value>soap:VersionMismatch</soap:Value>
         </soap:Code>
         <soap:Reason>
            <soap:Text>System.Web.Services.Protocols.SoapException:
                Possible SOAP version mismatch: Envelope namespace
                http://schemas.xmlsoap.org/soap1/envelope/ was
                   unexpected.
                Expecting http://schemas.xmlsoap.org/soap/envelope/.
                at System.Web.Services.Protocols.SoapServerProtocol.
                   ReadParameters()
                at System.Web.Services.Protocols.WebServiceHandler.
                   Invoke()
                at System.Web.Services.Protocols.WebServiceHandler.
                   CoreProcessRequest()
            </soap:Text>
         </soap:Reason>
      </soap:Fault>
   </soap:Body>
</soap:Envelope>
```

Chapter 15 Labs: Accessing Web Services with SOAP

These simple entry-level lab exercises show you how to use the information obtained from an XML Web service WSDL file and how to access some third-party Web services. These utility and help sites are good examples of what is available to test your SOAP server service. We use them to demonstrate just how generic SOAP client code is. We don't expect you to perform any coding here; just think about the types of requests you're sending and the responses you're getting. In fact, the code is so generic it can be auto-generated directly from the WSDL file. In the event that any of these third-party sites change, visit the book's Web site for new labs.

Lab 15.1: Time Service

1. Activate your Web browser. Type the following in the locator bar:

   `http://www.soapclient.com/soapmsg.html.`

2. Skip the top part of the page that has to do with the SOAP Message Builder. Navigate down to the SOAP Message Generator. Enter the location of the WSDL file for the Time Service Web service.

   a. For WSDL File, enter the following URL on one line with no breaks:

      `http://services.develop.co.za/GetLocalTime.asmx?WSDL`

   b. For Method Name enter GetTime.

3. Click Generate.

4. Move back to the top of the page. The Server Address, SOAP Action, and SOAP Message code has been auto-generated and is ready to use.

5. Click Execute to send the SOAP request. The SOAP response will be similar to Figure 15.6.

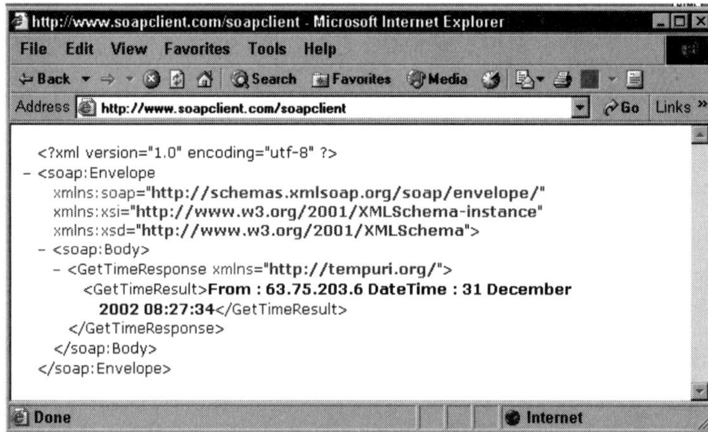

Figure 15.6 SOAP message results.

Lab 15.2: Daily Quote Generator

1. Activate your browser again and type the following in the locator bar:

   ```
   http://www.soapclient.com/soapmsg.html.
   ```

2. Skip the top part of the page that has to do with the SOAP Message Builder. Navigate down to the SOAP Message generator. Enter the location of the WSDL file for the Today's Quote Web service.

   a. For WSDL File, enter the following URL on one line with no breaks:

      ```
      http://webservice.effective--web.net/globalself/
      globalselfDailyThought.WSDL
      ```

   b. For Method Name, enter "getTodaysQuote".

3. Click Generate.
4. Move back to the top of the page. The Server Address, SOAP Action, and SOAP Message code has been auto-generated and is ready to use.
5. Click Execute to send the SOAP request. You should see a SOAP response similar to Figure 15.7.

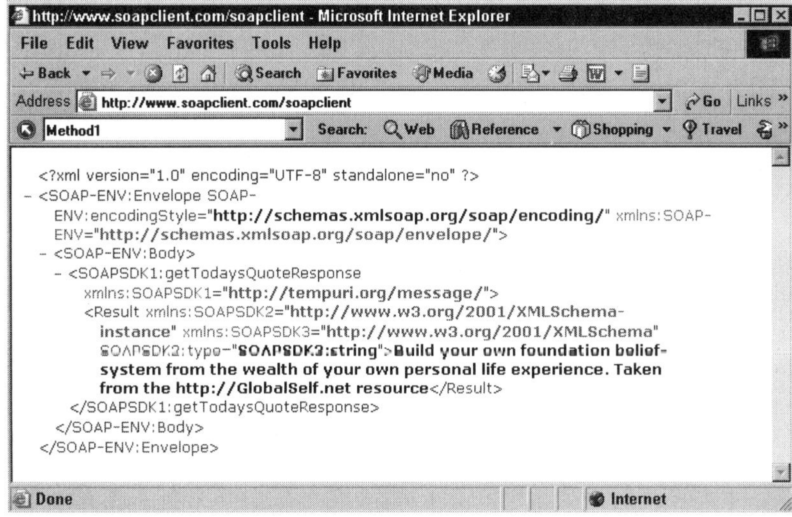

Figure 15.7 SOAP message results.

Lab 15.3: Email Verifier with Parameters

This XML Web service is interesting, since it ensures that you understand how to interpret a WSDL file well enough to pick out the required parameters.

1. Activate your browser and type the following into the locator bar:

   ```
   http://www.soapclient.com/uddisearch.html.
   ```

2. In the UDDI Browser, set the following search criteria:
   a. Operator: "Microsoft"
   b. Search for "email" in Service Names.
   c. Click Search.
3. Scroll down to Email Verify. Make sure that you have CDYNE (because we know it works).
4. Click Discovery URL to review the XML file.
5. Locate the Web Service Interface for Email Verify, and note exactly where the WSDL file for the Email Verify is. Hint: look for the <accessPoint ...> element that contains a URLType attribute whose value is http.
6. Go to the WSDL file for the Email Verify by entering the URL that you discovered in the previous step in your browser:

   ```
   http://ws.cdyne.com/emailverify/ev.asmx?wsdl
   ```

7. Inside the WSDL file, find the name of the method. It's called VerifyEmail. Make a note of it. You will need it later.
8. Inside the VerifyEmail method, a parameter is defined as "email" in a typestring where minOccurs= "0" and maxOccurs= "1". Make a note of it, too. You will need it later also.
9. In your browser, type the following in the locator bar:

   ```
   http://www.soapclient.com/soapmsg.html.
   ```

10. Skip the top part of the page that has to do with the SOAP Message Builder. Navigate down to the SOAP Message Generator. Enter the location of the WSDL file for the Email Verifier Web service.
    a. For WSDL File, enter the following URL on one line with no breaks:

       ```
       http://ws.cdyne.com/emailverify/ev.asmx?wsdl
       ```

    b. For Method Name, enter VerifyEmail.

11. Move back to the top of the page. The Server Address, SOAP Action, and SOAP Message code has been auto-generated and is ready to use—except for the one parameter, called *email*.

12. Enter a valid string value for the message to pass to the method to check. Modify the code so that it matches the code that follows, but insert your own email address. The modified line is highlighted.

```
<?xml version="1.0" encoding="UTF-8" standalone="no"?>
<SOAP-ENV:Envelope
     xmlns:SOAP-ENV="http://schemas.xmlsoap.org/soap/envelope/"
     xmlns:http="http://schemas.xmlsoap.org/wsdl/http/"
     xmlns:soap="http://schemas.xmlsoap.org/wsdl/soap/"
     xmlns:s="http://www.w3.org/2001/XMLSchema"
     xmlns:s0="http://ws.cdyne.com/"
     xmlns:soapenc="http://schemas.xmlsoap.org/soap/encoding/"
     xmlns:tm="http://microsoft.com/wsdl/mime/textMatching/"
     xmlns:mime="http://schemas.xmlsoap.org/wsdl/mime/"
     xmlns:xsi="http://www.w3.org/2001/XMLSchema-instance"
     xmlns:xsd="http://www.w3.org/2001/XMLSchema" >
   <SOAP-ENV:Body>
      <s0:VerifyEmail xmlns:s0="http://ws.cdyne.com/">
         <s0:email>linda@skillsinmotion.com</s0:email>
      </s0:VerifyEmail>
   </SOAP-ENV:Body>
</SOAP-ENV:Envelope>
```

13. Click Execute to send the SOAP request. First try sending a request that you know is correct; then send a request that you know is incorrect.

Summary

SOAP technology and concepts can't be isolated and explained alone. SOAP must be explained within the context of XML Web services, because it is a part of that environment. Meanwhile, more programming tools for SOAP are constantly being developed and introduced, since SOAP is rapidly increasing in popularity. Here are a few more SOAP-related facts you should take away with you:

- We provided two definitions for Web services. Both are acceptable. Essentially, Web services are business applications with Internet-related, standards-based technologies. They are accessed by existing or potential customers, suppliers, and partners using a variety of hardware and platforms.

- The UDDI Business Registry has endless potential and will probably be the key for successful business-to-business interoperability. UDDI provides a database of useful services: some for free, some for a fee. Developers and providers are responsible for creating the services and registering the services. Although the services themselves can be written in various languages like Visual Basic, C#, Java, and C++, they shall, by specification, include WSDL XML files and service descriptions on how to use the services.
- WSDL files are XML files and are the key to Web service consumption, forming a contract between the code and XML Web services. WSDL files are well structured, and although they can be coded by hand, they are more often auto-generated by the programmer's IDE or other development tool set.
- SOAP messages are XML files. Their root data element is <Envelope>. <Header> elements are optional but useful for containing metadata. The mandatory <Body> element contains the SOAP payload (whether request or response).
- Typically, there are SOAP requests and SOAP responses. SOAP requires the help of a transport protocol, usually HTTP, to move information from node to node.
- When we refer to XML Web services, we mean UDDI, WSDL, and SOAP messaging working together. Special Web extensions, APIs, and foundation classes are required to support XML Web services. A normal Web server will not have the capability to receive and respond to SOAP messages.
- XML Web services, with SOAP messaging, are the future of e-business.

Review Questions

1. Which of the following protocols is used to discover XML Web services?
   a. WSDL
   b. SOAP
   c. UDDI
   d. XMLP
   e. RPC
2. True or false? It is mandatory for Web services to be registered with a UDDI registry.
3. Which XML file describes the service in enough detail for a Web services consumer?
   a. UDDI
   b. tModel
   c. XMIDL
   d. WSDL
   e. All of the above
4. True or false? WSDL XML files are generated from the programmer's code using a supplied utility or tool.
5. The transport protocol for SOAP messaging is
   a. TCP/IP
   b. IIOP
   c. RPC
   d. HTTP
   e. None of the above
6. True or false? A SOAP request can be auto-generated from a WSDL XML file.
7. Which Web site would you visit to obtain the most recent status and information on the SOAP/1.2 specification?
   a. www.w3c.org
   b. www.uddi.org
   c. http://schemas.xmlsoap.org
   d. www.xmlsoap.org

8. What are the mandatory required elements of a SOAP message?
   a. <Envelope>
   b. <Header>
   c. <Body>
   d. <Fault>
   e. All of the above
9. True or false? It is a best practice to ensure that all attributes inside the <Envelope> element of the SOAP request be namespace-qualified.
10. Which of the following namespaces identifies the <Envelope> element as a SOAP envelope?
    a. http://schemas.xmlsoap.org/soap
    b. http://schemas.xmlsoap.org/wsdl/soap
    c. http://schemas.xmlsoap.org/soap/envelope
    d. http://schemas.xmlsoap.org/wsdl/envelope
    e. None of the above

Answers to Review Questions

1. **a.** UDDI. Universal Discovery, Description, and Integration. The root organization for UDDI services is http:/www.uddi.org.
2. False. By registering with a UDDI service, you can be discovered and uniquely classified. No rule out there says that you have to register the service.
3. WSDL. Once the WSDL XML file has been located, a considerable amount of information can be derived–in fact, enough to create a SOAP message to request information.
4. True. Yes, it is the responsibility of the programmer to create a working WSDL XML file. Although it can be auto-generated from the code, it is a good idea for a programmer to be familiar with WSDL files so that he or she can troubleshoot and tweak the WSDL XML file if necessary.
5. **d.** HTTP. However, it is not the only protocol, but rather the protocol of choice. Remember HTTP + XML = SOAP.
6. True. A technically correct WSDL file has enough information in it to create a valid SOAP request to a Web service.
7. **a.** www.w3c.org. Always!
8. **a.** and **c.** <Envelope> and <Body>. The <Header> is optional. There is no <Message> element, and <Fault> is a subelement of the <Body> element.
9. False. All attributes inside the <Envelope> element must be namespace-qualified, without question. It is not just best practice.
10. **c.** http://schemas.xmlsoap.org/soap/envelope.

MathML

This chapter introduces the Mathematical Markup Language (MathML), defined by the W3C as a ". . . specification for describing mathematics as a basis for machine-to-machine communication. It provides a much-needed foundation for the inclusion of mathematical expressions in Web pages." They further define it as ". . .intended to facilitate the use and reuse of mathematical and scientific content on the Web, and for other applications such as computer algebra systems, print typesetting, and voice synthesis. MathML can be used to encode both the presentation of mathematical notation for high-quality visual display, and mathematical content, for applications where the semantics plays more of a key role, such as scientific software or voice synthesis. MathML attempts to capture something of the meaning behind equations rather than concentrating entirely on how they are going to be formatted out on the screen. This is on the basis that mathematical equations are meaningful to many applications without regard as to how they are rendered aurally or visually."

MathML was developed to answer an issue that actually goes back long before the advent of the World Wide Web, perhaps to the very beginning of technical publishing. This issue encompasses the sharing of mathematical and scientific expressions in an unambiguous manner.

No matter what the final goal is—from the production of printed material to the creation of input for an automated research design or simulation program—number and symbol combinations lose their meaning, or even mislead the reader, if they are not coded or represented accurately.

This chapter explores the challenges faced by those who strive to make mathematical and scientific notation—the display and the underlying meaning—more ubiquitous across the Web. You will see that, while MathML is another XML-related application, it is one that has its own idiosyncrasies. We will introduce you to some basic MathML concepts and techniques, and then introduce you to three applications (of more than three dozen that have been developed) for developing math expressions that meet these challenges. By the end of this chapter, you will be able to create simple MathML expressions and integrate them into your Web page documents.

Mathematical Expression Issues

Those who want to communicate the meaning of mathematical or scientific expressions face several challenges, including these historic ones:

- Do my symbols mean the same to my readers as they do to me? Or do my symbols confuse my audience? For example, does the *A* in $A=\pi r^2$ mean "area" to them? Or do they think I'm talking about amperes (electricity) or acceleration (physics)? Or do they think I should use a lowercase *a*? Does the *r* stand for radius to them, or turn/rotate to the right, or resistance (electricity)? And what about π? Or what if they think I've included typographical errors? Or should I be using Greek, Cyrillic, Latin, Chinese, or any other characters?
- Are the units of measure that I use the same as my reader's or correspondent's? Or should I provide alternate versions of the expressions to accommodate them? Do most readers expect symbols and constants to be pertinent to the metric system or to the imperial system? Or to some system of weights and measures that they are more familiar with?
- Is the syntax I use for these expressions the same as the syntax my readers expect to use (or will the syntax change for the country, institution, or field of endeavor of my audience)? Or do they reorder the expressions, based on their own language or conventions? Are my superscripts the same as theirs?

Figure 16.1 introduces the equation that we will use as an example throughout this chapter. The equation on the left ($A=\pi r^2$) should be very familiar. If not, let us explain: It allows us to calculate the area (*A*) of a circle. The *r* is the length of the circle's radius (the distance from the center of the circle to its outer edge) and the π represents the ratio of the circumference of the circle to its diameter (π=c/d). The little superscript 2 indicates that the value of *r* must be multiplied by itself.

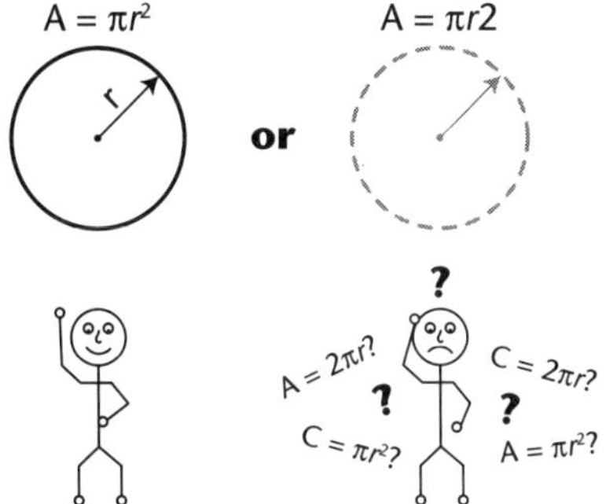

Figure 16.1 Ambiguity in expressions.

Thus, in Figure 16.1, the circle equation on the left should not be considered to be the same as, say, the equation on the right ($A=\pi r2$). We are not using the $A=\pi r2$ equation here to represent any other known scientific or mathematical concept but, oddly, many people—Web site developers among them—have difficulty expressing $A=\pi r^2$. The $A=\pi r2$ variation of the equation appears fairly frequently on the Web, as does $A=(\text{pi})r^2$ and other variations.

From an appearance perspective, interchanging A with a, or R with r, or "pi" for π doesn't matter much. The context usually clarifies the meaning. However, it could be a different story if mix-ups occur in a teaching, research, or other functional environment. If the literal underlying meaning of $A=\pi r2$ is mistakenly taught or used instead of $A=\pi r^2$, serious errors may occur.

Meanwhile, the development of the Internet and the World Wide Web has exacerbated the historic mathematical expression issues and introduced a few more:

- Will the printing/rendering technology I use be able to produce the symbols I have to use? Do I have to create or download fonts? Will the symbols and constants scale well?
- What if someone in my audience is handicapped visually? Will my expressions translate well into audio or some other compensatory medium?
- Once I have created and transmitted my expressions, can they be used quickly as input to other applications, without having to be re-created from scratch? That is, can I create *active* documents that not only display mathematical or scientific expressions, but actually communicate the semantics (that is, the underlying meaning) of the numbers, symbols, constants, and operations within those expressions?

Classroom Q & A

Q: Hold it a second. There's that word *semantics* again. Is this the same semantics we've seen in previous chapters, like Chapter 13, "RDF"?

A: No, the term semantics is one that appears in several XML contexts. It is used most generally when we just want to discuss the structure or display of a document versus the semantics of the document (that is, the content data found within the structure). In Chapter 13, we referred to the W3C's Semantic Web objective, wherein Web search agents can examine standardized metadata to learn about the subject matter in Web resources. *Semantics*, as we use it here, has a narrower focus: the actual meaning of numbers, constants, variables, and operators in the mathematical expressions in a document.

The Web community clearly needs a way to render and transmit mathematical expressions accurately and quickly. As more research and commerce are conducted and coordinated via the Web, the Web community has spotlighted the last issue: the development of math and science objects that are "active," that provide for the automatic processing and manipulation described previously.

Early Visual Presentation Solutions

Since the mid-1970s, the IT industry has developed several visual presentation solutions, such as:

eqn. Developed in 1975 by Bell Labs for use with the UNIX typesetting system named troff. It was an influence on EzMath, which is demonstrated in the Chapter 16 lab exercises.

TeX. Developed by D. Knuth of Stanford University in the late 1970s. Became the most popular method for electronic typesetting of mathematical expressions. Provides more control over typesetting details and relies heavily on macros. Available as freeware or shareware, or from commercial vendors.

LaTeX. Developed by L. Lamport in the mid-1980s. Available by anonymous FTP from the LaTeX3 Project (which has continued development) Web site at www.latex-project.org/ftp.html.

AMS-TeX. Developed by the American Mathematical Society in the 1990s. A set of fonts and macros for mathematical typesetting, above and beyond those available with TeX and LaTeX.

ISO12083:1994. A DTD for math expressions. One of four DTDs in ANSI/NISO/ISO 12083, the Electronic Manuscript Preparation and Markup standard.

Others. From the 1980s to the present, several word processing and graphics applications provide the capability to create math and science expressions, which are usually converted to proprietary formats or into graphics formats like JPEG, GIF, or TIFF.

However, those developments were capable only of visual presentation and were not capable of conveying the underlying semantics (that is, the actual meaning) of math and science expressions. Plus, the first five listed were considered a little too esoteric and complex for ordinary Web page developers and end users. That's why many opted for the "Others": commercial word processor and graphics applications that could be used to create mathematical expressions as graphic images, which would then be loaded as graphics into Web pages. In this way, browsers were less likely to misinterpret the code and would at least present *something*. This approach, however, is not ideal, since it has several drawbacks:

- Image-containing pages are slow to download and display in an end user's browser.
- Once displayed on the screen, the images may not be satisfactory to look at. (In Chapter 11, "VML," you learned that bitmap images especially are not scalable.)
- Extra graphic files must be administered.
- Once transmitted and displayed, the math expressions cannot be manipulated (e.g., you cannot cut and paste the whole expression or parts of the expression; you also can't fill in values and get answers).
- Expression fonts and formats are fixed and may not match an end user's display settings.
- No alternatives exist for people who are visually handicapped.

ISO 12083:1994 (the Electronic Manuscript Preparation and Markup standard) only describes declarations for presentation syntax; however, it represents a major step toward integrating presentation and semantic markup.

The W3C and MathML

From the discussion so far, it's no surprise that Web and other technical application developers were searching for a mathematical expression application that would facilitate the automatic processing of the underlying mathematics while unambiguously displaying the concepts, constants, and operators. Thus, documents would have to be clear and *active*. This basic requirement appears, on the surface, that it could be easily met, but it has proved to be a challenge. During the early 1990s, the W3C recognized the issues surrounding the expression of mathematics and the need for better support for scientific communication. In fact, Dave Raggett even included an HTML Math proposal in the Working Draft of HTML 3.0, in 1994.

The W3C Math Working Group

In mid-1996, the HTML Math Editorial Review Board was formed after a meeting of the Digital Library Initiative brought many interested parties together. That Board expanded and, in 1997, became the W3C Math Working Group. Over the years, the Working Group's membership has included representatives from many organizations: the American Mathematical Society, the Boeing Company, Design Science, Inc., Geometry Technologies, Inc., IBM Corporation, the French National Institute for Research in Computer Science and Control (INRIA), MacKichan Software, Inc., MATH.EDU, Inc., Microsoft Corporation, the Numerical Algorithms Group Ltd. (NAG), Radical Flow Inc., Stilo Technology, Universita di Bologna (Italy), University of Western Ontario (Canada), Waterloo Maple Inc., Wolfram Research, Inc., and others. MathML continues to be produced by the Math Working Group as part of W3C Math Activity.

MathML Design Goals

To the W3C, math expressions make up just one of several kinds of structured data that have to be integrated into the Web. Originally, to integrate math expressions, they envisioned just a simple, straightforward extension to HTML, one that could be easily implemented in Web browsers, office suites, and other applications. The design goals included the following:

- Easy to implement and easy to use.
- Sophisticated enough to meet all math-related requirements.
- Able to interact with other applications so that expressions do not lose their meaning and do not have to be reentered or reconstructed.
- Capable of producing high-quality renderings in several media.
- Markup that embeds seamlessly into Web page documents.
- Existing authoring tools should require few modifications to generate MathML.
- Flexible enough to provide for tailored input and output; a sort of "all things to all developers" solution.

Check the W3C Goals, too.

The design goals in the preceding list paraphrase those found at the W3C MathML Web site and in other literature. If you want to see a listing of the actual documented W3C MathML design goals, visit www.w3.org/TR/2002/WD-MathML2-20021219/chapter1.html#intro.goals.

As the Math Working Group's work progressed, it became apparent that the answer did not lie in extending HTML, but in extending XML instead. The W3C's Math Working Group produced the following W3C MathML Recommendations:

- Mathematical Markup Language (MathML) 1.0 Specification (MathML 1.0), which was endorsed by the W3C in April 1998.
- Mathematical Markup Language (MathML) 1.01 Specification, endorsed as a revision of MathML 1.0 in July 1999.
- Mathematical Markup Language (MathML) Version 2.0 (MathML 2.0), endorsed in February 2001.
- The first Working Draft of Mathematical Markup Language (MathML) Version 2.0 (2nd Edition)—the second edition of MathML 2.0—in December 2002.

The second edition of MathML 2.0 is a reissue of MathML 2.0 and incorporates corrections resulting from MathML 2.0 errata into the main text. Also, for the first time, it includes a W3C XML Schema. In this version of MathML, all examples are included in the text (see it at www.w3.org/TR/2002/WD-MathML2-20021219/).

MathML Implementations

A veritable explosion of MathML implementations has occurred in the past year or two. We demonstrate three implementations (Amaya, EzMath, and WebEQ) in the lab exercises. For a comprehensive list of MathML implementation, please visit the W3C MathML Software Web page (www.w3.org/Math/implementations.html). However, please read the following caution.

If you are looking for a MathML application/implementation, be careful to read the descriptions attached to those listed on the MathML Software Web page. Some are compliant with the most up-to-date MathML specifications (at this writing, MathML 2.0); some only comply with older versions, like MathML 1.01 or 1.0. Others provide both content and presentation markup, while others provide only one or the other.

To obtain a list of Web browsers that display MathML expressions, check the list provided by the W3C at their *Putting Mathematics on the Web with MathML* Web page at www.w3.org/Math/XSL/.

MathML document validation services are available at the W3C, too. These provide the MarkUp Validation Service at validator.w3.org/ or the original W3C MathML validation service at www.w3.org/Math/validator/. These validation services are especially handy if the editor you use does not validate your code.

What Is MathML?

MathML consists of XML tags that can be used to mark up expressions so that they display properly and maintain their semantics. Approximately 30 of its elements are presentation elements that describe notational structures. Another 150 or so elements (the content elements) specify the intended meaning of math expressions. MathML also has interface elements (the main one is the <math> element) that facilitate the embedding of MathML into Web page documents. MathML can be used to encode math expressions for the following:

- Presentation in high-quality visual displays
- Mathematical semantics, to be used with applications where semantics play a major role (as in scientific software or voice synthesis)

MathML expressions can be searched, indexed, and manipulated with a scientific or mathematical application; rendered with Web browsers; edited with office applications; displayed with projectors; and printed with printers or plotters. MathML is legible to humans but is not primarily intended for direct use by developers. In most cases, coding MathML data documents can be very complex—especially when a developer wishes to combine presentation and content elements—thus, it is better left to equation editors, conversion programs, and other specialized applications.

The W3C recognized early that any mathematical expression language that met all the design requirements would be complex. They concluded that a layered architecture approach, such as that represented in Figure 16.2, would be appropriate.

The bottom layer—Layer 1—provides a set of general, yet powerful platform-independent tools that Layer 2 applications use to exchange, process, encode, and render expressions. MathML constitutes Layer 1, since its features define a standard for interoperability, ease of implementation, ease of processing and rendering, and ease of maintenance. MathML is called a low-level XML application because its specification serves as a model and stimulus for writing and coordinating other math expression applications.

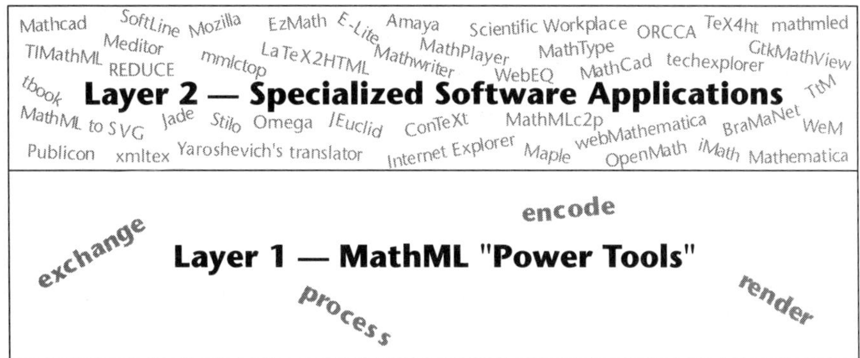

Figure 16.2 Layered architecture model.

The top layer of the Layered Architecture Model—Layer 2—consists of the specialized software tools used to generate coded mathematical data and expressions, such as those listed at the W3C's MathML Software page at www.w3.org/Math/implementations.html. When you read the descriptions on that Web page, you see that the applications are fairly specialized, aimed at specific user groups or toward accomplishing specific tasks. In fact, some of the MathML-compliant applications listed at the W3C Web site are already integrated into other office and technical application suites.

The Logical Structure of a MathML Document

If you build a dedicated MathML document, it should come as no surprise that it must have a prolog and root data element, just like other XML-related documents.

The Prolog

The only mandatory statement is the XML declaration, which should resemble:

```
<? xml version="1.0" encoding="iso-8859-1" ?>
```

All other statements are considered optional. However, to achieve various objectives, you may want to include document type declarations (DTDs), processing instructions (PIs), or comments.

MathML DTDs or Schemas

MathML does not provide the capability to create your own arbitrarily named element types. However, the W3C Math Working Group works continually to create new element types to provide us with more flexibility so that you can display and manipulate more math expressions. Those element types and other components are declared in two DTDs and one schema. The two MathML.DTDs correspond to MathML 1.01 and MathML 2.0. The schema was introduced with MathML 2.0, second edition. You can view and copy them from the following Web sites:

- DTD for MathML 1.01: www.w3.org/TR/REC-MathML/appendixA.html
- DTD for MathML 2.0: www.w3.org/TR/2002/WD-MathML2-20021219/appendixa.html#parsing.dtd
- Schema for MathML 2.0: www.w3.org/Math/XMLSchema/mathml2/mathml2.xsd

To create a MathML-dedicated data document, include the following in the DTD statement:

```
<!DOCTYPE math
    PUBLIC "-//W3C//DTD MathML 2.0//EN"
           "http://www.w3.org/Math/DTD/mathml2/mathml2.dtd">
```

If you copy the DTD to a local site, you should provide the appropriate URI instead of the www.w3.org URI that appears in the third line of code.

Most of the time, however, your MathML expressions will not require their own dedicated document. If the MathML expression will be used in an XHTML document, you can take advantage of the XHTML DTD, extended with this MathML module. This DTD includes all the necessary declarations included in one file. To use it, insert the following doctype declaration:

```
<!DOCTYPE html
    PUBLIC "-//W3C//DTD XHTML 1.1 plus MathML 2.0//EN"
           "http://www.w3.org/Math/DTD/mathml2/xhtml-math11-f.dtd">
```

Again, if you copied the DTD to a local site, you should provide the appropriate URI.

You can also validate MathML expressions using the XML Schema for MathML, located at www.w3.org/Math/XMLSchema/mathml2/mathml2.xsd. Although the declaration does not appear in the prolog, we think it's still appropriate to mention it here. Thus, to link our MathML expressions to the XML Schema for MathML, use the following declarations in the <math> element:

```
<mml:math xmlns:mml="http://www.w3.org/1998/Math/MathML"
          xmlns:xsi="http://www.w3.org/2001/XMLSchema-instance"
          xsi:schemaLocation="http://www.w3.org/1998/Math/MathML
            http://www.w3.org/Math/XMLSchema/mathml2/mathml2.xsd">
...
</mml:math>
```

If you need to review these terms, refer back to Chapter 5, "XML Schemas." Remember that the value of the schemaLocation attribute is a pair of URIs. The first is the MathML namespace URI; the second, the location of the schema for that namespace. If you use a local copy of the schema, you must adjust the second URI accordingly.

If you need to validate your MathML documents, validation services are available from the W3C. Please refer back to the *MathML Implementations* section earlier in this chapter.

MathML and Style Sheets

If you wish to use MathML in a dedicated document or in an XHTML document, insert the following processing instruction into the prolog:

```
<?xml-stylesheet type="text/xsl"
          href="http://www.w3.org/Math/XSL/mathml.xsl"?>
<html xmlns="....
```

Unfortunately, because of its security configuration, Internet Explorer will not allow an XSLT style sheet to be applied to a data document unless both documents are located on the same server. If that is possible, and the expression will be displayed without connecting to the Internet, consider using the following:

```
<?xml-stylesheet type="text/xsl" href="mathml.xsl"?>
```

For further information regarding styles and other MathML display issues, please visit the W3C's *Putting Mathematics on the Web with MathML* Web page at www.w3.org/Math/XSL/.

MathML Markup Specifications

MathML markup consists of presentation elements, content elements, and interface elements. Some specifications pertain to all MathML elements, and some pertain to each of the three component types.

Two main W3C markup specifications exist: MathML 1.0 and MathML 2.0. If you create small, uncomplicated math expressions according to either, the results are similar. Differences begin to appear when you try to create more complex expressions.

However, even with fairly simple expressions, you can see differences between the MathML 1.0 and MathML 2.0 specifications. For example, look at the MathML presentation markup examples in Figure 16.3.

The <math> Element

In Figure 16.3, all three of the MathML 2.0-compliant presentation markup examples contain top-level <math> elements, but the MathML 1.0 example doesn't. MathML 2.0 specifies the need for a single root <math> element, which provides a number of improvements:

- It provides for an island of MathML markup within a Web page document, resolves some presentation issues, and produces improvements in functionality and interoperability.
- It provides an attachment point for information, which affects a MathML expression as a whole (for example, in the future, a <math> element will be the logical place to attach style sheet or macro information, when these facilities become available for MathML).

$$A = \pi r^2$$

MathML 1.0/1.01

```
<mrow>
  <mi>A</mi><mo>=</mo><mi>&pi;</mi>
  <msup>
    <mi>r</mi>
    <mn>2</mn>
  </msup>
</mrow>
```

MathML 2.0
No namespace

```
<math display='block'>
  <mrow>
    <mi>A</mi><mo>=</mo><mi>&pi;</mi>
    <msup>
      <mi>r</mi>
      <mn>2</mn>
    </msup>
  </mrow>
</math>
```

MathML 2.0
m namespace

```
<m:math display='block'>
  <m:mrow>
    <m:mi>A</m:mi><m:mo>=</m:mo><m:mi>&pi;</m:mi>
    <m:msup>
      <m:mi>r</m:mi>
      <m:mn>2</m:mn>
    </m:msup>
  </m:mrow>
</m:math>
```

MathML 2.0
Default namespace

```
<math display='block' xmlns='http://www.w3.org/1998/Math/MathML'>
  <mrow>
    <mi>A</mi><mo>=</mo><mi>&pi;</mi>
    <msup>
      <mi>r</mi>
      <mn>2</mn>
    </msup>
  </mrow>
</math>
```

Figure 16.3 Presentation markup comparison: MathML 1.0 versus MathML 2.0.

- If the MathML document will be used by an application that conforms to the W3C Namespaces in XML Recommendation, you can place a MathML namespace declaration in the <math> element start tag, since the <math> element is an interface element. The namespace syntax would resemble the following:

```
<math xmlns="http://www.w3.org/1998/Math/MathML">
```

- It can contain various attributes that affect all the elements nested within the <math> element's entire enclosed expression (inward-looking attributes).
- It can contain various attributes that may be used to integrate with third-party rendering software, to render expressions properly in a browser, and to integrate them into XHTML documents (outward-looking attributes).

Table 16.1 lists the <math> element's attributes.

Table 16.1 The <math> Element Attributes

ATTRIBUTE	EXPLANATION
Inward-looking attributes	
class="value"	Provided for CSS support.
style="value"	Provided for CSS support.
id="value"	Provided for CSS support.
macros="URI"	Provides a pointer to external macro definition files. Macros are not part of the MathML specification, but a macro mechanism is anticipated as a future extension to MathML.
mode="display/inline"	Specifies whether the enclosed MathML expression should be rendered in a display style or an in-line style. The default is mode="inline". Deprecated in MathML 2.0.
display="block/inline"	Replaces the deprecated mode attribute. Specifies whether the enclosed MathML expression should be rendered in a display style or an in-line style. Allowed values are block and inline (default).
xref="URI"	With id, provided for use with XSL processing.

(continued)

Table 16.1 *(continued)*

ATTRIBUTE	EXPLANATION
Outward-looking attributes	
overflow="scroll/elide/ truncate/scale"	If size negotiation is not possible or fails (for example, a long equation), overflow can be used to suggest an alternative processing method. *scroll* instructs the processor to provide a viewport with horizontal or vertical scrollbars to allow the users to examine the entire expression. *elide* means that the expression is to be abbreviated by removing enough of it so that the remainder fits into the window (for example, a large expression might have only the first and last terms displayed, with '+ ... +' between them). *truncate* means the expression will be abbreviated by simply cutting remainders off at the right and bottom borders. *scale* means that, if the expression is too large, fonts will be chosen so that the full expression fits in the window.
altimg="URL"	Provides a fall-back for browsers that do not support embedded elements.
alttext= "text string"	Another fall-back for browsers that do not support embedded elements or images. It is recommended that an alttext attribute always be provided, so that an end user can at least get some information despite a MathML malfunction.

When providing values for any MathML attributes, you should consult with the W3C's MathML Web site, since the values must be listed in a particular format.

No nesting of <math> elements is allowed; one <math> element cannot contain another <math> element. It is considered an error if such nesting occurs.

MathML and Namespaces

Even when working with applications that help you create and display mathematical expressions in MathML, you must still consider how to use namespaces and DTDs, and how to validate your MathML code.

If the MathML expressions are to be used by an application that conforms to the Namespaces in XML Recommendation, then the following typical syntax should be used (note the use of the MathML 2.0-related <math> element for the namespace declaration, which we recommend unless the application will not support it):

```
<math xmlns="http://www.w3.org/1998/Math/MathML">
```

As with other XML-related languages, since the declaration is only being used for the purpose of creating unique element names, the XML Namespaces Recommendation does not require the existence of the URI that is used for the namespace name.

MathML Attributes

MathML is particular about its attribute syntax, even more so than normal XML. It has additional rules that must be observed by the MathML implementations, and it is considered an error to violate them. The MathML syntax and values for each attribute value are specified in each element's attribute table. We recommend consulting those attribute tables when composing MathML documents (another good reason to use MathML implementations when possible). We also recommend that you read the *MathML Attribute Values* section of the current MathML specification (for MathML 2.0, section 2.4.4, which can be viewed at www.w3.org/TR/2002/WD-MathML2-20021219/chapter2.html#fund.attval).

Bases, Scripts, Characters, and Symbols

When we discuss how the text, numbers, and other expression components are encoded in MathML, the instructions—here and in MathML specifications and tutorials—are often given in terms of bases, scripts, characters, and symbols. To understand these terms, look at the dissected equation for the area of a circle in Figure 16.4.

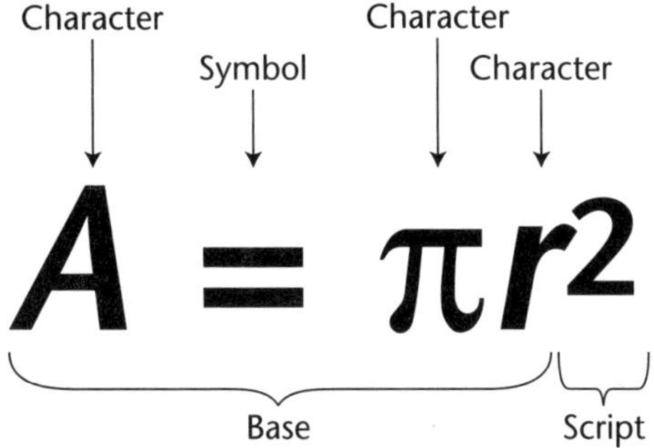

Figure 16.4 Dissected equation.

Expressions are broken into a *base* ($A = \pi r$) and a *script* (the single superscripted character 2). The base can be further dissected into a sequence of characters—A, π, and r—and symbols, like the equal sign (=).

Presentation Markup

Presentation markup element tag names generally begin with an *m* character, which is then followed by those additional characters that describe the content of the element.

Presentation elements create a syntactic structure for the math expression, in a manner similar to the way that titles, sections, and paragraphs describe the structure of a text document. These are the basic symbols and expression-building structures that we are most familiar with. They are usually focused on visual impression, so their element names usually appear to be visual in nature. However, they are also designed to contain information for audio renderings.

Thirty-one presentation elements and more than 50 attributes are grouped in five categories. We've listed the elements in Table 16.2. To view a list of and explanations for all the attributes that can be used with these elements, visit the W3C MathML 2.0 Web site at www.w3.org/TR/2002/WD-MathML2-20021219/chapter3.html and select any appropriate links.

If you are going to use more than a few presentation elements and attributes in an expression, do not attempt to code the expressions manually. Instead, use one of several available implementations to do that. For example, an abundance of potentially confusing elements, attributes, and other components exist. Further, token elements and general layout elements have specific rules, as defined in the DTDs. Following are a few examples:

- General layout schemata elements, like the outer <mrow> element, expect to only find token elements in their content.
- The <mi> and <mo> elements are tokens, and their content consists only of characters and symbols.
- Scripts and limits help to further define the content of the token characters and symbols.

It's even difficult for longtime experts to keep track of all the presentation markup rules.

Table 16.2 MathML Presentation Elements

ELEMENT NAME	EXPLANATION
Token elements	Represent the smallest units of meaningful mathematical notation (examples: characters and symbols).
<mglyph>	Adds new character glyphs to MathML.

Table 16.2 *(continued)*

ELEMENT NAME	EXPLANATION
<mi>	Identifier.
<mn>	Number.
<mo>	Operator, fence, or separator.
<ms>	String literal.
<mspace/>	Space (declared empty element).
<mtext>	Text.
General layout schemata elements	Describe basic notations (examples: fractions, radicals) or general functions (examples: style properties, error handling) not handled by other element types.
<menclose>	Encloses content with a stretching symbol (e.g., a long-division sign).
<merror>	Encloses a syntax error message from a preprocessor.
<mfenced>	Surrounds content with a pair of fences.
<mfrac>	Forms a fraction from two subexpressions.
<mpadded>	Adjusts space around content.
<mphantom>	Makes content invisible but preserves its size.
<mroot>	Forms a radical with specified index.
<mrow>	Groups any number of subexpressions horizontally.
<msqrt>	Forms a square root sign (radical without an index).
<mstyle>	Style change.
Script and limit schemata elements	Positions one or more scripts around a base level script.
<mmultiscripts>	Attaches prescripts and tensor indices to a base.
<mover>	Attaches an overscript to a base.
<msub>	Attaches a subscript to a base.
<msubsup>	Attaches a subscript-superscript pair to a base.
<msup>	Attaches a superscript to a base.
<munder>	Attaches an underscript to a base.
<munderover>	Attaches an underscript-overscript pair to a base.

(continued)

Table 16.2 *(continued)*

ELEMENT NAME	EXPLANATION
Table and matrix elements	For matrix, array, and other tablelike mathematical notation; similar to HTML table elements except that, with these, you can use specialized attributes for finer layout control.
<maligngroup/>	Alignment group marker (declared empty element).
<malignmark/>	Alignment point marker (declared empty element).
<mlabeledtr>	A row in a table or matrix with a label or equation number.
<mtable>	Table or matrix.
<mtd>	One entry in a table or matrix.
<mtr>	Row in a table or matrix.
Enlivening expression element(s)	Provides a mechanism for binding actions to expressions or subexpressions.
<maction>	Binds actions to a subexpression.

A basic presentation encoding for the sample area of a circle equation is shown in Figure 16.5.

The top-level structure in the figure starts with a general layout schemata element named <mrow>, which instructs the parser to lay the expression out horizontally. The base A, π, r characters are each inside their own <mi> token element; an <mi> element indicates that these are to be displayed as identifiers. The equal sign (=) sign is inside a <mo> token element, signifying that it is to be displayed as an operator. Finally, the character 2 is inside a <mn> token element that specifies that the 2 is a number (or value). This number is a superscript to the token element r, since the MathML markup shows that the <msup> and </msup> tags surround the variable r and its power value 2.

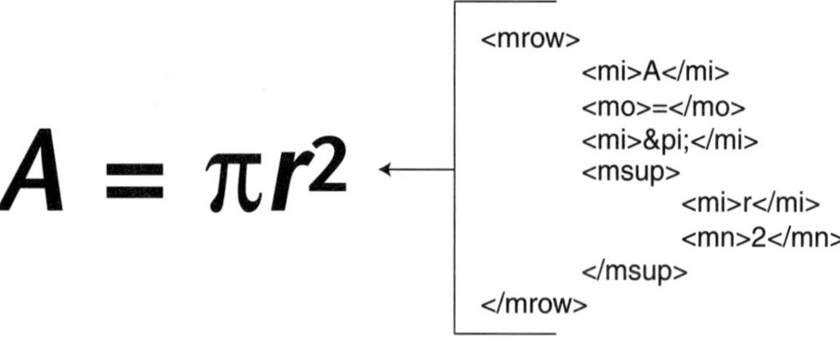

Figure 16.5 Presentation markup example.

Content Markup

Content markup (also referred to as semantic markup) elements differ from presentation elements, because they prescribe how their contents are to be manipulated mathematically, as opposed to prescribing how the content will be displayed. Content markup is intended for eventual transcription into input for computer applications that calculate and otherwise manipulate the expressions. Content markup looks like presentation markup, but it uses a different set of 150 elements and an even greater number of attributes to convey the same expressions while maintaining their mathematical semantics.

The MathML content markup elements available with MathML 2.0 are listed in Table 16.3, without descriptions.

These elements are constantly being added to, deleted, and modified with respect to function. For the latest list, along with explanations and examples, please visit the content element definitions at www.w3.org/TR/2002/WD-MathML2-20021219/appendixc.html#cedef.Constants.and.Symbol.Elements.

Table 16.3 MathML Content Elements

ELEMENT NAME	ELEMENT NAME	ELEMENT NAME
	Token elements	
<cn>	<ci>	<csymbol>
	Basic content elements	
<apply>	<codomain>	<compose>
<condition>	<declare>	<domain>
<domainofapplication>	<e>	<fn>
<ident>	<image>	<inverse/>
<interval>	<lambda>	<otherwise>
<piece>	<piecewise>	<reln>
<sep/>		
	Arithmetic, algebra, and logic elements	
<abs/>	<and/>	<arg/>
<ceiling/>	<conjugate/>	<divide/>
<exists/>	<factorial/>	<floor/>
<forall/>	<gcd/>	<idiv/>
<imaginary/>	<implies/>	<lcm/>
<max/>	<min/>	<minus/>
<not/>	<or/>	<over/>
<plus/>	<power/>	<quotient>
<real/>	<rem/>	<root/>
<times/>	<xor/>	

(continued)

Table 16.3 *(continued)*

ELEMENT NAME	ELEMENT NAME	ELEMENT NAME
	Relation elements	
<approx/>	<eq/>	<equivalent/>
<factorof>	<geq/>	<gt/>
<leq/>	<lt/>	<neq/>
	Elements related to calculus	
<bvar>	<curl/>	<degree>
<diff/>	<divergence/>	<grad/>
<int/>	<laplacian/>	<lowlimit>
<partialdiff/>	<uplimit>	
	Elements related to set theory	
<card/>	<cartesianproduct>	<in/>
<intersect/>	<list>	<notin/>
<notprsubset/>	<notsubset/>	<prsubset/>
<set>	<setdiff/>	<subset/>
<union/>		
	Elements related to sequences and series	
<limit/>	<product/>	<sum/>
<tendsto/>		

Elementary classical function (including trigonometric function) elements			
<sin/>	<sinh/>	<arcsin/>	<arcsinh/>
<cos/>	<cosh/>	<arccos/>	<arccosh/>
<tan/>	<tanh/>	<arctan/>	<arctanh/>
<sec/>	<sech/>	<arcsec/>	<arcsech/>
<cosec/>	<csch/>	<arccsc/>	<arccsch/>
<cotan/>	<coth/>	<arccot/>	<arccoth/>
<exp/>	<ln/>	<log/>	

	Elements related to statistics	
<mean/>	<median/>	<mode/>
<moment/>	<momentabout/>	<sdev/>
<var/>		
	Elements related to linear algebra	
<determinant/>	<matrix>	<matrixrow>
<outerproduct/>	<scalarproduct/>	<selector/>
<transpose/>	<vector>	<vectorproduct/>
	Semantic mapping elements	
<annotation>	<semantics>	<xmlannotation>

Table 16.3 *(continued)*

ELEMENT NAME	ELEMENT NAME	ELEMENT NAME
Elements related to constants and symbols		
<complexes/>	<emptyset/>	<eulergamma/>
<exponentiale/>	<false/>	<imaginaryi/>
<infinity/>	<integers/>	<naturalnumbers/>
<notanumber/>	<pi/>	<primes/>
<rationals/>	<reals/>	<true/>

We strongly recommend that you use an equation editor to code content markup equations. Manipulating all these elements and their attributes, while following all the coding rules, is a very complex operation to be done manually. Let the equation editors deal with the rules and components. However, to maintain a handle on the process, we suggest that you construct abstract trees of your markup projects; the abstract tree technique is discussed later in this chapter.

Figure 16.6 provides the content markup version of the $A=\pi r^2$ example. Note that there are twice as many lines of code as shown previously in the presentation markup example of Figure 16.5. You can see that conveying the semantics of the expression is a more involved process than conveying simply its display characteristics.

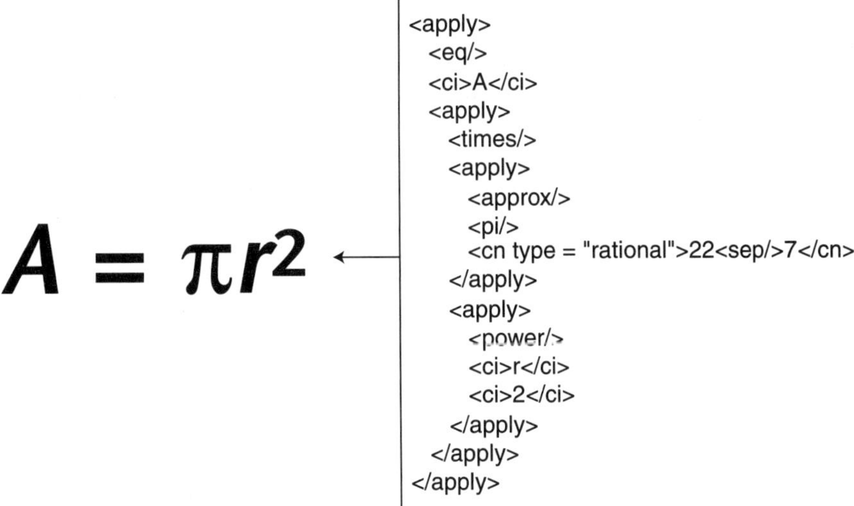

Figure 16.6 Content markup example.

The top-level structure in Figure 16.6 starts with an application marker. This is encoded with the outermost (that is, the top and bottom) <apply> and </apply> tags. This <apply> element explicitly applies a function to its argument(s); thus, the first thing after the <apply> start tag should be the function or operator (in this case, the equal sign), followed by its argument (the variable named *A*). The *A* data character is placed inside a <ci> element, which is a content identifier.

The next <apply> tag begins the πr^2 grouping, which won't be complete until the second to last </apply> tag. The <apply> start tag here is followed by a <times/> empty element, which activates a multiplication operator. Now the arguments to the multiplication operator must be provided. Since the next argument is the constant π and because MathML uses a function to define π, another set of nested <apply> and </apply> tags must appear. In this case, they surround the π function that begins with the binary function approximation (<approx/>) element, followed by the <pi/> element, which actually identifies the function to the parser. The function itself is enclosed within a numerical constant element <cn>. The parser is told that the constant will be a rational number of a value approximating 22 divided by 7. The <sep/> element tells the parser that two parts are needed to fully describe the constant, and the two parts appear on each side of that element.

The next <apply> element encloses the r^2 function. The operator <power/> element tells the parser that the first <ci> content identifier data, *r*, should be raised to the power indicated in the second content identifier (that is, 2).

Prefix Notation

The odd-looking MathML element nesting scheme is called *prefix notation* (PN), since it places the operators (the equal sign, the multiplication sign, the power notation) before the respective operands (the *A*, π, and *r*) in their respective elements. If they were in the opposite order (for example, <ci>A</ci><eq />, instead of <eq /> <ci>A</ci>), that is *postfix notation*. When we use pen and paper for arithmetic calculations, we usually use a scheme called infix notation, in which the operands and operators are mixed. In fact, the familiar $A=\pi r^2$ is an example of *infix notation*.

Consider the PN processing algorithm as a series of scans from left to right, as illustrated in Figure 16.7.

The first scan travels until it has passed the last operator: the power operator. It then applies that operation to the subsequent operands, *r* and 2, to get r^2. On the next scan, the last operator encountered is the multiplication sign, which is applied to the π constant and the r^2. On the third scan, the equality operation element is encountered; it is applied to the *A* and the πr^2 combination to obtain the final result.

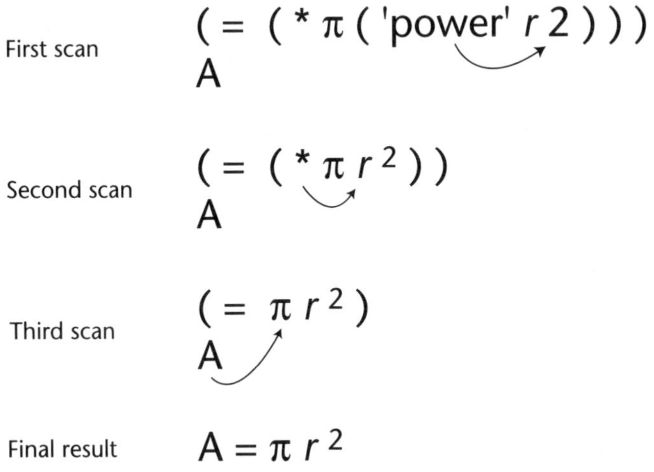

First scan	(= (* π ('power' r 2))) A
Second scan	(= (* π r 2)) A
Third scan	(= π r 2) A
Final result	$A = \pi r^2$

Figure 16.7 Prefix notation example.

Combining Presentation and Content Markup

Content markup is not altogether concerned with the display of our expression. For some expressions, the display must be almost inferred by an end user. Thus, those who are unfamiliar with the expression or its components may be at a disadvantage. Sophisticated rendering applications may soon be developed that use appropriate style sheets or other techniques, but as of this writing, rendering content expressions with all the necessary visual nuances still requires the developer to take extra steps. It is obvious that employing presentation tags alone limits the ability to reuse MathML expressions or to evaluate or manipulate them using another application. The question, then, becomes "can we combine the two techniques?" The answer is "yes."

Presentation markup and content markup can be combined in two ways: by using mixed markup, which intersperses content and presentation elements in a single abstract tree; or by using parallel markup, which requires separate presentation and content trees. If you are interested in learning more about mixed and parallel markup techniques, please visit the appropriate section of the latest MathML specification. As of this writing, the section is located at http://web3.w3.org/TR/MathML2/chapter5.html.

Two Basic Math-Expression Creation Techniques and Concepts

Before we examine an example math editor, we will introduce a couple of techniques or concepts that can help to create math expressions, regardless of the kind of markup structure (presentation, content, or both) or editor you ultimately use. Once you grasp these concepts, you will more easily use the math editor tools described in subsequent sections.

Abstract Expression Trees

The abstract expression tree was mentioned briefly in previous sections. Abstract expression tree diagrams are similar to file directory (or file folder) diagrams. They are good for both designing MathML expressions and for checking the progress or results of a MathML editor. Figure 16.8 shows an example of an abstract expression tree applied to the area of a circle example and depicting presentation markup elements (of course, either presentation or content markup elements can be illustrated).

To organize the tree so that it might be more meaningful and easier to work with, we segmented the math expression according to its <mrow> elements. If we use content markup, then segmenting expressions according to the <apply> elements may work.

Layout Boxes

The layout box is a concept that ought to be understood before we set out to create MathML markup. Layout boxes are used by several MathML editors as a kind of bounding box for certain math notations and are categorized according to their intended contents:

- Simple layout boxes contain individual characters, and their dimensions depend only on the character font being used.
- More complicated layout boxes arrange their child boxes—similar in concept to child elements—according to ready-made configurations that an author can choose from on the MathML editor's grid of symbol buttons.

A composition window from Design Science, Inc.'s MathType MathML editor is illustrated Figure 16.9.

The MathML editor provides a symbol grid with several (in this case two) rows of symbol buttons from which you can select the appropriate symbols to populate your expression. The working area of the editor contains a nearly complete expression; the only character that remains to be added is the power of 2, although a layout box has already been placed in the proper position. That layout box was placed by the developer who, after entering the other characters, clicked the superscript/subscript symbol button and selected, from the several option buttons displayed, a superscript button. All the developer has to do now is type in a "2". Meanwhile, the developer has also used the lowercase Greek symbol button to insert the π symbol. Some developers refer to the symbol buttons and other utilities as widgets (slang for programming subroutines, which is what they really are).

Layout boxes can be a little tricky for beginners, especially because they have to be selected in the proper order. The abstract expression tree technique can help here, but be prepared to practice with layout boxes until they feel more automatic to you.

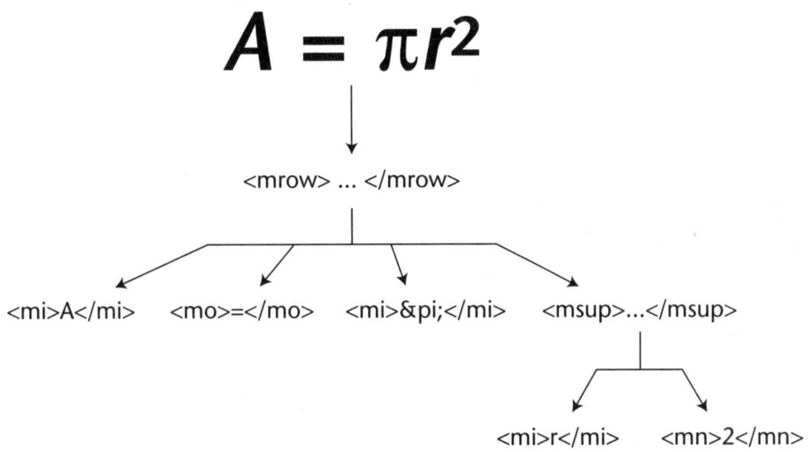

Figure 16.8 Abstract expression tree example.

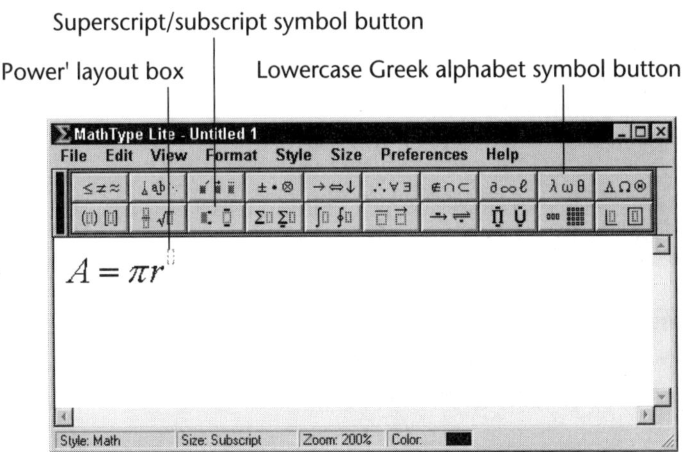

Figure 16.9 Layout boxes and symbol buttons.

Meanwhile, MathType can be used as a standalone math editor, or it can be integrated with other office suite applications, like Microsoft Word or Visio. If you would like more information about the MathType editor, or its siblings MathPlayer (a MathML display engine for Internet Explorer) or WebEQ (a MathML content markup editor), visit Design Science, Inc.'s Web site at www.mathtype.com/.

Chapter 16 Labs: Getting Started with MathML

MathML had something of a slow start, but development has accelerated recently. Two years before we published this book, it was difficult to find a MathML-compliant math editor. Now there are many different editors available that are compliant with the most recent specifications (an up-to-date listing resides at www.w3.org/Math/implementations.html). The major issue now is to find one that has the right combinations of features to best suit your uses. Despite varying features, all math editors are somewhat similar to use. The approach we chose for these labs is to demonstrate a few editors and demonstrate some very basic instruction so that you can quickly become familiar with them and productive.

Lab 16.1: Install and Use Amaya for MathML

In this lab, we download, install, and use the presentation-oriented Amaya editor, which was developed and is currently maintained by the W3C. It's free, so let's take a look at it to see what it can do. Be aware that currently only Netscape, Mozilla, and Amaya itself can display the MathML expressions we create with it.

1. Activate a browser and go to www.w3.org/Amaya/.
2. Locate the link on the side navigation bar called Distributions under the Download Amaya section.

The most current version as of this writing is 7.2. Download the most current release shown. Be careful not to link to non-Windows binary code. You must use the executable Windows code for this lab.

3. Click the amaya-WinNT-7.2a.exe link.
4. Download and save the executable file to your hard disk.
5. Go to the directory where the amaya-WinNT-7.2a.exe file is located and double-click the file to start the installation.
6. Accept all defaults during the installation.
7. Reboot if necessary.
8. Start the Amaya editor by clicking Start, Programs, Amaya, Amaya.
9. On the top menu bar, go to File, New, New MathML document.
10. Rename the file from New.mml to MathML-Lab1.mml and click Confirm.
11. Enter your example area of a circle expression: *A equals pi "r" squared*. To do this, first make sure that the Amaya editor window, now named MathML-Lab1.mml, is the active window. Type in an uppercase letter "A". If the window is inactive, click Edit on the top menu bar and make sure Editor Mode is check marked.
12. Click anywhere inside the editor window. You should see the editor stylize the uppercase *A* into italics.
13. Type in an equal sign (=) immediately following the *A*.
14. Click anywhere inside the editor window. You should see the editor stylize and space the equal sign.
15. Enter the pi symbol. Click the Maths icon on the top menu bar. The Maths icon looks like a yellow X over Y.
16. Click the Greek letter icon at the bottom of the second column (the alpha, beta, and gamma symbols).
17. Click on the pi symbol, as shown in Figure 16.10. A pi symbol should now appear inside the main editor window.

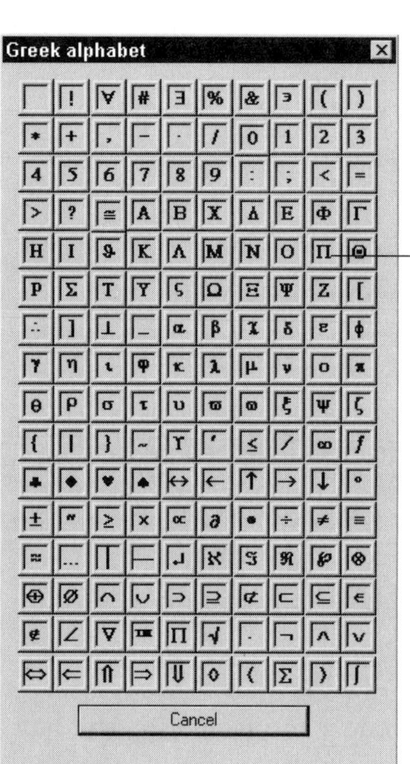

Figure 16.10 Use the pi symbol as indicated on the Greek Alphabet template.

18. Click Cancel to close the Greek Alphabet template.
19. Click anywhere inside the editor window to format the pi symbol.
20. Enter *r*2. To insert these symbols, click the Maths icon on the top menu bar. The Maths icon looks like a yellow X over Y.
21. Click the superscript format symbol, as shown in Figure 16.11. A generic format symbol should now appear inside the editor.

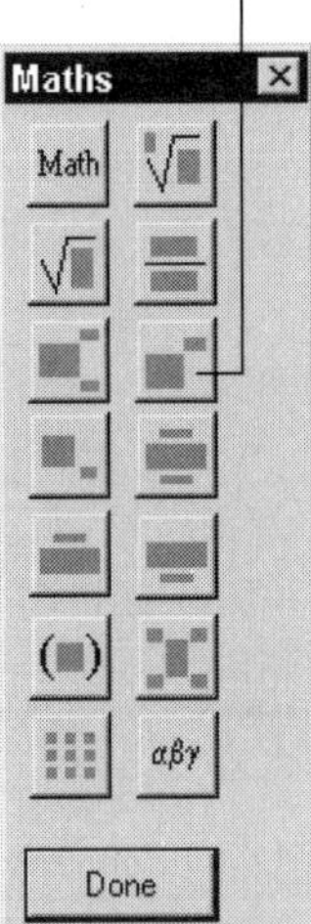

Figure 16.11 Click on this format symbol to create a power exponent.

22. Click the pink icon that represents the base number, and type a letter "r".
23. Click the pink icon that represents the power exponent, and type the number "2".
24. Click anywhere inside the editor window to format the entire equation. Your editor should resemble Figure 16.12.

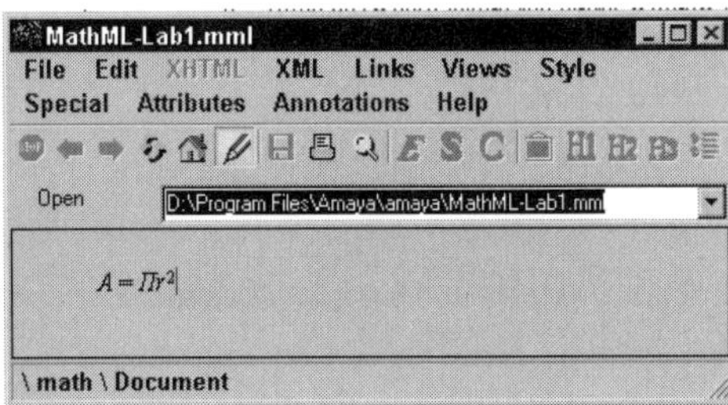

Figure 16.12 The area of a circle expression as depicted in the Amaya editor.

25. Save the file by clicking File, Save.
26. Review the MathML presentation source code for the file by clicking Views, Source code. Compare it to Figure 16.13.

MathML-Lab1.mml

File Edit XHTML XML Links Views Style Special Attributes Annotations Help

```
<?xml version="1.0" encoding="iso-8859-1"?>
<!DOCTYPE math PUBLIC "-//W3C//DTD MathML 2.0//EN"
      "http://www.w3.org/TR/MathML2/dtd/mathml2.dtd">
<!-- Created by amaya 7.1, see http://www.w3.org/Amaya/ --
<math xmlns="http://www.w3.org/1998/Math/MathML">
  <mi>A</mi>
  <mo>=</mo>
  <mi>&Pi;</mi>
  <msup>
    <mi>r</mi>
    <mn>2</mn>
  </msup>
</math>
```

Figure 16.13 XML source code (presentation format) for the area of a circle expression.

Lab 16.2: Install and Use WebEQ for MathML

Design Science, Inc.'s presentation-related WebEQ application has many more features than those we introduce in this lab exercise. The resulting source code is the same regardless of how the equation was built. In an effort to support Web browser presentation, WebEQ has an applet option that offers an opportunity to build an equation that will display inside Internet Explorer.

1. Go to www.dessci.com/en/. Click the WebEQ 30-Day Trial download link. The trial download link is located on the right-hand side of the window under Free Downloads.
2. Enter your email address as requested.
3. Download the Windows platform version of WebEQ, and save the file to your disk.
4. Go to the directory where the install.exe file is located and double-click the file to start the installation.
5. These instructions assume that you are using the English version, so choose English.
6. Accept all remaining defaults by clicking Next, Install, Done to the End.
7. Reboot if necessary.
8. Start the WebEQ editor by clicking Start, Programs, WebEQ 3.0 Evaluation, WebEQ Editor.

9. Enter the sample area of a circle expression $A=\pi r^2$. First make sure that the WebEQ editor window is the active window, and type in an uppercase letter "A".
10. Type in an equal sign (=) immediately after the A.
11. Insert the pi symbol. Click the Lowercase Greek Alphabet palette—the menu bar looks like an alpha/beta (α/β) symbol set—then click the pi symbol, as shown in Figure 16.14.

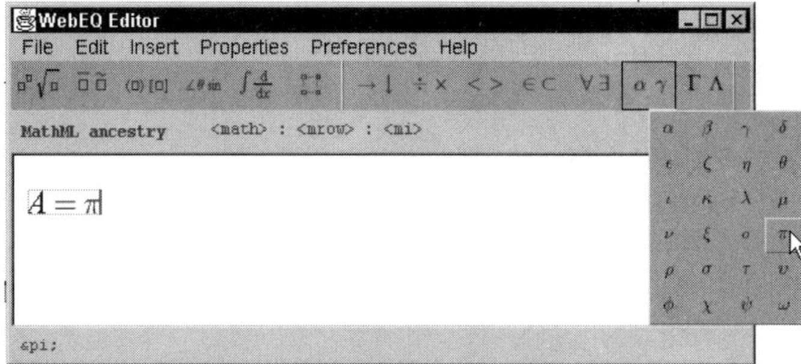

Figure 16.14 Lowercase Greek palette with pi symbol.

12. Enter "r^2". To insert these symbols, click the leftmost formatting icon on the top menu bar. The icon has a square root sign inside it, as shown in Figure 16.15.

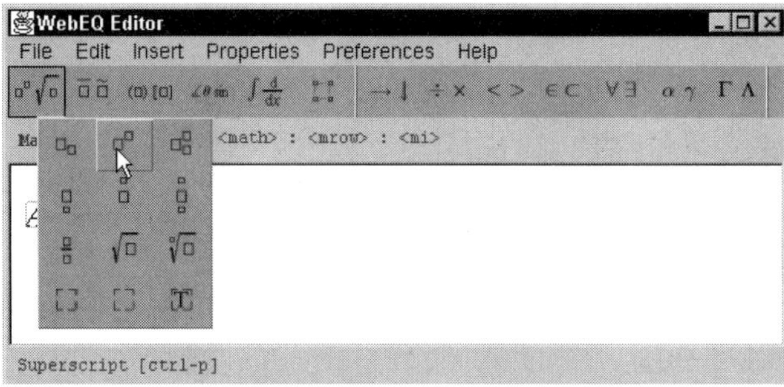

Figure 16.15 Formatting a base number with a power.

13. Choose the formatting symbol indicated in Figure 16.15.
14. Click inside the base number box, and type a lowercase *r* in the space.
15. Click inside the power number box, and type "2" inside the box. Your editor should resemble Figure 16.16.

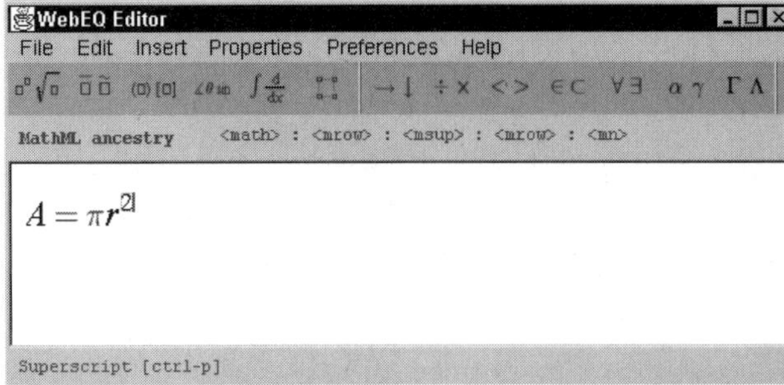

Figure 16.16 The area of a circle as depicted by the WebEQ editor.

16. Save the file by clicking File, Save As MathML, MathML-Lab2.
17. Use Notepad to review the MathML presentation-related source code for the file. Navigate to the directory where you saved the MathML-Lab2 file, open the file using the Notepad editor, and compare the code to that shown in Figure 16.17.

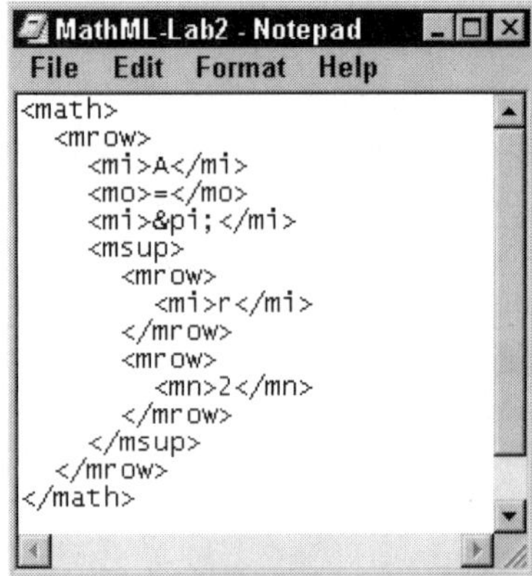


```
<math>
  <mrow>
    <mi>A</mi>
    <mo>=</mo>
    <mi>&pi;</mi>
    <msup>
      <mrow>
        <mi>r</mi>
      </mrow>
      <mrow>
        <mn>2</mn>
      </mrow>
    </msup>
  </mrow>
</math>
```

Figure 16.17 Source code (presentation format) as depicted by Notepad.

Lab 16.3: Install and Use EzMath for MathML

EzMath was developed by Dave Raggett and Davy Batsalle, with support from Hewlett-Packard Laboratories. We consider EzMath to be the easiest MathML editor to use. Its resulting source file will be in content format as opposed to presentation format. In an effort to support Web browser presentation, it has a plug-in option. In this lab, however, we will build an expression that displays inside Netscape but not Internet Explorer.

1. Go to www.w3.org/People/Raggett/EzMath/. Click the www.w3.org/People/Raggett/ezmath1_1.zip download link.
2. Download and save the file to your disk.
3. Go to the directory where the ezmath1_1.zip file is located and double-click the file to unzip file contents.
4. Extract *All Files* to the C:\ directory. This process creates an EzMath directory.
5. Start the EzMath editor. Click the C:\EzMath\EzMath.exe file; the editor appears, as shown in Figure 16.18.

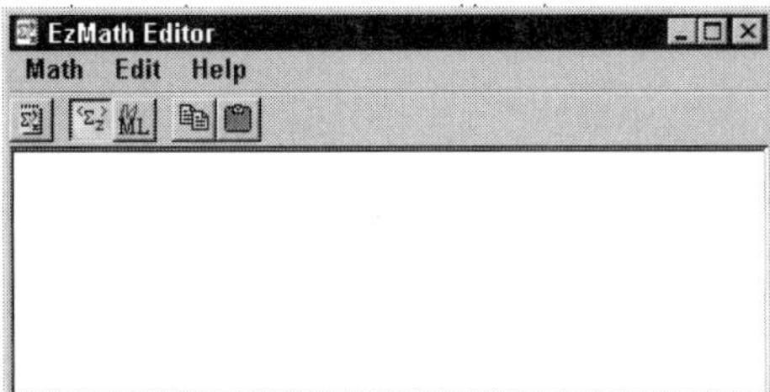

Figure 16.18 EzMath Editor.

6. Enter the example expression $A=\pi r^2$. To do this, first, on the EzMath menu bar, click Edit and then scroll down to and select View expression... Ctrl-S.
7. Inside the EzMath Expression Editor, type in the phrase "A equals pi r squared". Compare your input window to Figure 16.19.

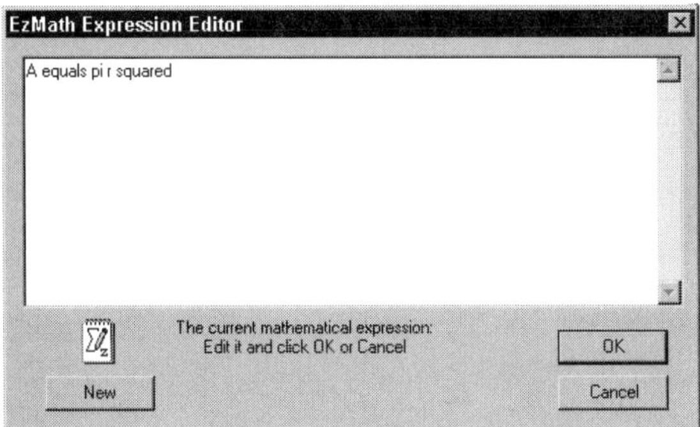

Figure 16.19 Example expression entered as a phrase or sentence.

8. Click OK. The EzMath editor should now look like Figure 16.20.

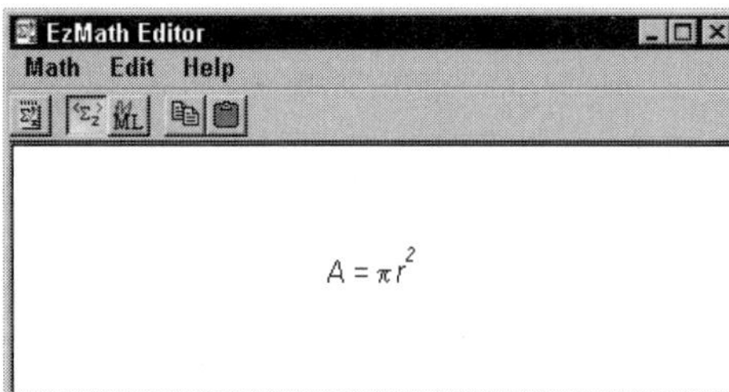

Figure 16.20 The area of a circle expression as shown by the EzMath editor.

9. Review the source code. To do so:
   a. Click the Set Clipboard Format to MathML button on the menu bar (the button looks like an M over ML).
   b. Click the Copy to Clipboard button (the Copy to Clipboard button looks like two pages side by side).
   c. Click the View Clipboard icon.
10. Compare your code to that shown in Figure 16.21.

If you click the Set Clipboard Format to EzMath button (which looks like a Greek letter sigma with a small subscript z next to it, both inside angle brackets), then you click Copy to Clipboard, View Clipboard, you will see the generated plug-in code to use for the Netscape browser.

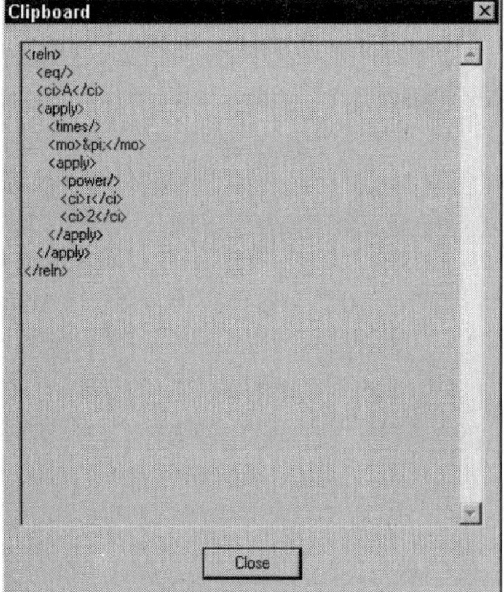

Figure 16.21 Content markup source code, as depicted by EzMath editor.

11. Normally, you would be expected to cut and paste the MathML code into a file of your choice to save the generated results. In this case, you can save the code to a file called MathML-Lab3 (using Notepad) if you think it may benefit you in the future.

Summary

MathML development is accelerating. Implementations are proliferating. MathML shows great promise as it begins to answer issues that have faced technical publishers for many years and the Internet since its inception.

Following are some key concepts to remember about the MathML specification:

- The W3C defines MathML as a ". . .specification for describing mathematics as a basis for machine-to-machine communication. It provides a much-needed foundation for the inclusion of mathematical expressions in Web pages."
- MathML allows technical publishers and developers to overcome historic issues regarding ambiguities and internationalism, as well as more recent issues concerning updatable or active documents and expressions that are accessible to visually handicapped persons.
- Since the mid-1970s, the IT industry has provided interim solutions, only capable of facilitating visual presentation and incapable of conveying the underlying semantics of mathematical equations. Several were too esoteric and complex for ordinary Web page developers and end users to use.
- In the early 1990s, the W3C recognized the issues surrounding the expression of mathematics. By 1997, the W3C established its Math Working Group, which developed four ever-improving MathML specifications from 1998 to the present. Their design goals included ease of implementation and use, sufficient sophistication to meet all math-related needs, the capability to produce high-quality renderings plus active documents, and the ability to embed MathML expressions into Web page documents.
- MathML consists of markup tags that create expressions that display properly and maintain their semantics. Approximately 30 presentation elements describe notational structures, 150 content elements specify the intended meaning of math expressions, and a few interface elements facilitate the embedding of MathML into Web page documents.

- MathML constitutes the lower Layer 1 of the mathematics-related Layered Architecture Model. It provides powerful platform-independent tools to facilitate interoperability, implementation, processing, maintenance, and processing. The top Layer 2 consists of specialized applications and other implementations.
- Many MathML implementations have been developed in the past few years. For a list of implementations, visit W3C's Implementations Web page at www.w3.org/Math/implementations.html. A list of Web browsers that display MathML expressions can be found at www.w3.org/Math/XSL/. MathML document validation services are available at validator.w3.org/ or www.w3.org/Math/validator/.
- The nesting scheme of content markup relies on prefix notation. It facilitates processing by a succession of scans, each involving relations around the operators in the expressions.
- Content and presentation techniques can be combined, since each is dedicated to semantics or display, respectively. Two methods are used: mixed markup or parallel markup.
- Abstract expression trees and layout boxes are valuable tools to use when designing MathML expressions, when checking the progress of MathML editor applications, or when using math editors.

Review Questions

1. Which of the following are issues faced by technical publishers regarding mathematical expressions?
   a. Do I share a common syntax with my readers?
   b. Are my symbols and constants the same as my readers'?
   c. Can visually handicapped people still benefit from my expressions?
   d. Are my documents active?
   e. All of the above.
2. True or false? Early IT expression solutions were capable of visual presentation and conveying the underlying semantics, but could not cope with internalization and other Internet-related concerns.
3. Which of the following were *not* MathML design goals?
   a. Seamless embedding into Web page documents
   b. Flexibility with respect to input and output
   c. Easy to implement/easy to use
   d. Capability of high-quality rendering in various media
   e. None of the above
4. True or false? MathML constitutes the upper Layer 2 of the Layered Software Architecture Model, where it facilitates interoperability, implementation, maintenance, processing, and rendering.
5. Fill in the blank: If a MathML expression is used in an XHTML document, we can use the ________________________________.
   a. XHTML DTD
   b. The XHTML DTD, extended with its MathML module
   c. MathML 2.0, second edition DTD
   d. Any MathML DTD or schema
   e. None of the above
6. True or false? Internet Explorer will not allow a MathML-related XSLT style sheet to be applied to a data document unless both documents are located on the same server.

7. In the expression, $A=\pi r^2$, in MathML terms, the *A* is called a ________________________.

   a. Character
   b. Symbol
   c. Script
   d. All of the above
   e. None of the above

8. True or false? Presentation markup is concerned with syntactic structure, whereas content markup is concerned with semantics.

9. Which notation scheme does MathML's content markup observe?

   a. Postfix
   b. Prefix
   c. Infix
   d. Suffix
   e. None of the above

10. The basic concepts that benefit MathML expression designers are________________________. (Choose all that apply.)

    a. Symbol buttons
    b. Abstract trees
    c. Layout boxes
    d. Widgets
    e. Process subroutines

Answers to Review Questions

1. **e.** These are all concerns faced with those who have developed MathML.
2. False. Early IT solutions were capable of visual presentation, but they could not convey semantics. Plus, they were often esoteric and tough to learn.
3. **e.** These are all design goals. Others are described in the text and at the W3C MathML 2.0 specification Web site.
4. False. Although the description is true, MathML actually constitutes the lower level of the model.
5. **b.** This question is taken directly from the text, in the *MathML DTDs or Schemas* section.
6. True. This was mentioned in the section titled *MathML and Style Sheets*.
7. **a.** The A, π, and r are all characters.
8. True. The answer is found in the text in the *Presentation Markup* and *Content Markup* sections.
9. **b.** This was discussed in the section titled *Prefix Notation*.
10. **b.** and **c.** These were discussed and demonstrated in the section titled *Two Basic Math Expression Creation Techniques and Concepts*.

About the 60 Minutes Web Site

This appendix provides you with information on the contents of the Web site that accompanies this book. On this site, you will find information that will help you with each of the book's chapters.

This Web site contains:

- Streaming video presentations that introduce you to each chapter of the book. These presentations provide overview information that can help you understand the content of the chapter.
- Sample code that is used throughout the book. The sample code is presented in separate simple text files, which will allow you to easily copy and paste the code when and where you need it.
- Data and solution files for the lab exercises in each chapter.
- There is also a case study Web site (www.spacegems.com) that facilitates the completion of the lab exercises.

To access the site, visit www.wiley.com/compbooks/60minutesaday.

System Requirements

Make sure that your computer meets the minimum system requirements listed in this section. If your computer doesn't match up to most of these requirements, you may have a problem using the contents of the Knowledge Publisher Studio.

- PC with a Pentium processor running at 266 Mhz or faster with Windows NT4, Windows 2000, or Windows XP.
- At least 256 MB of total RAM installed on your computer; for best performance, we recommend at least 512 MB.
- A high-speed Internet connection of at least 100K is recommended for viewing online video.
- Internet Explorer 6.0 or higher.
- Browser settings need to have Cookies enabled; Java must be enabled (including JRE 1.2.2 or higher installed) for chat functionality and live Webcast.
- Screen Resolution of 1024x768 pixels.

60 Minutes a Day Presentations

To enhance the learning experience and further replicate the classroom environment, *XML in 60 Minutes a Day* is complemented by a multimedia Web site which aggregates a streaming video and audio presentation. The multimedia Web site includes an online presentation and introduction to each chapter. The presentation, hosted by Linda McKinnon and Al McKinnon, includes a 10 to 15 minute video segment for each chapter that helps to deliver the training experience to your desktop and to convey advanced topics in a user-friendly manner.

Each video/audio segment introduces a chapter and details the important concepts and details of that chapter. After viewing the online presentation, you are prepped and primed to read the chapter.

Upon reaching the companion site that contains the video content for this book you will be asked to register using a valid email address and self-generated password. This will allow you to bookmark video progress and manage notes, email, and collaborative content as you progress through the chapters. All video content is delivered "on demand," meaning that you can initiate the viewing of a video at any time of the day or night at your convenience.

Any video can be paused and replayed as many times as you wish. The necessary controls and widgets used to control the delivery of the videos use strict industry standard symbols and behaviors, thus eliminating the necessity to learn new techniques. If you would like to participate in a complete five minute online tutorial on how to use all features available inside the presentation panel, visit http://www.propoint.com/solutions/ and click on the DEMO NOW link on the left hand side of the Web page.

This video delivery system may be customized somewhat to enhance and accommodate the subject matter within a particular book. In these cases, special effort has been made to ensure that all information is readily available and easy to understand. In the unlikely event that you should encounter a problem with the content on the site, please do not hesitate to contact us at Wiley Product Technical Support.

Code and Bonus Content

In addition to the presentations, you can download the sample code files and view additional resources.

Troubleshooting

If you have trouble with the Web site, please call the Wiley Product Technical Support phone number: (800) 762-2974. Outside the United States, call 1 (317) 572-3994. You can also visit our Web site at www.wiley.com/techsupport. Wiley Publishing, Inc. will provide technical support only for installation and other general quality control items; for technical support on the applications themselves, consult the program's vendor or author.

Index

, (comma) content operator, 133
<> (angle brackets), tags, 77
* (asterisk) content operator, 134
| (pipe) content operator, 133
+ (plus sign), content operator, 133–134
? (question mark) content operator, 133

A

<a> element, SMIL hyperlinking, 480–481
abbreviations, RDF, 515
absolute positioning
  CSS style rules and, 269–271
  VML figures, 436–437
<abstract> element, CDF documents, 554
abstract expression trees, MathML, 638
access
  channels, 564–567
  public, remote external DTDs, 125–126
Active channels, Webcasting, 532
Active Desktop, Webcasting, 532
actuate attribute, XLinks, 291–292
Adobe FrameMaker, 48
Advanced Text Management System (IBM), 9
algebra elements, MathML content markup, 633–634
align attribute, <div> element, 379
alignment, text, CSS style rules, 269
Amaya editor, installation, 640–644
Amaya software project, 227–228
AMS-TeX, MathML and, 618
<anchor> element, SMIL hyperlinking, 481–483
angle brackets (< >), 77
<animation> element, SMIL, 473
ANSI (American National Standards Institute), Computer Languages for the Processing of Text, 12
ANY keyword, 132
anyURI data type, definition, 182
Apache Web Server, 42
applications. *See* XML applications
Arbortext Epic, 55
arcs
  VML, 430
  XLinks, 286
    inbound, 286
    outbound, 286
    third-party, 286

arithmetic elements, MathML content markup, 633–634
asterisk (*) content operator, 134
ATTLIST keyword, 135
attribute declarations (DTDs)
  attribute list declarations, 134–135
  default values, 137
  definition, 119
  languages, 138–139
  types, 136
  white space preservation, 137–138
attribute node type, style sheets, 348
attribute normalization, definition, 149
attributes
  <a> element, SMIL, 481
  <anchor> element, SMIL, 481–483
  <channel> element, 551
  child elements and, 81
  datafld, 385–387
  datasrc, 385–387
  description, 80–81
  <Description> element, RDF, 513
  <div> element, 379
  elements and, 81
  global, XLinks, 287–299
  id, <layout> element, SMIL, 462–463
  ID attribute, selectors and, 263–264
  instances, lab, 110–111
  <item> element, 556–557
  <logo> element, 558
  <logtarget> element, 560–561
  <math> element, 627–628
  MathML, 629
  media object elements, SMIL, 475–476
  names, 80–81
  namespaces, declaring in DTD, 146–149
  nesting, 81
  notation declarations and, 143–145
  pseudo-attributes, 73
  resource attribute, RDF, 516
  SOAP messages
    encodingStyle, 601–602
    mustUnderstand, 600
    role, 600
  start tags, 80–81
  style sheets
    named set, 343
    output attributes, 344–345
  <switch> element test attributes, SMIL, 478
  <table> element, dataPageSize, 382
  type, <layout> element, SMIL, 462–463
  XHTML, 223–225
  XLinks, type elements combination, 292–293
  XML Schema, declaration, 165
<audio> element, SMIL, 473
authoring software. *See also* editing software
  classifications, 45
  definition, 40
  graphical editors, 45, 47–51
  integrated development environments, 45
  simple text editors, 45–47
axes, XPath, 304–306

B

backgrounds, images as, 264–266
behavior declarations, VML documents, 423–424
Berners-Lee, Tim, 15, 25
binary data type, definition, 182
binding. *See* data binding
binding agents, data binding and, 392–393
<binding> element, WSDL documents, 592–593
bitmap graphics
  advantages, 417
  disadvantages, 417–418

files, file format, 417
pixels, 416
raster graphic files, 416
BizTalk, DTDs and, 162
block-level boxes, VML, 425
<body> element, SMIL
media object elements, 472–477
<par> element, 470–472
<seq> element, 470–472
<switch> element, 477–479
<Body> element, SOAP messages, 602
boolean data type, definition, 182
borders, elements, 268
browsers. *See* Web browsers
pull technology and, 530
XLinks, display, 315–316
buttons, descriptions, recordsets, 398

C

CAD (computer-aided design), vector graphics and, 418
calculus-related elements, MathML content markup, 634
CALS (Continuous Acquisition and Lifecycle support), 14
cascading nature of style sheets, 272–273
case sensitivity, HTML-related tags, 221
cataloging Web content, RDF and, 503
CC/PP (Composite Capabilities/ Preferences Profile Specification), 512
CDATA section, reserved characters and, 100–101
CDF (Channel Definition Format)
channels
availability, 534–536
<channel> element, 548–549
description, 545–546
file modification, 570–572
files
creating, 569–570
posting to Web server, 564
generator, downloadable, 545
Internet Explorer 4, 532
introduction, 529
Microsoft Note, 544
resources, 544–545
specification development, 544–546
subscriptions, adding channels and, 536–541
XML differences, 546
CDF documents
channel definitions, 550
character encoding, 563–564
elements
<abstract> element, 554
<channel> element, 550–551
<earliesttime> element, 555–556
<http-equiv> element, 561
<intervaltime> element, 555
<item> element, 556–557
<latesttime>, 556
<log> element, 559–560
<login> element, 562–563
<logo> element, 558–559
<logtarget> element, 560–561
<schedule> element, 555
<title> element, 557
<usage> element, 561–562
prolog, 549–550
special characters, 563–564
CDF Generator, installation, lab, 568
<channel> element, CDF documents, 548–551
Channel value, CDF <usage> element, 562
channels
accessing, 564–567
adding to Favorites, CDF subscriptions and, 535–541
availability, 534–536
designing, 547–549
Favorites button, IE, 535
logo images, 549
overview, 532–534

channels *(continued)*
  synchronization
    activation, 542–543
    setup, 542–543
  viewing offline, 543
character data, definition, 71
character encoding, CDF documents, 563–564
character points, XPointer, 314
character references
  numeric
    parsing and, 98–100
    reserved characters and, 98–100
  XML Schema validation and, 190
characters
  MathML, 629–630
  reserved, 97
child elements
  asterisk (*) content operator, 134
  attributes and, 81
  comma (,) content operator, 133
  description, 78
  element content, 79
  pipe (|) content operator, 133
  plus sign (+) content operator, 133–134
  question mark (?) content operator, 133
CIM/XML, 511
classes
  pseudo-classes, 258–260
    CSS classes and, 260–263
  selector grouping, 256–258
classical function elements, MathML content markup, 634
clientless streaming, streaming media delivery, 456
closed elements, XHTML syntax, 221–223
<Code> element, SOAP <Fault> element, 604–605
coding, open source, 7
color
  hexadecimal values, 440
  predefined names, 440
  RGB function, 440
  shapes, VML, 440–441
comma (,), content operator, 133
comment node type, style sheets, 347
comments
  literal string, 76
  prolog, 76
  XML Schema prolog, 168
communications
  pull technology, 530
  push technology, 530
  Webcasting and, 531
complex content types, XML Schema, 165
compositors, element type declarations (XML Schema), 181
Conglomerate, description, 48
constant-related elements, MathML content markup, 635
content
  element content, 78
    child elements, 79
    mixed, 183–184
    mixed content, 79
  MathML markup elements, 633–636
    presentation markup mix, 637
  Web, RDF rating and, 503
content axes, XPath, 306
content handlers, XML parsers, 69
content model
  constraints, XML Schema, 166
  element type declarations, 129
  RDF documents, 510–512
  XML data, substituting, 515–516
content operators
  asterisk (*), 134
  comma (,), 133
  pipe (|), 133
  plus sign (+), 133–134
  question mark (?), 133

content separators, GML tags, 10
control codes (specific coding) in early documents, 7
Coombs, Renear, DeRose paper on markup, 5
Corel XMetal, description, 54
CSS (Cascading Style Sheets)
  cascading, 272–273
  classes, pseudo-classes and, 260–263
  Dave Raggett's Adding a Touch of Style Web site, 241
  inline style specifications, 242–243
  introduction, 239
  levels, 240–241
  parsing and, 247–248
  properties, 251–253
  Strict variant (XHTML) and, 215
  style rules
    absolute positioning, 269–271
    borders, 268
    declarations, 251
    images as backgrounds, 264–266
    images as discrete elements, 266–267
    indentations, 269
    margins, 269
    pseudo-classes, 260–263
    relative positioning, 271–272
    selectors grouped by class, 256–258
    selectors grouped by ID attribute, 263–264
    selectors grouped by pseudo-classes, 258–260
    selectors overview, 249–251
    selectors with pseudo-elements, 253–255
    syntax, 249
    text alignment, 269
  W3C CSS Validation Service, 241
  W3C CSS Working Group, 240–242
  XHTML and, lab, 273–274
  XML and, lab, 274–275
  XSLT and, 335
current template rule, style sheets, 349
curved lines, VML, 430

D

daily quote generator, SOAP lab, 607
DARPA (Defense Advanced Research Projects Agency), XML origins and, 17
data bindable elements, 376
data binding
  binding agent, 392–393
  data island storage, 389–392
  datafld attribute, 385–387
  datasrc attribute, 385–387
  definition, 374–375
  DSOs (data source objects), 393–396
  introduction, 373
  labs
    JavaScripts using IE's DSO binding, 405–409
    XHTML file with internal XML data island, 401–403
    XHTML file with reference to external data island, 403–405
  mapping and, 374
  nesting data, 387–388
  parser instructions and, 385–387
  placeholders and, 374, 376–378
  synchronization and, 374
  table repetition agents, 392–393
  two-level rule, 387–388
  variables, style sheet elements, 344
data consumer elements
  introduction, 376
  single-valued, 378
    overrestrictive data and, 382–385
  tabular data, 378
  XHTML data consumer elements, 378
data instance
  attributes, 80–82
  declared-empty elements, 77
  default namespace declarations, 90–91

data instance *(continued)*
elements
content, 78–79
creation lab, 105–109
element types, 77–78
empty elements, 78–79
empty string namespace declarations, 91–92
namespace declarations, inheritance and, 92
namespaces, 85–88
nested elements, 83–85
prefix namespace declarations, 89–90
tags, 77
XHTML documents' logical structure, 219–220
data island storage
external data islands, 389–391
internal data islands, 391–392
XHTML file with internal XML data island, 401–403
XHTML file with reference to external data island, 403–405
data placeholders. *See* placeholders
data type constraints, XML Schema, 166
data types
anyURI, 182
binary, 182
boolean, 182
date, 182
decimal, 182
ENTITY/ENTITIES, 182
ID, 182
int, 182
integer, 182
language, 182
Qname, 182
simple, element type declarations and, 181–182
string, 182
time, 182
datafld attribute, div element, 379, 385–387
dataPageSize attribute, table element, 382
datasrc attribute, div element, 379, 385–387
date data type, definition, 182
Dave Raggett's Adding a Touch of Style Web Site, 241
DCD (Document Content Description), DTDs and, 162
DCF (Document Composition Facility), 10
DCMI (Dublin Core Metatdata Initiative), RDF documents and, 511
decimal character references, table, 99
decimal data type, 182
decimal format, style sheet declaration, 343
declarations
DTDs, 127–134
namespaces, prefixes, 148
style rules, 251
declared-empty elements, 79–80
<definitions> element, WSDL documents, 589
delimiters, GML tags, 10
<Description> element, RDF documents, 512–513
descriptive markup, definition, 5
design
CDF channels, 547–549
MathML, 620–621
DesktopComponent value, CDF <usage> element, 562
DHTML (Dynamic HTML), DSOs and, 393
digital imaging
bitmap graphics, 416–418
vector graphics, 418–419
direction of links, XLinks, 286
discrete elements, images as, 266–267
distortion, SMIL objects, 466–467
<div> element
align attribute, 378
datafld attribute, 385–387

datasrc attribute, 385–387
HTML tables and, 379–380
<span> element and, 378
DMZs (Demilitarized Zones), network segments, 41–42
DNS (Domain Name Services), UDDI registries and, 583
DOCTYPE definition
declaration statement, Transitional variant (XHTML) and, 216
internal DTDs, 75
introduction, 74–75
VML document prolog, 422
DOCTYPE keyword, 74
document element, 78
document processing
applications, 68
definition, 4
errors, 70
XML parsers, 69–70
document root node type, style sheets, 347
document type declaration, 74–76
documentation, DTD suites, 121
domain names, mapping, 42
drawing
Bézier curves, 427–429
vector graphic images, 418
DrawML Specification, introduction, 446
DSOs (data source objects)
DHTML and, 393
recordsets, navigating, 396–401
DTD handlers, XML parsers, 69
DTDs (document type definitions)
attribute declarations, 119, 134–135
default values, 137
languages, 138–139
types, 136
white space preservation, 137–138
BizTalk and, 162
creating, 120–121
DCD and, 162
declarations, 127–134
element type declarations, 119
any content, 132
content model, 129
content operators, 132–134
declaration identifier, 128
empty elements, 131–132
mixed content, 130–131
names, 129
other element types, 130
parsed character data, 129
entity declarations, 119
general, 139–140
extensibility in design, 121
external, 118
lab, 149–153
private, 123–124
remote with public access, 125–126
subsets, 122–123
subsets on Web sites, 124–125
Frameset variant (XHTML), 217–218
history of, 118
instances, creating, 153–154
internal, 75, 118
external DTD combination, 126–127
subsets, 122
introduction, 117–118
locations, 121–122
MathML document prolog, 623–625
namespace declarations
attributes, 146–149
limitations, 149
notation declarations, 119, 143–146
overview, 118–119
parameter entity declarations, 140–141
reasons to use, 119–120
RELAX and, 162
Schematron and, 162
SGML and, 13
SMIL document prolog, 460–461
Strict variant (XHTML) and, 215
suites, documentation, 121
Transitional variant (XHTML) and, 215–216

DTDs *(continued)*
types, 121–122
valid documents and, 104
well-formed documents and, 120
XML Schema and, 162, 190
DTP (desktop publishing) applications
description, 11
TeX applications, 11
duration facet, description, 185
DVI (Device Independent) format, DTP and, 11

E

<earliesttime> element, CDF documents, 555–556
editing software, 40. *See also* authoring software
element content
child elements, 79
definition, 78
mixed content, 79, 183–184
operators, 132
element node type, style sheets, 347
element type declarations (DTDs)
any content, 132
content model, 129
content operators, 132
asterisk (*), 134
comma (,), 133
pipe (|), 133
plus sign (+), 133–134
question mark (?), 133
declaration identifier, 128
definition, 119
empty elements, 131–132
mixed content, 130–131
names, 128
other element types, 130
parsed character data, 129
XML Schema
compositors, 181
data types, 181–182
empty element content, 181
mixed content, 183–184
<sg1:catalog> element, 181–182
<sg1:diamonds> element, 178–181
<sg1:gem> element, 178–181
elements. *See also* individual elements
attributes and, 81
borders, 268
content, 78–79
creating, style sheet nodes 6-12, 348
data instance, creation lab, 105–109
declared-empty, 77
empty elements, 79–80
extent, 78
instances, lab, 110–111
MathML, 212–213
names, well-formed documents and, 102
nested, 83–85
sibling elements, 84
no content, 79–80
types
child elements, 78
description, 77
document element, 78
GI (generic identifier), 78
naming rules, 77
nested, 220–221
root element, 78
white space, 77
XML Schema, declaration, 165
Emacs, 46
email
push technology and, 530
verification, SOAP lab, 608–609
Email value, CDF <usage> element, 562
Emilé, 48
empty elements
declared-empty, 79–80
element type declarations (DTDs), 131–132
end tags, 80
no content, 79–80
start tags, 80
XHTML syntax, 221–223
XML Schema element type declarations, 181

empty string namespace declarations, 91–92
encodingStyle attribute, SOAP messages, 601–602
end tags
  definition, 77
  empty elements, 80
  SGML, 14
enlivening expression elements, MathML, 632
entities
  definition, 92–93
  external, 93–94
  general entities, 94–96
  internal, 93–94
  named entities, 98
  notation declarations and, 145–146
  parameter entities, 94–96
  parsing, 93
  predefined, 97–98
ENTITIES data type, 182
ENTITY data type, 182
entity declarations (DTDs)
  definition, 119
  general, 139–140
ENTITY keyword, 140
entity resolvers, XML parsers, 70
<Envelope> element, SOAP, 598–599
eqn, MathML and, 618
equation editors, MathML content markup, 635
error files, virtual hosting, 42
error handlers, XML parsers, 69
errors
  document processing, 70
  XML parsers, 70
expat XML parser, 70
expressions
  MathML
    abstract expression trees, 638
    layout boxes, 638–640
    planning and, 616–617
  XPath
    functions in, 308–311
    location paths and, 301–304
    predicates, 307–308
extended-type XLinks, 295–299
extent of element, description, 78
external data islands
  definition, 389–391
  XHTML files with reference, 403–405
external DTDs
  definition, 118
  lab, 149–153
  private, 123–124
  remote with public access, 125–126
  subsets, 122–123
    at Web sites, 124–125
external entities
  description, 93–94, 139
  parameter entities, 140, 143
external style sheets, document affiliation, 244–247
external subsets, 76
EzMath, 646–649

F

facets, XML Schema, 180, 184–185
<Fault> element, SOAP messages, 603–604
figure placement, VML
  absolute positioning, 436–437
  relative positioning, 437
  static positioning, 436
  z-index, 437–438
figures, VML
  coloring shapes, 440–441
  overlapping, 437–438
file formats, procedural markup and, 5
filenames, virtual hosting, 42
<fill> element, VML, 441–442
fills, VML
  gradient fills, 442–443
  pattern fills, 443
  pictures, 443
flat catalog structure, XML Schema documents, 186–189
flipping images, VML, 438–439
fonts, vector fonts, 418
formatting language, XSL, 333
fractionDigits facet, 185

Frameset variant (XHTML)
DTDs and, 217–218
introduction, 214
freeform XML, 103
functions
function elements, MathML content markup, 634
XPath expressions, 308–311

G

GCA (Graphic Communication Association)
GML and, 8
System X project (GenCode), 10
GenCode, 10
general entities, 94–96
generic coding, beginnings, 7–8
GetLocalTime Web service, WSDL files, 586–588
GI (generic identifier), 78
GIF image format, logo images, 558
global attributes, XLinks
actuate, 291–292
definition, 287–288
extended-type, 295–299
show attribute, 291–292
simple-type linking elements, 294–295
type attribute, 289–291
global references, XML Schema, 173–175
GML (Generalized Markup Language)
code examples, 9
origins, 8–9
portability, 10
tags, 10
GO (Gene Ontology) project, 512
Goldfarb, Charles, 9
gradient fills, VML, 442–443
graphic objects, VML path attribute, 427–429
graphical browsers, 43
graphical editors
Adobe FrameMaker, 48
Conglomerate, 48
Emilé, 48
GUIs, 47
Microsoft FrontPage 2002, 49
Microsoft Word, 49–51
Microsoft XML Notepad, 48
Peter's XML Editor, 48
structure checking, 47
XAE (XML Authoring Environment for Emacs), 48
graphics
bitmap graphics, 416
raster graphics, 416
graphs, RDF, 509–510
grouping shapes, VML, 444–446
GUIs (graphical user interfaces), 47

H

hardware requirements
authoring software, 40
editing software, 40
<head> element, SMIL
<layout> element, 462–463
<meta> element, 469
<region> element, 465–466
<root-layout> element, 463–465
<switch> element, 469–470
helper components, XML Schema, 165
hexadecimal character references, table, 99
hexadecimal color values, 440
hierarchies, virtual hosting, 42
HLink, XHTML development and, 210
HTML (HyperText Markup Language)
data and, 208–209
document conversion to XML, 55–56
DTP and, 11
extensibility, 208
history, 15–16
limitations, 208–209
SGML and, 14
styles
inline specifications, 242–243
internal style sheet specifications, 243–244
table, XSLT elements, 348

tables
<div> element, 379–380
first row, 349
tags, *versus* XML tags, 20
VML document prolog and, 422
W3C validation service, conversion and, 226–227
Web site conversion to XHTML, 225–226
XHTML history, 206–207
HTML-Kit, 229, 232–234
HTML-Tidy utility
HTML file validation lab, 230–232
introduction, 229
<http-equiv> element, CDF documents, 561
HTTP server, 40
HTTP streaming, streaming media delivery, 456
hyperlinks, SMIL elements, 479–483

I

IBM Http Server, 43
IBM Script, Advanced Text Management System and, 9
id( ) function, XPath/Xpointer, 310–311
id attribute
<div> element, 379
<layout> element, SMIL, 462–463
ID attribute, selectors and, 263–264
ID data type, 182
IDEAlliance, 8
IDEs (Integrated Development Environments)
Arbortext Epic, 55
Corel XMetal, 54
description, 52–53
Komodo, 55
TurboXML, 54
Xeena, 54
XML Spy, 55
IETF (Internet Engineering Task Force), 15–16
IIS (Internet Information Services)
configuration, 58–59
installation, lab, 57–60
software, 40
testing, 59–60
Web Server software, 43
image property names, 265
images
as backgrounds, 264–266
as discrete elements, 266–267
flipping, VML, 438–439
generating, with VML, 420
logo images, CDF channels, 549
rotating, VML, 438
shapes, VML, 431
XML-to-HTML transformations, 366–368
<img> element, SMIL, 473
importing
style sheet element for, 343
style sheets, 343
inbound arcs, XLinks, 286
indentations, CSS style rules, 269
infix notation, MathML, 636
inline style specifications, 242–243
installation
Amaya editor, MathML, 640–644
CDF Generator, lab, 568
EzMath, 646–649
IIS, lab, 57–60
TIBCO XML Transform software, 353–354
TurboXML, lab, 60–61
WebEQ, 644–646
instan, design, lab, 111–112
instances
creating, lab, 153–154
elements and attributes, lab, 110–111
instantiation, 349
int data type, 182
integer data type, 182
internal data islands, 391–392
XHTML files, 401–403

internal DTDs
definition, 118
external DTDs combination, 126–127
subsets, 122
internal entities
description, 93–94, 139
parameter entities, 140, 141–142
internal style sheet specifications, 243–244
internal subsets, 75–76
Internet browsers. *See* Web browsers
Internet Explorer
browser software requirements, 40
channels, 535
description, 44
media environment, lab, 485–486
<intervaltime> element, CDF documents, 555
inventory control, <xs:pattern> element and, 184
ISBNs (International Standard Book Numbers), <xs:pattern> element and, 184
ISO (International Organization for Standardization)
ISO12083:1994, MathML and, 619
SGML and, 13
<item> element, CDF documents, 556–557

J

JavaScript
code, recordsets, 396–397
DSO binding technology, 405–409
JPEG image format, logo images, 558

K

key declaration, style sheets, 343
keywords
ANY, 132
ATTLIST, 135
DOCTYPE, 74
ENTITY, 140
NOTATION, 144
Komodo, 55
Konqueror
browser software requirements, 40
description, 44

L

labs
authoring environment creation, 56–61
CDF
CDF Generator installation, 568
channel availability, 572–574
conventions, 27–32
CSS
combining with XHTML, 273–274
combining with XML, 274–275
data binding
JavaScript using IE's DSO binding, 405–409
XHTML file with internal XML data island, 401–403
XHTML file with reference to external data island, 403–405
data instance with elements, creation, 105–109
DTDs
creating external, 149–153
instance creation, 153–154
file creation, 569–570
file modification, 570–572
HTML file validation, HTML-Tidy and, 230–232
IIS Web server installation, 57–60
instances
design, 111–112
elements and attributes and, 110–111
instructions, 27–32
links, inserting in XML file that has DTD, 275–278
MathML
Amaya editor installation, 640–644
EzMath installation, 646–649
WebEQ installation, 644–646

RDF creation
code validation, 517–519
RDFedt editor, 519–523
SMIL
IE media environment, 485–486
media environment, 486–490
RealOne Media Player installation, 484
SOAP
daily quote generator, 607
email verifier, 608–609
time service, 606
Space Gems, 29
transformation software, 351–368
TIBCO XML Transform, 353–368
TurboXML installation, 60–61
VML document creation, VML example, 447–449
VML shapes, 450
Web service access, SOAP, 605–609
XHTML file creation, HTML-Kit, 232–234
XLink, 316
comparing types, 322–325
link creation, 317–318
multiple links in XML file, 318–319
outbound links, 319–322
third-party links, 324–325
XML, searches, 29–30
XML Schema
complex elements extended, 198
complex types, 196–198
creation, 191–195
instances, 195
XPath, 316
XPointer, 316
language data type, 182
languages
attribute declarations, 138–139
lingua franca, 8
subset languages, 18
<latesttime> element, CDF documents, 556
LaTeX, MathML and, 618
layout boxes, MathML expression creation, 638–640
<layout> element, SMIL <head> element, 462–463
left-flush tags, GML, 14
Length facet, 184
linear algebra-related elements, MathML content markup, 634
lines, VML, 431
lingua franca, 8
<link> element, 242–246
links. *See also* XLinks
XML files, DTDs and, 275–278
literal string, comments and, 76
local references, XML Schema, 173–175
location paths, XLinks and XPath expressions, 301–304
location steps, XPath
axes, 304–306
node tests, 306–307
predicates, 307–308
<log> element, CDF documents, 559–560
logic elements, MathML content markup, 633–634
logical devices, 88
logical structures
documents, 71–92
XHTML syntax, 218–220
RDF documents, 510–514
XLinks, 286–299
<login> element, CDF documents, 562–563
<logo> element, CDF documents, 558–559
logo images, CDF channels, 549
<logtarget> element, CDF document, 560–561
Lorie, Ray, 9

M

mapping
data binding and, 374
domains, 42

margins, CSS style rules, 269
markup
  definition, 6–7, 71
  descriptive, 5
  metamarkup, 5
  presentational, 5
  procedural, 5
  proprietary data formats, 12
  punctuational, 5
  reasons to use, 6
  referential, 5
  standards, 12
  tags, 6
  Text Description Language, 8
  types, 4
<math> element, MathML, 626–628
MathML documents
  MathML DTDs, 623–625
  schemas, 623–625
  style sheets, 625
MathML (Mathemat Markup Language)
  presentation markup, script and limit schemata elements, 631–632
MathML (Mathematical Markup Language)
  AMS-TeX, 618
  attributes, 629
  bases, 629–630
  characters, 629–630
  content markup, 633–636
    algebra elements, 633–634
    arithmetic elements, 633–634
    basic content elements, 633
    calculus-related elements, 634
    classical function elements, 634
    constant-related elements, 635
    linear algebra-related elements, 634
    logic elements, 633–634
    presentation markup mix, 637
    relation elements, 634
    semantic mapping elements, 634
    sequence-related elements, 634
    series-related elements, 634
    set theory related elements, 634
    statistic-related elements, 634
    symbol-related elements, 635
    token elements, 633
  display speed, 619
  download speed, 619
  elements, 212–213
  eqn, 618
  expressions
    abstract expression trees, 638
    layout boxes, 638–640
    planning and, 616–617
  fonts, 617
  infix notation, 636
  introduction, 615–616
  ISO12083:1994 and, 619
  labs
    Amaya editor installation, 640–644
    EzMath installation, 646–649
    WebEQ installation, 644–646
  LaTeX and, 618
  <math> element, 626–628
  namespaces, 212–213, 628–629
  overview, 622–623
  PN (prefix notation), 636–637
  postfix notation, 636
  presentation markup, 630–632
    content markup mix, 637
    enlivening expression elements, 632
    general layout schemata element, 631
    table and matrix elements, 632
    token elements, 630–631
  printing technology and, 617
  rendering technology and, 617
  scripts, 629–630
  symbols, 629–630
  TeX and, 618
  visual presentation solutions, 618–619
  visually handicapped persons, 619
  W3C and, 619–620
    design goals, 620–621
    implementations, 621–622
    Math Working Group, 620
  XHTML development and, 210

matrix elements, MathML, 632
maxExclusive facet, 185
maxLength facet, 184
media environment, Internet Explorer, 485–486
media object elements, SMIL <body> element, 472–477
memory, vector graphics files, 418
<message> element, WSDL documents, 590–591
<meta> element, SMIL <head> element, 469
meta tags, metadata and, 499–500
metadata
  initiatives, 511
  introduction, 499–500
  meta tags and, 499–500
  PICS and, 500–502
  RDF and, 500–502
  SOAP messages, 600
Metadata Activity
  Semantic Web Activity and, 504
  W3C, 500–501
metalanguages
  definition, 7
  description, 6
  introduction, 6
  meta-markup, 7
  XML as, 18
metamarkup, 5
Microsoft FrontPage 2002, 49
Microsoft Note, CDF and, 544
Microsoft Notepad, 46
Microsoft Word, HTML/XML creation, 49–51
Microsoft WordPad, 46
Microsoft XML Notepad, 48
minExclusive facet, 185
minLength facet, 184
mixed content
  description, 183–184
  elements, 79
modularity of XHTML, 213–214
Mosher, Ed, 9
Mozilla
  browser software requirements, 40
  description, 44
  Mozilla.org, RDF and, 506
MSXML XML parser, 70
multidirectional links, XLinks, 324
mustUnderstand attribute, SOAP messages, 600–601

N

name attribute, <div> element, 379
named entities, 98
namespace declarations
  default, 147
  default namespace declarations, 90–91
  definition, 85–86
  DTD limitations, 149
  empty string namespace declarations, 91–92
  inheritance and, 92
  prefix namespace declarations, 89–90
  RDF documents, 511
  <schema> element, 170–171
  SMIL documents, 461
  VML documents, 422–423
  XSLT style sheets, 341
namespace node type, style sheets, 347
namespaces
  attributes, declarations in DTD, 146–149
  definition, 85–88
  MathML, 212–213, 628–629
  qualifying URLs, 88
  RDF documents, 510–512
  universal name, 88
  XLinks, 287
  XML Schema
    target namespaces, 171–172
    xs prefix, 170
naming
  attributes, 80–81
  element types, 77

naming *(continued)*
elements, well-formed documents and, 102
links, XLinks, 287
NASSL (Network Accessible Services Specification Language), WSDL and, 585
nesting
attributes, 81
data binding and, 387–388
element types, XHTML syntax, 220–221
elements, 83–85
XML Schema document structure, 186
Netscape
browser software requirements, 40
description, 44
NITF (News Industry Text Format), 14
nodal structure, source document, 340
node points, XPointer, 313–314
node tests, XPath location steps, 306–307
nodes, style sheets
current template rule, 349
element creation, 348
filling out cells in table row, 350–351
HTML table initial row, 349
HTML table with XSLT element types, 348
individual name table cell, 350
matching to, 347–348
source node, 349
template patterns and table row, 350
template rule, 349
NONE value, CDF <usage> element, 562
normalization, attribute normalization, 149
notation declarations (DTDs)
definition, 119
non-XML data
attributes and, 143–145
entities and, 145–146
NOTATION keyword, 144
numeric character references
parsing and, 98–100
reserved characters and, 98–100

O

Oasis Cover Pages Web site, SGML-related languages, 13
object-oriented graphics
fonts, 418
vector graphic images, 418
objects, SMIL documents, 466–469
offline work, channel viewing, 543
open source
document coding, 7
OSI, 208
Opera, 44
operating system requirements, 40
OSD (Open Software Description Format), CDF development and, 544
OSI (Open Source Initiative), 208
outbound arcs, XLinks, 286
outbound links, XLinks lab, 319–322
outline fonts, vectors and, 418
output of style sheet elements
description, 343
output attributes, 344–345
ovals, VML, 431
overlapping figures, VML, 437–438

P

<par> element, SMIL <body> element, 470–472
paragraph breaks, <span> element, 380
parameter entities
declarations, 140–141
definition, 94
external, 143
internal, 141–142
parsing
character data, element type declarations, 129
character references, numeric, 98–100
CSS and, 247–248

entities, 93
expressions, XPath and, 301–303
predefined entities and, 97–98
reserved characters, 97
well-formed documents and, 101
path attribute
relative coordinates, 428
VML graphic objects, 427–429
<path> element, VML, 429–430
pattern fills, VML, 443
payload, SOAP, 594
PDF (Portable Document Format), DTP and, 11
Peter's XML Editor, 48
physical structure of documents, 92–96
PICS (Platform for Internet Content Selection), metadata and, 500–502
picture fills, VML, 443
piname in processing instructions, 74
pipe (|), content operator, 133
pixels
bitmap graphics and, 416
definition, 416
placeholders
data bindable elements, 376
data binding and, 374
data consumer elements, 376–378
<div> element, 378–380
plaintext applications, 12
plus sign (+), content operator, 133–134
PN (prefix notation), MathML, 636–637
pointers, internal document structure, 312–313
points, XPointer, 313
character points, 314
node points, 313–314
<port> element, WSDL documents, 593
portability
GML, 10
XHTML, 214
<portType> element, WSDL documents, 591
position( ) function, XPath/XPointer, 311
postfix notation, MathML, 636
posting CDF files to Web server, 564
Precision Graphics Markup Language, introduction, 446
predefined entities, 97–98
predefined entity references, data content, 563
predefined shapes, VML
description, 430–434
templates, 433–434
predicates, XPath, 307–308
prefix namespace declarations, 89–90, 148
presentation markup, MathML, 630–632, 637
presentational markup, 5
primary components, XML Schema, 165
primitive graphic objects, 426
PRISM (Publishing Requirements for Industry Standard Metadata), 511
private external DTDs, 123–124
procedural markup, 5
processing instruction node type, style sheets, 348
processing instructions, prolog, 73–74
prologs
CDF documents, 549–550
MathML documents
MathML DTDs, 623–625
schemas, 623–625
style sheets, 625
RDF documents, 510
SMIL documents, 460–461
VML documents, 422
WSDL documents, 589
XHTML documents, 219
XML documents
comments, 76
document type declaration, 74–76
processing instructions, 73–74
XML declaration, 72–73
XML Schema, 168–169

properties
  CSS language, 251
  image properties, 265
  RDF, 508–509
property elements, RDF, 512–514
proprietary data formats, markup languages and, 12
PS (PostScript) format, DTP and, 11
pseudo-attributes
  definition, 73
  style sheets, 339
pseudo-classes
  CSS classes and, 260–263
  grouping selectors, 258–260
pseudo-elements, selectors with, 253–255
public access, remote external DTDs, 125–126
public domain software, Web servers, 42
publication, Web, 498–499
publishing, CDF channel creation, 546–547
pull technology, 530
punctuational markup, 5
push technology, 530

Q

Qname data type, 182
qualified references, XML Schema, 173–175
qualifying URLs, namespaces and, 88
query contexts, style sheet node 5, 346–348
question mark (?), content operator, 133

R

radio broadcasting, push technology and, 530
ranges, XPointer, 314–315
raster graphic files, 416
RDF documents
  abbreviations, 515
  content model, 510–512
  <Description> element, 512–513
  namespaces, 510–512
  resource attribute, 516
  structure
    prolog, 510
    <RDF> element, 510–512
  URIs, 503
<RDF> element, RDF documents, 510–512
RDF (Resource Description Framework)
  code validation, lab, 517–519
  definition, 502–504
  file creation, RDFedt editor, 519–523
  graphs, 509–510
  implementations, 506–507
  introduction, 497
  metadata and, 500–502
  properties, 508–509
  resources, 508
  statements, 507–508
  values, 509
RDF Validation Service, 506
RDFedt editor, RDF file creation, 519–523
RealOne Media Player, SMIL installation lab, 484
recordsets
  button descriptions, 398
  DSOs and, 396–401
  JavaScript code, 396–397
  XHTML table definition, 398
  <xml> element, 397
rectangles, VML, 431
<ref> element, SMIL, 473
referential markup, 5
<region> element, SMIL <head> element, 465–466
relation elements, MathML content markup, 634
relative coordinates, VML graphics, 428
relative positioning
  CSS style rules and, 269
  VML figures, 437

RELAX (Regular Language description for XML), DTDs and, 162
remote external DTDs, public access, 125–126
reserved characters
CDATA sections, 100–101
numeric character references, 98–100
parser and, 97
predefined entity references, 563–564
resource attribute, RDF, 516
resources
CDF, 544–545
RDF, 503, 508
XLinks, 285–286
RGB color, VML, 440
Rice, Stanley, 8
role attribute, SOAP messages, 600
root directories
creating, 58
virtual hosts, 42
root element
definition, 78
nesting, 84–85
<sg1:diamonds> element declaration, 175–178
SMIL documents, 461–462
well-formed documents and, 101
rotating images, VML, 438
rounded rectangles, VML, 431
RSS (RDF Site Summary), 511
Ruby Annotation, XHTML, 209–210

S

scalability
shapes, VML, 443–444
vector graphics, 419
scalable fonts, vectors and, 418
<schedule> element, CDF documents, 555
<schema> element, namespace declarations, 170–171
schema handlers, XML parsers, 69
schemas, MathML document prolog, 623–625
Schematron (Schema for Object-oriented XML), DTDs and, 162
SCL (SOAP Contract Language), WSDL and, 585
screening, XML parsers and, 69
ScreenSaver value, CDF <usage> element, 562
scripts, MathML, 629–630
searches
labs, 29–30
VML, 421
Web searches, 498–499
secondary components, XML Schema, 165
selectors
grouping
by class, 256–258
by ID attribute, 263–264
by pseudo-class, 258–260
pseudo-elements, 253–255
style rules, overview, 249–251
semantic mapping elements, MathML content markup, 634
Semantic Web, 22, 504–505
<seq> element, SMIL <body> element, 470–472
sequence-related elements, MathML content markup, 634
series-related elements, MathML content markup, 634
<service> element, WSDL documents, 593
set theory related elements, MathML content markup, 634
<sg1:catalog> element declaration, 181–182
<sg1:diamonds> element declaration, 175–178
<sg1:gem> element declaration, 178–181
SGML (Standard Generalized Markup Language)
approval, 13
DTDs and, 13, 120

SGML *(continued)*
  end tags, 14
  first draft, 12
  SGML-based languages, 13–14
  start tags, 14
  Web site, 7
  XML and, 18
<shape> element, VML, 425–426
shapes, VML
  color, 440–441
  grouping, 444–446
  predefined, 430–434
  scaling, 443–444
<shapetype> element, VML, 435
show attribute, XLinks, 291–292
sibling elements, nesting, 84
simpl text editors. *See* text editors
simple content types, XML Schema, 165
SimpleText, 46
single-valued data consumer elements
  data binding agent, 393
  definition, 378
  overrestrictive data and, 382–385
  <table> element, 380–381
sitecrawlers, Webcasting and, 531
SKUs (stock keeping units), <xs:pattern> element and, 184
SMDL (The Standard Music Description Language), 14
SMIL documents
  <body> element
    media object elements, 472–477
    <par> element, 470–472
    <seq> element, 470–472
    <switch> element, 477–479
  <head> element
    <layout> element, 462–463
    <meta> element, 469
    <region> element, 465–466
    <root-layout> element, 463–465
    <switch> element, 469–470
  hyperlinks, 479–483
  namespace declarations, 461
  objects
    dimension matching, 466–469
    fitting to region, 466–469
  prolog, SMIL DTD, 460–461
  root element, 461–462
  <smil> element, 461–462
<smil> element, 461–462
SMIL (Synchronized Multimedia Integration Language)
  labs, RealOne Media Player installation, 484
  media environment lab, 486–490
  overview, 455, 456–457
  streaming media and, 455–456
  W3C and
    version 1.0, 457–458
    version 2.0, 458
  XHTML and, 459
  XHTML development and, 210
  XML applications and, 68
SOAP (Simple Object Access Protocol)
  Envelope, 598–599
  description, 594–595
  <Fault> element, 603–604
    <Code> element, 604–605
    <Value> element, 604–605
  introduction, 579
  labs
    daily quote generator, 607
    email verifier, 608–609
    time service, 606
  messages, 597–598
    <Body> element, 602
    encodingStyle attribute, 601–602
    header, 599–605
    mustUnderstand attribute, 600–601
    role attribute, 600
    sample, 605
  requests
    creating the client, 586
    example, 602–603
  response example, 603
  specification development, 595–596
  UDDI and, 579–580
  WSDL and, 579

software
browser software, 40
editing software (*See* editing software)
TIBCO XML Transform, 353–368
Web servers, 41–43
SoftwareUpdate value, CDF <usage> element, 562
source document
nodal structure, 340
style sheets, embedded, 339
transformations, 336–341
source node, style sheets, 349
Space Gems
labs, 29
Web server configuration, 41–42
Space Gems' Private Network, 41
<span> element
<div> element and, 378
element names, 378
paragraph breaks, 380
special characters, CDF documents, 563–564
specific coding, 7
start tags
attributes, 80–81
definition, 77
empty element, 80
SGML, 14
well-formed documents and, 102
static library, HTML, 21
static positioning, VML figures, 436
statistic-related elements, MathML content markup, 634
storage, data islands
external, 389–391
internal, 391–392
streaming media
clientless streaming, 456
definition, 455
HTTP streaming, 456
SMIL and, 455–456
true streaming, 456
Strict variant (XHTML)
CSS and, 215
DTDs and, 215
introduction, 214
string data type, 182
strings, empty string namespace declarations, 91–92
structure checking, graphical editors and, 47
style attribute, <div> element, 379
<STYLE> element, 243–244
<style> element, 243–244
style sheets. *See also* CSS (Cascading Style Sheets)
attributes, named set definition, 343
decimal format declaration, 343
elements, 343
embedding in source documents, 339
importing, 343
key declaration, 343
MathML documents, 625
namespace declarations, 341
nodes
6-12/element creation, 348
18-22/filling out cells in table row, 350–351
23-25/individual name table cell, 350
13/building HTML table with XSLT element types, 348
15/current template rule, 349
16/HTML table initial row, 349
5/query contexts and first template rule, 346–348
14/source node, 349
17/template patterns and table row, 350
15/template rule, 349
matching to, 347–348
output attributes, 344–345
processing instructions, pseudo-attributes, 339
root node, 341

style sheets *(continued)*
- templates, 343
- tree output, 343
- variables, binding, 344
- white space
  - preserving, 343
  - stripping, 343

styles
- inline specifications, 242–243
- internal style sheet specifications, 243–244
- rules
  - absolute positioning, 269–271
  - borders, 268
  - declarations, 251
  - images as backgrounds, 264–266
  - images as discrete elements, 266–267
  - indentations, 269
  - margins, 269
  - relative positioning, 271–272
  - selectors grouped by class, 256–258
  - selectors grouped by ID attribute, 263–264
  - selectors grouped by pseudo-classes, 258–260
  - selectors overview, 249–251
  - selectors with pseudo-elements, 253–255
  - syntax, 249
  - text alignment, 269

subset languages, 18

subsets
- external subsets, 76
- internal subsets, 75–76

Sun ONE Web Server, Web site information, 43

SVG (Scalar Vector Graphics)
- overview, 446
- VML and, 415
- XHTML development and, 210

<switch> element, SMIL <body> element, 477–479

symbol-related elements, MathML content markup, 635

symbols, MathML, 629–630

SYMM-WG (Synchronized Multimedia Working Group), SMIL and, 457–458

synchronization
- channels
  - activation, 542–543
  - setup, 542–543
- data binding and, 374

syntax
- grammar rules, 21
- RDF, abbreviations, 515
- style rules, 249
- XHTML, document logical structure, 218–220
- XLinks, browser display, 315–316

SYSTEM keyword, DTDs, 75

system requirements, authoring environment creation, 56

T

<table> element
- attributes, dataPageSize, 382
- single-valued consumer elements, 380–381
  - overrestrictive data and, 382–385
- tabular consumer elements, 380–381

table elements, MathML, 632

table repetition agents, data binding and, 392–393

tabular data consumer elements
- definition, 378
- <table> element, 380–381
- table repetition agent, 393

tags
- end tags, 77
- GML, 10
- introduction, 6
- start tags, 77

target namespaces, XML Schema, 171–172

TEI (Text Encoding Initiative), 14

television broadcasting, push technology and, 530
template rule
  current template rule and, 349
  style sheet node 5, 346–348
templates
  current template rule, 349
  patterns, table rows, 350
  predefined shapes, VML, 433–434
  <shape> element, VML, 425–426
  style sheet elements, 343
  template rule, 346–349
TeX applications
  DTP applications, 11
  MathML and, 618
text
  alignment, CSS style rules, 269
  definition, 71
  description, 3
Text Description Language, 8–9
text editors
  definition, 12
  design and, 21
  development and, 21
  displays, 46
  Emacs, 46
  Microsoft Notepad, 46
  Microsoft WordPad, 46
  origins, 45–46
  SimpleText, 46
  vi, 46
<text> element, SMIL, 473
text node type, style sheets, 348
<textstream> element, SMIL, 473
third-party arcs, XLinks, 286
third-party links, lab, 324–325
TIBCO XML Transform software
  installation, 353–354
  XML-to-HTML transformation, 360–366
    images and, 366–368
  XML-to-XML transformation, 354–360
time data type, 182
<title> element, CDF documents, 557
token elements
  MathML content markup, 633
  MathML presentation markup, 630–631
totalDigits facet, 185
transformations
  diamond list tabulation example, 336–351
  formatting, 336
  introduction, 331
  reasons to transform, 332–333
  software, labs, 351–368
  source document, 336–341
    nodal structure, 340
  structural transformation, 336
  style sheets, pseudo-attributes, 339
  XML Transform software
    XML-to-HTML transformations, 360–366
    XML-to-XML transformations, 354–360
  XPath and, 335
  XSL and, 333–334
  XSL parsers and, 334
  XSLT and, 334–335
  XSLT style sheet, root node, 341
Transitional variant (XHTML)
  DOCTYPE declaration statement, 216
  DTDs and, 215–216
  introduction, 214
traversal, XLinks, 286
true streaming media, streaming media delivery, 456
Tunnicliffe, William, 8
TurboXML
  description, 54
  installation, lab, 60–61
two-level rule in data binding, 387–388
type attribute
  <layout> element, SMIL, 462–463
  XLinks, 289–291
type elements, XLinks attributes combination and, 292–293

type linking elements, XLinks, 294–295
<types> element, WSDL documents, 589–590
typesetting technologies
 DTP applications, 11
 GML, 10
 mainframe publishing applications, 11
 plaintext applications, 12
 text editors, 12
 word processor applications, 11–12

U

UBR nodes, UDDI and, 583–584
UDDI (Universal Description Discovery, and Integration)
 business registry, 582
 project, 581
 registries, DNS and, 583
 SOAP and, 579–580
 specification, 581–582
 sponsoring organization, 581
 UDDI TC (Technical Committee), 584
<uline> element, 242–243
universal name, 88
UPCs (Universal Product Codes), <xs:pattern> element and, 184
URIs (Universal Resource Identifier), RDF documents and, 503
<usage> element, CDF documents, 561–562
use= attribute, 180

V

valid documents, 104
validating parsers, 69
validation
 CSS Validation Service, 241
 DTDs and, 120
 HTML files, HTML-Tidy utility and, 230–232
 RDF code, lab, 517–519
 XML Schema validation, character references and, 190
<Value> element, SOAP <Fault> element, 604–605
values, RDF and, 509
variables, style sheets, 344
vector graphics
 advantages, 418–419
 CAD systems and, 418
 disadvantages, 419
 fonts, 418
 memory, 418
 object-oriented graphics, 418
 scalability, 419
vi text editor, 46
<video> element, SMIL, 473
virtual hosting
 definition, 42
 error files, 42
 filenames, 42
 hierarchies, 42
 root directories, 42
virtual server, 42
VML (Vector Markup Language)
 advantages, 421
 arcs, 430
 block-level boxes, 425
 <body> element, 424
 CSS and, 420
 curved lines, 430
 custom figures, 435
 development of, 419–420
 documents
  behavior declarations, 423–424
  creating, lab, 447–449
  namespace declarations, 422–423
  prolog, 422
 element categories, 424
 figure overlap, 437–438
 figure placement, 435–436
  absolute positioning, 436–437
  relative positioning, 437
  static positioning, 436
  z-index, 437–438
 figures, coloring shapes, 440–441
 files, size, 421

<fill> element, 441–442
fills
gradient fills, 442–443
pattern fills, 443
pictures, 443
HTML and, 420
images
flipping, 438–439
rotating, 438
in shapes, 431
introduction, 415
lines, 431
ovals, 431
path attribute, 427–429
pen commands, 427–428
<path> element, 429–430
rasterizers, 421
rectangles, 431
relative coordinates, 428
rounded rectangles, 431
searches, 421
<shape> element, 425–426
shapes
grouping, 444–446
predefined, 430–434
scaling, 443–444
<shapetype> element, 435
specification document, 420
vector graphics definition, 420
XHTML and, 420

W

W3C
Amaya open source software, 227–228
CSS Validation Service, 241
CSS Working Group, CSS development, 240–242
HTML validation service, 226–227
MathML and, 619–620
design goals, 620–621
implementations, 621–622
Math Working Group, 620
Push Technology Workshop, CDF development and, 544
transformations and
XPath and, 335
XSL, 333–334
XSL parsers, 334
XSLT and, 334–335
XLinks and, 284–285
XML and, 25–28
XML document definition, 4
XPointer and, 311–312
Web browsers
definition, 43
graphical browsers, 43
Internet Explorer, 44
Konqueror, 44
Mozilla, 44
Netscape, 44
Opera, 44
software requirements, 40
XML parser and, 43
Web content, RDF rating, 503
Web resources, metadata, 499–500
Web searches, 498–499
Web servers
Apache Web Server, 42
CDF file posting, 564
definition, 40
IBM HTTP Server, 43
IIS (Internet Information Server) software, 43
public domain software, 42
root directory, creation, 58
software, configuration, 41
Sun ONE Web Server, 43
Web services, 580
Web sites
channel subscriptions, 541
converters, 55–56
converting to HTML
HTML-Kit, 229
HTML Tidy utility, 229
W3C validation service, 226–227
converting to XHTML, 225–226
Dave Raggett's Adding a Touch of Style, 241

Web sites *(continued)*
external DTD subsets, 124–125
XML in 60 Minutes a Day
DTD labs, 154
IIS installation files, 57
Web traffic, <log> element, CDF documents, 559–560
Webcasting
Active channels, 532
Active Desktop, 532
communications and, 531
overview, 531–532
sitecrawlers and, 531
WebEQ, 644–646
well-formed documents
composition, 101–103
DTDs and, 120
white space
attribute declarations and, 137–138
data instance and, 82–83
element types and, 77
preserving, style sheet element, 343
stripping, style sheet element, 343
whiteSpace facet, 185
word processor applications, WYSIWYG, 11
WSDL documents
<binding> element, 592–593
<definitions> element, 589
GetLocalTime sample file, 588–594
last line, 594
<message> element, 590–591
<port> element, 593
<portType> element, 591
prolog, 589
<service> element, 593
SOAP requests, creating the client, 586
<types> element, 589–590
WSDL (Web Services Description Language)
development of, 585–586
file structure, 588
GetLocalTime Web service, 586–588
introduction, 585
NASSL and, 585
SCL and, 585
SOAP and, 579
WYSIWYG (What You *See* Is What You Get), 11–12

X

XAE (XML Authoring Environment for Emacs), description, 48
Xeena, 54
Xerces XML parser, 70
XFrames, XHTML development and, 210
XHTML (Extensible HyperText markup language), 24
advantages, 211–214
CSS and, lab, 273–274
data consumer elements, 378
definition, 209
documents, external style sheet affiliation, 244–247
extensibility, 212–213
files
internal XML data island, 401–403
reference to external data island, 403–405
Frameset variant, 214, 217–218
history, 209–211
HTML history, 206–207
introduction, 205
modularity, 213–214
portability, 214
Ruby Annotation, 209–210
SMIL and, 459
Strict variant, 214, 215–216
syntax
attributes, 223–225
closed elements, 221–223
document logical structure, 218–220
HTML-related tags, 221
nested element types, 220–221
table definition, recordsets, 398
Transitional variant, 214, 216–217

Web site conversion
HTML-Kit, 229
HTML Tidy utility, 229
HTML validation service, 226–227
Web site conversion to, 225–226
Working Draft, 210
XHTML Modularization, 210
XML relationship, 211–212
XLinks
arcs, 286
inbound, 286
outbound, 286
third-party, 286
attributes, global, 287–299
direction, 286
extended-type, 295–299
inbound links, lab, 323
introduction, 283–284
labs, 316
comparing types, 322–325
creating links, 317–318
multiple links in XML file, 318–319
outbound links, 319–322
links
browser display, 315–316
naming, 287
logical structure, 286
namespaces, 287
multidirectional links, lab, 324
namespaces, 287
outbound links, lab, 323–324
resources, 285–286
simple-type linking elements, 294–295
syntax, browser display, 315–316
third-party links, lab, 324–325
traversal, 286
type elements, combining with attributes, 292–293
W3C and, 284–285
XPath and, 284, 300
location paths, 301–304
XPath/XPointer expression and, 300
XPointer and, 284–285, 300
XML applications
definition, 68
SMIL and, 68
XML declaration
pseudo-attributes, 73
VML document prolog, 422
XML documents, prolog and, 72–73
XML Schema prolog, 168
XML documents
attributes, names, 80–81
conversion, HTML to XML, 55–56
data instance
attributes, 80–81
default namespace declarations, 90–91
element content, 78–79
element types, 77–78
empty elements, 78–79
empty string namespace declarations, 91–92
namespace declarations and inheritance, 92
namespaces, 85–88
nested elements, 83–85
prefix namespace declarations, 89–90
white space, 82–83
definition, 67–68
description, 3–4
entities, 92–96
external, 93–94
internal, 93–94
parsing, 93
external style sheet affiliation, 244–247
prolog, 71–72
comments, 76
document type declaration, 74–76
processing instructions, 73–74
XML declaration, 72–73
structure
logical structure, 71–92
physical structure, 92–96

XML documents *(continued)*
styles
inline specifications, 242–243
internal style sheet specifications, 243–244
valid, 104
well-formed, 101–103
<xml> element, recordsets, 397
XML (Extensible Markup Language)
best practices list, 26
CSS and, lab, 274–275
DARPA and, 17
data substitution to data content models, 515–516
derivative languages, 7
files, inserting links, 275–278
goals list, 26
history of
control codes, 7
generic coding, 7–8
macros, 7
open source code, 7
introduction, 1
as metalanguage, 18
SGML and, 14
SGML heritage, 18
W3C and, document definition, 4
XML files, XLinks lab, 318–319
XML in 60 Minutes a Day Web site, labs, 154
XML parsers
content handlers, 69
definition, 43
description, 69–70
DTD handlers, 69
entity resolvers, 70
error handlers, 69
errors, 70
literal string and, 76
schema handlers, 69
screening and, 69
validating parsers, 69
XML-related applications, 22–25
XML Schema
abstract model, 164–166
attributes, declaration, 165
component groups, 165
content model constraints, 166
content types, 165
data type constraints, 166
definition, 24
document structures, 185–189
flat catalog structure, 186–189
introduction, 185
nesting, 186
DTDs and, 162, 190
element type declarations
complex data types, 175–178
compositors, 181
empty element content, 181
mixed content, 183–184
<sg1:catalog> element, 181–182
<sg1:diamonds> element, 175–178
<sg1:gem> element, 178–181
elements, declaration, 165
facets, 180, 184–185
global references, 173–175
introduction, 161–161
labs
complex elements extended, 198
complex types, 196–198
constraints, 192–195
creation, 191–192
instances, 195
local references, 173–175
logical structure, 166–175
main documents, 172
model construction, 165
models, constraints, 166
namespaces
target namespaces, 171–172
xs prefix, 170
overview, 162–163
prolog, 168–169
<schema> element, namespace declarations, 170–171

support documents, 172
validation, character references and, 190
version 1.0, 163–164
XML Schema WG, Web site, 163
XML Spy, 55
XML transformations. *See* transformations
XPackage (XML Package Specification), 511
XPath
axes, 304–306
expressions
functions in, 308–311
location paths and, 301–304
functions, 308–311
introduction, 300–301
labs, 316
location steps, 303–304
node tests, 306–307
predicates, 307–308
node tests, 306–307
transformations and, 335
XLinks and, 284, 300
XPointer and, 311–312
XSL and, 333
XPath/XPointer expression, XLinks and, 300
XPointer
functions, 308–311
internal document structure, 312–313
labs, 316
node tests, 306–307
points, 313
character points, 314
node points, 313–314
ranges, 314–315
W3C and, 311–312
XLinks and, 284–285, 300
XPath and, 311–312
xs prefix, namespaces, 170
XSD (XML Schema Definition) language, definition, 163
XSL (Extensible Stylesheet Language)
formatting language, 333
formatting objects, 333
transformation language, 333
XSL-FO (XSL Formatting Objects), XSL and, 333
XSL parsers, transformation and, 334
XSLT (XSL Transformation)
CSS and, 335
description, 334–335
elements, HTML table, 348
style sheets
elements, 343
example, 342
root node, 341
XSL and, 333

Z

z-index, VML figure placement, 437–438